Sound and Affect

Sound and Affect

VOICE, MUSIC, WORLD

Edited by
Judith Lochhead, Eduardo Mendieta,
and Stephen Decatur Smith

University of Chicago Press   Chicago and London

The University of Chicago Press, Chicago 60637
The University of Chicago Press, Ltd., London
© 2021 by The University of Chicago
All rights reserved. No part of this book may be used or reproduced in any manner whatsoever without written permission, except in the case of brief quotations in critical articles and reviews. For more information, contact the University of Chicago Press, 1427 E. 60th St., Chicago, IL 60637.
Published 2021
Printed in the United States of America

30 29 28 27 26 25 24 23 22 21   1 2 3 4 5

ISBN-13: 978-0-226-75183-2 (cloth)
ISBN-13: 978-0-226-75801-5 (paper)
ISBN-13: 978-0-226-75815-2 (e-book)
DOI: https://doi.org/10.7208/chicago/9780226758152.001.0001

This book has been supported by the General Fund of the American Musicological Society, funded in part by the National Endowment for the Humanities and the Andrew W. Mellon Foundation.

Library of Congress Cataloging-in-Publication Data

Names: Lochhead, Judith Irene, editor. | Mendieta, Eduardo, editor. | Smith, S. Decatur (Stephen Decatur), editor.
Title: Sound and affect : voice, music, world / edited by Judith Lochhead, Eduardo Mendieta, Stephen Decatur Smith.
Description: Chicago : University of Chicago Press, 2021. | Includes bibliographical references and index.
Identifiers: LCCN 2020047086 | ISBN 9780226751832 (cloth) | ISBN 9780226758015 (paperback) | ISBN 9780226758152 (e-book)
Subjects: LCSH: Music—Psychological aspects. | Affect (Psychology) | Music—Philosophy and aesthetics. | Music—Political aspects. | Emotions in music.
Classification: LCC ML3838.S63 2021 | DDC 780.9—dc23
LC record available at https://lccn.loc.gov/2020047086

♾ This paper meets the requirements of ANSI/NISO Z39.48-1992 (Permanence of Paper).

CONTENTS

Preface ix

Introduction *1*
JUDITH LOCHHEAD, EDUARDO MENDIETA,
AND STEPHEN DECATUR SMITH

PART 1. Sounding the Political

CHAPTER 1. Waves of Moderation: The Sound of Sophrosyne in Ancient Greek and Neoliberal Times *37*
ROBIN JAMES

CHAPTER 2. The Politics of Silence: Heidegger's *Black Notebooks* *56*
ADAM KNOWLES

PART 2. Affect, Music, Human

CHAPTER 3. Sign, Affect, and Musicking before the Human *71*
GARY TOMLINSON

CHAPTER 4. Human Beginnings and Music: Technology and Embodiment Roles *99*
DON IHDE

CHAPTER 5. The Life and Death of Daniel Barenboim *108*
JAMES CURRIE

PART 3. Voicings and Silencings

CHAPTER 6. The Philosopher's Voice: The Prosody of Logos *141*
EDUARDO MENDIETA

CHAPTER 7. Late Capitalism, Affect, and the Algorithmic Self in Music Streaming Platforms *159*
MICHAEL BIRENBAUM QUINTERO

PART 4. Affective Listenings

CHAPTER 8. Music, Labor, and Technologies of Desire *197*
MARTIN SCHERZINGER

CHAPTER 9. Musical Affect, Autobiographical Memory, and Collective Individuation in Thomas Bernhard's *Correction* *224*
CHRISTOPHER HAWORTH

PART 5. Temporalities of Sounding

CHAPTER 10. The "Sound" of Music: Sonic Agency and the Dialectic of Freedom and Constraint in Jazz Improvisation *239*
LORENZO C. SIMPSON

CHAPTER 11. Merleau-Ponty on Consciousness and Affect through the Temporal Movement of Music *253*
JESSICA WISKUS

CHAPTER 12. A. N. Whitehead, Feeling, and Music: On Some Potential Modifications to Affect Theory *268*
RYAN DOHONEY

PART 6. Theorizing the Affections

CHAPTER 13. Delivering Affect: Mersenne, Voice, and the Background of Jesuit Rhetorical Theory *289*
ANDRÉ DE OLIVEIRA REDWOOD

CHAPTER 14. Mimesis and the Affective Ground of Baroque
Representation 303
DANIEL VILLEGAS VÉLEZ

CHAPTER 15. Affect and the Recording Devices of
Seventeenth-Century Italy 325
EMILY WILBOURNE

CHAPTER 16. Immanuel Kant and the Downfall of
the *Affektenlehre* 342
TOMÁS MCAULEY

Acknowledgments 361
List of Contributors 363
Bibliography 365
Index 391

PREFACE

There is nothing like a political rally when it comes to experiencing the affective resonances of sound, music, and voice, the sheer loudness of thousands of humans being together, reveling in their noisiness, exuberantly inhabiting the dome of their being-with as they reverberate. The thunderously resonant intensity of the rally has heralded some of modernity's brightest and bleakest moments alike. Indeed, Leni Riefenstahl captured the power of the experience in her 1935 documentary *The Triumph of the Will*. This classic of propaganda, drawn from sixty hours of footage shot through the four days of the 1934 Nazi Party Congress in Nuremberg, is often credited with having created a visual grammar that aggrandized and mythologized Hitler and the Nazi party, becoming a role model for future political documentaries. Arguably, Riefenstahl also invented an aural grammar, presaging an "auditory" culture that went along with the optics and visual culture of the Nazis. The documentary, like the cover of Thomas Hobbes's *Leviathan* (1651), is now part of the political iconography of totalitarianism. But unlike the mute image that meets Hobbes's reader, Riefenstahl's film also traces what we call a "sonic affective regime" that included Richard Wagner, Herbert Windt, Hitler's thundering voice, columns of soldiers stamping on pavement, the rolling of military vehicles with their unique acoustic imprint, the chanting of masses, and the signature "Heil Hitler" yelled by thousands of people in unison, uniting the will of the people into one voice. It may echo today in Charlottesville. This anthology, however, is not a study of a totalitarian acousteme, the aural counterpart of an episteme; nor is it, following Veit Erlmann in his indispensable *Reason and Resonance: A History of Aurality*, what we could call "genealogy of totalitarian aurality." Instead, we are interested in the entanglements of tonal resonances and affective dispositions as they reverberate through distinct modern soundscapes. Rather than ask "Where are we when we think?," as Hannah Arendt did, or "Where are we when we listen to music?," as Peter Sloterdijk did, in this anthology we are asking: Where are we placed by the soundtrack that accompanies our lives? Obviously, that soundtrack is not merely sonorous, harmonious, even melodic; it is also cacophonous, syncopated, discordant, and at times screeching. Yet that sound envelope, that dome of sounds, places us somewhere.[1] Sound, music, voice create moods, affective dispositions. To be in the world is to be in a sonic landscape, to be in sound, to be in a knot of moods, emotions, and feelings. This is what we aim to explore in this rich anthology: how we are placed in certain affective attitudes, directionalities, and dispositions by the music, sounds, and sonority that envelop us, like the heartbeat inside the womb. We maintain that music studies, sound studies, and affect theory have reached levels of development and convergence that can enable us to develop new lines of research on the ways in which sound, music, and voice impact our individual and collective emotional lives and dispositions. Now more than half of humanity lives in cities, cathedrals of noise, and there is no place on the earth that does not echo with the near or distant sounds of human activity. Rather than a *Silent Spring*, Rachel Carson's haunting sonic image, we now live in what we could call an Acoustocene, the soundtrack of the Anthropocene, with its own death-march symphony. The chapters that make up this anthology are incisive and generative prolegomena to further research into what we have called "sonic affective regimes."

Judith Lochhead, Eduardo Mendieta,
and Stephen Decatur Smith

Note

1. For more on the idea of how music places, see Judy I. Lochhead, "Music Places: Imaginative Transports of Listening," in *The Oxford Handbook of Sound and Imagination*, vol. 1, ed. Mark Grimshaw-Aagaard, Mads Walther-Hansen, and Martin Knakkergaard (Oxford and New York: Oxford University Press, 2019), 683–700.

Introduction

Judith Lochhead, Eduardo Mendieta, and Stephen Decatur Smith

In the voice as it speaks, stutters, rustles, hesitates, chokes, cries, or projects an accent; in music, whether vocal, instrumental, or electronic; in our sonic environments, whether natural or manmade; and in the many modalities of listening that respond to our sonic worlds—the sounds we make and hear can externalize, reflect, evoke, recall, or catalyze affective states. Indeed, countless phenomena attest that sound and affect are linked, albeit in ways that are far from stable or autonomous. Race, class, age, gender and sexuality; ability and disability; social, cultural, and political experience; and diverse forms of historical change can all condition the relays and relations of sound and affect. If we live in a "tower of sound," to use an expression from Leonard Cohen, this tower is sometimes a battlement and sometimes a beacon, every bit as protean, contentious, and contradictory as the world in which it takes shape. It is the task of *Sound and Affect* to create a space in which music studies, sound studies, affect theory, and philosophy can think through these linkages, intersections, and entwinements.

Sound and Affect: Voice, Music, World originated in a conference of the same name held at Stony Brook University in April of 2014. Like its parent, this volume gathers work from several interdisciplinary trajectories in order to address a substantial lacuna at the intersection of sound and affect. Affect, emotion, feeling, and the passions have all been topics of intense research, interest, and debate in the humanities and neurosciences in recent decades. This work, often called the *affective turn*, has generated important scholarship across diverse fields of research in the humanities, social sciences, and biological sciences. Following writings by such authors as Sara Ahmed, Lauren Berlant, Antonio Damasio, Brian Massumi, Martha Nussbaum, John Protevi, Silvan Tomkins, and Patricia Ticento Clough, and finding theoretical roots especially in the philosophies of Henri Bergson, Gilles Deleuze, Martin Heidegger, Maurice Merleau-Ponty, and Baruch Spinoza, research in what we call the affective domain has assumed a central role in studies of literature, political theory, art history, anthropology, neuroscience, psychology, philosophy, and cultural studies.[1] The affective turn has been paralleled by a burgeoning interest in sound as a significant and understudied dimension of social, cultural, and political life. A new interdisciplinary field, that of sound studies, has blossomed in the wake of research by such foundational figures as R. Murray Schafer, Don Ihde, Steven Feld, Jonathan Sterne, and Emily Thompson.[2] Recent research in sound studies spans the disciplines of art history, media studies, cultural studies, philosophy, anthropology, and music. Finally, this scholarly interest in affect and sound has been matched in recent years by a philosophical turn in music studies, as scholars in musicology, music theory, and ethnomusicology develop rich new engagements with the history of philosophy and the history of musical thought, as well as new ways of interfacing with the work of contemporary philosophers. Philosophy has also seen a parallel turn in recent years toward sound as a focus of study, often in relation to its affective powers.

This anthology brings together these domains (affect studies, sound studies, music studies, and philosophy), and to that end it gathers together scholarship focused on what might be called the study of the "sonic affective regimes" that condition all societies in their unique historical configurations. Affect affects sound, and sound affects affect, in such a way that social agents are disposed and attuned, or indisposed and tuned out, to social events and forces. The philosopher Robin James, in her book *The Sonic Episteme: Acoustic Resonance, Neoliberalism, and Biopolitics*, uses Foucauldian analytics to coin an extremely generative concept: *sonic episteme*. With it she aims to provide an analysis of correlations among certain sounds, resonances, and ideas about the social order. The rhythms of sound have historically been represented mathematically through ratios. The sounds of the world thus become a mathematical equation, ordering a sonic panorama that gives a sense of wholeness and orderliness to what upon first hearing is cacophonous and chaotic. In James's work, neoliberalism finds expression in certain kinds of musical practices, technologies of the self, and mathematical orders that naturalize socioeconomic relations. The sound of neoliberalism is the tune of a biopolitical order. Our collection, which includes a chapter by James, seeks to map, to sound, to "sonar" the sonic affective regime, revealing the entanglements and echoes of sounds, affects, modes of agency, and ways of making and understanding music. We suggest that the nascent research and paradigm shifts in the four convergent areas covered in this collection at once enable and call for the deciphering of the sonic affective regime.

Part I of the Introduction examines entwinements of music, sound, and affect in four historical moments. This account is intended not to provide a comprehensive historical narrative, but rather to zoom in on four snapshots that can provide context for the essays gathered in this collection. In chronological order, these are (i) the entwinement of music, sound, and affect in the political thought of Plato and Aristotle; (ii) the theoretical approaches to musical organization that involved specific correlations between sonic structures and affective qualities in the seventeenth and eighteenth centuries; (iii) the role that music plays in the change from the passions to the emotions that occurs across the late eighteenth and nineteenth centuries and into the early twentieth; and (iv) the emergence of sound studies in the late twentieth and early twenty-first centuries and its own (still infrequent) turns to affect. Part II describes the turn to affect across the twentieth- and twenty-first-century humanities, presenting the conceptual debates along with the attendant ambiguities of terminology and the phenomena to which they refer. This part also marks out some landmark scholarship that allows us to map the territory of affect studies across a wide array of disciplines and interdisciplines. Part III introduces the essays of this collection in light of these conceptual and historical contexts.

Three Moments

AFFECT, EDUCATION, AND POLITICAL ORDER: ANCIENT PHILOSOPHIES OF MUSIC AND AFFECT

Sonic affective regimes are not new. They have been around since the beginnings of Western philosophy, when thinkers began to write about the relationships between music, reason, character, agency, and political order. The study of sonic affective regimes is at stake in the work of the alleged fathers of Western philosophy: Plato and Aristotle. Plato's *Politeia*, the *Republic*, sets out to describe Kallipolis, the well-ordered, beautiful, and just city, and how such a *polis* could be constructed and its citizens educated. Chapter 3 of the *Republic* focuses on the education of the guardians of the polis. For the moment let us bracket the issue of how other sections of the polis are to be educated, or how their education is passed over in silence. What is noteworthy is that the education of the guardians of the polis must begin with musical education, before the youngsters (both male and female) become the protectors of the polis. Physical or athletic education was not primary. Plato, speaking through the lips of Socrates, argues that education must follow this order for two reasons:

> First, because rhythm and harmony permeate the innermost element of the soul, affect it more powerfully than anything else, and bring it grace, such education makes one graceful if one is properly trained, and the opposite if one is not. Second, because anyone who has been properly trained will quickly notice if something has been omitted from a thing, or if that thing has not been well crafted or well grown. (401d–e)[3]

Plato compares Kallipolis to a just, ethical, and beautiful soul, and he conceives justice and goodness as a form of harmony. In the city, justice is harmony among the classes; in the soul, goodness is harmony among the parts of the soul (the appetitive, the spirited, and the rational or deliberative). Musical training is the first form of education in which the individual is introduced to the notions of virtue, balance, propriety, and harmony among parts. Socrates therefore also claims:

> Fine speech, then, as well as harmony, grace, rhythm, go along with naiveté. I do not mean the foolishness for which naiveté is a euphemism, but the quality a mind has when it is equipped with a truly good and fine character. (400e)[4]

This explains why chapters 3 and 4 of the *Republic* argue for the need to censor poets and musicians. They must produce only the kinds of poetry, narrative, and music that are conducive to the "right" kind of ethical dispositions. Plato's didacticism, and his outright censorship and persecution of artists, has become anathema to our modern sensibilities, even if we occasionally have eruptions of Platonic distaste for certain sounds and narratives. Plato's Kallipolis is predicated precisely on the formation of a sonic affective regime, one that sought to coordinate moral character, political obedience, and subordination to the rule of reason as promulgated by philosopher-kings, through the cultivation of certain harmonies and rhythms.

Aristotle, rejecting his teacher's didacticism and his plain misunderstanding of the autonomy and uniqueness of the arts, set out to give both poetics and rhetoric their due in his books with those very names. Both of these works are thinly veiled polemics against Plato's subordination of music, poetry, and rhetoric to the moral and political ends of the polis. In the *Poetics*, for instance, Aristotle provides a succinct and revealing definition of tragedy, one instance of the power and skill of artistic creation:

> Tragedy, then, is an imitation of an action that is serious, complete, and of a certain magnitude; in language embellished with each kind of artistic ornament, the several kinds being found in separate parts of the play; the form of action, not of narrative; through pity and fear affecting the proper purgation of these emotions. By "language embellished," I mean language into which rhythm, "harmony," and song enter. By "the several kinds of separate parts," I mean, that some parts are rendered through the medium of verse alone, others again with the aid of song. (6.1449b25–32)[5]

Forms of *poiesis* are implicated in the production and catharsis of affect through plot, character, diction, thought, and song. Sound is implicated in this affective productivity through both diction and song. For Aristotle, plot is the decisive element, the soul of tragedy. Artistic works, however, cannot be reduced to character, that is, to their moral elements and lessons. We can and should read Aristotle's *Poetics*, then, as a clear and explicit rejection of what we have called Plato's didacticism.

What about the effects of certain music and sounds on the disposition of citizens? Aristotle takes this up directly in book 8, chapter 5, of his *Politics*. There he claims:

> It is evident from these things, then, that music can render the character of the soul of a certain quality. If it is capable of doing this, clearly it must be employed and the young must be educated in it. The teaching of music is fitting in relation to the nature of those of such an age, for on account of their age the young do not voluntarily put up with anything that is not sweetened; but music by nature belongs among the sweetened things. Moreover, there seems to be a certain affinity on their part for harmonies and rhythms; hence many of the wise assert either that the soul is a harmony or that it involves harmony. (1340b12–20)[6]

Book 8, in general, is devoted to what we can call the "aesthetic education" of the polis, and in it Aristotle considers poetry, drama, and music. He seems to be in accordance with Plato on the positive role of musical education in the education of children, although it is not clear that this education has distinct and strict moral and political aims. Later, in chapter 7 of book 8, Aristotle will make his position explicit:

> Since we accept the distinction of tunes as they are distinguished by certain persons in philosophy, regarding some as relating to character, some to action, and some to inspiration (and they regard the nature of harmonies as akin to each of these, one of them to one part), and since we assert that music should be practiced not for the sake of a single sort of benefit but for the sake of several (for it is for the sake both of education and of purification [*Katharsis*]—as to what we mean by purification, we will speak of it simply at present, but again and more elaborately in the discourses on the poetic arts—and third, it is useful with a view to pastime, rest, and the relaxation of strain), it is evident that all the harmonies are to be used, but that all are not to be used in the same manner, but with a view to education those most relating to character, and with a view to listening to other performing those relating to action and those relating to inspiration as well. (8.7.1341b–1342a5)[7]

While music can have many uses and certainly can be enjoyed at different levels simultaneously, it nonetheless plays an important role in the moral education of individuals in general, and of citizens in particular. For Aristotle, with his more nuanced arguments and for more elaborate reasons, music plays a critical role in the production of an affective order, through both catharsis, which is sometimes translated as purgation, and purification or relief, often accompanied by pleasure. Plato's and Aristotle's treatises on politics turn out to be explorations of the relationships between sound, affect, and agency—that is, of the production of what we called a "sonic affective regime."

MOVING THE AFFECTIONS: EARLY MODERN MUSINGS ON THE AFFECTIVE POWERS OF SOUND

In his earliest written work, the *Compendium musicae* (1618), René Descartes sets out the goals of music: "Renatus Cartesius' Compendium of music, whose object is sound, whose end is to delight and move in us various affections. . . ."[8] Such musical goals have their source in the Neoplatonic thought of the Renaissance, as demonstrated by Claude Palisca, Penelope Gouk, and Gary Tomlinson.[9] Intellectual and aesthetic interest in the affections grew out of the Renaissance revival and development of early Greek and Roman thought about the spirits, humors, and temperaments.[10] The spirits were conceived as thin and airy vapors that communicate between soul and body. The four humors, the bodily substances of blood, yellow bile, phlegm, and black bile, were seen as being responsible for overall bodily health and for temperament. Too much blood would result in a sanguine temperament, too much yellow bile a choleric temperament, too much phlegm a phlegmatic temperament, and too much black bile a melancholic temperament. Spirits, humors, and temperaments all figure in Renaissance thinking about sound, music, and hearing. Here again, the ways in which these modes of experience are configured in this historical moment may be read as traces of a sonic affective regime, one that can condition the social interpretation of bodily health and illness, and also as visions of the cosmic order and its social reflection.

Two authors from this era provide some insight into sound and its affective dimensions: the music theorist and composer Bartolomeo Ramis de Pareia and the philosopher Marsilio Ficino. In his *Musica practica* (1482), Ramis de Pareia sets out a theory connecting the four church modes in their authentic and plagal dispositions to both the humors and to the planets, making broad connections among *musica humana*, *musica instrumentalis*, and *musica mundana*. For instance, the Dorian mode, associated with phlegm, combats sluggishness with a rousing character, and the Hypodorian mode enhances sluggishness with a doleful character. Ramis de Pareia sets out the powers of modes to affect human behaviors through their intervallic, melodic, and cadential characteristics, and he claims an all-encompassing link between these sonic powers and the cosmic forces controlling planetary motions.

Ficino went beyond the Neoplatonism of Ramis de Pareia, combining "it with two practical arts … medicine and music" in order to pursue a "musical magic" with therapeutic value.[11] In the commentary to his translation of Plato's *Timaeus* (1484), Ficino describes the affective power of musical sound: "Musical sound … moves the body by the movement of the air," and this movement "excites the airy spirit, which is the bond of body and soul." Thus "by its nature, both spiritual and material, [musical sound] at once seizes and claims as its own, man in his entirety."[12] The power of musical sound to affect a human being in her totality, both body and soul through the actions of the spirits, endows it with magical properties. In his *Da vita coelitus comparanda* (1489), Ficino claims that because the "very matter of song is altogether purer and more similar to the heavens," musical sound has more power than medicine.[13] As Tomlinson and others have argued, this power was a kind of "musical magic" that flowed from music's resonance with celestial harmony and its ability to affect both body and soul through the movements of the air.[14] By its effects on the spirits, musical sound's therapeutic value extends to both body and soul — and, significantly, to their interactions.

The influence of the thinking of such authors as Ramis and Ficino about the affective power of music is palpable in music theory and aesthetics until the middle of the eighteenth century. As Gouk observes, Ficino's *De vita comparanda* "became the *locus classicus* for sixteenth and seventeenth-century discussion of music's effects."[15] Gioseffo Zarlino, one of the most important music theorists of the sixteenth century, includes a chapter in his *Le institutioni harmoniche* (1558) addressing "how music can move the soul ... and induce ... in a human being various behaviors." Like Ramis, Zarlino links the modes to specific passions and observes that when a particular harmonic sound is heard there is a corresponding "mutation of the soul."[16] This focus on the capacity for sound and its sensations to affect human behaviors characterizes the writings of a wide range of authors during the sixteenth century. The Italian humanist Girolamo Mei is notable both for his observations about the role of pitch height for moving the affections and for his involvements in the aesthetic discussions in the Florentine Academy, which led to the emergence of a new "expressive" musical style at the beginning of the seventeenth century.

Writing on the passions and on the power of sound and music to move the affections continued through the seventeenth century and into the eighteenth. Neoplatonist approaches to the affective domain continued but were transformed. As Gouk observes, "Neo-Platonic and occult ideas were not so much rejected [in the seventeenth century] as simply taken over by mathematicians and natural philosophers."[17] This transformation is part of what Thomas Dixon argues was a gradual—yet incomplete—secularization and professionalization of the concepts of the passions and the affects (see part II, section 2 of this chapter).[18] For Dixon, this process entailed a more rationalist approach, in which the passions and affections were understood as "'mechanisms' designed by God."[19] Descartes's last published work, *On the Passions of the Soul* (1649), exemplifies this change, serving as (in Larry Jorgensen's words) a "bridge between the ancients and the later 'science' of aesthetics."[20]

Writings about music and affect in the eighteenth century reflect this move toward a greater rationalization. For instance, in his *Das neueroffnete Orchestre* (1713), Johann Mattheson employs a systematic taxonomy connecting keys and their affective characteristics. He lists the seventeen (out of the twenty-four major and minor) most practical keys and describes their characteristics. For instance, C major is "rude, bold, also tender," and C minor is "sweet, sad."[21] As George Buelow argues, Mattheson disavowed any simple correlation between affect and particular musical features, and he avoided formulating a consistent and complete *Affektenlehre* (i.e., Doctrine of Affects), despite occasional claims to the contrary; rather, Mattheson's theoretical writing, growing out of his own compositional creativity, reflected the then-widespread belief that the affective functions of music could be understood within the rationalistic thought of the eighteenth century.[22]

As a vibratory force, sound in its musical manifestation plays a central role in thinking about humans and the cosmos in the early modern era. Conceived as movement, musical sound served as a magical bridge between body and soul, operating in both the metaphysical and the physical realms. In the music-theoretical writings of Descartes and Zarlino, the affective qualities of musical sound are understood to reside in what today we might think of as the technical details of musical structure—the size of intervals and their temporal dispositions. For early modern thinkers, sound and affect are intricately intertwined. Although later music theorists could not agree on a specific correlation between particular sound configurations and affective qualities, the power of musical sound to generate such affects retained its magical aura.

ROMANTICISM AND EARLY MODERNISM: THE RELOCATION OF AFFECT

The transitions in musical thought and practice that took place around the beginning of the nineteenth century might be cast in terms of a new accent on individual emotion at the expense of transpersonal affect. If, for example, works such as Schumann's lieder and piano miniatures are taken to be exemplary, then the musical production of this moment might indeed appear to be shaped by structures of feeling that are principally personal, individual, interior, subjective, or psychological, as opposed to the more objective and nonindividuated notions of affect belonging to the seventeenth and eighteenth centuries. We suggest, however, that a fuller picture of this moment would encompass not only the emergence of new forms of musical emotion, but also new and shifting counterpoints among multiple forms of musical feeling. In such a picture, Romantic musical emotion would move in counterpoint with other shapes of feeling, including forms of affect carried over from earlier epochs.

Carl Dahlhaus's interpretation of Rossini can point to a way in which transpersonal or impersonal affect persists alongside a new individualization of emotion. In the whirling pile-ups of confusion that accumulate in the composer's comedies Dahlhaus hears "the demonic," an intensity of feeling that points beyond the circumstances of the drama and toward the audience's memories of recent wars, as well as the feelings of tension and anxiety left in their wake.[23] Conversely, in the "sugarcoated pathos of [Rossini's] serious operas" Dahlhaus finds hints of a "surreptitious gloom that sees the cogs churning mechanically at the root of tragedy." Thus, "the extremes meet," and Rossini's "cheerfulness is simply the obverse of a melancholy that afflicted not just himself but his entire age."[24] On this reading, the melancholy and demonic mania that pervade Rossini's operas are not reducible to individual characters onstage, or to the emotional consequences of the drama's events and actions. Instead, without naming it as such, Dahlhaus swerves here toward a conception of historical affect like that of Lauren Berlant. "The present," Berlant suggests, "is perceived, first, affectively"; and on Dahlhaus's reading, Rossini's operas register an affective field ("a melancholy that afflicted not just himself but his entire age") that belongs inextricably to *his* present.[25] Indeed, Dahlhaus develops a closely related account of late Beethoven and Schubert; in both he hears a resignation that goes beyond the circumstances of their individual biographical circumstances and stands more broadly as a trace of the affective fields of the restoration that followed the Napoleonic wars. Without attesting overtly to this thought, Dahlhaus's various analyses suggest that, in an age of musical emotion, musical affect persisted, tracing and recalling the contours of broad historical affective fields. Here again music can seem to adumbrate a sonic affective regime, this time a regime belonging to European culture in the wake of the Napoleonic wars.

Many of the most consequential philosophical analyses of music and sound dating from the first decades of the nineteenth century register this persistence of affect as it moves in counterpoint with new forms of musical emotion. These dynamics are discernible across the analyses of music in Hegel's lectures on aesthetics. In one sense, Hegel might easily be taken as an eminent example of the line of nineteenth-century musical thought that most strongly accents interior, individual, subjective life. Music, Hegel says famously, "takes as its subject-matter the subjective inner life itself"; its aim is to "presen[t] itself, not as an external shape or as an objectively existing work, but as that inner life."[26] In these formulations, Hegel appears to understand musical feeling not only to be radically interior, and in this sense personal and individual, but even as the height of subjectivity tout court, in which aural auto-affectivity communicates from within the ear to the subject her own subjective state.

At other junctures, though, Hegel's analysis of music acknowledges, indeed requires, forms of feeling that cannot be limited to this seemingly atomistic experience. One such moment appears amid a discussion of the ways that music can comport itself as the setting of a text. Here, Hegel describes a structure of feeling as "the ideal significance" (*ideellen Bedeutung*) of "the thing itself" (*die Sache selbst*):

> In old church-music, e.g. in a *Crucifixus*, the deep elements lying in the nature of Christ's Passion, e.g. this divine suffering, death, and entombment, are often so treated that what is expressed is not a *subjective* feeling [*subjektive Empfindung*] of sympathy or individual human grief at these events, but as it were the thing itself [*die Sache selbst*], i.e. the profundity of its meaning moves through the harmonies and their melodic course.[27]

In experiencing works of this kind, he goes on, a listener, in their deepest interiority (*in seinem innerste leben*), will live through (*durchleben*) the death and suffering of Christ; they will immerse their entire soul (*Gemüt*) in the experience, such that it "extinguishes everything else and fills the subject (*das Subjekt*) with this one thing (*Sache*)." The listener's inner life thus ceases to be entirely inner, as the gap vanishes between their individual affective experience and the "thing itself," with the latter appearing as a structure of feeling that is not limited to any one individual listener, performer, or composer, but that resides instead on the transindividual level of the religious and musical community.

The multiplicity and dynamism with which these forms of feeling appear in Hegel's philosophy of music might be taken as emblematic of the myriad constructions of feeling that appear throughout philosophical treatments of music in the early decades of the nineteenth century—constructions that are, as we have argued above, by no means limited to a simple transition from affect to emotion. Within the first and second generations of Romantic musical thought, the eighteenth-century doctrines of the affects have an ongoing life, sometimes taking the form of a spiritualized technology of feeling. Joseph Berlinger, the narrator of Wilhelm Heinrich Wackenroder's *Fantasies on Art*, calls music "the most marvelous" of the "various splendid inventions" that have been developed for "the preservation of the emotions."[28] This thought is echoed later in E. T. A. Hoffmann's famous review of Beethoven's Fifth Symphony, where he writes that Beethoven's music "sets in motion the machinery of awe, of fear, of terror, of pain"[29]—a determination that already suggests the affinities between Beethoven's music and Hegel's *Phenomenology of Spirit* (1807) that would be so richly significant for Adorno more than a century later. Around the turn of the nineteenth century, then, at precisely the moment when a new accent on instrumental music, with its aesthetic of longing, is sometimes said to mark an end to a musical aesthetic of distinct affects, these decisive texts seem to cast instrumental music as an instrument *of* affect, a technology of feeling, or a mechanism constructed to set individual affects in motion.

At mid-century, the highly influential polemics of Eduard Hanslick's *On the Musically Beautiful* (1854) were explicitly devoted to displacing the centrality of feeling in music aesthetics, in favor of a conception of music centered on its "tonally moving forms,"[30] which are addressed to the imagination, rather than the nervous system. But Hanslick can be read as reaffirming what he would seem to resist. As Dahlhaus has argued, Hanslick's gallery of musical affect theorists, which he presents in order to offer a clear picture of the opposition, suggests a continuity in musical thought running from avowed affect theorists of the eighteenth century—figures such as Mattheson, Johann Nicolaus Forkel, and Friedrich Wilhelm Marpurg—through the early nineteenth century and all the way to Wagner. The entire project of *On the Musically Beautiful* can thus seem dependent on Hanslick's sense that theories of musical feeling not unlike those of the eighteenth century retained a substantial currency in his own day.[31] The theorist who would dethrone musical feeling from its place of centrality offers a genealogy of musical affect that traces its relevance well into the nineteenth century. And indeed, this genealogy could be drawn through Hanslick's theory itself. Even as he insists that music's aesthetic substance lies in its form, he echoes centuries of earlier musical affect theory by locating a tremendous power in music's capacity, as sound, to move the body on the level of its materiality. Music's "intense action on our nervous system," he writes, "explains the characteristic force and directness with which music (as compared with arts that do not employ the medium of sound) is capable of exciting emotions."[32] Music, he insists, can never represent "definite emotions," or feelings shaped by their attachment to a specific image or idea.[33] Nonetheless, because he locates in music an intense power of feeling that begins with a material impact upon the nerves ("the mysterious links in the invisible telegraphic connections between mind and body"), his project contains a stratum that remains continuous with the tradition of affective thought from which it strains to distinguish itself.[34]

The affective moment of Hanslick's theory can also point to another kind of juxtaposition or counterpoint in the ways that nineteenth-century musical thought conceived affect or emotion. Hegel and the early Romantics could still treat the affects as relatively discontinuous. Hegel's Anthropology (appearing at the outset of his *Philosophy of Mind*, section I, "Subjective Mind," subsection A, paras. 388–412.³⁵) catalogues the feelings of the soul one at a time, and the technical metaphors of Wackenroder and Hoffmann can also suggest discrete levers attached to discrete affects, even if, especially in Hoffmann, these discrete feelings appear against the background of a single, overwhelming sense of yearning. But in Hanslick, sharp distinctions among the affects seem to collapse. As he mocks Mattheson's gridlike typology of musical feeling, and as he insists on the indefinite structure of music's powerful impact upon the emotions, Hanslick suggests a picture of musical affect that is distributed as a shifting and continuous qualitative multiplicity, rather than a quantitative multiplicity of separate and discrete shapes of feeling.

In this, Hanslick may be said to belong clearly to a new moment of affect, the emergence of which Fredric Jameson locates in the second half of the nineteenth century. For Jameson, Richard Wagner's famous 1859 letter to Mathilde Wesendonck is emblematic of this new formation of musical feeling.³⁶ In it Wagner connects his own "inborn" tendency to "swing from one extreme of temper to another" with the "art of transition," according to which his music would shift seamlessly, not only among sonic formations and events, but also across spaces of affect and desire.³⁷ For Jameson, this stream of shifting affects in Wagner places him alongside artists such as Gustave Flaubert and Charles Baudelaire (and we might add Hanslick, when he turns to affect), who mark the opening of a new phase of modernity by registering and documenting in their work a "sensory singularity, the unclassifiable and indeed unnamable *haeccitas* or 'this-ness'" of affective bodily life.³⁸ Jameson argues that this new, modern shape of affect is distinct from emotion: emotions, he believes, may be named, and in this sense interpreted, whereas affects present themselves as nameless, not only because they inhere in bodily life prior to consciousness, but also because they are continually shifting and shading, transitioning into new states, and thus resisting stable designation.

If Wagner's work presents affect in this sense, Schopenhauer's philosophy, when it turns to music, might be taken as another space of overlap and counterpoint, which prefigures this new field of affect while also carrying holdovers from an earlier epoch. On the one hand, Schopenhauer's notion of the Will—an aimless, irrational urge, fundamentally "one" but "at variance with itself," experienced in bodily life prior to its manifestation in the higher operations of the mind and objectified directly in music—might be understood as an obvious precursor to the new forms of affect that Jameson hears in Wagner's art of continuous transition.³⁹ This affinity would be signaled by Wagner's famous predilection for Schopenhauer's thought. And yet, on the other hand, because Schopenhauer insists that music is able express the "essential nature" of discrete and impersonal feelings that may be named, identified, and in this sense understood (music, he writes, "does not express ... this or that affliction, pain, sorrow, horror, gaiety, merriment, or peace of mind, but joy, pain, sorrow, horror, gaiety, merriment, peace of mind themselves"), his thought may be read as an echo of the notions of musical affect that prevailed in the eighteenth century and earlier—affect, that is, as a field of distinct intensities of feeling, which might be arrayed in a typology, a table, or a doctrine.[40] The picture of affect that Jameson finds in Wagner may be traced again in Nietzsche's writings on music, both before and after his break with Wagner. The dark churning of the Dionysian, and the sunny and fatal feelings Nietzsche finds in *Carmen*, all whirl beneath and before anything that might resemble the discrete forms of feeling that are the objects of the eighteenth-century affect theorists.

In the twentieth century, Theodor Adorno instantiates a kind of affective counterpoint not unlike the one at work in Schopenhauer, though in Adorno this dynamic is reshaped by a bleak vision of modern capitalist culture. If there is a stratum of Adorno's thought that converges with the vision of affect that Jameson sees emerging around the middle of the nineteenth century, it can perhaps be located in Adorno's notions of "mimesis" or "mimetic comportment," a realm of action and experience in which the living being makes itself like its other, without grasping that other on the level of conceptual reason. This mimesis is pre-mental, pre-rational, even pre-subjective, but it is nonetheless thoroughly mediated and transformed by historical life. Mimesis, Adorno believes, is at work in all art, not least in music: "as expression," he writes, "music behaves mimetically."[41] Stirring in the depths of bodily life (mimesis "reaches back into the biological dimension"), and irreducible to concepts, techniques, or artistic forms (though in constant dialectical tension with all of these), Adorno's mimesis can be grasped as the kind of shifting, qualitative, corporeal intensity that Jameson identifies as modernist affect.[42]

And yet, Adorno's thought can also be read to include what might be called an *Affektenlehre* of the culture industry. In his criticisms of popular culture writ large, and of popular music in particular, Adorno is persistently concerned with the ways in which feeling can be produced and circulated so as to maintain relations of power in unchanging and exploitative configurations. The popular song, in his most cynical interpretations, thus becomes something like a single-serving dose of affect, shaped and parceled out according to a gridlike structure of planning that echoes the affective typologies of the eighteenth century, and delivered with a technical precision that recalls Wackenroder's notion of music as a "splendid invention" for the "preservation of the emotions." Adorno's diatribes against jazz, Stravinsky, and Wagner make him sound like a Plato for late capitalism. Dark as this vision may appear, though, it is tempered in Adorno's work by a unflagging utopian strain, which also has roots in the affective depths of the body. When Adorno writes that "all music, with its first note, promises that which is different," he situates utopian promise in an experience that is too fast ("from its first note") for elaborate conceptual mediation, even if Adorno regards this promissory experience as always conditioned by past mediations, and always subject to mediations yet to come. In this passage and elsewhere, Adorno construes music as the site of a powerful affective intensity, which can attest that the world might change, profoundly, and for the better. Such moments in Adorno's work can strongly recall, and can be read in tandem with, the utopian philosophy of Ernst Bloch, who also wrote extensively on music, but with less of the animus against modern forms of music that directly appealed to affect, even in its most visceral, less cerebral, and more resonant forms. Finally, between Jameson's vision of nineteenth-century modernist affect in Wagner and Adorno's diagnosis of musical mimesis and feeling in the twentieth century, it is possible again to find traces of a sonic affective regime, as both writers examine the ways in which music registers and conditions the experience of affect in relation to power and hope.

THE VIBRATORY FORCE OF SOUND: SOUND STUDIES

The fourth moment we consider is the field of sound studies, which emerged around the turn of the millennium. Like affect studies itself, sound studies is an inherently interdisciplinary field, and its focus on sound as a topic of scholarly attention has parallels in other areas of research. This focus has been understood as both a corrective to the visualism and textualism in Western thought generally and as a result of the new sound technologies of the latter half of the twentieth century. The early history of sound studies is centered around three foundational texts from the 1970s by Don Ihde (one of the authors in this volume), R. Murray Shafer, and Jacques Attali.[43] These studies focused on sound and music, taking up issues of sonic experience, sounding environments, and sound as a reflection of social structures. Listening as a mode of sensory engagement with the world also became a central topic, one that is crucial in the era of new sound technologies, which change all aspects of listening—when, what, how, where, and so on. As Ihde pointed out in 1976, "By living with electronic instruments our experience of listening itself is being transformed."[44] The emergence of sound studies as a recognized field is often marked by the publication of Emily Thompson's *Soundscapes of Modernity* in 2002 and Jonathan Sterne's *The Audible Past* in 2003.[45] Here we briefly introduce three recent writings that address how sound operates in the affective domain in order both to exemplify differing approaches and to set up essays in this collection.[46]

In her *Music in Everyday Life* (2000), Tia DeNora takes up the question of how people "mobilize music as a resource of producing the scenes, routines, assumptions and occasions that constitute 'social life.'"[47] In conceptualizing the "power" of music in everyday life, DeNora focuses on musical sound as a force that operates in the generation of affective meaning. She argues that "musical affect" results from "'human-music interaction'"—in other words, that it is constituted "reflexively in and through the practice of articulating or connecting music with other things."[48] Although DeNora understands the force of musical experience as a complex, nondeterministic, and contingent relation between sound and human, she also recognizes the physicality of music's vibratory force, maintaining that music "enable[s] different relocations and levels of awareness, heightening and suppressing bodily energies and capacities, modes of attention and feeling."[49]

Building explicitly on affect theory from Brian Massumi and from Gilles Deleuze and Félix Guattari, Steve Goodman addresses the "acoustic violence of vibration" in *Sonic Warfare: Sound, Affect, and the Ecology of Fear* (2010). He traces how sonic vibrations are deployed not only to impact people, including their "individualized, subjective, personal emotions" and their "collective moods," but also the "structure of the built environment ... connect[ing] every separate entity in the cosmos, organic or nonorganic."[50] Goodman addresses a wide array of historical and fictional events, interlaced with philosophical accounts of sound, across thirty-four chapters. These range from how U.S. soldiers in World War II simulated the sounds of troops to fool the enemy about both the whereabouts and the size of their forces (chapter 7), to the use of infrasound in movies, below the threshold of hearing, to induce nausea and fear (chapter 12), to the use of capitalist sonic branding to "modulate the auditory nervous system through contagious vibration" (chap. 27).[51]

In "Sensing Voice: Materiality and the Lived Body in Singing and Listening" (2011), Nina Eidsheim considers the underwater operatic project of Juliana Snapper with respect to the "body's physical relationship with sound."⁵² Because sound waves travel more quickly through water than through air, the experience of both singing and listening in water differs significantly from the same experience in air. As Eidsheim points out, the human eardrum does not register most sounds when submerged in water, but the sound vibrations are registered by skull bones, and hence the "sound resonates in the body, going directly to the inner ear."⁵³ From this observation about how the physical circumstances of musical experience play a central role in the qualitative features of sound, Eidsheim argues that music itself should be considered as a "triangulation of events": "sonic vibrations . . . , our bodies' encultured capacity to receive these vibrations, and how we have been taught to understand them."⁵⁴

These three authors—DeNora, Goodman, and Eidsheim—treat sound and affect from differing perspectives, but each addresses sound as a bodily presence whose significance arises from the reflexive relations among vibrations, cultures, and subjectivities, thus exemplifying what we call genealogies of "sonic affective regimes." They give a taste of differing approaches, among the several that have emerged over the last several years. And they provide a sampling of work in music and sound studies that overlaps historically with a broader affective turn across the humanities.

Concepts and Debates

The turn to affect since World War II was a slow revolution, emerging from a scholarly investment in "the body" across the humanities, social sciences, and biological sciences. It must be underscored that fertile ground was cultivated by the work of early twentieth-century phenomenologists, above all Eugen Fink, Edmund Husserl, Martin Heidegger, Jean-Paul Sartre, Maurice Merleau-Ponty, and Simone de Beauvoir, to mention a few. Some of this work was taken up by philosophical anthropologists, such as Arnold Gehlen, Helmut Plessner, Karl-Otto Apel, and the young Jürgen Habermas, who focused on the distinct characteristic of the human body, its expression of emotion, and its cognitivist interests in coping with the world. Arguably, the more recent affective turn in the humanities is a belated response to the work on body, affect, and emotive expression that was pioneered by earlier phenomenologists.⁵⁵

Central to the debates developed in these literatures is a seemingly simple question of terminology—for example, affect, emotion, passions, feeling—as well as the question of what kinds of phenomena these terms designate. While some scholars insist on hard distinctions between these terms and their referents, others maintain an essential ambiguity. Further, philosophers and historians who consider earlier uses of these terms and others—for example, the appetites, agitations, affections, and sentiments—sometimes argue that these terminological distinctions refer to deep cognitive and conceptual distinctions, claiming that, for instance, passions and emotions are distinct phenomena, where in one case the subject is passive and in the other active. We use the term the "sonic affective regime" to refer to the broad array of phenomena referenced in both historical and more recent writings. This allows us to recognize what might be described as Wittgensteinian family resemblances among these terms and emotive phenomena, but also to allow the distinctions between them to emerge. This introduction to the concepts and debates about the affective domain is not meant to be exhaustive; instead, we hope to provide a framework of ideas that will orient the essays in this collection.

LANDMARKS

In the humanities, work in feminist theory, queer theory, cultural studies, and philosophy set the stage for this focus on the body and its relation to social structures. Likewise, in the social-physical sciences, the emergent fields of cognitive science and neuroscience approached the body from materialist perspectives while maintaining a sense of the relations between the body its social environment. Brief thumbnails of three works can serve here as landmarks for delineating a map of the primary concepts and debates in the affect theory of the present. One is Eve Kosofsky Sedgwick and Adam Frank's 1995 article, "Shame in the Cybernetic Fold: Reading Silvan Tomkins," in which the authors turn to a theory of affect promoted by the psychologist Silvan Tomkins.[56] Arguing against social constructionist theories of affect employed by literary scholars, Sedgwick and Frank adopt Tomkins's bodily/materialist perspective on affect. According to Tomkins, there are a fixed number of affects, which are rooted in the physiology of the body and which arise in response to external stimuli along a polarity of shame and interest. These affects, Tomkins believes, operate prior to or beneath consciousness. Also appearing in 1995, Brian Massumi's "The Autonomy of Affect" builds upon the philosophy of Gilles Deleuze, who develops a concept of affect from his reading of two other philosophers, Baruch Spinoza (1632–1677) and Henri Bergson (1859–1941).[57] For Massumi, affect is an intensity of the body, which conditions behavior. Massumi also locates affect prior to consciousness, and he makes a hard distinction between emotions and affects, emotions being a "subjective" and "socio-linguistic fixing of the quality of an experience ...," whereas affects are "unqualified"; they are "not ownable or recognizable," and as such, they are "resistant to critique."[58] Another landmark text on affect from this period is Antonio Damasio's 1994 *Descartes' Error: Emotion, Reason, and the Human Brain*.[59] Characterizing his work as the conjoining of neuroscience and psychology, Damasio argues that emotions play a central role in human rationality. For Damasio, "high reason" is a conscious activity of the higher brain centers that involves a logic-based cost-benefit analysis. This rational, conscious mind is affected, however, by the operation of the innate "primary emotions," which are hardwired into the brain's limbic system. It is the job of "somatic markers" to link the primary emotions, through the feelings of secondary emotions, to the high-reason deliberations of the conscious mind. Each of these landmark works promotes the idea of a system of bodily intensities that, although they play a determinative role in human behavior, operate outside of human consciousness. These intensities are variously referred to as emotions, feelings, passions, or affects by these authors and others, while some maintain a distinction between emotions and affect. Perhaps the most significant debates within affect theory nowadays revolve around the issues that underlie this distinction.

Throughout the "turn to affect" exemplified in these studies, one may note interdisciplinary or even multidisciplinary strands. Sedgwick and Frank read the work of Tomkins as a basis for approaching affect in literary studies. Massumi builds his approach to affect from the work of three well-known philosophers—Spinoza, Bergson, and Deleuze—and relies on existing psychological research for case studies. Damasio not only alludes to Descartes but uses neuropsychology to take on fundamental philosophical questions about truth, logic, and consciousness. It is also possible to discern, as Gross and Dixon point out (see page 20), a transition from thought in philosophy dealing with passions and affections to thought in psychology dealing with emotions and affects. Indeed, questions about the nexus of ideas regarding the body and mind have often circled around to phenomena related to *feelings* of bodies and minds. In a sense, the "turn to affect" of the recent past may be understood as a reconceptualizing of phenomena that have long vexed and fascinated writers in a wide range of disciplines, arguably since Plato berated the poets in his *Politeia* and Aristotle aimed to develop, and redeem, a philosophy of affect in his *Poetics*, *Rhetoric*, and *Politics*.

In addition to these major interventions from the end of the twentieth century, numerous writers have developed various forms of historical inquiry into affect and emotion. Rob Boddice has argued insightfully that the practice of doing historical work has always been invested in the affective. To write history, he claims, is not only to narrate the past, but also to aim to inculcate a certain affect about what has transpired.[60] Other writers have worked to track the transformations in notions of affect and emotion across long historical arcs. Amélie Oksenberg Rorty, for example, has shown how changes in the concepts and examples of the passions have proven central to philosophical accounts of the "mind and its powers" in the history of European philosophy.[61] She notes that "from Descartes to Rousseau, the mind changed."[62] Across this period, she argues, the "emotions ... cease[d] to be merely turbulent commotions: among them appear sentiments, ways of feeling pleasures and pains as evaluations, and so as the proper guides to action."[63] Making a somewhat different but equally historicizing move, Daniel M. Gross has argued that the largely political rhetoric of the passions in the seventeenth century was transformed into an "implicit epistemology" in the eighteenth-century.[64] Or, more colorfully, Gross writes that across this historical transition, "emotions that were once treated by everybody as externalized forms of currency and world investments [were] sucked, as it were, into the brain."[65] As Gross suggests, modern approaches to emotions have located them in the brain and by extension in the body, in opposition to earlier political and/or economic concepts of the passions. Thomas Dixon similarly traces the conceptual change from passions to emotions in the late eighteenth and early nineteenth centuries.[66] He argues that this transformation involved not simply a change of terminology but the creation of a new category of psychological thought. As Dixon observes, by the middle of the nineteenth century emotions were set up as categories of "morally disengaged, bodily, non-cognitive and involuntary feelings," as opposed to pre-nineteenth-century notions captured by such terms as "passions," "affections," "sentiments," and "appetites."[67] These earlier notions, he argues, involved the "movements or actions of a will or self" and were embedded in theological concepts of the soul.[68]

Several recent studies relate contemporaneous thinking about emotion and affect to longer historical trajectories, creating snapshots of recent thought on affect and how we got here. In *The History of Emotions*, the historian Jan Plamper addresses the question "what is an emotion?" in part by noting the conceptual slippage between emotion and affect from Charles Darwin's references in 1872 to Massumi's in 2002.⁶⁹ Suggesting that Darwin and Massumi, as well as others, may not even be referring to the same phenomena, Plamper points out the essential dilemma of a history of emotion—an inquiry in which terms and objects shift dizzyingly. Plamper does, however, show that since the late nineteenth century, it is possible to locate research in one of two poles: hard versus soft, essentialist versus antiessentialist, determinist versus antideterminist, universalism versus social constructivism—all of which can be mapped in various ways onto nature versus culture. In their *What Is the History of Emotions?* (2018), Barbara H. Rosenwein and Riccardo Cristiani cover several centuries of how different affects have been demoted or promoted to the status of emotions. They, too, ask what it means to do the history of emotions, and their inquiry is oriented especially around the question of what the future holds in store, given the rise of new modes of sociality and new technological mediations (video games, chat rooms, and obviously, social media).⁷⁰

In *The Ascent of Affect: Genealogy and Critique* (2017), the historian of science Ruth Leys gives a genealogical account of thought about the emotions since World War II, mostly from the perspectives of psychology.⁷¹ She demonstrates how research during the period toggled between the cognitivists' and the noncognitivists' approaches, both sides including psychologists and philosophers. The cognitivists argue that emotions are intentional and shaped by contexts of understanding, while the noncognitivists claim that there are basic, hardwired emotions triggered by sensations operating at subpersonal levels in the body. As Leys shows, the cognitivists have "trouble accommodating the existence of emotions in nonhuman animals (or in infants before they acquire language)," and the noncognitivists "have difficulty explaining how it is that emotions have meaning."⁷² While Leys devotes most of her book to a review of debates about emotion in psychology and philosophy, and their intersection (including the work of Damasio), she also takes up the question of the "turn to affect" initiated by such authors as Sedgwick and Frank and Massumi. She shows that the affective systems they propose are closely linked with the work of the noncognitivist emotion researchers, especially through their reliance on autonomic corporeal processes (conceived either as emotions or as affects). It is worth noting that both Leys and Plamper trace polarizations in emotion research as universal versus social constructionist or cognitive versus noncognitive, polarizations that themselves resonate with mind/body distinctions. More recently, the long history of philosophical thought about the affective domain has received increased attention with two essay collections: *The Oxford Handbook of Philosophy of Emotion*, edited by Peter Goldie (2010), and *Thinking About the Emotions: a Philosophical History*, edited by Alix Cohen and Robert Stern (2017), the latter an "overview of the history of the philosophy of the emotions."[73]

COORDINATES OF RECENT WORK

A brief sampling of authors who have contributed to the affective turn since the middle years of the twentieth century demonstrates the breadth of this turn and the variety of interventions that have been made. As is demonstrated by the very titles of articles and books, there is no terminological consensus: the specific meanings of feeling, emotion, and affect continue to arise from their contexts. The conceptual openness for this domain of experience — what we call the affective domain — is not unique to work in the current turn to affect in the humanities; rather, it speaks to the centrality and richness of this domain across great swaths of intellectual history. Along with this conceptual openness, we may also note that, when the affective domain is taken up, disciplinary boundaries become wonderfully porous. In this sampling, we make no attempt to demonstrate how affect, emotion, or feeling plays a role in any particular disciplinary context. Rather, we provide a few additional landmarks illustrating the turns and even zigzags within affect studies, which are supplemented by the present collection of essays on the sonic. Raymond Williams's "Structures of Feeling," a chapter in his 1977 *Marxism and Literature*, has served as an early model for cultural approaches to affect.[74] For Williams, the styles of "manners, dress, building, and other similar forms of social life" are not "epiphenomena[a]"; rather, they are indicative of structures of feeling that "exert palpable pressures and set effective limits on experience and action."[75] Similarly focused on affective experiences of the everyday, Kathleen Stewart's *Ordinary Affects* (2007) takes account of "public feelings" that inhabit social and personal experiences, with the goal of painting the picture of an "emergent present." For Stewart, affects circulate through the "practices and practical knowledges" of the ordinary, bestowing the specific and changing quality of public and intimate experience.[76]

Sara Ahmed's *The Cultural Politics of Emotions* (2004) similarly takes up questions of the social circulation of emotions. Asking what "emotions do" rather than what "emotions are," Ahmed conceives them as the "effects" arising from specific encounters or situations. These emotion effects then circulate amongst things in the world, establishing an "affective economy," produced as the "effects of circulation."[77] Already in 1983, Arlie Russell Hochschild's *The Managed Heart: Commercializa-*

tion of Human Feeling argued that feelings are social and cultural practices and that management of these feelings has capitalist economic benefits.[78] This turn toward the capitalization of emotion is also thematic in Michael Hardt's "Affective Labors" (1999).[79] Building on the work of various feminist authors investigating what was deemed "labor in the bodily mode," Hardt demonstrates the dominant role of "affective immaterial labor ... in the production of capital."[80]

Scholars in the fields of feminist and queer studies have been central contributors to the late twentieth- and early twenty-first-century turn to affect. After encountering the work of Tomkins (as discussed above), Sedgwick published *Touching Feeling: Affect Pedagogy Performativity* (2003), a collection of essays exploring how affects "attach to things, people, ideas, sensations, relations, activities, ambitions, institutions, and any number of other things." This is a wide-ranging collection that, in refusing "to become linear," plays out Sedgwick's thoughtful feelings as she encountered the circumstances of breast cancer.[81] The topics of the essays vary from the performativity of shame in the writing of Henry James, to the reparative undercurrents of "paranoid readings" of critical theory, to thought about the pedagogies of life and death in Buddhist practice. Working through her reading of Tomkins, Sedgwick reflects on the differing sorts of affective experiences that populate one's life.

Lauren Berlant's work similarly addresses cultural issues, with a focus on life in the United States since the nineteenth century. In a series of books tracing the roles of affect in social events, literature, and popular culture, Berlant demonstrates how matters of intimate life of the individual have become public vehicles of citizenship and national identity. In The *Queen of America Goes to Washington City: Essays on Sex and Citizenship* (1997), Berlant introduces the concept of the "intimate public sphere" while tracing the uncanny similarities between the cases of Harriet Jacobs in the nineteenth century and Anita Hill in the late twentieth century.[82] In Jacobs's 1861 autobiographical narrative of her life as a freed slave, and in Anita Hill's testimony to the U.S. Senate in 1991, the "claims for justice against racism and claims for justice against both patriarchal and heterosexual privileges were made to compete with each other." As Berlant argues, these cases reveal the "unsettled and unsettling relations of sexuality and American citizenship—two complexly related sites of subjectivity, sensation, affect, law, and agency."[83] In *Cruel Optimism* (2011), Berlant addresses the "affective structure of an optimistic attachment," such as the optimism attached to fantasies of the "good life" in some situation comedies. Addressing issues of precarity in the neoliberalism of late capitalism, these situation comedies hold open the possibility of the "good life," allowing viewers to sustain and feel the fantasy of a better life.[84]

Negative affects of trauma, guilt, and shame, or affects associated with the bodily outcomes of violence in various forms, have been the focus of several important studies in response to, for instance, wars in the twentieth and twenty-first centuries, the Holocaust, the AIDS epidemic, and 9/11. Like other affect studies, these incorporate a range of disciplines, from psychiatry and medicine to cinema and literature. Ruth Leys's *Trauma: A Genealogy* (2000) and *From Guilt to Shame: Auschwitz and After* (2007) trace the historical changes in concepts of trauma, guilt, and shame over the twentieth and twenty-first centuries, demonstrating that the concepts are unstable and respond to social and theoretical pressures. For instance, in the years since the end of World War II, concepts of "survivor guilt" as felt by Holocaust survivors have been replaced by concepts of "shame," marking a shift from an "intentionalist or cognitivist paradigm" to one of an "anti-intentionalist" mode of being.[85] Similarly, Daniel Gross argues for a historically informed and methodologically diverse approach in *Uncomfortable Situations: Emotion between Science and the Humanities* (2017).[86] Arguing against an unnecessary dualism in the debate over universalist versus social constructionist accounts of the affective domain, Gross articulates a "phenomenology of emotion" in which he, like Ahmed, understands emotion as transactional. Building on Aristotle's *Rhetoric* and combining it with insights from recent scientific work in situated cognition, Gross develops a "rhetoric of emotion" organized around seven relationship types.[87]

Sianne Ngai's masterful *Ugly Feeling* (2005) traces another dimension of negative affects in a work that is as much transatlantic in its archives as it is interdisciplinary in the uses it makes of different texts — not just novels and works of theory, but also movies and television series. Ngai describes her text as a "bestiary of affects."[88] It is a most apt description, for a bestiary brings together not just "noble" but also "ignoble," endearing but also terrifying, beasts. And the emotions are not only, or always, pleasant; they are just as often terrifying and revolting. Her investigation locates itself at the intersections of aesthetics and politics in order to unfurl a series of studies on negative emotions and their political use and misuse, emotions such as envy, anxiety, paranoia, and irritation, as well as a set of emotions, one that she labels "animatedness" (a distinct form of racialized affect), and the other "stuplimity" (a combination of shock and boredom). In this way, Ngai offers us a vocabulary with which to wade through the tonalities of affect that reverberate in "ugly" ways throughout our public world, with its comforting sounds but also with the abject sounds of pseudo-populist demagogues with their doublespeak and grade school–level diction and grammar.

Finally, Martha Nussbaum's work combines historical and philosophical perspectives in order to analyze the role of affect in ethical and political life. Nussbaum's *The Fragility of Goodness* (1986) mined the thought of ancient Greek philosophers and literary writers on matters concerning the well-being of individuals and the "role of emotions" in ethics.[89] In a later work, *Upheavals of Thought: The Intelligence of Emotions* (2001), Nussbaum argues more directly that emotions are "part and parcel of the system of ethical reasoning."[90] Building on ideas from Greek Stoic philosophy, she develops a cognitivist model of the emotions, claiming that "emotions are appraisals or value judgments."[91] In some of her more recent work, Nussbaum has turned to what she calls "political emotions," namely the way in which affect informs or misinforms the political realm. Emotions may be cognitive, she argues, but they also have political efficacy.[92]

This brief sampling of the concepts and debates of recent ventures into affect theory makes no claims to comprehensiveness, but it does suggest the range of thought that has informed the essays of this collection. These essays make specific incursions into how sonic affective regimes have operated not only in the historical past but also in the present.

Chapter Summaries

The essays collected in this volume vary widely, in ways that reflect the extreme diversity among conceptions of affect, passion, emotion, and feeling, both historically and within contemporary affect theory. Part 1, "Sounding the Political," includes essays by Robin James and Adam Knowles. James's "Waves of Moderation: The Sound of Sophrosyne in Ancient Greek and Neoliberal Times" (originally one of the keynote lectures at the conference on which this volume is based) argues that, as neoliberalism takes the market as a universal model for all thought, life, and experience, it produces an imperative for a kind of "moderation" or "self-mastery," which echoes the Platonic notion of sophrosyne. Through analyses of Platonic treatments of harmony, the logics of neoliberalism, and Ludacris's "The Rest of My Life," James shows how this neoliberal self-mastery takes sound and music as sites where the cost/benefit calculations of the market can be "translated into nonpropositional form . . . at the level of affect." Knowles's "The Politics of Silence: Heidegger's *Black Notebooks*" argues that silence provides the "weft and warp" of Heidegger's infamous notebooks. Though the reception of these texts, published only in 2014, has been dominated by their odious politics and anti-Semitism, Knowles insists that they cannot be read only as a moment of Heidegger's biography. Instead, he interprets them as a crucial moment in Heidegger's "sigetics," or interrogation of silence, and reconstructs ways in which the *Black Notebooks*, with all their profoundly disturbing moments and themes, are indispensable in reading Heidegger's thought writ large, especially his understanding of language and politics.

Part 2, "Affect/Human/Music," includes essays by Gary Tomlinson, Don Ihde, and James Currie. Tomlinson's essay, "Sign, Affect, and Musicking before the Human," which grew out of another of the keynotes at the original conference, is rooted in his recent work tracing the emergence of music across vast evolutionary time scales. Tomlinson leverages research in biosemiotics in order to intervene in debates about music and affect. The production of meaning, he argues, is neither limited to human life and language, nor entirely distinct from the intensities of feeling that are the principal theme of much affect theory; instead, Tomlinson shows how a biosemiotic analysis extending well beyond the human can illuminate entwinements of feeling and signification that remain crucial in modern musicking. Ihde's "Human Beginnings and Music: Technology and Embodiment Roles" takes up a deep evolutionary perspective not distant from Tomlinson's, sketching an overview of the technologies used in human musicking from the earliest bone flutes to the present day, and offering speculations on the first emergence of musicking among our prehuman ancestors. From a deconstructive close reading of Daniel Barenboim's 2006 BBC Reith Lectures, Currie's "The Life and Death of Daniel Barenboim" weaves a meditation on music, life, affect, and professionalism. Music, Barenboim contends, can offer models for, and even lessons on how to lead, a certain kind of life. Currie brings this thought into dialogue with contemporary Deleuzian affect theory (especially via Elizabeth Grosz) and asks what kind of life this would be, what kind of person would live it, and what impact profession and discipline (not least the professions of music studies) might have upon it.

Part 3, "Voicings and Silencings," includes essays by Eduardo Mendieta and Michael Birenbaum Quintero. Mendieta's "The Philosopher's Voice: The Prosody of Logos" calls for a philosophy of language that is materialized on the level of the voice, all the way down to its embodied accents. Through readings that range from Homer through Rousseau and Derrida to Habermas, Mendieta theorizes vocal accent, with all its affective overtones, as a "bodily hexis" that always accompanies and conditions logos. In "Late Capitalism, Affect, and the Algorithmic Self in Music Streaming Platforms," Birenbaum Quintero considers how streaming services in the twenty-first century, with their reliance on algorithms to both discern and replicate listener's taste preferences, have the potential to shape new musical subjectivities in the twenty-first century. He counters the hard distinction between affect and emotion (as posed by Massumi), looking instead for the productive relation between them "to examine culturally and historically specific processes of entrainment of emotion, perception, and self-conceptualization." Reading both Theodor Adorno and Tia DeNora from the historical perspectives of their implicit accounts of affect and emotion, Birnbaum Quintero shows how Adorno claims a "jazz subject" who "choose[s] popular music as a kind of explanatory mechanism" for the current moment, and how DeNora claims that music allows for a sonic "self-identity" in which music "qualifies affective experience." Further, Birenbaum Quintero demonstrates that the positions of Adorno and DeNora are both historically situated by the mode of listener access to the musical sound that was prevalent when they wrote. Reflecting on the present affective moment, Birenbaum Quintero shows that new streaming-service algorithms based on listener taste basically remove choice as an element of freedom, relying on algorithms that reaffirm identities and listener taste.

Part 4, "Affective Listenings," includes essays by Martin Scherzinger and Christopher Haworth. Haworth's "Musical Affect, Autobiographical Memory, and Collective Individuation in Thomas Bernhard's *Correction*" reads Bernhard's novel alongside the music of Phil Collins and films by Robert Altman, all with an eye to contemporary music studies' thematization of affect. Echoing Tomlinson, Haworth traces a formulation of affect that is not strictly autonomous from subjectivity or semiosis; instead, he sees affect entangled with the formation of identities and sense, especially on a transpersonal, social level that he follows Gilbert Simondon in calling "collective individuation." Scherzinger's "Music, Labor, and Technologies of Desire" speculatively and critically diagnoses new forms of labor, affect, and technology that have taken shape in recent decades, arguing that musical practices are at once historical precursors of current mutations across these domains, key players in the crystallization of their new contemporary forms, and sites where their new shapes may be may be discerned and critiqued today. In particular, Scherzinger is keenly critical of ways in which the indeterminacy of affect, along with the kinds of connection that such open affective experience can facilitate, might now fall prey to new forms of harvesting, extraction, and exploitation, which were unforeseen in earlier affect theory and in some musicological literature that valorized affective and emotional experience. Writing with an eye to recent developments at intersections of machine learning, advertising, and cognitive science, Scherzinger cautions that, "left unsupervised on account of its inarticulate nonsignifying intensity, affective arousal stands to be colonized by all manner of militarized adaptation, just as interactive instincts stand to be colonized by all manner of industrial interpellation."

Part 5, "Temporalities of Sounding," includes essays by Lorenzo Simpson, Jessica Wiskus, and Ryan Dohoney. In his "The 'Sound' of Music: Sonic Agency and the Dialectic of Freedom and Constraint in Jazz Improvisation," Simpson investigates timbre and freedom in jazz, focusing especially on the ways in which what he calls "the fitting response" in jazz improvisation can both echo and model ethical action in life outside music. Wiskus's "Merleau-Ponty on Consciousness and Affect through the Temporal Movement of Music" shows how music comes to exemplify crucial themes in Maurice Merleau-Ponty's late work. She argues that, as Merleau-Ponty reads Proust's description of musical experience in *À la recherche du temps perdu*, he shows how music can demonstrate with special vividness the ways in which expression, creativity, and affect arise from a separation (*écart*) and negativity that are at the heart of time-consciousness. Like Tomlinson's and Haworth's essays, Dohoney's "A. N. Whitehead, Feeling, and Music: On Some Potential Modifications to Affect Theory" proposes a picture of affect that differs in crucial ways from the Deleuzian account presented by Massumi. By reading Whitehead's philosophy—and especially in his rarely studied reflections on music—alongside Eric Wubbels's Viola Quartet, Dohoney reconstructs a conception of affect, not as an intensity radically autonomous from subjectivity, but rather as "relational evidence for the processes of subject formation itself."

Finally, part 6, "Theorizing the Affections," turns to the seventeenth- and eighteenth-century precursors of the contemporary turn to affect in the humanities writ large, and in music studies in particular. This section includes essays by André Redwood, Daniel Villegas Vélez, Emily Wilbourne, and Tomas McAuley. In "Delivering Affect: Mersenne, Voice, and the Background of Jesuit Rhetorical Theory," Redwood studies the ways in which Mersenne's fascination with a mechanistic picture of the physical world powerfully (but incompletely) shaped his understanding of the voice, its power to move the affections, and the mobilization of this power in rhetoric. Villegas Vélez's "Mimesis and the Affective Ground of Baroque Representation" mobilizes contemporary affect theory à la Deleuze and Massumi in order to address a historiographical problem—namely, how it might be possible to understand Athanasius Kircher's 1650 *Musurgia Universalis*, and especially the constructions of musical affect that it presents, as belonging at once to what Foucault has called the Renaissance and classical epistemes, epochs of thought that, in Foucault's work, are conceived as sharply discontinuous and distinct. With an eye to contemporary affect theory, Villegas Vélez suggests that "the epistemic problem of situating the *Musurgia* can be productively addressed by approaching it as an ontological one." Wilbourne's "Affect and the Recording Devices of Seventeenth-Century Italy" studies the relationship between two kinds of affect in mid-seventeenth-century Venetian opera—affect as an emotional state, and affect in the sense of the *affeti*, or conventional vocal ornaments used often in the music of this period. Following Monique Scheer and Pierre Bourdieu, Wilbourne theorizes the *affeti* as a form of recording technology, a means by which affect might be inscribed, catalyzed, disseminated, and consumed. McAuley's "Immanuel Kant and the Downfall of the *Affektenlehre*" ends the collection by asking about the end of the musical doctrine of affects around the close of the eighteenth century. In Kant's *Critique of the Power of Judgment*—and especially in the new emphases on cognition, disinterestedness, and freedom that it introduced to aesthetics—McAuley locates an epochal shift, in the wake of which early notions of musical affect could no longer be valued as they had been before. As McAuley notes, though, and as the studies gathered here continue to attest, this "may have been the end of the *Affektenlehre* ... but that does not mean that it was the end of affect."

Notes

1. Full bibliographic information on these foundational figures in affect studies may be found in the bibliography of this essay collection.
2. Full bibliographic information on these foundational figures in sound studies may be found in the bibliography of this essay collection.
3. Plato, *Republic*, trans. C. D. C. Reeve (Indianapolis, IN: Hackett, 2004), 84.
4. Ibid., 83. Here "naiveté" translates the term *euêtheia*, which can also be translated as "good ethical disposition."
5. Aristotle, *Poetics and Rhetoric*, trans. S. H. Butcher and W. Rhys Roberts, introd. and notes Eugene Garvey (New York: Barnes & Noble Classics, 2005), 17.
6. Aristotle, *Aristotle's Politics*, trans. and with an introduction, notes, and glossary by Carnes Lord, 2nd ed. (Chicago: University of Chicago Press, 2013), 232.
7. Ibid., 235–36.
8. Descartes, *Compendium musicae*, quoted and translated in Claude Palisca, *Music and Ideas in the Sixteenth and Seventeenth Centuries*, Studies in the History of Music Theory and Literature 1 (Urbana: University of Illinois Press, 2006), 302.

9. Palisca, *Music and Ideas*; Penelope Gouk, *Music, Science, and Natural Magic in Seventeenth-Century England* (New Haven, CT: Yale University Press, 1999); and Gary Tomlinson, *Music in Renaissance Magic: Toward a Historiography of Others* (Chicago: University of Chicago Press, 1993).

10. Palisca gives a good summary of the Renaissance distinctions of such terms as "passions," "affections," "spirits," "humors," and "temperaments," considering their origins and issues of translation with respect to thought about music. See Palisca, *Music and Ideas*, 291–92.

11. Tomlinson, *Music in Renaissance Magic*, 84–85.

12. Ficino, *Commentarium in Timaeium* in *Opera omnia*, 1453, trans. D. P. Walker in *Spiritual and Demonic Magic from Ficino to Companella*, 2nd ed. (Notre Dame, IN: University of Notre Dame Press, 1975), 8–9; quoted in Tomlinson, *Music in Renaissance Magic*, 111.

13. Tomlinson, *Music in Renaissance Magic*, 132.

14. Tomlinson's rich and complex argument about Ficino's musical magic is not directly focused on affect, but his account of Ficino and other Renaissance authors is illuminating for those interested in historical accounts of the affects and the passions. It is also worth noting that Ficino's thoughts about music and sound in particular were promoted by Heinrich Cornelius Agrippa in *De occulta philosophia* (1533).

15. Gouk, *Music, Science, and Natural Magic*, 226.

16. Gioseffo Zarlino, *Le institutioni harmoniche* (1558), quoted in Palisca, *Music and Ideas*, 296.

17. Gouk, *Music, Science, and Natural Magic*, 229.

18. See Thomas Dixon, *From Passions to Emotions: The Creation of a Secular Psychological Category* (Cambridge: Cambridge University Press, 2003).

19. Ibid., 22.

20. Larry M. Jorgensen, "Descartes on Music: Between the Ancients and the Aestheticians," *British Journal of Aesthetics* 52, no. 4 (2012): 407.

21. George J. Buelow, "Johann Mattheson and the Invention of the *Affektenlehre*," in *New Mattheson Studies*, ed. George J. Buelow and Hans Joachim Marx (Cambridge and New York: Cambridge University Press, 1983), 401.

22. Palisca views Mattheson's writings about the affections as outdated. See Palisca, *Music and Ideas*, 290. Both Palisca and Buelow point out that eighteenth-century composers and music theorists, including Mattheson, did not have an operative, fully worked out theory of *Affektenlehre*; rather, this concept was proposed by German musicologists writing in the early years of the twentieth century. Nonetheless, eighteenth-century theorists and composers did make associations between modes and specific affects.

23. Carl Dahlhaus, *Nineteenth-Century Music*, trans. J. Bradford Robinson (Berkeley and Los Angeles: University of California Press, 1989), 64.

24. Ibid.

25. Lauren Berlant, *Cruel Optimism* (Durham, NC: Duke University Press, 2011), 4.

26. G. W. F. Hegel, *Aesthetics: Lectures on Fine Arts*, trans. T. M. Knox (Oxford: Clarendon Press, 1975), 909.

27. Ibid., 935.

28. Wilhelm Heinrich Wackenroder, *Confessions and Fantasies*, trans. Mary Hurst Schubert (University Park: Pennsylvania State University Press, 1971), 180.

29. E. T. A. Hoffmann, *E. T. A Hoffmann's Musical Writings: Kreisleriana, The Poet and the Composer, Music Criticism*, trans. Martyn Clarke (Cambridge: Cambridge University Press, 1989), 98.

30. Eduard Hanslick, *On the Musically Beautiful: A Contribution towards the Revision of the Aesthetics of Music*, trans. and ed. Geoffrey Payzant (Indianapolis, IN: Hackett, 1986), 29.

31. Carl Dahlhaus, *The Idea of Absolute Music*, trans. Roger Lustig (Chicago: University of Chicago Press, 1989), 71.

32. Eduard Hanslick, *The Beautiful in Music: A Contribution to the Revisal of Musical Aesthetics*, trans. Gustav Cohen (London: Novello, 1891), 122.

33. Hanslick quotes Mattheson with disdain: "'A Couranto should convey hopefulness.' 'The Saraband has to express no other feeling than awe.' 'Voluptuousness reigns supreme in the Concerto grosso.'" Ibid., 55.

34. Ibid., 109.

35. G. W. F. Hegel, *Philosophy of Mind*, rev. and with an introduction by Michael Inwood, trans. W. Wallace and A. V. Miller (Oxford and New York: Oxford University Press, 2007).

36. Fredric Jameson, "Wagner as Dramatist and Allegorist," *Modernist Cultures* 8, no. 1 (2013): 18.

37. Richard Wagner, *Richard Wagner to Mathilde Wesendonck*, trans. William Ashton Ellis (New York: Charles Scribner's Sons, 1905), 184.

38. Jameson, "Wagner as Dramatist and Allegorist," 16.

39. Arthur Schopenhauer, *The World as Will and Representation*, trans. E. F. J. Payne (New York: Dover, 1969), 1:113, 146.

40. Ibid., 261.

41. Theodor Adorno, *Mahler: A Musical Physiognomy*, trans. Edmund Jephcott (Chicago: University of Chicago Press, 1992), 22.

42. Theodor Adorno, *Aesthetic Theory*, ed. Gretel Adorno and Rolf Tiedemann, trans. Robert Hullot-Kentor (New York: Continuum, 2002), 329.

43. Don Ihde, *Listening and Voice: Phenomenologies of Sound*, 2nd ed. (Albany, NY: State University of New York Press, 2007); R. Murray Schafer, *The Tuning of the World: A Pioneering Exploration into the Past History and Present State of the Most Neglected Aspect of Our Environment—the Environment*, 1st ed. (New York: A. A. Knopf, 1977); and Jacques Attali, *Bruits: Essai sur l'economie politique de la musique* (Paris: Presses Universitaires de France, 1977), trans. Brian Assumi as *Noise: The Political Economy of Music* (Minneapolis: University of Minnesota Press, 1985).

44. Ihde, *Listening and Voice*, 5.

45. Emily Thompson, *The Soundscape of Modernity: Architectural Acoustics and the Culture of Listening in America, 1900–1933* (Cambridge, MA: MIT Press, 2002); and Jonathan Sterne, *The Audible Past: Cultural Origins of Sound Reproduction* (Durham, NC: Duke University Press, 2003).

46. While we do not address it here, Marie Thompson and Ian Biddle, eds., *Sound, Music, Affect: Theorizing Sonic Experience* (New York: Bloomsbury Academic, 2013), should be acknowledged as an important predecessor to this volume.

47. Tia DeNora, *Music in Everyday Life* (Cambridge and New York: Cambridge University Press, 2000), xi.

48. Ibid., 33.

49. Ibid., 160.

50. Steve Goodman, *Sonic Warfare: Sound, Affect, and the Ecology of Fear* (Cambridge, MA: MIT Press, 2010), xiv.

51. Ibid., 147.

52. Nina Sun Eidsheim, "Sensing Voice: Materiality and the Lived Body in Singing and Listening," *Senses and Society* 6, no. 2 (2011): 135. Parts of this article appear in Eidsheim,

Sensing Sound: Singing and Listening as Vibrational Practice (Durham, NC: Duke University Press, 2015).

53. Eidsheim, "Sensing Voice," 147.

54. Ibid., 149.

55. See Donn Welton, ed., *The Body: Classic and Contemporary Readings* (Malden, MA: Blackwell, 1999).

56. Eve Kosofsky Sedgwick and Adam Frank, "Shame in the Cybernetic Fold: Reading Silvan Tomkins," *Critical Inquiry* 21, no. 2 (1995): 496–522. The primary work of Silvan Tomkins that Sedgwick and Frank read of is *Affect, Imagery, Consciousness*, 4 vols. (New York: Springer, 1962–92).

57. Brian Massumi, "The Autonomy of Affect," in "Politics of Systems and Environments, Part II," *Cultural Critique* 31 (Autumn 1995): 83–109. Massumi's article was subsequently included in his *Parables for the Virtual: Movement, Affect, Sensation* (Durham, NC: Duke University Press, 2002), 23–45.

58. Massumi, "The Autonomy of Affect," 88.

59. Antonio Damasio, *Descartes' Error: Emotion, Reason, and the Human Brain* (New York: G. P. Putnam's Sons, 1994).

60. Rob Boddice, *The History of Emotions* (Manchester: Manchester University Press, 2018).

61. Amélie Oksenberg Rorty, "From Passions to Emotions and Sentiments," *Philosophy* 57, no. 220 (1982): 161.

62. Ibid.

63. Ibid., 159. This shift in how emotions are considered integral to both knowledge and meaning is also tracked in Robert C. Solomon's still indispensable work *The Passions: Emotions and the Meaning of Life* (1976; Indianapolis, IN: Hackett, 1993).

64. Daniel M. Gross, *The Secret History of Emotion: From Aristotle's "Rhetoric" to Modern Brain Science* (Chicago: University of Chicago Press, 2006).

65. Ibid., 7–8.

66. Dixon, *From Passions to Emotions*.

67. Ibid., 3.

68. Ibid., 251.

69. Jan Plamper, *The History of Emotions: An Introduction*, trans. Keith Tribe (Oxford: Oxford University Press, 2015), 10–11.

70. Barbara H. Rosenwein and Riccardo Cristiani, *What Is the History of Emotions?* (Cambridge, UK, and Malden, MA: Polity Press, 2018).

71. Ruth Leys, *The Ascent of Affect: Genealogy and Critique* (Chicago: University of Chicago Press, 2017).

72. Ibid., 4.

73. Peter Goldie, ed., *The Oxford Handbook of Philosophy of Emotion* (Oxford and New York: Oxford University Press, 2010); and Alix Cohen and Robert Stern, eds., *Thinking about the Emotions: A Philosophical History* (Oxford: Oxford University Press, 2017), 2.

74. Raymond Williams, "Structures of Feeling," in *Marxism and Literature* (Oxford and New York: Oxford University Press, 1977), 128–35.

75. Ibid., 131–32.

76. Kathleen Stewart, *Ordinary Affects* (Durham, NC: Duke University Press, 2007), 1–2.

77. Sara Ahmed, *The Cultural Politics of Emotion* (2004; Edinburgh: Edinburgh University Press, 2014), 4, 8.

78. Arlie Russell Hochschild, *The Managed Heart: Commercialization of Human Feeling* (Berkeley and Los Angeles: University of California Press, 2012).

79. Michael Hardt, "Affective Labor," *boundary 2* 26, no. 2 (1999): 89–100.

80. Ibid., 96. Here Hardt is quoting Dorothy E. Smith, *The Everyday World as Problematic: A Feminist Sociology* (Boston: Northeastern University Press, 1987), 78–88.

81. Eve Kosofsky Sedgwick, *Touching Feeling: Affect, Pedagogy, Performativity* (Durham, NC: Duke University Press, 2003), 1. Sedgwick died of breast cancer in 2009.

82. Lauren Berlant, *The Queen of America Goes to Washington City: Essays on Sex and Citizenship* (Durham, NC: Duke University Press, 1997).

83. Ibid., 243.

84. Berlant, *Cruel Optimism*, 2.

85. Ruth Leys, *Trauma: A Genealogy* (Chicago: University of Chicago Press, 2000); and Leys, *From Guilt to Shame: Auschwitz and After* (Princeton, NJ: Princeton University Press, 2007); quotation in *From Guilt to Shame*, 11–12.

86. Daniel M. Gross, *Uncomfortable Situations: Emotion between Science and the Humanities* (Chicago: University of Chicago Press, 2017).

87. Ibid., 9–10.

88. Sianne Ngai, *Ugly Feelings*, 1st Harvard University Press paperback ed. (Cambridge, MA: Harvard University Press, 2005), 7.

89. Martha C. Nussbaum, *The Fragility of Goodness: Luck and Ethics in Greek Tragedy and Philosophy*, rev. ed. (1986; New York: Cambridge University Press, 2001).

90. Martha C. Nussbaum, *Upheavals of Thought: The Intelligence of Emotions* (Cambridge and New York: Cambridge University Press, 2001), 1.

91. Ibid., 4.

92. Martha C. Nussbaum, *Political Emotions: Why Love Matters for Justice* (Cambridge: Belknap Press, 2013); and Nussbaum, *Anger and Forgiveness: Resentment, Generosity, Justice* (New York: Oxford University Press, 2016).

PART 1

Sounding the Political

CHAPTER 1

Waves of Moderation

THE SOUND OF SOPHROSYNE IN ANCIENT GREEK AND NEOLIBERAL TIMES

Robin James

Postdemocra[cy] . . . is the perfect realization of the empty virtue Plato called **sophrosune***: the fact of each person's being in their place, going about their own business there, and having the opinion identical to the fact of being in that place and doing only what there is to do there.*[1]

The ear serves as the organ of balance, readily "making sense" of things and recognising resonances and proportions between the frequencies of sound waves—as with an octave, for example. The eye can make very accurate alignments, but has no way of telling the proportional relationships between the frequencies of light.[2]

Neoliberalism has a specific concept of the market, and it treats that idea of the market as the universalizable model for everything: parenting, the environment, even (biopolitical) "life" itself. As Jason Read explains, neoliberals like Gary Becker think that "everything for which human beings attempt to realize their ends, from marriage, to crime, to expenditures on children, can be understood 'economically' according to a particular calculation of cost for benefit."[3] This cost/benefit calculus is characteristic of a specific type of neoliberalism, one that uses probabilist math to predict future success and maintain market equilibrium. (This contrasts with the kinds of postprobabilist or "possibilist" neoliberalisms identified by scholars such as Lisa Adkins, Louise Amoore, and Melinda Cooper, which use different types of math and aim for market disequilibrium.)[4] But how does this probabilist concept of the market get translated into nonpropositional form, into a type of implicit knowledge, into a discourse or convention that works at the level of affect?

This is where "moderation" comes in. In the first epigraph, Jacques

Rancière claims that "postdemocracy" (his term for what I'm calling neoliberalism) — in particular, the sorts of statistics and forecasting used in opinion polls — is a postmillennial inflection of Platonic sophrosyne. *Sophrosyne* is a term from ancient Greek that generally is rendered as "moderation" or "self-mastery." Cost/benefit calculus is a kind of moderation, a historically and technologically specific type of moderation that updates ancient Greek concepts of moderation or sophrosyne to accord with the kind of probabilist, Gaussian math used by twenty-first-century economists and statisticians. Though it worked primarily as an ethical and political concept, some ancient Greek philosophers — including Plato — grounded their notions of sophrosyne in then-current notions of musical harmony as geometric proportion. Moderation brought your existence into proper proportion, such as the proportions illustrated in the *Republic* by the myth of the metals (gold:silver:bronze) or the theory of the divided line (visible:intelligible). Geometry was the most advanced mathematics available to Plato, Pythagoras, and other ancient Greek thinkers, but it's obviously not the math people in the twenty-first century use to think about either economics or acoustics. Like Plato, we still think about sounds and society in terms of ratios — but instead of using geometry to determine proportionality, we use statistics to calculate frequencies and probabilities. Updating the science behind our concept of sophrosyne to reflect contemporary mathematics and acoustics, I argue that sophrosyne can help us understand how the neoliberal market works politically and ethically, especially at the level of affect. As was the case for Plato, neoliberal sophrosyne is still a kind of self-relation, and more specifically a type of self-mastery, which is modeled on musical harmony. Neoliberal market logics, in particular, *Homo economicus*'s cost-benefit calculus, are embodied as a type of affective self-relation modeled on *sound waves*. The neoliberal version of sophrosyne, additionally, belongs to what I called elsewhere the "sonic episteme."[5] Thus, just as Plato's notion of sophrosyne was implicated in an episteme that established relations between proportion and ratio so as to project a hierarchy of subordination, neoliberal sophrosyne envelops social agents in an acoustic chamber that also establishes an order of subordination and domination, but one based on statistical and probabilistic distributions. Like Plato's *polis*, neoliberal biopolitical governmentality has its rhythm and acoustic resonance (that is, it sounds both a frequency and oscillating pattern of varying intensity).

Acoustic harmony is a relationship among sound waves: frequencies (harmonics and partials) emerge from the interaction of other frequencies; signal emerges from noise. In order to have signal, there must be noise. Unlike in modernity, in which noise is destabilizing, in probabilist neoliberalism noise (or, in more market-oriented terms, risk) is beneficial—up to a point: the wrong quantity or quality could impede the emergence of healthy, successful signal. Similarly, as Jonathan Sterne has shown, over the course of the twentieth century audio engineers and architects came to understand noise as beneficial and necessary—something to be managed rather than eliminated.[6] Signal/noise and cost/benefit calculations are practices of moderation. Neoliberal moderation locates the ever shifting point of diminishing returns and determines whether it is more profitable to (a) maximize everything to this asymptotal limit, or (b) crash past this point and resiliently bounce back in a whirl of shock-doctrine creative destruction.

I use the concept of waves—both this image of a cresting wave, taken from the Atlanta rapper Ludacris's 2012 video for his song "The Rest of My Life," and the ideas of waveforms in acoustics and the similarly wave-shaped normal curve in statistics—to unpack what neoliberal sophrosyne is and how it works. In what follows, I will first discuss Plato's concept of sophrosyne and show how this concept is grounded in the music theory of the ancient Greeks, specifically, their understanding of harmony as geometric proportion. I will then use Jacques Attali's work on music and Michel Foucault's late work on both ancient Greek thought and neoliberalism to first (a) establish that moderation is important to neoliberalism's marketization of everything and then (b) show that this neoliberal concept of moderation is, like Platonic sophrosyne, grounded in a concept of harmony, but one that's different from Plato's geometric one. This neoliberal concept of harmony is acoustic and algorithmic. I will conclude with an example of acoustic sophrosyne, both as a structure of subjectivity and as a musical gesture: the aforementioned Ludacris song.

Platonic Sophrosyne

Sophrosyne was a common concept, and various philosophers theorized it in different ways. I focus narrowly on Plato's understanding of it, because, as Jacques Rancière argues in the quote presented as the epigraph to this chapter, that is the version embodied by neoliberalism (what he calls "postdemocracy" or "consensus").

SOPHROSYNE AS A PRACTICE

For Plato, sophrosyne is what makes citizens free: specifically, free from enslavement to the pleasures, and thus fit to be politically free from enslavement to another human master. You freed yourself from enslavement to the pleasures by following the authority of the True.[7] The free man is not liberated from mastery; rather, he follows the best master of all, the truth.[8] He orders his life according to the True and its logos. Just as the Logos is the "beautiful itself," sophrosyne is, as Plato says in the *Republic*, "*beautiful order* and continence of certain pleasures and appetites, as they say, using the phrase 'master of himself.'"[9] Sophrosyne is the True put into practice; this is why Foucault calls sophrosyne an "orthos logos," a practice of truth.

Moderate lives replicate, as accurately as possible, the order or logos of the Truth itself. This logos is *proportionate*. For example, Plato's divided line doesn't just separate the visible from the intelligible, but expresses a ratio between them, "the ratio of their comparative clearness and obscurity."[10] This same ratio, then, is what the practice of sophrosyne allows one to embody. "Acquiring moderation," Plato writes, means bringing every aspect of your existence "*in proportion* as soul is more honorable than body."[11] The soul or the intelligible isn't the main focus here—it's the proportional relationship between soul and body; that proportion is the "logos" in soprhosyne's "orthos logos." Here, the proportion is to stand in the "right" relation to logos. This is why Foucault describes sophrosyne/self-mastery as "the right sense of proportion."[12]

Proportion, for Plato as for the Greeks more generally, is both a ratio and a hierarchical ordering. Plato's myth of the metals, for example, describes a proportional relationship that is both a ratio (the gold get the most responsibility) and a hierarchy at the same time (the gold are on the top).[13] Thus, moderation is not just a geometric or material distribution; it's also a distribution of authority or status. As Foucault explains,

> in the individual who is *sophron*, it is reason that commands and prescribes, *in consonance* with the structure of the human being: "it is fitting that the reasonable part should rule," Socrates says ... and he proceeds to define the *sophron* as the man in whom the different parts of the soul are in agreement and *harmony*, when the part that commands and the part that obeys are at one in their recognition that it is proper for reason to rule and that they should not contend for its authority.[14]

Moderation really is about mastery, about making sure the part that should rule—the soul, the guardians—is in command. Sophrosyne, then, is the practice of embodying this hierarchical ratio. A body so ordered expresses a "harmonious" order among its parts.[15] Immoderate bodies are leaky—they overflow with noise, fluids, and so on. As Ann Carson explains, "Woman as a species is frequently said to lack the ordering principle of sophrosyne," and is thus "given to disorderly and uncontrolled outflow of sound," often represented as "a loud roaring noise as of wind or rushing water ... 'she who pours forth.'"[16] Moderation keeps sound waves, fluids, all that is condensed in Carson's metaphor of running water—moderation is what keeps them in check.

Foucault's use of musical language to describe sophrosyne—consonance, harmony—is not accidental. Plato, like many ancient Greek philosophers, explicitly modeled sophrosyne on musical harmony. Sophrosyne "bears more likeness to a kind of concord and harmony than the other virtues" because it, like ancient Greek notions of musical "harmony" is a type of hierarchical proportionality.[17] If sophrosyne is modeled on musical harmony, then understanding how the ancient Greeks calculated musical proportions will help us to understand more fully their concept of sophrosyne.

MUSICAL HARMONY

There is no one theory of harmony in ancient Greek philosophy; it was actually a matter of much contention. Everybody disagreed about what the proper proportions and ratios were and how to determine them. However, this means that everyone agreed that musical harmony was "something balanced, proportional, ratio-like."[18] They also all understood proportion as something one calculated geometrically. This is why Plato says "a man experienced in geometry would ... grasp the truth about equals, doubles, or any other proportion."[19] Ratios aren't calculated arithmetically but derived from the geometric division of a line, like a monochord's string. For example, fretting a string in a 1:1 ratio (basically dividing it into two equal parts) produced the interval of an octave, and dividing a string according to a two-thirds/one-third ratio produces the interval of a fifth. Proportion was fundamentally mathematic, and a specific type of math at that: geometry.

Though contemporary Westerners commonly understand harmony as a relation among sounds themselves, the ancient Greeks thought the relationships among an instrument's parts and between the instrument and the sounds it produces were also important factors in musical harmony. For example, Plato thought sounds could be harmonious only when they were produced by instruments whose structural features were geometrically proportionate. Manipulating an instrument in geometrically disproportionate ways in order to produce sonically proportionate sounds, as one would do to play the flute or the ancient Greek double-reed instrument called the aulos, produced an inferior form of harmony and a deception akin to sophistry.[20] A logically ordered body produces logically ordered sounds.[21] Harmonic proportionality was not a measurement of sound frequencies (as we would consider it today), but a measurement of the physical construction of the vibrating body or instrument making the sound. Remember, this is geometry, not acoustics. The assumption—or ideal—is that visually, geometrically proportionate instruments should produce acoustically proportionate sounds ... because the same *mathematical* proportions ought to govern them both.[22]

Plato thinks the relationship between visual/auditory proportion and mathematical/philosophical proportion must itself be proportionate, putting greater weight or emphasis on the intellectual than on the perceptual. This is why he disagrees with Pythagoras's theory of harmony, which reverses the proper order between material structure and audible output. According to Plato, Pythagoras "put[s] ears before the intelligence,"[23] placing disproportionate emphasis on auditory perception, and insufficient emphasis on intellectual proportion (e.g., the "consideration of ... numbers").[24] For Plato (unlike for Pythagoras), the relationship between perceptual and intellectual proportion is itself harmonious: both a ratio and a hierarchical ordering. Whatever correctly embodies this hierarchically ordered series of ratios will be harmonious; the way a person did this was by practicing sophrosyne. For example, Richard Stalley argues that "Sōphrosunē will consist in an agreement and harmony among the parts, whereby appetite and spirit willingly accept the rule of reason (442c–d). There is an important link between the order and harmony of the soul and that of music, but it is not to be understood, in Eryximachus's way, as a balance between opposites. The key point is that reason must be in control."[25] Practicing sophrosyne put your body and soul in the proper geometric proportion, which is again both a ratio and a hierarchical ordering with reason. Plato takes the principles behind the idea of musical harmony—a hierarchically ordered geometric ratio with reason on top—and applies them to non-musical phenomena, like individual behavior or civic order; when he applies them in non-musical contexts, he calls these principles moderation or sophrosyne.

Plato's concept of sophrosyne was grounded in a very specific concept of musical harmony—a concept that is nowadays considered foreign at best, obsolete at worst. Twenty-first-century Western music theory and science understand harmony acoustically, not geometrically. They use calculus-based mathematics to measure and describe sound frequencies. Neoliberal sophrosyne is a theory of moderation or self-mastery modeled on acoustic harmony, harmony measured with neoliberalism's privileged forms of mathematics (statistics and calculus). What neoliberalism takes from Plato is (a) the idea of sophrosyne, and that it's a good thing, and (b) that sophrosyne is a type of harmony. However, neoliberalism departs from Plato in its definition of harmony, and thus also in what counts as sophrosyne and how it is measured. Shannon Winnubst reminds us that "neoliberals are not ancient Greeks" because "neoliberal practices of pleasure, freedom, and truth ... diverge widely from those of the ancient Greeks."[26] Both neoliberals and ancient Greeks (in this case, Plato) focus pleasure, freedom, and truth around practices of harmonious sophrosyne—but "harmonious" means something entirely different in each context.

WHAT NEOLIBERAL SOPHROSYNE TAKES FROM MODERNITY

Winnubst argues that the "critical difference" between the ancient Greek and the neoliberal practice of freedom and truth "is that one comes much before modern Christianity and the other ... springs out of it."[27] Like neoliberalism generally, neoliberal sophrosyne draws on and upgrades aspects of modernity. In particular, it combines what Foucault calls modernity's "epistemological" notion of truth with the Platonic "structural" and "ontological" model of truth.[28] A structural or ontological relationship to truth is one in which truth is something whose organization you come to embody—your *form* is isomorphic with that of the truth. An epistemological relationship to truth is one in which truth is something whose *content* you know. Just as neoliberal sophrosyne updates the logic you ought to become isomorphic with, it also updates the epistemological content that logic allows you to know.[29]

For neoliberals, the "enterprising market" combines both the ontological character of ancient Greek moderation with the epistemological character of modernist discipline.[30] The economic rationality of investment, risk, and reward is both an epistemological and an ontological model: both the content and form of the truth that one must both know and embody. To use Foucault's language from the last lectures at the Collège de France, neoliberalism structures a historical ontology of ourselves in which technologies of the self are entangled with neoliberal economic rationality. As Winnubst explains, "The market, not the contract, becomes the site of veridiction," such that "human capital becomes the barometer for all of life's activities."[31] Neoliberalism thinks everything, from parenting to marriage to education to personal appearance, ought to behave like a market—and not just any old market, but a market premised on entrepreneurial investment. Every transaction is an investment, and actors use cost/benefit calculus to decide whether a venture is worth it. As Gary Becker puts it, "Individuals decide on their education, training, medical care, and other additions to knowledge and health by weighing the benefits and costs."[32] Unlike the modern subject, whose inner self could be known through interpretation (e.g., psychoanalysis), *Homo economicus*'s behavior is knowable because it is predictable.[33] The cost/benefit calculus is what makes him predictable: he will always maximize his interests. According to Becker, "Now everyone more or less agrees that rational behavior simply implies consistent maximization of a well-ordered function, such as a utility or profit function."[34] There's that "well-ordered" language again, language that echoes Plato's discussions of sophrosyne, as well as Rancière's argument that neoliberal society embodies Platonic sophrosyne. Balancing maximum reward with acceptable risk, cost/benefit calculus is a practice of moderation. In its probabilist form, neoliberal market logic is a kind of sophrosyne.[35]

Neoliberal Sophrosyne

Neoliberal market logic is a kind of sophrosyne (again, as a self-relation of mastery; a technology of the self, to use Foucault's language), but it departs significantly from the ancient Greek version, both in what counts as moderation and in how moderation is measured.

ECONOMIC RATIONALITY AS SELF-MANAGEMENT

An enterprising market understands relationships and value in terms of investment, risk, and reward: the riskier the investment, the greater the reward. However, every venture has a point of diminishing returns, at which the cost just isn't worth the benefit. For example, Foucault says that neoliberals apply this thinking to policing and frame the task of criminal justice as minimizing rather than eliminating criminality: "Society does not need to conform to an exhaustive disciplinary system. A society finds that it has a certain level of illegality and it would find it very difficult to have this rate indefinitely reduced."[36] In other words, there's a point at which further investment in policing and crime prevention doesn't produce results that justify that investment. Neoliberal biopolitics is not a zero-sum calculus aimed at eliminating problems, but an economic ratio-nality that tries to balance the rates at which problems occur (crime, mortality and morbidity, unemployment, school dropout); the normal or acceptable rate would be that reached at whatever point the cost/benefit equation for policing and prevention tips into the red. This balancing act is the crux of neoliberal economic rationality. Cost/benefit calculus is a type of moderation.

Twenty-first-century physics and Western music theory understands harmony in terms of mathematical relationships among interacting sound frequencies. These relationships—frequency ratios, Fourier transforms (which can be used to measure the harmonics that compose a signal, or the various frequencies in a chord)—can be modeled, mathematically, with the tools that economists utilize to model the market. Just as contemporary economists don't use geometry to model the market—they use statistics—data scientists model individual (and population) behavior with adaptive algorithms that are designed to predict your next choice or click. Both probability functions and sound frequencies are visually modeled as wave-shaped curves. There's resonance between the math we use to understand acoustic harmony and the math we use to understand the market.

In his 1977 book *Noise* or *Bruits*, its title coming from a term that, in either English or French, can refer to both sonic and statistical phenomena, Jacques Attali makes this very connection: "The laws of acoustics," he argues "displa[y] all of the characteristics of the technocracy managing the great machines of the repetitive [i.e., neoliberal] economy."[37] Primary among these characteristics is the statistical modeling of risk, noise, or chance. In an interview with Fredric Jameson and Brian Massumi, Attali describes this characteristic as

> a more properly statistical vision of reality, a macrostatistical and global, aleatory view, in terms of probabilities and statistical groups. This last seems to me to be organically related to that whole dimension of non-harmonic music ... which involves the introduction of new rules and in particular those of chance ... and that is in its turn the same kind of theorizing one finds in macroeconomics—namely, statistical and global conceptions of the movement of masses and of mass production. So the most appropriate terminology for all these developments on so many distinct levels remains that of statistics proper: namely, the management of mass.[38]

According to Attali, the physics of sound, open work–style composition, and neoliberal political economy all converge around a common logic or "kind of theorizing," namely, the statistical modeling of chance or aleatory processes, the "noise" that arises from the interaction of sound waves and/or people. For example, in 1962 Becker wrote that even irrational market behavior can be "represented by a probabilistic model" according to which "the average consumption of a large number of independent households would almost certainly be at the middle of the opportunity set."[39] In other words, the normal curve ("the middle of the opportunity set") makes even economically irrational behavior—like impulse buys—statistically rational at the level of the market. Distinguishing his probabilistic theory from "arithmetical" theories of the market, Becker argues that "hence the market would act as if 'it' were rational not only when households were rational, but also when they were inert, impulsive, or otherwise irrational." Probabilistic forecasting and Gaussian normal curves are statistical ratios that allow economists to harness noisy behavior, to control for it, indeed, to normalize it as part of a rational market.

Between *Noise* and this 1983 interview with Jameson and Massumi, Attali is making the overall claim that the kinds of math that audio engineers and acousticians use to measure signal and noise, the kinds of compositional practices that mid-twentieth-century avant-garde Western art music used to harness chance and aleatory sounds (i.e., noise), and the kinds of math that late twentieth-century economists (like himself) use to describe markets and market behavior—in particular, noisy "abnormal" behavior that isn't statistically normal or economically "rational"—are all the same underlying thing. That underlying thing is a specific technique or technology for managing noise, chance, or irrationality: the statistics neoliberal economists use and the frequency ratios acousticians use produce what Attali calls a "simulacrum of *self-management*" that characterizes a nominally "free" deregulated market.[40] No matter how irrational or noisy individual choices or frequencies are, the overall market or signal remains normal and rational. Key here is the idea of self-management, or self-mastery, or, indeed, moderation—sophrosyne.

Like Platonic sophrosyne, neoliberal sophrosyne is a type of ratio, but it's measured statistically and probabilistically rather than geometrically and mathematically. As Mary Beth Mader argues, "With the spread of the statistics of population and their role in the constitution of subjects, then, social relations literally become rationalized, or more precisely, ratio-ized."[41] Statistics measure the frequency of a variable across a population—or, in the case of acoustics, across time; they're not geometric ratios, but frequency ratios. And the normal (or Gaussian) curve visualizes these frequencies. As Mader explains, "In its social scientific employment, it is a graphic representation of the distribution of frequencies of values for a given measured property, with the most frequent values being those in the distribution that cluster around a mean or average in a single peak."[42] Statistical norms are ratios of ratios: it takes individual measurements of the rate at which a given property X appears in a population (this is the first set of ratios) and then aggregates these and finds the most common or "normal" rate, the average rate Y at which X rate occurs. Similarly, neoliberal moderation isn't a static, invariant hierarchy (as it is for Plato), but a dynamic probability—and probabilities are things you measure with statistics. Under constantly changing conditions, what is the probable success or failure of an investment? What will be the likely return on ventured risk? Just how far can you maximize risk (and thus also return) before passing the point of diminishing returns? As Foucault explains, although, on the one hand, the point of entrepreneurship is to take investments and "somehow push them to their limit and full reality,"[43] on the other, we have to recognize that "there is a threshold that cannot be crossed."[44] This limit is also the central issue in Nate Silver's book on data forecasting, *The Signal and the Noise*. The book asks: how do we get the most out of data crunching without being *too* inaccurate? Practicing sophrosyne means pushing oneself, or any venture, to your limit and full reality. It's a practice that allows you to maintain peak performance, to Zeno's-paradox it ever closer to that asymptote that marks the point at which a cresting wave crashes in on itself. Only what *doesn't* actually kill you will make you stronger. Moderation is an essential virtue of the truly entrepreneurial life; it's how you balance the ratio of risk and reward.

The moderation or self-mastery embodied in neoliberal cost/benefit calculus is a practice of sophrosyne because its concept of what counts as "moderate" correlates with contemporary understandings of musical harmony. For Plato, musical harmony was calculated with geometric ratios; contemporary acousticians use frequency ratios. As Mader shows, frequency ratios are also the fundamental mathematical element of neoliberal biopolitics, the probabilistic calculus behind economic forecasting, and *Homo economicus*'s cost/benefit calculus. Rancière's claim that neoliberal societies embody Platonic sophrosyne is, for the most part, correct. Neoliberal cost/benefit calculus and concepts of economic rationality are ratios that allow markets and individuals to be deregulated and self-managing—they're just ratios calculated statistically rather than geometrically. Neoliberal self-management is sophrosyne and not some other type of balancing or moderation because sophrosyne is a concept of moderation grounded in the science of sound and concepts of musical ratios. The difference between Plato and neoliberals such as Becker is that they're using different kinds of math to calculate what is ultimately the same overall principle—the principle of self-mastery within a social order of ranked ratios.

Sophrosyne is a nonnumerical, affective way of understanding all that math. It translates neoliberal economic rationality, in particular, the ratio of cost to benefit, into the qualitative, nonquantified behaviors and experiences cost/benefit calculus supposedly quantifies. Sophrosyne helps people feel, intuit, and understand neoliberalism's statistical tools—frequency ratios, Gaussian distributions, predictive analytics, market forecasts, etc.—in affective, qualitative terms. "Moderation" is the affect that we feel when we successfully practice cost/benefit calculus.

A concept of self-mastery, sophrosyne makes it easy to hold individuals responsible for work that is actually done at the structural level: if you fail, it must be your fault for miscalculating. The sneaky thing about cost/benefit calculus is that it naturalizes existing relations of privilege and inequality while on the surface appearing to function independently from them, and even as a remedy to them. The more privilege you have, the more risk you can tolerate. For example, as a cis white woman, I can move through space with less vulnerability to arrest, harassment, or assault than most people experience, so I can engage in riskier behaviors (driving with a broken tail light, carrying illegal drugs) with less likelihood of negative repercussions. And even if I do experience some costs, my privilege makes it easier to tolerate and bounce back from the losses. Ludacris's 2012 song, "Rest of My Life," illustrates just this point.

JUST LUDACRIS ENOUGH

Ludacris's "Rest of My Life" is about him being just Ludacris *enough*. Neoliberal sophrosyne is evident in both the song's lyrical content and its musical composition.

First, the lyrics. Ludacris raps the verses and Usher sings the hooks. Both men repeatedly speak about you-only-live-once (YOLO, as the then-trendy acronym puts it) risk taking that generates crisis or transgression. With a nod to Friedrich Nietzsche and probably also to Kanye West's 2007 song "Stronger," Ludacris opens with the line "What don't kill me will only make me stronger." Risk and transgression are good, but only when they're not actually lethal. It's not a coincidence that this line is accompanied, in the video, by an image of a cresting wave, a wave whose energy is itself maxed out but has not yet crashed past the point of diminishing returns. Rhetorically asking, "Why tiptoe through life to arrive safely at death?," he suggests that a life without risk isn't really lived; to live is to venture risks, to push limits. The lyrics describe this way of living as a type of gambling, wagering, and balancing: "living... on the edge," "I go for broke," "I'm winning the bet." This song is about cost/benefit calculus—venturing risk, making a bet in an attempt to maximize one's payoff. Powering through the pause between phrases to squeeze in even more words, that last line *performs* the risk taking and limit pushing the words describe. The need to "game" it is evidence of the fact that there are still limits, specifically, points of diminishing returns. Life is best lived when we surf this "edge," when we ride the crest of burnout. Sophrosyne, then, is the art of gaming it, of "going for broke," of predicting what our point of diminishing returns will be.

However, as we know, in all gambling ventures, the house always wins. Ludacris's bets aren't that risky, because society is structured to support his so-called transgressions, because, in turn, his transgressions stabilize the relations of privilege and domination that allow hegemonic social institutions to function most efficiently. Just consider the transgressions he names in the song: "Tryin to keep my balance, I'm twisted, so just in case I fall / written on my tombstone should be 'women, weed, and alcohol.'" Women, weed, and alcohol. Hmm. These are all safe and, mainly, legal. The neoliberal state profits from all of them. And what is more safe than practicing heterosexuality? Now, this picture is complicated by Luda's blackness—these transgressions aren't as safe for Black men as they are for whites. I'll pick this argument back up after I talk about the song's musical climax, because something happens in the video during this part of the song that's relevant to this point about race.

The video's repeated image of the cresting wave is a visual symbol for the musical device called a "soar." As I discuss in more detail in my book *Resilience and Melancholy*, the soar is a Zeno's paradox–like intensification up to, or sometimes past, an asymptote, usually by speeding up the frequency of rhythmic events. Soars take a repeated rhythmic event (word, drumbeat, handclap) and exponentially intensifies these repetitions until they sound like one solid tone or silence; they are the sonic equivalent of the phenomenon that allows us to see twenty-four frames (or more) per second as one continuous film projection. Soars push and sometimes transgress the limit of aural perception. The soar is a sonic transgression that pays off because it intensifies the pleasure we feel on the downbeat "hit" or climax. With the soar, as with casino gambling, when individuals go over the limit and press their luck too far, the house wins. Individual transgression boosts the song's overall bottom line.

Only certain kinds of individual transgressions have a positive cost/benefit outcome. The video makes this more than clear. Two things show up in the main soar that appear nowhere else in the video: a white guy (David Guetta, a French DJ and EDM artist, who did the instrumentals) and an American flag. At the moment of maximum musical and sonic transgression, the video shows us white identity and institutional whiteness. The video uses Guetta's whiteness and the institutional whiteness of American nationalism and nationalist inclusion to contextualize Ludacris's transgressions, to show that these risks are indeed economically rational ventures. Without such evident whiteness, these risks would produce losses rather than profits; they'd be a bad bet. As some scholars of neoliberalism have argued, blackness comes to be identified with and as risk.[45] Given the general criminalization of blackness, being Black is generally risky enough in itself, and it intensifies the risk of other transgressions. For example, in a May 30, 2015, report, the *Washington Post* found that in the first six months of 2015, of the 385 fatal shootings by police, "about half the victims were white, half minority. But the demographics shifted sharply among the unarmed victims, two-thirds of whom were Black or Hispanic. Overall, blacks were killed at three times the rate of whites or other minorities when adjusting by the population of the census tracts where the shootings occurred."[46] It's three times as risky to be Black as it is to be any other race. And cases such as Jonathan Ferrell's (killed by a Charlotte, North Carolina, police officer after requesting assistance following a car accident) demonstrate, Black people don't have to do anything illegal, or even questionable, to be treated as an unacceptable risk in need of quarantine. Blackness may be so risky that it makes neoliberal cost/benefit calculus an impossible venture. This is perhaps why, as Lester Spence argues, non-bourgeois Blacks are generally thought to be "exceptions unable to be re-formed ... according to market logic."[47]

In order for Ludacris's bets to appear to be profitable, economically rational decisions, his transgressions need to look and feel white ... enough. Just as his bets need to be just ludicrous enough to maximize profits, they need to be just white enough to appear merely ludicrous and not dangerously pathological. Cost/benefit calculus is a racialized (as well as gendered) and racializing (as well as gendering) technology. Neoliberal sophrosyne isn't just individual self-mastery, the practice of regulating one's flows; it's also a matter of how power flows through you. Or rather, individual practices of sophrosyne occur in and on a field that distributes risk and reward in carefully calculated ways so that no matter how much noise anybody makes, the (white supremacist, patriarchal) house always wins.

From Ratio to Affect

Neoliberal sophrosyne is the practice of being as noisy, as "gaga," as "manic-pixie-dreamy," as "ludacris" as we can—without upsetting the overall signal.[48] It's "healthy" risk-taking that doesn't pass over into pathological over- or underuse. From the perspective of probabilist neoliberalisms, to be successful entrepreneurs of ourselves, we must be moderate. And as the Ludacris video suggests, being "moderate" means being just white, masculine, and homonormative enough that your self-entrepreneurship doesn't distort the overall distribution of wealth and privilege.[49]

If human capital is, as Angela Mitropoulos puts it, "the unfolding of (capitalist) economic logic onto putatively non-market behaviours,"[50] sophrosyne explains how market mechanisms—that is, algorithms—can manifest in and across bodies as affects. Sophrosyne translates algorithms into affect, mathematical propositions into kinesthetic and aesthetic properties. It is a tool neoliberalism uses to make affect, corporeality, and nonpropositional/drastic/implicit knowledges legible to, and thus controllable by, market logics. That is, sophrosyne allows us to think of and/or experience affect, bodies, habit, nonpropositionalizable phenomena in terms that are translatable into actual statistics, probabilities, and forecasts, namely, in terms of moderate or immoderate cost/benefit ratios. Whereas Plato's Kallipolis was a tower of harmonious sound, to riff on Leonard Cohen, neoliberalism's social ontology of *Homo economicus* vibrates with its own acoustic resonance. Yet—and this is a theoretical desideratum—the concept of neoliberal sophrosyne brings apparently objective mathematical operations into a format that can be critically theorized. In the West, and arguably in every culture, music, and sound in general, have been used to translate math into qualitative relations that vibrate deep in the very structure of agency. Plato's *polis* is one example, and so is neoliberal's "sonic episteme," a term I coined to precisely disentangle the relations among forms of governmentality, technologies of the self, and site of veridiction.[51] Such critical theorizing as I have done in my analysis of Ludacris's song reveals that cost/benefit calculus is just as hierarchical as Platonic ratio-nality was: risk is always disproportionately shouldered by nonwhite, non-cisheteromasculine, disabled populations, just as reward always disproportionately accrues to white cisheteromasculine able-bodied ones.

Notes

1. Jacques Rancière, *Disagreement: Politics and Philosophy* (Minneapolis: University of Minnesota Press, 1999), 106.
2. Julian Henriques, *Sonic Bodies: Reggae Sound Systems, Performance Techniques, and Ways of Knowing* (New York: Continuum, 2011), xxix.
3. Jason Read, "A Genealogy of Homo-Economicus: Neoliberalism and the Production of Subjectivity," *Foucault Studies* 6 (February 2009): 28.
4. Lisa Adkins, *The Time of Money* (Stanford, CA: Stanford University Press, 2018); Louise Amoore, *The Politics of Possibility* (Durham, NC: Duke University Press, 2013); Melinda Cooper, *Life as Surplus: Biotechnology and Capitalism in the Neoliberal Era* (Seattle: University of Washington Press, 2008).
5. Robin James, *The Sonic Episteme: Acoustic Resonance, Neoliberalism, and Biopolitics* (Durham, NC: Duke University Press, 2019).
6. Jonathan Sterne, *MP3: The Meaning of a Format* (Durham, NC: Duke University Press, 2009), 1–32.
7. As Foucault summarizes, "Moderation implied that the logos be placed in a position of supremacy in the human being and that it was able to subdue the desires and regulate behavior." Michel Foucault, *The Use of Pleasure*, vol. 2 of *The History of Sexuality*, trans. Robert Hurley (New York: Vintage Books, 1988), 86.
8. As Shannon Winnubst explains, "The ethical problem of *aphrodisia* for the Greeks was the ongoing effort 'to be free in relation to pleasures . . . to be free of their authority'; to do so, one must cultivate a particular relation to truth that 'constituted an essential element of moderation.'" Winnubst, "The Queer Thing about Neoliberal Pleasure: A Foucauldian Warning," *Foucault Studies* 14 (September 2012): 90. Plato's *Phaedo* also extensively discusses freedom as submission to the mastery of the "Truth."
9. Plato, *Republic*, in *The Complete Works of Plato*, trans. Benjamin Jowett, Kindle ed. (Kirkland, WA: Latus ePublishing, 2012), 430e. Unless otherwise specified, all citations of Plato in this chapter are made to this edition.
10. Ibid., 509d. Plato continues: "Represent them then, as it were, by a line divided into two unequal sections and cut each section again in the same ratio (the section, that is, of the visible and that of the intelligible order), and then as an expression of the ratio of their comparative clearness and obscurity.".
11. Ibid., 591b; emphasis mine.
12. Foucault, *The Use of Pleasure*, 83.
13. The theory of the divided line is a hierarchical order grounded in a metaphorics of proportion. For example, the intelligible gets a bigger proportion of space on the line because it is more "real" than the visible: "Take these four affections arising in the soul in relation to the four segments: intellection in relation to the highest one, and thought in relation to the second; to the third assign trust, and to the last imagination. Arrange them in *proportion*, and believe that as the segments to which they correspond participate in truth, so they participate in clarity" (Plato, *Republic*, 611d). Foucault's understanding of proportion is consistent with Plato's (and also, interestingly, with Rancière's reading of Plato in *Disagreement*). For Plato, a harmonious city was one in which "each man does one thing" (*Republic*, 397e), and there is a "proper order for each of the things that are" (*Gorgias*, 506d); when each thing follows its own proper logos, the whole will be harmonic, consonant, balanced, well ordered, etc. Thus, as Plato argues in *Republic*, "for all well-governed peoples there is a work assigned to each man in the city which he must perform" (*Republic*, 406c). A harmonic

city is one in which the gold souls do gold things, the silver ones do silver things, and so on. Those who are "mixed," who do more than one thing and have more than one role, have no place in Plato's ideal city because they would disrupt its harmonious attunement. As Plato says, "He doesn't harmonize with our regime because there's no double man among us, nor a manifold one, since each man does one thing" (*Republic*, 397e).

14. Foucault, *The Use of Pleasure*, 87; emphasis mine.

15. For example, *Republic*, 410c, describes a "harmoniously adjusted" or "attuned" soul as "moderate." Or, as Judith Peraino puts it, the ancient Greeks thought moderation "tunes the soul to the cosmic scale" which, as Plato says in "Timaeus" [trans. Jowett], 32c, "was harmonized by proportion." Peraino, *Listening to the Sirens: Musical Technologies of Queer Identity from Homer to Hedwig* (Berkeley and Los Angeles: University of California Press, 2005), 33.

16. Ann Carson, "The Gender of Sound," in *Glass, Irony and God* (New York: New Directions, 1995),126.

17. Plato, *Republic*, 430e. As Helen North explains, "*Sophrosyne* and its cognate forms were ... closely identified with the feeling for harmony." North, "The Concept of *Sophrosyne* in Greek Literary Criticism," *Classical Philology* 43, no. 1 (1948): 2. North speculates that "the term *sophrosyne* passed from ethics first to music"; ibid. According to A. A. Long, "Aristotle observes (*Top*. IV.3 123a37) that *symphōnia* [loosely, 'consonance'] may be predicated of 'moderation' (*sōphrosynē*) but such a usage is metaphor since strictly all *symphōnia* pertains to sounds." Long, *Stoic Studies* (Berkeley and Los Angeles: University of California Press, 1996), 204. Drawing a more macro-level analogy or isomorphism, "the Stoics envisaged a virtuous character as directly analogous to a harmonic system" (ibid., 218). Working with smaller-scale comparisons, "Ptolemy and Aristides Quintilianus ... se[t] up correspondences between specific virtues and harmonic intervals" (ibid., 215).

18. Long, *Stoic Studies*, 207.

19. Plato, *Republic*, 530a.

20. See Plato, *Symposium*, 215b–22c, where, for example, Alcibiades says that Socrates, "if you opened his inside, you cannot imagine how full he is, good cup-companions, of sobriety [σωφροσυνης]" (216d–e). See also 209a–b, 196c ("Love, by controlling pleasures and desires, must be eminently temperate (σωφρονοι)," and 187d–88e. Plato is arguing that philosophy is the moderate, temperate pursuit of wisdom. Loving wisdom means attuning your body to The Good so that when you vibrate your body to make it speak, the sounds, words, and ideas that come out of it are themselves properly tuned. To be "attuned" to The Good means reflecting the proportionality or harmony among its various parts (e.g., between "divine" and "common"). Sophistry, on the other hand, is an immoderate love, a knowing that is disproportionate and literally ir-ratio-nal. What comes out of the mouth of sophists may sound identical to what comes out of the mouth of philosophers; the difference is in the relationship between the body/soul of the speaker and the sounds that come out of his mouth. A sophist is immoderate because the "wisdom" of his words does not correspond to a proportionately ordered body—he can produce words that sound wise, but only through immoderate bodily practices (i.e., bodily practices that don't reflect the proportions expressed in The Good as represented on the divided line).

21. So one's outward appearance served as evidence of one's moderate—or immoderate—ethos. As Foucault puts it, "The individual fulfilled himself as an ethical subject by shaping a precisely measured conduct that was plainly visible to all." Michel Foucault, *The Birth of Biopolitics: Lectures at the Collège de France, 1978–79*, ed. Michel Sennelart, trans. Graham Burchell (New York: Palgrave Macmillan, 1990), 91; emphasis mine. The point was to display a properly ordered body that, like a properly proportionate musical instrument,

would reliably produce proportionate sounds/speech. As Plato explains, "if the fine dispositions that are in the soul and those that agree and accord with them in the form should ever coincide in anyone, with both partaking of the same model, wouldn't that be the fairest sight for him who is able to see?" (*Republic*, 402d; emphasis mine). This is why Foucault says that sophrosyne's "hallmark, grounded in truth, was both its regard for an ontological structure and its visibly beautiful shape" (*The Use of Pleasure*, 89; emphasis mine). Outwardly visible harmony should be the manifestation or expression of inner harmony. Inner harmony ought to produce outward beauty.

22. As Tobias Mathiesen explains, ancient Greek musical thought was "an attempt to present all the instruments—flute, reed, and string—as manifesting the *mathematical* principles of harmonics in the same *visual* manner." Mathiesen, *Apollo's Lyre: Greek Music and Music Theory in Antiquity and the Middle Ages* (Lincoln: University of Nebraska Press, 2000), 210; emphasis mine.

23. Plato, *Republic*, 531a.

24. Ibid., 531c.

25. Richard Stalley, "Sophrosyne in Symposium," in *X Symposium Platonicum: The "Symposium"; Proceedings I, Pisa, 15th–20th July, 2013*, 203.

26. Winnubst, "The Queer Thing," 91.

27. Ibid.

28. "The relation to truth was a structural, instrumental, and ontological condition for establishing the individual as a moderate subject leading a life of moderation; it was not an epistemological condition enabling the individual to recognize himself in his singularity as a desiring subject and to purify himself of the desire that was thus brought to light" (Foucault, *The Use of Pleasure*, 89).

29. One significant difference between probabilist and postprobabilist neoliberalisms is their respective relation to truth: it matters in the former case, but not in the latter. Probabilisty, after all, is an attempt to calculate what is actually most likely to occur. The point is to get it right, or as close to right as possible. Postprobabilist neoliberalisms don't care about getting it right because a demand for truth or accuracy limits the ability to accumulate surplus value. As Cooper argues in *Life as Surplus*, postprobabilist neoliberalisms operate according to what she calls a "capitalist delirium" (12). The idea is that because reality will certainly at some point radically reorganize itself, and its reorganizational capacities far surpass the power or severity of any crisis, our actions don't have to respect the hard limits to our present reality.

30. Winnubst, "The Queer Thing," 91.

31. Shannon Winnubst, *Way Too Cool: Selling Out Race and Ethics* (New York: Columbia University Press, 2015), 35, 37.

32. Gary Becker, "A Theory of the Allocation of Time," *Economic Journal* 75, no. 299 (1965): 503.

33. See Read, "A Genealogy of Homo-Economicus"; and Andrew Dilts, "From 'Entrepreneur of the Self' to 'Care of the Self': Neo-Liberal Governmentality and Foucault's Ethics," *Foucault Studies* 12 (October 2011): 130–46.

34. Gary Becker, "Irrational Behavior and Economic Theory," *Journal of Political Economy* 70, no. 1 (1962): 1.

35. Winnubst argues that neoliberalism doesn't have an "orthos logos": "neoliberalism functions as a normalizing technology of power without exerting a normative rationality" (*The Queer Thing*, 89). The competitive, deregulated market is the normalizing technology she speaks about. In the competitive market, everything is fungible, and nothing stands

firm as a normative grounding or limit. However, I want to suggest that acoustic harmony, manifested in such metaphors as the "sine wave" or the "audio equalizer," is neoliberalism's consistent, material, and perhaps even "objective," normalizing rationality or "orthos logos." Just as the ancient Greeks understood sophrosyne according to a proportional harmonics, neoliberal sophrosyne is a calculation of signal:noise ratio, measured in terms of frequency and amplitude. So it's like a proportion (a ratio), but it's visualized as an asymptote, as a statistical rather than a geometric distribution.

36. Foucault, *The Birth of Biopolitics*, 256.

37. Jacques Attali, *Noise: The Political Economy of Music*, trans. Brian Massumi (Minneapolis: University of Minnesota Press, 1984), 113.

38. Jacques Attali, "Interview with Jacques Attali," interviewed by Fredric Jameson and Brian Massumi, *Social Text* 7 (Spring 1983): 11.

39. Becker, "Irrational Behavior," 5.

40. Attali, *Noise*, 114; emphasis mine.

41. Mary Beth Mader, *Sleights of Reason: Norm, Bisexuality, Development* (Albany: State University of New York Press, 2011), 45.

42. Ibid.

43. Foucault, *The Birth of Biopolitics*, 138.

44. Ibid., 136.

45. As Che Gossett argues, in public health discourse in the United states, "the dominant regime of risk categorization always already mark[s] Black people ... as 'vulnerable,' 'at risk,' 'a statistic.'" Gossett, "We Will Not Rest in Peace: AIDS Activism, Black Radicalism, Queer and/or Trans Resistance," in *Queer Necropolitics*, ed. Jin Haritaworn, Adi Kuntsman, and Silvia Posocco (New York: Routledge, 2014), 43.

46. Kimberly Kindy, and reported by Julie Tate, Jennifer Jenkins, Steven Rich, Keith L. Alexander, and Wesley Lowery, "Fatal Police Shootings in 2015 Approaching 400 Nationwide," *Washington Post*, May 30, 2015, accessed accessed June 1, 2015, http://www.washingtonpost.com/national/fatal-police-shootings-in-2015-approaching-400-nationwide/2015/05/30/d322256a-058e-11e5-a428-c984eb077d4e_story.html.

47. Lester K. Spence, *Stare in the Darkness: The Limits of Hip-Hop and Black Politics* (Minneapolis: University of Minnesota Press, 1999), 15.

48. Jack Halberstam, *Gaga Feminism: Sex, Gender, and the End of Normal* (Boston: Beacon Press, 2012); and Nathan Rabin, "I'm Sorry for Coining the Phrase 'Manic Pixie Dream Girl,'" *Salon*, July 15, 2014, accessed June 1, 2015, http://www.salon.com/2014/07/15/im_sorry_for_coining_the_phrase_manic_pixie_dream_girl/.

49. In probabilist neoliberalisms, sophrosyne functions analogously to the way family responsibility functions in postprobabilist neoliberalisms, i.e., to guarantee the ongoing reproduction of white supremacist patriarchal distributions of personhood and property.

50. Angela Mitropoulos, *Contract and Contagion: From Biopolitics to "Oikonomia"* (New York: Minor Compositions, 2012), 149.

51. James, *The Sonic Episteme*, esp. chap. 4.

CHAPTER 2

The Politics of Silence

HEIDEGGER'S *BLACK NOTEBOOKS*

Adam Knowles

As long as we do not know more than we write,
as long as we do not think from the unsayable,
as long as we do not belong to beyng, every word is too much.
Once again to know more than we say and speak. Once again to keep
  silent, to silence over the language of metaphysics through saying.
  Once again the word. Once again the listening answer.
Instead of noise, stillness—through writing and speaking?[1]

Introduction

Since the publication of the first three volumes of Heidegger's *Black Notebooks* in 2014, an uneasy form of academic normality has begun to settle around a set of texts that justifiably sparked perplexity and outrage when they came to light.[2] As the cycle of routine academic exegesis, translation and commentary has taken hold of Heidegger's peculiar testimony, the philosophical contours of these texts have begun to reveal themselves more clearly. While the earliest responses to the *Notebooks* focused on the troubling and deeply pernicious anti-Semitic passages that are most prevalent in the volumes of 1938–41,[3] a second layer of responses by Heidegger scholars has tended to downplay the philosophical value of the *Notebooks*.[4] In the midst of the initial wave of philosophical and journalistic responses, Günter Figal, the former head of the Heidegger Gesellschaft, issued a sagacious proclamation: "The first results are not the best ones."[5] Heeding Figal's warning in this essay, and while still engaged in what I characterize as an active reading and rereading of the *Notebooks* that remains necessarily open to revision, I will argue that the *Notebooks* are a central element of Heidegger's "sigetics" (*Sigetik*). Sigetics, derived from *sigē*, one of the Greek words for silence, is a term Heidegger develops for experimentation with a silent thinking in the 1930s and beyond.[6] In order to demonstrate the sigetic operation of the *Notebooks*, I will focus on a term that is central to Heidegger's understanding of silence: the capacity for silence (*das Schweigenkönnen*).

By focusing on Heidegger's treatment of silence, this essay will show that the *Notebooks* are not ancillary to Heidegger's thinking, but instead function as a series of signposts and guides that serve to lead readers through his thinking to what Heidegger in various terminological formulations calls "the preserved destiny of the hidden Germans" (*die aufbehaltene Bestimmung der verborgenen Deutschen*) (*GA*, 97:31).[7] The core of Heidegger's politics in the *Notebooks* involves recovering a capacity for listening to the silent call of the hidden Germans, a people whose history "possesses a power for keeping silent through which another form of communication is grounded" (*GA*, 97:31). According to Heidegger, this communication, silent but not wordless, is only possible for those who have the strength to "wile daily and nightly in the unnameable" (*GA*, 97:35) as a manner of preserving the essential force on the "invisible front of the secret spiritual Germany" (*GA*, 94:155/114). By being attentive to Heidegger's vast repertoire of methods of silence and silencing, as well both worded and wordless forms of saying in the *Notebooks*, I will show that they constitute a central component of Heidegger's thinking and not merely—as those deeply invested in the value of Heidegger's thinking may be tempted to believe—a philosophically irrelevant private project.

As he announces early in the first volume, Heidegger intends to "write out of a great reticence" (*GA*, 94:28/22), and, as he states sometime around 1940, they are written in "the time of the essential active silence" (*GA*, 96:54). What does this active silence say? How does this silence speak? And what does this silence *not* say, either because Heidegger chooses not to say it, or because Heidegger's thinking points to something unsayable? Perhaps most importantly and most troublingly, what are the ethical implications of turning to Heidegger to deal with these questions? After all, it is well known that he brutally implemented the Aryanization laws during his time as rector of Freiburg University in 1933–34 during *Gleichschaltung*, the forced ideological assimilation of German institutions of higher education.[8] And what would it mean to inadvertently silence the *Notebooks* by assuming defensive postures that depict them as a mere biographical curiosity?

I will provide some provisional answers to these questions in two sections. In the first section, I analyze Heidegger's development of the capacity for silence in his 1933–34 lecture course "Being and Truth," taught contemporaneously with the earliest volumes of the *Notebooks*. In the second, I will focus on selected passages from the first three volumes of the *Notebooks* in order to demonstrate how silence functions as the matter and the medium of Heidegger's thinking in order to illuminate a discussion of the capacity for silence in the third volume of the *Notebooks*. This chapter will therefore move from the ontological analysis of silence to the analysis of the performance of silence, though for Heidegger these two are always deeply intertwined. This brief essay intends not to offer a comprehensive account of silence in Heidegger's work, but rather to trace some important thematic and terminological continuities between the *Notebooks* and Heidegger's larger project of thinking, while also arguing for the continued importance of Heidegger's work, not despite, but because of, the purportedly "dangerous" element of Heidegger's thinking.[9]

The Capacity for Silence as the Exercise of Power

Although we are often accustomed to thinking of silence in terms of disenfranchisement, the silence that Heidegger becomes increasingly concerned with in the 1930s is a matter of power. Far from resulting from a lack of power, this silence is something one is capable of, something with which one empowers oneself and for which acquires a capacity.[10] As we will see in the following section, Heidegger's politics involves vesting oneself with this silence as an endowment bestowed only on select few listeners.

In his 1933–34 lecture course "Being and Truth," held while he served as *Rektor-Führer* of Freiburg University, Heidegger calls this power, in a section entitled "The Ability to Keep Silent as the Origin and Ground of Language," the "capacity for silence" or the "ability to keep silent" (*das Schweigenkönnen*).[11] The passage seeks to ground a claim that completely reverses the priority of speech and silence established in *Being and Time*: "The ability to keep silent is the origin of language" (das Schweigenkönnen ist der Ursprung der Sprache) (*BT*, 84). How is the *capacity* for silence the origin of language? And what kind of language emerges from silence?

Heidegger begins unfolding this claim in a properly Aristotelian fashion by acknowledging the circularity of the process, for "we are supposed to speak about keeping silent" (*BT*, 85). Yet even as he poses this question, he draws back, asking instead what would it mean to *not* speak about keeping silent. What form of silence would it presuppose if one were to preserve silence in reverence? Is it not possible that "one could sell oneself short all too cheaply and relegate keeping silent, as a dark 'mystical' thing, to the so-called emotional premonition and intimation of its essence"? Hence, Heidegger concludes, we will speak about silence but not believe that "with the help of a 'definition' we have come to grips with keeping silent" (BT, 85). Silence can be known, and known to a certain degree, but it is known through speech. This speech, moreover, is not contrary to silence, even if it is the interruption of silence. At this point Heidegger turns to a question that obsesses him from the late 1920s onward: the status of language in distinguishing the human from the animal.[12]

At first Heidegger seems to suggest that, if the animal does not have to or simply cannot speak, and if the animal is constantly silent, then the animal must be "prepared for and capable of speaking to a much a higher degree, because it can keep silent more—indeed, constantly" (BT, 85). But something even more fundamental distinguishes human from animal, namely that, even while silence is the origin and ground of language, animals have no capacity to speak. Humans, those creatures who have a deficient capacity for silence because they do in fact speak, and do so constantly and resoundingly, are the only creatures able to keep silent as a capacity for silence. Hence Heidegger concludes: "Human language arises from the inability to keep silent, and consequently from a lack of constraint. The *miracle* of language is therefore based on a *failure* [*Versagen*]" (BT, 85). How can we speak through a failure?

This justification for this strange "miracle" is found in a phrase that echoes like a refrain throughout Heidegger's thinking: "Only what can speak can be silent" (Schweigen kann nur, was sprechen kann).[13] The capacity for silence thus emerges as a complex, manifold concept somewhere in the distinction between muteness and silence. On the one hand, the capacity for silence can be meaningfully applied to analyze particular instances of silence. This, however, does not mean that every act of silence is equal, for "a mute is unable to keep silent, even though he says nothing" (BT, 109). The mere act of nonvocalization is not sufficient to determine the distinction between muteness and the capacity for silence; instead, something else must be known, namely whether or not the speaker is *empowered to choose* silence. The secret spiritual Germans come into their own as the people empowered to choose silence.

As his own performances of silence show, Heidegger is well attuned to the distinction between silencing and the power to choose silence. Heidegger's capacity for silence as an act or deed requires this prior sanctioning of the possibility of choosing silence as an arrangement, attunement, or structure that distinguishes muteness from silence. Thus Heidegger concludes: "Keeping silent is rather, at the very least, the not-talking of someone who can talk. As we said before, it is a definite, exceptional way of being able to talk" (*BT*, 86).

We thus begin to see that the *Notebooks* are Heidegger's peculiar performance of this form of not-talking as an exceptional way of being able to talk. They are the performance of a willfully chosen silence whose medium is the word. Layered over with manifold registers of silence, they are perhaps most important not for what they do say, but for what they do not say. Moreover, they fill a gap in Heidegger's work at which he hints as he summarizes the significance of silence for his understanding of language:

> Note that with this proposition, I pass decisively beyond what is said in *Being and Time*, § 34, page 164 and following. There, language was indeed brought into an essential relationship with keeping silent; the starting point for a sufficiently originary conception of the essence of language was laid down, in opposition to the "philosophy of language" that has reigned until now. And yet I did not see what really has to follow from this starting point: keeping silent is not just an ultimate possibility of discourse, but discourse and language arise from keeping silent. In recent years, I have gone back over these relationships and worked them through. This obviously cannot be explained here. Not even the different manners of keeping silent, the multiplicity of its causes and grounds, and certainly not the different levels and depths of reticence [*Verschwiegenheit*]. Now only as much will be communicated as is needed for the advancement of our questioning. (*BT*, 87)

This quote is significant for a number of reasons. Beyond announcing a decisive reversal of a critical element of his own conception of language in *Being and Time*, it also provides significant hints at how silence operates within Heidegger's work.[14] Firstly, when Heidegger curtly remarks that "this obviously cannot be explained here," that does not necessarily mean that there is an appropriate place to explain this conception of silence. Indeed, it is not so much a matter of silence not being explained in such a large lecture course, but more that this silence cannot be explained at all. Hence Heidegger announces that, even though he has "gone back over" and "worked through" the "the different manners of keeping silent, the multiplicity of its causes and grounds, and certainly not the different levels and depths of reticence," he will not rehearse these manifold registers at the moment. Instead, he will only communicate as much as "is needed for the advancement of our questioning."

The *Notebooks* are the continuation of that questioning, but also the performance of the very silence that is being questioned.

The *Black Notebooks* as the Performance of Silence

Whether on account of the nature of the philosophical diary, a lack of care, or a deeply seated ironic gesture on Heidegger's part, the *Notebooks* are not easy to read. This is not merely because one so often gnashes one's teeth at the outlandish politics Heidegger represents before, during, and after World War II. The difficulty lies also on a purely aesthetic level: they are repetitive, mundane, and too often lacking in the exuberant prose that marks Heidegger's writing in its most vital moments. Indeed, reading the *Notebooks* from beginning to end is such a grueling and odious task that it will likely be their fate to be poached for particular passages, especially since their structure of seemingly unrelated entries seems to lend itself to this strategy.[15]

Despite these problems, with time the attentive reader begins to recognize not so much a guiding thread throughout the *Notebooks*, but a fabric woven together by means of a web of terms. At times this fabric is held together with great cohesiveness, and at times it seems to intentionally unravel. It binds together many different tentative alliances of words, with a number of fundamental terms emerging repeatedly at critical junctures and then often disappearing without warning. The weft and warp of this fabric is silence. Even in his most direct, obtuse, and offensive moments, Heidegger still holds something in reserve. Thus one might say that the mantra of the *Notebooks* is an entry from the fourth volume: "I only trust in one thing: that we have been given the gift of knowing more than we say. Otherwise the word has no weight" (GA, 97:57). Yet even if Heidegger intends to lend weight to the word in the *Notebooks*, that does not mean that they are not overburdened by a great amount of dead weight that must be sifted through. By stressing this repeated thematization of silence, I do not mean to say that the *Notebooks* are *about* silence, for it is hard to say that they are about anything. Instead, it is more appropriate to say that they are *of* silence, or that they emerge out of silence, the necessary silence with which Heidegger lends weight to the word. In this section I will explore some of the modalities of the capacity for silence expressed in the *Notebooks* according to the rough organizing principle of chronology.

In the earliest entries of the first volume of the *Notebooks*, Heidegger stages a conversation with himself as he ponders entering what he calls the "situation" (GA, 94:7/7). Silence is at the center of many of the questions he poses to himself. Thinking on how a man comes to himself, for example, Heidegger asks: "Must he not have kept silent for a long time, in order to once again find the force and power of language and to be borne along by it?" (GA, 95:6/6). Shortly thereafter he follows up: "Must the great lone path be ventured, silently—into Da-sein, where beings become more fully beings?" (GA, 94:7/7). Once again, only a few pages later Heidegger reminds himself: "Yet 'say' it to yourself daily in your taciturnity: be silent about bearing silence" (GA, 94:10/8). Remaining silent about silence is the fundamental mode of attunement that sets the ground for listening, a listening that must be learned anew by those attuned to its voice. This listening is not intended for all, but is instead intended for the originary listeners, whom Heidegger christens with such names as "the most solitary ones" (*die Einzigsten*), "the most futural ones" (*die Künftigsten*; GA, 94:338/246), "the questioners" (*die Fragenden*; GA, 94:285/209), "the few" (*die Wenigen*; GA, 94:198/145), "the invisible ones" (*die Unsichtbaren*; GA, 94:370/269), and "the race to follow" (*das übernächste Geschlecht*; GA, 94:346/252).[16] Heidegger describes the listening attained by these solitary few in a characteristic passage: "The *Originary silence* as *further* silence in and out of the presentiment of language. But that silence is not inactive—rather, the initially open listening into (beings)" (GA, 94:78/59).

The few, solitary, and silent ones listen to something quite specific: the emergency (*Not*).[17] "The emergency" is an ontological term that is at best tangentially related to the actual state of Europe's destruction during World War II. For Heidegger, listening to the call within the emergency is the only essential political task, for it is useless to "try and improve any aspect whatever of that which lies on the surface, instead of bringing into salience the most extreme and broadest plight: the decay of being" (GA, 94:88/67). Hence politics for Heidegger does not involve making adjustments to what has already come to be, but instead involves an essential questioning rooted in an attuned listening that speaks through a silent saying in tune with this listening. Moreover, Heidegger intends to portray his own very public and often boisterous involvement in politics not as the manifestation of this essential saying, but instead as the expression of its necessary failure. Why is this failure necessary? Is it necessary because—to draw on a language quite foreign to Heidegger—politics must always tell *the noble lie*?

> But how to experience this plight? Is it necessary that many, the many, experience it? No—that is even impossible. The "situation"—not what passes for that today, but the place of the track of the essence of being—should and can be known only to a few, and they must be

silent if they are to act in the power of this knowledge.... Because nothing escapes contemporary people, because they have a facile and correct answer for everything, whereby they throttle everything as already having been, the essential must therefore remain in silence now and for the future—but all the harder and all the clearer may be what is said in the power of that silence. (*GA*, 94:88/67)

Heidegger's ontological politics is a politics of decomposition. More precisely, it is a politics of hastening the decomposition of that which is already in a state of putrefaction. Heidegger lays out these relations in a schematic depicting the relation between philosophy, language, and humanity:

> *Philosophy*! Finally its essence is up for discussion. It is to bring:
> Dasein to silence (positively)
> being into words (language—truth)
> and the pretense about humanity into silence—thus it is to put
>   humanity at risk (positively)
> However: bringing being to the word means everything but setting
>   up and popularizing an "ontology." (*GA*, 94:1815)[18]

The painful difficulty involved with reading passages such as this is that Heidegger both does and does not mean that philosophy literally ought to put humanity at risk. That is to say, Heidegger posits something under the guise of an ontological claim that cannot but have deeply troubling ontic consequences, even if Heidegger does not expressly commit to them. Heidegger's silence often operates in this gap, as can be seen in his initial hope that World War II will result in an essential confrontation that might bring about the "purification of being from its deepest disorder" (*GA*, 96:283). There is obviously much more to be said about this politics of decomposition, but for the moment I would like to remain on the topic of silence.

The decomposition of being is accompanied by a decomposition of language, which for Heidegger has degraded into so many used-up, spent, and worn-out words that have lost all vitality through the "ruination of language" (*Sprachverhunzung*; *GA*, 96:238). The ruination of language is brought about by the tendency of the masses to easily draw equivalences and to muddle what is unique with comparisons. Hence the listening few hold back in a silence that will not shy away from expressing itself through false, apparent equivalences offered up for the sake of the many who could and should not understand what is held in silence. A language that necessarily fails does not preserve itself by keeping silent, yet it can at least influence the particular formation of its failure by controlling the way it speaks. This is how Heidegger would like us to understand his voice as the *Rektor-Führer*, but also his voice of reckoning in the *Notebooks*: the necessarily elusive attempt to control a discourse that tries to write the story of its own failure. I mean this not at all as a defense of Heidegger, but as an attempt to translate the complexity of his multilayered attempt at self-representation through the writing, preservation, and disclosure of the *Notebooks*—works that Heidegger intended to be the capstone of his *Complete Works*.

This complex play between failure, the essential word, and the deed of silence is illustrated in a particularly dense entry from the third volume of the *Notebooks*, which I will first translate in full and comment on:

> The stages which rise up to the essential occurrence of the word beginning from the most immediate use of the word are these: *the word signifies, the word has meaning, the word says, the word is*. The last one means: the word belongs to the essential occurrence of beyng itself and in that belonging achieves the highest loyalty to its own essence.... Hence the contemplation of language in the "philosophy of language" goes astray instead of forging ahead to rescue the word. The first "act" of this rescue consists in the capacity for silence [*das Schweigenkönnen*], the second in learning to hear the rare conversation [*das seltene Gespräch*], the third in the attempt to hint at the essential word. However, any effort in this direction becomes ensnared in the vicinity of the things that have recently been written and spoken; and even if this effort does rise above this ensnarement, it remains in the grips of the common distortion of the essence of language [*Sprachunwesens*]. (GA, 96:288–89)

Here Heidegger traces the steps from the use of the word, which always fails in what it intends to say, to the essential occurrence of the word. Yet even restoring the relation to the essential occurrence in the three-step process of developing the capacity for silence, hearing the rare conversation, and experimenting with forms of written and spoken silence is not sufficient to rescue the word. This is because the word has always already been abandoned, having fallen victim to the chatter of things already spoken—the material for so many hasty comparisons. Whether or not any philosopher of language agrees with this ontology of decline is irrelevant to the interpretive task at hand, for, independent of whether or not Heidegger has provided a convincing description of language, what is of interest here is recognizing that Heidegger offers critical interpretive hints for understanding the relation between his public political persona and the place of his thinking in that persona.

Among the many things that the *Notebooks* are and might be, they are in part a continuously evolving set of directions on how to read the *Notebooks* and, by extension, Heidegger. This does not mean to say that we as readers of Heidegger are beholden in any way to the interpretive scheme of the master, yet it does compel us to recognize that any attempt to come to terms with Heidegger's politics must begin to unravel the complicated and manifold manners in which Heidegger embedded his politics within a complex set of strategies of veiling, occlusion, evasion, and well-chosen silences for which he himself provides hints on how to unravel, especially in the *Notebooks*. In other words, Heidegger remains an essential resource for understanding his own failure.

Conclusion

To summarize the results of this exploration of Heidegger's strategies in the most succinct form possible, it is necessary to draw the following contradictory conclusion: Heidegger both did and did not mean what he said in the *Notebooks*. In other words, when Heidegger writes in 1945, among many other travesties of thinking contained therein, that misrecognizing the destiny of the German people was "a more essential 'guilt' and a 'collective guilt,' the magnitude of which could not be measured against the atrocities of the 'gas chambers,'" and that the "German people and land are already a single '*concentration camp*,'" he both did and did not mean what he said (*GA*, 97:99–100). Pointing out this ambiguity is potentially a very dangerous statement that risks sounding flippant. Hence, it is necessary to state as clearly as possible that, by saying that Heidegger, at least in some way, did not mean what he said because what he said is itself a distortion and falling away from what cannot be said, I do not intend to defend Heidegger or absolve him of any responsibility for his loathsome political views. Indeed, I intend to do the contrary, for in reading Heidegger we must always remain vigilantly attentive to the possibility that what Heidegger did not say, that what he did not relinquish to the essential distortion of language, may even be *far more disturbing than what he did say*. As Heidegger writes: "Those who are deadly silent [*Totgeschwiegenen*] have seemingly been reputed to have the greatest impact" (*GA*, 96:70). The danger of not reading the *Notebooks* as an integral part of Heidegger's philosophical project is that we prevent ourselves from drawing even more radical (and radically disturbing) conclusions about Heidegger's politics than is possible simply by recreating Heidegger's political deeds or searching—in the manner of Emmanuel Faye—for a superficial philosophical National Socialism.[19]

By way of closing, I want to reiterate the ethical stakes of arguing for the *Notebooks* as having philosophical and not merely biographical value. I am deeply concerned with the possibility that labeling the *Notebooks* as philosophically irrelevant serves as an unintended apology for Heidegger that, in effect, allows for the easy resumption of business as usual in the world of Heidegger scholarship. This unwitting apology goes something along these lines: these terrible texts are Heidegger's words, they tell us about the man, but they are not his thinking and therefore have no impact on his thinking. Moreover, I am equally concerned about the possibility of taking recourse in chronology and retreating back to *Being and Time*, a work that—in Jeff Malpas's words—seems to be accorded a degree of "quarantine," as if it were untainted merely because it was written before Heidegger's public entry into right-wing politics.[20] Yet there is, as Malpas notes, something even more problematic about the very use of the language of quarantine, purity, and contamination, "a language so characteristically employed by the Nazis and anti-Semites themselves."[21]

The *Notebooks* must be reckoned with by every responsible Heidegger scholar for their impact on Heidegger's thinking as a whole. What is so fascinating about the *Black Notebooks* is that, in so many ways, they beg not to be read. They seem written so as to be written off. This is not incidental to their structure, but is instead embedded and folded within the texture of the work, within its fabric of silences. The *Notebooks*, for all of their rambling screeds, droning meditations, and slack-jawed commentary on contemporary events (with Heidegger necessarily at the center of them), are saying something else beneath all of those feints. Have we found the language to say what Heidegger could not or did not say? And what will it mean to find it? What will it mean to be the audience for this terrible performance of silence? What—in other words—is Heidegger's capacity for silence a capacity for?

Notes

1. Martin Heidegger, *Anmerkungen I–V (Schwarze Hefte, 1942–48)*, vol. 97 of *Gesamtausgabe*, ed. Peter Trawny (Frankfurt am Main: Vittorio Klostermann, 2015), 56; "Beyng" is the conventional translation of Heidegger's use of the outdated German spelling of *Sein* (being) as *Seyn*. *Seyn* indicates the use of the term in the being-historical sense developed in Heidegger's thinking in the 1930s.

2. Martin Heidegger, *Überlegungen II–VI (Schwarze Hefte 1931–1938)*, vol. 94 of *Gesamtausgabe: IV. Abteilung; Hinweise und Aufzeichnungen*, ed. Peter Trawny (Frankfurt am Main:

Vittorio Klostermann, 2014); *Überlegungen VII–XI (Schwarze Hefte 1938–1939)*, vol. 95 of *Gesamtausgabe: IV. Abteilung; Hinweise und Aufzeichnungen*, ed. Peter Trawny (Frankfurt am Main: Vittorio Klostermann, 2014); *Überlegungen XII–XV (Schwarze Hefte 1939–1941)*, vol. 96 of *Gesamtausgabe: IV. Abteilung; Hinweise und Aufzeichnungen*, ed. Peter Trawny (Frankfurt am Main: Vittorio Klostermann, 2014); hereafter cited parenthetically as "GA" with the German/English pagination. Translations from vol. 94 the *Black Notebooks* are taken from *Ponderings II–VI: Black Notebooks,1931–1938*, trans. Richard Rojcewicz (Bloomington: Indiana University Press, 2016). All other translations from the *Black Notebooks* are my own.

3. The scholarly and journalistic literature on the *Black Notebooks* is already quite extensive. The first volume to appear in English was Ingo Farin and Jeff Malpas, eds., *Reading Heidegger's "Black Notebooks 1931–1941"* (Cambridge, MA: MIT Press, 2016). For a bibliography that covers contributions until mid-2015 see Andrzej Serafin, "A Reception History of the *Black Notebooks*," *Gatherings: The Heidegger Circle Annual* 5 (2015): 118–42. On Heidegger's anti-Semitism, see Peter Trawny, *Heidegger and the Myth of a Jewish World Conspiracy*, trans. Andrew J. Mitchell (Chicago: University of Chicago Press, 2015), and "Heidegger, 'World Judaism' and Modernity," in *Gatherings: The Heidegger Circle Annual* 5 (2015): 1–20; and Jesús Adrián Escudero, "Heidegger's *Black Notebooks* and the Question of Anti-Semitism," *Gatherings: The Heidegger Circle Annual* 5 (2015): 21–49.

4. David Farrell Krell, "Heidegger's *Black Notebooks, 1931–41*," *Research in Phenomenology* 45, no. 1 (2015): 127–60.

5. "Philosoph Günter Figal tritt als Vorsitzender der Martin-Heidegger Gesellschaft zurück: Kritische Forschung nötig" (radio interview, WDR3), accessed September 20, 2015, http://www.wdr3.de/zeitgeschehen/guenterfigal106.html.

6. On Heidegger's sigetics, see Daniela Vallega-Neu, "Heidegger's Reticence: From *Contributions* to *Das Ereignis* and toward *Gelassenheit*," *Research in Phenomenology* 45, no. 1 (2015): 1–32; Vallega-Neu, "Heidegger's Poietic Writings: From *Contributions to Philosophy* to *Das Ereignis*," in *Heidegger and Language*, ed. Jeffrey Powell (Bloomington: Indiana University Press, 2013), 119–45; and Francisco Gonzalez, "And the Rest Is *Sigetik*: Silencing Logic and Dialectic in Heidegger's *Beiträge zur Philosophie*," *Research in Phenomenology* 38, no. 3 (2008): 358–91. On *sigē* and silence in the Greek world, see Silvia Montiglio, *Silence in the Land of Logos* (Princeton, NJ: Princeton University Press, 2000).

7. On secret spiritual Germany, see Theodore Kisiel, "The Siting of Hölderlin's 'Geheimes Deutschland' in Heidegger's Poetizing of the Political," in *Heidegger und der Nationalsozialismus, II: Interpretationen*, ed. Alfred Denker and Holger Zaborowski, Heidegger-Jahrbuch 5 (Freiburg: Karl Alber, 2009), 145–54; and Richard Polt, "The Secret Homeland of Speech: Heidegger on Language, 1933–34," in *Heidegger and Language*, ed. Jeffrey Powell (Bloomington: Indiana University Press, 2013), 63–85.

8. Hugo Ott, *Martin Heidegger: A Political Life*, trans Allen Blunden (London: HarperCollins; New York: Basic Books, 1993), esp. part 3; and Rüdiger Safranski, *Martin Heidegger: Between Good and Evil* (Cambridge, MA: Harvard University Press, 1998), chaps. 13–18.

9. Heidegger's former friend and collaborator Karl Jaspers described Heidegger's thinking as "dangerous" (*verhängnisvoll*) in a report that he wrote to the French denazification commission in 1945. The report is in the form of a letter written to Friedrich Oehlkers on December 22, 1945. A translation of the letter can be found in Ott, *Martin Heidegger: A Political Life*, 336–41. Peter Trawny probes the limits of this dangerous element in *Freedom to Fail: Heidegger's Anarchy*, English ed. (Cambridge, UK, and Malden, MA: Polity Press, 2015); the "danger" of Heidegger is likewise at stake in Jacques Derrida's many readings of Heidegger, including, most importantly in this context, *Of Spirit: Heidegger and the Question*, trans. Geoffrey Bennington and Rachel Bowlby (Chicago: University of Chicago Press, 1989).

10. For more on this conception of silence see my essay "A Genealogy of Silence: *Chōra* and the Placelessness of Greek Women," in *PhiloSOPHIA: A Journal of Continental Feminism* 5, no. 1 (2015): 1–24.

11. Martin Heidegger, *Being and Truth*, trans. Gregory Fried and Richard Polt (Bloomington: Indiana University Press, 2010), 84–88; hereafter cited parenthetically in the text as BT. For a detailed analysis of this lecture course, see Polt, "The Secret Homeland of Speech." I deviate from the translators' rendering of *Schweigenkönnen* as "ability to keep silent" and instead choose the more Aristotelian "capacity for silence." For a detailed explanation of this decision, see my essay "Steresis and Silence: The Aristotelian Origins of Heidegger's Thinking of Silence," in *Sources of Desire: Essays on Aristotle's Theoretical Works*, ed. James Oldfield (Newcastle upon Tyne: Cambridge Scholars, 2012), 94–110.

12. Heidegger's most extensive treatment of the question can be found in *The Fundamental Concepts of Metaphysics: World, Finitude, Solitude*, trans. William McNeill and Nicholas Walker (Bloomington: Indiana University Press, 1995).

13. Martin Heidegger, *Plato's "Sophist,"* trans. Richard Rojcewicz and André Schuwer (Bloomington: Indiana University Press, 1997), 11; see also Heidegger, *Being and Time: A Translation of "Sein und Zeit,"* trans. Joan Stambaugh (Albany: State University of New York Press, 2010), 159 ff.

14. For more on this reversal see Daniela Vallega-Neu, *Heidegger's "Contributions to Philosophy": An Introduction* (Bloomington: Indiana University Press, 2003), 7–52.

15. Jeff Malpas confirms this assessment in "On the Philosophical Reading of Heidegger: Situating the *Black Notebooks*," in *Reading Heidegger's "Black Notebooks 1931–1941,"* ed. Ingo Farin and Jeff Malpas (Cambridge, MA: MIT Press, 2016), 12: "Although hermeneutically problematic, this tendency toward what amounts to a form of selectively focused reading is partly a result of the nature of the *Considerations*, and of the *Notebooks*, as a disparate collection of reflections on a wide range of topics, and so as lacking the sort of overarching thematic or organizational unity that would normally be associated with a single work."

16. I have deviated here from many of Rojcewicz's renderings.

17. For more on the emergency, see Richard Polt, *The Emergency of Being: On Heidegger's Contributions to Philosophy* (Ithaca, NY: Cornell University Press, 2006).

18. Translation modified.

19. Emmanuel Faye, *Heidegger: The Introduction of Nazism into Philosophy in Light of the Unpublished Seminars of 1933–1935*, trans. Michael B. Smith (New Haven, CT: Yale University Press, 2009).

20. Malpas, "On the Philosophical Reading of Heidegger," 17.

21. Ibid., 10.

PART 2

Affect, Music, Human

CHAPTER 3

Sign, Affect, and Musicking before the Human

Gary Tomlinson

Introduction

The thoughts offered here were set in motion in the course of a project to describe the emergence of music (or musicking) across evolutionary time scales,[1] but they range across several topics and disciplinary terrains. Musicking points with exemplary clarity, first, toward an intersection of evolutionary thinking in biology with the humanistic enterprise of semiotics. This crossing will lead to another, conflicted one: the crossing of an *affect theory* that proposes an extended phenomenology with the *realism* that recently has, in certain precincts of philosophy, advanced an innovative ontology. I will aim to spotlight both certain missteps of the phenomenology and opportunities afforded by the ontology. The starting point of musicking will recede, but it will not be lost from sight.

If we take the defining project of that strain of the humanities now labeled "posthumanism" to be a thinking-beyond the human and anthropocentrism,[2] we can readily see that, deployed historically, such an effort will encounter not only the nonhuman but also the prehuman. For reasons that will be surveyed later on, aligning musicking along such a deep-historical axis offers a leverage to this effort that is the more powerful because of the ways musicking stands apart from language and symbolic cognition. These latter two activities are often taken to demarcate and distinguish the human from the non- and prehuman, but musicking, properly understood, can blur this line. The blurring is achieved not especially (as might be assumed) by attending to the putative nonhuman "music" found in the world today — birdsong, whale songs, and much more; thinking of these complex communicative activities as music has for a long time confused more than it has clarified. Instead, the blurring stems from *human* musicking: from scrutinizing it for access to a broad communicative stream in the biosphere that encounters much more than the human alone, a *parahuman* stream that will further some aims of the posthumanist project.

This understanding of musicking does not, however, approach all the conformations in the biosphere that might be thought of as communicative. Rather, it runs toward biosemiotic questions that will draw distinctions even while urging parahuman inclusiveness. Human exceptionalism is seen to fade, but broader exceptions in the biosphere take shape. These exceptions, then, oppose certain moves in the recent theorizing of affect, which have tried to knock down distinguishing markers in the world of lived experience and to create a single spectrum of affective intensities extending across the whole biosphere (and even beyond it). Musicking has been a touchstone for some who have thus extended vague notions of affect or experiential intensity, in part because it figures importantly in one of their founding texts, *A Thousand Plateaus*.[3] However, they have misunderstood musicking and read Deleuze and Guattari incompletely; our adjusted view once again has an effect opposed to far-flung extensions of affect.

Something related to posthumanism's attempt to think beyond human exceptionalism has also characterized the recent turn in philosophy called *speculative materialism* or *speculative realism*. The stakes of this turn are a refuting of the correlation between thought and the world by which the latter was taken to conform to the former—Kant's Copernican Revolution in epistemology. According to Quentin Meillassoux, a leader in the new direction, this "correlationism" has been since Kant the founding premise of the Western tradition, the humanism that has determined and beleaguered the ontologies of Hegel, Heidegger, Wittgenstein, and many others down to our own day. To overturn it requires recalling an earlier mathematization of knowledge (if with a new mathematics, unknown to Galileo or Descartes or even Leibniz and Newton) and using this other dispensation to locate a place for a knowledge of events for which there could be no sentient observer, no possibility of a Kantian correlation (the Big Bang, for example). In pursuing this strategy, Meillassoux moots the possibility of knowledge of past events conceived as *of the past* rather than as a retrojection of present correlational consciousness—the mode of most twentieth-century historicisms, which have in general followed in the Kantian tradition.[4] Both the impetus to break down correlationism and the reconceiving of historicism intersect with the posthumanist superseding of humanism. As we will see, the second of these moves in particular can profit from an erecting of distinctions that some posthumanist work, particularly concerning affect, flattens.

The direction taken here, finally, is not toward effacing differences but instead toward shifting the lines drawn and the terms that enable us to draw them.

Biosemiosis and Musicking

To present musicking in a way that facilitates an approach different to the usual human/nonhuman frontier is to raise the question of its connections to a broad biosemiotics. This, in turn, broaches other frontiers: far reaches of the sign, agency, and affect. At the farthest reach, we witness these phenomena emerging from a universe of information indifferent to the presence of organic life; to this place we will return. More locally, a biosemiotic approach, in developing a general theory of the sign in the biosphere, loosens the grip of language and the symbol on our views of the emergence of the human. From a historical vantage point this is necessary because any view of the emergence of humanity must find ways to conceive pre-sapient hominins equipped with nothing like modern musicking, language, or symbolic cognition, but instead deploying protolinguistic and protomusical behaviors in sophisticated social negotiation. Linguocentric and symbolocentric approaches to deep histories of the human are ubiquitous, but they build barriers, posit revolutionary shifts, and encourage catastrophism where instead continuities are called for. Biosemiotics helps us to envisage a more far-reaching semiosis, a nonsymbolic making of signs that embraces but exceeds the human.

To analyze this sign making, biosemioticians have turned to the ideas of Charles Sanders Peirce.[5] The leverage Peirce offers comes in general from his focus on the process of signification, rather than the structure of the sign.[6] This process involves nested relations among his three famous types of signs (icon, index, and symbol), such that indices rely on icons and symbols rely on indices and therefore icons as well. Peirce's thinking on these relations was shifting and complex, but it pointed toward a stable foundation for signification, an ontological a priori to it that he termed "thirdness." He realized that signification of whatever kind involves not only the relation of sign to object (secondness), but also *a relation to this relation* of a third element. This third element is arguably Peirce's signal contribution to semiotics; he called it "interpretant."[7]

The biosemioticians' interpretant builds on this Peircean concept. It names an element of organismal activity or experience, an attending to stimuli that connects them and makes one of them a sign in relation to the other, the object. The interpretant marks an organism's experience of a relation external to itself, the fold or wrinkle that constructs a relation to a relation and thereby draws bits of information into a semiotic process. The attending aspect here is central.[8] It points up the relation of Peircean semiosis to what philosophers working in the phenomenological tradition call intentionality, the capacity of mind to be directed toward something; and it extends this capacity and its semiotic concomitants very far beyond human minds—however far, indeed, we extend the phenomenon of attention itself.

In evolutionary terms, this sweeping semiosis is always niche constructive, though niche construction need not be semiotic. The biocultural evolution of hominins and some other lineages (especially, though arguably not only, mammals and birds) may be thought of as one among several general types of niche construction. Biocultural evolution is necessarily semiotic, given the nature of culture, defined minimally as the transmitting of behaviors learned in one generation to successive generations; but most instances of niche-constructive evolution are nonsemiotic (I'll come back to examples later). This difference between semiotic and nonsemiotic evolution marks in the biosphere the limit of signs and the distinction of sign from information (to which I'll also return). The interpretant defines, ultimately, ecological entailments circumscribing certain kinds of organisms—sentient organisms, let us imprecisely say. It thus extends semiosis far out through the biosphere, rendering large reaches of it—but not all of it—a *semiosphere*:[9] the vast network of semiotic acts mediating between certain organisms and the surrounding world of information, including other organisms.

Through the interpretant, the sign becomes for both Peirce and the biosemioticians a constructive, poietic moment of the perceiver's projection of itself into its environment. The engagement of the perceiver is a reactive making of signification, not a passive registering of it or a happening upon it. This making is a two-way street, as is all niche construction: the organism, opening out to aspects of its environment, is shaped and constituted at the same time as it shapes and constitutes. The nature of this poietic mutuality can take several forms, as Peirce made clear in discerning three hierarchically ordered kinds of interpretant. "In all cases," he wrote, the interpretant "includes feelings; for there must, at least, be a sense of comprehending the meaning of the sign. If it includes more than mere feeling, it must evoke some kind of effort. It may include something besides, which, for the present, may be vaguely called 'thought.' I term these three kinds of interpretant the 'emotional,' the 'energetic,' and the 'logical' interpretant."[10] Note two things here: the alliance of feelings and meaning in *all* signs, and therefore even in the most basic, far-flung kind of interpretant; and the distinction of meaning, present in all interpretants, from *thought*, limited to the third, rarest type.

If Peirce's semiotics has been foundational in extending signification and describing a semiosphere, its impact on music studies has hardly been less important. As early as 1944, Susanne Langer's *Philosophy in a New Key* employed Peircean categories in an attempt to reconcile Eduard Hanslick's musical formalism with Ernst Cassirer's philosophy of symbolic forms.[11] Langer exercised a strong influence on Leonard Meyer's watershed study *Emotion and Meaning in Music* and thus initiated a whole genealogy in studies of musical expression and perception.[12] Recent outgrowths of this family tree with explicit Peircean orientation include the works of the music theorists Jean-Jacques Nattiez and Naomi Cumming, the ethnomusicologist Thomas Turino, and the philosopher Charles Nussbaum.[13]

These writers have emphasized the index and indexicality—Peirce's semiotic function of pointing, deixis, contiguity, in-touch causality, and embodiment—as basic to musical expression, far more so than Peirce's other sign types, icons and symbols. Some of the writers, Cumming in particular, have also considered the interpretant. This is not to say that they ignore symbolism. They cannot do so, for musicking, like all other aspects of human culture, is always suspended in symbolic webs and transformed by them, and it is only in deep-historical perspective that we encounter anticipations (not musicking and language in their modern forms) of musicking and language in a presymbolic space. Nevertheless, the effort of these theorists is at heart one of describing how musical signification is rooted in indexicality rather than symbolization and conveys meaning without semantics and many other features that language requires. Peirce's emphasis on semiosis as a process of construing perceptions and constructing signs, rather than on the sign as representation, has suited this effort well.

In its overweening indexicality, modern musicking is allied with our ancestors' presymbolic communicative sociality—their protolanguage, protomusic, and technosociality—all of which relied on the burgeoning of a deictic and proximate signification long before symbolic cognition or human modernity.[14] Modern musicking adds much to this ancient indexicality, especially a systematizing of indices, through combinatorial and hierarchic organization, that presapient hominins 300,00–500,000 years ago could not command.[15] This systematizing is akin to the indexical formalization Michael Silverstein recognizes in the pragmatics of modern language, which creates a metapragmatic level manifested in all discourse and especially pronounced in activities such as ritual,[16] except that metapragmatics hovers close above the symbols of language, while the musical systematizing of indices points away from them. Musicking in its modern form thus offers a circumstance close to unique in communication: a complex, combinatorial, and hierarchic formalization of nonsymbolic signs. But let me be clear about the import here of modernity: much evidence indicates that this formalization marshals a constellation of panhuman capacities that have existed for some 40,000–70,000 years, if not more.

Modern musicking (in this sense) relies on the kind of indexical semiotic labor broadly dispersed through the semiosphere, far beyond humans or the hominin lineage alone. For nonhuman animals, indexicality represents no half measure of semiosis, but instead semiotic fullness, the consummation of the sign. The index, for biosemioticians, marks the moment when experience and learning reshape a sign making that would otherwise remain flatly iconic, a question of difference or its absence; and in nonhuman signification in the world today, there is arguably no semiosis other than these—that is, no symbolism. Human musicking, then, merges a systematic cognition characteristic of our species with an indexical response to experience that is far more widespread. In this it restrains the human sign-making machine even from a place in the midst of a hypertrophied symbolism, beckoning toward both the parahuman and the prehuman. Musicking stands *before* the human, both chronologically and in the sense of a coeval challenging of human exceptionalism.

Sign and Information

What Peirce called the *emotive* interpretant, his most basic and widespread type, adduces a foundational affective aspect of semiosis—and of musicking too, as an aspect or kind of semiosis. This affect of biosemiotics, however, cannot be reconciled easily with that described by affect theorists such as Brian Massumi. Massumi, translator of Gilles Deleuze and Félix Guattari's *A Thousand Plateaus*, followed them in defining affect as a pre- or protoemotional experience of intensity, "a prepersonal intensity corresponding to the passage from one experiential state of the body to another and implying an augmentation or diminution in that body's capacity to act."[17] This seems to be on the right track, separating affective experience from Cartesian-style catalogs of discrete emotions; and the idea of a shift in experience recalls the interpretant-generating wrinkle and organismal engagement of biosemiotics. But Massumi takes pains to dissociate his affect from consciousness—hence, it would seem, from agency—and especially from signification all told. In an influential essay of 1995 he described intensity or affect as "a non-conscious, never-to-conscious autonomic remainder." The "autonomous system" of affect "is not semantically or semiotically ordered"—not ordered, that is, "as a conventional system of distinctive difference."[18]

We can see that Massumi has engaged here in some sleight of hand, substituting a local precinct of signification for the whole of it: his idea of conventionalized difference pertains only to the Peircean symbol, not to semiosis in general. "Signification" and "semiosis" in Massumi's account seem thus to circle back toward language, and it is on the basis of this linguocentrism that he opens his divide between them and affect. Language, he writes later, creates a level of "qualification" that does not correspond to the plane of intensity but instead typically interferes with it; it can only "amplify intensity" by "making itself functionally redundant."[19] Massumi's nonconscious intensities, meanwhile, offer up a strange kind of experience, one that shifts without awareness or attention and then "implies" altered capacities. For higher animals, his affect includes processes such as those of the autonomic nervous system; but can we reasonably maintain that autonomic changes are always experiential, or are they so only when they bring about a shift of attention? Is my peristalsis experiential and affective, or does it come to be such only when my indigestion or my postprandial torpor makes itself felt or known?

The biosemiotic interpretant, instead, involves meaning in its shift of experience or attention; "there must," as Peirce said, "be a sense of comprehending the meaning of the sign." The interpretant also incorporates an irreducible element of agency, for it is a function of the organism's relation to its surroundings, a reaction to or imposition on it by which the organism produces sign and object. Such consciousness or awareness marks the moment of shifting attention; by another name it marks a salience that rises up in the relation of the animal to itself and its environment, through processes we understand only imperfectly.[20] The biosemiotic approach recognizes the shifting intensities of Massumi's affect and certainly allows for organismal shifts without awareness or consciousness; but it encompasses affect within the semiotic process, involving it always in agency and meaning. It extends agency and meaning as far as poietic interpretants can be found in the animal kingdom.

How far can we track this animate making of signs? To answer this question will be to define the emergence of semiosis from information.[21] It is clear, to start, that the sign cannot be coextensive with information;

the sign is not environmental stimulus alone, but instead results from a particular process enacted *upon* information that makes a relation to a relation. This difference is described, from other angles, by several approaches to an understanding of information. "Shannon information," for example, as described and quantified in Claude Shannon's famous article of 1948,[22] reserves no place for anything like Peirce's interpretant. It could not do so, because Shannon's account was one of secondness, not thirdness, as is made clear by his disregard of any content or "meaning" transmitted. Shannon information entails no relation to a relation but is instead relation alone, a correspondence distanced along a channel. In framing the fundamental problem of communication as "reproducing at one point either exactly or approximately a message selected at another point," Shannon captured the essential reduplicative nature of informational secondness. Information can be quantified prior to any content it might carry, but not prior to its transmission from sender to receiver. The very phrase "information transmission" is a tautology, for information comes about only in a doubled existence.

More recently, Jerry Fodor emphasized this reduplication and gave us something closer to a definition of information. Again, the key term of contrast is meaning: "There is a lot less meaning around than there is information. That's because all you need for information is reliable causal covariance.... Information is ubiquitous but not robust; meaning is robust but not ubiquitous."[23] Reliable causal covariance captures the tautology of all information. As a postulate of minimal requirements, it sets the bar very low, pervading the cosmos with information in all manner of simple and complex systems. From our Peircean vantage we might say that in a situation of secondness nothing more than reliable covariance is possible—but a good deal less. As there is no third term to intervene and connect two terms—that connection producing the sign—there remain only two possibilities: a conformation/ correspondence/ covariance or its absence.

Information in Fodor's sense, then, is ubiquitous far beyond the biosphere—and necessarily, then, foundational within it. In a conversation some years ago I asked the evolutionary theorist Stuart Kauffman for a biologist's definition of information, and he paused only briefly before responding: "A bacterium swimming up a glucose gradient"— not a definition, but an adroit and exemplary instance. To say that the bacterium is not processing information would defeat any useful definition of the term. But at the same time, it makes little sense to think of a bacterium forming meanings or indulging in interpretant poiesis, or to assign to it agency (I'll come back to this point). It makes little sense, in other words, to think of a bacterium in terms of thirdness; its relation to the world is one of sheer secondness, informational through and through. This contrast between the bacterium and animals distinguishes a fundamental pair of overlapping functions in the biosphere. Since Fodorian information characterizes all organized systems, all living things are information processors; but only some living things, a slim minority at that, are sign makers.

Orchid and Wasp

Placing limits on signs in the far broader field of information opens fascinating questions regarding the emergence and proliferation of semiosis in a portion of the biosphere and a slice of its history. What thresholds needed to be crossed in the complexity of living organisms in order for thirdness to appear? Was the crossing inevitable in a biosphere burgeoning in complexity about 550 million years ago? Was there a certain kind of complexity within organic design that could not but be accompanied by an emergent semiosis?

Entertaining these questions, posed here in deep-historical terms, illuminates a divide between types of coevolution that the evolutionary theorist Richard Prum exemplifies in a different way: by contrasting the roots of a plant with its flowers.[24] To describe the natural selection that resulted in plant root systems, he notes, we need little more than knowledge of the nutrient requirements of plants and of the physical conditions in which many of these nutrients may be obtained—solubility of nutrients, osmosis and diffusion mechanisms across cell membranes, and so forth. This is true notwithstanding the coevolutionary feedback dynamics of many sorts that arose in the course of root-system evolution among different species of plants, other organisms, and the nonliving environment, all of which would figure in a fuller account of the niche-constructive history of any species. The flower, on the other hand, requires from the start a different kind of explanation, one that takes account of coevolutionary feedback. This is because the selection for flowers depended in some measure upon the interactions of plants with animate organisms—pollinators, such as flying insects and birds. As these constructed their niches, so flowers constructed theirs, in a shifting mutuality of selective pressures.

The Peircean perspective allows us to see something further about Prum's phylogeny of flowers. It is not merely coevolutionary from the start; it is also *fundamentally but not wholly* semiotic. The animate organisms creating the feedback loops whereby selective pressures were altered and reshaped were not mere information processors; the cells of the root system were this, covarying reliably with gradients and other factors in the soil around them. The pollinators, instead, were sign makers, generating interpretants that guided their behaviors. For them, the flowers pointed to—were indices of—their own requirements. This semiosis, then, entered as a crucial aspect into the coevolutionary feedback by which flowers, information processers but not sign makers, evolved.[25] I observed before that not all coevolution need be semiotic; now we see that many nonsemiotic organisms emerged from niche-constructive interactions with semiotic ones.

The relation of flower and animal pollinator can also be described without reference to semiosis, and Steven Shaviro, working from Deleuze and Guattari's *A Thousand Plateaus* and Alfred North Whitehead's *Process and Reality* to put Kant's aesthetic judgment on a Darwinian footing, has recently pursued this avenue.[26] Shaviro's key term is beauty, which, he agrees with his sources, arises as a process enacted between flower and pollinator. Beauty does not inhere in an orchid, and neither is it a pure projection onto the flower by a wasp; instead, it comes about as a relation between the two or through an "aparallel evolution" of them (to use a phrase from *A Thousand Plateaus* that seems to do the same work as the more transparent "coevolution" of the biologists).

Shaviro follows Whitehead deeply into this process. Orchid and wasp are connected to one another through what Whitehead called *prehensions*, "concrete facts of relatedness" by which the two are brought into a nexus that mutually constitutes both as "actual entities" or "actual occasions."[27] Such networks of mutual constitution stand at the heart of Whitehead's processualism: *"how* an actual entity *becomes* constitutes *what* that actual entity *is"* (PR, 23). A prehension, then, is "referent to an external world," and thus it has a "vector character"; this directedness involves purpose, valuation, causation and, most basically, emotion or feeling (PR, 19). A flower's beauty results from what Whitehead termed a *proposition*, a prehension in action along which change in the world comes about (paraphrasing Shaviro) or (quoting Whitehead) "an element in the objective lure *proposed for feeling"* by the prehension, which, "when admitted into feeling...constitutes *what is felt."* Shaviro concludes simply: "Something *happens to* the wasp" that "encounters the orchid"; from this prehension, or proposition of feeling, arises felt beauty.[28]

I will return to Whitehead's prehensions and feelings below, but for now I note that in Shaviro's nonsemiotic analysis of the wasp and the orchid we once again veer toward affect theory—and also toward its discontents. We end up with something like Massumi's agentless affect, since the wasp's active changing of the world seems to disappear in its experience of the flower's proposition. The wasp is swept up in a process that alters it (as an occasion in the world) and from which emerges its feeling; only then, perhaps, does its agency kick in, as it flies to the flower. To be sure, Whitehead's phrase "admitted into feeling" needs here to be taken into account, as it seems to hint at an agency like that in the Peircean interpretant. In the interpretant, however, the agency of the semiotic partner is never obscured.

An additional difficulty concerns the term *beauty* itself. Shaviro's notion of a wasp experiencing beauty cannot be mere poetic license, for its implications are large. They are so because affect theory, when it is not busy divorcing agency and meaning from animal experience and thus narrowing semiosis toward the human (a stance of anthropocentrism), pursues an almost opposite course along which capacities and percepts of a distinctly human cast are widened implausibly beyond the human (anthropomorphism). Shaviro moves in this direction when he likens wasp to gardener in the full version of a quotation excerpted above: "The orchid is not beautiful in itself: but something *happens to* the wasp, or to the gardener, who encounters the orchid and feels it to be beautiful." Both gardener and wasp perceive or construct beauty, and we can see that it is Whitehead who has sponsored Shaviro's rejection of human exceptionalism in the assimilation of the two. The move is a laudable one, in keeping with the best aims of posthumanism in general; but if not carefully made, it comes at a price. Let us see how this price is paid in a strain of affect theory different from Massumi's.

Difficulties of Ubiquitous Agency

With its distinction of signs from information, the approach I have outlined makes apparent the continuity between humanity and a broader community of life as well as an equally evident discontinuity: the uneven, partial distribution of agency and meaning in that community. It extends agency and meaning as far as the sign itself, far beyond the human, but at the same time not as far as all life, and certainly not beyond the biosphere. This is a position of exceptionalism, but of a broad, latitudinarian sort.

Rejecting this position leaves two alternatives, both unacceptable. I have already suggested the first: a retreat to a narrow exceptionalism in which signs and semiosis (often confused, in this position, with symbolism) are the sovereign attainment of humans alone, or perhaps of humans and a few other species. In this move the rich, complex experiential world of animal poiesis far beyond the human is effectively reduced to causal covariance, information-alone, nonsemiotic secondness. The implausibility of this reduction is apparent to any observer of that poiesis among higher animals in the world today, which evinces agency and experience of meaning, two hallmarks of thirdness and the interpretant.

The second alternative to the biosemiotic approach avoids this anthropocentrism but swings far in the other, anthropomorphic direction. It proposes a fantastical extension of meaning and agency through the whole of the biosphere, and in some cases beyond it. This option has been taken by some recent affect theorists, who seem to react to the exclusion of consciousness and agency from Massumi's affective intensities by filling the cosmos with both. The option has found advocates also in a broader attempt to rethink the object on philosophical grounds—an "object-oriented ontology" that shades often into a revival of an ancient panpsychism. I will consider these one at a time.

A good example of the hyperextension of meaning and agency comes in William Connolly's response to Ruth Leys's critique of affect theory.[29] Wishing to save his view of affect, Connolly extends agency and intentionality very far indeed—and far beyond consciousness. To do so he cites Kauffman's bacterium-and-glucose gradient, the example of information from my dinner-table conversation, which Kauffman later worked up in a book. Kauffman wrote: "Let us stretch and say it is appropriate to apply [agency] to the bacterium. We may do so without attributing consciousness to [it]. My purpose in attributing actions (or perhaps better, protoactions) to a bacterium is to try to trace the origin of action, value, and meaning as close as I can to the origin of life itself."[30] We note immediately Kauffman's qualifications of the notion even of bacterial action, let alone agency: "Let us stretch and say ..."; "actions, or perhaps better, protoactions." We note also Kauffman's frank special pleading. He wants to make not just agency but value and meaning as closely coterminous with life and its origin as he can manage. There is a metaphysics at work here, one signaled in the title of Kauffman's book, *Reinventing the Sacred: A New View of Science, Reason, and Religion*.[31]

More important, however, is the fact that Kauffman's definition of agency is sweepingly broad—too broad, finally, to be of use in affect theory; Kauffman makes this clear, but Connolly does not cite this part of the discussion. An agent, Kauffman specifies, is any system of self-generating, self-sustaining complexity, able minimally to carry out thermodynamic work, bounded by a membrane, and with receptors to detect food or avoid poison. "Virtually all contemporary cells," he says, "fulfill this expanded definition."[32] It may be that the catchment of "agency" can be usefully applied to all cells—to a cell in my liver, for example, or to a cell in a leaf, as well as to the bacterium; if it is, however, the word loses its power to characterize the more local affective experiences of more complex organisms.

We can underscore this point with a Kauffmanesque thought experiment. Imagine with Connolly that a single bacterium, without central nervous system, nucleus, or any other bounded organelles, evinces an agency linked to affect. What mechanisms would experience or express this? The answer would need to be the receptors and the mechanisms of action they involve: the flagella and their molecular controls that enable the cell to swim toward increasing glucose concentration. But then how do we avoid extending agency further? We would need to think, for example, of the agency of the mechanism of coding and translation that builds the proteins for the flagellum—amino acids locking in order to translating messenger RNA. But if we extend agency this far, mustn't the regress continue, to the atomic valences in the molecules that bring about the bonding on which protein coding depends? We are getting close to the electrons-with-feelings of some of the wildest affect theorists.

But we have at hand a category other than affect or intentionality for all these phenomena. It is information, reliable causal covariance. The bacterium is an information processor par excellence, indeed, a miniature miracle of information processing. We may wish to follow Kauffman and, by lexical convention, apply the term *agency* to all this complexity. But the disadvantage of doing so, as I have said, is that the term ceases to do useful work in our conversations about the far less widespread phenomena of affect, interpretant making, and meaning; and the advantages of doing so are unclear at best, except in the service of a metaphysics like Kauffman's. So let us say again: Information is basic to life, and much else beyond, while semiosis is more narrowly distributed, and only within the biosphere. Distinguishing between the two offers a way of modeling fundamental differences that have emerged across the history of the cosmos. Agency, meanwhile, may be coterminous with semiosis (in the Peircean view) or there may be some other way of thinking about it, but it cannot both be extended to the limit of life or, beyond that, the limit of information and at the same time be usefully related to affect.[33]

The extension of agency is allied in Connolly's thinking, as it is in that of other affect theorists, with a narrowing misapprehension of the idea of signification. (We have already witnessed this narrowing at work in Massumi's position.) In these views, the sign often comes to seem synonymous with *representation*, a term, in this usage, opposed to embodiment and embodied experience; or with *conventionalization*, which seems to some of these writers to define the sign but of course is limited in Peircean semiosis to one (rare) type of sign, the symbol; or even with *ideology*, an effect of human culture and society and their patterns. If signification is made coterminous with ideology or even conventionalized signs, it certainly cannot be extended far beyond the human. Meanwhile, accepting a representational view of the sign pushes us once again back toward human exceptionalism and Kant's epistemological revolution.

No such limitations are found in the approach I've advocated here, combining a broad extension of the sign, conceived as relation-to-relation, with an ontological distinction of signs from information. The semiotic realm is seen to be vast but not without limit; from these features the model gains a power not only to efface the border between the human and the nonhuman but also to describe biocultural, coevolutionary processes that arise in all cultural animals and from which human modernity may plausibly be supposed to have emerged.

Whitehead's Feeling, Harman's Relations

On the other hand, suppose rocks have feelings. Then we might as well attribute to them agency also. Such a revival of panpsychism is the direction in which some have carried the new ontologies of objects. This brings us to the second anthropomorphic trend named above: the philosophical extension of affect, experience, agency, and even mind.

Both modest "object-oriented" ontologists and more radical panpsychists have relied on Whitehead's post-Kantian, processual ontology, introduced above. The crux of the matter involves Whitehead's vectorlike prehensions, activated in the form of propositional feelings, and the emotional experience that results from them. Remember the orchid, the wasp, and the gardener, and imagine now (as Whitehead did) that the entity-constituting emotional involvement extends not only to the gardener or even to the gardener and the wasp, but to the orchid also. Now extend the realm of feeling with another example: a lizard seeking the warmth of a rock that has been sitting in the sun. In this circumstance, Whitehead would say, prehensions or propositional vectors extend in several directions: between lizard and rock, between rock and sun, and between lizard and sun. These prehensions alter in greater or lesser degree the actuality as entity-in-process (or as *occasion*) of lizard, rock, and sun, and they do so in ways involving causation, valuation, purpose, and, most basically, feeling. Whitehead thus gave the term *feeling* a new, technical status: he meant it to capture an aspect of the mutual, causal alterations that shape all entities.

Now take a further step with the object-oriented ontologist Graham Harman. For him, these feelings or prehensions are indistinguishable, whether it is the lizard or the rock or even the sun that prehends. Their categorical sameness challenges the Kantian tradition, in which "human access" to reality has been privileged; now we describe equivalencies to human access: lizard access, rock access, sun access.[34] In Shaviro's reading of Harman, this position is tantamount to panpsychism; "'human access,'" Shaviro writes, "is no different in kind from the sort of mental or epistemological access that all entities have to whatever other entities they encounter. I prehend the sunlight that warms me ... in much the same way that ... fire prehends the cotton that it consumes." Here the granting to fire of a "mental access" is arresting (at least), but for hard-core panpsychists it follows, as Shaviro shows, from Whitehead's defining of cognition, thought, and mentality as outgrowths of his fundamental feeling. Affective relation is a component of all the constitutive relationality in the world and, as such, sponsors all these other relations and their breadth.[35]

It is evident, however, that there is a wide gap between Whitehead's "feeling" and the "affect" of the affect theorists. Likening the two runs the obvious risk of an unintended category switch, in which a colloquialism ("feelings") is mistakenly taken to be synonymous with a carefully defined technical term. Feeling, in Whitehead's sense, cannot aid in attempts to define and distinguish affect from such things as Cartesian emotions; at least, if it is posited to do so, its efficacy will need to be established from the ground up according to the principles of Whitehead's ontology. In this, Whitehead's feeling is like Kauffman's agency: Each term has been coopted to denote so encompassing an aspect of reality that it has been made inapt for the more quotidian uses to which affect theorists put it.

Harman's position, on the other hand, amounts to much more than inadvertent category switching or wide-eyed panpsychism. For him, objects "perceive" insofar as they stand in relation to one another, not as a simple fact of their existence or their endowment with some soul-like quality (*QO*, 122). He uses the example Shaviro cites of fire and cotton related through prehensions—it is a favorite of his—to advance not an all-out panpsychism, but a "polypsychism" in which all objects might relate to one another (thereby "perceiving") but do not necessarily do so.

This points to a fundamental tenet of Harman's object-oriented ontology: its division of real and sensual objects. Real objects are autonomous from what encounters them, standing outside of relationality and withdrawing from the "experience" of other objects; Harman relies on Heidegger's tool analysis to describe this category. Sensual objects are objects as they enter into relations with other objects, "encrusted with accidental qualities" as a result of those relations; this category Harman adapts from the intentionality or attending-to of Edmund Husserl and Franz Brentano (QO, chaps. 2 and 3 and pp. 47–48). In relation to Whitehead, we could put Harman's position this way: his sensual objects are, like Whitehead's objects, connected by prehensions and emerging as occasions through relational processes; but his real objects propose something essential about objects that departs from Whitehead's thinking.

The fundamental "ontological rift" (QO, 119) for Harman, then, comes not between human perceptions and the rest, in the Kantian manner, but between real objects and relationality—that is, sensual objects. The power of this formulation is considerable, but so also is its tendency to flatten the other rift I have pointed to: the rift—or, better, deep-historical rupture—that introduced signs into a cosmos of informational causality alone. There is little place in Harman's ontology for the difference between Peircean secondness and thirdness, little place also for the difference in the biosphere between more and less complex organisms. Insofar as his sensual object is a matter of an intentionality made ubiquitous—objects directed toward or attending to other objects, thereby "encountering" or "experiencing" them—it is like Whitehead's prehensional feeling. Both conceptions aim to characterize all relationality at a foundational level; in this they converge on my information, sharing with it both conformational and causal aspects.[36] But neither conception has much to say about semiotic agency and its particular, redoubled relationality or thirdness.

Assimilated to information, Whitehead's feeling and prehensions and Harman's perceptions and encounters among objects might be seen as solidifying the borderline between information and sign, helping us to pinpoint a categorical difference in relations of entities in the world, rather than as dissolving the cosmos into a puddle of undifferentiated affect. This difference, as we can now reaffirm from another vantage point, intersects obliquely with the old border between the living and nonliving. Information and its relationality range freely across this border; semiosis, meaning, affect, feeling (in the affect theorists' various senses), experience, and consciousness all are far more narrowly circumscribed.

Biosemiosis and Musicking Again: *A Thousand Plateaus*

The close bond of semiosis with affect, feeling, or emotional intensity that I have advocated should come as no surprise to the affect theorists, since it is basic to *A Thousand Plateaus*, a foundational text for their approach. Deleuze and Guattari start from a position akin to Whitehead's processualism, defining affect as the forces of "becoming-animal," the animal drives that are the de- and reterritorializations of assemblages.[37] From Spinoza's *Ethics* they borrow a distinction of active and passive affects, reframing these as the capacities for action and for undergoing that characterize any animal and connect it to the network of intersecting assemblages making up the abstract machine of nature. Affective assemblages themselves are coalescences of relations that resemble Whitehead's networks of entities connected by prehensions or Harman's relations of objects—or at least resemble the small portion of these that form within the animal/animate realm. Deleuze and Guattari see no objectification or frozen representation here; indeed, they single out, as a primary failing of psychoanalysis, its view of the (human) animal as a fixed representation of its drives, rather than as a becoming-animal shifting with the flux of its assemblages. For them, in sum, "affects are becomings."

Representation and objective fixity, then, are foreign to affect as well as the assemblages it de- and reterritorializes; but must signification also therefore be divorced from affect, in the manner of Massumi? By no means. Deleuze and Guattari define affect as what an animal can do in its assemblages; the assemblages themselves, in which becoming-animal occurs and to which that becoming gives shape, appear as arrays of environmental entailments or affordances in which animals' capacities intersect with each other and with the inanimate world. The sum of an animal's affects, all its capacities for acting and undergoing, provide the measure of its becoming; and for this reason, counting or tallying animal affects is for Deleuze and Guattari nothing other than ethology itself. To make and exemplify this point they rely on Jacob von Uexküll and his famous analysis of the *Umwelt* of the tick.[38] With this move, their position on affect migrates from a source of affect theory to a reflection on biosemiotics, since Uexküll is a forefather of that field and his tick its semiotic, interpretant-generating exemplar. Uexküll's *Umwelt* is not a territory in which a distinct animal eats, mates, and defends itself. Instead, it is an assemblage, affectively and semiotically made and unmade in the relations of becoming-animal.

Deleuze was well aware of this semiotic orientation. In an interview with Catherine Clément on the 1980 publication of *Mille plateaux*, he explicitly connected animal assemblages, ethology, and semiotics. "We are trying," he said, "to substitute the idea of assemblage for the idea of behavior: whence the importance of ethology, and the analysis of animal assemblages, e.g., territorial assemblages.... In assemblages you find states of things, bodies, various combinations of bodies, hodgepodges; but you also find utterances, modes of expression, and whole regimes of signs."[39] Here fixed "animal behavior" is transformed into becoming-animal and assemblage making, and these in turn are allied to semiosis. Deleuzians and affect theorists alike are quick to connect "affect" in A Thousand Plateaus with Spinoza. Fair enough. They are considerably slower to explore its rich, essential connection to Uexküll's semiotic ethology—a cherry-picking that has obscured much.

Peircean semiotics in A Thousand Plateaus is not restricted to the becomings of nonhuman animals, of course. One of the central chapters in the book is devoted to distinguishing the several "regimes of signs" Deleuze mentioned in the interview, and it starts from ideas of Peirce, "the true inventor of semiotics."[40] From my parahuman, biosemiotic perspective this chapter is of limited relevance, since it concerns the need to reassert a specifically linguistic pragmatics submerged during the post-Chomskyan era and hence attends mostly to language and symbol. But one distinction drawn here stands out for our purposes: an arrangement that aligns the index with territorialization ("the territorial states of things constituting the designatable"), the icon with reterritorialization ("operations ... constituting the signifiable"), and the symbol with deterritorialization ("a constant movement of referral from sign to sign").[41] It would be a mistake to oversolidify or rigidify this scheme, since territorialization, deterritorialization, and reterritorialization are, throughout A Thousand Plateaus and beyond, not opposed to one another but linked as processes of formation and change in assemblages. (Deterritorialization, Adrian Parr has written, "inheres in a territory as its transformative vector"; again we drift close to Whitehead's prehensions.)[42] Nevertheless, we can push the indexicality/territoriality alliance here in directions that will allow us to follow Deleuze and Guattari's discussion of musicking and the refrain along a specifically semiotic path.

It is important to do this because musicking attracts affect theorists like moths to a flame, usually because they think it accommodates their vague ideas of intensities unfettered by sign, meaning, or agency. Here is Jeremy Gilbert, for example: "Music has *physical effects* which can be identified, described and discussed but which are not the same thing as it having [sic] *meanings*, and any attempt to understand how music works in culture must ... be able to say something about those effects without trying to collapse them into meanings."[43] Here a hoped-for, embodied affect-without-meaning is mooted; but "meaning" seems restricted to something representational or symbolic, in the Massumian manner of linguistic meaning—a bird or a cat could not have it. With Gilbert's mention of culture, also, we are on the verge of rehabilitating the pernicious old nature/nurture chasm (which Whitehead and Massumi, along with many others, had wisely thrown out).[44] It is hard to tell how close to the edge Gilbert comes, but Eric Shouse, elaborating Gilbert's views, jumps over:

> Music provides perhaps the clearest example of how the intensity of the impingement of sensations on the body can "mean" more to people than meaning itself.... In a lot of cases, the pleasure that individuals derive from music has less to do with the communication of meaning, and far more to do with the way that a particular piece of music "moves" them. While it would be wrong to say that meanings do not matter, it would be just as foolish to ignore the role of biology as we try to grasp the cultural effects of music.[45]

What is missing from both Shouse and Gilbert, obscured by their eagerness to discover embodied intensities without meaning, is any appreciation of the complex, hierarchized, formalized, and combinatorial cognition, perception, and action that must be in play for musicking to emerge from the more general stream of acoustic stimuli. The effects they value in musicking could just as well pertain to the impact of a foghorn blaring unexpectedly in the darkness or the explosion of a volcano, the bark of a dog or the buzz of a mosquito. We may welcome such terminological expansiveness, like a band of Italian Futurists, and want to extend thus the catchment of "music." As in the cases of Whitehead's *feeling* and Kauffman's *agency*, however, we do so only by disqualifying the term for other, more discerning uses.

Deleuze and Guattari, for their part, instead tried to take account of such musical formalizations. They concluded their chapter linking Spinozist affect, becoming-animal, and Uexküll's tick with a section on becoming-music, and they followed this with a long chapter on music and the refrain (*ritournelle*).[46] The gist is that the refrain is a frozen territoriality—here we come back to Uexküll, since it is birdsong and its territorial imperatives that Deleuze and Guattari play upon—which poses a block of content captured in an assemblage that stands at the heart of music, but *is not itself* music. Music comes about with the deterritorializing of the refrain in a process in which machinic transversals cut across its assemblage: the Beethoven machine, the Berio machine, the African shrike machine.[47] An assemblage is thus opened to other assemblages; interassemblages result that are at once new structurings of refrains, remaking their selective pressures or territories. The voice poses the refrain, but the "machining" of the voice (*machination de la voix*) creates music. Musicking is a surmounting of the fixed imperatives of vocal repetition, the frozen "mate with me" or "get off my land" messages of the birdsong. Or, to allude to one of the recurring issues in Deleuze and Guattari's thought, the refrain is actual, but musicking virtual: a set of immanent vectors of sound formalizations that undermine all tendencies to sameness of that-which-returns (the *ritournelle*).

Musicking, then, affirms the becoming and change immanent in all repetition and signification; this is its exemplary force for Deleuze and Guattari. The indexicality of the refrain, its alliance with territoriality, is seen to be subject, like all other becomings-animal tallied in ethology, to the transformations of the assemblage. Indexicality and musicking alike are caught up in the parahuman, semiotic play of transversals that *re*territorialize as they *de*territorialize. These transversals constitute new territorial outcomes, in the interassemblage, of machinic operations. There is something systematic about this animate building of interassemblages; semiosis broaches new possibilities for order in the biosphere's machinic transversals. For musicking's part, the transversals are well described as the formalizations of its indexical signs. These are never static, always becomings; they arise in all the things we might call musicking, human and nonhuman, but they assume outlines of advanced formalization in human musicking, marking large differences between a Beethoven machine and a shrike machine. (To underscore these differences, minimized in Deleuze and Guattari's account, and not to devalue the immense complexities of nonhuman communication, I have here pursued parahuman semiosis through human musicking alone.) Because these formalizations assume fleeting, territorial arrangements, they indexically affiliate human musicking with rites and religion, with social difference and transcendence, perhaps with fascist force, as Deleuze and Guattari assert. This is the effect of the refrain-as-actual, but it is unmade by musicking-as-virtual. This power of musicking opens onto affective and signifying realms that are characteristically human but that extend continuously far beyond the human. Deleuze and Guattari never lost sight of these continuities of affect, sign, and meaning, and musicking is one of their signal exemplifications of all three. These are lessons affect theorists who tarry in musical locales need to take to heart.

History versus Historicism: Meillassoux

The revival of Whitehead and his prehensions and the new object-oriented ontology of Harman are aspects of the recent development of speculative materialism I described briefly in the introduction to this chapter. This line of thought counters Kantian humanism and its aftermaths, especially the fundamental correlation in which knowledge of the world is seen to arise from the nature of human access to it, given only through our being. It is evident why this move away from the Kantian base would appeal to all the positions encountered above opposing human exceptionalism: not only panpsychism but affect theory, Shaviro's aesthetics, and my biosemiosis.[48]

But there is, I think, a special connection between the biosemiotic approach and Quentin Meillassoux's brand of speculative materialism, introduced in his manifesto *After Finitude*. This connection concerns life and the life sciences, and in it the import of biosemiosis can be seen in a bright light while an opportunity not seized by Meillassoux can be defined. I conclude with a gesture toward this double opening: toward parahuman biosemiosis philosophized, and toward an adjusted view of the question, central to Meillassoux's project, of the relation of science to a nonhuman past or future.

This question, though it cannot be answered simply, can be simply put: if all knowledge is shaped by human access to the world, what is the nature of the knowledge created by modern science concerning the world at a time when there were (or will be) no humans to gain this access? Less plainly: if knowledge is subject to the limits and conditions laid out in Kant's transcendental idealism, in this way given to human comprehension and made in it, how is it that "science thinks [it is] ... *a time which, by definition, cannot be reduced to any givenness which preceded it*" and allowed it to emerge (*AF*, 21)? Meillassoux pursues this puzzle by reconsidering several starting points for post-Cartesian thought: not only Kantian correlationism, but, before it, Hume's questioning of the grounding of causality and Leibniz's principle of sufficient reason. The resolution Meillassoux sketches is mathematical, for mathematics (he argues) offers access to the world that is absolute without being transcendental or relying on metaphysics. He exemplifies this through Georg Cantor's set theory (also developed by his teacher Alain Badiou), which demonstrates the "transfinite," that is, the impossibility of totalization even in a set of infinite members (*AF*, 103–5). The point is neither easy nor fully explicated by Meillassoux, but we can attempt to sum it up this way: the world is contingent because in it causality and laws can find no stable ground. Mathematics can model this contingency without recourse to metaphysical presumptions because it can model absolute realities that are nontranscendental (i.e., nontotalizable). Without this mathematical means, we are cast back onto the attempt to sidestep or evade contingency, a project inevitably reliant on illusions of transcendentalism and special human access. "Whatever is mathematizable," in sum, can be posited as an ontological fact without involving thought or the transcendentalism of its correlations; therefore, mathematization defines a thought "able to think a world that can dispense with thought" (*AF*, 116–17).

This role for mathematics, according to Meillassoux, renovates the mathematization of nature that defined the Galileian and Cartesian inauguration of modern science. It reasserts the noncorrelational thought of science in its pre-Kantian form and moves to close the schism between philosophy and science opened by Kant. His shaping of knowledge according to the conditions of human access to it was not, after all, the Copernican Revolution he thought it to be, since it was not a decentering of humanity in the cosmos like the real Copernican Revolution, from which the Galileian and Cartesian mathematization followed. It was instead the opposite: a reinstalling of humanity in its central place, nothing less than a "Ptolemaic counter-revolution" (*AF*, 118–19).

In the wake of this Kantian "reversal of the reversal" (*AF*, 119), this recentering of decentered humanity, historicism assumed its modern shape. Historicism, for Meillassoux, is a "topsy-turvy" affair, in which the temporality of thought of the past is always reversed by correlational access to it: "You thought that what came before came before?," the Kantians ask; "Not at all: for there is a deeper level of temporality, within which what came before the relation-to-the-world is itself but a modality of that relation-to-the-world." For the correlationist, "the deep meaning of the pre-human past consists in its being retrojected on the basis of a human present." Historicism and the philosophy that sponsors it both fail to face squarely the "*paradox of manifestation*" presented by science, the sheer fact of "empirical knowledge of a world anterior to all experience" (*AF*, 123).

Meillassoux's critique of correlationist historicism suggests an opportunity hidden in his argument to define further this kind of knowledge-before-experience. He does not seize the opportunity, for it depends on recognizing two revolutionary turns in modern science, not just one, and he attends only to the first. In addition to his Galileian mathematization of nature, arising from the Copernican decentering of the human, there is, no less powerful, the Darwinian historicization of life.[49] If Galileian and Cartesian mathematics proffered a contingent but absolute *means* for understanding nature-without-humanity,

Darwin's variation-with-selection discovered a *process* leading to a parallel but independent understanding. It is an abstract machine in the Deleuzian sense, a virtual operation immanent in the realm of life by which life *must* manifest itself to thought as a linearity that reaches back to a time before thought. Natural selection and variation built a time machine that opposed the formation of history as retrojection even as this historicism was taking shape. Thinking the machine manifested previously inconceivable dimensions and categories of pastness (though, in the midst of the Kantian regime, these needed to be disguised under labels such as a historicist "prehistory").

Darwin's, modified and enriched across the last century, spawned others that widened his historicization from life to nature as a whole, from the speciation of living things to the Big Bang. These other Darwinian machines, defined as often as not by Meillassoux's mathematics, generate chaotic recursivity, spontaneous order, and emergent complexity of all sorts. They also are time machines, involve processes of feedback and/or selection, and are indifferent to humanity and its being-in-the-world. (Meillassoux may conceive his mathematics as just such a virtual time machine, though this is not clear in *After Finitude*; however this may be, when he asks, "What is it that happened 4.56 billion years ago? Did the accretion of the earth happen, *yes or no?*" [AF, 16], the opportunity signaled in his question is a Darwinian more than a Cartesian or Galileian one.) In the operation of all these machines, the upside-down temporality of Kantian historicism is turned right side up again. The reversal of the reversal is reversed. The past recovers its pastness, and mind is understood not as that which grants access to the world, but as one among numberless end points arising from what came irrevocably *before*.

The Darwinian and post-Darwinian machines are at root anti-Kantian. Indeed, they point up a real irony of correlationism: Transcendental thought thinking its history—that is, thinking how transcendental thought could arise in a biosphere without it—requires models of process and continuity that it itself threatens to make inconceivable. The catastrophism I mentioned before, by which many models of the emergence of human modernity assert a sheer human difference, is a gauge of the effectiveness of the threat, and also a measure of ineffective understandings of Darwin's achievement. Rightly conceived, that achievement amounts to a qualitative challenge as radical as the Galileian/Cartesian quantitative one to the defining of knowledge by means of human access.

The drawing of wide, parahuman borders that I have attempted in this essay is therefore not a reinstituting, on another scale, of metaphysics or Kantian epistemology—not merely an extension to dolphins or crows of the correlational access assigned by others only to humans. Instead, it stakes an ontological claim afforded by these two scientific revolutions—especially by the second, since this was the turn in our thought that guaranteed a historicism beyond the human. What is to be gained in not allowing such borders to be effaced is a precision in describing an empirical past that poses us as its future—which is to say that the borders delineate a deep-historical projection that is something other than a retrojection. What would it be like, finally, to *think* the burgeoning of semiosis from within a cosmos organized by information alone? Or the emergence of affect and mind from a biosphere without them? Or the advent of the human from a nonhuman world? This is the history of the future that Darwin's machine holds out to us.

Notes

1. See my *A Million Years of Music: The Emergence of Human Modernity*, 1st ed. (New York: Zone Books, 2015); also, my "Evolutionary Studies in the Humanities: The Case of Music," *Critical Inquiry* 39, no. 4 (2013): 647–75. I am grateful to Jairo Moreno and Gavin Steingo for their close reading of an earlier version of this essay and perceptive comments on it. That version appeared in *boundary 2*, no. 43 (2016), a special issue they edited entitled "Econophonia: Music, Value, and Forms of Life," pp. 143–72. The essay originated as an address to the conference "Sound and Affect: Voice, Music, World," SUNY Stony Brook, April 18–19, 2014; I am grateful to the organizers, Judith Lochhead, Eduardo Mendieta, and Stephen Smith, for the invitation to participate.

2. Three important accounts, among many, are Cary Wolf, *What Is Posthumanism?* (Minneapolis: University of Minnesota Press, 2010), for an approach along Derridean lines with a large admixture of the systems theory of Niklas Luhmann; Rosi Braidotti, *The Posthuman* (Cambridge, UK, and Malden, MA: Polity Press, 2013), for a Deleuze/Guattarian vantage informed by feminist and postcolonial theory; and Donna J. Haraway, *Staying with the Trouble: Making Kin in the Chthulucene* (Durham, NC: Duke University Press, 2016), for an unsettling of some already hardening posthumanist truths.

3. Gilles Deleuze and Félix Guattari, *A Thousand Plateaus: Capitalism and Schizophrenia*, trans. Brian Massumi (Minneapolis: University of Minnesota Press, 1987); first published as *Mille plateau*, vol. 2 of *Capitalisme et schizophrénie* (Paris: Éditions de Minuit, 1980).

4. Quentin Meillassoux, *After Finitude: An Essay on the Necessity of Contingency*, trans. Ray Brassier (London and New York: Continuum, 2008), esp. chaps. 1, 4, and 5. Hereafter, this work is cited parenthetically in the text as *AF*.

5. See, e.g., Thomas A. Sebeok, *Signs: An Introduction to Semiotics*, 2nd ed. (Toronto: University of Toronto Press, 2001); Sebeok, *Global Semiotics* (Bloomington: Indiana University Press, 2001); Terrence Deacon, *The Symbolic Species: The Co-Evolution of Language and the Human Brain* (New York and London: W. W. Norton, 1997); Deacon, "The Symbol Concept," in *The Oxford Handbook of Language Evolution*, ed. Maggie Tallerman and Kathleen R. Gibson (Oxford and New York: Oxford University Press, 2012), 393–405; Deacon, "Beyond the Symbolic Species," in *The Symbolic Species Evolved*, ed. Theresa Schilhab, Frederik Stjern-

felt, and Terrence W. Deacon, Biosemiotics 6 (Dordrecht: Springer Netherlands, 2012), 9–38; Paul Kockelman, "Biosemiosis, Technocognition, and Sociogenesis: Selection and Significance in a Multiverse of Sieving and Serendipity," *Current Anthropology* 52, no. 5 (2011): 711–39; and Kockelman, *Agent, Person, Subject, Self: A Theory of Ontology, Interaction, and Infrastructure* (Oxford and New York: Oxford University Press, 2013).

6. See Kockelman, *Agent, Person, Subject, Self*, 13–14.

7. For Peirce's views discussed in this section, see Charles S. Peirce, *The Essential Peirce: Selected Philosophical Writings*, vol. 2, *1893–1913*, ed. Peirce Edition Project (Bloomington: Indiana University Press, 1998), 4–11, 161–64, and 401–21; Peirce, *Philosophical Writings of Peirce*, selected and ed. with an introduction by Justus Buchler (New York: Dover, 1955), chap. 7 ("Logic as Semiotic: The Theory of Signs"); and Peirce, *Selected Writings (Values in a Universe of Chance)*, ed. with an introduction and notes by Philip P. Wiener (New York: Dover, 1966), 381–93.

8. See Gary Tomlinson, *Culture and the Course of Human Evolution* (Chicago: University of Chicago Press, 2018), chap. 4. Kockelman describes the interpretant simply as a "change in attention"; see *Agent, Person, Subject, Self*, 14.

9. The term was coined by Juri Lotman in the early 1980s; see Lotman, "On the Semiosphere," trans. Wilma Clark, *Sign Systems Studies* 33, no. 1 (2005): 205–26.

10. Pierce, *The Essential Peirce*, 409.

11. Susanne K. Langer, *Philosophy in a New Key: A Study in the Symbolism of Reason, Rite, and Art* (Cambridge, MA: Harvard University Press, 1942). Hanslick's *Vom musikalisch-Schönen: Ein Beitrag zur Revision der Ästhetik der Tonkunst* (Leipzig: Rudolph Weigel, 1854), reprinted many times into the twentieth century, described a uniquely musical formalism that has remained a strong current in musical thought. It is by the measure of this formalism that other arts, from poetry to architecture, came more and more to be seen as "aspir[ing] to the condition of music," to recall Walter Pater's famous phrase. Hanslick's formalism engendered new conceptions of the distance between music and language; Langer's important book attempts to draw together many strands, including a Wagner-derived theory of myth and an early anthropological theory of ritual, but its chief ingredients are Hanslickian musical formalism and a theory of signs that joins Peirce with Cassirer.

12. Leonard B. Meyer, *Emotion and Meaning in Music* (Chicago: University of Chicago Press, 1956).

13. Jean-Jacques Nattiez, *Music and Discourse: Toward a Semiology of Music*, trans. Carolyn Abbate (Princeton, NJ: Princeton University Press, 1990); Naomi Cumming, *The Sonic Self: Musical Subjectivity and Signification* (Bloomington: Indiana University Press, 2000); Thomas Turino, "Peircean Thought as Core Theory for a Phenomenological Ethnomusicology," *Ethnomusicology* 58, no. 2 (2014): 185–221; Turino, "Signs of Imagination, Identity, and Experience: A Peircean Semiotic Theory for Music," *Ethnomusicology* 43, no. 2 (1999): 221–55; Turino, *Music as Social Life: The Politics of Participation* (Chicago: University of Chicago Press, 2008), esp. chap. 1; and Charles O. Nussbaum, *The Musical Representation: Meaning, Ontology, and Emotion* (Cambridge, MA: MIT Press, 2007).

14. See my *A Million Years of Music*, esp. chaps. 3 and 5.

15. Ibid., chap. 4. For more on systematized indexicality and its general role in recent hominin evolution, see Tomlinson, *Culture and the Course of Human Evolution*, esp. chaps. 5–7.

16. See Michael Silverstein, "Metapragmatic Discourse and Metapragmatic Function," in *Reflexive Language: Reported Speech and Metapragmatics*, ed. John A. Lucy (Cambridge: Cambridge University Press, 1993), 33–58; Silverstein, "Indexical Order and the Dialectics of Sociolinguistic Life," *Language and Communication* no. 23, no. 3 (2003): 193–229.

17. Massumi, in Deleuze and Guattari, *A Thousand Plateaus*, xvi.

18. Brian Massumi, "The Autonomy of Affect," in "Politics of Systems and Environments, Part II," *Cultural Critique* 31 (Autumn 1995): 83–109; the essay was republished as chap. 1 of Massumi, *Parables for the Virtual: Movement, Affect, Sensation* (Durham, NC: Duke University Press, 2002). Here also is Eric Shouse, glossing Massumi's position: "An affect is a nonconscious experience of intensity; it is a moment of unformed and unstructured potential. Of the three central terms in this essay—feeling, emotion, and affect—affect is the most abstract because affect cannot be fully realized in language, and because affect is always prior to and/or outside of consciousness (Massumi, *Parables*). Affect is the body's way of preparing itself for action in a given circumstance by adding a quantitative dimension of intensity to the quality of an experience. The body has a grammar of its own that cannot be fully captured in language because it 'doesn't just absorb pulses or discrete stimulations; it infolds contexts…' (Massumi, *Parables* 30)." See Shouse, "Feeling, Emotion, Affect," *MC Journal* 8, no. 6 (2005): para. 5, http://journal.media-culture.org.au/0512/03-shouse.php.

19. Massumi, "The Autonomy of Affect," 86.

20. See, e.g., Duane M. Rumbaugh, James E. King, Michael J. Beran, David A. Washburn, and Kristy L. Gould, "A Salience Theory of Learning and Behavior: With Perspectives on Neurobiology and Cognition," *International Journal of Primatology* 28, no. 5 (2007): 973–96.

21. For an extended discussion, see Tomlinson, *Culture and the Course of Human Evolution*, chap. 4.

22. C. E. Shannon, "A Mathematical Theory of Communication," *Bell System Technical Journal* 27, no. 3 (1948): 379–423, http://cm.bell-labs.com/cm/ms/what/shannonday/shannon1948.pdf; see esp. 379–80.

23. Jerry Fodor, *A Theory of Content and Other Essays* (Cambridge, MA: MIT Press, 1990), 93.

24. Richard Prum, "The Evolution of Beauty," talk given at the Whitney Humanities Center, Yale University, January 2013; see also Richard O. Prum, *The Evolution of Beauty: How Darwin's Forgotten Theory of Mate Choice Shapes the Animal World—and Us*, 1st ed. (New York: Doubleday, 2017).

25. In saying this of the flower I am aware of—if not convinced by—recent extensions to plants of semiotic agency (as opposed to complex information processing and transmission). For an overview of early work in this field, see Kalevi Kull, "An Introduction to Phytosemiotics: Semiotic Botany and Vegetative Sign Systems," *Sign Systems Studies* 28, no. 1 (2000): 326–50. For an introduction to current debates concerning plant cognition, learning, and more, see Michael Pollan, "The Intelligent Plant," *The New Yorker*, December 23, 2013, https://www.newyorker.com/magazine/2013/12/23/the-intelligent-plant.

26. Steven Shaviro, *Without Criteria: Kant, Whitehead, Deleuze, and Aesthetics* (Cambridge, MA: MIT Press, 2009), 2–4; also chap. 3.

27. Alfred North Whitehead, *Process and Reality*, ed. David Ray Griffin and Donald W. Sherburne, corrected ed. (New York: Free Press, 1978), 22.

28. Shaviro, *Without Criteria*, 3; see Whitehead, *Process and Reality*, 187.

29. William E. Connolly, "The Complexity of Intention," *Critical Inquiry* 37, no. 4 (2011): 791–98; see also Ruth Leys, "The Turn to Affect: A Critique," *Critical Inquiry* 37, no. 3 (2011): 434–72.

30. Quoted from Connolly, "The Complexity of Intention," 793.

31. Stuart A; Kauffman, *Reinventing the Sacred: A New View of Science, Reason, and Religion* (New York: Basic Books, 2008).

32. Ibid., 78–79. Kauffman has devoted much of his career to describing autocatalytic systems in aggregates of molecules, or, as they are also termed, autopoietic systems. See esp.

his earlier books *The Origins of Order: Self-Organization and Selection in Evolution* (Oxford and New York: Oxford University Press, 1993) and *Investigations* (Oxford and New York: Oxford University Press, 2000). For a classic account of autopoiesis, see Humberto R. Maturana and Francisco J. Varela, *Autopoiesis and Cognition: The Realization of the Living* (Dordrecht and Boston: Reidel, 1980).

33. There is another possibility regarding the agency of bacteria, one that is mooted by Connolly ("The Complexity of Intention," 793): that it can be an emergent product of bacterial collectivities and their internal relations. The complexity of such aggregates is great (and fascinating), but the burden of demonstrating the heuristic advantage that comes from the application to it of the term "agency" is a large one. Moreover, invoking "emergence" as a magic word wherever complexity appears in the world or when old-style, reductionist causal accounts falter is an increasingly frequent expedient in humanistic and social-science accounts, one that seems to me to lurk in Connolly's recourse to the emergent agency of bacterial colonies. This is not to doubt in general the importance of emergent complexity in explanatory accounts across many disciplines, only to insist that it amounts to more than an incantatory invocation — as it does in Kauffman's earlier work (see n. 32 above) or in the thought of Terrence Deacon, e.g., "The Hierarchic Logic of Emergence: Untangling the Interdependence of Evolution and Self-Organization," in *Evolution and Learning: The Baldwin Effect Reconsidered*, ed. Bruce H. Weber and David J. Depew (Cambridge, MA: MIT Press, 2003), 273–308. For my modeling of emergent processes involved in the biocultural evolution of *Homo sapiens*, see *A Million Years of Music*, chaps. 1, 6, and 7; and *Culture and the Course of Human Evolution*, chaps. 5 and 7.

34. See Graham Harman, *The Quadruple Object* (Winchester, UK, and Washington, DC: Zero Books, 2010), 44–47 and 118–19. This work will be cited parenthetically in the text as QO.

35. Steven Shaviro, "Consequences of Panpsychism," http://www.shaviro.com/Other texts/Claremont2010.pdf, 6, 13–14. Whitehead was more careful than some modern-day panpsychists to distinguish the special way he used the word "mental": "Mental activity is one of the modes of feeling belonging to all actual entities in some degree, but only amounting to conscious intellectuality in some actual entities" — in effect, another Whiteheadian redefinition for special purposes of a commonplace term; see *Process and Reality*, 56.

36. On the "conformal" "phase" of feelings, see Whitehead, *Process and Reality*, 164. For Harman, causation must of course originate in the sensual (i.e., relational) realm, but it asymmetrically involves real objects also; see Harman, *The Quadruple Object*, 74–76.

37. See Deleuze and Guattari, *A Thousand Plateaus*, chap. 10; for the following two paragraphs, esp. pp. 254–60.

38. See Jakob von Uexküll, *"A Foray into the Worlds of Animals and Humans,"* with *"A Theory of Meaning,"* trans. Joseph D. O'Neil (Minneapolis: University of Minnesota Press, 2010).

39. From "Eight Years Later: 1980 Interview," in Gilles Deleuze, *Two Regimes of Madness: Texts and Interviews, 1975–1995*, ed. David Lapoujade, trans. Ames Hodges and Mike Taormina (Los Angeles, CA: Semiotexte, 2006), 175–80, at 177. My thanks to Jairo Moreno for drawing this interview to my attention.

40. Deleuze and Guattari, *A Thousand Plateaus*, chap. 5; for Peirce the inventor, see n. 41 (p. 531).

41. Ibid., 112.

42. Adrian Parr, ed., *The Deleuze Dictionary* (New York: Columbia University Press, 2005), 67.

43. Jeremy Gilbert, "Signifying Nothing: 'Culture,' 'Discourse' and the Sociality of Af-

fect," *Culture Machine* (2004), accessed August 19, 2014, https://culturemachine.net/deconstruction-is-in-cultural-studies/signifying-nothing/.

44. "It is meaningless to interrogate the relation of the human to the nonhuman if the nonhuman is only a construct of human culture.... The concepts of nature and culture need serious reworking, in a way that expresses the irreducible *alterity* of the nonhuman in and through its active *connection* to the human, and vice versa. It is time that cultural theorists let matter be matter, brains be brains, jellyfish be jellyfish, and culture be nature, in irreducible alterity and connection." Massumi, "The Autonomy of Affect," 100.

45. Shouse, "Feeling, Emotion, Affect," para. 11.

46. Deleuze and Guattari, *A Thousand Plateaus*, 299–350.

47. "A machine," they write, "is like a set of points that insert themselves into the assemblage undergoing deterritorialization, and draw variations and mutations of it." Deleuze and Guattari, *A Thousand Plateaus*, 333 (trans. modified; see *Mille plateaux*, 411). Manuel De Landa ranks among the most important commentators on the Deleuzian/Guattarian abstract machine; of his several accounts, my favorite is the least systematic: *A Thousand Years of Nonlinear History* (New York: Zone Books, 1997). For De Landa's recent thoughts on the assemblage, see *Deleuze: History and Science* (New York: Atropos, 2010), esp. chaps. 1, 3, and 4.

48. These affinities, however, might in some cases prove illusory. I have suggested, for example, how the extension of affect far beyond the human can amount to anthropocentrism or anthropomorphism—neither one an effective countering of Kant's humanistic idealism.

49. I am not the first to point to a Darwinian inadequacy in Meillassoux's conception of science; for a response along different lines than mine, see Martin Hägglund, "Radical Atheist Materialism: A Critique of Meillassoux," in *The Speculative Turn: Continental Materialism and Realism*, ed. Levi Bryant, Nick Srnicek, and Graham Harman (Melbourne: re.press, 2011), 114–29.

CHAPTER 4

Human Beginnings and Music

TECHNOLOGY AND EMBODIMENT ROLES

Don Ihde

For many years, I have tried to keep up with the latest developments in science. One exercise has been to regularly read *Science, Scientific American,* and for a long time, *Nature.* Supplementing these I include *The New York Times, Science Times, The Economist,* and *National Geographic.* I am also a dedicated watcher of science documentaries. But, of course, all of science is too much, and so my favored clippings are thematic: human origins, human migrations, and the newest in human archaeology and anthropology. Another favorite is acoustics, or anything related to the experience of sound—including music and animal sounds—and musical technologies or instruments.

So no one should be surprised to learn of my fascination with the human origins of music and musical practices and instruments. This essay will thus begin in the prehistoric past with questions about humans and their musical experience. If we begin with physiology and the current fads deeply related to neurology, we can presume that as soon as we humans could move and vocalize, bodily music and dance were part of what we did. But since, lacking any material remains, we have no direct empirical evidence for these activities, the best we can do is speculate from current physiological and neurological findings.

Ice Age Music

We do not even know for sure which hominids first attained language; debates are currently raging about whether Neanderthals had it. But in this regard, maybe musical praxis—or at least archaeological remnants of it—preceded language, since there is some evidence they had musical instruments. Although some DNA has been extracted, the fossil remains of the Neanderthals are not good enough to prove that their laryngeal development was sufficient for speech. Yet current animal studies now show that many creatures of the animal kingdom produce songs, have learning patterns similar to ours for learning songs, have cultures of song with different dialects, and have songs that evolve (many birds, most cetaceans, mice, possibly a few primates, etc.).[1]

So here is my own relatively conservative speculation: I suspect the first human musical praxis was bodily, at least singing and dancing, and was practiced by our predecessors the Neanderthals and possibly their newly discovered contemporaries the Denisovans. Possibly the earliest physical evidence of a dance may be the clay floor of the roughly 40,000 BP Chauvet Cave,[2] on which footprints indicate what appears to be a dance pattern. The site is in the deepest part of the cave, thus the scene had to include torches and likely some form of singing.[3] Others surmise that since many of the cave rooms are large and acoustically excellent, they may have served regularly for ritual singing and dancing. Iegor Reznikoff, a French acoustical scientist, visited a number of Ice Age caves and found a good number of acoustically excellent cavern spaces with animal paintings on the walls (including Niaux, a cave I have also visited). Of Niaux, Reznikoff says, "Most of the remarkable paintings are situated in the resonant Salon Noir, which sounds like a Romanesque chapel," and he concludes that in a prehistoric parallel to cathedrals, a musical ritual may have been a part of cave practice.[4]

Instruments are also introduced at about this time, although they too are surrounded by controversy. The oldest of the "bonewinds," as I call them, dates to 45,000 BP and is associated with a Neanderthal site.[5] This four-hole flute, broken at the ends, is usually considered a human-made flute, and a physical analysis of the hole separation indicates that it was tuned to the upper tones of a diatonic scale. The counterargument is that the holes were made by an animal bite, not human drilling. I side with the flute interpretation because I think a tuning system as suggested is unlikely from an animal bite; it is hard for me to imagine a hyena-tooth spacing that produces a diatonic tuning. However, birdbone flutes from 36,000 BP are clearly flutes, since the holes show drill marks more clearly. Interestingly, the hole spaces yield a very close tuning system encompassing the upper tones of a diatonic scale. These are associated with *Homo sapiens* sites in the Hohe Fels Cave in Germany.[6] I do not think it a far stretch to speculate that while not yet discovered, there may have been not only singing, dance, and flutes, but percussion instruments as well. Later horns were invented, probably first using an animal horn as an instrument, and I have described prehistoric evidence of simple string instruments, some of which were simply a multistable use of a bow under tension or a hunting bow used musically. The earliest depiction of this is 15,000 BP, but arrows date back to at least 22,000 BP.[7] Bushman cliff paintings show groups playing hunting bows under tension with gourd resonators. These simple single-stringed instruments were still played into modern times by Bushmen and, owing to the ancient slave trade, in Brazil. Ancient one- and two-stringed ancient instruments are also still played in Chinese music. As with all instruments, to play with skill calls for learned bodily motions, and with these simplest instruments very subtle overtones may be produced that give the music an unexpected complexity.

Ancient Instrumentation

Now, making nearly a ten-thousand-year leap, I want to look at a very old group of stringed instruments which, interestingly, could be considered multicultural in form and practice: these are known as the lute in the West, the oud in Asia Minor, the sitar in India, and the shamisen in Japan—four geographically distant cultures. The single-stringed bow, sometimes with a gourd resonator, goes back to the late Ice Ages; the lute/oud/sitar/shamisen group—all with multiple strings, a resonator sound box, and a neck with or without frets and played by plucking either with the fingers or a plectrum—dates to antiquity. Instruments in this group are depicted in representations from Babylonian, Egyptian, and other ancient cultures starting roughly 4000–3000 BP. While there is no clear evolution and developmental history or set of artifacts that would span the ten-thousand-year leap, once multiple-stringed instruments begin to be used, it is rather amazing to note the parallelism of design.

I first want to look at some of the variations, developments, and convergences in design. Very early lutes, ouds, sitars, and shamisen were often three-stringed, a fact frequently reflected in the etymology of the names. Strings multiplied over time, with most classical variations of these instruments having from three to seven strings. Interestingly, Eastern instruments often had an uneven number of strings, while Western instruments were more likely to have an even number; however, there were exceptions in each case. There was an also discernible movement toward more and more strings—up to eighteen in Europe and twenty-one in India. The original narrow necks of these instruments were widened as more strings were added, but only a small number of strings, between three and six, were used to play melodies. The added strings often served in the role of drones, usually at lower or bass pitches. This evolution happened in all the cultural streams I examined. Instrument necks varied in shape, with different bends or curved shapes, and necks could be fretted or unfretted. Strings were usually gut at first; later metal was used, and later still, nylon.

Resonators also followed interesting variational lines. Indian instruments often used large gourds—not unlike the prehistoric gourd resonators—whereas Chinese and Japanese variants used drumlike, skin-covered resonators. The favored materials were often dog or cat skins. European lute and Persian oud sound-box resonators were usually constructed, hollow, wooden boxes.[8] In all cases, small variations in instrument construction were associated with the different musics to be played. These varied from ritualistic and meditative styles to more raucous and louder street and dance musics. What strikes me is that both the variations and the convergences occur in all four of the cultural strands I am identifying, yet the different musical styles remained distinctly varied. From the microtones of Indian raga to the distinctive tuning system of Asian classical music, to Renaissance musics—each music was unique.

Given the subtle differences, even within a given cultural strand, the performers had to hone different playing skills. Multiple-stringed instruments, like other musical instruments, take hours and years of practice to attain a virtuoso level of performance. And in the case of multiple-stringed instruments, this includes delicate tuning. One saying in the field is, "If you have played for eighty years, sixty of those have been spent tuning." And there is also a very ancient association here with notation. The earliest notation, which goes back to approximately 4000 BP, is a Babylonian tablature incised on a clay tablet, which was then baked. Tablature is an isomorphic depiction of a stringed neck with marks to show finger placements at the proper frets. This notation can be found in a number of cultures and was the earliest in our own tradition, although it eventually gave way, at least in classical music, to the two-staff systems we now predominantly use.[9]

Finally, before leaving almost a millennium of this group of multiple-stringed and plucked instruments, I want to turn to lessons learned from a broader history of technologies. I claim that all technologies have "shelf lives." The most ancient stone technologies seem to have had the longest shelf lives—such as the case of the Acheulean hand axe, a bi-faced, multipurpose tool most likely invented by *Homo erectus* 1.8 million years BP. This form and style of tool remained basically unchanged for 1.4 million years and seems to have been abandoned at the time of Neanderthals. The lute-style multiple-stringed instruments I have been describing, assuming we begin with their depictions, lasted several millennia, with peak use in all the areas noted from roughly 800 BP until the more complicated keyboard music of the Western classical period 250 years ago.[10] Of course multiple-stringed instruments are still played, if no longer in lute forms, then in classical instrumental forms (violins, violas, cellos, string bass, etc.) and the use of many guitar variants, mostly electrified today.[11]

Synthesizers

My next leap is not so vast in time, but in technology it is a much greater one than the previous ten-thousand-year jump. Synthesizers are contemporary and electronic, and they entail very different technologies, embodiment practices, and constructed sounds. The first synthesizer is usually considered to be the theremin, invented by Leon Theremin in 1920. It came into being by accident. Theremin intended to make a machine that could measure gas pressures and diffusions. It included an L-shaped antenna that produced an electromagnetic field in the space between the arms of the L. Theremin found to his surprise that when he moved his hands in this space, strange and eerie sounds were produced. After playing and experimenting, he discovered he could produce melodies.[12] This was a radical departure for a musical technology — it electronically produced its own sounds, which were unlike those of any extant instrument. As a musical instrument, it did not really catch on, although a few virtuoso players did perform on it, and it was added to a few orchestra ensembles. Where it became popular — and this was to be the fate of many early synthesizers — was in film scores as nondiegetic music or a sound effect, particularly in the genres of science fiction and horror. The electronic sounds were not produced by strings or by the physical processes of traditional instruments; rather, they resulted from electromagnetic processes. Unlike traditional instruments, the theremin was not played physically by touching the instrument itself, but by moving one's hands in empty air in the L space of the antenna. Thus, while it is clear that the learned bodily skills required to play the theremin remained a requirement, these were more dancelike than even keyboard embodiment skills. Still, the absence of physical contact with the instrument is a transformation in embodiment relations, one that relates to subsequent developments as well.

Before I continue the focus upon synthesizers, I need to make a brief aside to another development of digitally produced music. The mid-twentieth century saw a vast expansion of recorded music. Today's nostalgia for vinyl (analog) LPs looks back at what was once the most popular recording technology, that form later replaced by digital CDs, for which studio manipulation could construct sounds, remove noise, and change the music to be heard. And while both LP and CD recordings were at first home-centered musics, the coming of portability produced yet another transformation. The Walkman and related portable technologies allowed individual users to take music with them—on walks, as the name suggested, but also while jogging or just sitting in a park. Today, of course, digital musics are no longer tied to discs but are played through MP3 or other portable and earbud players. This was music dissociated from wider social or concert settings.[13]

I have discussed synthesizer development more extensively in *Acoustic Technics* (2015) and shall not repeat that work here; rather, I shall turn to the most contemporary form, the digital synthesizer. The contemporary synthesizer—like so many of our electronic technologies—looks more like a computer, with screen, keyboard, and speakers, than like any traditional musical instrument. Its "innards" are transistors, wires, and a complex of electronic sound *and visual* producing technologies. One can experimentally manipulate and shape each sound, which is also displayed on a screen, often in oscillograph waves, now in glowing multicolor. The output or display is usually audio-video, parallel to the whole spectrum of such technologies (televisions, cinema, computer displays, etc.). Early synthesizer players often liked the ability of the synthesizer to mimic any sound. Even cheap digital pianos could be made to sound like an organ, a koto, a harpsichord, or whatever. Soon, however, experts moved to prefer the non-isomorphis of electronic acoustic sounds and began to explore the range of the synthesizer's never-before-produced sound qualities.

I have attended many synthesizer "concerts," which are, compared to traditional orchestra, chamber, or even rock concerts, *disconcerting*. A series of electronic boxes fill the stage, and usually the musical piece is already recorded. Thus while there is a concert technician who may be the composer, there is no actual human player. This implies a very different kind of embodiment for performance. It is not gone, but has occurred offstage, as it were. The actual production of the music—and usually the composer is also the player—has occurred in a studiolike setting. Most of the drama of a live performance has simply been displaced. To counter this, many contemporary composers utilize a multimedia show. My own experience of such events has been many events at the Brooklyn Academy of Music featuring the compositions of Philip Glass or Steve Reich—*Hindenburg, Einstein on the Beach*, and similar musical and screen displays that include synthesizer music. The drama is restored, but in a new genre very distinct from any traditional concert. But such a hybrid multimedia concert also places the synthesizer back in an instrumental role. It is but one sound strand alongside the live performers; thus, like the theremin, it becomes only a part of the ensemble.

Earlier analog synthesizers, well described in Trevor Pinch and Frank Trocco's *Analog Days* demonstrates that the Moog and Buchla synthesizers follow two different shapes and playing styles.[14] The Moog had a keyboard and was the forerunner of the proliferation of digital keyboards that followed. The Buchla was more like a music studio and had buttons, switches, and moveable rheostat-type levers. Today, in an interesting development, a set of new hybrid synthesizers is available specifically for doing music online. These machines have both a keyboard and a studiolike control board and can be programmed to place music online or stored in the cloud. Such a transformation changes what counts as an audience, since they are played by manipulating the combined keyboard-studio control panel, and they open onto a global listening audience (without being a concert). It is the online, multi-listener counterpart to the smaller, carry-around, earbud music machines that grew out of Walkman-like devices. This diffusion onto the Internet brings with it variations on collaborative composition. One can sing on—with up to nine others—such a site at MIT.

Summary and Conclusions

Now, taking a long view of the time slices surveyed here, one can imagine human music originating even before modern humans, *Homo sapiens*. If, as surmised, our first music might have been instrumentless, having been instead an embodiment action probably encompassing singing and dance, then origins are fully embodiment actions. Instruments, too, are clearly prehistorical, going back at least to the early Ice Ages, since the discovered instruments, flutes, go back that far. Was the music as sophisticated as the visual art—cave paintings—and sculpture of the times, 40,000+ BP? If a (diatonic) tuning system was employed, there obviously had to be some sophistication on the part of the makers. The bodily skills, with these earliest instruments, directly held and played, had to have been experienced in what I call *embodiment relations*, in which the instrument is taken as a kind of extension and transformation of bodily expression. Flute playing, with spaced holes for fingering, and later proliferations into all sorts of woodwinds beginning with recorders, maintained a very long trajectory of both playing and sounding. By the end of the Ice Age, of course, many other instruments were used, some known only through depictions.

My second time slice, mostly from depictions but also from tablature notation, goes from 4,000 BP to 250 years ago, with the instruments still being played today but in small numbers. I began with one small class of plucked, multistringed, lutelike instruments, but horns, percussion, and keyboards (although later in this period) were also played. Yet in this several-millennia-long duration, most embodiment involves direct physical playing, with tactile use of the instrument. Each calls for, minimally, nuanced differences in skills, and much practice is needed for virtuosity. In researching this selective history, I was surprised to see how parallel developments occurred in the full range of different cultures I described. However, the musics in the selected cultures remained distinctly different. Only in late modernity do significant hybridizations seem to occur. One good example is the mid-twentieth-century impact of the sitar and Indian raga music on Euro-American popular musics—Ravi Shankar and George Harrison come to mind.[15]

My third, contemporary, and electronic music slice showed, in some ways, the most radical transformations of music. I indicated that by digitizing and using electronic technologies, deep modifications of embodiment, of sounds, and of social practices take different forms in today's world. I shall point to only a few aspects of this transformation. First, sounds. Each period emphasizes and focuses on different sound qualities. For example, in the very simple instrumentation of prehistory, the quality of overtones assumes great importance in performance, listening, and playing. Two examples would be the one- or two-stringed Chinese instruments and similarly, the single-stringed hunting bows of Africa or Brazil. In later periods, the change from gut to metal strings produced very different tones. And in electronic music, timbre is often forefronted.

I have not here forefronted a well-known phenomenon of music history, although this has been well documented by, for example, Trevor Pinch and Karin Bijsterveld.[16] That is, with each change of instrumental technologies there is a protesting outcry. Pinch and Bijsterveld focus upon the introduction of mechanical keys for woodwinds, and one can see why. Each change of technology brings with it a different selectivity of musical possibilities. To add mechanical keys is to gain precision, speed, and the like, while lessening the previous vibrato fingering skills.

In this exposition I hinted at the introduction of keyboard music, roughly the time of Bach, which made possible a much wider range and complexity of music than is possible on the lute. But there were also those who complained about how "mechanical" the keyboard was in comparison to the harp. My years of retirement spent listening to keyboard virtuosos in Carnegie Hall leaves me doubtful that with the keyboard has come any loss of virtuosity.

Notes

1. I address this phenomenon in greater detail in *Acoustic Technics* (Lanham, MD: Lexington Books, 2015).

2. I use the scientific dating convention of "before present."

3. Jill Cook, ed., *Ice Age Art: Arrival of the Modern Mind* (London: British Museum Press, 2013), 45–47.

4. Reznikoff, quoted in Ker Than, "Stone Age Art Caves May Have Been Concert Halls," *National Geographic News*, October 28, 2010, 1.

5. Nicholas J. Conard, "A Female Figurine from the Basal Aurignacian of Hohle Fels Cave in Southwestern Germany,." *Nature* 459 (June 2009): 248–52. doi:10.1038/nature07995.

6. Cook, *Ice Age Art*, 46–47. An updated and more accurate dating analysis was applied in 2012 and showed that this flute dates from 43,000 BCE.

7. Don Ihde, *Experimental Phenomenology: Multistabilities*, 2nd ed. (Albany: State University of New York Press, 2012). See the chapter titled "Under Bow Tension."

8. "Lute" and "Oud," Atlas of Plucked Instruments, accessed February 13, 2020, http://www.atlasofpluckedinstruments.com/index.

9. Thomas Forrest Kelly, *Capturing Music: The Story of Notation*, 1st ed. (New York: W. W. Norton, 2014), 59.

10. "Lute," Atlas of Plucked Instruments, accessed February 13, 2020, http://www.atlasofpluckedinstruments.com/lutes.htm.

11. Don Ihde, "Sound beyond Sound," in *The Routledge Companion to Sounding Arts*, ed. Marcel Cobussen, Vincent Meelberg, and Barry Truax (New York: Routledge, 2017).

12. Albert Glinsky, *Theremin: Ether Music and Espionage* (Urbana: University of Illinois Press, 2000).

13. Stacey O'Neal Irwin, *Digital Media: Human-Technology Connections* (Lanham, MD: Lexington Books, 2016;, see esp. chaps. 5–8.

14. Trevor Pinch and Frank Tocco, *Analog Days: The Invention and Impact of the Moog Synthesizer* (Cambridge, MA: Harvard University Press, 2002).

15. "Sitar," Wikipedia, accessed May 17, 2016, https://en.wikipedia.org/wiki/Sitar.

16. Trevor Pinch and Karin Bijsterveld, "'Should One Applaud?' Breaches and Boundaries in the Reception of New Technologies in Music," *Technology and Culture* 44, no. 3 (2003): 536–59.

CHAPTER 5

The Life and Death of Daniel Barenboim

James Currie

In a quite literal sense, a great deal of excitement accompanied the development of affect studies within the Anglo-American academy. As pertinent as the ideas and concepts that were starting to accumulate within these developments was the tangible impression of the sensations, feelings of intensity, and force momentums that scholars themselves now seemed able to access by giving their attention to such ideas and concepts. It was as if the ideas and concepts were, to a degree, as much a ruse, and the collateral of excitations the scholars' real prize. Keeping this in mind, and aligning it with the basics of Deleuzian notions of affect—whose proclivities are similarly toward sensation, intensity, and force, and which will be my primary theoretical orientation in this essay—I might then make the following proposal: that the development of affect studies was itself affectively charged to a high degree, as if something of the very content of affect theory were being replicated recursively at the qualitative level of scholarly life experience. As a result, the distinct markers under which academic work had, at the basic, pragmatic level of action, been relatively happy to operate—in which subjects (academics) investigate objects (such as affective life) according to professionalized standards for validating the reality of findings—seemed to have undergone some kind of transformative cross-fertilization. Once more, scholarly practice was therefore marked recursively, since one of the absolute basics of affect theory across the board has been to dissolve autarkic conceptualizations of the thinking subject into a more fluid, relational, and dialogic mode. In the words of the geographer Nigel Thrift, to take but one such formulation, "Individuals are generally understood as effects of the events to which their body parts (broadly understood) respond and in which they participate."[1] Subjectivity no longer preexists its objective confrontations, but is rather an emergent property of the productive contagion between the human and objects (human or otherwise).

Of course, one could put the whole thing down to fashion and write it off as yet another example of the mimetic hysterics attendant on yet another academic fad—scholars "acting out" in the manner of the very theories under whose spell they have fallen. If by "fashion" something tangible is meant—for example, the inordinate degree to which the forces of the market and commodification, and the social and political pressures on which they feed, can penetrate right to the very center of academic production—then I would, with qualifications, concur. Indeed, under the aegis of professionalism, this will constitute in part one of the lines from which the counterpoint of this essay will be composed. But the condemnation is usually meant as a one-liner to curtail further discussion, like swatting an irritating fly, and a full sociopolitical understanding of the forces influencing the academic production and dissemination of ideas, for example, is not so easily concluded, nor the point so easily quashed. More often than not "yet another academic fad" is shorthand for world-weary assumptions that there is nothing new under the sun, and that any aspiration otherwise will eventually find itself subject to gravity and be forced back down to earth. As with professionalism, I will have more to say about gravity later on. For the moment, however, we should note that there is nothing inherently meaningless about something that happens repeatedly and with a similar affective charge, such as when academic fashions shift and scholars get excited. In psychoanalysis, for example, such things are of the essence, and I would argue likewise. Academic fads might thus be thought of as highly charged symptoms: manifest through them is the full degree to which academic practice (which seeks to know) is subjected to the gamut of social, political, and economic forces that press in upon it but are simply too extensive to be kept fully present as knowledge to academic consciousness when it is at work. The time of academic fashions' full intensity is both the best and worst of times, where the darkest of ideological obfuscations entrap academic discourse unawares from behind, but also where thwarted utopian hopes rise up from the dead once more.

Regarding affect studies and their relationship to the study of music and sound, I will be interested more in the latter question of thwarted hopes and dreams. Keeping to my first theme of the recursive replication of affective intensity at the very level of the scholarly practice that investigates affective intensity, I will be seeking to make inroads into opening up the following: what might be gained for musicological discourse if it were somehow to become like music, understood here as a certain form of affective sonic intensity? In this essay, the realization of this aspiration—the becoming-music of musicology, to speak the speak for a moment—will imply that musicology has managed to find a means of inhabiting what I will call *musical life*. In this condition, something that is learned first within the boundaries of the musical then passes over, like an infection, to act as a transformative contagion in aspects of life, which I will refer to as *extramusical* life, that are not usually identified as being musical per se. As I will endeavor to illustrate, with this edifying transgression of the conceptual boundaries that enable us to demarcate some things as music and others as not, a number of our normative categories come to be seriously challenged. The three main ones that my argument will address itself are: (1) *professionalism* and the attendant division of labor that it imposes upon the various activities (such as work and leisure) that constitute our life; (2) *language* and the often highly instrumentalized values we bring to bear on judging its usage; and (3) *the human* and the assumptions we make about what ground is foundational in order that it might be unambiguously identified. As will become clear quite rapidly, the potential influence of affectively conceptualized notions of music upon each of these categories acts as a catalyst for a kind of metastasization of interdependent transformations between them. By the end of this chapter, the utopian aspect implicit in affect's ability to realize such transformations will have been drawn to the surface. In the conclusion, I will suggest reasons that the utopian possibility in relationship to affect studies in the academy was nevertheless missed, and what this might imply about the future of academic life, understood (shamelessly and without apology) in its broadest, existential sense.

Although this essay will be concerned with addressing such immodestly epic themes as life and death, it will nevertheless proceed at the much more intimate level of close reading. My analysis will be focused (almost exclusively, and at an often micrological, deconstructive level) on the opening remarks made by the conductor and pianist Daniel Barenboim in the first of the BBC's Reith Lectures that he gave in 2006. The blithe reason I address myself to this discourse is that it contains a theory of live musical performance (what I will refer to as a theory of *sonic gravity*) that shares strong homologies with Deleuzian notions of art as a form of affective intensity. On the one hand, since Barenboim is more what I would call a Romantic Existentialist, it is of simple interest to see how such a theory arises from within proclivities to which it would seem antithetical. The explication of Barenboim's theory and its affective resonances will be made in part 3 of this essay. More provocative, however, is Barenboim's repeated assertion that he has learned more about how to live in extramusical life from having had to master the art of making music according to such an affectively charged theory of sonic gravity. If this is indeed the case, then Barenboim (in his very being and action) allows us to test my abiding theme here regarding what happens when a discursive interest in affect is recursively replicated as part of the very life of the subject producing that discourse. And so, working according to a literal-minded fidelity, I test the claim out on the very language that Barenboim employs and inhabits in the lecture itself. As this essay proceeds, Barenboim, in all his hubris, difficulty, glibness, and bravura, becomes a provocative metaphor for musicological potentialities: for the possibility of a life both lived in music and also in the (musical) life of making discourse about music. It is precisely Barenboim's unevenness, the sometimes perplexing mixture with him of the burnished alongside the tarnished, that will allow something of the real antagonistic valence of what is at stake here to be seen with clarity.

I

For the academic critic seeking to parcel out and identify different strands of thinking, philosophy, and influence, Barenboim's discourse, whether live talks, published interviews, or written texts, can be frustrating and worse. At times, he can seem to be an example of that most treasured of academic insults, the dilettante. After all, for academic readings to identify as professional, they must uphold an ability successfully to prove a series of basic intellectual equations. For example, when an academic reads a certain statement (X) in, say, a letter by a composer, she might then show that it is actually a symptom or expression of something else (Y) — perhaps some aspect of context, or a manifestation of that composer's reading of a certain philosopher, or the influence of a particular politics, and so on. With Barenboim, however, there is the impression that the relationship between Xs and Ys has gotten wild, perhaps even chaotic. It is as if we move from one side to the other of the various equations by means of leaps of faith, the seduction of a metaphor, or that most suspicious aspect of argument, the forms of rhetoric that Plato termed sophistry. As perhaps befits his success as a conductor, such means, rather than being the tools of elucidation, can sometimes seem with Barenboim to be part of the arsenal of shamanic arts, even charlatanism. When this is so, his speech becomes more passion-fueled dynamic than faithful representation, grabbing at whatever can be easily reached for as clarification and indulging its appetite for the pleasures to be gained from its own forward propulsion, in and of itself. Its fidelities at such moments are to force rather than meaning, and if we take pleasure in being seduced by such proclivities we may have no cause for complaint. Nevertheless, a sort of detritus of names, references, and definitions is left in his wake, like fast-food containers chucked from the window of a speeding car. In a smear, as he dashes by, come flying metaphysics, tragedy, existentialism, neuroscience, Busoni, Nietzsche, Beethoven piano sonatas, the ethics of Spinoza—and this I found just by skimming my eye across a couple of pages of a lecture transcript.

When I read more in the traditional modes of my professional intellectual training, many of these signs invoke skepticism. And so when I read Barenboim it is not unusual for me—and not irrelevant for this essay—to be reminded of students in the early stages of their academic training, a full tank of excitement and a somewhat unruly bag of names and concepts. This can be touching and also cause for anxious hopes: that the gas tank will come to be full of worked-out ideas, and that such clarifications will then continue to fuel excitement, rather than causing it to wither and die, its departure marked merely by the remaining death's head of professional pedantry. But when, as with Barenboim, we are dealing with a publicly influential figure—one who has on a certain level authorized himself to make what in some people's opinion are controversial claims about agonized political situations in the eastern Mediterranean and how music might intervene—the stakes in our judgments are more loaded, and calls for critical condemnation perhaps more pressing.

Or maybe the problem is less Barenboim's and more our professionalism. This being the case, then Barenboim is inadvertently critiquing us, since a consistent feature of Barenboim's discourse over the years has been to circulate a distinction between music as a profession and music as a way of life. Within this distinction, music as a way of life is what has value. I leave for later in this essay the question as to what Barenboim might mean exactly here by "life"; elucidation of Barenboim's usage of this word will slowly reveal ways in which his discourse productively resonates with basic aspects of Deleuzian affect theory. For the moment, though, we can note that the inhabiting of music with such an intention is for Barenboim what then opens musical practice up to the possibility of creating pragmatic possibilities within the zones of the world that are not, strictly speaking, musical—in what I will hereon refer to as *extramusical life*.

On a certain level, then, Barenboim's discourse resonates sympathetically with some of the predominant tendencies of Anglo-American musicological values over the past quarter of a century. Through its vehement rejection of the music in-itself, musical autonomy, and the legacies of nineteenth-century notions of absolute music, Anglo-American musicology has repeatedly sought to valorize the idea that music does tangible things in the world, and that it self-evidently performs cultural, ethical, and political work that empirically invalidates any attempt to conceptualize it as a hermetically sealed object, through the practices, for example, of musical formalism. If my professional academic sensibilities might, therefore, be offended by the sometimes raw and unseasoned manner in which Barenboim can seem to conscript concepts in order to fuel his discourse, I am also faced with a certain dialectically convoluted challenge: that the discourse that results from Barenboim's lack of professionalism (academically defined) is in the service of his rejection of professionalism as he defines it elsewhere, and that such a rejection in turn supports the very values that our professionalism as academics helps us articulate by means of our examples. It is for such reasons that reading and listening as an academic to Barenboim speak can be uncomfortably riveting, both attractive and repellent, for one is being both validated and rejected at one and the same time. I am kept in place by paradoxes and contradictions that allow me to glimpse the possibility (sometimes vertiginous) of liberating my own intellectual practice from the deathly rote of the professional qualifications in which it can so frequently find itself mired. For truly, what would academia as a way of life, rather than academia as a profession, look like? In the present climate of neoliberal austerities within the academy, which have inspired the growth of a veritable jungle of overprofessionalized symptoms, it is hardly irrelevant to ask. And so, to pose the question broadly in its obvious Nietzschean formulation, we might wonder: what are the uses and abuses of professionalism for life?[2]

In order to negotiate such questions, I would like to draw attention to the first of Barenboim's 2006 Reith Lectures ("In the Beginning was Sound," presented at Cadogan Hall in London). At the very outset of this lecture, music and life appear more as separate phenomena, both of which function as constituent parts of a single economy but which nevertheless do not collide fully enough in order to make the transformation into the symbiosis that is musical life. Barenboim admits that music can be a form of respite from the world: "It gives us formidable weapons to forget our existence and the chores of daily life." And thus there are "millions of people who like to come home after a long day at the office, put their feet up, if possible have the luxury of somebody giving them a drink while they do that, and put on the record and forget all the problems of the day."[3] Music, scripted here by Barenboim as part of the world of leisure, has a kind of basic instrumental and, we might say, medicinal value; it alleviates the immediate symptoms resulting from the labor we must perform in order to survive financially.[4] Life here is more what I have called extramusical life; and music is that which enables us, through an act of forgetting that works by temporarily disabling memory, to move the realities of such life to the emotional distance necessary to allow us to be sufficiently rejuvenated to return efficiently to our extramusical employments. Music in this formulation is palliative rather than curative, a temporary relief from the smart created by the wound of "the problems of the day," rather than a long-term commitment to heal that wound, enact any kind of far-reaching critique, or offer an alternative mode of being.

Since one of the forms that such employments might take is that of the practice of our professional life, we can already intuit an implicit critique of professionalism herein. To continue with the medical metaphors, professionalism would seem to be en route to being guilty of inhibiting the realization of the holistic; it is the symptom of a world that seeks to sustain itself as an array of constitutive parts kept in a condition of suspended alienation from each other. The "problems of the day" are to be kept quarantined within the day itself by means of the barrier created by musical forgetting; they cannot be allowed too effectively to infect our consciousness elsewhere. Similarly, the music that enables this act of forgetting—and which, by definition, must also be mediated by such "problems"—is nevertheless also to be kept in a certain state of quarantine, as mere supplement to the professional day and its travails. There is a frozen dialectic in place between music and professional life. Each position is placed in a relation of neutralized mutual dependency whereby the lines of interaction between them merely work to keep each in its respective place, thereby allowing neither for the possibility of a positive transformation to occur, nor for either position to act so radically as just to abandon the other. As I implied before, they are employed less for themselves and more for the sustaining and stabilizing of the economy within which they function. It is a stalemate. And progeny born of such mating are perhaps always more withered than vibrant.

We can start to justify such a seemingly hyperbolic expression of Barenboim's brief and seemingly innocuous remark if we note how likewise hyperbolic are the words Barenboim himself uses to introduce the innocent scene of having a drink and listening to some music at the end of a difficult day. Music, "through its sheer power, and eloquence, gives us formidable weapons to forget our existence and the chores of daily life."[5] There is a profound rhetorical incommensurability here between the elevated stylistic register of the initial words assigned to music—"sheer power," "eloquence," "formidable weapons"—and the more mundane words of the "chores of daily life" that cower with mild embarrassment at the tail end of the sentence. It is as if music's potential to exceed the boundaries assigned it within this quotidian economy of neutralized mutual dependency that I just articulated were already making its pressures felt. Why would one employ something of dignity in relationship to mere rote activity? If the chores are merely quotidian, then surely something more modest than the "formidable" could just as well act as the instrument of our forgetting of them. The manner in which music's magnitude is being employed here seems profligate, like demanding a tank for the purpose of squashing a pea. Something of music within this formulation must therefore remain inert, unemployed, unexercised. And if one allows something to be kept inactive for long enough, it will potentially lose its vibrancy and wither away—like those progeny born of stalemating, just invoked. Professionalism, it would seem, can trap music in a depressing economy that leads to its evisceration.

If we allow our own speculations to be productively infected by Barenboim's incipient hyperbole, then we can predict whether music itself might not revolt. After all, there is something insulting about forcing the magnificent to tend to the mundane, of pressing nobility into service. Why should music have to clean up the psychological detritus left over from the day's "chores"? The question of servitude is strongly present figuratively in Barenboim's language at this point; who are those people who are tired from the office, then return home, put their feet up, and "if possible have the luxury of somebody giving them a drink"? Is this "somebody" (made oddly ambiguous by Barenboim at this moment) also a servant, like the music? If so, we should remind ourselves that servants have been known to turn, grabbing whatever is at hand and suddenly wielding it as a weapon. So why not just grab the music that Barenboim has already both identified as such ("formidable weapons") and handily positioned within the environs in the form of a record that might be played? The fact that Barenboim at this moment is conceptualizing the musical weapon mildly as a positive kind of palliative *technē*, one that allows us to recuperate by means of a gentle forgetting, does not preclude that it might not do otherwise—more violently, for example. Indeed, later in the question-and-answer session of this particular lecture, Barenboim propounds this possibility directly as part of his own existentially tinged belief system: "I believe that things, creations, objects, are neither moral nor immoral."[6] To illustrate this point, he turns once more to this question of the weapon: "What is a knife?" His continuation precludes from us the comfort of certainty: "Is that [knife] an instrument with which you can murder someone, therefore an instrument of violence, or is it something with which you cut the bread and feed your neighbor?"[7] Barenboim's answer is, neither: "It's when the human being makes use of it that he, this is the free will, he decides whether it is moral or whether it is immoral."[8] Thus, "the knife in itself is perfectly innocent"—a point that Barenboim then immediately applies to music, momentarily bringing the tendency in this lecture of aligning the musical in relationship to the instrumentality of weapons to a certain stability of clarification: "The music is innocent— it is what the human being makes of it."[9] So under what conditions might the human pick up the musical weapon for violent purposes? And whom might it attack?

The latent answer sleeping innocently within Barenboim's seemingly inconspicuous opening remarks is both shocking and far-reaching: we ourselves will pick up the weapon that is music, and we will then turn it against our own breast. We are dealing with a kind of suicide attempt. Before music helps us forget "the chores of daily life," it is first, as the text makes quite clear, a formidable weapon "to forget our existence." This statement allows a counterpoint of deathly logics to make its pressure felt. We can notice, for example, the odd implications unleashed from the making of the short two-item list: "our existence and the chores of daily life." We are dealing once more with the strangeness of rhetorical incommensurability, such as we saw earlier in the imbalanced equation of "sheer power," "eloquence," and "formidable weapons" to the "chores of daily life," or between the "magnificent" and the "mundane," or in the image of "nobility" in "service." The all-encompassing aspiration of the term *existence* is simply in an embarrassing condition of excess in relation to mere "daily life." What kind of cynical ennui could make us speak of both in the same breath without flinching at the equating of the two? If the alignment is not to function pathologically, either the mundane must be hiding untapped sublimities, or, in keeping with tendencies already noted, "existence" itself has withered to a mundane pittance. Continuing, we could also observe that "daily life" makes more sense as a *subset* of "existence" (our existence, *including* the chores of daily life) rather than what exists *as well as* something else ("our existence *and* the chores of daily life"). If our chores are somehow not part of our existence, then where on earth (quite literally) are they performed?

Following the logic's grim momentum, the answer is that they take place outside of existence, and so once again we are faced with the unlikely option either of imagining them in some kind of transcendent splendor, or (more likely, considering Barenboim's proclivities) of figuring them in some kind of nonexistence, perhaps somewhere in death. More perplexing still, if music allows us "to forget our existence"—and yet it seems logical to presume that such existence is still somehow sustained whilst we are listening to music on our recording—then, reading with a certain harsh fidelity to Barenboim's words, the following must be the case: when listening to music in this way, we would have to answer the question "Are you alive?" with a blank, "I don't know, I've forgotten." If you don't know whether or not you are alive, then surely you are a little dead. Unraveling this further, we are a little dead when we are in the process of dying—increasingly we are less and less alive. And finally, adopting the revelatory logic of linguistic play, we can take things one mad last step and note that another kind of "little dead" is "an insignificant ghost"—something too small to be of import (insignificant), and yet, since dead but only a "little," caught in a kind of no-man's land between living and death, and so not completely sure if it be one or the other, either/or. Ghosts, indeed, are often confused in this regard.

We can now collect all of this together and more precisely answer the earlier question regarding under what conditions the human might pick up music and use it for the purposes of violence: when the majority of our activities are not part of our existence and so are partly dead; when we ourselves are more dead than alive; when, out of shame perhaps over what might be revealed from being inconsistent, we retain perverse fidelity to the consistency of death's presence in our life and so make music partly dead too. It is when such conditions prevail that we will pick up music and use it for violence. We use music then to perform violence against ourselves, to make sure that we too are, once and for all, dead. As I characterized it above, this is an economy of neutralized mutual dependencies, a whole whose constituent parts sustain their bare minimum of magnetic attraction to each other through the meager current generated by their concerted commitment toward being as close as they possibly can to nonexistence—to having "forgot" their existence, to return once more to Barenboim's words. It is just enough to sustain the minimum of basic vital signs; it is the homeostasis of the life support machine. For Barenboim, its motor is professionalism, the rote activities we perform in support of depleting our lives so that, paradoxically, we can support them just enough in order that they might survive. And so in response to our initial Nietzschean question as to what might be the uses and abuses of professionalism for life, we now can answer quite clearly: the uses are *as* abuses. Faced with life, professionalism functions as insult.

Following the dialectical variability of Barenboim's notion of the weapon, the cure for this life-in-death condition is in part the poison too; it is constituted, as we shall see, by the music that we have just used in order to try to kill ourselves. The suicidal aspirations of music making that I outlined above—the fact that it inspires us "to forget our existence"—can now be strategically reinscribed into a different economy, a sacrificial one. With sacrifice, music is no longer used for violence merely so that that which remains of us will be grateful to limp along at the homeostatic level granted by the clemency of professionalism. Rather, the results of the violence are potentially fatal enough that we will be forced now to live in our entirety, and in each instance of that life to live more rather than less. Sacrifice is here the prelude to tumescence, not the inflicting of a wound and resultant production of castrating lack. And so, as Barenboim continues, "music has *another* weapon that it delivers to us."[10] Remaining consistent with the underlying existential heroics of his position, we will receive this weapon only "if we *want* to take it"[11]—in other words, only if we are prepared to make that sacrifice. This is a weapon through which "we can learn a lot about ourselves, about our society, about the human being, and politics, about society about anything that you choose to do."[12] It is therefore a pedagogical weapon, one that increases our knowledge of the world. By means of this expansion, it reinforces further our understanding of what was lethal in the preceding inscription of music as a "formidable weapon." Literally speaking, it helps us to understand that when we use music to "forget our existence," the musical weapon encourages us to know *less*. Or, to conclude more bluntly, we come to realize that instrumentalizing music in a low-grade medicinal fashion in relation to "the chores of daily life" makes us stupid. We spare ourselves the shame of this condition by reversing how the current runs within the circuit of the musical and the nonmusical. And so, instead of deciding to live in a certain inane way and then employing music merely to nurse the minor illnesses resulting from that decision, we decide, rather, to live in music, and to luxuriate in our nonmusical lives in the collateral resultant from that specific form of habitation. As Barenboim states: "I learn more about living from music than about how to make a living out of music."[13] But only, as he repeats in a later lecture, "so long as you don't view music only as a pastime, no matter how enjoyable, or as something to forget the world,"[14] only if we allow the repercussions of opening ourselves up to music's lessons fully to infect the rest of our lives. If there is to be life, then there must be contagion.

II

So what kind of human would be produced from a full opening up to the repercussions of music's pedagogy? If we proceed once more by means of a brutal fidelity to Barenboim's own discourse, a logical answer would be: a human like Daniel Barenboim. His Reith Lectures are, after all, repeatedly scripted as communications of what he himself has learned from music—that he "can only speak from that point of view in a very personal way,"[15] and this "because I learn more about living from music than about how to make a living out of music."[16] So what kind of human is Daniel Barenboim? What kind of being, in his instance, has been born of music?

The questions are important, because attempting to answer them makes us aware of how rarely it has been considered necessary to speculate in this regard—or at least how rarely in Anglo-American musicology, and at least until quite recently. The web of forces—historical, political, ecological, institutional, and economic—in which the discourses of academic music studies have to date been able to nestle have been snug enough to make the human question not much of a question. Approaching the issue from the perspective of pragmatism, we might simply say that there has been no need. Inquiry, after all, has a tendency toward being provoked into being mostly when the ground constituted by our assumptions is no longer stable or expansive enough to support our confidence comfortably. Without the threat of such instability, the human, as Lacan was known frequently to quip, will simply not want to know; and one of the names under which this highly functioning and often spectacularly erudite mode of ignorance has carried out its business is humanism.[17] So rather than asking questions on the order of "what kind of human is Daniel Barenboim?" we have tended to commence further down the line—beyond the station where we picked up our humanist assumptions—and from there simply to have asked: "Who is Daniel Barenboim?" Default settings repeatedly fire up inquiry always already at the level of subjectivity, or rather—and particularly if we continue to keep in mind Lacan, for whom the subject is emphatically not a category of humanistic discourse—further along the path at the level of the ego.[18] Stepping straight up onto this well-trod stage, we have then begun performance of its oft-posed questions, which, when the human under consideration is filtered through this optic, often bespeak meanings, agency, and intentions as expressed through language. So, we pore over writings, pronouncements, and acts of speech, such as the very lecture by Barenboim under consideration here. And from behind the weight of our labors, a sense of who this person might be will, if we remain committed enough to the hard-won skills of our professional training, start to shine, like sunlight streaming forth through openings made as the clouds depart. Viewed positively, we are able to put people in place, to locate them; and this desire for clear placement haunts the humanist drive toward understanding others and thus resonates throughout the next stages of my analysis.

Barenboim's discourse often makes it difficult to illuminate the question of who he might be. As I stated up front, there are frustrations, a sense of chaos, a perhaps unadmirable dilettantism; concepts and ideas slip, slide, and rather randomly short-circuit one another. Instead of being able to fix locations on a map and then join the dots in order to create a picture of him, one can find oneself preoccupied with a breathless pursuit of the points themselves, as if Barenboim were a being so consumed by movement that images of him cannot form. Or perhaps our problem with stabilizing our understanding is more the symptom born of an opposite problem—that there is simply nothing much there to understand in the first place. For example, reviewing Barenboim's Reith Lectures for *The Guardian*, Guy Dammann judged that in his attempt to fulfill his purported agenda (to communicate the true nature of the power of music), Barenboim "was pretty unsuccessful":

> If you peel away the layers of confused metaphysics, the beguiling but largely irrelevant musical examples, and the sprinkling of badly digested neuroscience, you are left with something that amounted to little more than a few disjointed conjectures. These ranged from the apparent nonsense that listening to good music counteracts political correctness to the true, but none the less, highfalutin observation that muzak degrades the value of musical experience, placing a vital aspect of our cultural life farther and farther from our reach. However valid such observations might be on their own terms, leaving them stranded without even the trappings of logical, theoretical or empirical support simply weakens their appeal and opens them up to charges of art snobbery.[19]

The conclusion Dammann draws from this is simply that "Barenboim emerges from the series looking somewhat foolish."[20] And there is a certain comfort to be taken from the proficiency with which the certainty of this condemnation fixes our understanding, thereby resolving the question regarding who Daniel Barenboim might be. From Dammann's vantage, Barenboim is less beyond the conceptual capacities of humanism, and more just unworthy of its consideration: he is a buffoon.

Attendant on the comforts of such a clarification is a rather depressing form of Platonism, in which musicians, in the name of the Good, must be cautioned against transgressing their place. As Socrates states in the *Republic*, "Does it not follow . . . that one man does only one job well, and that if he tries to take on a number of jobs, the division of effort will mean that he will fail to make his mark at any of them?"[21] And later, "So ours is the only state in which we shall find (for example) the shoemaker sticking to his shoemaking and not turning pilot as well, the farmer sticking to his farming and not taking on court work into the bargain, and the soldier sticking to his soldiering and not running a business as well."[22] Since for Plato, in this particular argument, the artist's mimetic capacity for imitation is precisely what threatens to seduce the human into losing his socially expedient unitary professional focus, then, likewise, a conductor should stick to playing music rather than playing at intellectual, for fear of turning us all into fools. We are back once more with the question of professionalism that had preoccupied us in the earlier stages of the arguments of this essay, but we are now looking at it from the other side of the fence. Musicians should know their place. Any proposition that music might teach us something about how to survive in extramusical life should be subject to rigorous scrutiny; or, if we happen to live in Plato's republic, it should be arbitrated by a philosopher.

But in offering us the comforts that a clear answer so effectively provides, I wonder if Dammann is not only unmasking Barenboim's failure to follow through, but also distracting us from a more disturbing antagonism that arises in this particular instance of professional place having been transgressed. For when Barenboim speaks—and thus when a musician shape-shifts into a public intellectual—there arises a strange holographic superimposition of an extraordinary (if idiosyncratic) rhetorical confidence of vocal tone and delivery occurring simultaneously with an extraordinary destabilization of meaning in the form of an endless proliferation of questions (intended or otherwise). For Dammann, this contradiction cannot stand; if rhetorical force cannot be aligned with conceptual clarification, then we are dealing with a brand of scam. But maybe that is precisely the challenge posed by the musical human: in other words, to inhabit confidently a world where meanings are never stabilized, to somehow manage to be sure-footed even when the ground is never stable. Perhaps the idea that Barenboim is a "buffoon" is therefore less a failed conceptualization of the musical human when out of its musical element (such as when a conductor gives a public lecture), and more a conceptualization so direct it obliterates the revelation being made. In short, the musical human enforces upon our lives a certain comic injunction. And that injunction would be congruent with the provocation that I have just made: that we must learn to live confidently in a world of questions. Barenboim at a certain moment enacts this point himself in full comic mode: "You understand that all of what I'm telling you now is what I have learned to feel, and hope to have learned through all these years of making music. I'm in no way pretending to give you a fundamentalist theory that provides all the answers, even for those things that there are no questions about."[23] This is almost a Groucho Marx–style joke, one that eats its own tail. And in the live recording, it makes the audience laugh. For not only will Barenboim not give us grounding answers to our questions; neither will he give us grounding answers to our answers. Like all great comics, it is as if he wants to put a banana peel under every pronouncement, yet, at the same time, he seeks to encourage us not to fall over.[24]

Even in the very opening of the first of his Reith Lectures, there is something on the cusp of being comically awry. An initially innocent impression might be that we are merely being set up to go through the pro forma motions of a rhetorical exordium, whereby the speaker introduces the lecture to come by adopting the stance of modesty. This stance in turn functions to acknowledge the perhaps insurmountable difficulties of the proposed subject itself: "Ladies and gentlemen, I'm perfectly aware of the great honor to be asked to deliver the Reith Lectures. It is with some trepidation that I do that, because I firmly believe that it is really impossible to speak really deeply about music. All we can do then is speak about our own reaction to the music. So maybe the honor is dubious, or maybe the BBC thought it would be very short."[25] As if to punctuate, the audience then laughs, acknowledging Barenboim's concluding witticism—which knowingly works to soften both the slightly stiff formality of his opening sentence and the potentially disingenuous self-effacement of its follow-up, and also helps to underline, through mild relief, that the subject of the lecture has been established: a discussion of music in terms of "our own reaction." Up to this point, we proceed at the level of civility, an almost courtly dance of considered gesticulations: three subtly applied stylistic maneuvers (formality, modesty, and comedy) and we all are now in place to begin, bonded together communally through the solvent created by our laughter.[26] What we know is that speaking about music is impossible, and that by recognizing that fact we both act with modesty— which in itself is another means of knowing one's place—and also, by implication, allow for the possibility of logically coherent discourse.

Barenboim therefore begins somewhat like the early Wittgenstein, respecting where we cannot speak ("that it is really *impossible* to speak really deeply about music") by means of an acknowledgment of the logical limits of discourse; for Wittgenstein, when we find ourselves at such a threshold we realize that "in that place one must be silent."[27] But territorial courtesies are rapidly forgone, and the space where silence might have been is overwhelmed: "In any case, the impossible has always attracted me more than the difficult. The impossible, if there is some sense behind it, has not only a feeling of adventure, but a feeling of activity which I do admit I enjoy very much. I will therefore attempt the impossible and maybe try and draw some connection between the inexpressible content of music and, maybe, the inexpressible content of life."[28] The passage begins in seeming continuity with the practice of courtesy already noted in the lecture's opening gestures—"in any case." The immediate aim of this quotidian formulation is to draw attention away from the potentially insulting cheekiness as to whether "the honor is dubious" to have been asked by the BBC to deliver the Reith Lectures. "In any case" therefore affirms the institutional validity of the frame by which the lectures are constituted (the BBC) and once more shows a certain respect for the already-noted discursive sense of place in effect. Yet imagine for a moment that Barenboim had begun this sentence with an equivalent adverbial construction: "Irrespective." This can easily function simply as an unmarked substitution for "in any case." But its now relatively obsolete usage (implying disregard and the negation of respect) would have worked to color Barenboim's innocent continuation with intimations that he is about to abandon what had come before. And in order to make such an exit, logically he would have to step across (as in the Latin *transgressus*) the perimeter marking the very place whose confines he has seemingly just affirmed.

This transgression is indeed what Barenboim immediately enacts. And by doing so he validates an aspect of the comic theory that I here in part put into practice: that sometimes it is precisely in the kinds of linguistic play just performed (between "in any case" and "irrespective") that responsibilities toward understanding the world are to be most forcefully encountered. Therefore, irrespective of what has just been said with regard to hubris, for Barenboim it is "the impossible that has always attracted me more than the difficult." And this changes everything, sacrificing all that has immediately gone before. Through a radical shift in proposal regarding linguistic function, questions as to whether an "impossible" discourse is logically feasible in relationship to speaking about music now become moot. Barenboim discards previous claims of being driven by a logical pragmatics of meaning: by what language can say about music. Language is no longer an instrumentalized form of humanist *technē*, one that the subject employs in order, for example, to answer the question "who is Daniel Barenboim?" Its energies are no longer consumed solely with articulating the truth of the object, but are now also channeled into activating something for the subject too, perhaps even something beyond the boundaries of subjectivity per se. Language is driven here by an appetite for something, and appetite privileges one of the affect theorist's most frequently valued conditions: intensity, which I shall begin to elaborate upon shortly. Thus, for Barenboim, the pursuit of the impossible is validated by the fact that, in comparison with the "difficult" (which one assumes refers to the lecture's first proposal, which was to "speak about our own reaction to the music"), "the impossible has always attracted me more." In other words, "the impossible" intensifies the activities of our attention when it makes itself present to this faculty. Broadly speaking, we are dealing with desire rather than meaning, taste and aesthetics rather than ethics and pragmatics. And so, if we return to our presiding question here and ask once more what kind of human is produced by making oneself open to musical contagion, a provisional answer based on Barenboim's behavior at this moment would be: a human who in part has recalibrated language in such a way.

In the West, one of the privileged names we have had for such a human is poet. The poet is a being whose proclivities, amongst other things, have the effect of sublimating language's explicative functions into lyrical force; or, to activate the common trope, a being who exacerbates into prominence *the musical within the linguistic*. Language is here less communication than a means of creating (once more) affective intensification, and so is redolent, as I began to suggest in the previous paragraph, of a certain Deleuzian strain in affect theory. As Elizabeth Grosz has put it, for Deleuze "the arts produce and generate intensity, that which directly impacts the nervous system and intensifies sensation. Art is the art of affect more than representation, a system of dynamized and impacting force rather than a system of unique images that function under the regime of signs."[29] To this I would add that, rather than disciplining language so that it can then be made to follow straight the path of the project unfurling from the ego's articulated goals, the poetic being disciplines itself so that it can then be taken by the routes of desire and forces of intensity that language activates—in Barenboim's case, by fueling speech into being through the attractions exerted by the impossible. "Art proper," to cite Grosz once more, "emerges when sensation can detach itself and gain autonomy from its creator and its perceiver."[30] Or, to apply an Adornian formulation, the poet has "the capacity for being voluntarily involuntary" and so—returning to our abiding humanist question here—easily unnerves us as we attempt to understand, by application of the notion of agency and intention, who she might be.[31] Entry into the mode of poiesis comes with the threat and/or promise of a certain disillusionment of the self; in payment for being allowed to pass over, some of the ropes must be cut that keep language grounded enough to constitute an ego. As Arthur Rimbaud put it in a famous letter to Georges Izambard of May 13, 1871, "Je est un autre."[32] The "I" is here an Other thing, less part of the subject (*Je suis un autre*) than an object from which the subject is now displaced. And for the humanist scholar this comes with a certain darkness, because it means that attendant upon the illumination that is granted the poet in her *ekstasis* is that she starts as an individual to become a nobody. And so a well-functioning society in which everyone lived according to what they had learned affectively from music would, to all extents and purposes, be like an orchestra of nobodies.

Barenboim, of course, has rarely struck his critics as a being in flight from his ego. It is completely credible to hear his profession that "the impossible has always attracted me more than the difficult" less as exilic or transgressive in relationship to such constitutive psychological parameters than as colonial—an act of hubris in which a productive risk might be taken to seize a vastly expanded purview for his sense of self. So not only is Barenboim perhaps not beyond his ego, but worse, even more fully entrenched than the depressing norm; less a challenge to the humanist question of *who* he might be, for many he has appeared rather as a parody of its implied object of inquiry: not just an individual, but, worse, an egotist.

This starts to seem credible in the immediate qualification he gives to his confessed attraction to the impossible; it now becomes "the impossible, if there is some *sense* behind it." If the subject can still access sense—using language to make meaning, understand, and locate—then the agency and identity of the humanistic ego is still in action; and if such sense can remain activated even in the presence of forces ("the impossible") by which it should by rights be eclipsed, then this ego is, moreover, projected into a sublime register. In a manner pervasive in Barenboim's discourse, the human now becomes the heroic, and the collateral of jubilant narcissism attendant upon this upgrade thereby appears to energize what immediately follows. Thus, the mastery attained by subtending the impossible with articulate meaning allows pleasurable affects to accumulate, "not only a feeling of adventure, but a feeling of activity which I do admit I enjoy very much." And from here, the leap to apotheosis can finally be made and connections drawn "between the inexpressible content of music and, maybe, the inexpressible content of life." The normative linguistic fact—that if the content of both life and music is inexpressible, then it must surely also be impossible to enact the conceptual maneuver that would allow connections between these two impossibilities to emerge—simply does not register in Barenboim's discourse at this moment. It is either eclipsed by his hubris or works according to a different linguistic logic that distinguishes itself from this potential embarrassment by means of a certain nuance that does not immediately draw attention to itself.

But if we still believe in the validity of Barenboim's fundamental claim regarding music's ability to teach us something about life—a claim, we should remind ourselves, that is also basic to many ways in which Anglo-American musicology justifies the need for an intellectual discourse on music, and thereby justifies its own existence—then it is beholden unto us to try and articulate what this nuance might be. For if we simply accept, like Dammann, that Barenboim's Reith lectures fail to create coherent discourse, and yet simultaneously we try to sustain that negative judgment along with the relatively uncontroversial proposition that Barenboim is a human who has learned to live by retaining an inordinately close proximity to music throughout his life, we will be faced, unless we simply decide to inhabit contradiction blithely, with some stark choices.

For example, on the one hand, and most cynically, we might simply have to conclude that a life lived in proximate fidelity to music teaches one next to nothing about how to live well, and it is for that reason that Barenboim is unable sufficiently to substantiate his claims. The failure of his discourse is thus less the product of a lack of conceptual discipline and more of the limits of his imagination, since he has burdened himself with the task of employing language to invoke something that doesn't exist. Indeed, scanning the biographies of great musicians, there is ample evidence to suggest that success in music is often purchased with a total failure in extramusical civilian life. And that being the case, most of us will need to go back to the drawing board and seriously rethink our line of defense with regard to the relevance of this art form. Otherwise, we will be left with only the most spartan and self-referential forms of aesthetic autonomy: that music's value lies simply in the value of taking part in music. On the other hand, if it is indeed the case that a life lived in close proximity to music does in fact help one to live better, then in Barenboim's case the sustaining of that proximity proves itself to be potentially detrimental to the very language that could communicate such a truth. If our musical fidelities have any ethical value, it seems logical that part of their exercise should involve conscription of others to the cause, necessitating effective explanation. And so perhaps Barenboim's problem, if we can talk about it as such, arises from the fact that his fidelities are simply too strong; he is not prepared to betray music's influence in relation to language so that language might sharpen its wits enough to effectively encourage others to be persuaded of music's value. Returning to the metaphors of an earlier part of this essay, music must therefore die a little (in relation to language) so that the truth of how it emboldens life can be told (through language). The professionalism of intellectual discourse marks the location for such a moribund pragmatism. Or, to put it otherwise, in this instance musicology is the necessary death in life—which is hardly the best sales pitch at a time when the value of such intellectual pursuits is so continually contested in the neoliberal academy. So what would it mean for talk about music to be a bit of life instead?

III

If we accept that Barenboim is unable to conceptualize effectively the claims he would wish to make for music in relation to life, it is nevertheless the case that he is frequently able to enact and embody them in the present moment of the live lectures themselves. And so the fact that his language does not function well according to certain linguistic criteria of explanation is in part compensated for by the fact that it functions exceedingly well homologically in relation to how Barenboim himself (ideally) envisions music phenomenologically. Leaving aside the question of whether it is even desirable for language to undergo such musical contagion, we can here credibly propound the influence of music onto an aspect of extramusical life (language), from there set about assessing the resultant production of a moment of musical life (to return to the terminology in part 1 of this essay), and establish more fully connections with affect theory.

In order to proceed, we must put to one side the idea that language is first and foremost a bearer of meaning and return to the more poetic orientation already touched upon in part 2. We can then note that Barenboim's spoken use of language in these lectures is characterized by two interrelated and mutually supportive aesthetic qualities: seamlessness and intensity. Misgivings about terminological clarification notwithstanding, it is nevertheless the case that the mode in which Barenboim moves us from topic to topic and idea to idea is, on the whole, that of a kind of continuous and unfalteringly lubricated transition, one that, earlier in this essay, I had characterized in the pejorative as a smear, but that I would now rather think of here metaphorically, taking my lead, as we shall see, from Barenboim's own words, as a kind of legato flow. Indeed, we might argue that the specificity of each particular idea or topic, and the articulation of the markers that might distinguish one from another on the level of meaning, are decidedly secondary in Barenboim's live speech to the desire for effective production of this liquid sense of movement within which the sequence of points continuously gestates and blooms forth. For better or worse, his language is that of an unending gestural becoming, rather like the Prelude to Wagner's *Tristan und Isolde*, with its imbrications of wavelike forms, which in a myriad array of proportions, nested within and endlessly outgrowing, continue to overflow without respite.

Such being the case, it is then no surprise that the opening notes of the *Tristan* Prelude in fact provide one of the very first musical examples that Barenboim plays live on the piano during the course of this first Reith Lecture.[33] Having concluded his opening remarks with his assertion of the pedagogical import of music for life ("I learn more about living from music than about how to make a living out of music"), Barenboim then switches register in order to look at the physical phenomenon of sound itself. The sudden change in topic, from grand talk of "the impossible content of life" and such to the nuts and bolts of sound production, would seem at first to belie my assertion that Barenboim's spoken discourse progresses by means of an aesthetics of smooth continuity. However, the aesthetic inconsistency created by this particular sharp shift in topic is recouped positively at the level of content and meaning in the form of a discussion of how notes in music never exist in isolation, but only ever in a state of becoming: "The physical aspect that we notice first is that sound does not exist by itself, but has a permanent constant and unavoidable relation with silence. And therefore the music does not start from the first note and goes onto the second, etc., etc., but the first note already determines the music itself, because it comes out of the silence that precedes it."[34] If, conceptually, Barenboim's spoken discourse avoids isolation and specification, opting instead for a constant opening out of one concept into another, so likewise musical notes are always already en route, never absolute or singular. Even if "we achieve a total silence, and we start a piece of music that becomes rather than is there—it's not about being but about becoming."[35] And so, with regard to the opening of the *Tristan* Prelude, "the music is not from the A to the F, but from the silence to the A,"[36] and then by implication onward, ad infinitum. With the opening of Beethoven's Piano Sonata Op. 109, the example that immediately follows, "the pianist has to create the feeling that the music has already been here, it's already going, and now much as you step on a train that is already in motion, you join it."[37] In other words, you join its already existent ongoing state of becoming.

As it presently stands, even with all its philosophical atmosphere of becoming over being, this is not much more than the articulation of an aesthetic preference. After all, there are plenty of other musics (most of Thelonious Monk and Igor Stravinsky, for example) in which the proclivity is toward a kind of brittle atomization of singular notes in brutal isolation from their surroundings. And if that kind of music were where Barenboim's language had learned how to live, then he might have presented his audience at the first of his Reith Lectures with a cooler mode of finely etched irony in the style of Karl Kraus, or with a nonnegotiable volley of gunshots in the style of an avant-garde manifesto. The next move in Barenboim's argument, however, elevates this aesthetic preference for legato over staccato to the level of an existential challenge, in which the inextricable threading of one musical moment to the next becomes the mode by which music attempts to defy death. In doing so, Barenboim's discourse will help me to start returning my argument back to its initial concerns with the deathly quality of professionalism, and from there to its tentative conclusions about when and where it might be possible to inhabit musical life.

Barenboim is able to achieve his somewhat outrageous short circuit, in which a performance indication (legato) comes to be equated with life itself, through recourse to a rather provocative theory of how sound relates to silence, which I will term his theory of *sonic gravity*:

> Sound reacts to silence much like the law of gravity tells us, that if you lift an object from the ground you have to use a certain amount of energy to keep it at the height to which you have brought it up to. You have to provide additional energy, otherwise the object will fall back to the law of gravitation on the ground. But this is exactly what sound does with silence. I play again the same note, I play it, I give a certain amount of energy, and if I do nothing more to it, it will die.[38]

Without the continued application of energy to sound, a sound will decay back into the silence whence it came. Barenboim's implication is that this is the status of sound outside of the terrain established by musical art. To recast the point in Deleuzian terminology, this is the status of sound within chaos, which is not to be thought of as some kind of formless horror, but rather as just the multitude of forces of the cosmos in all their continuous comings and goings, efflorescence and retraction, interweavings and fragmentation, potentiality and undoings. In Grosz's words, chaos occurs "not as absolute disorder but rather as a plethora of orders, forms, wills—forces that cannot be distinguished from each other, both matter and its conditions for being otherwise, both the actual and the virtual indistinguishably."[39] Thus, a coordination of forces allows a sound to blush forth; that energy passes on into something else, and the logic of sonic gravity then makes that sound decay.

It is only in art or music that the nomadic fragility of the sonic within the chaos of the cosmos (or, for Barenboim, its vulnerability to silence) can come to be sustained in a more continuous fashion. For Gilles Deleuze and Félix Guattari, this happens through the creation of a frame, or through an act of framing by means of which a quality of the undifferentiated chaos of the cosmos gets isolated out from the undifferentiated miasma: "Art takes a bit of chaos in a frame in order to form a composed chaos that becomes sensory."[40] As a result of this specification, the quality thereby undergoes the process of affective intensification that we have already encountered in our earlier discussion of the poetic, creating a new kind of intensity (called *sensation*) that only exists within the frame of art: "not the repetition of sensations already experienced or available beyond or outside the work of art, but those very sensations generated and proliferated only by art."[41] And so art does not "map this chaos so much as draw strength, force, material from it for a provisional and open-ended cohesion."[42] This open-ended cohesion is a framed territory that we might (with many careful qualifications) term art's *formal relations*, broadly conceived.

In Barenboim, at least at this stage of his explication, a frame starts to be created for sound by means of the application of an "additional energy," a metaphorically upward-moving force supplied by the human, in excess of what is simply already there sonically, that delays chaotic obsolescence, keeping the sound alive and stopping it from sinking back down. Once this is put into effect, a distinction between sound (as part of chaos, and thus subject to sonic gravity) and music (as a form of art) can start to come into focus. For Barenboim, this focus that we call music is then kept alive beyond the duration of one single note by means of the broadly expanded logic of legato that I have already discussed. The overall result is what he then calls *expression*—which I am prepared to at least make analogically available to the Deleuzian concept of *sensation*.

For expression to happen, Barenboim states:

> The notes in music cannot be allowed to develop their natural egos, so that they hide the preceding one, but the expression in music comes from the linkage, what we call in Italian legato—bound. When we play five notes that are bound, each note fights against the

power of silence that wants to make it die, and is therefore in relation to the preceding note and to the note that comes after that.[43]

It is as if the notes were somehow stitched together using a thread constituted by the very "additional energy" that initially had been brought to bear in keeping a single note afloat. This additional energy, this necessary prerequisite for the framing of chaos and the production of musical art, therefore moves both vertically, in counterpoint to the tendency of sound to fall back down to the ground, and horizontally, as a means of linking a series of notes together over a more extended time period. The combination of these movements of energy weave the different sonic components together, allowing them to create an entity that can then be distinguished from chaos—such a mark of distinction between one state (chaos) and another (art) being precisely what constitutes a frame. As Deleuze and Guattari state: "It is said that sound has no frame. But compounds of sensation, sonorous blocs, equally possess section or framing forms each of which must join together *to secure a certain closing off.*"[44] The resultant music thereby works somewhat like the domed roof of a cathedral, in which each stone is drawn down by gravity toward the ground, and yet held in suspension by the way in which each also leans into its neighbor. If for some reason this balance of forces were lost, the roof would fall down back into the chaos from which it was initially enticed. And for Barenboim, the pressure created by this constant threat of the collapse of expression within musical performance marks "the beginning of the tragic element in music."[45]

IV

If we now combine Deleuze and Grosz with Barenboim, we can make the following formulation: that for musical performance, life is the form of energizing focus that arises when we continue to hold our gaze steady, even when extraordinarily powerful forces (such as death) threaten to distract us from doing so. This being the case, what then is the value of this almost existentially tinged practice of affective intensification for extramusical life—for example, for the life of language in a lecture about music? To repeat my earlier question: what would it mean for talk about music to be a bit of life instead?

In Deleuzian theory, one of the answers that can be given to the question of what it might mean to participate in the affective intensity of artistic sensation is: one has become wealthy. In Grosz's words: "Art and nature, art in nature, share a common structure: that of excessive and useless production—production for its own sake, production for the sake of profusion and differentiation. Art takes what it needs—the excess of colors, forms, materials—from the earth to produce its own excesses, sensations with a life of their own, sensation as 'non organic life.'"[46] This Deleuzian kind of wealth is one that breaks contract with the economy of forces through which the idea is usually conceptualized. It is no longer the case here that the necessities for life must first be established and then we can indulge in a bit of luxury. It is rather that this luxury is life itself, and that the homeostatic sustaining of certain forces that we usually consider foundational are, in many instances, secondary. Grosz, through careful reading of Charles Darwin, is able to take such notions all the way back to questions of sexual selection. Thus, for its evolution, life itself can only happen "to the extent that there is something fundamentally unstable about both its milieu and its organic constitution."[47] If there were no such instability, nothing in excess of life's ability merely to sustain itself, transformation and proliferation of diversity in life would simply not occur. And so, evolution happens in life forms "becoming-artistic, in their self-transformations, which exceed the bare requirements of existence."[48] Contrary to our generally instrumental interpretation of things like the "haunting beauty of birdsong, the provocative performance of erotic display in primates, the attraction of insects to the perfume of plants," where the aesthetic phenomena are reduced to the level of tools for getting something else done, Grosz (via Darwin and Deleuze) states that they are "all in excess of mere survival."[49] They are testament to "the excessiveness of the body and the natural order, their capacity to bring out in each other what surprises, what is of no use but nevertheless attracts and appeals."[50] To speak tautologically for a moment, life is therefore the luxury we cannot afford to live without.

Following through on this, if we now apply such affectively charged notions of music to an evaluation of the aesthetic qualities of Barenboim's spoken discourse about music, we might easily feel that we have gotten too close to some serious posthumanist whimsy. Daniel Barenboim as Big Bird: a flash of color, a flap of wing, and a plummy middle-class British audience selected by the BBC thereby accesses "the opening up of life to the indeterminacy of taste, pleasure, and sensation."[51] But above and beyond how crass we might find such a perverse and glib conclusion—and, moreover, how it might validate some of our suspicions (not all of them unjustified) regarding some of the jargon-drenched silliness of the veritable industry of Deleuzian work in the contemporary academy—what else might be motivating our discomfort at this moment? If we continue with our experiment, following through on the logic of the affective position that I have been laying out here and asking what its deflection from music onto language about music might imply, one of the conclusions we might reach is that talk about music that refuses the life-enhancing contagion of music itself results not only from a necessary sacrifice of enjoyment (the miseries of whose labors being justified in terms of their ability to bring us to conceptual stabilization about music), but also from a condition that is a peculiar mixture of being both profoundly lacking in pragmatism and dreary, a sort of joyless waste of time. For as we have seen, the seeming luxuries of such excited aestheticized discourse are, from the position of Grosz's Deleuzian argument, fundamental. In the frame of nature and art, their absence would simply result in a halting of the production of species diversification and possibility of as yet unknown forms of sensation. And in the frame of discourse, as for example in the world of musicology, we might proffer likewise—that without such life, play, theatrics, display, and periodic loosening of conceptual precision for affective productions of sensation—the space cannot be made in musicology for the production of the new and the diversification of the field, which may be central to its possibilities of a successful future. This, I propose, is what is at stake in musicology's being part of musical life.

V

At the beginning of this essay, I noted that the emergence of affect as a focal topic in academia was accompanied recursively by an affective intensification of scholarly life itself. I suggested that we might view such excitement symptomatically as a register for how academia can be caught up, somewhat unknowingly, in the hopes and devastations of its own time, and before I conclude I would like to return briefly to this point.

If affect studies in music have likewise been affectively charged— so that musicology at times has been able to appear as part of musical life, rather than simply its professional outside observer—that would seem to be cause for hope. It would suggest that musicology is vibrant: vibrant enough to have been able to exceed the merely pragmatic instrumental economy of academic thought, and vibrant enough to access the realm of "excessive and useless production."[52] As such, musicology would not only be life-affirming, but also fundamental for future diversification and the production of the new. But as the force of the turn to affect in academia itself starts to wane, and "but another academic fad" no doubt steps forward to take its place, we might benefit from viewing this now-passing affective vibrancy from the shadows for a moment. From this vantage we should note that the coming to the fore of affect studies has run relatively parallel in the academy to increasingly unambiguous neoliberal agendas. Such agendas set up instrumentality as their ultimate value: research has to proceed first and foremost from an evaluation of its extradisciplinary applicability, relevance, and ability to attract grants and funding. Teaching, likewise, must now be curved in terms of the skill sets it will offer students as they negotiate the brutal fragility of the job market; the rising ranks of contingent faculty in exploitative labor situations and the inroads that are slowly but steadily being made into the dismantling of the tenure system (in the United States) make academics themselves vastly more vulnerable to basic pragmatic questions of subsistence than used to be the case. In such an environment, the space available for the excessive, the useless, and the serious work of play that characterizes affective life must, by definition, be shrunk or misconstrued, out of fear, as decadence. For in order for such life to be activated into its practice, the academy would in part have to forget the material concerns that neoliberalism both forces upon it and pressures into reimagining as inspiration rather than drudgery.[53] Viewed symptomatically, we might therefore say that the excitement that accompanied affect studies was as much a means of registering that the moment had already passed when such a charged vision of life could actually have been realized in the academy as it was a celebration of the immanent arrival of such a better world. And so, if Daniel Barenboim makes us uncomfortable, that may be the result not so much of his shortcomings as a thinker as of the impossible antagonism his example forces upon us: that we can no longer afford the musical life that we cannot afford to live without.

Notes

1. Nigel Thrift, "Intensities of Feeling: Towards a Spatial Politics of Affect," *Geografiska Annaler: Series B, Human Geography* 86, no. 1 (2004): 60.

2. I refer of course to the second of Friedrich Nietzsche's *Untimely Meditations*, first published in 1874, "On the Uses and Disadvantages of History for Life," in Nietzsche, *Untimely Meditations*, ed. Daniel Breazeale, trans. R. J. Hollingdale (Cambridge: Cambridge University Press, 1997), 57–123.

3. Daniel Barenboim, "In the Beginning Was Sound," transcript, *Reith 2006—Daniel Barenboim: In the Beginning Was Sound*, BBC Radio 4, April 7, 2006, www.bbc.co.uk/radio4/features/the-reith-lectures/transcripts/2000/#y2006, 3. All quotations, unless otherwise

stated, are from this transcript; the page number is given as it appeared on the transcript when I accessed it on August 24, 2017.

4. Barenboim's concept of music is here resounds with one of Aristotle's categories in the *Politics* for music's function of *paidia*, or amusement. As Aristotle writes, "Amusement is for the sake of relaxation, and relaxation is of necessity sweet, for it is the remedy of pain caused by toil." Cited in Mechthild Nagel, *Masking the Abject: A Genealogy of Play* (Lanham, MD: Lexington Books, 2002), 52.

5. Barenboim, "In the Beginning Was Sound," 3.

6. Ibid., 13.

7. Ibid., 14.

8. Ibid., 13–14.

9. Ibid., 14.

10. Ibid., 3, my emphasis.

11. Ibid., my emphasis.

12. Ibid.

13. Ibid.

14. Daniel Barenboim, "Meeting in Music," transcript, *Reith 2006—Daniel Barenboim: In the Beginning Was Sound*, BBC Radio 4, April 28, 2006, www.bbc.co.uk/radio4/features/the-reith-lectures/transcripts/2000/#y2006, 3–4, accessed August 24, 2017.

15. Barenboim, "In the Beginning was Sound," 3.

16. Ibid.

17. "As for us, we consider ourselves to be at the end of the vein of humanist thought. From our point of view man is in the process of splitting apart, as if as a result of a spectral analysis, an example of which I have engaged in here in moving along the joint between the imaginary and the symbolic in which we seek out the relationship of man to the signifier, and the 'splitting' it gives rise to in him. Claude Lévi-Strauss is looking for something similar when he attempts to formalize the move from nature to culture or more exactly the gap between nature and culture." Jacques Lacan, *The Seminar of Jacques Lacan, Book VII: The Ethics of Psychoanalysis, 1959–1960*, ed. Jacques-Alain Miller, trans. Dennis Porter (New York: W. W. Norton, 1997), 273–74.

18. For a concise summary of the issue in Lacan, see Bruce Fink, *The Lacanian Subject: Between Language and Jouissance* (Princeton, NJ: Princeton University Press, 1995), esp. chap. 4 ("The Lacanian Subject," 35–48), the first three subheadings of which capture clearly what is at stake: "The Lacanian Subject Is Not the 'Individual' or Conscious Subject of Anglo-American Philosophy" (36), "The Lacanian Subject Is Not the Subject of the Statement" (37), and "The Lacanian Subject Appears Nowhere in What Is Said" (38).

19. Guy Dammann, "Rules of Engagement," *Guardian*, May 13, 2006, accessed August 22, 2017, www.theguardian.com/music/2006/may/13/classicalmusicandopera.

20. Ibid.

21. Plato, *The Republic* (London: Penguin, 1987), 152.

22. Ibid.

23. Barenboim, "In the Beginning Was Sound," 5.

24. A traditionally conservative mode of thinking about comedy argues that when we witness someone caught up in their own self-importance slip up on a banana peel, we come to a more humble idea of who we are; comedy, in such a formulation, is on the side of human finitude. However, in a brilliant analysis of the comic mode, Alenka Zupančič argues that the banana peel cliché actually speaks in the opposite direction: "Regardless of all accidents and catastrophes (physical as well as psychic or emotional) that befall comic characters,

they always rise from the chaos perfectly intact, and relentlessly go on pursuing their goals, chasing their dreams, or simply being themselves. It seems that nothing can really get to them, which somehow contradicts the realistic view of the world that comedy is supposed to promote." As illustration, she points to Sir John Falstaff in Shakespeare's *The Merry Wives of Windsor*. Zupančič, *The Odd One In: On Comedy* (Cambridge, MA: MIT Press, 2008), 28–29.

25. Barenboim, "In the Beginning Was Sound," 2.

26. The communal function of laughter has often been noted. For example, in a discussion of what he calls "Laughter's Messianic power," the philosopher Simon Critchley states that "the tiny explosions of humour that we call jokes return us to a common, familiar world of shared practices, the background meanings implicit in a culture." Critchley, *On Humour* (London and New York: Routledge, 2002), 16. For Henri Bergson, taking this trope further, laughter can start to suggest something sinister. As he states in his famous essay of 1900, "Le Rire": "Laughter always implies a kind of secret freemasonry, or even complicity, with other laughers, real or imaginary." Bergson, *Laughter: An Essay on the Meaning of the Comic*, trans. Cloudesely Brereton and Fred Rothwell (Rockville, MD: Arc Manor, 2008), 11.

27. I refer, of course, to the famous final proposition (7:1) of the *Tractatus Logico-Philosophicus*: "Wovon man nicht sprechen kann, darüber muß man schweigen" (Whereof one cannot speak, thereof one must be silent). Ludwig Wittgenstein, *Tractatus Logico-Philosophicus*, trans. C. K. Ogden (London: Routledge & Kegan Paul, 1922).

28. Barenboim, "In the Beginning Was Sound," 2.

29. Elizabeth Grosz, *Chaos, Territory, Art: Deleuze and the Framing of the Earth* (New York: Columbia University Press, 2008), 3.

30. Ibid., 8.

31. Theodor Adorno, *Minima Moralia: Reflections from Damaged Life*, trans. E. F. N. Jephcott (London and New York: Verso, 1994), 222. The full aphorism reads: "Artistic Productivity is the capacity for being voluntarily involuntary."

32. A translation of this letter can be found in Arthur Rimbaud, *Selected Poems and Letters*, trans. Jeremy Harding (London: Penguin, 2004), 236. Harding translates the line, somewhat misleadingly, as "I is somebody else." "I is an other" would be a more effective rendering,

33. Barenboim, "In the Beginning Was Sound," 4.

34. Ibid., 3.

35. Ibid., 4.

36. Ibid.

37. Ibid.

38. Ibid., 4–5.

39. Grosz, *Chaos, Territory, Art*, 5.

40. Gilles Deleuze and Félix Guattari, *What Is Philosophy?*, trans. Hugh Tomlinson and Graham Burchell (New York: Columbia University Press, 1994), 206.

41. Grosz, *Chaos, Territory, Art*, 18.

42. Ibid., 8.

43. Barenboim, "In the Beginning Was Sound," 5.

44. Deleuze and Guattari, *What Is Philosophy?*, 189 (my emphasis).

45. Barenboim, "In the Beginning was Sound," 5.

46. Grosz, *Chaos, Territory, Art*, 9.

47. Ibid., 6.

48. Ibid.

49. Ibid., 7.

50. Ibid.
51. Ibid., 6.
52. Ibid., 9.
53. David Blake, "Musicological Omnivory in the Neoliberal University," *Journal of Musicology* 34, no. 3 (2017): 319–53, presents an excellent discussion.

PART 3

Voicings and Silencings

CHAPTER 6

The Philosopher's Voice

THE PROSODY OF LOGOS

Eduardo Mendieta

Every sound we make is a bit of autobiography. It has a totally private interior yet its trajectory is public. A piece of inside projected to the outside. The censorship of such projections is a task of patriarchal culture that . . . divides humanity into two species: those who can censor themselves and those who cannot.[1]

Bodily hexis *is political mythology realized, em-bodied, turned into a permanent disposition, a durable manner of standing, speaking, and thereby of feeling and thinking.*[2]

We women notice that a "deep" (masculine) voice prevails more easily than a soprano timbre. But this is because "deepness" is a sign of the positively marked social status of the utterer (as also is a voice which is "distinguished," "free of provincial accent," etc.), and an audience reacts to the materiality of the voice as a sign which is immediately interpretable within a grid of social positions and oppositions. The social importance crystallized around the speaker's name and the social values which govern reaction to the voice's timbre work together to form an unconscious hearing which hierarchizes individuals' utterances.[3]

It is not enough to tune into the sonority, into bodily pleasure, into the song of the flesh, or into the rhythmic drives from which this song flows; this attunement alone will not suffice to pull speech itself from the deadly grip of logocentrism. The metaphysical machine, which methodologically negates the primacy of the voice over speech, should be dismantled by transforming this primacy into an essential destination–and by keeping in mind that the metaphysical strategy that neutralizes the power of the voice is also a strategy in which the spoken of "more than one voice" [à piu voci], each one different from the other, remains unheard for millennia.[4]

Physiognomy of the Voice

Few films capture as powerfully and accurately the drama of not having a voice, of not having the proper voice, of having a broken voice, as the British historical drama *The King's Speech*, a film released in 2010 to widespread acclaim, nominations, and prizes. Colin Firth plays Prince Albert, Duke of York, the future king George VI; Geoffrey Rush plays Lionel Longue, an Australian speech and language therapist. The performances are truly stellar. Firth's "Bertie" is a troubled, irascible, and shy, but also loyal, tender, and loving father, friend, and husband. King George VI took up the challenge of inspiring and sustaining Britain through World War II and became the British voice of resistance and endurance in the face of the Axis powers. At the same time, we see Longue struggle in xenophobic, accentocentric, vocal-chauvinist London, which demeans him because of his colonial accent. It is difficult not to feel sympathy for both men, and as I watched the film I found myself moved by the almost insurmountable challenges both faced. More than sympathy, I felt empathy, as someone who has been told that he speaks "broken English"—I was told this by a woman in a pub in England—and who has never shed his accent, although I have lived most of my life in the United States, and who thus also speaks his "mother" tongue with an accent.

The film, however, is also an investigation in what we can call the *physiognomy of the voice*.[5] Physiognomy is an ancient discipline that aimed to derive insights into the interior lives of individuals by their outward appearances, such as the shape of the nose, the height and width of the forehead, the shape of and distance between the eyes, the fullness of the lips, and the tone and tightness of the skin; the length of the legs, the shape of the calves, and the size of the chest; and also the timbre, depth, and tone of the voice.[6] Just as the eyes are windows into the soul, the voice reveals the entire depth of a person's moral character. The voice not only projects what is internal, but also places us in the midst of webs of relations, both physical and ideological. If the face is the visible sign of the soul, the voice is the sonorous envelope that creates a social canopy of relationality.[7]

In *The King's Speech*, we see Longue using a variety of exercises to help the future king, who as a second son had never expected to be king, overcome his severe stammer. These include disrupting his speech by swearing, singing, and reciting ditties and tongue twisters. The ascesis of the voice is as much a physical regime as it is a psychic drama. To overcome and manage his speech impediment, Albert must disrupt his own speech. Here speech therapy appears as a disruption of a vocal disruption. We also see Longue using different bodily comportments to help Prince Albert, take control of his voice—to have his voice. These include breathing exercises, swaying to create a bodily rhythm, yelling vowels, and dancing while singing. What makes this film uniquely illustrative is that it is also the staging of the sonic, vocal, auditory drama of class, gender, and colonialism. Prince Albert is made fun of, even by his brother and father. He is painfully unregal. Longue is a colonial subject, derided and deauthorized. Both are voice orphans. Both are in some respects without voice. Their broken voices, it should not go without saying, elicit a whole plethora of feelings, passions, and dispositions–what Pierre Bourdieu calls a "political mythology" and what the artist and thinker Brandon LaBelle calls an "oral imaginary" that interpellates our whole sonic embodiment.[8]

This ideological opera of the ascesis of the proper, masculine, authorized, and revered voice has been played since the birth of so-called Western philosophy. The philosopher's voice has been implicated in the political mythologies and oral imaginaries of the rational, civilized, and domesticated voice since its birth in ancient Greece. We learn from Diogenes Laertius's *Lives of Eminent Philosophers*, for instance, that Plato had a "weak voice," which Socrates in a dream had likened to the sweet sound of a swan.[9] So when Socrates was introduced to Plato, he recognized him as the cygnet from his dream.[10] We learn that Aristotle "spoke with a lisp," and with an accent, because he was from Macedonia. In addition—and here is a bit of physiognomy applied to Aristotle—"his calves were slender (so they say), his eyes small, and he was conspicuous by his attire, his rings, and the cut of his hair."[11] We learn that Socrates, who was perhaps infamous for his lack of good looks, was the son of a sculptor, and he himself, it is claimed, was a mason, whose sculptures were in the Acropolis. In fact, Socrates occupies a distinct place in the history of physiognomy in general, as the special case of a face that did not reveal the truth of a superior moral character.[12]

It would be tempting to call this dramatic opera of the ascesis of the voice "The Noble, the Ugly and the Foreign," where Plato is the noble, as he was from an Athenian noble family; Socrates is the ugly, not simply because he had the most un-Athenian facial and bodily characteristics; and Aristotle is the foreign, as he was a metic, a resident alien, from Macedonia, a region of the Hellenic world that was peripheral to Athenian culture. This dramatic staging of the voice of the philosopher continues unabated to this day.[13] We have numerous recordings of Michel Foucault, with his metallic, sharp, quick voice, as well as some of Heidegger, with his soft, deep, meditative, mercurial German. Finally, while we don't have access to John Rawls's voice, we do know from his students that he spoke with a stammer, which apparently developed from the trauma of having two of his brothers die from illnesses they caught from him.

The Soundless Voice of Unaccented Philosophy

The linguistic turn of modern philosophy has made it impossible for us to accept the Cartesian/Kantian/Hobbesian monological and autarkic subject. Modern philosophy now departs from an intersubjectively constituted self. We can only think in terms of dialogic, relational, thoroughly linguistified selves and agents. Whereas the motto of modern philosophy was "Cogito ergo sum," the motto of modern post-linguistic-turn philosophy is "We speak, thus I can relate." One of the consequences of the linguistification of agency and selfhood was that we became more attentive to the material phenomenology of embodiment. To be a relational subject, which dwells in language, means we have to be ever sensitive to how that dwelling is always materially mediated. This mediation, of course, is not simply corporeal; it is also technoscientific. Linguistic mediation is thus technosomatic (to trade in some Derridean coinage). Yet, surprisingly, attention to the materiality of the human voice has remained neglected. I argue in this essay that the linguistic turn of modern philosophy remains still too idealistic, too unmediated, too solipsistic. That modern, linguistified philosophy remains without voice. Logos remains tethered to some Platonic version of "language."

When linguistic-turned philosophers speak of language, they mean something like an immaterial, almost purely grammatical, abstract system of putting signs together. Language, even for these philosophers, is no more than a theoretical activity, the performance of a Chomskyan calculus. Even when they attend to the pragmatic dimension of semiosis, they neglect the very materiality of signifying. For humans to use a language means to speak. But to speak means to utter words with one's lips, tongue, larynx, and lungs. The voice in most of modern philosophy is a disembodied one. To the extent that the "grain of the voice," to use Roland Barthes's wonderful expression, remains neglected, we fail to reflect on the limits of language.[14] Or, more precisely, when we do not listen to the prosody of language, that is, to the cadences, rhythms, accents, the tonality, and pitch of spoken language as it is spoken by bodies with and in language, we limit what language communicates not simply through grammar and syntax. How something is said, with what tone and intonation, communicates more, and certainly faster and sooner, than what the sentence may say grammatically. This chapter will focus on the analysis of voice, the materiality of voice, as it is reflected in the voice of certain philosophers, and how they dealt with that accent, their own prosody. The general claim is that modern philosophy needs to make a phonological shift so that it can begin to hear the prosody of reason. Karl-Otto Apel wrote famously that there is no metaphilosophical language of philosophy. We can say that there is no philosophy that is not unaccented. All philosophy is always the philosophy of a philosopher, that philosopher's language, that philosopher's own accented pronunciation of her logos.

How Logos Lost Its Voice

All account of the emergence of logos in the West, at the very least, must begin with a bow in the direction of Homer. Every study of orality must begin with the transition from the oral to the written, and of course Homer is at the center of that transition. We must remember that the *Iliad* and the *Odyssey* were sung as poems, as performed poetry, before they were written down by "Homer," the blind bard, the metonym for a tradition of itinerant bards. Even as we read it, we can't circumvent the cadences of the text. We approach the story through a text that is the trace of the domesticated voice, but even then we still feel the force of voice in its rhythms. Of course, we also have gotten used to reading these original songs/poems in a prose version, one more brace on the voice of the poet. It is no longer the sound that weaves us the story, but the linearity of a narrative imposed by the impatient mind of the reader who has forgotten how to hear the voice of another. Before we were readers, we were listeners. Before logos was language as a system of signification, it was voice.

In the *Iliad*, the poem of force, to use Simone Weil's expression, there is one supreme force, and that is logos, logos as speech.[15] There are the logoi of the gods, the logoi of the warriors, and the logoi of the women. Before there is the force of the spear and sword, the rock and the arrow, there is the force of the speech that always accompanies an agon, a confrontation. As Alessandro Baricco put it in the epilogue to his twentieth-century version of the *Iliad*, logoi appear in Homer's *Iliad* as shields against the violence of war: "The word is the weapon with which men freeze the war. Even when they are discussing how to carry on the war, they're not carrying it on, and this is always a way of saving themselves."[16] Words arrest the onslaught of the certain death of soldiers, but they are also testimony to their reason, eloquence, to their presence of mind. These are not grunts, cannon fodder, skulls to be crushed by the violence of war, but speakers of logos, who must move from the agon of speech to the agon of struggle to expose themselves to the logic of iron and bronze. Logos in the *Iliad* is a way of being humanized, just as the gods are humanized by their speeches to one another and to mortals.

In the *Odyssey*, the power of logos as voice is articulated not simply in Odysseus's numerous speeches. Odysseus the cunning is Odysseus the *logorroico*. He does not cease to speak, and in fact, to save himself, he must speak to himself. His wits and his cunning are but his listening to the voice of his inner self speaking. Yet, there are two distinct passages in the *Odyssey* that merit careful attention. The first is the famous passage in which Odysseus ties himself to the mast of his ship, while his sailors, who must continue to row, have had their ears plugged so that they can't succumb to the beautiful, enchanting, terrifying voices of the sirens. Voice, as song, can be destructive, as it is also the means for singing the praise of the gods and the valor of heroes. But if their singing is terrifying, their greatest weapons, greater yet than their voice, as Franz Kafka wrote in his parable "The Silence of the Sirens," is their silence. For the silence of the sirens is the silence of voice, the silence of logos.

The second very telling and important section in the *Odyssey* is when Odysseus finally, after his many travails and circumnavigations, arrives back in Ithaca. Upon his return, he is misrecognized, or rather is not recognized by anyone, except Argos, his faithful dog. Argos, now old, decrepit, arthritic, and covered in fleas, is lying on a pile of dung, forgotten and uncared for. Yet despite his destitute condition, Argos nonetheless "presences" Odysseus:

> Now, as they talked on, a dog that lay there
> lifted its muzzle, pricked his ears ...
> It was Argos, long-enduring Odysseus' dog
> he trained as a puppy once, but little joy he got
> since all too soon he shipped to sacred Troy.
> In the old days young hunters loved to set him
> coursing after the wild goats and deer and hares.
> But now with his master gone he lay there, castaway,
> on piles of dung from mules and cattle, heaps collecting
> out before the gates till Odysseus' serving-men
> could cast it off to manure the king's estates.
> Infested with ticks, half-dead from neglect,
> here lay the hound, old Argos.

> But the moment he sensed Odysseus standing by
> he thumped his tail, nuzzling low, and his ears dropped,
> though he had no strength to drag himself an inch
> toward his master. Odysseus glanced to the side
> and flicked away a tear, hiding it from Eumaeus,
> diverting his friend in a hasty, offhand way:
> "Strange, Eumaeus, look, a dog like this,
> lying here on a dung-hill ...
> what handsome lines! But I can't say for sure
> if he had the running speed to match his looks
> or he was only the sort that gentry spoil at table,
> show-dogs masters pamper for their points. (Book 17,317–41)[17]

What does Argos recognize, or rather, how does Argos recognize his master? It is Ulysses's voice that he recognizes, and it through his ears that he welcomes the wanderer. He pricks up his ears, attentively, watchfully, and then wags his tail. Voice as signing can be terrifying, ethereal, angelic, but voice is also what makes us singular. And hearing ourselves is in many ways a rejection of how we have been individualized by our language and our voice. It is our voice that individualizes us. There is language, and there is sound, and words in language may be pronounced in a certain way, and each language may be distinct in its grammar. But it is voice that plunges us into the abyss of particularity and uniqueness. Each of us is a unique voice.

The Accents of the Passions

In an article published in the journal *Mind* in 1877, Charles Darwin, partly in response to one by Hippolyte Taine on children's mental development translated in an earlier issue of the same journal, provides us with ample evidence of his powers of both observation and scientific discipline. The article, titled "A Biographical Sketch of an Infant," is based on very close observations of his own children that he wrote down over many years. He detailed, day by day, week by week, year by year, the signs of his children's development: from the earliest reflex reactions (sneezing, yawning, hiccupping, stretching) to the most advanced manifestations of senses of justice, shame, and gratitude. Toward the end of this essay, Darwin confirms Taine's observation that children learn to inflect sounds even before they have acquired language. This is noted by the way children can intone a basic sound such as "mum" when either asking for food or acknowledging gratitude. What Darwin writes next is especially worthy of extensive quotation:

> The wants of an infant are at first made intelligible by instinctive cries, which after a time are modified in part unconsciously, and in part, as I believe, voluntarily as a means of communication,—by the unconscious expression of the features,—by gestures and in a marked manner by different intonations,—lastly by words of a general nature invented by himself, then of a more precise nature imitated from those he hears; and these latter are acquired at a wonderfully quick rate. An infant understands to a certain extent, and as I believe at a very early period, the meaning or feelings of those who tend him, by the expression of their features.[18]

Three things are worth underscoring in Darwin's passage. He notes that as first children make "instinctive" sounds, but very early on they begin to modulate, articulate, shape those sounds with tone and pitch. Second, these sounds are accompanied by gestures. Voicing is already accompanied with gesturing; we could also say that gesturing helps to articulate the voice. Finally, even before they have acquired language, or learned a language, children have already begun to master the language of gesture and affect. Gesturing is a gateway to the state of the soul, to stick with Aristotle and Hegel's metaphors. But additionally, this gesturing that communicates affect is linked before language is present to the voicing that is prior to speaking. As noted above, before a child arrives in the world, he or she is already in a world of sound. The rhythms, tones, pitch, volume, and cadences of the world that she is entering have been communicated to her not just by the mother's voice, but by the mother's own world. Even before we speak, we have an ability to distinguish the sound of that which is familiar from what is strange. We come to the world enveloped in sound, already ready to voice at its rhythms.

A philosopher who, like Darwin, paid close attention to the relationship among language, voice, affect, and gesture was Jean-Jacques Rousseau. Today we study him mostly for his pioneering insights into the foundations of political justice, but he also contributed to pedagogy, music theory, and the philosophy of language. More to the point, however, Rousseau linked affect, language, race, and politics in ways that are directly relevant to the main argument of this essay. In the *Discourse on the Origin and Basis of Inequality* (commonly known as the *Second Discourse*), he intimated some views about language that he had developed more extensively in an essay apparently written around the same time, namely the "Essay on the Origin of Languages." In it, Rousseau claimed that languages evolved from the passions, and not from needs. Needs, as he put it, "dictated the first gestures and that the passions wrested the first voices."[19] Indeed, in the state of nature, need drove humans away from one another, for they all would have been competing for the little that was available: "We did not begin by reasoning but by feeling. It is claimed that men invented speech in order to express their needs; this opinion seems untenable to me. The natural effect of the first needs was to separate men and not to bring them together. This had to have been so for the species to spread and the earth to be populated promptly, otherwise mankind would have been crammed into one corner of the world while the rest of it remained deserted."[20] Inasmuch, then, as it was passion and not need that drove humans to develop language, then the first languages were not those of geometers, but of poets.[21] The first languages, which were directly linked to the expression of passion and not need, were perforce full of force, allegory, metaphor, and above all intonation and sonic affect:

> The passions have their gestures, but they also have their accents, and these accents, which make us tremble, these accents, from which we cannot shield our organ, penetrate by it to the bottom of the heart, and in spite of us carry to it the movements that wrest them, and make us feel what we hear. Let us conclude that visible signs convey a more precise imitation, but that interest is aroused more effectively by sound.[22]

In fact, Rousseau notes, the earliest languages were always rich in images that were linked to passionate, forceful, rhapsodic, and allegorical speaking. Language phonetically communicated what used to be signified through gesture. Language, in fact, takes over gesture without ever abandoning it, or sublimating it. In Rousseau's view, spoken language is a synthesis of gesturing, affect, and voicing. The power of language emanates from the way it synergizes the gesturing body, with voice, in words that are raised to a higher power precisely because they can be heard in their full intensity. For Rousseau, language communicates before meaning is deciphered in the structure of the spoken sentence. Even before we fully grasp what someone has said, we understand what they meant.

For Rousseau, additionally, the force of a language is also the expression of a people's temperament. In fact, Rousseau distinguished the southern and northern languages. Here Rousseau is not digressing far from either Condillac or Montesquieu, both of whom embraced a geographic differentiation of nations with their respective temperaments. Rousseau, however, provides a bridge between the two, for he links geography to ethnicity/race to politics. For him, languages are directly linked to the political justice of a specific political system. As he put it at the end of the "Essay on the Origin of Languages": "I say that every language with which one cannot make oneself understood by the assembled people is a servile language; it is impossible for a people to remain free and speak that language."[23] To anticipate something he will claim with respect to climates in *The Social Contract*, only some languages can provide the proper soil on which the tree of freedom can grow. These are that languages that are "sonorous, prosodic, harmonious languages, in which discourse can be made out from a distance."[24]

We know from Jacques Derrida's extensive, thorough and insightful analysis of Rousseau's "Essay" in *Of Grammatology* (*De grammatologie*, 1967) that there are many oxymorons and supplements that play a double role in Rousseau's economy of language and social evolution.[25] Rousseau, in fact, epitomizes what Derrida calls "phonocentrism," the philosophical belief that presence is guaranteed by the immediacy of voice. Yet, as incisive as Derrida's exegesis is, he fails to acknowledge a very important dimension of Rousseau's work. Rousseau is less interested in whether some truth about being, the world, or consciousness is revealed in and through language than he is in ordinary language, the human voice—not the metaphysical voice (to use Stanley Cavell's formulations from *A Pitch of Philosophy*).[26] Rousseau may have been the first sociolinguist inasmuch as he was really interested in the historical relationship between the geographically determined body comportment of peoples, the types of temperament and moods that these give rise to, and how they imprint and shape that people's language. At the same time, he was also interested in the ways in which literacy had an adverse effect on the power and effectiveness of language. In the same way that "civil" society had a pernicious effect on the natural goodness of humans, writing—a tool of priests, kings, the nobility, and philosophers—became a tool in the domestication of the tongue, the strangling of the human voice. The more writing mediated between the voice and language, the more grammar made a language syntactically precise and efficient by means of rules and diacritics, and the more the vitality of a language was attenuated, the more a people were turned over to the retainers of language academies. The grammarians of language, so to speak, aim not simply to make a language more precise and clear, for those who read, but also directly to domesticate both the tongue of a people and the expression of their passions. The more a language is domesticated by syntax and grammar, the more it becomes a whip of servility and despotism. Liberty indeed must have its tongue, and its passion must be voiced with all of its vital accents.

Sonic Self

To hear may be inevitable for humans, and only injury or congenital disorders can prevent us from entering the world sonically. Voicing, the twin of hearing, on the other hand, commands an incredible array of skills that must be learned, slowly and deliberately. Compared to all the other skills a child must learn, learning to voice is simply amazing. Anne Karpf captured well the wide range of skills we have to learn in order to be able to speak:

> To speak, you need to control the movements of the larynx, glottis, soft palate, jaw, lips, and tongue, as well as the able to synchronize the respiratory cycle with the activity of the vocal cords. Saying, "Hello, how are you?" alone requires the coordinated use of more than 100 muscles. It's scarcely surprising, then, that newborns can't do it, especially since their vocal tract is very different from adults'.[27]

These one hundred muscles evidently are growing and maturing, as the child goes from infancy through puberty and adulthood, to old age. Our voice is continuously changing precisely because so many different muscles are in play. Most important, learning to speak is the acquisition of what Bourdieu called a "bodily hexis," by which he meant something like bodily comportment and sets of corporeal dispositions that have been imposed and acquired through approbation or censure. A bodily hexis is the way in which the body is both branded and domesticated to stand, walk, eat, laugh, yell, and above all speak in certain authorized ways. Before we arrive in the world, we are all being socialized and domesticated into distinct bodily hexes. Bourdieu, however, is not interested simply in the history of bodily hexis, even as he demonstrates how the body is the "site of incorporated history," to use John B. Thompson's felicitous formulation.[28] He is above all interested in how a certain historically produced body practices are intricately linked to what he calls "linguistic habitus."[29] Thus, the way in which we speak—how we speak, to whom, under what conditions, with what tone, with what accent—is intricately entwined with our bodily comportment. Bourdieu demonstrates why it is practically impossible to disentangle the use of language, as the alleged performance of a set of abstract linguistic rules, from the way in which we "execute" or "perform" language to voice it, to speak it. Language is never simply a formal calculus that regulates how certain variables combine in a set of determined ways. It is always a bodily performance, and as such, it is also the trace of history.

For Bourdieu, "language is a body technique, and specifically linguistic, especially phonetic, competence is a dimension of bodily hexis in which one's whole relation to the social world, and one's whole socially informed relation to the world, are expressed."[30] How we produce language, that is, how we voice it, is determined by one's entire relationship to the social world. This is why when we utter any word, we betray our full social history and social status. Part of the bodily hexis that determines the linguistic habitus of individuals is what was called by Pierre Guiraud "articulatory style," meaning how vowels and consonants are articulated to produce certain phonetic markers. The articulatory style is most revelatory of class, ethnicity, race, and of course region and country of origin. It is in the articulatory style, the way we dispose, flex, tighten, and flare up all of the organs that make the human voice box, that history becomes flesh.[31] In other words, we cannot *not* speak with an accented voice. Indeed, we all have a distinctive voice, for we all intone and vocalize differently. All languages have their own prosody, but so does each one of us. Just as a finite number of rules can give an almost limitless variety of syntactical variations (made more numerable by the pragmatic dimension of language use), so can there be innumerable prosodic variations. Karpf put it beautifully: "Prosody is the audio version of our personality, our sonic self."[32] There is no language without voice, and there is no voice without accent, and there is no accent that is either not derogated or not overvalorized. Linguistic habitus is also the site for the transmittal and renewal of social hierarchy. Prosody is the locus of social contestation. Prosody is also the tower of sound where singularizations take place.

The Accented Voices of Logos

Before his death, Italo Calvino was working on a book that he intended to be made up of five stories, each of which would focus on one of the senses. He was only able to finish three of them: those on taste, hearing, and smell. The story on hearing, which is really an allegory for the sovereign philosopher who has become prisoner of his own voiceless reason, includes a powerful passage:

> A Voice means this: there is a living person, throat, chest, feelings, who sends into the air this voice, different from all other voices. A voice involves the throat, saliva, infancy, the patina of experienced life, the mind's intentions, the pleasure of giving a personal form to sound waves. What attracts you is the pleasure this voice puts into existing: into existing as voice; but this pleasure leads you to imag-

ine how this person might be different from every other person, as the voice is different.³³

Philosophy comes in many styles, genres, and formats. Philosophy is literature, or a certain performance of our capacity to weave stories. Each philosopher has a distinct style, and their philosophy can't be dissociated from that style. Their philosophy *is* partly that style, the style they crafted. From Plato to Judith Butler, philosophy is a matter of style, for to think is to think in a certain way. Logos comes dressed in the style given to it by the philosopher *qua* writer. But a philosophical style is the enactment of a certain relation to one's voice. The style a philosopher ends up adopting is one that results from negotiating how they hear themselves speak in public and in private. In philosophical style we can find a shield to attenuate the accents in our voices. Style may also be a megaphone for an infatuation with the sound of our voice. Style may be a rein on a runaway voice. Style may be the agon of philosophy, but it is also the agon of voice.

We should approach the agon, the struggle, the *polemos* of philosophy with style and voice through the one philosopher who has meditated on this relationship as very few have: Derrida:

> One entered French literature only by losing one's accent. I think I have not lost my accent; not everything in my "French Algerian" accent is lost. Its intonation is more apparent in certain "pragmatic" situations (anger or exclamations in familial or familiar surroundings, more often in private than in public, which is a quite reliable criterion for the experience of this strange and precarious distinction.) But I would like to hope, I would very much prefer, that no publication may permit my "French Algerian" to appear. In the meantime, and until the contrary is proven, I do not believe that anyone can detect by *reading*, if I do not myself declare it, that I am "French Algerian." I retain, no doubt, a sort of acquired reflex from the necessity of this vigilant transformation. I am not proud of it, I make no doctrine of it, but so it is: an accent—any French accent, but above all a strong southern accent—seems incompatible to me with the intellectual dignity of public speech. (Inadmissible, isn't it? Well, I admit it.)³⁴

This is quite an admission by someone who also writes: "The accent indicates a hand-to-hand combat with language in general; it says more than accentuation. Its symptomatology invades writing."³⁵ There are several things here that need to be foregrounded: Derrida bemoans that he never lost his French Algerian accent, and thus, that he never properly entered the canon of French literature. But is this a sustainable claim? Is not Derrida already part of French literature, *qua* French writer, who granted both French and non-French entry to much of French literature? Was not Derrida already part of French literature, when he was in a *polemos* with Foucault, and when he published within a year three books that would shift the direction of French philosophy in irreversible ways? And since he never lost his accent, then, it is also implied, he could not ascend to the heights of dignified public speech. Additionally, unless he declared himself to be a French Algerian, no one would detect his accent in his writing; but this claim is vitiated by the stronger one, namely that it is the symptomatology of accent, which is more than mere accentuation, that invades writing. Writing itself is the stigmata of the hand-to-hand combat that is all accent. Finally, deconstruction is precisely the enactment of a certain ethos which says that all texts speak with many voices, and that there is no language that does not speak without an accent.

Like Derrida, Jürgen Habermas has become the paragon of post-linguistic-turn philosophy. Unlike Derrida, however, Habermas has focused his philosophical energies in thinking through the implications of the linguistification of reason for social theory, which is why there is a particular sociological category that is pivotal to all this thinking. I am of course referring to the category of the public sphere: *Öffentlichkeit*, which refers both to a social space and to the condition of something being public. So publicness and public sphere are entwined not simply in the German language but also in Habermas's entire theory of communicative action. Tellingly, the roots of this entwinement are also biographical. When Habermas was awarded the Kyoto Prize, he was asked to give a speech in which he should talk about the autobiographical roots of his thinking. It is probably one of Habermas's most confessional and autobiographical texts. In his speech, now included as the opening chapter of *Between Naturalism and Religion*, he begins by making a distinction between "public" and "publicity," in light of the rise of the "media society," with its craving for stars, personalities, and celebrities.[36] Thus, while the public sphere can be used by celebrities and public intellectuals, the former are engaging in publicity, while the latter appear in the public sphere not on a stage but within its space of reasons, in order to give or take reason. If in the one case everyone else's gaze is focused on the star, in the other people's ears are focused on the reasons and opinions being exchanged. The public sphere, with its connotations of light, brightness, and clearing, is also a space of air, of sound, of echoes and reverberations. The public sphere is the horizon of visibility as much as of orality and aurality. In this context, Habermas claims: "In discourses that focus on issues of common concern, participants turn their backs on their private lives. They have no need to talk about themselves. The line between public and private spheres does not become blurred but instead the two domains complement each other."[37] This is a fascinating passage, not to say problematic. I flag it at this moment because from the outset I want to have it read in conjunction with Derrida's passage quoted above, which also appeals to the distinction between the private and the public, and how there is a shielding, a sheltering behind the wall that separates the private from the public. It is also a passage that calls for heavy exegesis. In what sense do these two spheres have a "complementary relationship" (*komplementäres Verhaltnis*), when one calls for turning one's back on one's motives for stepping into the brightly lit and noisy debate of the public sphere?

A little later in the text, Habermas gives us the "biographical roots" of his obsession with the "conceptual triad" of "public space," "discourse," and "reason": "I shall begin with my early childhood, with an operation that I underwent directly after I was born. I do not believe that this surgery, as one might suppose, enduringly shook my faith in the world around me. However, the intervention may well have awakened the feelings of dependence and vulnerability and the sense of relevance of our interactions *with others*."[38] And then, he adds, later, linking his childhood experiences to his philosophical outlook: "The approach to the philosophy of language and the kind of moral theory that I developed within this framework may have been inspired by two experiences I had as a schoolboy: first, that other people did not understand me very well (a) and, second, that they responded with annoyance or rejection (b)."[39] A few paragraphs later he expands on what people's reaction to his speech impediment did for his own relationship to philosophical texts: "Incidentally, my speech impediment may also explain why I have always been convinced of the superiority of the written over the spoken word."[40]

As with Derrida, so with Habermas: written texts are shields behind which to conceal a certain perceived or imagined weakness or fault with one's voice. It is a perceived or imagined fault by virtue of the voices' publicness. We are vulnerable to either the approbation or the disapproval, misunderstanding, or annoyance of those in the public sphere, who have expectations about how we should sound. Our voices at home are smooth, soft, reassuring, unguarded, unchecked. In the public sphere we never know if our language will sound broken, foreign, uncouth, fearful, choked. At the same time, it is to be noted, how what Derrida calls the symptomatology of the public "invades" or "colonizes" the space of intimacy. It is because of how both Derrida and Habermas thought their voice would be heard that they adopted a certain orientation to their thinking and to writing their thinking. The sound of their voice in public reverberated into the practice of their writing and their own philosophical style. The symptomatology of a sanctioned "articulatory style," the amplification of an authorized prosody, invades the performance of philosophical style. This style is either the silencing of one's public voice or a revenge on that censure.

At the same time, however, both Derrida and Habermas exemplified what I at the outset identified as a certain idealism and etherealization of post-linguistic philosophy. Inasmuch as both of these thinkers emphasize language, the language they have in mind is one without materiality, without the "grain of the voice," without the "patina of experience" that gives voice its inflection and timbre. In this, then, they are complicit in contributing to what Adriana Cavarero calls the "strategic deafness" of philosophy,[41] which is at the same time the silencing of voice's plurality and the neglect of its materiality.

In *Monolingualism of the Other*, Derrida wrote this striking sentence: "For never was I able to call French, this language I am speaking to you, 'my mother tongue.' These words do not come to my mouth. I leave to others the words 'my mother tongue.'"[42] In Habermas's Kyoto speech, appropriately titled "Öffentlicher Raum und politische Öffentlichkeit: Lebensgeschichtliche Wurzeln von zwei Gedankenmotive" (Public Space and Political Public Sphere: The Biographical Roots of Two Motifs in My Thought), he writes: "We invariably find ourselves within the element of language. Only someone who can speak can remain silent."[43] It can be said that no one has a mother tongue that they can claim is theirs alone, in the way our mother and father may be—theirs and only theirs. It is intrinsic to the mother tongue that it is the tongue of many, and thus, it is the tongue of many accents. The mother tongue has not one sound; its sound is the sound of its children. Indeed, perhaps our mother tongue can claim us, but no one can claim her in an exclusive and possessive way. Voice is the horizon of the singular, the particular, because this is what the mother tongue commands. A mother tongue without its plurification in and through voice would be impossible. Only because we speak in some mother tongue, or an adopted one, can we speak as we speak but also remain silent. Only someone who speaks with an accent can speak. There is no speaking without an accent. Logos has a voice, and that voice cannot but be accented. It is not without interest that Derrida's and Habermas's voices are the accented voices of two philosophers who experienced estrangement from their voices in their alleged mother tongues.[44]

Notes

1. Anne Carson, "The Gender of Sound," in *Glass, Irony & and God* (New York: New Directions Books, 1995), 119–142, at 130.

2. Pierre Bourdieu, *Outline of a Theory of Practice* (Cambridge: Cambridge University Press, 1977), 93–94.

3. Michèle Le Dœuff, "Philosophy in the Larynx," in *The Philosophical Imaginary*, trans. Colin Gordon (London and New York: Continuum, 2003), 129–137, citation at 136.

4. Adriana Cavarero, *For More than One Voice: Toward a Philosophy of Vocal Expression*, translated by Paul A. Kottman (Stanford, CA: Stanford University Press, 2005), 15–16.

5. My thinking on the physiognomy of the voice has been deeply influenced by Maud W. Gleason's superlative study, *Making Men: Sophists and Self-Presentation in Ancient Rome* (Princeton, NJ: Princeton University Press, 1994), esp. chap. 4, "Aerating the Flesh: Voice Training and the Calisthenics of Gender."

6. See Aristotle's spurious treatise "Physiognomics," in *The Complete Works of Aristotle: The Revised Oxford Translation*, ed. Jonathan Barnes (Princeton, NJ: Princeton University Press, 1984).

7. For an expansion on this theme, see my article "The Sound of Race: The Prosody of Affect," *Radical Philosophy Review* 17, no. 1 (2014): 109–31.

8. Brandon LaBelle, *Lexicon of the Mouth: Poetics and Politics of Voice and the Oral Imaginary* (New York: Bloomsbury, 2014).

9. Diogenes Laertius, *Lives of Eminent Philosophers*, trans. R. D. Hicks, vol. 1, books I–V (Cambridge, MA: Harvard University Press, 1925), 281.

10. It would be interesting to read this anecdote in conjunction with the myth told in the *Phaedrus* that tells of the origin of cicadas, who were at first men who were taken to their deaths by the pleasures of singing. As Cavarero notes, the myth of the human origin of cicadas links to the Homeric Sirens, and thus to the mythopoesis of the power of the singing voice; see Cavarero, *For More than One Voice*, 101–2.

11. Ibid., 445.

12. See Gernot Böhme, *Der Typ Sokrates*, expanded ed. (Frankfurt am Main: Suhrkamp Verlag, 2002), 210–33 (chapter titled "Über die Physiognomie des Sokrates und die Physiognomik überhaupt").

13. Two works that fill in the gaps are David Appelbaum, *Voice* (Albany: State University of New York Press, 1990), and Andrew Fiala, *The Philosopher's Voice: Philosophy, Politics, and Language in the Nineteenth Century* (Albany: State University of New York Press, 2002). See also Jonathan Rée, *I See a Voice: Deafness, Language and the Senses; A Philosophical History* (New York: Metropolitan Books, 1999).

14. Roland Barthes, *Image, Music, Text*, essays selected and translated by Stephen Heath (New York: Hill & Wang, 1977), see the essay "The Grain of the Voice," 179–89.

15. Simone Weil and Rachel Bespaloff, *War and the Iliad*, trans. Mary McCarthy, introduction by Christopher Benfey, afterword by Herman Broch (New York: New York Review of Books, 2005).

16. Alessandro Baricco, *An Iliad*, trans. Ann Goldstein (New York: Vintage International, 2007), 154.

17. Homer, *The Odyssey*, ed. Bernard Knox, trans. Robert Fagles, Bibliotheca Homerica Langiana (New York: Viking, 1996), 363–64.

18. Charles Darwin, "A Biographical Sketch of an Infant," *Mind* 2, no. 7 (1877): 292–93.

19. Jean-Jacques Rousseau, *Essay on the Origin of Languages and Writings Related to Music*, trans. and ed. John T. Scott (Hanover, NH: University Press of New England, 1998), 293.

20. Ibid., 293–94.

21. Ibid., 293.

22. Ibid., 292.

23. Ibid, 332.

24. Ibid.

25. Jacques Derrida, *Of Grammatology*, trans. Gayatri Chakraborty Spivak (Baltimore, MD: Johns Hopkins University Press, 1976).

26. Stanley Cavell, *A Pitch of Philosophy: Autobiographical Exercises* (Cambridge, MA: Harvard University Press, 1994).

27. Anne Karpf, *The Human Voice: How this Extraordinary Instrument Reveals Essential Clues about Who We Are* (New York: Bloomsbury, 2006), 99–100.

28. Pierre Bourdieu, *Language and Symbolic Power*, ed. John B. Thompson, trans. Gino Raymond and Andrew Adamson (Cambridge, MA: Harvard University Press, 1991), 13. The quote is from Thompson's introduction to this selection of essays.

29. Ibid., 81–89.

30. Ibid., 86.

31. Ibid., 86.

32. Karpf, *The Human Voice*, 33.

33. Italo Calvino, *Under the Jaguar Sun*, trans. William Weaver (New York: A Harvest Book, Harcourt, 1988), 54.

34. Jacques Derrida, *Monolingualism of the Other, or, The Prosthesis of Origin*, trans. Patrick Mensah (Stanford, CA: Stanford University Press, 1998), 45–46.

35. Ibid., 46.

36. Jürgen Habermas, *Between Naturalism and Religion: Philosophical Essays*, trans. Ciaran Cronin (Cambridge, UK, and Malden, MA: Polity Press, 2008).

37. Ibid., 12.

38. Ibid., 13.

39. Ibid., 15.

40. Ibid., 16.

41. Cavarero, *For More than One Voice*, 14.

42. Derrida, *Monolingualism of the Other*, 34.

43. Habermas, *Between Naturalism and Religion*, 15.

44. See my essay "The Jargon of Ontology and the Critique of Language: Adorno and Philosophy's Motherless Tongue" in *The Aesthetic Grounds of Critical Theory: New Readings of Benjamin and Adorno*, ed. Nathan Ross (Lanham, MD: Rowman & Littlefield, 2015), 47–65.

CHAPTER 7

Late Capitalism, Affect, and the Algorithmic Self in Music Streaming Platforms

Michael Birenbaum Quintero

Theorists since Theodor Adorno have turned to music and the music industry to discuss the ways in which capitalism molds subjects.[1] More recently, Tia DeNora has offered that music is a "technology of the self" by which listeners bend the affective and perceptual flow of daily life into coherent—and marketable—narratives of identity.[2] But the nature of musical experience has changed radically since the publication of DeNora's turn-of-the-millennium landmark in ways that musicologists have yet to account for. This shift arises in part from the rise of platforms such as Spotify, Pandora, YouTube, Songza, and others, streaming formats that have moved music beyond the bounded materiality of such twentieth-century media as CDs and LPs and even the less material boundedness of the MP3 file. With this change, the music industry has recovered from the threat of peer-to-peer (P2P) file sharing ("piracy") by reentrenching copyright regimes, while listeners have traded ownership of discrete downloadable files for access to the seemingly limitless "celestial jukebox." Music scholarship is only beginning to apply an Adornian reading—that is, to inquire into the ramifications for individual self-making and capitalist interpellation of subjects—to the new modalities of music listening that these technological and industrial shifts are engendering.

One way to imagine the link between musical experience and sense of self in capitalist society in both Adorno's and DeNora's thought is as a relationship between affect and emotion, although neither uses these terms. It is at the point at which human experience of the raw intensities of sensation or experience (what some theorists call "affect") are processed and rationalized as biographizing, socially conditioned desires, self-descriptions, or emotions that capitalist modernity finds its ground zero.

I find these delineations between affect and emotion, between experiential intensity and biographical rationalization, useful, but I should state from the beginning that I have no particular ontological stake here. I am not interested, as affect theorists such as Brian Massumi seem to be, in discovering a more pure or authentic, prerational or natural mode of being-in-the-world.[3] Rather, the difference between undifferentiated sensation (broadly, affect) and socially intelligible narrativization of that sensation (emotion), as analytical categories, is important for my argument because the gap between them provides a space in which to examine culturally and historically specific processes of entrainment of emotion, perception, and self-conceptualization. This offers the possibility of examining the relationship between individuals at the intimate level of experience and broader societal regimes of power, in that it prizes apart the seemingly self-evident nature of emotion into an experiential component and a narrative, social, or biographic component that admits, and indeed gives a specific site of intervention, for the workings of ideology, interpellation, and subject formation.

In this chapter, I would like to read Adorno from an affect perspective, using the vocabulary of the processing of musical affect into recognizable and actionable emotion to understand his description of the workings of the culture industry. In doing so, it is also necessary to maintain the historical specificity of the music industry of Adorno's moment so that an understanding of false individualism and the homogenization of musical taste can be grasped in the context of the Fordist mode of production of the deeply consolidated music industry of the time.[4] An affect approach is also enlightening for reading DeNora's work; her observations about what we might call listeners' "soundtracking" of specific contexts and activities such as work, exercise, and lovemaking can be understood as using music reflexively to shape their affective experience and to frame that experience in self-making narratives. Like Adorno's account, DeNora's is historically specific, in her case to the more flexible modes of production and neoliberal forms of self-crafting at the turn of the millennium, although the specific affordances of streaming music had yet to arrive. And like Adorno's account, hers has broad political ramifications for the ways in which the relationship between individual subjectivities and the broader social, political, and economic order are structured by music. Thus, a fairly detailed discussion of Adorno's and DeNora's work gives us a vocabulary and set of concerns to bring to the study of streaming music platforms.

In other words, I am interested in the ways in which music, which has long functioned to reinforce forms of subjectivity that reproduce capitalism (for example, the individual), has been transformed by the recent proliferation of streaming platforms. What I would like to suggest in this essay is that streaming platforms and the forms of listening they afford comprise still other dispositions, in which taste, that all-important component of the capitalist subject, has been farmed out to algorithms. These new algorithmic modalities of listening, by shaping the manifestation of undifferentiated affect as socially meaningful emotion, intervene radically into listeners' spinning of musical experience into narrations of who they are. As such, describing these new processes of self-narration limns the particularities of the new instantiations of capitalism within which streaming music platforms and their users operate.

Affective Experience and Entrained Qualification

Key to understanding music's role in processes of self-making, I suggest, is a close examination of the relationship between the raw experiences and the intensities of sensation that theorists have called "affect," on the one hand, and the culturally conditioned and socially recognizable conceptualization and narration of affective experience on the other.[5] Massumi's Deleuzian/Spinozist notion of affect describes the flow of intensities and stimuli and perturbations over and through the body, which are felt, in both the physioperceptual and the emotional senses of the word, in real time.[6] It is significant that affect, unlike emotion, is posited as preconscious and prelinguistic, indeed, as autonomous:

> Intensity [or affect] is ... a nonconscious, never-to-conscious autonomic remainder. It is outside expectation and adaptation, as disconnected from meaningful sequencing, from narration, as it is from vital function. It is narratively de-localized, spreading over the generalized body surface, like a lateral backwash from the function-meaning interloops traveling the vertical path between head and heart.[7]

This real-time experience of the play of affective-physiological intensities over the body is anterior to and separate from the process by which affect is narrativized and made socially meaningful, a process Massumi calls "qualification."[8] This takes place when raw affective sensation is identified and explained using the conventionalized language of emotion: joy, melancholy, anger, and the like.

There are corollaries in experimental psychology to this distinction between affect/intensity and emotion/qualification. The psychologists Stanley Schachter and Jerome Singer suggested in 1962 that emotion is a process of interpreting and attempting to attribute a felt but still unspecified bodily condition. That is to say, people feel bodily stimuli and subsequently use contextual information to identify the specific emotion their body is showing itself to be influenced by. This "two-factor" theory of emotion (comprised of physiological arousal and cognitive labeling) clearly lends itself to the notion of a gap between undifferentiated affective intensity and the socially recognizable and contextually appropriate emotions to which that intensity is attributed.[9]

For anthropologists of the senses, the space between the felt and the attributed is also the place where culture and epistemology can be located. Rather than an abstract symbolic or intellectual concern, culture acts in the process of qualification. Take, for example, the account of the anthropologist Paul Stoller in the African Sahel, who was utterly blind to a phenomenon that was absolutely concrete for his Songhay teacher Djibo, seated right next to him:

> He turned toward me. "Did you hear it?" "Hear what?" I asked dumbfounded. "Did you feel it?" "Feel what?" I wondered. "Did you see it?" "What are you talking about?" I demanded. Sorko Djibo shook his head in disbelief. He was disappointed that I had not sensed in one way or another the man's [spirit] double as he, Djibo, had liberated it. He said to me: "You look but you do not see. You touch, but you do not feel. You listen, but you do not hear."[10]

Sorko Djibo's explanation of the anthropologist's insensibility is not much different from Massumi's description of the qualification of affect—that raw perceptual sensation (seeing, feeling, hearing) is so incommensurate with or alien to Stoller's enculturated processes of interpreting that sensation (looking, touching, listening) is impossible to imprint on, or even enter, his consciousness, even though, according to Djibo, it is nonetheless sensible to him.

Again, I am less concerned with arguing for the existence of a prerational perception, or with rehearsing familiar Romantic narratives about the inauthenticity of modern sensorial experience, than with understanding how the particular relationship of affect and its qualification is contingent, such that differently acculturated human beings, wearing different sets of perceptual goggles and earphones, as it were, at the level of qualification, inhabit phenomenologically different worlds. This applies not only to nonmoderns like the Songhay but also to us moderns. We too are entrained to perceive precisely as moderns;

put more succinctly, modernity colonizes and entrains our sensorium. Nadia Berenstein's history of artificial flavoring, for example, shows the contingent and arbitrary nature of the process by which, for example, the taste of synthetically derived methyl anthranilate and the color purple have come to stand in for—indeed, to be actively entrained as—grapes, and how diacetyl has become so pervasive a taste element in synthetic margarine that manufacturers have begun to add it into natural butter to make it taste more like . . . itself.[11] Stoller's teacher Djibo would likely be as baffled by the entrained perceptual equivalency between a banana and a "banana"-flavored candy laced with isoamyl acetate as Stoller was by the assertion that had he known how to listen he would have just heard a ghost.

Affect in Adorno's "Jazz Subject" and DeNora's "Self-Identity"

Theodore Adorno's work on the role of popular music might seem like a strange place to begin a discussion of affect or subjectivity. After all, Adorno's analysis has been long critiqued for its seemingly deterministic representation of listeners as stripped of agency by a monopolistic culture industry—as *objects* more than subjects. "There is nothing left for the consumer to classify. Producers have done it for him," he and Max Horkheimer write in *Dialectics of Enlightenment*.[12] This perspective suggests that listeners play no particular role in interpreting musical commodities—the interpretation is already done for them by the culture industry, which could be described as interpreting *listeners* in order to offer them the most appropriate products. This line of thought links Adorno's thought to Marxist notions of ideology and false consciousness, and to Adorno's contemporary Louis Althusser's description of interpellation, the process by which subjects are constructed ideologically when they are "hailed," as by the police in Althusser's example, or in Frantz Fanon's account of his racialization as a Black man in France ("Look, a Negro!"),[13] or Butler's of the gendering of a baby at birth ("It's a girl/boy!").[14]

But Adorno's thought does not dispense with the interiority of the mass subject (or *Jazz-Subjekt*, as he calls it) in favor of a totally exogenous interpellation.[15] For Adorno, it is not that the capitalist system dispenses with or obviates individuals; rather, it "alters the composition of individuality itself."[16] A reading from the perspective of affect is surprisingly useful in understanding exactly what comprises this new form of individuality—this jazz subject, in Adorno's thought.

In this light, one might even understand his theory as *beginning* with affect. In "On Popular Music," Adorno posits a kind of affective disposition as the definitive experience of capitalist modernity and mass society. In particular, labor "on the assembly line, in the factory, or at office machines" produces a generalized affect of anxiety, combined with boredom and physical and mental exhaustion.[17] The undifferentiated nature of this realm of feeling, its bodily experience—combining the disquiet of anxiousness with the overstimulated numbness of fatigue and boredom—would seem to mark it as closer to the realm of free-flowing affective intensity than socially narratable emotion.[18] Indeed, Adorno marks precisely this undifferentiated character, and people's incapacity to be reflexive about it, as fundamental to the affective structure, marked by distraction and inattention, upon which popular music works:

> The frame of mind to which popular music originally appealed, on which it feeds, and which it perpetually reinforces, is simultaneously one of distraction and inattention. Listeners are distracted from the demands of reality by entertainment which does not demand attention either. ... Distraction is bound to the present mode of production, to the rationalized and mechanized process of labor to which, directly or indirectly, masses are subject. This mode of production ... engenders fears and anxiety.[19]

For Adorno, the ideological effect of popular music is its channeling of this distracted anxiety into particularly identified—in Massumi's terms, "qualified"—emotional modes. The culture industry offers a kind of emotional infrastructure for understanding and acting on that anomie (although not, Adorno asserts, curing it). It is not only that popular music acts as a bodily and affective "stimulant" that provokes a feeling of "effortless sensation," that is, that it heightens affect sensation already perturbed by the experience of mass society.[20] More important, it works by herding that affective play of intensities into a prefabricated set of emotional categories that are as standardized as the genres of music themselves. It is in this sense that we can understand the two (implicitly gendered) variants of listeners that Adorno focuses on, which he describes as "emotional" and "rhythmic obedient" types.[21]

Adorno's emotional listener, embodied by "the poor shop girl," consumes the kitschy sentiment of romantic music and film:[22]

> When the audience at a sentimental film or sentimental music become aware of the overwhelming possibility of happiness, they dare to confess to themselves what the whole order of contemporary life

ordinarily forbids them to admit, namely, that they actually have no part in happiness.... They consume music in order to be allowed to weep.... The actual function of sentimental music lies ... in the temporary release given to the awareness that one has missed fulfillment.[23]

In other words, the "girl behind the counter" listens to sentimental music to channel her affective intensity into recognizable and actionable sadness.[24] She seeks "to be allowed to weep" because the music's sentimental sadness gives a generic recognizability to an affective disposition that is otherwise the undifferentiated and unnamable feeling of daily life, giving the emotional listener a way to make it intelligible and to act upon it.

The "rhythmically obedient" type, on the other hand, is the jazz-crazed jitterbug dancer, who claims his fury and "frenzied enthusiasm" on the dance floor as an expression of his individuality (the gendered pronoun is Adorno's).[25] But Adorno describes the affective disposition of the jitterbug, despite its intensity, as ambiguous, in that it is not easily settled into particular emotional genres (fury, enthusiasm) or even directed in a single direction: "No one who has ever attended a jitterbug jamboree or discussed with jitterbugs current issues of popular music can overlook the affinity of their enthusiasm to fury, which may first be directed against the critics of their idols but which may tilt over against the idols themselves."[26] In Adorno's analysis, the unsettled affective disposition of the jitterbug reveals how contingent the process is by which the jitterbugs attribute their emotional state to one of enthusiastic individualistic freedom. In fact, Adorno suggests, this is a fairly flimsy rationale or emotional labeling patterned on the conventionalized emotional genres offered in the mass media:

[Their] mass hysteria, fanaticism and fascination themselves are partly advertising slogans after which the victims pattern their behavior. This self-delusion is based upon imitation and even histrionics. The jitterbug is the actor of his own enthusiasm or the actor of the enthusiastic front page model presented to him. He shares with the actor the arbitrariness of his own interpretation.[27]

There is in Adorno's interpretation a complex kind of agency, evident in what he calls the jitterbugs' "pseudo-individualizations" and crystallized in the image of the masses of supposedly individual jitterbugs dancing to the same underlying rhythm. This scene is metaphorically loaded for Adorno: a profound moral passivity masked by the outward appearance of frenetic movement, a mass homogenization disguised as self-expression. On the one hand, the political quiescence popular music provokes is profoundly dangerous:

> Their response to music immediately expresses their desire to obey. However, as the standardized meter of dance music and of marching suggests the coordinated battalions of a mechanical collectivity, obedience to this rhythm by overcoming the responding individuals leads them to conceive of themselves as agglutinized with the untold millions of the meek who must be similarly overcome. Thus, do the obedient inherit the earth.[28]

It is important to note, however, that Adorno's jazz subjects, as unreflective, masochistic, and politically quiescent as they may be, are not without agency. They are not coerced into their passivity, or even beguiled into it; they themselves choose it. The jazz subject is "only under a spell of his own making":[29]

> Enthusiasm for popular music requires willful resolution by listeners, who must transform the external order to which they are subservient into an internal order. The endowment of musical commodities with libido energy is manipulated by the ego. This manipulation is not entirely unconscious therefore.... [The jitterbugs] "join the ranks," but this joining does not only imply their conformity to given standards; it also implies a decision to conform. The appeal of the music publishers to the public to "join the ranks" manifests that the decision is an act of will, close to the surface of consciousness.[30]

If passivity is in fact chosen, the nature of political will, and therefore of freedom and agency, reveals rather more complexity in Adorno's thought than he is usually given credit for. The political effects of popular music on its listeners arise neither from blunt coercion nor from some kind of subliminal rhythmic mesmerism. Rather, and again with recourse to the distinction between undifferentiated affect and narrativized emotion, they *choose* popular music as a kind of explanatory mechanism. For Adorno, this takes place when listeners hear music that sounds familiar (both because of its formulaic nature and because of listeners' own inattention), and they place it in some socially recognizable genre of those offered in the mass media. In doing so, "one not only identifies it innocently as being this or that, subsuming it under this or that category, but by the very act of identifying it, one also tends unwittingly to identify oneself with the objective social agencies or with the power of these individuals who made this particular event fit into this pre-existing category and thus 'established' it."[31] The work of DeNora, one of Adorno's most prominent commentators (and critics) in contemporary musicology, is useful for understanding how music works to "qualify" affective experience in ways that reflect the complexities of Adorno's discussion of agency and of the "composition of individuality" in capitalist modernity. Her *Music in Everyday Life* (2000) takes up Adorno's project of examining musical subject formation under capitalism but breaks with it both in method and scope. Indeed, she is quite critical of Adorno's lack of attention to listeners, with whom she conducts interviews as the fundamental basis for her study, and she is far more reticent to make the kind of broad systemic analysis to which Adorno is inclined. Despite approaching the subject from the other direction, as it were, her more granular analysis sheds light on music's provision of an explanatory emotional grid for locating undifferentiated affect in ways that make sense for understanding Adorno.

DeNora is concerned with two broad sets of listeners' practices. The first, "self-regulation," refers to strategies that are focused on a particular moment or scene: mood setting, emotional self-expression, or motivation. Her interviewees use music to regulate their affective states, whether doing exercise, concentrating at work, venting anger, setting the mood for romantic rendezvous, and the like. The tools by which music works for these purposes are varied, including somatic beat matching, the semiotic bearing of meaning, generic intertextuality, delineating physical space, mnemonics, and more. Secondly, she describes music as a tool for the construction of what she calls "self-identity."[32] In this, she borrows from constructivist understandings of the modern self as a "reflexive project" that stitches together lived experiences into biographical narratives that work to construct the self as coherent and enduring over time. As with the processes of self-regulation, music works in diverse ways in projects of self-narration, but I want to turn to some of the ways in which DeNora's accounts of music's role in both the contextually specific regulation of the self and the broader and longer-term narrative construction of the self might be understood through an affect framework.

In its role as a technology of self-regulation, music's functionality is clearly tied to affect. In DeNora's analysis, this works in two directions: that of "instigator" and that of "container."[33] As instigator, music provides a means for a person desirous of a particular emotional disposition—enthusiasm at the moment of leaving for a party, say, or tenderness for a romantic setting—to create a particular level of affective intensity that lends itself to being felt in the desired way. In container mode, on the other hand, music can operate (as I suggest is the case with Adorno's model) as a means of interpreting and acting on one's affective disposition in the terms of conventional genres of emotion, as when one of DeNora's informants "describes how she uses music to induce and heighten a sad emotional state, in a way that is akin to 'looking at yourself in a mirror being sad.'"[34] In neither case is emotion self-evident. When music acts as an instigator, whereby a particular affective disposition is provoked in order that it may be channeled into the conventions of a particular emotion, this is a reflexive process by which an individual ascertains what the appropriate emotion for a given context is. That is, music does not merely "act upon individuals, like a stimulus. Rather music's 'effects' come from the ways in which individuals orient to it, how they interpret it and how they place it within their personal musical maps, within the semiotic web of music and extra-musical association."[35]

When music works as a container (as in the sad music), this is not a matter of expression of a self-evident emotion, but its reflexive narrativization:

> Music is not simply used to express some internal emotional state. Indeed, that music is part of the reflexive constitution of that state; it is a resource for the identification work of "knowing how one feels"—a building material of "subjectivity." This is to say that a candidate simulacrum of feeling is also a template for fleshing out feeling, a material against which the aspects of "how I feel" may be elaborated and made into an object of knowledge. One may say to one's self, "this music is how I feel" and one may grow tense and relax as the musics codes, when the music does.[36]

This use of music to conventionalize and narrativize affect, to "qualify" it, in Massumi's terms, is also key to the way in which DeNora understands its role in the ongoing process of self-making. Self, she argues, is not an essence but a product of the reflexive, socially embedded work of making meaning out of experience:

> individuals engage in a range of mostly tacit identity work to construct, reinforce, and repair the thread of self-identity. This work is what makes that thread appear continues throughout the varied moments of day-to-day living whenever one formulates accounts of self to self and others. A great deal of identity work is produced as presentation of self to other(s)—which includes a micro-politics—through the enactment of a plethora of mini "documents-dramas'"

over the course of a day.... But the "projection" of biography is by no means the only basis for the construction of self-identity. Equally significant is a form of "introjection," a presentation of self to self, the ability to mobilize and hold on to a coherent vision of "who one knows one is."[37]

In many ways, music's capacity for structuring listeners' "self-narrativization" emerges from the accrual over time of its functioning in the role of "self-maintenance"; as it creates a kind of socially intelligible framework for affect, music works as "a technology for spinning the apparently continuous tale of who one is ..., a device for the generation of future identity and action structures, a mediator of future existence."[38]

The conclusions that arise from this seem to differ greatly from Adorno's:

> Music is an active ingredient in the organization of self, the shifting of mood, energy level, conduct style, mode of attention and engagement with the world. In none of these examples, however, does music simply *act upon* individuals, like a stimulus. Rather, music's "effects" come from the ways in which individuals orient to it, how they interpret it and how they place it within their personal musical maps, within the semiotic web of music and extra-musical associations.[39]

Here, importantly, music itself is not an agent: "The individual experience of culture is a topic that cannot ... be addressed by the idea that music inculcates, instigates or nurtures particular mind-sets."[40] Yet neither does DeNora grant listeners total agency in their processes of musical signification. This is because the range of meanings of which a given musical listening is capable is bounded by social convention and by prior listenings.[41] On the one hand, "music's meanings and effects are constructed and dependent upon how they are appropriated." On the other, "patterns of appropriation—associated with particular styles within particular settings—emerge and accrue over time." Prominent among the socially meaningful patterns of appropriation are those "propounded by mass-distributed culture forms (for example, what music is used to signal intimacy and romance in films)." The power these mass-mediated conventions have over musical meaning is not the result of industrial representations' *determining* interpretation, but of the fact that when mass-mediated cultural texts "appropriate aesthetic materials as ordering devices," they disseminate "resources for action and experience" that people find easy to use:[42]

> Human action is assembled at least in part by a practical appropriation of models and resources for action's configuration. We see this perhaps most clearly in examinations of situated discourse, for example in how actors may draw upon conventional narratives, registers and manners of speaking to generate a voice and point of view locally.... This need not imply the absence of a subject but, rather, that subjects, if they are to realize themselves as speakers, must find the words and so cast about for available and appropriate linguistic techniques. So, too, subjects may find available auditory structures with which to configure themselves.[43]

As we have seen, Adorno's jitterbug is described as being "under a spell of his own making," which also suggests that the affects of mass culture are more than a matter of raw coercion. What else it might be is illuminated by DeNora's insistence that mass-mediated categories of musical meaning—in the form of already conventionalized emotional concepts—provide keys for interpreting the rawer stuff of musical affect in ways that affect processes of subject formation. Thus, DeNora's thought is quite useful for thinking through Adorno's understandings of listeners' affective and interpretive agency, despite the considerable differences in methodology, scope, and emphasis between the two. The complexities of this understanding of agency—the active surrendering, through the use of popular music as a means of "qualifying" affective experience, of possibilities for unconventional ways of understanding it—are particularly salient for examining the subject of music streaming.

From Industry Consolidation to Techno-Optimism to Corporate Retrenchment

The 1930s and 1940s context of the political economy of popular music on which Adorno was writing is very different from that of today's late modernity. Even DeNora's fieldwork at the close of the 1990s is in many ways different from the present moment, particularly given the 2000s crisis and the 2010s' reentrenchment of the music industry, and in the concurrent emergence of social media. Accordingly, some of the ways they describe musical subject formation, the role of affect, and questions of agency are necessarily products of those moments.

The period Adorno was describing, that of the 1930s and '40s, was marked by the definitive urbanization of society and the successful creation of the laboring, commodity-consuming masses, borne out in political models ranging from European fascism to Latin American national-populism to the progressive populism of New Deal–era United States. Key to Adorno's writing was the centrality of then-new media technologies to these transformations and the political and subjective forms that accompanied them. Adorno's account of popular culture's homogenizing effects, ideological consistency, and overwhelming scale are clearly representations of the culture industry of that moment—highly concentrated and tightly integrated both vertically and horizontally.[44] For most of the twentieth century, music labels were not only directly responsible for production, because they funded time in expensive recording studios, but also built marketing decisions into production, for example as record companies decided whether to produce certain artists lavishly for heavy marketing to the largest possible audiences, a tactic popular during Adorno's day but more recently also responsible for the careers of such artists as Michael Jackson.[45] The same corporate infrastructure was responsible for what Adorno calls "plugging"—incessantly repeating hit songs—on radio programs also usually owned by the same conglomerates that controlled booking, touring, composition, and copyright.[46] Music, then, fit within a Fordist business model that governed the production and consumption of material commodities in the twentieth century: mass-scaled production of standardized commodities for the broadest possible swath of society, which Adorno and Horkheimer call an "insatiable uniformity."[47] Indeed, even the variety that the culture industry does provide is illusory:

> Sharp distinctions like those between A and B films, or between short stories published in magazines in different price segments, do not so much reflect real differences as assist in the classification, organization, and identification of consumers. Something is provided for everyone so that no one can escape; differences are hammered home and propagated. The hierarchy of serial qualities purveyed to the public serves only to quantify it more completely. Everyone is supposed to behave spontaneously according to a "level" determined by indices and to select the category of mass product manufactured for their type.... The schematic nature of this procedure is evident from the fact that the mechanically differentiated products are ultimately all the same.[48]

It is in this sense that there "is nothing left for the consumer to classify. Producers have done it for him."[49]

The late 1990s, however, when DeNora carried out her research, were characterized less by mass-scale labor than by the differentiated and multidirectional mini-hustles of neoliberalism. This is a very different context from Adorno's moment, as production was increasingly becoming flexible, offering services and such intangible commodities as finance, management, and the production of intellectual property rather than material goods. In the 1930s, labor time and leisure time were clearly delineated from each other temporally; Adorno's work on the culture industry intended to describe how capitalism infused both sides of the divide. The context DeNora describes, however, is one in which work and leisure time are hopelessly muddled, such that one is always potentially working. The affective fine-tuning necessitated by this oscillation between work and leisure (among other social settings) figures prominently in DeNora's idea of musical self-maintenance. Indeed, she notes that "emotional flexibility ... [is] an increasingly characteristic tendency, in late modernity, to experience emotion vicariously and according to the parameters of feeling that are placed on offer within specific situations."[50]

Along with those changes in the modes of production, the turn of the millennium has been marked by shifts in modes of consumption. The music industry of the late 1990s (in its last hurrah before the digital disruptions of the new millennium) was beginning to take on a narrowcasting model, driven less by the consumption of a few broadly marketed commodities than of a broad diversity of products, each microtargeted to small social sectors that, taken together, made up a huge market. This is not to say that the corporate structure of the music industry is not concentrated—indeed in terms of ownership structures it may have been as monopolistic by the 1990s as it was in Adorno's day, and perhaps more so. The large number of specialist indie labels owned by a small number of media conglomerates exemplifies this state of affairs.[51] But it does offer a variety of taste niches and genre subcultures perhaps unimaginable under the taste standardization of Adorno's day.

This invokes and provokes new forms of subjectivity; indeed, DeNora, in her chapter on music and shopping, describes a generational shift between older shoppers (who came of age during the moment Adorno describes), for whom music in stores is a nuisance, and younger consumers, who readily identify with music in stores and the particular brand identity for which it is curated. For the latter, "identity construction and maintenance has [sic] become a leisure pursuit in its own right, through the various activities of self-care and cultivation such as body shaping, grooming procedures, therapy and the appropriation of 'style,' where a good part of the pleasure associated with these pursuits is linked to the playing out of fantasy life."[52]

If music, as DeNora would have it, was a raw material for the formation of self, both the sheer quantity of music available and the new possibilities for engaging with it creatively were believed by the techno-optimists and copyright anarchists of the decade of the 2000s to provide the components of more complex, active, and creative selves. This argument is taken up in a specifically musical and social media context in the Mexican sociologist Rossana Reguillo's essay on youth cyberculture.[53] Breaking with a long history of Latin American cultural studies focused on the often obsessively monogeneric musical tastes of discrete youth subcultures or "urban tribes," Reguillo finds a liberating new eclecticism in young people's posting of YouTube music videos on Facebook, which for her amounts to a kind of derangement and intermingling of popular-music canons and a capacity for experimentation and identification across the aesthetic boundaries between the kinds of exclusive subcultural identities—metalhead, hippie, punk—that structure the sociality of the youth in Latin American cities.[54] Gone are the days in which listening to, say, punk rock (which of course, involved walking into a store spatially partitioned by genre and publicly purchasing a media object from a cashier) practically required a kind of elaborate self-presentation that marked one off as not a poseur apt to have their subcultural loyalty tested by "real" punks. Reguillo, inspired by Alessandro Baricco's notion of the new "barbarians," uses this insight to offer that the musical hyperabundance that characterizes streaming platforms (specifically, for Reguillo, YouTube) seems to facilitate the making of more complex selves unburdened by the overdetermined identity work of subcultural genre loyalties, in which posting YouTube videos on Facebook provides a means for a more horizontal kind of identity pedagogy, a break from fossilized canons and norms, and a more playful, experimental, and capacious musical life for young people.[55] Or, more broadly (and perhaps exaggerating Reguillo's point), the subjects of musical streaming orient themselves less to the consistency and stasis of identity than to the flexibility and immediacy of experience.

While much has been made of the techno-optimism of the decade of the 2000s, it is important to note that the conditions from which it arose are essentially gone. If that previous decade was the one in which recorded music transcended the material media of its transmission and in doing so troubled the regime of copyright that governed it, the current decade is one in which music has transcended even the discrete quasi-object of the digital audio file to take a new and more dematerialized form—the stream. The object form, whether the physical CD or 8-track or 45, or the digital MP3 or WAV file, was owned, and therefore bought, sold, traded, given, stockpiled, or downloaded. This transcendence of a propertylike relationship with an objectlike unit of music is particularly important given its structural importance in Adorno's argument: "[Listeners] invest the song with an object-like form that makes it possible for them to feel as if they own it and to derive validation of their own good taste. This is the tendency to transfer the gratification of ownership to the object itself and to attribute to it, in terms of like, preference, or objective quality, the enjoyment of ownership which one has attained."[56] Adorno is not necessarily talking about ownership of material musical artifacts; the songs he discusses might just as easily be heard on the radio. The important part is their power to narrativize the self through a relationship of ownership as much as through real-time experience. Certainly, however, the liberation of specific songs from discrete technological artifacts, and the concomitant proliferation of musical pieces to a seemingly infinite quantity could not but promote a move away from ownership as the primary relationship. This is a sweeping change; many people who came to musical maturity before the rise of streaming find the lack of ownership of specific tracks almost ontologically disconcerting.

Although she could not have known it at the time, DeNora's 2000 publication date marked a crucial moment in the history of the music industry, punctuated by the 1999 release of Napster and the rise of P2P file sharing. After 2000, the recorded and commoditized widgets of the commercial music industry gave way to the liberated postcommodity of the freely circulating MP3, the convergence of practices of consumption and production in mashup and remix culture, and the decline of the record labels' monopoly on music production and distribution. During the decade of the 2000s, huge swathes of the body of recorded sound that had previously been effectively unavailable became accessible, as did the technological means to remix those sounds and create new ones, potentially democratizing musicianship and making consumption less passive.

The rise of streaming, beginning with Internet radio and increasingly customizable on platforms such as Pandora and Spotify, involve a whole new form of engagement, in which music is not a set of tracks to be owned, but an experience in which one immerses oneself. Crucially, however, this disposition has not decommodified music, but has in fact intensified corporate control over music and copyright regimes. What is at stake in music streaming is an entirely different central economic figure—not property to be owned, but experience to be accessed.[57] And, crucially, unlike the decade of the 2010s, in which the existence of the formal music industry was obviated by the file-sharing musical exchange that bypassed it, streaming platforms have arisen as a reentrenchment of the commercial music industry's ability to act, through technological access and intellectual property ownership, as a gatekeeper for listeners' access to music, for the price of subscription, listener data, or targeted advertisements.

The streaming moment, then, demands a different understanding of music listening: neither the material-bound listening of the music industry of the previous century nor the infinite and cost-free ownership and creative repurposing of musical objects imagined by the techno-optimists of the decade of the 2000s. Instead, streaming platforms such as Spotify have reentrenched proprietary control over music as listeners have traded ownership of discrete files for license to stream the seemingly limitless "celestial jukebox." Daniel Ek, Spotify's founder, has described the platform as emerging from the need to match post-Napster consumer expectations for musical access to the enforcement of the copyright regimes underwriting music creation (although more in favor of traditional rightsholders such as publishing companies than of creative artists, who are asked to bear the pinch until the subscription-advertising model becomes sustainable).[58] Streaming platforms — even the relatively disorderly YouTube — are closely policed for copyright violations, and in general, streaming platforms' bypassing of specific downloadable files mitigates against the mashup, remix, and repurposing of media that was understood during the 2000s as revolutionizing and democratizing music consumption.

The role of the music industry in the age of streaming is different from its role at its twentieth-century heights. The wide accessibility of low-cost production for artists beginning around the 1990s has made the record industry less necessary as a means of production than as a way to market musical products. Marketing music, too, became much more complicated when P2P networks essentially made all music ever recorded both available and free, but provided no guidance on how to navigate a catalog that was practically limitless but that nonetheless required a significant time investment, both for downloading itself and for deciding what to download in the first place. The availability on P2P networks or iTunes of huge music catalogs led to an aporia-inducing amount of choice with no real means to work through it. Indeed, the British researcher Will Page found that rather than exulting in the esoteric, most file downloads on P2P networks in the mid-2000s hewed quite closely to the Billboard Top 40.[59] Increasingly, the music industry began to recognize its value-added contribution to be the kind of guidance that would help consumers find their way through the catalog. Music streaming, in which copyright holders rely on platforms with deep sedimented knowledge about music listeners both as blocks and as individuals to siphon music directly to them — gaining more demographic and consumption information in the process—arose as the means for the music industry to consolidate as listener guides through the musical wilderness.

Music-streaming services followed early adopters, such as Amazon and Netflix, of algorithms that nudged users toward what they might like. These recommendation algorithms use a number of distinct criteria, set to activate hierarchically and at different moments (the specific ordering of the different filters is what makes these systems algorithms). Some algorithms focus on characteristics of the music to gauge musical similarity and difference to recommend similar tracks to those a listener has already enjoyed. They identify, tag, and code sonic characteristics such as tempo or timbre, sometimes supplemented by nonsonic metadata and text or discourse produced in reviews or scraped from social media on other platforms. Still others focus on the specific characteristics of the listener, tying her musical selections to those of other users judged to have similar listening habits, even as her own musical choices are used to flesh out ever more detailed accounts of the kinds of listeners she purportedly resembles. This also involves triangulation of demographic and ad-based information in order to draw particular kinds of psychographic portraits combining musical taste with information useful to advertisers.[60] Many services simply provide curated playlists, which, although technically not algorithms, provide useful information for a given listener's overall taste profile. Some platforms, such as Spotify, combine these forms, providing curated playlists and user-controlled playlists, as well as algorithmically generated playlists and streaming radio, between which the user can toggle. Most platforms allow for some degree of variability between molecular and molar choice—that is, skipping an individual song or passing to an entirely new playlist. Almost all develop profiles, with varying degrees of detail, of listeners' musical choices that enable increasingly sophisticated recommendations.

I'm less concerned with the inner workings of the streaming platforms, however, than with their effects in producing subjects, to which I now turn.

Streaming the Self

The "new emotional flexibility and the aesthetic reflexivity to which it is linked" beg comparison with the questions of power and agency put forward by Adorno and Horkheimer.[61] Is the pursuit of identity through consumerism in fact merely borrowing the prefabricated identities into which the culture industry interpellates the masses, as Horkheimer and Adorno would have it; or is identity more open, and do people have more agency in taking on their identity concepts than in the heyday of Adorno's hyperconcentrated culture industry? DeNora writes, "Retailers no longer cater to pre-existing 'lifestyle' groups but actually instigate the image of such groups by fabricating and placing on offer images of agency that are achievable in and through participation in retail scenes, in and through the purchase of significant items."[62] Her argument that entire "lifestyle groups" are not prefabricated goes against Adorno and Horkheimer's argument about A and B films, magazine stories, and other cultural products being marketed to subgroups constituting the culture industry.[63] Clearly, the more standardizing and normative interpellations of the culture industry described by Adorno do not seem to hold, given the more open, fluid, and creative processes by which the culture industry puts forward not full-blown "identities" but more contingent "stances," which are not incorporated as a totalizing "self" but rather incorporated into "repertoires" of self. But the distinction is a fine one:

> The retail outlet produces potential sources of identification for the consumer, who may visit such a location as a kind of identity repository, as a storehouse of possible ways of being and possible stances. By making a purchase, the consumer is exporting a way of being from the shop and importing it into her or his personal repertory of modes of being, where it becomes a resource for the production of self-identity.[64]

That is, her assertion that consumption-activated "images of agency" and "ways of being" are in fact put forward by capitalism and incorporated into the repertoire of the self does not seem radically different from Adorno's evocation of popular culture as a means of putting narrativizing affective experience into conventional forms.

Although DeNora is reticent to embrace top-down accounts of power, the comparison seems particularly apt when she gestures toward the work of scholars such as Baudrillard to describe "the proliferation of a particular kind of emotionality proffered by and in the interests of administration," going on to cite Stepjan Mestrovic's *Postemotional Society*:[65] "What appears to be postmodern disorder or the circulation of random fictions, as depicted by Jean Baudrillard, turns out to have a hidden order of its own, and to be highly automated, rehearsed, and planned."[66] The question, then, is how even these more flexible "ways of being" can be tied to "the interests of administration" and the specific kind of "hidden order" they might have, and how—

or if—this is substantially different from the top-down, interpellating force of Adorno's culture industry.

After all, both YouTube and Facebook, the platforms discussed by Reguillo, surveil their users to a historically unprecedented degree, assembling ever more granular profiles of who they are, what they do, and what they want (and which advertisers might want to sell them those things). These platforms argue that this surveillance exists in order to "tailor user experience," giving users what they want. This is in some ways reminiscent of what Adorno describes: "The promoters of commercialized entertainment exonerate themselves by referring to the fact that they are giving the masses what they want."[67] But for Adorno, "what they want" is a result of the culture industry's teaching them to desire what is for sale: "The less the mass discriminates, the greater the possibility of selling cultural commodities indiscriminately.... The people clamor for what they are going to get anyhow."[68] Thus, Adorno's critique is of the masses' alienation from their own true desires. Today's social media platforms extrapolate what those desires are, often before the individual even knows, hailing vendors to help the consumer satisfy them.

Another way to get at the question is to return to Adorno's assertions about the muddling of distinctions between the realms of labor and leisure by the forms of subjectivity that capitalism promotes. If, as DeNora recognizes, self-making has become a leisure pursuit, the more recent rise of social media has made self-making an imperative, even a peculiar kind of intellectual and emotional labor: "identity labor" or "personal branding."[69] As "a form of self-presentation singularly focused on attracting attention and acquiring cultural and monetary value,"[70] identity labor is, on the one hand, a function of the flexibilization of the labor market, valuing "entrepreneurs of the self" within the "enterprise culture" of the labor market values.[71] Thus "the soul of the worker must be culturally legible, arguably in the form of an resonant image or brand,"[72] making "the acquisition of an image ... a singularly important element in the presentation of self in labour markets."[73] But what is presented "is to be always pursuing some sort of activity, never to be without a project, without ideas, to be always looking forward to, and preparing for, something."[74] Curiously, this is as valuable in posturing for the labor market as it is in the exteriorizing self-representation of how interesting one's leisure life is on social media—what Christine Rosen calls "egocasting."[75] Thus, self-care is taken to be the maximization of marketable skills, and our emotional lives are structured by the exteriorizing display of the intimate and/or banal details of our felt interiority on social media, creating what Hearn describes as "the erosion of any meaningful distinction between notions of the self and capitalist processes of production and consumption," a concern already present in Adorno's closed system of capitalist labor and leisure.[76] Jason Read describes this as a relationship between the subjective and social realms: "Capital's direct involvement in the production of subjectivity ... scrambles the division between production, as the production of things, and reproduction, as the reproduction of the relations of production."[77]

This same principle of involution tracks alongside a broader shift in the structures of power, as neoliberal governance has catalyzed a shift from Foucauldian disciplinary societies to what Deleuze called societies of control,[78] or from normative, regulative, rigid, top-down forms of power to the factive, self-organizing, flexible, and immanent forms Scott Lash calls "post-hegemonic."[79] Here, the model of submission to power has been replaced by the taking up of limited options for freedom and self-realization in ways that are both more lightly felt and more powerfully straitjacketing than the old disciplinary regimes (for example, commodity consumption). Again, emotion is key, especially as it resonates within categories of culture. If culture in the disciplinary society was held out by Matthew Arnold and Schopenhauer as a refuge from the philistinism of the workaday world by the rigorous cultivation of feelings in line with the masterworks of the great geniuses, today culture meets us more than halfway, shaping our feelings for us, offering us the emoticons we use to represent our emotional state almost before we even have a chance to experience the feelings they purportedly represent.

Certainly, some streaming platforms (such as Spotify) permit reflexive self-building and active, attentive, or what are referred to as "lean-in" forms of listening through such practices as the designing of publicly available playlists or the ability to choose or skip songs in real time. Other popular services, such as Pandora, are more constrained. YouTube has begun to choose the next video to be shown for the user based on similarities with material already viewed, allowing for a more passive listening mode, and even Spotify also includes "lean-out" listening modalities structured experientially by algorithms that choose music for listeners based on what it knows about their taste and mood. It seems logical enough that the lean-in modality is imagined as freedom, in that it grants the user the quintessential capitalist freedom of choice of the musical products she will consume. But increasingly, streaming platforms and other tech companies are describing lean-out modalities as a freedom *from* choice, as freeing listeners from the exhausting intrusion of the imperative for attentive musical selection into their fields of awareness.

This is not to say that an algorithmically aided, lean-out listening modality cannot be understood as imposing homogenizing mass taste on the individual, as in Adorno's day. These algorithms are in fact deeply individualized, organized, in the case of Spotify, by the user's own taste (gleaned from her playlists and a detailed register of her song skipping), a real-time log of her activities (based on her geolocation, the movement of her cell phone's accelerometer, and her selection of activities-based playlists for work, study, or exercise, or mood-based playlists explicitly designed, as were the soundtracks of DeNora's informants, to accompany celebration, sex, socializing, or heartbreak) and comparison with other users who share her musical taste and affinities. Thus, attending to algorithmic listening does not mean rehearsing wellworn and values-laden demarcations between the technological and the human, such as the claim that algorithms are an artificial distortion of human authenticity. The algorithms are in some ways an augmentation of individual authenticity, designed precisely to intensify users' natural sense of themselves, not from outside, as through Adorno's authoritarian music industry, or through their intentional action, as in DeNora's soundtracking listeners, but almost as an emanation of the self. One Twitter user captured both the uncanniness and the emotional accuracy of Spotify's algorithmically personalized weekly playlist: "It's scary how well @Spotify Discover Weekly playlists know me. Like former-lover-who-lived-through-a-near-death experience-with-me well."[80] (Spotify responded by sending the user a consent form to grant use of the tweet in an ad campaign that also used playlist names and other listener information). However, the uncanniness of being understood by an algorithm is generally less prominent in listeners' experience than its frictionless incorporation into their lives. A brief delay in its weekly update in 2015 was bemoaned by one Twitter user: "It's 10:41am on Monday and my @Spotify Discover Weekly playlist hasn't updated yet and I'm doing my best not to have an existential crisis."[81]

Rather than a dialectic relationship between self and other or structure and agency, the algorithmic generation of musical experience simply confirms the self to the self, within which the algorithm itself is only a technique. There is not even an explicit hailing, but simply a selection of generally agreeable musical experiences. Fanon's latter-day Afro-Caribbean is racialized not (only) by a French child's unwelcome hailing ("Look, a Negro!") but by the entirely welcome appearance of *zouk* music in her Spotify Discover Weekly playlist.

Both the more structure-oriented notion of interpellation as being hailed by an institution and readings that emphasize possibilities for resistance assume at least some separation between the interpellated subject and the hailing institution. This structure-agency dialectic is called into crisis by corporate technologies of personalization under neoliberal capitalism. A brief but prescient essay by Gilles Deleuze describes this break.[82] For Deleuze, the binaries of the individual and the anonymous masses or anonymizing institutions that were of such deep preoccupation of the political and economic philosophy of the twentieth century result from the processes of "enclosure" and concentration of individuals and the channeling of their force and their labor into such institutions as the prison, hospital, school, factory, and family, as described by Foucault. These enclosures function as "molds, distinct castings" that bend the individual in keeping with the needs of the institution. Deleuze opposes to this the rise of "controls" that do not mold, shape, or restrict but work as "a modulation, like a self-deforming cast that will continuously change from one moment to the other, or like a sieve whose mesh will transmute form point to point."[83] That is, the mechanisms of late capitalism do not coerce individuals into specific spatial and temporal configurations, stifling their individualism, but rather work inside them, utilizing their individualistic movements, cannibalizing the energy they are already producing through those movements as a hydroelectric plant derives energy from the downhill flow of water or as a geothermal plant conducts heat from inside the earth. The locus of power is immanent rather than hierarchical, in Lash's terms.[84] One is interpellated, in other words, in oneself, as oneself, even by oneself, albeit always in terms intelligible within the logic of capital.

Jeremy Rifkin has suggested that the technologically enabled commodification of the human lifeworld is a historic juncture, as momentous as "the enclosure and privatization of land and labor into property relations" at the dawn of modernity.[85] If music indeed anticipates historical change, as Attali famously affirmed, it would seem to be a useful place to inquire into the new kinds of selves emerging from hypercapitalism, and for its place in mediating between affect and emotion.

These examples suggest an interpretation that is agnostic to narratives of the inviolability of the categories of the human and the nonhuman. But sanguine techno-optimism also seems misplaced because the degree to which the specific user data upon which the algorithm is crafted—not only every song in a user's playlist, but also a real-time log of every song skip, location ping, and accelerometer jostle, as well as media, photos, and contacts stored on the user's mobile device and information from third-party "service providers and partners"—itself becomes a rent-producing commodity.[86] As with commercial radio, the business model is less about selling music to listeners than about selling listeners to advertisers—selling them in real time (such that advertisers can make their pitches, for example, as the listener is exercising) and with far more finely grained profiles than broadcast radio is able to aggregate by means of genre-associated demographic data on age and income. As with Amazon and Facebook (the latter a Spotify partner), the detailed data produced by the totality of streaming platform users as they consume music in their daily lives can be used to predict their preferences and desires: people who listen to Pink Floyd are more likely to vote conservative, we learn,[87] and people who don't like to listen to unfamiliar songs are more likely to buy energy drinks.[88] This data, in turn, is used to create more data about user preference in order to market ads and experiences to users whose assimilation of those experiences (for example, adding a song from an algorithmically produced Spotify playlist to a user-created playlist, or listening to Songza's "Hillbilly Workout" playlist or Pandora's "Bachata" station) confirms the user's sense of him- or herself and contributes to the fine-tuning of data profiles that will offer future ads and experiences, creating a feedback loop of confirmation bias. In other words, not only do streaming algorithms mediate between musical experience and the narrativization of the listening self, they also commodify the data points and relevant statistical correlations of that narrative.

Clearly, digital platforms are not just the virtualization of an already constituted public sphere. They bring their own affordances, which, in the case of music discovery tools, are heavily mediated by the particular dispositions of discovery. Some platforms curate music discovery by gently guiding users across similar tracks toward various kinds of difference. Similarity and difference, in this case, are determined through the use of particular sonic characteristics tagged by human listeners. Some platforms supplement this information by mining nonsonic information and even a certain kind of discursive force field around particular tracks from information on other parts of the Internet to determine relationships among artists, songs, and genres. The pretense here is nothing less than a map of musical relationship among all recorded sound featured on Spotify, which among other things can be used to calibrate listener discovery. The website Every Noise at Once, for example, seeks to quantify every musical genre (as of August 2018, more than 1900, including "danish jazz," "deep chiptune," "sound effects," and "african percussion" [all *sic*]), arranging them along two axes—vertically from "organic" to "mechanical and electric" and horizontally from "denser and more atmospheric" to "spikier and bouncier."[89]

The contingent delineations of genre ("monastic" vs. "liturgical"), the questionable classification of songs within them (the "vallenato" playlist includes more cumbia and salsa than vallenato), and the arbitrary pseudo-quantification by which such qualities as organicism are coded (why is "classical guitar" more "mechanical" than "classical tuba"?) are less important to the endeavor than the assumption that a spacious and comprehensive representation and organization of all recorded sound is possible or meaningful—what Amanda Modell, channeling Donna Haraway, calls a "god trick."[90]

The Every Noise project is an offshoot of Echo Nest, the music quantification program purchased by Spotify and used in some of their algorithms (such as "Similar To" playlists). But, as is the case in other recently publicized algorithm snafus, like the inability to tag the faces of nonwhites in photos or the advertising of lower-paying jobs to women, all-too-human biases creep through. The apportioning of defining categories such as "danceability" or "spiky rhythm," as well as genre delineations, is done by particular humans, but so too are the specific algorithmic filters through which these categories are applied. Given the demographics of Silicon Valley, these techniques tend to work well on English-language music consumed by young, middle-class white men, but less well as we venture further afield from this unmarked musical center. More perniciously, while platforms such as Echo Nest are open and can be used for other projects (like Every Noise), the specific parameters gathered under the umbrella of a category such as "atmospheric" are not available for tinkering, which essentially universalizes one set of musical criteria.

All of this said, however, musical discovery tends to assume that music is to be amassed, or, in Attali's terms, stockpiled, as a means of bolstering a sense of self or as evidence for claims about the self. However, as I have suggested with recourse to Reguillo's essay, the kind of subject at stake in late capitalism is less a clearly defined and temporally enduring "self" than contingent, changeable, and more ad hoc structures of experience. This is not to say that the two are mutually exclusive—certainly some categories of experience are regulated by or compared with perduring senses of the self—but rather that the contingencies of the moment seem to bear more heavily on musical choice than does a more restrictive sense of musical taste or identity. Unlike members of the subcultural "urban tribes" of the twentieth century, for whom a musical affinity for, say, metal or jazz was nothing less than a life choice, the millennial surfers of musical streams choose metal to go to the gym and jazz to host a dinner party.

Rather than stockpiling music as a means of sedimenting identity, then, people are rather more often engaged in soundtracking their real-time experiences. This is essentially a continuation of the behavior DeNora describes, in which her informants use music as a kind of emotional or cognitive prosthesis to motivate themselves or create the proper headspace or atmosphere for this or that activity. These activities, again, are tied to the no-collar workplace, as well as to the practice of rebroadcasting activities outward on social media, in a manner that suggests that both experience and self-recognition of the content of that experience are central. One is called upon, in choosing and then experiencing activity-linked playlists for "Study" or "Playing in the Autumn Leaves," or the emotive/expressive "Sad-Breakup Songs," to recognize one's own emotions in the ways in which the playlists' music is isomorphic with a reasonable-seeming attribution for the underlying affect.[91] Interestingly, some playlists on Songza include temporally fleeting activities or moods with seemingly more durable social identities in playlists, like "Hillbilly Workout," the country-music gym playlist, and "Girl Hold My Earrings," an playlist of all-Black women rappers and singers under "Moods: Angry" heading, seemingly designed to allow the listener to temporarily inhabit the persona of the Angry Black Woman. Thus, the streaming platform encourages not only an attribution of emotion from affect, but also some aspects, however temporary, of identity.

This is not necessarily the kind of self-conscious cultivation of a more complex self in the sense celebrated by Reguillo. Indeed, streaming listening is often structured experientially by algorithms engaged precisely to *avoid* the intrusion of attentive musical choice into listeners' fields of attention. The algorithm, then, emerges as a technology that intervenes radically in the relation between raw affect and biographizing emotion. So if discovery aids the stockpiling of music to formulate a notion of the self, the mood-based and activity-based playlists and pay option on services such as Spotify and Songza are built around a kind of management and recognition of emotional experience, a kind of authorization. The mood- or activity-based playlists or filters make all the more efficient the kind of emotional prostheses DeNora describes, and the mood playlists act to emotionally entrain the self in a way that Schachter and Singer would likely recognize.

Clearly, desire and feeling have long been essential to capitalism, which has increasingly colonized the inner reaches of our lifeworlds through the ways in which it both provokes affective perturbations and offers tools to narrativize them—processes in which music is particularly salient. The shift from the prepotency granted by musical ownership to the immersive experience of the bespoke musical stream reflects a break in the kinds of interpellation or self-building that take place under late capitalism. That these processes are historically contingent is clear; the question, though, is one of power and agency. What do we make of the willing delegation of musical agency to the algorithm? Should we describe it apocalyptically as the algorithmic subject's self-subjugation or focus on more liberating prospects of transcending fixed notions of the subject altogether?

But perhaps the question is misguided, in that it assumes a fairly stable notion of the human subject, which may or may not have agency. If taste and feelings, as basic characteristics of human personality, should be farmed out to an algorithm, the question is principally one not of agency, but of the nature of the human subject itself, after which agency is a second-order question. At the same time, this is not a matter of the inhumanity of the machine, in which the algorithm steps in as a threat to an inviolable humanity. If listening, as Jean-Luc Nancy would have it, is always relational, a space of interiorizing the exterior, of mutual resonance between subjects,[92] it is not entirely clear what the ramifications are of resonating alongside not another subject, but alongside an algorithm that is designed precisely to interpellate oneself to oneself as oneself, to narrativize one's affective experience as both emotion and more broadly, identity, especially when the ultimate purpose behind the mechanism for subjectivizing the user is reducing her to a data profile.

Again, affect and its narrative qualification are key here, and it is worth comparing streaming algorithms with the processes identified by Adorno and DeNora. We will recall that for Adorno, popular music worked both to exacerbate the affective perturbations caused by the overstimulation of modern life and to provide a framework for harnessing that affective experience to conventionalized narratives of emotions and the supposedly independent and even rebellious self. The problem, for Adorno, is not so much that the qualification of affect is conventionalized — after all, human interaction and even language are based on the adoption of social conventions — but that the conventionalized narratives of mass musical experience cloak political quiescence and conformity under a specious individualism that allows musical experience to supplant political agency: "What should be close at hand, the 'consciousness of suffering,' becomes unbelievably alien. The most alien thing of all, however, the process that hammers the machinery into men's consciousness and has ceased to contain that which is human, invades them body and soul and appears to be the nearest and dearest thing of all."[93]

For her part, DeNora is also not worried that the narrativization of affect (either in the experiential interpretation of affective experience or in the broader processes of identity construction) utilizes socially conventionalized forms. She does distinguish, however, between two different processes whereby this might take place:

> It is easy to see music's role in relation to the processes of [social] administration ... indeed, music's role in relation to the "dialectic of enlightenment" was the subject of Adorno's life work. As an ephemeral and subtle medium, one that can be changed in an instant, music's role is key here in helping to instantiate scenarios of desire, styles of (momentary) agency, and in fostering a new and "postmodern" form of communitas—a co-subjectivity where two or more individuals may come to exhibit similar modes of feeling and acting, constituted in relation to extra-personal parameters, such as those provided by musical materials. Such co-subjectivity differs in important ways from the more traditional (and modern) notion of "inter-subjectivity," which presumes interpersonal dialogue and the collaborative production of meaning and cognition. Inter-subjectivity—even if understood in the ethnomethodological sense ... involves a collaborative version of reflexivity. By contrast, co-subjectivity is the result of isolated individually reflexive alignments to an environment and its materials.[94]

That is to say, it is one thing when processes of subject formation arise from collaborative, inter-subjective interaction between humans. It is something quite different, and something more closely tied to darker processes of social administration, when subject formation emerges from the co-subjective interaction of isolated interactions with a media environment. Algorithmic experiences of streaming music provide scripts for the narrativization of affect that are external to intra-subjective collaboration. In this, and in their use of unknowable, black-boxed criteria they are far closer to co-subjective. But the fact that they operate precisely at the place where the subject constitutes itself, through the narrativization of affective experience, they might even be closer to a solipsistic and *intra*-subjective process. If there is any dialogue at all, it is between the inchoate subject of affective experience and the identity and emotional scripts that are both constituted externally and provide an even more enhanced, augmented version of the self, more authentic than the self could come up with on its own.

Conclusions

Two sets of final questions might be drawn from all of this, the first methodological and the second more broadly philosophical. In terms of methodology, certainly, as DeNora recognizes, exclusive focus on either musical texts, generic intertextuality, or the meaning-making processes of mass mediation do not touch the place where meaning making actually happens, which is among listeners. But DeNora's own research, while focused on listeners, was not strictly ethnographic. Most of her work was based on interviews, which allows access to people's accounts of their own experiences but is always mediated by their own interpretive frames—a problem when what is being analyzed is precisely music as one of those interpretive frames. Ethnographers have engaged in participant observation as providing a broader sense of local experience, particularly in its nonlinguistic registers. This is complicated in often solitary technological practices such as music streaming, but digital ethnography has become increasingly sophisticated in its methods since around the 2010s. Among those methods is close attention to the specific poetics and the specific sets of affordances offered by streaming platforms themselves. In her theoretical overview, DeNora mentions the ways in which specific material practices of listening have constraints and affordances that narrow or widen the possibilities for particular sets of significations but never takes up the precise question.[95] Where it is accessible, a close reading of code could help us understand the criteria and filters utilized in particular algorithms, as well as the way they are ordered hierarchically to preclude or maximize certain kinds of experiences. Unfortunately, most of the code for these algorithms is usable but "blackboxed" at best, entirely inaccessible at worst. Taina Bucher offers methodologies for examining how people engage with the "known unknown" of inaccessible algorithms as they try to second-guess these shapers of their online experience.[96] A similar tracking of people's real-world negotiations of music algorithms in an ethnographic vein seems appropriate for this study.

More broadly, the notion of the algorithm as steward of musical taste and tool for the negotiation of affect invites philosophical debates not only of agency, but of the category of the human. Discussions of technologically augmented humans in late capitalism are fairly common, as in Donna Haraway's well-known account of cyborgs.[97] As Frédéric Vandenberghe points out, human body parts, formerly viewed as inviolable, are increasingly understood as fungible and apt for replacement when they wear out.[98] But cyborg augmentation is usually understood as operating on the flesh, which is still under the command of the intellect and as such does not violate any understanding of the human in which the Cartesian binary is assumed. But what is at stake in the algorithmic management of emotion and affect is the augmentation not of a body under control of a human mind but of precisely that mind, and of precisely the aspect of the mind that is the most human: feeling.

Louis Chude-Sokei, relying on the work of Silvia Wynter, links questions about the nature of the humanity of robots and artificial intelligence with the foundational delineation of humanity at the dawn of Atlantic modernity to exclude nonwhites.[99] In this light he relates Donna Haraway's cyborg, as an emblem of liberating hybridity and the exceeding of categories, to Caribbean notions of creolization. If racial miscegenation, imagined by white supremacists and eugenicists as an enervating backsliding, can instead be thought through as a revitalizing and civilizationally foundational creolization, than perhaps, he suggests, the increasingly intimate entanglements of the human and the robotic might be thought of in the same light. This is, however, complicated by the fact that, whereas the restriction of nonwhites to beyond the pale of humanity for the purposes of race-based slavery was in service to the profit motive, and structurally creolization could be understood as counteracting that dehumanizing exclusion, the technological development that has driven the merging of human and artificial bodies and intelligences is itself a function of the corporate pursuit of lucre rather than the reenchantment of human personhood, and is driven by kinds of surveillance and capture that have rather different political ramifications.

It is curious that the category of the human in terms of its adjacency to nonhuman technologies has become so blurred at precisely the same moment as the category of the human has been blurred in the political sphere of the Trump-era United States, which expels asylum-seeking refugees, trans people, Black and Latino people interacting with police, and colonial subjects in Puerto Rico from the category of the human and as deserving subjects of human rights. That is, humanity is being called into question on two fronts: on the one hand, notions of the human are supplemented by algorithmic management of musical affect; on the other, humanity is undermined by the denial of the rights that are subsumed within the category of the human in liberal democracies. Returning to Wynter, it is worth noting that these are humans whose place in the economic order vacillates between the cheap labor inherited from slavery and the precursor to robotic automation—or as the "wasted lives" understood as excess in relation to formal and corporate capitalism.[100] Clearly, the posthumanist perspective that scholars have applied to understanding our society does not preclude an examination of affect; rather, it elicits the question of how affect, and its algorithmically enabled management, can be understood in a posthumanist setting.[101]

It should be apparent by now that the qualification and narration of raw affective or perceptual experience is both fundamental to the construction of self and socially and historically specific. It follows, then, that we can identify the specific technologies by which affective experience is bent into narratives under late capitalism in its current manifestation. Music streaming platforms operate at the semiattentive zone of experience at which music listeners conceptualize undifferentiated affect as socially meaningful emotion. Music streaming's operations — the withdrawal of discrete music commodities such as the album or the song to the more immersive experience of the playlist; the farming out of taste, that all-important component of the capitalist subject, to music selection algorithms; the hyperpersonalization of musical experiences that are both intimately felt and artificially produced — suggest ruptures in the very notion of personhood from the ways that music can be understood as interpellating subjects in earlier capitalist forms.

Notes

This project arose from supervising the undergraduate senior thesis and honors project of Walker Kennedy at Bowdoin College. Walker's "under-the-hood" analysis at the level of coding was helpful in sparking my questioning of the broader set of questions addressed in this essay, which I presented at a symposium, "Political Economy of Sound," at the American Comparative Literature Association meeting at Harvard University in March 2016. The other participants in that forum were especially helpful to my work on this project, especially Eric Drott, Michael Gallope, Sumanth Gopinath, Martin Scherzinger, Jim Sykes, Ben Tausig, and Naomi Waltham-Smith. I'm also very grateful to the editors of this volume for their patience and support.

1. Theodor Adorno, "On Jazz," trans. Jamie Owen Daniel, *Discourse: Journal for Theoretical Studies in Media and Culture* 12, no. 1 (1990): 45–69, https://digitalcommons.wayne.edu/discourse/vol12/iss1/4; Adorno, with George Simpson, "On Popular Music: III. Theory about the Listener," *Journal on Media Culture* 2 (January 2000), http://www.icce.rug.nl/~soundscapes/DATABASES/SWA/On_popular_music_3.shtml; and Max Horkheimer and Theodor W. Adorno, *Dialectic of Enlightenment* (London: Allen Lane, 1973).

2. Tia DeNora, *Music in Everyday Life* (Cambridge and New York: Cambridge University Press, 2008).

3. Brian Massumi, "The Autonomy of Affect," in "Politics of Systems and Environments, Part II," *Cultural Critique* 31 (Autumn 1995): 83–109, https://doi.org/10.2307/1354446.

4. Max Horkheimer and Theodor W. Adorno, *Dialectic of Enlightenment: Philosophical Fragments*, ed. Gunzelin Schmid Noerr, trans. Edmund Jephcott (Stanford, CA: University of Stanford Press, 2002). On the music industry of the time, see Scott DeVeaux, *The Birth of Bebop: A Social and Musical History* (Berkeley and Los Angeles: University of Califor-

nia Press, 1999); Reebee Garofalo, "From Music Publishing to MP3: Music Industry in the Twentieth Century," *American Music* 17, no. 3 (1999): 318–54; and Richard A. Peterson, "Why 1955? Explaining the Advent of Rock Music," *Popular Music* 9, no. 1 (1990): 97–116.

5. Massumi, "The Autonomy of Affect," 83–109.

6. Brian Massumi, "Introduction," in Gilles Deleuze and Félix Guattari, *A Thousand Plateaus: Capitalism and Schizophrenia*, trans. Brian Massumi (Minneapolis: University of Minnesota Press, 1987), xvi; and Massumi, "The Autonomy of Affect," 83–109.

7. Massumi, "The Autonomy of Affect," 85.

8. Ibid., 84–85.

9. Stanley Schachter and Jerome Singer, "Cognitive, Social, and Physiological Determinants of Emotional State," *Psychological Review* 69, no. 5 (1962): 379–99.

10. Paul Stoller, *The Taste of Ethnographic Things: The Senses in Anthropology* (Philadelphia: University of Pennsylvania Press, 1989), 115.

11. Nadia Berenstein, "Flavor Added: The Sciences of Flavor and the Industrialization of Taste in America" (Ph.D. diss., University of Pennsylvania, 2018).

12. Horkheimer and Adorno, *Dialectic of Enlightenment* (1973), 123.

13. Frantz Fanon, *Black Skin, White Masks* (London: Pluto Press, 2008), 82.

14. Judith Butler, *Bodies That Matter: On the Discursive Limits of "Sex"* (New York: Routledge, 1993), 241.

15. Adorno, "On Jazz," 64. See also J. Bradford Robinson, "The Jazz Essays of Theodor Adorno: Some Thoughts on Jazz Reception in Weimar Germany," *Popular Music* 13, no. 1 (1994): 1–25.

16. Adorno, "On Popular Music," para. 40. Note that all citations for this work are given with paragraph numbers.

17. Ibid., para. 24.

18. See Susan Buck-Morss, "Aesthetics and Anaesthetics: Walter Benjamin's Artwork Essay Reconsidered," *October* 62 (Autumn 1992): 3–41.

19. Adorno, "On Popular Music," para. 21.

20. Ibid., para. 24.

21. These might also correlate with the romantic/lyrical "sweet" and danceable "hot" variants of popular jazz at the time.

22. Adorno, "On Popular Music," para. 34.

23. Ibid., paras. 33–34.

24. Ibid., para. 33.

25. Or perhaps his translator's.

26. Adorno, "On Popular Music," para. 46.

27. Ibid., para. 50.

28. Ibid., para. 30.

29. Ibid., para. 50.

30. Ibid., para. 47.

31. Ibid., para. 11.

32. The curiously redundant term is borrowed from Anthony Giddens, *Modernity and Self-Identity: Self and Society in the Late Modern Age* (Cambridge: Polity Press, 1991).

33. DeNora, *Music in Everyday Life*, 58.

34. Ibid., 58.

35. Ibid., 61.

36. Ibid., 58.

37. Ibid., 62–63.

38. Ibid., 63.
39. Ibid., 61.
40. Ibid., 126.
41. She also concedes that "the use of music as a device of scene construction may elide rational consciousness. Without being aware of how they are responding to and interpreting music, actors may latch on to and fall in with musical structures." Ibid., 123.
42. Ibid., 125–26; italics in original.
43. Ibid., 123.
44. DeVeaux, *The Birth of Bebop*; Garofalo, "From Music Publishing to MP3"; and Peterson, "Why 1955?"
45. Garofalo, "From Music Publishing to MP3."
46. Peterson, "Why 1955?"
47. Horkheimer and Adorno, *Dialectic of Enlightenment: Philosophical Fragments*, 97.
48. Ibid.
49. This last quote is from a 1973 version of the same work as the one cited above. The 1973 translation of the quoted passage is more straightforward than the 2002 Stanford version. Horkheimer and Adorno, *Dialectic of Enlightenment* (1973), 123.
50. DeNora, *Music in Everyday Life*, 148.
51. Garofalo, "From Music Publishing to MP3."
52. DeNora, *Music in Everyday Life*, 131.
53. Rossana Reguillo, "Errant Surfing: Music, YouTube, and the Role of the Web in Youth Cultures," trans. Peggy Westwell and Pablo Vila, in *Music and Youth Culture in Latin America: Identity Construction Processes from New York to Buenos Aires*, ed. Pablo Villa (New York: Oxford University Press, 2014), 106–31.
54. Michel Maffesoli, *The Time of the Tribes: The Decline of Individualism in Mass Society*, trans. Don Smith (London and Thousand Oaks, CA: Sage, 1996).
55. See Alessandro Baricco, *The Barbarians: An Essay on the Mutation of Culture* (New York: Rizzoli, 2014).
56. Adorno, "On Popular Music," para. 14.
57. Jeremy Rifkin, *The Age of Access: The New Culture of Hypercapitalism, Where All of Life Is a Paid-For Experience* (New York: Jeremy P. Tarcher/Putnam, 2000). This is not to say that property has ceased to be important, as Martin Scherzinger's observations about recent developments in the intellectual property—both its increased reach into previously unimaginable spheres such as genomics and the expansion of a plunderable commons in the global South—make clear. Scherzinger, "Alchemies of Sanctioned Value: Music, Networks, Law," in *Artistic Citizenship: Artistry, Social Responsibility, and Ethical Praxis*, ed. David J. Elliott, Marissa Silverman, and Wayne D. Bowman (Oxford and New York: Oxford University Press, 2016), 359–80. More properly, music, as a property, has become increasingly concentrated in the hands of rightsholders, while listeners have forsaken claims to ownership of material musical artifacts for access to music experiences.
58. John Seabrook, "Spotify: Friend or Foe?" *The New Yorker*, November 24, 2014, https://www.newyorker.com/magazine/2014/11/24/revenue-streams.
59. Will Page and Eric Garland, "The Long Tail of P2P," *Economic Insight* 14 (2008): 1–8.
60. Dawn Papandrea, "Spotify's CMO on Using Data to Create Content Marketing Hits," *NewsCred Insights*, June 5, 2017, https://insights.newscred.com/spotify-cmo-data-content-marketing/; and Omari Stringer, "The Sound of Politics: An Examination of Political Orientations and Musical Preferences among College Aged Adults" (honors undergraduate thesis, University of Central Florida, 2017), http://stars.library.ucf.edu/honorstheses/159.

61. DeNora, *Music in Everyday Life*, 148.

62. Ibid.

63. Horkheimer and Adorno, *Dialectic of Enlightenment: Philosophical Fragments*, 97.

64. DeNora, *Music in Everyday Life*, 146.

65. Jean Baudrillard, "Consumer Society," in *Selected Writings*, ed. Mark Poster (Stanford, CA: Stanford University Press, 1988.

66. DeNora, *Music in Everyday Life*, 149. DeNora cites Stjepan G. Meštrović, *Postemotional Society* (London and Thousand Oaks, CA: Sage, 1999).

67. Adorno, "On Popular Music," para. 22.

68. Ibid., paras. 22–23.

69. Alison Hearn, "'Meat, Mask, Burden': Probing the Contours of the Branded 'Self,'" *Journal of Consumer Culture* 8, no. 2 (2008): 197–217; and Ivana McConnell, "Identity Labor: Self-Concept in the Age of the Personal Brand," *The Learned Fangirl*, August 19, 2016, accessed June 31, 2018, http://thelearnedfangirl.com/2016/08/identity-labor-personal-brand.

70. McConnell, "Identity Labor," 213.

71. Paul du Gay, *Consumption and Identity at Work* (Thousand Oaks, CA: Sage, 1996), cited in Hearn, "'Meat, Mask, Burden,'" 203.

72. Hearn, "'Meat, Mask, Burden,'" 203.

73. Ibid., 204.

74. Luc Boltanski and Eve Chiapello, "The New Spirit of Capitalism," paper presented at the Conference of Europeanists, March 14–16, 2002, Chicago, IL; cited in Hearn, "'Meat, Mask, Burden,'" 203.

75. Christine Rosen, "The Age of Egocasting," *New Atlantis* 7 (2004–5): 51–72; and Hearn, "'Meat, Mask, Burden,'" 210.

76. Hearn, "'Meat, Mask, Burden,'" 197.

77. Jason Read, *The Micro-Politics of Capital: Marx and the Prehistory of the Present* (Albany: State University of New York Press, 2003), 159; and Hearn, "'Meat, Mask, Burden,'" 20, 204–5.

78. Gilles Deleuze, "Postscript on the Societies of Control," *October* 59 (1992): 3–7; and Frédéric Vandenberghe, "Deleuizian Capitalism," *Philosophy and Social Criticism* 34, no. 8 (2008): 877–903.

79. Scott Lash, "Power after Hegemony: Cultural Studies in Mutation?," *Theory, Culture & Society* 24, no. 3 (2007): 55–78; see also David Beer, "Power through the Algorithm? Participatory Web Cultures and the Technological Unconscious," *New Media & Society* 11, no. 6 (2009): 985–1002.

80. Quoted in Adam Pasick, "The Magic That Makes Spotify's Discover Weekly Playlists So Damn Good," *Quartz*, December 21, 2015, https://qz.com/571007/the-magic-that-makes-spotifys-discover-weekly-playlists-so-damn-good/.

81. Ibid.

82. Deleuze, "Postscript," 3–7.

83. Ibid., 4.

84. Lash, "Power after Hegemony," 55–78.

85. Rifkin, *The Age of Access*, 14.

86. Thomas Fox-Brewster, "Location, Sensors, Voice, Photos?! Spotify Just Got Real Creepy with the Data It Collects on You," *Forbes*, August 20, 2015; and "Understanding People through Music: Millennial Edition," Spotify, accessed September 14, 2017, https://www.spotifyforbrands.com/sv-SE/news/understanding-people-through-music-millennial-edition/.

87. Stringer, "The Sound of Politics."

88. "Understanding People through Music."

89. Glenn McDonald, "Every Noise at Once," EveryNoise, accessed February 14, 2020, http://everynoise.com/engenremap.html#otherthings.

90. Amanda Modell, "Only God Can Make a Genome: Pandora Internet Radio, God Tricks and 'The Music Itself'" (paper presented at the Society for Ethnomusicology National Meeting, Austin, TX, December 8, 2015). See also Donna Haraway, "A Cyborg Manifesto: Science, Technology, and Socialist-Feminism in the Late Twentieth Century," in *Simians, Cyborgs, and Women: The Reinvention of Nature* (New York: Routledge, 1991), 149–81.

91. These are playlists available in 2015 on the Songza platform, subsequently purchased by Google and now defunct.

92. Jean-Luc Nancy, *Listening*, trans. Charlotte Mandell, 1st ed. (New York: Fordham University Press, 2007).

93. DeNora, *Music in Everyday Life*, 149, citing Theodor W. Adorno, *Sound Figures*, trans. Rodney Livingstone (Stanford, CA: Stanford University Press, 1999), 14.

94. DeNora, *Music in Everyday Life*, 149–50.

95. Ibid., chap. 1.

96. Taina Bucher, *If . . . Then: Algorithmic Power and Politics* (New York: Oxford University Press, 2018).

97. Haraway, "A Cyborg Manifesto."

98. Frédéric Vandenberghe, "Deleuzian Capitalism," 895.

99. Louis Chude-Sokei, *The Sound of Culture: Diaspora and Black Technopoetics* (Middletown, CT: Wesleyan University Press, 2016); and Sylvia Wynter, "Unsettling the Coloniality of Being/Power/Truth/Freedom: Towards the Human, after Man, Its Overrepresentation—An Argument," *CR: The New Centennial Review* 3, no. 3 (2003): 257–337.

100. Zygmunt Bauman, *Wasted Lives: Modernity and Its Outcasts* (Malden, MA: Polity/Blackwell, 2004).

101. See Cary Wolfe, *What Is Posthumanism?*, Posthumanities 8 (Minneapolis: University of Minnesota Press, 2010).

PART 4

Affective Listenings

CHAPTER 8

Music, Labor, and Technologies of Desire

Martin Scherzinger

Pornopticon: Surveillance, Networks, and Desire *Incognito*

The so-called affective turn in the humanities at the turn of the twenty-first century was both historically and conceptually coterminous with a mutation in the economics of cultural production. In this chapter, I argue that the contemporary valorization and validation of affect could be weaponized against social, political, and economic struggles that demand systemic solutions (outside of the logic and grasp of affect theory) and served as an alibi for new forms of labor extraction. I present a speculative diagnosis of contemporary relations of production with reference to musical labor in an age of digitally networked subjects. Music, I argue, became a central vehicle for advancing not only surveillance networks innervated by affect, but also novel formations of labor in the contemporary sociotechnical moment.

The chapter outlines a hidden connection between desire (tethered to digital habitus) and labor (tethered to digital extraction techniques) before turning to musical production, construed as a kind of prescient vertex for recent transformations in labor relations. Along the way, I cast doubt on (1) the traditional Marxist construal of these relations, (2) the new cultural portrayals of desire, and (3) recent music scholarship that vindicates intensifications of affect. The chapter concludes with a brief description of recent developments in biotechnification (with a special interest in machine-measured tonal inflection for gauging preconceptual states of mind), arguing that a decontextualized universe of affects has both dangerously proliferated and at the same time is statistically clustered into anarcho-vitalist (dis)information networks. The flow of culture and information online is thereby centrifugally set adrift from the disciplinary apparatuses of the past and—through the ubiquitous tracking of user behavior—centripetally reconfigured by algorithmically mediated networks of the evolving present.

Affect, a key driver of behavioral surplus in this kind of surveillance economy, is regarded by humanist theorists as a subpersonal force—independent of reason, elusive of meaning, embodied, nonintentional, free-floating or autonomic, triggered, innate, and so on. As a material embodiment (instead of an idea), affect is thereby kept undefined—as a matter of methodological course—by this brand of humanist critique. A determined lack of interest in definitions, gnostic meanings, and semiotic interpretations, I argue, is a curious interpretive disavowal that effectively cedes the terrain of its digital representation—no less than its monitoring, manipulating, and modifying—to monopolized proprietary centers of computing. I argue against the kind of *analog paradigm* asserted by the material embodiment of affect, demonstrating that affect studies became a kind of nostalgic resistance to digitality itself. In other words, the ostensible resistance to any rule-governed system of thought of affect—its resistance to a *digital paradigm*—is shown to inhabit a kind of ineffable materiality, which, in a speculative final gesture, renders it a post-truth phenomenon. This essay is intended not as an exhaustive study of either affect, music, or labor, but as a schematic—and speculative—think piece directed toward reframing the vexed relationship between these terrains in our times.

It is now generally accepted that technological developments at the beginning of the twenty-first century have produced distinct anthropologies of the body.[1] In particular, the development of networked communication media (grounded in large-scale digital infrastructures) was coeval with a mutation in the tactile, visual, and audile body techniques that emerged from interaction (and feedback) with these media. As a subjective, practical experience, for example, quotidian online life—characterized by clicking and liking, linking and listening, swiping and scrolling—became enjoined, on an unprecedented scale, to techno-economic platforms that were designed to amplify networked affect. Contemporary technical design—from the screen itself and the blueprints of Web-based interfaces and applications to the algorithmic routines and subroutines that generated constantly refreshed content, timeline-based engagement, reposting, interactive audiovisual feedback, messaging streaks, recommendations, and so on—reflected the affective demands of an economy that came to regard human attention as a revenue-generating resource. An Internet-wide surveillance network produced detailed data dossiers on users (adopters and consumers) across the globe.

The methods used for data gathering derived from techniques adapted from criminology, policing, psychology, and psychiatry—technologies of control originating in the nineteenth and twentieth centuries. But by the beginning of the twenty-first century, these techniques had come to be deployed on a widespread scale, with a mass public that had (for the most part voluntarily) agreed to being tracked and measured. The technical proliferation of unique identifiers—cookies, scripts, APIs, content customization services, business intelligence services, and identification resources—had transformed the contemporary Internet into a wholesale technology of surveillance. In other words, online individuality became microdifferentiated into barcode-like metrics that were once the provenance of criminology.[2] These metrics intersected broad categories such as ethnicity, age, income, gender, and sexuality, as well as specific information pertaining to social status, mental stability, political affiliation, creditworthiness, health profile, and so on. Not only were users being tracked so that they could be targeted by marketing and advertising, thereby supplying the data animating metrics for algorithmic tools (such as recommendation systems, social media feeds, and streaming services), but they were increasingly subject to automated decisions based on their political, economic, and psychographic profiles. The owners of applications (social media and streaming services, on the one hand, but also search engines and service providers, on the other) adopted privacy policies that granted broad permission to collect user data, including personal information, device information, log information, location, local storage data, search history, and other information derived from tracking technologies.[3]

Did the widespread surveillance technologies produce the "disciplined" bodies—cautious, compromised, empowered—imagined by Michel Foucault, who, in *Discipline and Punish* (1977), famously deployed Jeremy Bentham's image of the panopticon to capture an essential element of both the penal system and the carceral elements of modern life itself? Or did the ubiquitous spyware hitched to digital devices correlate with exactly the opposite? Was this a kind of *inverted* panopticon effect? Contemporary subjects no longer experienced the *possibility* of being subject to the disciplining gaze of a centralized locus (thereby comporting their behavior to accommodate authority accordingly); instead, they experienced the *certainty* of being watched. They were nonetheless enjoined to experience, act, adopt, and produce in a mostly unfettered private way—a shift from disciplined to *de*-disciplined experience. Every post, comment, blog, wiki entry, invited friend, forwarded petition, destroyed (virtual) enemy, liked tweet, and uploaded photo produced what Jodi Dean considers a moment of surplus enjoyment; a momentary pleasure that provides a brief figure of jouissance to the experiential ground of the everyday. The feedback loop on social networks, video and music sharing sites, blogs, and so on "produces and circulates affect as a binding technique ... layering and interconnecting myriad communication platforms and devices."[4] The circuits of contemporary affect—broadly construed as desire, drive, appetite, enjoyment, and so on—became more and more strongly tethered to the communication technologies of contemporary capitalism. These new forms of affectively enriched surveillance served as a kind of digital entrapment—the instrumentalization of our noninstrumental capacities, or, perhaps most presciently, the financialization of what Gilles Deleuze and Félix Guattari famously called "desiring-production."[5]

The twentieth-century postmodern insight that commodity distribution and consumption were not merely passively imprinted by institutional power relations—that is, that reception was itself partly coproductive—has rung uncannily true in the twenty-first century. However, far from resisting hegemony by reading its messages against the grain—as was once implied by its "decoding" stance—such "prosumption" began to march in step with the ideological demands of digital capitalism.[6] Consumption itself, in its heterogeneous diversity, was transformed into a form of digital labor, extracted by technical interfaces designed for the capture of granular user data. From the perspective of the user, networked communication capabilities proffered, on the one hand, new modes of autonomy and individuality, and, on the other, enhanced means for social interaction, collaboration, and connectivity. In fact, social interactivity itself mingled with individuality in qualitatively new ways. As Adam Gopnik noted, social circles were largely supplanted and supplemented by social networks.[7] What was once internalized desire and appetite (more or less restrained in the context of social circles) was upended by circuits of connection and circulation that externalized and amplified desire and appetite in the context of digital networks. The quasi-cordoned-off space that characterized online human-screen interaction rewired the social interpellations once associated with traditional group interaction. Paradoxically, the online individual was at once both abstracted from established social coordinates, emerging within some version of incognito, and hyperbolically materialized within them, emerging within intensified zones of desire.

Networked communications thereby tipped the balance between the inside and the outside of the individual psyche. What were once internal desires—tastes, preferences, and attitudes, as well as secrets, hatreds, obsessions, paranoias, fixations, and fetishes—were granted expanded geographic and psychic reach behind closeted screen spaces. In other words, the enjoinment of cultural, sexual, and political content that was heliotropically guided by a kind of incognito desire could be instantly externalized and then also affirmed and amplified by the solicitude of user interfaces—super-user-friendly clicks, swipes, shares, likes, and links. It is as if desire—from pleasure and enjoyment to outrage and indignance—became incentivized and validated across distributed screen spaces of the attention economy. In short, the business model for online interaction depended on engagement, and uninhibited affective intensity became chiefly lucrative. From a Freudian perspective, one might loosely speak of the profit-driven digital interface as the instant affirmation of the id by the paradoxical intervention of a hyperactively solicitous superego—a case of the primitive drive less resisted (or educated by external objects, guidelines, and standards) than paradoxically affirmed (or educated by external objects of its own projection). Freed from the tempering effects of conventional sociality, the communications networks created the conditions for rapaciously atomized desire—a fantasy universe of affects, for better or worse—unburdened by the collective. The disciplined subject was replaced by the technical externalization of desire.

Labor Today: All Work Aspires to the Condition of Musical Work

Music, considered as a contemporary cultural practice, lay at the heart of this mutation in affective networking. This fact is revealed alone by corporate history, notably the acquisitions, mergers, and partnerships between online social media platforms and the evolving music industry. For example, a quick glance at the relationship between music delivery systems and social networking platforms in the first two decades of the twenty-first century reveals a pattern that demonstrates a recognition of music's value for generating attention and amplifying affect within those networks. The three dominant social media platforms of the first decade of the twenty-first century—Myspace, Google+, and Facebook—actively integrated industrial music production with social interaction, thereby conjoining emerging databases with recommendation vehicles. Myspace initially launched its own record label in 2005 and later integrated operations with major music labels in 2008; Google+ linked to an online music store and signed major deals with Citibank's EMI and Vivendi's Universal from its inception in 2011; and Facebook partnered with Spotify on a music streaming service when

Spotify first launched in the United States, also in 2011. Likewise, in the second decade of the century, the dominant music streaming services were geared toward building diversified media platforms that would move beyond music alone, including video and download functionality, social interactivity, and, eventually, virtual reality.[8] In other words, economic stakeholders on the dominant social media and streaming platforms of the early twenty-first century were demonstrably invested in incorporating musical listening as a revenue-generating resource.

This is why music's direct appeal to affect—grounded almost by definition in creative, expressive, authentic, emotional, and spiritual values—was a useful alibi for the restructuring of immaterial labor production more generally. At the dawn of the era of mainstream digital interaction, for example, Richard Stallman—one of the founding figures of the free-software movement—appealed to the power of love and inherent fascination to describe the future value of human labor in the context of free software on a mass scale. Tellingly, Stallman deployed music to clinch the argument in his well-known GNU ("Gnu's not Unix!") Manifesto: "There is no shortage of professional musicians who keep at it though they have no hope of making a living that way."[9] Likewise, nearly twenty years later Clay Shirky explained that musicians were likely to voluntarily deliver musical content without compensation because they were willing to "replace . . . greed with love."[10] Music's richly affective associations with creativity, emotion, and expression became an exemplary case of what Paolo Virno called "post-workerist" subjectivity.[11] In sum, the historical shift in music's commodity status in the first decade of the twentieth century—a decade that witnessed a kind of "commodity inversion," whereby the "compensable musical unit had transformed into an ephemeral node in a dense network of transmission lines"—was generously enabled by music's association with the figure of affectively rewarding labor.[12]

It is important to note that the political economy of digital music was less a radical break from the past than an intensification of some of its inherent historical tendencies. In fact, economists from Joseph A. Schumpeter to Frederic M. Scherer had detected the paradoxical nature of musical labor as it entered the market economy in the late eighteenth century. Construed as intrinsically rewarding, the economic outcomes for composers and musicians were highly variable—the reward system resembled "a lottery" more than reflecting any actual effort of labor.[13] The "prizes thrown to a small minority of winners" functioned as an alibi for the reproduction of musical work—musicians "do their utmost because they have the big prizes before their eyes and overrate their chances of doing equally well."[14] Music, in short, provided a natural alibi for the self-motivated expressive subject characterizing then contemporary relations of production. Although this economic scenario had been lamented from its outset—even Beethoven complained that he was a poor "business man and reckoner" and called for a centralized "artistic depot" for the proper remuneration of musical works—it remained the de facto remuneration system for music in the two centuries to come.[15]

And yet, there was something premodern about the character of musical labor in the second decade of the twenty-first century. The Harvard legal scholar Yochai Benkler—an avid defender of commons-based collaborative labor in the era of Web 2.0—recommended a restructuring of the music industry in the age of digital networks in terms that were instructively symptomatic. In his "Voluntary Payment Models," he recommended that musicians fulfill four requirements for the successful implementation of their remuneration schemes. Musicians should (1) communicate with fans (via blogs and tweets); (2) foster community among fans (via chat functions and forums); (3) collaborate with fans (offering incomplete tracks for remixes and mashups and soliciting input for lyrics, visuals, etc.); and (4) trigger reciprocity (because, according to findings in the behavioral sciences, "the population reciprocates trust with trust, and generosity with generosity").[16] Recognizing the role of the creative and expressive dimension of music, no less than its collaborative and communal social character, Benkler essentially argued in favor of a kind of karmic logic: if musicians acted like good communalists, more or less, they could expect to receive a voluntary contribution from listeners—like a tip. Benkler's model followed in the slipstream of America's considerable tipping culture, a result of an amendment to the Fair Standards Labor Act in 1991 wrought by the restaurant industry lobby, which fixed the minimum wage for servers and bartenders below $3. But for music, unlike the service industry, this economic scenario eliminated even this minimal minimum-wage requirement. Instead, it precariously redirected clients' and consumers' capacities for enjoyment and kindness toward the single revenue stream for artists and the producers' creative work to an additional layer of quasi-mandatory administrative labor (keeping in touch online, soliciting feedback, etc.). While the sentimental attachments of their fans were scripted as financial indicators, musicians—as in the age of Beethoven—were actually diverted from their primary creative work in the process. As in the age before technical reproducibility, in other words, Benkler's ideal musicians had become digital troubadours—enjoined both to the labor of online public relations (in addition to their creative work) and to the labor of performing live (which, by the second decade of the twenty-first century, had become the only substantive site of remuneration for musicians). The digital network thereby produced a paradoxical inversion of music's value, throwing remuneration practices back to a premodern time.

This kind of inversion of economic value became a relevant feature of the economy at large. In the digital age, the labor practices for information workers—in advertising, design, photography, journalism, fashion, and so on—were gradually coalescing around the lotterylike model for remunerating musicians. Traditional job placement was systematically replaced by precarious forms of self-employment. From call workers monitoring hotlines and free agents of service delivery systems to designers, software developers, and even lawyers, economic productivity became associated with the flexible, innovative, and expressive values—rich with affective nuance—undergirding precarious labor practices. Postindustrial capitalism—marked by an increasing shift in corporate culture from hierarchic to "participative" management—emphasized flexible workers and adaptable logistics. In his *Nice Work If You Can Get It: Life and Labor in Precarious Times*, Andrew Ross described job insecurity (or the labor precariat) as a systematic new norm.[17] The neoliberal subject was no longer the figure of law-abiding servility, but rather the figure of creative self-employment—innovative, flexible, networked, adept at multitasking, communally oriented, entrepreneurial, and so on. All work, it seems, was aspiring to the condition of musical work.

Pornucopia: Gamifaction in Cinema I

Can this kind of construal of the productive libido be regarded as a progressive category today? Or does the subject of capital—of increasing necessity enjoined toward erratic potential—already reflect a new reservoir of affective surplus for expropriation? There is a scene in Gary Ross's iconic film *The Hunger Games* (2012), a science-fiction thriller based on the novel by Suzanne Collins, in which the protagonist, Katniss Everdeen, displays her talents before an audience of gossiping, indulged, and powerful adjudicators in the capital of a society sharply stratified into districts. Katniss, a skilled sharpshooter from the poorest district, has volunteered herself as a contestant for the deadly annual Hunger Games, a high-stakes game show enforced by the nation of Panem as retribution for a past rebellion. The scene is grounded in a series of surprises. First, against the odds (well understood by the cinema audience at this point in the film), Katniss, under the gaze of her judges, actually *misses* the center of the target. Perhaps nerves interfered with her reaction time. Perhaps the interpellations of performance disrupted the innocent ease with which she honed her skill set. In contrast, of course, her failed shot looks wholly predictable to her onscreen aristocratic audience, who laugh and jeer in ridicule and contempt. Taken aback by her own misfire, Katniss, accompanied now by a mounting soundtrack that recalls the distant tolling of bells, digs deep. Reflectively, she lines up the target in the crosshairs once more. This time, true to form, she strikes the bullseye. However, there is an unexpected problem. The judges, at this point wholly absorbed in dismissive distraction, are no longer looking; they fail, once again, to bear witness to the protagonist's extraordinary skill. The second surprise comes next. Perplexed by her unreactive audience, Katniss lines up her target a third time; and, in a feat of clarity and determination, she fires another perfect shot. But this time she has taken aim not at the official competition target but at the apple wedged in the mouth of the roast pig on the table encircled by the judges of the Capitol. The apple is deftly dislodged from the dead pig's mouth. There is a thwack and then there is silence. The aristocrats, dumbstruck, stare down in shock.

The massive box-office success of *The Hunger Games*—the largest-grossing film released outside a summer or holiday period—is often described in terms of its resonance with twenty-first-century millennial anguish in the context of a technologically automated, postrecession world. The film's themes are paradoxically marked, on the one hand, by a ubiquitous entertainment apparatus riveted to spectacle and, on the other, by new realities of structured economic inequality. The gladiatorial death matches—Hunger Games—align these paradoxical themes by broadcasting *for consumption* the very struggle for survival. In the standard interpretation of Katniss, she represents a kind of indignant resistance to the rigged institutions of government and employment, struggling for what is fair and just. In short, Katniss embodies the kind of rebellion of a moral outsider ensnared in the brutal rules of an immoral dystopia. This official script, however, fails to register the texture of the signifying associations implicit in her characterization. Katniss, unofficially but perhaps more precisely, represents not the outsider at all, but the paradoxical *heroic insider* in the era of ubiquitous computation. What is fascinating about the scene painted above is that her wealthy adjudicators from the Capitol do not, it turns out, recoil in alarm at her menacing act of rebellion. They do not punish her. The intensity of their horror registers instead—in a filmically extended split second—sheer delight. This is pure affect—"a state of suspense, potentially of disruption"—and it signals a swerve toward the virtual.[18] In other words, the moment embodies a swerve from official signification (an act of dangerous rebellion) to asignifying intensity (a performance of embodied spectacle). One may even say that the reaction of the aristocrats is, to invoke Brian Massumi, physiologically "split" (about which more below).[19]

The paradox of affect is that it is said to be simultaneously autonomic (it "cannot but be experienced," it "cannot but be perceived," etc.) and radically incipient (it is "an unleashing of potential"); it "escapes confinement in the particular body whose vitality, or potential for interaction, it is."[20] This raises some questions: What aspect of affect does this moment in the film prominently signal? Does it signal the potential of affect to "veer off in another direction," to register delight in danger?[21] Does it thereby register a mode of embodiment that opens "empiricism into ethical experimentation"?[22] Or does it, on the other hand, register "a nonconscious, never-to-be-conscious" remainder, the production of a kind of autonomic presence?[23] Massumi of course allies the agonic relation of these parallel levels of affect. Official signification simply persists — at odds — with embodied intensity.

But what if the autonomic reaction of the adjudicators is less *non*conscious than it is *un*conscious? In other words, what if Katniss's risky maneuver actually signals the deeper unwritten rules of the game in contemporary society? Katniss thinks outside the box, innovatively breaking official rules. She acts the part of the master-entrepreneur in a hyperconnected world. Katniss, it turns out, eventually both wins the brutal competition to the death and simultaneously stakes out the ethical high ground. In fact, by forging an unholy conceptual alliance between love and ethics, on the one hand, and savagery and contest, on the other, the movie phantasmically suggests that it is her very loyalty, love, and strong ethical standing that somehow deliver her to victory in the deadly game. This is victorious savagery cloaked as ethics, heaven made in hell. She seizes the moment in the age of the moment — "every second is the ultimate *zeitgeist*" says Josh Ostrovsky, the Internet sensation known as the Fat Jew — with a perfect sense of timing.[24] In a fleeting flash of insight, she performs a gamble that officially challenges institutional authority, but unofficially, and more importantly, obeys the "post-Fordist" injunction toward innovation and entrepreneurialism.[25] She rewrites the rules, blending "fundamentally heterogeneous elements" to produce the obligatory "new": the obedient innovation.[26] Katniss is the true subject of contemporary capitalism: the visionary who sees in the pig's apple a bull's-eye.

I narrate this scene in some detail to illustrate that affective production has no inherent link to progressive politics. In fact, in the context of contemporary cultures of computing and consumption, desublimated energies became a condition for the possibility of data capture and harvest. In other words, the capitalist surveillance economy required granular data on subjects for its efficient functioning. Data doubles were best built of *de*standardised data—personalized cookies, banners, scripts, and clicks that lay both inside and outside the symbolic box (custom, convention, decorum). The Internet's data doubles were both memetic and secret, neurotic and orgiastic, civilized and uncivilized, true and fake. The Internet—at once the de facto information library and a "giant weird orgy" (in the words of Ostrovsky)—connected platforms, devices, and networks in what can be described as the algorithmic clustering of affect: the pornification of the library.[27] Desire was thereby put in the service of detailed (personalized, customized) metrics for software applications, search engines, content providers, and (later) service providers. This was the goal of the third-party trackers, the surveillance networks, and the ubiquitous spyware that instantly connected every visit to almost every site to several third-party servers. This was the age of the Internet as dragnet. The online user had metamorphosed into a producer: surplus labor.

Marxism in Ruins: From Alienation to Disalienation

There is a common argument about free-market economies that dialectically connects capitalist cycles of production with processes of subjective abstraction. For the subject of capitalism, economic activities become disembedded from social and cultural activities; workers' identities become alienated in the context of industrial production cycles—a "factory desert," in the words of Marco Revelli.[28] In other words, social bonds, kinship relations, and friendship obligations, as well as collective norms, historical debates, ethical systems, customs, and habits, are suspended in service of the efficient functioning of economic activity. The true subject of capital, the argument went, is rational, autonomous, and internally motivated—an abstraction that is brought into conformity with an economic reality that appears as a naturalized closed circuit. As Karl Marx and Friedrich Engels note, the economic system "has drowned the most heavenly ecstasies of religious fervour, of chivalrous enthusiasm, of philistine sentimentalism, in the icy water of egotistical calculation. It has resolved personal worth into exchange value, and in place of numberless indefeasible chartered freedoms, it has set up that single, unconscionable freedom—free trade."[29] Hannah Arendt expanded this theory of the subject—shorn of the capacity for meaningful experience, rendered atomized and lonely—in the context of totalitarianism.[30] Most theories of subject formation in the twentieth century (especially those crafted by writers in Western democracies) generally paid homage to this process of abstraction and alienation—the capitalist subject emerging in contexts of habituated subjection. For example, Marcel Maus's and Norbert Elias's examinations of body technique as a function of social power, Max Horkheimer and Theodor W. Adorno's lament about the standardization of cultural artifacts and social subjects under monopoly capital, Louis Althusser's theories of interpellation associated with ideological state apparatuses, Pierre Bourdieu's analysis of the economic determinants of the habitus, Henri Lefebvre's diagnosis of human comportment as dressage, Michel Foucault's famous analysis of discipline in the context of various institutional regimes, and Jacques Lacan's theories of the gaze all bear the marks of the classic Marxist inflection of the abstracted capitalist subject. Standardization, training, technique, interpellation, dressage, discipline: catchwords for a contemporary theory of the subject forged in the context of contemporary economic systems, disciplinary apparatuses, and power relations.

Could it be that this persistent, albeit variously inflected, allegiance to abstraction has lost its fundamental diagnostic value in the contemporary moment? What if the exact inverse were true? Could it be that the networked subject of the twenty-first century was structured less by the forces of uniformity, standardization, normativity, and discipline than by those of fluctuation, personalization, innovation, and erratic deregulation? On the model of affective networks outlined above, the disembedding from traditional social bonds in the twenty-first century was a result not of abstraction and alienation, but of the microtargeting of rapaciously externalized desire for vast databases characterized by a high level of granularity. Is the contemporary networked subject the figure not of alienation but of disalienation—a kind of de-discipline? This is the hyperbolically individualized subject tethered to the content customization of meticulously designed technological feedback loops. In fact, it is likely that the classic Marxist model (which provided the basic coordinates for twentieth-century theories of the subject) has been corroded by an irreducible recent ethnographic reality: namely, the expansive economic imperative to trawl surplus value from expression, freedom, reciprocity, autonomy, and above all desire. The classic model, which assumed a constitutive dialectical link between material labor and industrial production, could foresee neither the autonomy of subjects nor the independence of networks in the twenty-first century. The reign of the (once oppressive) symbolic order has in fact buckled under the weight of technically amplified desire. Along with democratizing access to large swaths of the world's information and knowledge, the digital network—by automating streams and feeds according to the financial logic of the attention economy—has afforded unedited access to monetized disinformation, wild and ruthless free speech, networks of viral indignation, politics as theater, limitless pornography, brutal fantasy, genuinely fake news, and of course a cornucopia of wall-to-wall music, algorithmically curated for personalized digital streaming. In short, one may speak here of the privatization of the libidinal economy, which (for all the instrumental operations of raw power and wealth driving it) may have played a role in undermining collective symbolic interaction and public reason, instead technically amplifying externalizations of desire.

Pornucopia: Gamification in Cinema II

Popular culture frequently bears the marks of this theoretical shift from an ideological apparatus that enforces discipline to one that enjoins desire. For example, the fantasy of being entangled in a virtual world beyond human control has been an ongoing theme in film for decades. In the first decades of the twenty-first century, movies ranging from the *Matrix* trilogy (1999–2003) and *Inception* (2010) to *Hunger Games* (2012), the *Westworld* series (2016–18), and *Get Out* (2017) explored this prototypical genre. The genre tends to depict variants on a general theme of an all-encompassing alternate reality to which human behavior comports in a kind of hallucinatory consensus. The prototypical plot engages protagonists caught in synthetic, machine-generated worlds that are nonetheless real seeming and difficult to escape or expose. The fictional fantasy of a virtual world enveloping the real one is occasionally transplanted to explain life itself. The Oxford philosopher Nick Bostrom, for example, no less an entrepreneur-innovator than Elon Musk, argued that our current lived reality has a relatively high probability of being a simulation; or, more precisely stated, "the odds that we are in base reality is one in billions."[31] Given the meteoric rise of wearable apps and the imminent arrival of invisible technologies characterized by data-streaming sensors on networked subjects—flexible electronic circuits have already been injected successfully into living mice, for example, offering a way for electronics to interface with brain activity and thereby theoretically making games indistinguishable from reality—this argument tends to take signs of techno-human evolution as an indicator of the likelihood of previous such evolutions.[32]

Aside from the persistence of this fantasy, however, in recent years there has been a noteworthy cultural shift regarding its actual significance in relation to power and desire. In *The Matrix*, for example, humans are subservient beings, incubated in pods to produce bioelectricity and thermal energy for the machines of artificial intelligence that govern them. Their minds are controlled by cybernetic implants, and their reality is completely simulated. The basic picture of the world portrayed in this popular film is recapitulated with some seriousness by a certain brand of academic discourse. As it is with the interpellations of Althusser's ideological state apparatus, or the disciplining effects of Foucault's institutional ones, the human subject in *The Matrix* is ensnared in webs of signification and reality that are more or less indifferent, oppressive, or hostile toward individual freedom. As a result, resistance to this hegemonic simulacrum entails resistance to the version of reality to which the matrix and its constructs subject humanity. Indeed, Jean Baudrillard's book *Simulacra and Simulation*, which makes an infamous cameo in the film, is tellingly opened (by the character Neo, played by Keanu Reeves) onto a page advancing an argument for theoretical nihilism and terrorism in the context of *The Matrix*'s weaponized hegemony. In short, the matrix is more or less a claustrophobic virtual reality to be resisted by gradually peeling away its layers of illusion. The film itself fictionally inhabits the dramatized (and exaggerated) figure of the oppressive institutional apparatus that abstracts, standardizes, disciplines, and interpellates the individual. The contemporary subject is ultimately subject to the uniform circuits of a virtual reality: hyperalienation.

In the wildly popular series *Westworld*, released nearly two decades later, like those in *The Matrix* humans play out life as puppet-avatars in a technologically advanced simulacrum of the world. This time, however, the virtual reality is an amusement park known as "Westworld"—a construct that reflects a kind of future telos in the evolution of game design. Wealthy humans coinhabit the park with androids in a nostalgically themed set recalling the early American West. As in *The Matrix*, both the set and the androids of *Westworld* are technologically augmented to the extent that they are indistinguishable from actual places and people. Machine lives commingle with human ones. But unlike the matrix, Westworld can be inhabited by its visitors without fear of retaliation from the hosts. As a result, these gamers experience Westworld not as a constraining, claustrophobic, or disciplining force, but as intense, liberating, and de-disciplining. Far from adjusting their behavior according to the demands of their matrix-like reality, inhabitants of Westworld unleash their deepest fantasies and most protean desires. In fact, visitors to Westworld (we are informed by one of its designers) come to act out their most violent urges and pornographic fantasies, shooting, looting, and screwing their way through the park. Instead of inducing fear and alienation as it does in *The Matrix*, the recognition in *Westworld* that the (game) world is but a virtual simulacrum of life lowers the symbolic stakes considerably. In other words, the takeaway for characters interacting with simulated worlds in *Westworld* is the antithesis of that found in *The Matrix*. The lesson of *Westworld* is that if reality amounts to mere string pulling in an elaborate game of puppetry, the doors to radical freedom and total desire are flung wide open. Far from the exaggerated Foucaultianism of *The Matrix*, in other words, we find in *Westworld* an unhinged Nietzscheanism—in total determination, one might say, total freedom reigns. *Westworld* of course soon complicates the border between human and machine, but the fundamental lesson concerning desire is sustained throughout. Not surprisingly, even the androids are soon enjoined to this paradoxical mode of freedom as the series progresses. By episode 6, the chief designer of Westworld, Dr. Ford (Anthony Hopkins), offers an uncanny echo of Friedrich Nietzsche: "In a way," he starkly proclaims, "the hosts [androids] are more free [sic] than us."

Affect: The Sonotropic Default

The contrast between these films registers a broader shift in the cultural order of things. In place of the disciplining forces of a previous era we now find, under the same cinematic rubric, new enjoinments to desire. Likewise, as argued in the opening passage of this essay, across the terrain of communication technologies of contemporary capitalism, digital networks have enabled and accelerated the technical externalization of desire in a literalization of Gilles Deleuze and Félix Guattari's "desiring machines." It is no wonder that theorists in the humanities—ranging from political philosophers to literary theorists—turned theoretical attention to the question concerning affect during this historical period. Examples abound. As described above, in the Deleuze-inflected political philosophy of Brian Massumi, affect registers as a kind of preconscious intensity, emerging autonomously, free from conventionally understood expression, feeling, or communication.[33] Similarly, for the literary critic Hans-Ulrich Gumbrecht, the notion of presence suspends the traditional focus of communication—figured as the transmission of meaning—and instead engages its material processes, embodied in particular media.[34] Given the rich metaphysical legacy of sound and music in the history of philosophy, it should come as no surprise that affect theory finds fertile ground in music scholarship and sound studies. Even nonmusicological approaches to the subject draw liberally upon sonic and musical phenomena to capture the peculiarities of affect. It is noteworthy, for example, that Gumbrecht's descriptions of the production of presence draw mostly on examples from the world of sport and music. Typical of his approach is this description of musical phenomena: "I wanted my students to know, for example, the almost excessive, exuberant sweetness that sometimes overcomes me when a Mozart aria grows in polyphonic complexity and when I indeed believe that I can hear the tones of the oboe on my skin."[35] Physiological responses such as this—a shiver down the spine, a widening of the eyes, or a tremor of the skin—are allied with the affective intensities of embodied experience. For Massumi, these kinds of involuntary autonomic reactions in fact betray a physiologically split experience— a "two-sidedness"—in which "the skin is faster than the word."[36] The word operates according to convention, reflection, content, and linearity, while affect is incipient, instantaneous, inchoate, and nonlinear.

The idea that "the word" (language) partakes of a divergent— indeed slower—physiological order than "the skin" (affect) is a recent incarnation of a lengthy philosophical dichotomy that is particularly well rehearsed in relation to music and sound. This antithetical construal—the conceptual order of language as opposed to the sensory orders of sonority—became particularly pronounced in the wake of seventeenth- and eighteenth-century theories of affect. For theorists such as Lorenzo Giacomini and René Descartes, the basic affects— ranging from admiration and love to sorrow and sadness—were legible as outwardly visible or audible phenomena. Revealingly, their attempt to schematize the physiological effects of external factors with recourse to a theory of the humors could never be exhausted by declarative nomenclatures. Music was a particularly powerful medium for eliciting through sound vibration these kinds of distinct corporeal experiences—clammy hands, flushed cheeks, watery eyes, raised heart rates, and so on—leading philosophers and music theorists such as Johann David Heinichen (1683–1729), Friedrich Wilhelm Marpurg (1718–1795), and Johann Joachim Quantz (1697–1773) to gesture toward, but ultimately fail to confirm, correlations between musical gestures, modes, and keys to listeners' internal states. As Roger Grant has convincingly shown, even Johann Mattheson, whose eighteenth-century *Affektenlehre* most famously taxonomized basic affects (rude, bold, despairing, sad, and so on) and correlated them with musical characteristics (melodic profiles, pitch ranges, harmonic sequences, rhythmic behaviors, dynamic intensities, musical keys) ultimately encountered a limit when it came to their substantive description.[37] Of the affects, Mattheson wrote: "The more one aspires to determine something positive about them, the more contradictions one may find, since the opinions about this material are almost numberless."[38]

Toward the end of the eighteenth century, theorists of musical affect began to turn away from a correlationist conception of affect altogether. The workings of affect were thereby separated from any associated representations and tethered instead to a kind of direct sympathetic responsiveness of the human nervous system to sound vibrations. This tendency to delink affect from representation (and to link it, in turn, to the physiology of sensation), became a hallmark of Romantic conceptions of music and its relation to the body. For nineteenth-century theorists of musical affect, the compulsion to rationalize the emotional profile of music's expressive capacity—and its concomitant fixing of affective taxonomies—tended to be called into question and doubt. In other words, in the postrevolutionary period, affective states elicited by sound tended to be inflected by a more complex metaphysics of becoming, set adrift of the linguistic taxonomies of affect ostensibly associated with centuries past. Language and representation were held to be conceptually severed from music's affective register. In the early Romantic imagination of Wilhelm Heinrich Wackenroder, for example, music was a kind of divine miracle grasped not by the intellect, but by emotion alone. Friedrich Schelling argued that music's ability to combine cognitive and sensuous experience should stand as a model for philosophy itself. Arthur Schopenhauer allied music with the primordial will, a concept of embodied becoming that was construed as the very antithesis of representation. Likewise, Søren Kierkegaard associated music with the endless striving of the pure unmediated life force, later reinterpreted by Nietzsche as music's Dionysian strain. In sum, the figure of music in nineteenth-century philosophy was characterized by its peculiarly ineffable embodiments, which gave representational taxonomies designed to capture them the slip.

The tradition that associated music's relationship to language as refractory and broken persisted throughout the twentieth century. The open-endedness of music even paved the way for a politics of hope in the thinking of Ernst Bloch; or, framed in a more negatively dialectical way, for the appearance of the nonexistent in the thinking of Theodor Adorno. Later in the century, theorists ranging from Pierre Schaeffer to Michel Chion (by way of Jean-François Lyotard, Roland Barthes, and many others) extracted the peculiarities of musical listening (variously construed as acousmatic, timbre oriented, material, reduced, and so on) from other habituated modes of listening—those that were oriented toward indices, for example, or toward either semantic or syntactic comprehension. Once again, the protocols of language-based communication were construed as antithetical to those of musical communication. As in the first half of the twentieth century, in the second half of the century as well the politics attendant upon music's nonsignifying capacity were frequently given a productive inflection. Deleuze and Guattari's transposition of modernist musical terms (borrowed from Olivier Messiaen, Pierre Boulez, and Luciano Berio), for example, laid the groundwork for a political philosophy grounded in the productive powers of assemblage and, of course, affect. Even the Marxist philosophers Alain Badiou and Slavoj Žižek granted pride of place to music's nonsignifying capacities. Badiou argued that music's immanent development, especially in the context of Wagnerian polyphony, imaginatively transcended the conceptual limits of linguistically mediated models for political change. As against the substitutive surrogacy of words, musical tones in this historical tradition were freed of propositional nomenclatures, instead ushering in variants of political hope, transformation, acousmatics, materiality, sensuality, and above all affective intensity. This is the sonotropic default of the modern philosophical understanding of music.[39]

Throughout the twentieth century, one could additionally detect frequent eruptions of nonmusical scholarly skepticism toward meaning-oriented theories of communication and art. Movements in the arts and music were often oriented as much toward presence, tangibility, and materiality as they were to meaning, interpretation, and ideas. From Walter Benjamin's interest in tactility and the optical unconscious, as in his classic 1935 essay "The Work of Art in the Age of Technical Reproducibility," to Susan Sontag's embrace of an erotics of art, resistant to the rough grip of interpretation in her classic 1966 essay "Against Interpretation," the idea that the senses resist orders of semiotic communication was not new. What is new and noteworthy in the twenty-first century is the sheer scope and authority of this way of understanding sound. In early twenty-first-century journalistic writing, music scholarship, and sound studies, the concept of affect became a key category for theorizing sonic experience. Scholars, composers, journalists, and DJs—ranging from Carolyn Abbate, Julian Henriques, Marie Thompson, Ian Biddle, Patricia Clough, and Will Shrimshraw to David Toop, Kode9 (aka Steve Goodman), Brian Hulse, and Adam Harper, among many others—confronted the peculiarly paradoxical power of sonic encounter construed as at once vividly material and ephemeral, present and unlocatable, intense and ineffable. At the same time, musicological studies frequently turned away from musical texts and toward musical performances, embodiment, and sensuous listening, while ethnomusicological ones turned away from musical contexts and toward an anthropology of the senses, questions concerning timbre, affective politics, sensuous ethnography, and even "acoustemology."[40]

Industrialized Affect: The Nanochronemics of Human Embodiment

What are we to make of the many claims associating sound and music with nonsignifying intensity—or affect—especially in relation to the above-discussed sociotechnical networks of contemporary capitalism? Can one afford to associate music with indeterminate, ineffable, intense, ephemeral, incipient, nonconscious, drastic, or nonsignifying characteristics in the context of the digital era, where affect is increasingly mapped, measured, and modified? Or is this kind of association—including the production of presence, the privileged audility of the drastic, and so on—symptomatic of a misleadingly hyperbolic construal of the opposition between language and music held firmly in the inertial grip of a centuries-old Western dialectic? In the context of ubiquitous biotechnification today, where surveillance is increasingly leveraged by artificial intelligence and machine learning toward predictive ends, is it not crucial to gain some understanding of the precise contents of affect—a seemingly autonomic sensory habitus—in relation to their capacity for machinic adaptation? Music scholarship, no less than the humanities at large, plays a critical role in exposing the social, historical, cultural, geographical, political, and economic underwriting of the so-called affective experiences that innervate the advance of contemporary biotechnology. In contrast, a philosophical position that insists on the radically nonsignifying openness of the body cannot hope to summon sufficient evidence to either accept, resist, or even redirect the terms massaged into the algorithmic model of experience to come.

Stakeholders abound. Aside from the various entrainment technologies developed for musical streaming—such as groove tracking and beat tracking—the military-industrial complex, for example, is paying increasing attention to human affect.[41] A new generation of militarized prosthetics, to take a single case among many, seeks to mobilize computing in conjunction with electrochemistry at the cellular level as it intersects with frequencies.[42] Here the quest is to improve reaction times in the handling of ballistic weapons in combat. These technologies deploy human thought alone—recorded and graphed by an electroencephalogram (EEG) and then formatted according to encoded characteristics of brain waves—to circumvent the neurological feedback between hands and brain. The extracted brain-wave patterns are transformed into various domain signals (frequency, etc.) to facilitate a series of calculations and characterizations, which in turn are digitally encoded for analysis. In other words, brain-wave signal analysis is recruited for technologies whose task it is to accelerate the instinctive galvanic response time for human agents in high-stakes military contexts of decision making.

Likewise, in lower-stakes technologies, such as those designed to predict states of health, depression ratings, mood categories, and typologies of well-being, microtemporalities are likewise measured against the background of affective behavior through music, sound, and voice. Companies such as Nemesysco, Semaine, Beyond Verbal, Cogito, and Interspeed, for example, offer analytics for emotional profiles and personality types using diagnoses grounded in vibration patterns of human vocalization. These computational evaluations—based on microtremors in the larynx, vocal intonations, intervallic patterns, and so on—ostensibly offer insight into psychological states, stress levels, and depression ratings, which in turn inform decisions about a person's trustworthiness, hirability, state of health, fitness for service, creditworthiness, criminal proclivities, and the like.[43] For example, research teams made up of engineers and psychiatrists are developing artificial intelligence–enabled technologies to test for the presence of mental illness grounded in the sound (dissociated from the content) of human utterances. These "vocal biomarkers" of a mental condition are claimed to register faulty body mechanisms directly, rather than circulating within human sociocultural meaning.[44] Not surprisingly, the data-driven categorizations deployed by these evaluations frequently rely on a basic interpretation of premodern taxonomies of emotional types said to be found in music. For example, the basic taxonomy deployed in Beyond Verbal's patent 8078470 B2 (2006), which outlines a procedure for measuring emotional attitudes through intonation analysis, directly conjures a premodern taxonomy for musical affect—the "tone" *do* (C) is associated with "the need for activity in general and for survival activity in particular"; *re* (D) is associated with "impulsiveness and/or creativity"; *mi* (E) is associated with "self-control, action within restraints"; and so on.[45] This kind of noninvasive prognostic of affective states uncannily recapitulates a simplified grasp of the basic categories of early eighteenth-century *Affektenlehre*, reconfigured in the context of microtemporal fluctuations of voice. With origins in lie detection (associated with military operations, law enforcement, and corrections), these decontextualized twenty-first-century measurements of affect, fundamentally opaque to users and adopters, are the calibrated microseconds that constitute the nanochronemics of human embodiment in an age of networked computation.[46]

Instead of giving free rein to the meticulous and declarative language of computing, historians, musicologists, sociologists, anthropologists, and social scientists might be in the best position to contextualize the experimental modalities mapping neural circuits in the brain down to the cortical lobes and amygdalae neurons, and therefore to demonstrate the precise ways in which engineers and computer scientists institute ontological commitments about the body today. In other words, as computing is tangibly brought into the realm of the human body, the humanities cannot afford to set affective experience adrift from all signifying. For all its promise as affectively intense, the desiring-production of an abstract machine, this kind of position actually marks a retreat into radically embodied openness—an impoverished method for leveraging productive engagement. Even if it is somehow true that affective states cannot, in the final analysis, accurately be grasped by fixed meanings, basic categories, and gnostic determinations, the economic demand for data-streaming sensors affixed to networked subjects and objects will ensure that these affective states are nonetheless measured and programmed as if they could be. In other words, left unsupervised on account of its inarticulate nonsignifying intensity, affective arousal stands to be colonized by all manner of militarized adaptation, just as interactive instincts stand to be colonized by all manner of industrial interpellation. For both theoretical and practical reasons, it is in the interests of militarized/industrialized machine learning and artificial intelligence to keep human affect as unrestrained—at once externalized and undefined—as possible. Against the validation of affect, then, the time may have come for disciplined restraint.

Studies of affect in music studies flourished in the first two decades of the twenty-first century. Whereas the fields of music theory, historical musicology, and ethnomusicology generally inhabited distinct methodological domains at the turn of the century, the question of affect had, by the second decade of the twenty-first century, witnessed a rare kind of methodological convergence among them. Indeed, the affect phenomenon took up considerable residency in theoretical, historical, and anthropological reflections on music, and while its precise conclusions were driven toward different ends, it did so on remarkably similar methodological terms. The likely reason for this is that the turn to affect, at the same time, bore the marks of a wider turn in philosophy (no less than the theoretically oriented humanities) toward *materialism*. This was a new kind of materialism—not to be confused with historical materialism or Marxism—that was largely catalyzed by a brand of Deleuze-inspired thought that took root in Anglophone academia in the late 1990s. In short, the new materialism was decisively pitted against analytics directed toward human consciousness and supposedly toward nonintentionality, physical life, real objects, direct sensations, and empirical reality itself.

In crude terms, this shift marked a revived valuation of empiricism, realism, and pragmatism and the concomitant devaluation of rationalism, abstraction, and reflection. As if to recapitulate European debates of the eighteenth century, empirical studies and ontological explanations gradually gained ascendancy over critical and conceptual ones. In Badiou's useful terms, this period marked the emergence of a kind of "democratic materialism," where *being*—construed as real objects, perceptions, and agents, paradoxically related by way of contingent, flexible, and fluid networks and assemblages—reigned supreme, at the expense of *event*: the possibility of material transformations borne of dialectical diagnosis and critical reflection.[47] The rise of affect studies in music was considerably enmeshed in this broad turn to non-Marxist materialism. If irreducible contextualism was the law of the new musicology of the late twentieth century, this brand of materialism became a guiding method for music studies in the early twenty-first century. The turn to affect as an object of investigation was a symptom of this general shift.

What is interesting about the materialist swerve toward affect was the striking extent to which it was fundamentally at odds with the contemporary consumer-electronics model of the world—the material infrastructures of digitality—which are characterized by discretization, abstraction, statistical and symbolic orders, and the modeling of formal systems directly. In other words, although these kinds of theoretical reflections on affect tended opportunistically to deploy insights from a free market of disciplines (ranging from acoustics to neuroscience and entangled in precarious, messy assemblages), the coalescence around a materialist position was curiously delinked from the primary modus of its own technological age: statistical analysis, formal modeling, digital abstraction, and so on. At the height of the digital paradigm, we paradoxically witnessed what Benjamin Boysen and Alexander Galloway call "semiophobia"—a fear of signs, symbols, and forms—and the privileging of embodiment and materiality, exemplified in the innards of affect.[48] By trusting material perception above semiotic abstraction, affect theory thereby generally missed the discretized aspects of sound that, as often as not, are the conditioning ground for digital analogs of affect. It is as if the affect phenomenon—its ineffable material gravitas—nostalgically resisted assimilation to the digital in the heyday of the digital. It is within the ruling paradigm of the analog, one might say, that contemporary affect lies.

Notes

I would like to thank Judith Lochhead and Steve Decatur Smith for their considerably helpful edits of the first draft of this chapter. Additional interlocutors include Finn Brunton, Lily Chumley, Eric Drott, Jessica Feldman, Alexander Galloway, Roger Grant, Benjamin Kafka, Ruth Leys, and Stephán-Eloïse Gras, whose work inspired much of my thinking here. Sections of this chapter draw on work that has appeared in previous publications, notably "The Executing Machine: Deleuze, Boulez, and the Politics of Desire," in *The Dark Precursor: Deleuze and Artistic Research*, ed. Paulo de Assis and Paolo Giudici (Leuven: Leuven University Press, 2017), 36–55; and "Political Economy of Music Streaming: Distributed Networks, Surveillance, and Automation," in *The Cambridge Companion to Music in Digital Culture*, ed. Nicholas Cook, Monique M. Ingalls, and David Trippett (Cambridge and New York: Cambridge University Press, 2019), 274–97. Paraphrases and citations are reprinted with permission.

1. The literature on the subject is vast, ranging from the social and subjective effects of technology on the physical and mental functioning of the body to the way technology can be designed to amplify compulsion in an environment of risk and reward. See, e.g., Linda F. Hogle, ed., *Regenerative Medicine Ethics: Governing Research and Knowledge Practices* (New York: Springer, 2014), or Natasha Dow Schüll, *Addiction by Design: Machine Gambling in Las Vegas* (Princeton, NJ: Princeton University Press, 2012). More recently, with the algorithmically amplified spread of online disinformation and political propaganda, questions surrounding subjective engagement with civic discourse (particularly as it relates to the free exchange of ideas, on the one hand, and data privacy, on the other) have become hotly debated in popular writing as well. See, e.g., Kathleen Hall Jamieson, *Cyberwar: How Russian Hackers Helped Elect a President; What We Don't, Can't, and Do Know* (New York: Oxford University Press, 2018); or Lee Rainie, Janna Anderson, and Jonathan Albright, "The Future of Free Speech, Trolls, Anonymity, and Fake News Online," Pew Research Center: Internet, Science & Tech, Washington, DC, March 29, 2017, https://www.pewresearch.org/internet/2017/03/29/the-future-of-free-speech-trolls-anonymity-and-fake-news-online/. This is but a small, random sample of an outpouring of commentary and writing toward the end of the second decade of the twenty-first century.

2. Of interest here are technical advances for policing that criminologists and criminal justice scholars call information-based (or "soft") technologies, which are contrasted with material-based (or "hard") ones. Soft technologies introduced into policing in America range from on-the-ground law-enforcement technologies (including mobile data centers, automated field reporting systems, computer-aided dispatch tools, record management systems, and software for automated fingerprint identification) to predictively oriented technologies (including automated risk and threat assessment instruments, classification and crime analysis software, tools for data sharing and system integration, and systems for monitoring the geolocation of populations). For a description of commonly acquired soft technologies toward the end of the twentieth century (and the scope of their federal funding), see Elizabeth Groff and Tom McEwen, "Identifying and Measuring the Effects of Information Technologies on Law Enforcement Agencies" (Washington, DC: U.S. Department of Justice, Office of Community Oriented Policing Programs, 2008). For a critical assessment

of contemporary policing technologies, see James Byrne and D. Rebovich, eds., *The New Technology of Crime, Law and Social Control* (Monsey, NY: Criminal Justice Press, 2007). For an investigation of the wholesale incorporation of surveillance technologies into the basic economic functioning of capitalism, see Shoshana Zuboff, *The Age of Surveillance Capitalism: The Fight for a Human Future at the New Frontier of Power* (London: Profile Books, 2019).

3. The literature examining the relationship between digital data capture and privacy policy is vast. While the exact catalysts for the vast data-collection practices of private companies in the first decades of the twenty-first century are not definitely settled, laws including Section 230 of the Telecommunications Act (1996) and Section 512 of Title 17 of the U.S. code (known as the "safe harbor" provision) of the 1998 Digital Millennium Copyright Act (DMCA) paved the legal way for the uploading of free user-generated content (UGC) with little legal liability for platform providers. Providers neither paid for, nor were they responsible for, the quality or veracity of uploaded content. These proprietary platforms were further entitled to track users and harvest their online data without restrictions. These new rulings effectively relocated the legal and financial risk from online platforms to users. For an account of data privacy, data security, the management of user data, and procedures for third-party requests for data and metadata in the context of *music* streaming platforms, see section IV ("Internet-Dragnet") of Martin Scherzinger, "Political Economy of Music Streaming: Distributed Networks, Surveillance, and Automation," in *The Cambridge Companion to Music and Digital Culture*, ed. Nicholas Cook, Monique Marie Ingalls, and David Trippett (Cambridge and New York: Cambridge University Press, 2019), 274–97. For an excellent account of the harvesting, aggregation, and selling of data on music streaming platforms, see Eric Drott, "Music as a Technology of Surveillance," *Journal of the Society for American Music* 12, no. 3 (2018): 233–67.

4. Jodi Dean, "Affective Networks," *Media Tropes* 2, no. 2 (2010): 19–44, https://mediatropes.com/index.php/Mediatropes/article/view/11932.

5. Gilles Deleuze and Félix Guattari, *Anti-Oedipus*, vol. 1 of *Capitalism and Schizophrenia*, trans. Robert Hurley, Mark Seem, and Helen R. Lane (Minneapolis: University of Minnesota Press, 1983), 1. First published as *L'Anti-Œdipe*, vol. 1 of *Capitalisme et schizophrénie* (Paris: Éditions de Minuit, 1972).

6. On the concept of "decoding," see Stuart Hall, "Encoding, Decoding," in *The Cultural Studies Reader*, ed. Simon During (London and New York: Routledge, 1993), 477–87. On the concept of "prosumption," see Marshall McLuhan and Nevitt Barrington, *Take Today: The Executive as Dropout* (New York: Harcourt Brace Jovanovich, 1972); and Dan Tapscott, *The Digital Economy: Promise and Peril in the Age of Networked Intelligence* (New York: McGraw-Hill, 1995).

7. Adam Gopnik, "The Information: How the Internet Gets Inside Us," *The New Yorker*, February 14 & 21, 2011.

8. Toward the end of the second decade of the twenty-first century, the dominant streaming platforms all tended to diversify their media platforms in an effort to secure a proprietary network-based monopoly. YouTube's system for streaming media included films (on YouTube Premium, initially known as YouTube Red) as well as a download functionality. At Apple Music, the streaming service included video programming (such as James Corden's "Carpool Karaoke"), while Facebook's Instagram introduced long-form video onto its platform. Spotify, known for its signature playlists (such as RapCaviar), also began to include podcasts and video in 2018, with aspects of virtual reality soon to follow.

9. Richard Stallman, "The Gnu Manifesto," gnu.org, first published 1983, accessed November 23, 2018, https://www.gnu.org/gnu/manifesto.en.html.

10. Clay Shirky, "The Music Business and the Big Flip," January 21, 2003, "Networks, Economics, and Culture" mailing, accessed November 23, 2018, http://www.shirky.com/writings/music_flip.html.

11. Paolo Virno, "Post-Fordist Semblance," trans. Max Henninger, *SubStance* issue 112 (vol. 36, no. 1) (2007): 42–46.

12. Martin Scherzinger, "Alchemies of Sanctioned Value: Music, Networks, Law," in *Artistic Citizenship: Artistry, Social Responsibility, and Ethical Praxis*, ed. David J. Elliott, Marissa Silverman, and Wayne D. Bowman (Oxford University Press, 2016), 363.

13. F. M. Scherer, *Quarter Notes and Bank Notes: The Economics of Music Composition in the Eighteenth and Nineteenth Centuries* (Princeton, NJ: Princeton University Press, 2004), 115.

14. Joseph A. Schumpeter, quoted in Scherer, *Quarter Notes and Bank Notes*, 115. For a discussion of the dialectic of chance and planning, see Max Horkeimer and Theodor W. Adorno, "The Culture Industry," in *Dialectic of Enlightenment* (New York: Continuum, 1997).

15. Ludwig van Beethoven, quoted in Scherer, *Quarter Notes and Bank Notes*, 85. See also Martin Scherzinger, "Toward a History of Digital Music: New Technology, Business Practices, and Intellectual Property," in *The Cambridge Companion to Music and Digital Culture*, ed. Nicholas Cook, Monique Marie Ingalls, and David Trippett (Cambridge and New York: Cambridge University Press, 2019), 33–57.

16. Yochai Benkler, "Voluntary Payment Models" (Boston, MA: Berkman Center for Internet & Society at Harvard University, 2011), accessed November 23, 2018, https://pdfs.semanticscholar.org/4c24/8de51703584c27f82814ea116e7a350c51d3.pdf. See also Benkler, *The Wealth of Networks: How Social Production Transforms Markets and Freedoms* (New Haven. CT: Yale University Press, 2006).

17. Andrew Ross, *Nice Work If You Can Get It: Life and Labor in Precarious Times* (New York: New York University Press, 2009).

18. Brian Massumi, *Parables for the Virtual: Movement, Affect, Sensation* (Durham, NC: Duke University Press, 2002), 26.

19. Ibid., 25.

20. Ibid., 33, 35, 36.

21. Ibid., 40.

22. Ibid., 33.

23. Ibid., 25.

24. Jon Ronson, "Josh Ostrovsky: 'The Internet Is Like a Giant Weird Orgy.'" *Guardian*, November 7, 2015, accessed June 13, 2017, https://www.theguardian.com/technology/2015/nov/07/josh-ostrovsky-fat-jew-jon-ronson-instagram.

25. Virno, "Post-Fordist Semblance," 42.

26. Gilles Deleuze and Félix Guattari, *A Thousand Plateaus: Capitalism and Schizophrenia*, trans. Brian Massumi (Minneapolis: University of Minnesota Press, 1987), 109.

27. Ronson, "Josh Ostrovsky."

28. Marco Revelli, "Worker Identity in the Factory Desert," trans. Ed Emory, in *Radical Thought in Italy: A Potential Politics*, ed. Paolo Virno and Michael Hardt (Minneapolis: University of Minnesota Press, 1996), 116–22.

29. Karl Marx and Frederick Engels, *Manifesto of the Communist Party* (1848), Marxists Internet Archive, 2010, 16, accessed on November 23, 2018, https://www.marxists.org/archive/marx/works/download/pdf/Manifesto.pdf.

30. Hannah Arendt, *The Origins of Totalitarianism* (1951; New York: Harcourt Brace Jovanovich, 1976).

31. Elon Musk, "Is Life a Video Game?" Code Conference, 2016, accessed November 23, 2018, https://www.youtube.com/watch?v=2KK_kzrJPS8.

32. Devin Powell, "A Flexible Circuit Has Been Injected into Living Brains," *Smithsonian*, 2015, accessed November 23, 2018, https://www.smithsonianmag.com/science-nature/flexible-circuit-has-been-injected-living-brains-180955525/.

33. Massumi, *Parables for the Virtual*.

34. Hans Ulrich Gumbrecht, *Production of Presence: What Meaning Cannot Convey* (Stanford, CA: Stanford University Press, 2004).

35. Ibid., 97.

36. Massumi, *Parables for the Virtual*, 25, 35.

37. Roger Mathew Grant, "Music Lessons on Affect and Its Objects," *Representations* 144, no. 1 (2018): 34–60.

38. Johann Mattheson and Reinhard Keiser, *Das neu-eröffnete Orchestre, oder Universelle und gründliche Anleitung, wie ein Galant Homme einen vollkommenen Begriff von der Hoheit und Würde der edlen Music erlangen . . . möge* (Hamburg: Benjamin Schillers Wittwe, 1713), 252.

39. On the concept of sonotropism, see Martin Scherzinger, "On Sonotropism," *Contemporary Music Review* 31, nos. 5–6 (2012): 345–51.

40. The latter term—a curious conjunction of the terms "acoustics" and "epistemology"—was coined by Steven Feld in 1992. See Feld, "Acoustemology," in *Keywords in Sound*, ed. David Novak and Matt Sakakeeny (Durham, NC: Duke University Press, 2015), 12–21.

41. On musical entrainment in software, see Martin Scherzinger, "Algorithmic Audition: Modeling Musical Perception," in *Imagined Forms: Modeling Material Culture*, ed. Martin Brueckner, Sandy Isenstadt, and Sarah Wasserman (Chicago: University of Chicago Press, 2020).

42. See "Future Soldier 2030 Initiative," *Wired*, 2009, https://www.wired.com/images_blogs/dangerroom/2009/05/dplus2009_11641-1.pdf.

43. The literature on the subject is too vast to summarize here. In the contemporary arena of clinical psychology, theories of the emotions are axiomatically grounded in the idea that the nervous system functions autonomically. For a typical account of this idea, see, e.g., Robert W. Levenson, "Emotion and the Autonomic Nervous System: A Prospectus for Research on Autonomic Specificity," in *Social Psychophysiology and Emotion: Theory and Clinical Applications*, ed. Hugh Wagner (Chichester and New York: John Wiley & Sons, 1988), 17–42. As to the practical deployment of voice analysis in matters pertaining to creditworthiness, health assessment, crime prevention, etc., the literature is again too vast to summarize here. For one example of the use of layered voice analysis in the context of lie detection in service of law enforcement, see "Layered Voice Analysis Test Report Finds Arjul Rai Guilty," webindia123, 2013, accessed November 23, 2018, https://news.webindia123.com/news/Articles/India/20131113/2283258.html.

44. Beth Semel, "Listening Like a Computer: Computational Psychiatry and the Re-Coding of Psychiatric Coding," presentation delivered at the Science, Technology and Society Seminar: STS Circle at Harvard, December 2, 2019.

45. Yoram Levanon and Lan Lossos-Shifrin, System for Indicating Emotional Attitudes through Intonation Analysis and Methods Thereof, US Patent 8078470 B2, filed December 20, 2006, and issued December 13, 2011, 1. See also Levanon and Lossos-Shifrin, System and Method for Determining a Personal SHG Profile by Voice Analysis, US Patent 7917366 B1, filed September 28, 2006, and issued March 29, 2011.

46. For an example of federally funded research into technologies for voice stress analysis (VSA) to detect deception in voice communications, see Darren Haddad, Sharon Walter, Roy Ratley, and Megan Smith, "Investigation and Evaluation of Voice Stress Analysis Technology," Final Report, February 13, 2002, https://www.ncjrs.gov/pdffiles1/nij/193832.pdf.

47. Alain Badiou, *Logics of Worlds: Being and Event, 2*, trans. Alberto Toscano (London and New York: Continuum, 2009).

48. Benjamin Boysen, "The Embarrassment of Being Human: A Critique of New Materialism and Object-Oriented Ontology," *Orbis Litterarum* 73, no. 3, (2018): 225–42; and Alexander Galloway, "Peak Analog," March 22, 2019, http://cultureandcommunication.org/galloway/peak-analog.

CHAPTER 9

Musical Affect, Autobiographical Memory, and Collective Individuation in Thomas Bernhard's *Correction*

Christopher Haworth

Introduction: Refuting the Subjectivization of Affect

Much recent critical debate in affect theory has centered on the question of affect's autonomy. Does affect operate independently of signification and semiosis, or is it always mediated by higher-level systems of meaning? On one side of the argument lie those theorists, such as Brian Massumi and Steve Goodman, for whom affect serves as a means to analyze human receptivity in parahuman terms. In an influential article from 1995, Massumi emphasizes the disconnection between a human "content" and a pre- or extrahuman "effect": "The primacy of the affective is marked by a gap between content and effect: it would appear that the strength or duration of an image's effect is not logically connected to the content in any straightforward way."[1] Goodman, too, insists on this separation: "Interoception, which is sensitive to intensity minus quality . . . preempts exteroception in that it makes decisions *before* the consciousness of extensive sensory objects fully emerges."[2] Both writers take a cue from Gilles Deleuze and Félix Guattari (who in turn take their cue from Baruch Spinoza) in defining affect in terms of a quantifiable power that is shared between living and nonliving things of the natural and cultural world.

> A body is not defined by the form that determines it nor as a determinate substance or subject nor by the organs it possesses or the functions it fulfills. . . . [A] body is defined only by a longitude and a latitude: in other words the sum total of the material elements belonging to it under given relations of movement and rest, speed

and slowness (longitude); the sum total of the intensive affects it is capable of at a given power or degree of potential (latitude).³

Flowing between human and nonhuman, living and nonliving, affect here is indifferent to the "semiotic regimes" it undergoes in the body that "captures" it.⁴

But there are those for whom affect cannot be decoupled from cultural processes of meaning making. Brian Kane has critiqued the "ontological turn" in sound studies, which he sees as bound up with a material-affective understanding of sound.⁵ Picking up Goodman's assertion that there is a disjunction (a "split second") between the autonomous affective system and conscious experience, Kane seeks to demonstrate that the affective capacity of sound is mediated by knowledge.⁶ His example is drawn from Franz Kafka's novel *The Burrower*, in which a mole is tormented by a sound that he cannot name or localize. *Pace* Goodman, Kane argues that resolving the location and source of this sound would diminish the affect of fear and anxiety that it caused:

> Since the ontological situation has not changed, the only way to account for the change in affect would be to appeal to something other than ontology, namely a change in the burrower's knowledge about the situation, or a change in the status of the sound's signification. Yet, if affect is ontological, operating at an imperceptible level beneath the subject's representation, how can a change in knowledge produce a change in affect?⁷

Kane later argues that the material-affective ontology that Goodman (alongside Greg Hainge and Christoph Cox) describes is actually a form of *ontography* rather than ontology: a description of the ontological commitments or "world-making" practices of particular culturally local groups.⁸

Gary Tomlinson goes even further in his insistence on the integral links between affect, culture, and consciousness. Although following Kane in arguing against those who "have tried to knock down distinguishing markers in the world of lived experience ... to create a single spectrum of affective intensities extending throughout the biosphere," he does not only do this by insisting on the codependency of knowledge and affect.⁹ Instead, he widens the field of signification to protolinguistic and protomusical behaviours, viewing the transmission of affect as part of a "far-reaching" semiosis, "a nonsymbolic making of signs that embraces but exceeds the human."¹⁰ Drawing on the interdisciplinary field of biosemiotics, he speculates that the "burgeoning of semiosis" may have emerged "from within a cosmos organized by information alone"—a world "beckoning toward both the parahuman and the prehuman."[11] The challenge for Tomlinson, then, is to understand how sign making emerges from within a wider informational cosmos and extends across a wider range of information-processing species.

This move to understand affect in terms of a nonsymbolic semiosis, inseparable from thought and reason, opens onto a wider musicological tradition. Both Naomi Cumming's Gadamerian hermeneutics of musical subjectivity and Tia DeNora's work on music as a "technology of the self" offer important precursors to the cool-headed critiques of Kane and Tomlinson.[12] Running through these authors' works is a question not only of signification but also of subjectification. How does art come to assume emotional significance in the lives of those that it touches? And how, recursively, can aesthetic experiences be said to *constitute* subjects such that music is integrated into everyday processes of affective and emotional self-maintenance, iteratively shaping individuals' immediate and future senses of self? DeNora's work in particular makes important moves toward answering these questions. Her ethnographic subjects frequently describe using music to help them constitute a coherent sense of self and identity, whether as an aide-mémoire linked to particular places and times or as resource for structuring and regulating aesthetic agency.[13] As DeNora provocatively argues, these uses of music are not merely expressivist—they are not simply a case of individuals delegating their internal feeling states to music and then using music to recall them, as in the case of a mirror that simply reflects what is in front of it. Rather, music for DeNora is a "magic mirror," for at the same time as it "allows one to 'see one's self' . . . its specific material properties also come to configure (for example, transfigure, disfigure) the image reflected in and through its (perceived) structures."[14]

The idea that music may partially constitute the intrapersonal associations that are attributed to it seems to contradict our most intimate musical experiences. In such a formulation, music is much more than simply the "soundtrack to your life," as the commonplace goes. Instead, it is granted a constitutive agency, having the power to actively shape the image (to use DeNora's mirror metaphor) that it is assumed to passively reflect. Such a view is consistent with the semiotics of affect that Cumming and Tomlinson advance, and at odds with notions of the autonomy of affect. If a particular piece of music has an affective "grammar," then it follows that individuals may search for and discover themselves within it. Furthermore, other individuals may do this as well: seeing ourselves in the "surface" of the mirror would then constitute a form of "individuation," in the Simondonian sense.[15] Thus, rather than imagining an individual surrounded by their individual music tastes, as implied by the "soundtrack to your life" metaphor, it may be more useful to envisage particular instances of music surrounded by individual subjects, each "transducing" the music's affective contours. Following Gadamer's refutation of the "subjectivization of aesthetics,"[16] the lesson from Cumming, Tomlinson, and Simondon is that we should also refute the "subjectivization of affect," turning our attention instead to its shared grammars and capacities for collective individuation.[17]

This chapter represents a germinal attempt to understand these shared grammars and collective individuations. I begin my inquiry by analyzing a fragment from *Correction*, a 1975 novel by the Austrian author Thomas Bernhard. Although ostensibly focused on "nature" rather than music, the fragment offers a new means by which to understand the interplay between musically evoked affect, memory, and the constitution of self. The focus of my analysis is specifically on the capacity of recorded music to act as a technology for memory recall. Variously referred to as "musically evoked autobiographical memory," "sonic déjà vu," "involuntary memory," or "sonic anamnesis," the effect, as Jean-François Augoyard and Henri Torgue put it, is one of "a reminiscence, in which a past situation or atmosphere is brought back to the listener's consciousness, provoked by a particular signal or sonic context."[18] The scholarly and literary interest in these experiences has so far been in the insights they provide into the phenomenology of temporal experience. This chapter departs from first-person phenomenology, however, to probe the extent to which recorded music affords the autobiographical experiences that it seems to neutrally house. Alongside *Correction*, the examples of collective affective individuation I draw upon come from a wide range of cultural referents, from Robert Altman's *Nashville* to the "divorce albums" of Phil Collins. While I do not hope to put these questions to rest in a chapter of this length, I intend at least to open up the problem for future research on music and affect.

"Our Way to School": Affect, Subjectivity, and the Life Course

Bernhard's *Correction* details the reunion of two childhood friends, Hoeller and the unnamed narrator, in the wake of their mutual friend Roithamer's suicide. Roithamer's story is told posthumously: the first half through the narrator's reacquaintance with Hoeller, with whom Roithamer was staying when he killed himself, and the second half through the notes and diaries he left behind. As children they had walked to school together through a wild and apparently dangerous stretch of mountainous and forested countryside in rural Austria. Roithamer was born into a rich aristocratic family living on an estate called Altensam, whilst the other two boys were less privileged. But Roithamer's childhood was by far the most difficult of the three, full of familial hatred, violence, and misunderstanding. The story is told from Hoeller's garret, part of a fantastic house overlooking a rushing river in the remote Aurach gorge that had inspired Roithamer. Later, the garret was the scene of his suicide.

Despite its having become something of a cliché to say it, the protagonist of the story is as much the absent Roithamer as it is the landscape that surrounds them: the black woods of Carinthia. Much of the literary description is bound up in the explication, correction, and rewriting of the incredible places within these woods, as though Bernhard were trying to outstrip language and bring the reader into unmediated contact with the affective experience. In a particularly exhilarating passage, the narrator finally breaks the reticence between the Hoeller and the narrator to offer an interpretation of their friend's suicide. What follows is an unbroken outpouring spanning four pages in which he details with increasing momentum how the three friends used to walk to school together, Roithamer coming down from Altensam to meet Hoeller and then finally himself:

> It was on our way to school that we had our most intense experiences, I said, when we think of everything on that way to school over the rocks and through the woods, along the Aurach, past the mine workers' cottages and on past Stocket, that is, right through the village, where we noticed all sorts of things, *things that would determine our lives*, rich in meanings, already determining the whole shape of our future and in fact already controlling it, since actually everything we are today, everything we see and observe and encounter on its way toward us, is influenced by what we saw and observed on our way to school then, if it isn't altogether made up of it.... did he, Hoeller, also remember our way to school so well, did he remember many thousands and hundreds of thousands of details, sensations, perceptions, feelings, intimations of feelings, those earliest important beginnings of thought on our way to school ... I could remember those thousands, hundreds of thousands of weather conditions on our walk to school, abrupt shifts in the weather, I felt them suddenly take place, transforming our way to school from one minute to the next and thereby transforming us inside from one minute to the next, and the incessant changing of colors in the woods and in the

Aurach as it tumbled headlong from the woods down to the plain, everything on our way to school had always been changes of color and of temperatures and of our moods, that muggy atmosphere in the summertime that sickened us on our way to school so that we came to be horribly sick later in school; or the cold in winter that we could cope with only by attacking it all along the way to school, we had to counterattack the cold, *stomping* all bundled up and scared through the deep, the deepest snow.... Our way to school took its course just as our subsequent life did, I said, with all its passages through darkness, back to light, with all its habits and unexpected coincidences, our way through life like our way to school kept being subjected to abrupt changes of weather, kept following the course of torrential river always to be feared, for as we always lived in fear on our way to school, fear of falling into the raging Aurach among others, so on our way through life we always lived in extreme fear of falling into this river where we lived, always terrified of this river which is invisible but always torrential and always deadly.[19]

Henri Bergson noted an "invincible tendency" of the mind that "impels us to think on all occasions of things rather than movements," and this is nowhere more apparent than in the customary tendency of the narrative arts to describe formative experiences in terms of epiphanies: transformative experiences that come, retroactively, to be associated with singular influential figures and events from one's life.[20] What the narrator of *Correction* depicts in the above account is a captivating challenge to this narrative mode. Far from being reducible to a single event or person, the narrator recalls a system of affects, set in motion by his movement through the world. Weather systems, flows, changes of temperature, colors, and moods: the force of the characters' formative experiences is affective, not representational, and this is underlined when later the narrator concludes that "the most conspicuous thing about the three of us walking to school together was our taciturnity."[21]

Although the affects are attributed to nature, it does not require a great interpretive leap to read this passage as an account of subjective musical experience. The changes in color, temperature, and atmosphere that the author recounts are sensory-affective qualities of the here and now whose meaning effects, like those of music, are predominantly indexical rather than symbolic. It is also possible to identify a formal correspondence between the prose in the passage and musical organization.[22] The repetition of "our way to school"—ten mentions in the quote—operates as a motif that is subsequently modified and altered in order to cement particular rhetorical associations (way to school/way through life). However, the connection I wish to examine concerns a more fundamental relation between the experience recounted and musical subjectivity. A more conventional narrative would have the narrator return to his childhood home and retrace the steps of the way to school, the sensory experience triggering involuntary memories in the mode of Proustian recollection or anamnesis. In this trope, the ritual of the walk to school would be like musically evoked autobiographical memory, where revisiting a particular record induces an instantaneous recollection of the people and events it originally accompanied. Yet although the prose in this extract belongs to the literary trope of revelation or epiphany, the narrator does not describe a sensory-driven anamnesis here. Instead, his realization is that the autonomic affective responses engendered by the walk to school actually determined the form that these experiences would later take in recollection. More than this, these experiences and their later recollections would partially determine the future courses that the protagonists' lives would take.

Considered as an account of musical experience, this marks a critical difference from the customary accounts of feeling and autobiographical detail that we frequently hear rehearsed in response to music. Traditionally, arguments against these accounts fix on their arbitrariness. The memory that music evokes—be it of a past event, place, or relationship—is "there" inside us anyway. The fact that music summons it, bringing it into consciousness, is a quality or otherwise of the art form, albeit one that has no bearing on the essential detail it recalls. Music is therefore cast as simultaneously a recording and a playback device, capturing the present and playing back the past.[23] Furthermore, it is supposedly neutral; if it weren't then, others would recollect the same memory—we would each experience images and recollections equally. *Correction* is interesting because it strenuously positions the affective experience as the determining force of the associations it conjures, rather than wild nature (or music, in my reading) receiving its significance via the events it witnessed. When the narrator suggests that the walk to school had controlled everything they would become, he is implying that the emotional themes of their later lives—the sense of fear they would grow up with, for example—have their basis in this daily ritual. More bleakly, it also implies that the tragedy of Roithamer's suicide was already in a sense "written" by his having "experienced too much" in having the farthest to travel.

Bad Vibes: In the Air Tonight

However, if we extend this speculation that the present is implicit in the past to musical experience, we find ourselves in a delicate area. The interpretation above seems to recall the determinate "subliminal messages" that it was once popular to insert into rock and pop music. How is the ending of *Correction* different to the infamous Judas Priest suicides of 1990, where two teenage heavy metal fans believed they had heard the subliminal message "do it!" in one of the band's tracks and, tragically, interpreted it as a directive to kill themselves?[24] In its common formulation, affect shares with the subliminal message a bipartite structure—a "gap between content and effect," in Massumi's words— and this affinity can occasionally lead to a tendency to elide the two.[25] Like affect, the subliminal message operates independently of the explicit narrative, often seeming to contradict it. However, unlike affect, the content that is "revealed" fully conforms to semantic interpretation; if it did not, then there would be no message to be decoded. The specificity of affect, then, if not its autonomy, is derived precisely from the fact that it does not submit to this cryptographic game of appearances. As already stated, this does not mean that affect is without meaning, but rather that incorporating it into semiotics requires that we step outside of symbolic communication.[26]

Somewhere between Massumian autonomy and the cryptographic subliminal message lies the filmmaker Robert Altman's notion of "subliminal reality."[27] Altman's films neatly conform to the bipartite structure identified by Massumi, but the attendant theory is more amenable to the emergence of tacitly understood collective meaning that I want to pursue. Similarly to Bernhard, Altman has described his approach as a kind of antinarrative, in which the explicit structure is not linear; instead, a certain "atmosphere" or "feeling" is created. He writes that audiences should "walk away ... not being able to articulate what they think about it. ... I'm more interested in touching people on an unconscious basis to where they sense something rather than intellectually know or agree to something."[28] In *Organs without Bodies*, Slavoj Žižek offers a memorable analysis of Altman's subliminal reality. Concerning the director's 1975 film *Nashville*, he writes: "When violence explodes at the end (the murder of Barbara Jean at the concert), this explosion, although unprepared and unaccounted for at the level of the explicit narrative line, is nonetheless experienced as fully justified, since the ground was laid at the level of signs circulating in the film's 'subliminal reality.'"[29] Yet, persuasive though it is, Žižek's analysis here suffers from a tendency to tell more than it shows—we have to take his word for it that audiences experience the meaning effects he describes. A swerve into popular-music scholarship can help fill some of the lacunae in his account. At one level, popular music is distinctive in the extent to which it prioritizes feeling over thinking. Writing about electronic dance music, Luis-Manuel Garcia calls this an "affective epistemology," where "feeling someone/something provides more authentic access to truth than disinterested rationality."[30] But more than this, collective feeling in popular music can often seize hermeneutic control of music, standing in for its explicit meaning. Joshua Clover, for example, describes how "Groove Is in the Heart" by the U.S. band Deee-Lite was swept up by the feeling of renewal in Europe in 1989, as the song's line "no walls, only the bridge" took on its own meaning in reception.[31] In a more recent example, Black Lives Matter protesters in downtown Los Angeles used Kendrick Lamar's "Alright" to channel and propagate collective resistance toward the incoming Trump administration.

Yet as the way-to-school section of *Correction* show, affective contagion can also be a negative social force, and musically induced affect is no different. To draw this into focus, my final example is a case study in negative affective consensus, or "affect as bad vibe": the so-called divorce albums of Phil Collins. These albums, specifically *Face Value* and *Hello I Must Be Going*, have over time become synonymous with a certain manifestation of the "soundtrack to your life" trope cited earlier. Released in 1981, both are credited with soundtracking the tail end of the "divorce boom" that started in the 1970s—hence their colloquial name. Yet neither of the two records explicitly touches on divorce as a theme. In fact, the only song Collins wrote on the subject was "Doesn't Anybody Stay Together Anymore?," which appeared much later, on 1985's *No Jacket Required*. In an interview for *Playboy* in 1986, he talked about the inspiration for the song: "You know, I was very happily married to Jill, my present wife, when I wrote it, but I had been divorced, my manager was getting divorced, a couple of good friends were getting divorced, and I thought, What's going on? Doesn't anybody stay together anymore? The song came from that."[32] Drawing on Žižek's analysis of *Nashville*, we might mischievously speculate that the seed for this potent contagion, seeming to indiscriminately wreck the marriages of those around him, was planted at the level of *feeling*—in the unvocalized, affective signs that structure the earlier "divorce" records. The divorce anthem par excellence is "In the Air Tonight," from *Face Value*. The object of his grief is never stated, his interlocutor is never named, its bitterness just hangs there, "in the air." Let's not kid ourselves, though: everything is there if we care to look for it. If the passable opening metaphor—"well if you told me you were drowning, I would not lend a hand"—is too obscure, then by the end of the verse we are clear as crystal: "I saw what you did, I saw it with my own two eyes, so you can wipe off that grin, I know where you've been, it's all been a pack of lies." In the video Collins is featured alone, facing a corridor of closed doors and opening them one by one until he is blinded by light, cementing the cuckolded-lover subtext. All the same, none of this can account for the way this song has come to stand for what it does, as a soundtrack to so many marriage breakups in the early 1980s, calling up unpleasant memories in the minds of an entire generation of children of the late twentieth century. Its capacity to *affect* is there in its subtext of marriage breakdown as feeling, its capacity to *be* affected filled by its having been made retroactively into a cultural signifier for divorce. Put more bluntly, its huge chart success was helped by divorce as a sociocultural trend, and its atmosphere, affect, and subliminal reality helped the trend develop as divorce rates in the United Kingdom and the United States hit a new peak in the early 1980s.

Conclusion

Augoyard and Torque's notion of sonic anamnesis, as a "reminiscence, in which a past situation or atmosphere is brought back to the listener's consciousness, provoked by a particular signal or sonic context," is a deliberate play on the Platonic concept of *anamnesis*, meaning "loss of forgetfulness."[33] Speculatively opening up the relationships among contagion, affect, and collective individuation in popular music, as I have done in this chapter, offers an even more audacious engagement with this problematic concept, gesturing as it does toward loss of forgetfulness—even a Jungian synchronicity—wherein a contingent and transcendent shared meaning overdetermines the explicit narrative of a song or album. Kodwo Eshun has referred to the affective experience of hearing recognizable samples in popular music and hip-hop as "abduction"—a temporary loss of self—and his stress on the strangeness of anamnesis is valuable.[34] For even if we consider the effect of musically evoked anamnesis as something relatively benign and innocent, surprising us with a long-forgotten place or person, one can still be unsettled by what it tells us about ourselves. How did something so trivial come to take on this symbolic form, as though a flattened memory image had survived the raw contingency of present experience, coming to fixedly represent a time, person, or place retrospectively? For Deleuze, this marked disconnect is possible because it was fixed in the first place: "The past and the present do not denote two successive moments, but two elements which coexist."[35] Put into Deleuze's words, what we have is essentially a present that never becomes the past, and a past that never was present. The two elements do not "touch" in the manner of a hand continually taking a baton and passing it back. Rather, they are distinct and contemporaneous, which Deleuze sees as a disjunction between being and becoming:

> We have great difficulty in understanding a survival of the past in itself because we believe that the past is no longer, that it has ceased to be. We have thus confused Being with being present. Nevertheless, the present is not; rather, it is pure becoming, always outside itself. It is not, but it acts. Its proper element is not being but the active and the useful. The past, on the other hand, has ceased to act or to be useful. But it has not ceased to be. Useless and inactive, impassive, it IS, in the full sense of the word: It is identical with being in itself.[36]

Referring back to *Correction*, we can see the walk-to-school passage as an attempt to capture in writing the present that is "always outside itself" rather than the "useless and inactive" past, which would be the autobiographical memory that a song, album, or change in weather evokes. The excerpt from *Correction* reminds us that the body is the proper site of the present: the sphere of action, emotion, and affectivity. When music affects us, it does not "refer" to emotions or feelings in the abstract. They take place now and are the very grain of being present. The past, having ceased to act or be useful, becomes an icon; it never was ("the present is not") but now it "is," as a memory image. And it is this double passing that we mourn when music regresses us to a previous time: the present's never having been, and the past's having lost its usefulness. This is how it becomes possible for contemporary revivalist popular-music genres to produce vivid nostalgia for periods of history that the audiences and artists themselves are not old enough to have experienced firsthand. "It is *all* our past," writes Deleuze: cultural memory and individual memory merge to form the one surplus.[37] And musical affect interpolates the process, lessening the friction with which personal and collective memory may coalesce.

Notes

1. Brian Massumi, "The Autonomy of Affect," in "Politics of Systems and Environments, Part II," *Cultural Critique* 31 (Autumn 1995): 84.

2. Steve Goodman, *Sonic Warfare: Sound, Affect, and the Ecology of Fear* (Cambridge, MA: MIT Press, 2010), 48.

3. Gilles Deleuze and Félix Guattari, *A Thousand Plateaus: Capitalism and Schizophrenia*, new ed. (London: A & C Black, 2004), 260.

4. Ibid., 227.

5. Kane takes the "ontological turn" to be evidence of a sound studies/auditory culture divide; Brian Kane, "Sound Studies without Auditory Culture: A Critique of the Ontological Turn," *Sound Studies* 1, no. 1 (2015). However, it is more plausible when understood as a split between sound art theory and sound studies. Christoph Cox, Greg Hainge, Steve Goodman, Seth Kim-Cohen, and Salomé Voegelin (the last of whom he addresses in a different article) are united by their shared commitment to theorizing sound as an aesthetic material, even if Goodman is more focused on electronic music than sound art. See Cox, *Sonic Flux: Sound, Art, Metaphysics* (Chicago: University of Chicago Press, 2018); Hainge, *Noise Matters: Towards an Ontology of Noise* (New York: Bloomsbury Academic, 2013); Goodman, *Sonic Warfare: Sound, Affect, and the Ecology of Fear* (Cambridge, MA: MIT Press, 2010); Kim-Cohen, *In the Blink of an Ear: Toward a Non-Cochlear Sonic Art* (United States: Continuum, 2009), and Voegelin, *Listening to Noise and Silence: Towards a Philosophy of Sound Art* (New York: Continuum, 2010).

6. Kane, "Sound Studies without Auditory Culture," is indebted to an earlier critique of Brian Massumi by Ruth Leys; see Leys, "The Turn to Affect: A Critique," *Critical Inquiry* 37, no. 3 (2011): 434–72.

7. Kane, "Sound Studies without Auditory Culture," 6–7.

8. Ibid., 16.

9. Gary Tomlinson, "Sign, Affect, and Musicking before the Human," this book: 72.

10. Ibid., 73.

11. Ibid., 76.

12. Naomi Cumming, *The Sonic Self: Musical Subjectivity and Signification* (Bloomington: Indiana University Press, 2000); and Tia DeNora, *Music in Everyday Life* (Cambridge: Cambridge University Press, 2000).

13. DeNora, *Music in Everyday Life*, 66.

14. Ibid., 70.

15. Gilbert Simondon argues that the unity of the individual does not preexist the processes of individuation that act upon it, nor does an individual ever reach the stage of being fully "individuated." An individual is always between individuations—always becoming— and this process is always relative to the individual's social and collective milieu. In this essay, music listening is conceived as a process of individuation. See David Scott, *Gilbert Simondon's Psychic and Collective Individuation: A Critical Introduction and Guide* (Edinburgh: Edinburgh University Press, 2014).

16. Hans-Georg Gadamer, *Truth and Method*, trans. rev. Joel Weinsheimer and Donald G. Marshall (London and New York: A & C Black, 2013), 39.

17. DeNora, *Music in Everyday Life*, 68.

18. Jean-François Augoyard and Henry Torgue, *Sonic Experience: A Guide to Everyday Sounds* (Montreal: McGill–Queen's University Press, 2014), 21.

19. Thomas Bernhard, *Correction*, trans. Sophie Wilkins (New York: Vintage International, 2010), 87–92.

20. Henri Bergson, *Matter and Memory* (Chelmsford, MA: Courier, 2012), 154.

21. Bernhard, *Correction*, 88.

22. Bernhard's love of music is well-known; his interest in the life and work of Glenn

Gould and the influence of musical form on his prose serve as common points of entry into his often forbidding literary style. Reading Bernhard's prose in music-analytical terms has also become something of a trope of literary criticism: see Andrea Reiter, "Thomas Bernhard's 'Musical Prose,'" in *Literature on the Threshold: The German Novel in the 1980s*, ed. Arthur Williams, Stuart Parkes, and Roland Smith (New York: Berg, 1990), 187–207; and Michael P. Olson, "Thomas Bernhard, Glenn Gould, and the Art of the Fugue: Contrapuntal Variations in *Der Untergeher*," in "Form and Style in Contemporary Austrian Literature," special issue, *Modern Austrian Literature* 24, no. 3/4 (1991): 73–83.

23. Steve Goodman expresses similar sentiments when he writes: "In other words, in that momentary flash, an instruction is communicated—record me! The flash abducts us into a past, potentially fictional but real, in that it forces an attitude of receptivity by compelling a vacation from the self—or, rather, a takeover of the body by an exterior entity, an audio virus programming your desire. Branding increasingly makes use of such memory glitches in which the distinction between past, present, and future becomes blurred." Goodman, *Sonic Warfare*, 150.

24. Nick Deriso, "Revisiting Judas Priest's Subliminal Lyrics Trial," Ultimate Classic Rock, accessed July 10, 2018, http://ultimateclassicrock.com/judas-priest-suicide-trial/.

25. Massumi, "The Autonomy of Affect," 84. In *Sonic Warfare*, Goodman deploys a host of auditory effects that he deems to take place subliminally—"affective tonality," "audio virology," "bass materialism," "subbass materialism," "logistics of affection," "subpolitics of frequency," "subliminal messaging"—yet the distinctions between these concepts is frequently elusive.

26. Tomlinson, "Sign, Affect, and Musicking," 74.

27. Cf. Robert T. Self, *Robert Altman's Subliminal Reality* (Minneapolis: University of Minnesota Press, 2002).

28. Hasti Sardashti, *"Short Cuts" and American Life and Society in Early Nineties*. Central Milton Keynes, UK: AuthorHouse, 2011), 29.

29. Slavoj Žižek, *Organs without Bodies: On Deleuze and Consequences* (New York: Routledge, 2004), 6.

30. Luis-Manuel Garcia, "Beats, Flesh, and Grain: Sonic Tactility and Affect in Electronic Dance Music," *Sound Studies* 1, no. 1 (2015): 60.

31. Joshua Clover, *1989: Bob Dylan Didn't Have This to Sing About* (Berkeley and Los Angeles: University of California Press, 2010), 101.

32. David Sheff, "Phil Collins Interview," *Playboy*, October 1986, accessed September 24, 2011, https://www.davidsheff.com/phil-collins.

33. Augoyard and Torgue, *Sonic Experience*, 21.

34. Kodwo Eshun, *More Brilliant than the Sun: Adventures in Sonic Fiction* (London: Quartet Books, 1998), 180.

35. Gilles Deleuze, *Bergsonism*, trans. Hugh Tomlinson and Barbara Habberjam (New York: Zone Books, 1988), 59.

36. Ibid., 55.

37. Ibid., 59.

PART 5

Temporalities of Sounding

CHAPTER 10

The "Sound" of Music

SONIC AGENCY AND THE DIALECTIC
OF FREEDOM AND CONSTRAINT IN
JAZZ IMPROVISATION

Lorenzo C. Simpson

It is a commonplace that jazz performers are characterized by the individuality of their style. This is often referred to as a musician's "sound"—the sensible embodiment of a player's artistic personality—which embraces both the player's quality of tone and their distinctive approach to rhythm and harmony.[1] If in "classical" or concert music our tendency is to think of a particular *instrument*, each associated with a body of historical knowledge genealogically handed down, in jazz we think instead of a particular *player*—that is, we have in mind not a trumpet, but a Miles Davis, Clifford Brown, or Nicholas Payton. That is because in jazz a performer's sound is a central component of musical expression. Yet, scant attention is paid to the sound of music in musicological discourse. I suggest that this lacuna can be linked to prevailing conceptions of the nature of the musical work. After focusing on the distinctiveness of sound as a matter of timbre or sound quality itself, I go on to consider the improvisational component of a musician's stylistic individuality, and I do so by developing the idea of the "fitting response" as a way to conceptualize how the jazz player intelligibly negotiates the dilemma that I characterize as the dialectic of freedom and constraint.

It is common to valorize stylistic individuality in jazz now, but of course it has not always been so. In 1926 the conservative German composer Hans Pfitzner, in his subtly titled book *The New Aesthetic of Musical Impotence*, deployed the trope of "soulless machinism" to describe jazz and was later joined, from the other end of the political spectrum, by Theodor Adorno in decrying the lack of musical agency found in jazz performance, a lack of agency that was signaled for them by this music's nonstandard sonorities.[2] As Adorno infamously put it: "The aim of jazz is the mechanical reproduction of a regressive moment, a castration symbolism. 'Give up your masculinity, let yourself be castrated,' the eunuchlike sound of the jazz band both mocks and proclaims, 'and you shall be rewarded, accepted into a fraternity which shares the mystery of impotence with you.'"[3]

Now, my aim here is not to set Adorno up as a straight man to be derisively dismissed—others have done that, and I have done a bit of it myself elsewhere—but rather to use him to foreground a blind spot that has impoverished accounts of performative agency in jazz. Timbre, or sonority, is a crucial component of stylistic individuality. I argue that in jazz, timbre is a central vehicle for the expression of musical agency and for the performance of identity; indeed, it is a sonic fingerprint of musical personality. Yet, though we do not lack musicological accounts of melody, understood as organized sequences of pitches, harmony, and rhythm—one might say, of those aspects of music that can, at least in principle, be notated or graphically encoded—relatively little attention seems to have been devoted to the purely sonic aspect of music. Discussions of the "sound" of music tend to be marginalized.[4]

I have suggested elsewhere that Adorno's relative silence on the issue of sonority—with the noted exception of his dismissing jazz's nonstandard sonority as a symptom of musical impotence—impoverished his musical analysis in general, but especially so when it came to jazz.[5] His attitude was perhaps symptomatic of a broader silence that had the effect of naturalizing or normalizing Western art music's sonority, making of it a kind of default sound, a sonority that was not heard as any particular or distinctive sonority per se but rather as a general or generic sonic presence, as a kind of white sound that, perhaps not unlike whiteness itself as a racial category, came to signify an absence of impurity. Of course, this is not actually true. Indeed, if it were, why not have orchestras that are made up only of instruments from one family—all strings, or all brass or all woodwinds? But the emphasis on the uniformity of a "standardized purity" (within a given instrumental family) has encouraged a view, largely unexamined, that sonority is a neutral element in classical concert music and hence can be taken to have little of significance to contribute to the expressive quality of the music.[6] In the case of the classical repertoire, this failure to thematize sonority is perhaps not fatal. But this is not the case for jazz.

This relative silence on the issue of sonority is no doubt also related to prevailing views about the nature of the musical work, about its ontology, about what kinds of thing a musical work and its constitutive components are. Correlated with the rise of musical notation in Western music has been the codification of a distinction between a performance and the thing performed, the work itself.[7] The work itself is singular and is ontologically distinct both from its score, which can exist in multiple copies, and from its performance. It has become common to think of a work as a type of abstract sound structure, of its score as an encoded set of instructions for realizing that abstract structure as a sonic event, and of its performance as a score-compliant instance of the work. The work is then an abstract kind or *type*, and its performance is taken to be a concrete instance, a score-compliant *token* of the type. In this conception, the work's abstract sound structure consists of a sequence of pitches, their duration, and their degree of loudness (of course, in the case of a Bach work for harpsichord, even dynamic components might be omitted).[8]

Now, a pitch of a specified duration, say, a concert A sixteenth note—which will be notated by the corresponding symbol in the second space of a treble staff—is also a type of which there are as many tokens or instances as there are occasions where a sound is produced by causing air to vibrate at 440 cycles per second for the requisite duration. But of course an A 440 produced by a zither is not the same sound as an A 440 produced on a French horn, or on a clarinet. By focusing on pitch as a sound *type*, these distinctions in tonal *quality* are elided.

Why should this relative indifference to sound per se—an indifference that is facilitated by what I have called the graphocentrism that haunts much of Western musical analysis—trouble us? What is lost? One reason for viewing timbre as an independent variable in the construction of a musical event is that it can have a significance that goes beyond or even contradicts the meanings typically associated with the melodic, harmonic, or rhythmic nature of the music performed. The sociologist John Shepherd has suggested that vocal timbre is an especially powerful case in point here, as different vocal timbres can, for example, be deployed in order to be read as projecting a variety of different gender locations or images.[9] Further, as I have suggested, such timbral individuality is a distinctive component of a jazz musician's voice, of his or her identity.

In jazz, the premium placed on having one's own sound means that musical spontaneity is often mediated through idiosyncratic instrumental timbre. Indeed, a varied timbral palette and an expectation that soloists will develop a unique personal sound are acknowledged to be prominent among African American musical values.[10] (To take but a few representative examples: within a couple of bars, one can fairly easily distinguish the sweet and fluid sound of Johnny Hodges on the alto saxophone from the tartness of Jackie MacLean or the heavily blues-inflected sound of Cannonball Adderley or the plaintive rawness of Ornette Coleman; or, on the tenor, the breathiness of Ben Webster from the almost metallic and vibratoless hardness at the center of a John Coltrane tone, or the lightness of Lester Young, or the swagger of Stanley Turrentine, or the slight dryness seasoned with a bit of grit found in Dexter Gordon.) Moreover, *vocalized* tonal qualities and pitch inflections are staples of jazz practice.[11] Though Adorno's compositionalist orientation allowed such modifications of "objective" sound to appear as at most a "whimpering which is helplessly testing itself," these "modifications" are constitutive not of musical impotence but rather of a corresponding agency.[12]

Not only is instrumental timbre a marker of artistic identity and musical agency, but it can also be reflective of social positioning. In this regard, I am reminded of the remark attributed to Coltrane when he was asked what he thought of Stan Getz's playing. Coltrane is reputed to have said something like "we all want to sound like Stan Getz." The beauty of Getz's sound notwithstanding, I take this to mean that Coltrane was socially positioned in such a way that playing with the cool, airy, diaphanous timbre of Getz, a timbre that suggested a kind of laid-back assuredness, was something that he, Coltrane, could not afford—that it would not be expressive of Coltrane's dry urgency. In other words, Coltrane *could* have sounded like Getz, but he would not have been Coltrane in doing so.

If we broaden our scale from the individual to the ensemble, we find a paradigmatic exemplar in Duke Ellington's orchestra. One of the features that set it apart from others was its distinctive timbral palette, leading one commentator to refer to the "timbral harmonies" of that band.[13] Ellington regarded members of his band as a gathering of distinctive "tonal personalities." A given note, when played by different members of his trombone section, could take on as many different colors as there were players. Consequently, *without altering the actual notes played*, this allowed Ellington to change the sound of a given harmonic voicing within a section merely by moving the players around to different chord tones.[14]

Indeed, in my view, a major component of what made Ellington a distinctively *jazz* composer was his recognition that sonority is the very medium of musical agency in jazz. Ellington did not write for instruments; he wrote for players. He is reputed to have said that when he contemplated writing a particular note, he always had to decide *whose* note it would be.[15] As a matter of fact, the charts he wrote for his band were not labeled, say, first or second alto saxophone, as is customary, but rather "Rabbit" (Johnny Hodges's nickname) or "Harry" (for Harry Carney). In the relationship between composer and performer, agency is thought to reside largely with the composer. But Ellington was a jazz composer not only in that he wrote swing rhythms with an underlying blues feeling and left openings for soloists, but also, and perhaps most important, because although he himself played the piano, his real instrument was his orchestra. Furthermore, each member of his band was to Ellington a specific tone color, so that he was really an aural painter—he painted in sound. And those colors were embodied in specific musical personalities. So he was a jazz composer in part because he wrote in such a way as to engage the musical agency of his players. In writing for the player rather than the instrument, his agency as a composer was mediated through the musical agency of his players.

Ellington gives us a striking example of the use of tone color to bear the weight of expressing musical spontaneity in one of his few completely through-composed works, *Concerto for Cootie*, written in 1940. (Note that it is not entitled "Concerto for Trumpet" but is a concerto written for a specific person.) This is a case where there was virtually no alteration of the composed melody by the solo trumpet player, Charles Melvin "Cootie" Williams. Rather, it is one whose improvisatory character was carried exclusively by the timbral variety deployed by "Cootie" Williams. It is a *timbral* improvisation, created through the use of a broad spectrum of tone colors in the various sections of the piece, making Williams a sort of second composer.[16] For a more recent example, I would regard the virtuoso saxophonist James Carter as explicitly practicing timbral improvisation superimposed upon more typical melodic, harmonic, and rhythmic spontaneity.

Now, I shall briefly turn to the other components of a jazz player's sound, that is, to the distinctive approaches to melody, rhythm, and harmony one finds in improvisation. An improvisatory performance is an expression of agency that typically unfolds within the context of the musical intentionality of other agents. I now want to address the question of what the conditions are that govern the improviser's negotiation between the twin demands of, on the one hand, the individuality of musical assertion and, on the other, musical responsibility. Harmonizing the competing demands of self-assertion and responsibility is one of the perennial concerns of ethics; accordingly, any attempt to answer this question will lead to an appreciation of the points of intersection between improvisation in ethics and the ethics of improvisation. What I would call a dialectic of freedom and constraint informs both, a dialectic that is expressively realized in what I shall call the "fitting response."

To begin with ethics: it is useful to recall Arthur Schopenhauer's response to Immanuel Kant's ethical theory. Kant, as it is well-known, claimed that an action is moral if and only if it conforms to a principle or rule that could be universalized; morality demands that we perform those and only those actions that conform to what Kant called the categorical imperative. Schopenhauer found Kant's context-indifferent universalist conception of morality to be tantamount to a kind of pedantry or rigorism, to be indeed a form of folly, the folly of being in the grip of a concept or maxim or rule and applying it doggedly no matter how different the situations of its application may be.[17] To understand our moral obligations to be discharged by our conscientious adherence to rules alone overlooks, Schopenhauer averred, the role of our discretion in discerning what is right, what is in my terms the *fitting response* in a particular case.[18]

Kant's deontological ethical theory has informed one of the two dominant currents in modern ethical theory. The other one is the utilitarian/consequentialist tradition associated with Jeremy Bentham and John Stuart Mill, where the concern is to act so as to seek the greatest good for the greatest number. Despite the manifest differences between the deontological and consequentialist traditions, both arguably assume that the role of the moral theorist is to seek "a fully explicit decision procedure for settling moral questions," to seek "explicit and univocal decision procedure[s]," so that what is morally right can be fully specified by rules.[19]

Insofar as this is so, neither tradition, in this sense, heeds Schopenhauer's complaint. Moreover, even if we decided that such a rule-based approach to ethics (whether a caricature of these traditions or not) was the best game in town, there is a conceptual issue that is insufficiently addressed, if not overlooked, by these traditions—namely, the problem of how general rules are to be applied to particular situations. Only if these rules were such that a full understanding of them would be sufficient for their correct application, only if they could be formulated in such a way that they required nothing in the way of contextual or indexical supplementation, could we apply them without having to exceed them in some way. But the rules associated with ethically mandated duties cannot be self-interpreting. Their necessarily schematic character will always leave underdetermined just how and when we are to fulfill those mandates. And this would be the case as well for any proposed "meta-rule" for following such rules. There can be no rules for the application of rules. Looking for further rules governing the application of rules would inexorably lead us to circularity or to a vicious infinite regress. Accordingly, the correct application of such first-order ethical rules will require capacities of discernment that exceed our understanding of the content of the rules in question. This capacity is typically denoted by such terms as *phronesis* or *judgment*, referring to the faculty concerned with the appropriate application of general rules.[20] So, the application of general moral rules in particular circumstances requires our ability to judiciously exceed what those schematic rules alone can tell us about our duties.[21] And indeed, we can be said to have grasped the rules only when we can perform their application in concrete situations. Insofar as the verdict of such a judgment cannot preexist the performance itself, moral judgment is not a taxonomic but, to some degree at least, a creative faculty.

While it is true that the schematic nature of rules necessitates the use of judgment in our application of them, we can nevertheless give reasons—reasons not drawn exclusively from the rule we are applying—for the choice we have made. Moral judgment can appeal to reasons, but it does not do so by virtue of any rule that makes them a reason.[22] These reasons can perhaps be stylized as rules, but only after the fact. They would not be rules that preexisted the choice, but would rather emerge in the situation of application. The moral rationality of a given action can be underwritten by its relationship to salient moral examples. Moral exemplars can in this way provide reasons.[23] Now, though it may be a matter of some controversy just how moral examples function as reasons, I believe that examples can be shown to function as reasons by virtue of the very same type of analogical reasoning from precedents that is used in common law legal reasoning.

Without getting too far into the weeds here, what these considerations suggest is that we must acknowledge that neither rigidly applying fully determinate rules, on the one hand, nor resigning ourselves to a sheer arbitrariness, on the other, exhausts the modalities through which we make moral decisions. I have adumbrated three possibilities: (1) algorithmically guided choice, where reasons are conclusive, and where there is a decision procedure with a unique result and an agreed-upon mechanism for definitively resolving disputes; (2) the condition of normless relativism or arbitrariness, where reasons are utterly irrelevant and, accordingly, there are no agreed-upon mechanisms for resolving disagreements; and (3) the hermeneutic domain of judgment, where reasons are relevant but not conclusive and there is a more or less shared set of criteria to which one can appeal when giving reasons, though the appeal to no single criterion nor the assignment of weights to criteria can be decisive. The idea of what I am calling the fitting response finds its place in this third space, the space between rule-dictated practice and the arbitrariness of "anything goes."

Schopenhauer generalized his vituperative objection to rigidly rule-based practice in ethical conduct to include such practice in life and art as well, claiming that in art it leads to the production of "lifeless, stiff, [and] abortive mannerisms."[24] The creative insight that characterizes moral judgment—discernment guided by the general rules that it seeks to apply in particular circumstances and by the form of life or ethos in which it is enacted—is equally requisite for generating the "fitting response" within artistic practice. The creative insight requisite to judgment places such judgment at the site or topos of freedom. Because it requires a perception that always, in a sense, "runs ahead" of orientational guidelines that cannot, by themselves, tell us how to proceed, such insight always puts us at risk of losing our way, of going astray. This is an unavoidable consequence of the freedom that it affords. But this does not force us to resign ourselves to the arbitrariness of an aimless meandering, no more than it does in the case of ethics.

Now, to speak of an "ethics of improvisation" is to speak to the ethos of improvisation, to speak of the way of life proper to improvisational practice—and to such practice within diverse contexts of improvisatory styles or traditions, from, say, New Orleans polyphony to the so-called avant-garde or "free" jazz and beyond; it is thus to speak to the mores that guide improvisatory behavior. Etymologically, *improvisation* itself refers to something done with a want (lack) of provision or forethought and so produced in the moment as a response to events in real time. So, to ask after the ethics of improvisation is to ask about the rules of thumb that should guide the production of relatively unpremeditated action undertaken in response to events in real time, the rules of thumb whose observance assures musical intelligibility.

What light does the idea of the fitting response shed on the phenomenon of improvisation? Musical improvisation is usefully viewed as a social and dialogical undertaking, as a dialogue both with the musical theme and with the community of other commentators on the theme. In this sense, improvisation is collaborative deliberation. What, then, are the guidelines for performing the fitting response? The faculty of judgment, as I have presented it, informs the production of a musical intervention that is fitting with respect to a common project, and it does so along two dimensions: (1) *formally* with respect to the harmonic or melodic structure of the composition that may serve as the basis of improvisation; and (2) *performatively* with respect to what others have done before and to what others are doing, a response to the community of performers. For instance, insofar as there is general agreement among the performers in an ensemble to remain tied to normal tonal harmony, formally one would respect the harmonic and melodic structure of the piece serving as the theme upon which improvisations are based (typically, for example, by acknowledging certain rules regarding relationships between chords and scales as one builds an improvisation). To be more explicit here, the rule would be to employ pitches selected from the scales corresponding to the harmonic context, but in such a way as to shape a melody. Because ethical guidelines function as constraints that condition the intelligibility and communicability of ethical decisions, the harmonic constraint would function here as a condition of musical intelligibility. It would serve as a matrix of intelligibility that allows us to recognize the production of a sequence of sounds as a move in a particular musical practice, to recognize such a production as a musical move, that is, as a move in a meaningful practice, rather than an arbitrary gesture. Analogous to the relationship between a linguistic utterance and its assertability conditions, a musical phrase can be assessed in terms of its appropriateness, its fittingness.[25] The harmonic structure, viewed as a constraint or as a mutually acknowledged backdrop, can in this way provide a metalinguistic frame that enables members of an ensemble to communicate with each other, to respond to one another and participate in a common conversation. This condition on musical intelligibility allows improvisatory acts — acts that, after all, are expected to be idiosyncratic or novel — to nevertheless be communicative. And they can have such communicative meaning not only by virtue of their conformity to expected harmonic and rhythmic structures, but also by dint of their surprising, but nonetheless intelligible, violation of those patterns.

The rules of thumb are guidelines, but, of course, they are neither necessary nor sufficient. The rule "use notes from the scales that correspond to the chords, but in a melodic fashion" is neither a necessary (one doesn't have to choose notes only from the stipulated scales) nor a sufficient (one shouldn't repeat the same sequence of notes each time one encounters the same chord) condition for a musically compelling improvisation. This rule thus has a schematic character and must be applied within particular contexts and in various performance traditions. It is schematic in that it leaves unspecified when to flout the chord-scale correspondence and, when it is acknowledged, how the rule is to be applied in various performance contexts and traditions. So the performer must find a way to be musically compelling in her application of the rule in order to produce the fitting musical gesture. A player may play a phrase that does not instantiate that rule, but she may nevertheless be able to give reasons for what she played — for example, in this particular musical situation, it would have been repetitious and tedious to have done so. This would be to act on a reason, but not on a reason that was drawn from the rule; rather, her reason would have been one that emerged in the course of her appraisal of the musical situation. This points to the importance of musical examples: jazz improvisers learn by listening to recordings.

The schematic nature of rules necessitates the use of judgment in our application of them. However, as I have pointed out, we can give reasons that are *not* drawn from the rule we are applying for the choice we have made. These reasons embody or imply rules (they can be stylized as rules), but these rules do not preexist the choice. Rather, they emerge during application. Thus, when a player justifies not applying a rule in the same way as before because to do so would be too repetitious, her reasoning might imply the rule "select your musical phrases or sequences so as to provide variety" (a decision that must be made in the context of what has already been played or is anticipated to be played). This is not a rule for the application of a rule. It is not a rule specifying how the rule is to be applied, how the application is to be effected. Rather, it is an ex post facto rule articulating how the rule was applied on this particular occasion. It emerges as a rational reconstruction of the reasons that would be given or of the rule that was implicit in the choice to which judgment led.

Such judgment is rationality eligible in that it is susceptible to such a reconstruction, and the rules that are implicit in its justification can be assessed as reasons. We can provide rational reconstructions of such musical gestures because reasons can be adduced for them. However, such reconstructions cannot be used predictively because we will not know what will *be* a reason for a particular musical agent. Hence, there is a sense in which a compelling solo can be characterized as displaying a "retrospective inevitability" without predictability.

In other words, freedom or originality can be found, at least in the first instance, in what the musician fashions within the constraints of form and material, in the distinctiveness of the story that can be articulated using that musical vocabulary, in her ability to liberate the music from the formal material in much the way that Michelangelo demanded that the sculptor liberate the figure from the block of stone in which it is potentially present.

For a particularly illuminating analysis that both confirms and illustrates my claims about the formal dimension of the fitting response, I would recommend a recent study of the musical achievement that made Louis Armstrong the central figure in the history of the jazz solo.[26] The analysis fixes upon the relationship of the constraints or boundaries provided by fixed musical structures to the freedom expressed in the variable improvised structures that Armstrong produced in the context of those constraints. In Armstrong's "Potato Head Blues," the fixed structure is a stop-time harmonic and rhythmic format that is characterized by the regularity and predictability of chords sounding every eight beats, a regularity and periodicity of punctuation that provided the background against which Armstrong improvised rhythmically complex and melodically compelling solos, and that allowed for improvisational surprises as the soloist moves in and out of phase, both rhythmically and harmonically, with the fixed structure. The constraint of this fixed structure allowed the freely produced solo to be understood as a meaningful gesture.[27]

Now, when we remember that improvisation, at least when done well, is typically also a social and collaborative process, we must acknowledge that thematizing this formal aspect alone would not be sufficient performatively. One could, for example, choose to perform tritone substitutions over dominant seventh chords when no one else on the bandstand is treating those chords in that way. Such chord substitutions are formally correct, but they may be performatively unfitting. They might be experienced as clashing, as flirting with a grating dissonance. Indeed some of Thelonious Monk's chord voicings were perceived in just this way by members of the ensembles in which he played at Minton's Playhouse or Monroe's Uptown House, in the early part of his career before bebop had been consolidated into a distinctive musical paradigm.[28] Further, though again formally correct, it would be considered a violation of performance convention for the pianist to play, in the left hand, the roots of the chords constituting the harmonic foundation of a given tune. To do so would be to step on the bass player's toes. When the rhythm section is "comping" or accompanying a soloist, its responsibility is to complement the solo and provide a foundation and frame replete with landmarks and points of reference for the soloist, sometimes commenting upon the soloist's phrases, often offering encouragement or perhaps even suggesting ideas, but not getting in the soloist's way. And members of the rhythm section must themselves engage in a constant negotiation with each other in an attempt to weave together mutually complementary strands in their contribution to the musical conversation.[29] The same applies when other front-line instrumentalists are playing background riffs behind soloists. For all, it is fundamental to negotiate a groove, to achieve a shared sense of the beat, to be "in the pocket."[30] One might say that the ethical component implied here is that one enters into an *aesthetic contract* that is based in part upon performatively being with Others (what Heidegger called *Mitsein*), a contract that requires each to adjust to the presence and actions of others. Thus, the ethics of improvisation would consist in fulfilling the requirement of responsiveness, placing a premium on attentive listening. And this is especially so in the case of so-called free jazz improvisations where the tonal center, because it is constantly renegotiated, may move around serendipitously.[31] The author Paul Gilroy has spoken of an "ethics of antiphony" in referring to Black creative and musical expression. Here we might in addition speak of an ethics of polyphony in talking about the shared responsibility in the contrapuntal conversation, which is a collaborative improvisation. Therefore, what I have called a dialectic of freedom and constraint is also one of agency and responsibility. To invoke an explicitly hermeneutic formulation: to improvise in concert with others is to participate in a conversation about a topic or, in H. G. Gadamer's terms, *Sache* (some harmonic and/or melodic structure), a conversation with side constraints articulated in the aesthetic contract. They will entail such maxims as "stay on topic" (the formal aspect) and "co-ordinate your comments with those of others" (the performative dimension). The fitting response is the result of the timely, responsible decision about how intelligibly to extend the "theme" (I use this term loosely) of the improvisation, a decision about how to carry on within the context of commitments to structure, genre, and collaborators, to preserve and invent, in Kierkegaardian fashion, to repeat and to carry forward, to enact what *could be* within the constraints of responsiveness. Improvisation in a collective is such a risky business that—to paraphrase Tennessee Williams's Blanche DuBois—the performers must always depend upon, perhaps not the kindness of strangers, but certainly the responsiveness of others.

I have tried to suggest that paying careful attention to what is distinctive of jazz will illuminate aspects of musical agency that might otherwise go unremarked—the individuality of styles of tone production and, especially given the performative dimension of the aesthetic contract, the role of conversational interplay.

Notes

1. See Ben Ratliff, *Coltrane: The Story of a Sound* (New York: Farrar, Straus & Giroux, 2007), x, 155.

2. Cf. Stephen Cottrell, *The Saxophone* (New Haven, CT: Yale University Press, 2012), 323.

3. Theodor Adorno, "Perennial Fashion—Jazz," in *Prisms*, trans. Samuel Weber and Shierry Weber (Cambridge, MA: MIT Press, 1967), 129.

4. See Cottrell, *The Saxophone*, 336.

5. See my *Unfinished Project: Toward a Postmetaphysical Humanism* (New York: Routledge, 2001), 42–59.

6. Cottrell, *The Saxophone*, 336. Again, this is a distinction in degree rather than in kind. But it has been pointed out that at least since the time of J. S. Bach, European concert music has established rather strict tonal criteria for the instruments that make up a symphony orchestra, a practice that has led to a considerable standardization of tone production; see

William P. Nye, "Theodor Adorno on Jazz: A Critique of Critical Theory," *Popular Music and Society* 12, no. 4 (1988): 72. Jazz musicians often refer to this as a "legit" sound. Stories abound about musicians who aspire to positions in classical orchestras but have been turned away because their sound was thought too distinctive for a given orchestra (see, e.g., Joseph Robinson, "What I Learned in the Lenoir High School Band," *Wilson Quarterly* 19, no. 4 [Autumn 1995]): 106. In symphony orchestras, a premium is placed on blending, and therefore on standardization, within instrumental families. Further, for most instruments there are sonic models that historically have set de facto tonal standards for the instrument, for example, the very dark sound of the Chicago Symphony's principal oboist. Of course, such *orchestras* often have distinctive sounds (e.g., that of the Philadelphia Orchestra or the Chicago Symphony or the Vienna Philharmonic), and this is in large measure a result of conductors' having at their disposal the spectrum of tonal variation allowable in a "legit" sound. To oversimplify somewhat, if the characteristic tonality of a particular symphony orchestra is the result of a particular, vertically imposed tonal standardization, then the characteristic tone colors of, say, Ellington's orchestra were the result of a particular mixture of *instrumentalists*. I am grateful to my former colleague the composer Alfred Cohen for a helpful conversation about some of these matters. The conclusion that I draw is, however, my own.

7. Peter Kivy, *Introduction to a Philosophy of Music* (Oxford and New York: Oxford University Press, 2002), 204.

8. It is a matter of some dispute whether other elements should be included—for instance, the tone color of a designated instrument. The composer might specify which instrument is to play a given sequence of pitches. Even if this consideration did incline us to include instrumental timbre in the sound structure, it is still the case that *controlling* for instrumental family, there is no acknowledgment of timbral variety within that family. In any event, it is not always the case that specific instrumentation is necessary for the preservation of work identity. As Kivy puts it, "What this strongly suggests is that sound structure, unspecified as to instrumentation, which is to say, timbre or tone color, lies far closer ... to our deepest intuitions about what makes the musical work the type that it is." Ibid., 217.

9. Cited in Cottrell, *The Saxophone*, 336.

10. Paul Berliner, *Thinking in Jazz: the Infinite Art of Improvisation* (Chicago: University of Chicago Press, 1994), 261.

11. Ibid., 108, 126–27.

12. Adorno, "On Jazz," trans. Jamie Owen Daniel, *Discourse: Journal for Theoretical Studies in Media and Culture* 12, no. 1 (1990): 67.

13. Stanley Crouch, *Considering Genius: Writings on Jazz* (New York: Basic Books, 2006), 138.

14. Ibid.

15. Ibid.

16. Cf. Mark Tucker, ed., *The Duke Ellington Reader* (Oxford and New York: Oxford University Press, 1993), 286. The details in Cootie's soloing that are different are precisely the locus of musical spontaneity. So, even though the notes were decided before the performance, Williams was given wide latitude in *interpreting* them; his variation of sonority makes of him a sort of second composer.

17. Arthur Schopenhauer, *The World as Will and Representation*, trans. E. F. J. Payne (New York: Dover, 1969), 1:59–60.

18. Ibid., 60.

19. See Charles Larmore, *Patterns of Moral Complexity* (Cambridge and New York: Cambridge University Press, 1987), ix, 4, 10.

20. Ibid., 7.
21. Ibid., 9.
22. Ibid., 14.
23. Ibid., 8.
24. Schopenhauer, *The World as Will and Representation*, 1:60.
25. Cf. also Robert Kraut, "Why Does Jazz Matter to Aesthetic Theory?" *Journal of Aesthetics and Art Criticism* 65, no. 1 (2005): 11–12.
26. Thomas Brothers, *Louis Armstrong: Master of Modernism* (New York: W. W. Norton, 2014), 270.
27. Ibid., 148, 266, 271.
28. See Robin D. G. Kelley, *Thelonious Monk: The Life and Times of an American Original* (New York: Free Press, 2009).
29. Berliner, *Thinking in Jazz*, 336.
30. Ibid., 349.
31. See Ronald M. Radano, *New Musical Figurations: Anthony Braxton's Cultural Critique* (Chicago: University of Chicago Press, 1993), 105–8.

CHAPTER 11

Merleau-Ponty on Consciousness and Affect through the Temporal Movement of Music

Jessica Wiskus

The French philosopher Maurice Merleau-Ponty was active in the middle of the twentieth century, pursuing a practice of thought—phenomenology—that had only recently been brought forth by Edmund Husserl. Introduced to Husserl's work in the 1920s through his studies at the École normale supérieure with Léon Brunschvicg, a slow but continuous dissemination of Husserl's thought throughout Paris intellectual circles culminated in Merleau-Ponty's own journey to the ancient university town of Leuven, Belgium, in April of 1939, shortly before he was called up for military service in World War II.[1] At Leuven, Merleau-Ponty came into contact with typescripts of Husserl's *Crisis* as well as volume 2 of *Ideas* (a work that would not be published until 1952); these manuscripts would have a formative influence on Merleau-Ponty's work during the war years, when a transformation of Husserlian phenomenology would find its expression in Merleau-Ponty's *Phenomenology of Perception* (published in 1945).[2] In Husserl's work, Merleau-Ponty felt himself to have discovered the foundation for a "manner or style of thinking" that could overcome dichotomies of object and subject, real and ideal, existence and expression.[3] Phenomenology overturned this dualism insofar as it made a study of the relation through which things disclose themselves, with the structures of consciousness—and, in particular, time-consciousness—a primary focus of investigation.[4]

Merleau-Ponty's role as a philosopher in his own right consisted in articulating for the project of phenomenology a framework through which the significance of our existence as embodied conscious beings—not merely rational beings—could be taken into account. According to Merleau-Ponty, there is a relationship of intertwining between the realm of existence and that of our consciousness, and this relationship is manifest according to our embodiment. "The body expresses existence at every moment," he writes in *Phenomenology of Perception*, and through this claim he moves to undermine the mind/body dualism of René Descartes and the self-reflective, solipsistic world of the *cogito*.[5] Indeed, one comes away from *Phenomenology of Perception* convinced of the necessity of a radical reassessment of the Cartesian thinking of consciousness, and one would not hesitate to offer that much of the exciting interdisciplinary research being conducted today (in neuroscience and psychology, for example) builds upon the foundation of Merleau-Ponty's call for an embodied approach to our understanding of mind. *Phenomenology of Perception* is therefore justifiably considered a work of contemporary significance—and the single book by Merleau-Ponty with which scholars from an array of disciplines are most likely to be familiar.

Puzzling then, perhaps, is the critique that Merleau-Ponty lodged in his later years against *Phenomenology of Perception*. Puzzling, but not insignificant, because Merleau-Ponty's later work makes this critique of *Phenomenology of Perception* precisely with respect to the question of consciousness—the central theme of phenomenology itself.[6] What Merleau-Ponty comes to see as problematic in *Phenomenology of Perception* is that the text allows for the possibility of reading a notion of consciousness as a positive entity—as some *thing*, as something like an identity or essence of self, or as self-possession (albeit one that might be extended throughout the body, according to the power of sensation in my fingertips or the posture of my spine). *Phenomenology of Perception* proposes a kind of consciousness situated in the reflective identity of the embodied "I-can" that would be juxtaposed against the identity of the object. Intentionality in this sense is understood in terms of a directed object of consciousness—an intention to something, toward something.

In July of 1959, nearly fifteen years after the publication of *Phenomenology of Perception*, Merleau-Ponty writes in a working note of his draft manuscript, *The Visible and the Invisible*: "The problems posed in *Phenomenology of Perception* are insoluble because I start there from the 'consciousness'—'object' distinction."[7] The note articulates the essence of Merleau-Ponty's critique: according to the later Merleau-Ponty, consciousness is not to be understood as set against objects; consciousness is not consciousness-of something. What Merleau-Ponty comes to see by the late 1950s is that in his early work, his investigation of perception remains tied to a particular notion of consciousness as *that before which the things* (including mental "things" such as ideas or images) *present themselves*. His early work can therefore be described as a "philosophy of consciousness" (albeit embodied consciousness)[8]—the very same complaint that Merleau-Ponty, in the working notes of *The Visible and the Invisible*, also lodges against Husserl's more Cartesian leanings.[9] It is this philosophy of consciousness that Merleau-Ponty takes great pains to reject through an extended critique of Descartes (and Jean-Paul Sartre) in the first two chapters of *The Visible and the Visible*. According to Merleau-Ponty, the world is not posited before consciousness nor even before the body (as embodied intentionality or an "I-can"); on the contrary, the world is always already there as the ground beneath us.[10] Thus, rather than thinking through consciousness in terms of its intentional content—that is to say, consciousness as a positive capacity or a grasping of mind—he tries to think of consciousness in terms of a lack or a separation (*écart*). The meaning of existence to which we are opened through consciousness, he claims, "is not [one of] coincidence, fusion with." He continues: it is a meaning inaugurated by separation.[11] By understanding separation (and not possession—that is to say, not consciousness-of something) as the locus of meaning, Merleau-Ponty feels that he will finally be able to overcome the so-called philosophy of consciousness and the dualist framework that it presupposes. In a part of an extensive working note of *The Visible and the Invisible* dated May 20, 1959, he writes, "Understand that the 'to be conscious' = to have a figure on a ground ... the figure-ground distinction [itself] introduces a third term between the 'subject' and the 'object.' It is *that separation* (*écart*) first of all that is the perceptual *meaning*."[12] That is to say, it is the figure-ground distinction or separation—as a dimension of depth—that "forms meaning."[13] How depth functions as a site but not a possession of expressive content is what Merleau-Ponty explores in his very last writings. "The solution," Merleau-Ponty writes in another working note of *The Visible and Invisible* (again from May 1959), "is to be sought in vision itself."[14] Of particular significance for Merleau-Ponty is the phenomenon of visual depth, explored as a dimension arising through the cohesion of separate or divergent points of view. A few months after he writes that "it is *that separation* first of all that is the perceptual *meaning*," he sketches out a general approach pertaining to his investigations in a working note dated November 1959:

> This *separation* (*écart*) which, in first approximation, forms meaning, is not a no I affect *myself* with, a lack which I constitute as a lack by the upsurge of an *end* which I give myself—it is a *natural* negativity, a first institution, always already there—Consider the right, the left.... Consider the *two*, the *pair*, this is not *two acts, two syntheses*, it is a fragmentation of being, it is a possibility for separation

(two eyes, two ears: the possibility for *discrimination*, for the use of the diacritical).[15]

In other words, this separation is not something that we possess or intend; the separation is a bodily constituted field, already there, beneath the opening of consciousness. When, for example, we employ our two eyes—the structure of which allow for "the possibility for *discrimination*"—we experience not two conscious acts (one intention of the right eye and one of the left eye) that give rise to vision; we experience a whole sense of depth. While it is evident that Merleau-Ponty investigates this experience of depth over a broad range of his writings (indeed, from *Phenomenology of Perception* to *The Visible and the Invisible*), it is in his later account of binocular vision that Merleau-Ponty sketches an analog for his final notion of consciousness.

On Consciousness, Part I: Separation and Depth

I look out upon an object before me (perhaps a bell tower), and my body is immediately implicated in the look. For what I notice is that my vision does not give me one single version of the tower revealed in its positivity. Rather, there are two versions, as in the double image of a stereoscope; the world before my left eye does not coincide exactly with the world before my right eye. There is a separation. Moreover, like the two-dimensional pictures placed before the stereoscope, what I see with each eye individually appears flat, lifeless. I may approximate a sense of depth by taking account of the relative size of objects that I see with monocular perception and then calculating a certain distance between the objects. But clearly, with only one eye I am not able to see depth in itself, which would be given to me without synthesis; rather, I employ a dimension of breadth in measuring the gap between objects. All of this takes place under the careful attention of the mind: grasping, comparing, and calculating. Yet, this is not how we actually experience the dimension of depth; when I look at the bell tower with both eyes, I do not sense conflict between the image of the left eye and the image of the right eye. There is no need for a calculating consciousness to measure as breadth the difference between the two images.[16]

On this point, the early and late work of Merleau-Ponty agree: the given experience of depth is distinct from the experience of breadth. The important difference lies in how the early and late Merleau-Ponty explain the sense of the phenomenon itself. In *Phenomenology of Perception*, Merleau-Ponty writes that "we pass from double vision to the single object, not through an inspection of the mind, but when the two eyes cease to function each on its own account and are used as a single organ by one single gaze."[17] For the early Merleau-Ponty, then, it is the body that effects a synthesis of the two points of view: depth arises when two parts of the body, functioning properly, work together as a "single organ." Thus, what is important for the early Merleau-Ponty is not the separation of the two eyes so much as the synthesis performed by the body as a whole. It is the body, first of all, that serves as the center for the "unity of binocular vision." He continues:

> When I look in the stereoscope, a totality presents itself in which already the possible order takes shape and the situation is foreshadowed. My motor response takes up this situation. Cézanne said that the painter in the face of his "motif" is about "to join the aimless hands of nature." The act of focusing at the stereoscope is equally a response to the question put by the data, and this response is contained in the question.[18]

Here, the intertwining and interpenetration of world and body is what gives rise to an experience of depth; above all, it is the painter's body that performs the synthesis and "'join[s] the aimless hands of nature.'"

Yet, when Merleau-Ponty takes up the question of perceptual depth again in *The Visible and the Invisible* and later course notes (especially the *Notes de cours sur "L'origine de la géométrie" de Husserl* of 1959–60), his sense of the "solution [that] is to be sought in vision itself" has subtly changed.[19] It has shifted from an emphasis on the synthesis of the body to an emphasis on transcendence. In the beginning of *The Visible and the Invisible*, he writes that "binocular perception is not made up of two monocular perceptions surmounted; it is of another order."[20] As he continues in the same paragraph, "It is not a synthesis; it is a metamorphosis."[21] Thus, the perception of depth is not the perception of a *thing*—not the perception of a "unity" or a "synthesis." Depth is of "another order," "a metamorphosis," or, as Merleau-Ponty writes frequently in the working notes of *The Visible and the Invisible*, a "transcendence."[22] Here, it is the *separation itself* that receives emphasis (and not the synthesis of the separated parts through embodiment). Again, in a working note from May 20, 1959, Merleau-Ponty claims, "We have to pass from the thing (spatial or temporal) as identity, to the thing (spatial or temporal) as difference, i.e., as transcendence, i.e., as always 'behind,' beyond, far-off… the present itself is not an absolute coincidence without transcendence."[23]

Spatial or temporal: we begin to understand how a renewed examination of the phenomenon of depth provides the later Merleau-Ponty with a model for investigating consciousness itself.[24] Recall that, for Merleau-Ponty drafting the notes for *The Visible and the Invisible* in May of 1959, consciousness "is not coincidence, fusion with."[25] Consciousness, like depth, offers a meaning that is articulated through separation or transcendence. Yet the depth of consciousness is not a spatial depth but a temporal depth, as the series of working notes from May 1959 clearly articulates (with headings such as "Husserl *Zeitbewusstsein*" and "(Bergson) Transcendence—*forgetting*—time"). Consciousness, Merleau-Ponty continues in that same series of working notes, is "a contact with Self *through* the divergence (*écart*) with regard to Self."[26] This divergence takes place through time. What Merleau-Ponty proposes for examination here is the structure not of separate images (as in binocular vision) but of separate times—the transcendent structure of the divergence that we know as past, present, and future. When, in May of 1959, Merleau-Ponty writes that "the present itself is not an absolute coincidence without transcendence," he could not be further from the claim that he had advanced in *Phenomenology of Perception*: "The present (in the wide sense, along with its horizons of primary past and future) nevertheless enjoys a privilege because it is the zone in which being and consciousness coincide."[27] Thus we see how the subtle change in Merleau-Ponty's approach to depth has been undertaken, in the late work, together with an unequivocal reworking of his ideas on temporality.[28]

On Consciousness, Part II: Transcendence and Time

When we speak about divergence or separation from self, we are speaking about the way that time pushes and pulls apart at our identity, both on a macro-level—with respect to the span of years between experiences and our retrieval of them through memory—and on a micro-level—with respect to the gap (of perhaps a few nanoseconds) between local sensation and the conscious registering of an event. Our self-presence is never a "coincidence, [a] fusion with," because our consciousness is never only awareness of the infinitely thin "now," moving swiftly along a line of oblivion and nonbeing. The traditional view of time—where we consider the present to be an infinitely thin point (i.e., lacking in all depth) yet somehow possessed of everything that is (that is to say, possessed of a fullness of presence)—is what Merleau-Ponty always works against. A lack of depth in the present would mean that we would have no means of understanding the different qualities of the present—the way that time seems to pass more quickly or slowly, for example, depending upon the activity in which we are engaged. To take the present as a "point" of time is to measure it from the outside, from the point of view of one who would not be involved in time—from the point of view of the eternal. A phenomenology of time-consciousness resituates the problem of time by specifically investigating temporality—how the past, present, and future are experienced for us—rather than the objective time of calendars and clocks. Thus, it is little surprise that Merleau-Ponty would discover in the work of Husserl a way to rethink the problem of time. In *Phenomenology of Perception*, for example, he adopts a model of time first proposed by Husserl in which the present is imbued with a certain extension according to a retention-protentional structure: the experience of the present would take place within a sort of background or reverberation of the immediate past and future. It is in this way that the present itself would be characterized by a certain kind of depth—a depth that, in *Phenomenology of Perception*, Merleau-Ponty associates with the body. It is as if time itself were almost a substance, with quality and volume: "In every focusing movement my body unites present, past and future, it secretes time."[29] Yet, as we have seen, it is just this kind of depth that Merleau-Ponty challenges in his later work when he shifts his focus from the experience of depth itself to the experience of the separation or divergence that gives rise to the phenomenon of depth; likewise, in his investigation of temporality, he moves away from an emphasis on the fullness or dimension of the present to a sense of the present as divergence and transcendence. Thus, in a working note of *The Visible and the Invisible* from the spring of 1959 entitled "Time," he begins by ruling out his earlier notion of time as a kind of bodily presence.[30] "The upsurge of time would be incomprehensible as the *creation* of a supplement of time that would push the whole preceding series back into the past. That passivity is not conceivable," he writes; "On the other hand every analysis of time that views it from above is insufficient" (that is to say, every analysis of time that attempts to look at it from the outside, as objective time). He continues, "Time must *constitute itself*—be always seen from the point of view of someone who *is of it*." Here he affirms the necessity of the phenomenological approach: "But this seems to be contradictory, and would lead back to one of the two terms of the preceding alternative." That is to say, even as we adopt a phenomenological approach, if in any way we conceive of the present as a positive—as a presence—whether as a sort of voluminous present or as the possession of consciousness, we are still not able to escape the concept of time as a kind of object. And here Merleau-Ponty sketches out his solution:

The contradiction is lifted only if the new present is itself a transcendent: one knows that it is not there, that it was just there, one never coincides with it--It is not a segment of time with defined contours that would come and set itself in place. It is a cycle defined by a central and dominant region and with indecisive contours—a swelling or bulb of time—A creation of this sort alone makes possible 1) the influence of the "contents" on time which passes "more quickly" or "less quickly," of *Zeitmaterie* on *Zeitform* 2) the acceptance of the truth of the transcendental analysis: time is not an absolute series of events, a tempo—not even the tempo of the consciousness—it is an institution, a system of equivalences.[31]

It is only by thinking through the present (as well as the past and future) as transcendence—as that which is never fully possessed or within our grasp—that we can come to understand time, both according to its qualitative character (i.e., as we experience it) and according to its function as the institution or rise of consciousness itself (i.e., as "the truth of the transcendental analysis"). That is to say, we experience time as a nonpossession: it is expressed according to differentiation or separation. And our consciousness—our sense of self—is also a nonpossession; *we* are expressed according to differentiation or separation. In sum, the principle structure of our being (or "institution," as Merleau-Ponty writes, above, drawing from Husserl's notion of *Stiftung*), from a phenomenological standpoint, is that of time-consciousness.[32]

And so perhaps we should not puzzle over Merleau-Ponty's critique of *Phenomenology of Perception*'s emphasis on the intertwining of the body's directedness toward and perception of the world; it was, in a sense, too present—too full—as it was portrayed in this early work. In *The Visible and the Invisible*, he seeks to describe a sense of the body as "that divergence between the within and the without"[33]—"the inauguration of the *where* and the *when*."[34] It is this that he refers to as the "flesh." The flesh is not the material body: "The flesh we are speaking of is not matter."[35] It is a new kind of embodied consciousness, one that expresses the divergence or nonpossession characterizing the understanding of time consciousness that he had worked out in the spring and summer of 1959. He searches for analogies: it is a "hinge" and "a being of depths, of several leaves or several faces, a being in latency, and a presentation of a certain absence," always characterized by "dehiscence or fission."[36] He continues: "What we are calling flesh, this interiorly worked-over mass, has no name in any philosophy."[37] As he sketches out his notion of the flesh for the first time (and, unfortunately, for the last time—the chapter of *The Visible and the Invisible* in which this discussion of flesh appears is the final chapter to have been completed in draft form before Merleau-Ponty's death in 1961), Merleau-Ponty turns, surprisingly, to music.

Why, in the last completed chapter of *The Visible and the Invisible*, did he engage—so radically for a philosopher of vision and visibility—with music? We should attend carefully to the surprising role that music plays in Merleau-Ponty's work at the very end of his oeuvre—the role that it plays at the precise moment when Merleau-Ponty seems to have grappled sufficiently with a critique of his earlier work and to be pushing ahead with his new program of philosophical research. A musical melody (as was also well appreciated by Husserl) shows us precisely how "a being in latency, and a presentation of a certain absence" can be expressive.[38] In music, time is the very material of meaning. In a melody, it is not the individual, present note that lends expressivity to a performance; rather, the movement or distension of time that occurs, in a sense, *between* the notes (as a "hinge") creates a phrase—in other words, the rhythm or groove. Ordinarily, we tend to think of rhythm as a measurement of duration—as a quantity that can be grasped—and we treat a rhythm as an object. In expressive music performances, we do not actually experience rhythm as the calculated sum of two different events in time (any more than we experience binocular vision as the studied synthesis of the images of the right and left eyes). We *move* to the rhythm; we *feel* the groove. We dance; we gesture; we organize ourselves to it. We do not seize it, possess it, or grasp it as we would an object. It flows through us even as, in some sense, it is present only in its absence. That is to say, a rhythm is not a positive entity or an object fashioned through intellectual synthesis of a past, present, and future; rather, it emerges according to the separation or differentiation of articulated events. The expressivity of music, as rhythm, is a "negativity or absence circumscribed," as Merleau-Ponty writes in the final completed chapter of *The Visible and the Invisible*.[39] And again he writes, with music there is "not the positing of a content, but the opening of a dimension"—the dimension of transcendence that we understand as temporality.[40] Thus, music as a site of phenomenological research offers us the means through which we might glimpse the inner framework of transcendence at the heart of time-consciousness. Moreover, it is abundantly clear through the experience of music that this transcendence is "a negativity that is not nothing," as Merleau-Ponty writes in *The Visible and the Invisible*.[41] It is not "a lack which I constitute as a lack" (as, we recall, Merleau-Ponty writes with respect to consciousness); it is not a volitional act of *no* or a negativity that would in any way be understood as a deprivation. It is, rather, a birthplace of meaning—the source of a feeling for life. Through music we begin to appreciate the sense in which consciousness as separation from self—that is, time-consciousness—discloses the very source of creative and affective expression.

On Consciousness, Part III: Music and Affect

We are now in a position to reexamine Merleau-Ponty's descriptions, in the final chapter of *The Visible and the Invisible*, of a musical melody and its effects through the *petite phrase* of Marcel Proust. Proust's *À la recherche du temps perdu* features the story of Swann—one of the principal characters of *Recherche*'s third volume, *Du côté de chez Swann* (*Swann's Way*)—and his musical obsession with a sweet and simple little phrase. In this account, the phrase is accorded a certain dynamic power of expression through which it eventually achieves an association with the turbulent development of Swann's love for Odette. The *petite phrase* becomes, as Proust writes, the "national anthem" of this love, such that it not only comes to represent Swann's affections but in fact seems to call him to action—to awaken him from his general lethargy and make possible his very ambition to love.[42] How is it that music stands at the center of Swann's affective world?

For Merleau-Ponty, it is the phrase understood in relation to its temporal and affective qualities that merits philosophical attention. The last few pages of *The Visible and the Invisible*—the pages immediately following his introduction of the notion of the flesh—are dedicated to the exploration of this *petite phrase*; they can be thought to develop the temporality of the flesh as it relates to the "spread" or "incessant escaping" of the "general manner"[43] of our being or consciousness.

In his account of the *petite phrase*, Merleau-Ponty is careful to distinguish between the audible notes of the melody and what he refers to as the "musical idea"—an idea "that is not the contrary of the sensible, that is its lining and its depth."[44] (In musical terms, this "idea" might be understood as the rhythm or the phrasing of the performance.) From Merleau-Ponty's descriptions, it is clear that the musical idea operates according to a temporal structure of transcendence. The musical idea is not contained within or bound to the limits of the sounding notes; rather, it is "behind the sounds or between them."[45] He explains, "We do not see, do not hear" the musical idea, "not even with the mind's eye."[46] The musical idea, Merleau-Ponty tells us, "presents to us what is absent."[47] And in writing this, Merleau-Ponty is not claiming that the musical idea "presents to us" something that was otherwise obscured from view, as if, through a repositioning of some sort, we become able to grasp what had simply escaped us. It "presents to us what is absent," insofar as it presents to us *that* there is an absence: separation or divergence itself—the transcendental structure of time-consciousness.[48] We are therefore never able to possess the musical idea. Merleau-Ponty writes: "Each time we want to get at it immediately, or lay hands on it, or circumscribe it, or see it unveiled, we do in fact feel that the attempt is misconceived, that it retreats in the measure that we approach. The explicitation does not give us the idea itself; it is but a second version of it, a more manageable derivative."[49] He continues:

> Swann can of course close in the "little phrase" between the marks of musical notation, ascribe the "withdrawn and chilly tenderness" that makes up its essence or its sense to the narrow range of the five notes that compose it and to the constant recurrence of two of them: while he is thinking of these signs and this sense, he no longer has the "little phrase" itself, he has only "bare values substituted for the mysterious entity he had perceived, for the convenience of his understanding."[50]

It is not Swann and his lack of musical training that explains the elusiveness of the *petite phrase*—it is, rather, due to the temporal movement of the music. With Swann's every effort to close in upon the essence of the phrase, it is as if his mental efforts were circling around a hollow of meaning.[51] Merleau-Ponty writes, "We do not possess the musical or sensible ideas, precisely because they are negativity or absence circumscribed; they possess us."[52] And so it is not only that the musical idea manifests the transcendence of the present; it is a performance of the generativity and creativity—the very possibility of expression—that is born of this transcendence. It is a "negativity or absence" that possesses us in the strong sense—we can have a possession of self only as "a contact with self *through* the divergence (*écart*) with regard to Self."[53]

Thus, it is not only that, for Merleau-Ponty, consciousness must be considered a nonpossession—an absence or negativity—but that this structure of transcendence gives rise to the very richness of conscious experience itself: its qualia, its affective stirrings. The divergence or transcendence of temporality is the source of creativity, and expression is not simply the representation of some other thing, transferred into a different mode; it is possible thanks to the very slipping away of time itself.

And this is what music demonstrates. Proust writes: "This music seemed to me something truer than all known books. At moments I thought that this was due to the fact that, what we feel about life not being felt in the form of ideas, its literary, that is to say intellectual expression describes it, explains it, analyses it, but does not recompose it as does music, in which the sounds seem to follow the very movement of our being."[54] The recomposition to which Proust refers is what we understand, through phenomenology, to be the constituting process of time-consciousness itself (as that which follows "the very movement of our being"). And thus it is that music expresses "what we feel about life," not only in the subjective sense but as a structure of our existence. Merleau-Ponty writes that the musical idea "is the invisible *of* this world, that which inhabits this world, sustains it, and renders it visible, its own and interior possibility, the Being of this being."[55] That is to say, a phenomenological analysis of the musical experience suggests not only a way of understanding the affective capacity of music but even time consciousness itself, and Merleau-Ponty's late work, in its turn to the *petite phrase* of Proust, stands as an important contribution to the overall phenomenological project and the repositioning of consciousness in terms of nonpossession.

Notes

1. For an account of the smuggling of Husserl's *Nachlass* out of Nazi Germany for safekeeping in Belgium, see H. L. Van Breda, "Le sauvetage de l'héritage husserlien et la fondation des Archives-Husserl," in *Husserl et la pensée modern / Husserl und das Denken der Neuzeit*, ed. H. L. Van Breda and J. Taminiaux (The Hague: Martinus Nijhoff, 1959).

2. For a concise summary of Merleau-Ponty's contact with Husserl's lectures and manuscripts, see Dermot Moran, *Introduction to Phenomenology* (London and New York: Routledge, 2000), 406–7. This book also serves as an excellent resource especially for those outside of continental philosophy who are interested in phenomenology. Likewise, Sebastian Luft and Søren Overgaard, eds., *The Routledge Companion to Phenomenology* (London: Routledge, 2014), highlights key figures and concepts of phenomenology in clear and accessible prose. For an in-depth engagement with phenomenology that focuses exclusively on Husserl, see Rudolf Bernet, Iso Kern, and Eduard Marbach, *An Introduction to Husserlian Phenomenology* (Evanston, IL: Northwestern University Press, 1993).

3. Maurice Merleau-Ponty, *Phenomenology of Perception*, trans. Colin Smith (London: Routledge, 1981), viii.

4. As it stands at the beginning of the twenty-first century, the term "phenomenology" is in frequent use — employed not only by philosophers of the continental tradition but also by philosophers of mind, neuroscientists, social scientists, therapists, and ethnographers of various disciplines — and its definitions are wide-ranging. In this particular essay, I consider phenomenology as it was understood by Merleau-Ponty, i.e., through the phenomenological reduction. The phenomenological method does not consist simply in the gathering of a report of subjective experience; it aims at tracing the structures that lie behind and inform that experience. In the preface to *Phenomenology of Perception* (itself one of Merleau-Ponty's

most fascinating essays on the work of Husserl), Merleau-Ponty writes, "It is because we are through and through compounded of relationships with the world that for us the only way to become aware of the fact is to suspend the resultant activity, to refuse it our complicity (to look at it *ohne mitzumachen*, as Husserl often says), or yet again, to put it 'out of play.' Not because we reject the certainties of common sense and a natural attitude to things—they are, on the contrary, the constant theme of philosophy—but because, being the presupposed basis of any thought, they are taken for granted, and go unnoticed, and because in order to arouse them and bring them to view, we have to suspend for a moment our recognition of them." Merleau-Ponty, *Phenomenology of Perception*, xiv–xv.

5. Ibid., 192.

6. Much of this critique takes place in the form of working notes (i.e., notes that Merleau-Ponty made to himself—notes that were not intended for publication, and so are not fully fleshed out). Most of the notes relevant to our inquiry were composed during the summer of 1959, just two years before his untimely death; they were brought to publication only posthumously.

7. Maurice Merleau-Ponty, *The Visible and the Invisible: Followed by Working Notes*, trans. Alphonso Lingis (Evanston: Northwestern University Press, 1968), 200.

8. Ibid., 244.

9. His critique of Husserl in the later working notes of *The Visible and the Invisible* should thus be understood as a kind of self-critique; in effect, he is criticizing his own early reading of Husserl. As mentioned, it was under an initial influence of Husserl's phenomenology that Merleau-Ponty composed *Phenomenology of Perception*. It was an "initial" influence insofar as Merleau-Ponty's engagement with the work of Husserl would span the whole of his academic life, as evidenced by the essay "The Philosopher and his Shadow" and an entire course at the Collège de France (*Husserl at the Limits of Phenomenology*, offered in 1959–1960). However, Merleau-Ponty's actual time at Leuven in 1939—the time when he read the (unpublished) complete manuscript of the *Crisis* and also *Ideas* II—was a mere six days (though, to be sure, he remained in touch with Van Breda at the Husserl Archives throughout the Second World War).

10. Indeed, in a working note from November of 1960, Merleau-Ponty distinguishes between the philosophy of Sartre, which takes "being and the imaginary" as "objects" (a view that he rejects), and the philosophy of Bachelard, which takes them as "elements" (a view that he embraces). Merleau-Ponty, *The Visible and the Invisible*, 267.

11. Ibid., 191. Rather poetically, he writes about "the *self* of perception as 'nobody,' in the sense of Ulysses." Ibid., 201. Such oblique approaches to consciousness are not, for Merleau-Ponty, disingenuous: consciousness never can possess itself, and so there must be this circuitous path toward an understanding. See, e.g., ibid., 179.

12. Ibid., 197.

13. Ibid., 216.

14. Ibid., 194.

15. Ibid., 216–17.

16. For another analysis of this phenomenon of depth, see Bettina Bergo, "Philosophy as *Perspectiva Artificialis*: Merleau-Ponty's Critique of Husserlian Constructivism," in *Maurice Merleau-Ponty, Husserl at the Limits of Phenomenology*, ed. Leonard Lawlor with Bettina Bergo (Evanston. IL: Northwestern University Press, 2002). See also chap. 2 of Jessica Wiskus, *The Rhythm of Thought: Art, Literature, and Music after Merleau-Ponty* (Chicago: University of Chicago Press, 2013).

17. Merleau-Ponty, *Phenomenology of Perception*, 270.

18. Ibid., 305.
19. Ibid., 194.
20. Ibid., 7.
21. Ibid., 8.
22. Indeed, "transcendence" is the term that he employs to describe consciousness itself. See esp. Merleau-Ponty, *The Visible and the Invisible*, 195, 196, 210, 225, 228, 229, 243–244.
23. Ibid., 195.
24. Indeed, in the course notes prepared for his lectures on Husserl of 1959–1960, Merleau-Ponty affirms that "philosophy is nothing other than the unconcealment of the depth dimension of all other activities." Merleau-Ponty, *Husserl at the Limits of Phenomenology*, 18.
25. Merleau-Ponty, *The Visible and the Invisible*, 191.
26. Ibid.
27. Merleau-Ponty, *Phenomenology of Perception*, 492.
28. In this context, therefore, it is perhaps useful to consider that Merleau-Ponty seeks "nuclei of meaning which are in-visible, but which simply are not invisible in the sense of the absolute negation (or of the absolute positivity of the 'intelligible world'), but [are invisible] in the sense of the *other dimensionality*, as depth hollows itself out behind height and breadth, as time hollows itself out behind space." Merleau-Ponty, *The Visible and the Invisible*, 236.
29. Merleau-Ponty, *Phenomenology of Perception*, 278. Interestingly, it is this very notion of time that Merleau-Ponty later refutes by turning to the example of the melody. In a lecture course given in 1957–58, we find Merleau-Ponty writing: "The melody gives us a particular consciousness of time. We think naturally that the past secretes the future ahead of it. But this notion of time is refuted by the melody." Maurice Merleau-Ponty, *Nature: Course Notes from the Collège de France*, trans. Robert Vallier (Evanston, IL: Northwestern University Press, 2003), 228.
30. The entire passage is from a working note of Merleau-Ponty, *The Visible and the Invisible*, 184.
31. Ibid.
32. A succinct analysis of Husserl's position with respect to the experience of time is provided by Nicolas de Warren, "Time," in *The Routledge Companion to Phenomenology*, ed. Sebastian Luft and Søren Overgaard (London: Routledge, 2014), 193. De Warren writes: "The *a priori* correlation between intentional acts of consciousness and intentional objects is ultimately constituted in original time-consciousness, or transcendental temporality. The difference and opening between 'subject' and 'object,' mind and world, is in this fashion grounded in the transcendental accomplishment of time-consciousness. In Husserl's technical vocabulary, the structure of 'transcendence in immanence' is constituted in original time-consciousness." For an in-depth examination of the topic, see de Warren, *Husserl and the Promise of Time: Subjectivity in Transcendental Phenomenology* (Cambridge: Cambridge University Press, 2009).
33. Merleau-Ponty, *The Visible and the Invisible*, 135.
34. Ibid., 140.
35. Ibid., 146.
36. Ibid., 148, 136, and 146.
37. Ibid., 147.
38. Ibid., 136.
39. Ibid., 151.

40. Ibid.
41. Ibid.
42. Marcel Proust, *Remembrance of Things Past*, 3 vols., trans. C. K. Moncrieff, Terence Kilmartin, and Andreas Mayor (New York: Vintage Books, 1981), 1:238.
43. Merleau-Ponty, *The Visible and the Invisible*, 148 and 147.
44. Ibid., 149.
45. Ibid., 151.
46. Ibid.
47. Ibid., 150–51.
48. It is in this sense that Merleau-Ponty writes in the working notes of *The Visible and the Invisible*, "The transcendence of the present makes it precisely able to connect up with a past and a future." Ibid., 196.
49. Ibid., 150.
50. Ibid., 150.
51. When, on p. 151 in *The Visible and the Invisible*, Merleau-Ponty describes the musical idea as "a certain hollow, a certain interior, a certain absence, a negativity that is not nothing," it is useful to reference the sense of "hollow" that he develops from an earlier passage of *The Visible and the Invisible* (123). In this earlier passage, Merleau-Ponty discusses time-consciousness with respect to the gap or separation that characterizes the experience of the present, describing it as "an overlaying, as of a hollow and a relief which remain distinct."
52. Ibid., 151.
53. Ibid., 192.
54. Marcel Proust, *Remembrance of Things Past*, 3:381.
55. Merleau-Ponty, *The Visible and the Invisible*, 151.

CHAPTER 12

A. N. Whitehead, Feeling, and Music

ON SOME POTENTIAL MODIFICATIONS TO AFFECT THEORY

Ryan Dohoney

In one of the most enigmatic sections of his magnum opus *Process and Reality*, Alfred North Whitehead posits the "category of the ultimate" that undergirds his metaphysical system.[1] This is the principle of creativity understood as "the advance from disjunction to conjunction." The movement produces something that "is at once the togetherness of the 'many' which it finds, and also it is one among the disjunctive 'many' which it leaves; it is a novel entity, disjunctively among the many entities which it synthesizes."[2] In an aphoristic formulation of the same idea, Whitehead writes that "the many become one, and are increased by one."[3] As he says elsewhere, "the basis of experience is emotional," such that any becoming from many to one is marked by an "affective tone" arising from the specific interactions of a given "many" resulting in a fragile "one."[4]

It was a novel musical entity that got me thinking with these Whiteheadian ideas, specifically Eric Wubbels's Viola Quartet (2007). I've experienced the piece both live at its premiere and several times since on the recording, which features Victor Lowrie, Max Mandel, Tawnya Popoff, and Miranda Sielaff.[5] Though Wubbels hasn't read Whitehead, his music nonetheless dramatizes the process of "many becoming one" that the philosopher identifies as the production of feeling. Wubbels himself describes his music as an exploration of various kinds of synthesis: "The building block of what I focus on is unison, both rhythmically and pitch-wise.... I want to find interesting ways of creating unisons which means examining instruments physically, gesturally from their technique so you can find ways of matching them, find[ing] intersections in space."[6] The play of the many and the one in Wubbels's Viola Quartet is inscribed across musical features: the shared gestural repertoire between the violas, the complex hocketing, and the

Fig. 12.1. Gestural enmeshments and the four violas as "meta-instrument." Eric Wubbels, Viola Quartet, p. 1. Reprinted with permission of the composer.

form itself, which moves from complex unisons in which the musicians form a "meta-instrument" from interlocking patterns (fig. 12.1) to reduced moments of pitch and rhythmic unison (fig. 12.2). Wubbels deftly moves between these types of unison through a sense of organic transformation—even mutation—as the players merge, diverge, and converge again over the course of the piece's sixteen-minute duration.

Affectively, the piece is riotous and enthralling. Wrenching, relentless flows of sound bark and spit from the violists' bows. Lowrie, Mandel, Popoff, and Sielaff are mangled into some sort of monstrous organism whose energy pulsates, explodes, and collapses, drawing me into their tenuous and strained collective. I join this many and become one with it as a first-person plural *we* bound up through sound and affect. But where is this *we* when we feel? The question of location is fundamental to any experience of affect, and indeed, the affect theory that has drawn on Whitehead has accounted for the relationships between subjectivity, sound, and sentiment in ways that seem not entirely congruent with Whitehead's radical relationality.

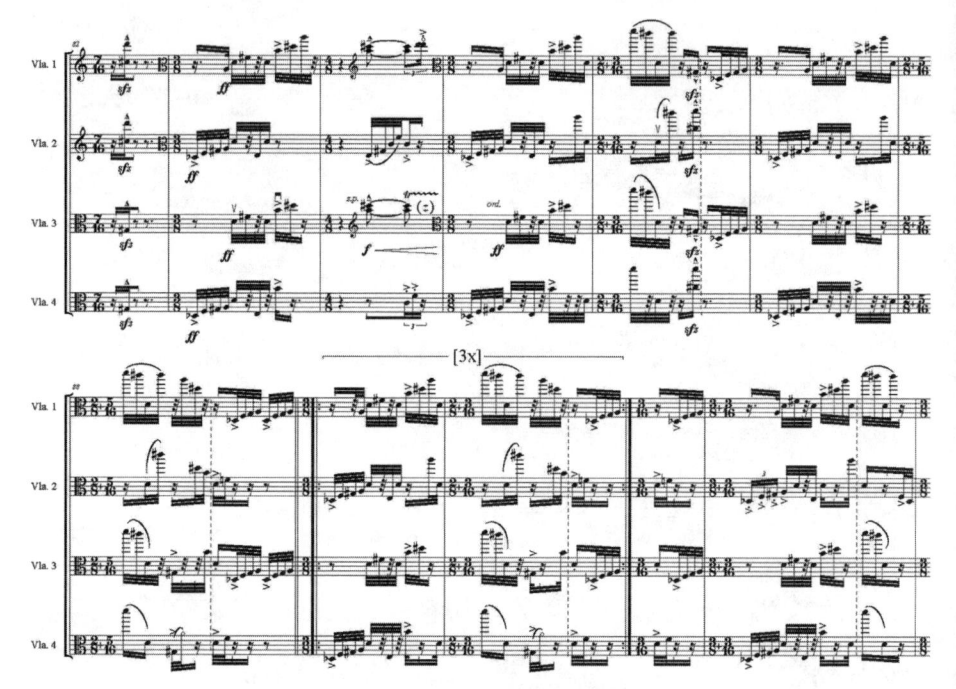

Fig. 12.2. Rhythmic and pitch unison with hocketing. Wubbels, Viola Quartet, p. 10. Reprinted with permission of the composer.

Glossing Whitehead in a larger reflection on semblance, art, and temporality, Brian Massumi writes:

> What is actually said and done from one moment to the next is discontinuous by nature. But something continues, thought-felt across the gaps. In Whitehead's words, it's a "nonsensuous perception," a virtual perception of "the immediate past as surviving to be again lived through in the present." Every situation, whatever its lived tonality, is sundered by these nonsensuously lived micro-intervals filled only qualitatively and abstractly by affect. Like the vanishing point, they wrap back around to surround. What Whitehead calls affective tonality is something we find ourselves in, rather than finding in ourselves. An embracing atmosphere that is also at the very heart of what happens because it qualifies the overall feel. Affective tonality is what we normally call a "mood."[7]

Here, Massumi enrolls Whitehead in his larger argument for "the autonomy of affect" that the former has developed over the last two decades.[8] Stated in this extract is the idea that "affective tonality" is something external to us and impersonal. Moreover, the larger assumption made by Massumi is that Whitehead's theory of emotions unequivocally supports his insistence on affect's autonomy.

Affect, as Massumi conceives it, is distinct from emotion, which is the form that affect takes once it has been domesticated by productions of subjectivity. For Massumi and others who have taken up his conception of affect—such as Jasbir Puar and Kathleen Stewart—affect is politically valuable inasmuch as it offers access to a world outside the current state of affairs or maps a potential plane upon which radical change is possible.[9] As such, it produces novelty and provides an energetic background flow whose virtuality and possibility are arrested once captured as personal emotion, thought, or language. As Massumi writes, "The primacy of the affective is marked by a gap between *content* and *effect*"—that is to say, there is no direct causation between what affect is and how a subject responds to it.[10] Affect is autonomous in that it exists prior to our sense of self or any sense of *we*. It follows, then, that both concrescence and community limit affect's circulation and political potential.[11]

It is this conception of affect that poses a problem for thinking the location of the *we* produced in listening. The complex becoming dramatized by Wubbels's Viola Quartet—its mangling together of bodies, technologies, listeners, and feelings—is too intertwined, too much of the same event to ascribe any autonomy to the affects engendered. I am not the first to find fault with Massumi's insistence upon affective autonomy. He has been critiqued in light of his work's grounding in misread experimental evidence as well as for its failure to account for the asymmetrical distribution of affects (both positive and negative) among persons.[12] Although I am in agreement with much in these critiques, I want to turn the question toward matters of music and emotion that are elided in the appropriation of Whitehead by Massumi, as well as Deleuze, from whom Massumi derives his theory of affective autonomy.[13] At issue is whether Whitehead can be understood to support a view of affective autonomy. I argue that his philosophy cannot, and, indeed, that Whitehead's theory of feeling describes affect as relational evidence for the processes of subject formation itself. Feelings result from becomings on all levels of worldly organization, from the atomic, to the human, to the technoscapes of global capitalism. The *we* that we are concretizes through affective mediation, through our mutual feeling of the world. The process of feeling is dramatized specifically in Whitehead's comments on music which have, until now, received little attention.

Whitehead, though, is hardly unknown to musicology and music theory. He was among Susanne Langer's professors at Harvard and shaped her thought in some important ways, especially in regard to Langer's ideas of significant form.[14] Beyond Langer, the aesthetician F. David Martin has explored Whitehead's concepts of "presentational immediacy" and "causal efficacy" in relation to musical experience.[15] In music theory, Christopher Hasty and Jonathan Bernard have productively engaged with Whitehead's philosophy.[16] Yet both theorists confine themselves to commentary on temporality and, in Hasty's case, the philosopher's understanding of beauty. Neither reflects on Whitehead's comments about musical experience. As I'll discuss below, Whitehead establishes explicit connections among music, emotion, and aesthetics, yet such connections are rejected out of hand by the composer-theorist Richard Elfyn Jones, who has emphasized Whiteheadian conceptions of temporality at the expense of emotion and affect. Jones has gone even further in his appropriation of Whitehead, refusing to "indulge" in questions of emotion while "confin[ing] ourselves to a rational, Whiteheadian approach."[17] That the temporal insights of Whitehead's thought are of interest for certain kinds of music-theoretical work is unsurprising, yet attempts such as Jones's to radically separate forms of experience (feeling from rationality) dismiss one of the most basic goals of Whitehead's philosophy: avoiding the fallacy of misplaced concreteness, in which we elevate abstract rationality over enmeshed emotional experience.[18]

While these scholars and others, such as Steve Goodman, have shown the potential of Whitehead's philosophy for thinking about musical and sonic experience, they have not noted that at important moments in his philosophy Whitehead turns to music to develop his theory of feelings—what he generally terms "prehensions."[19] These references are few, but they are striking for their heuristic value as well as their potential for thinking of emotional relations as indices of collective sociality.[20]

I

Whitehead's scholarly work falls roughly into three periods: an initial period of mathematics, a second period lasting from approximately 1910 to 1924 in which he worked in the philosophy of science and education, and then from 1924 to his death in 1947, which saw him turn to metaphysics and the development of process philosophy, or, as he called it, "the philosophy of organism."[21] In this last period Whitehead took up a professorship of philosophy at Harvard, where Susanne Langer became his student in 1924. Through his late philosophical works, Whitehead aspired to construct "a critique of pure feeling" that he hoped would "supersede the remaining *Critiques* required by Kantian philosophy."[22] In addition to Kant, Whitehead's main interlocutors were René Descartes, David Hume, Isaac Newton, Henri Bergson, and William James. Whitehead's philosophy is exceedingly complex, and even a simple summary of its contours is beyond the scope of this essay, yet in order to situate his theory of feelings, we must draw out a few central concepts: (1) the revision of the subject-object relation figured as an emotional encounter, (2) the founding of such emotional relations as the fundamental events building the world, and (3) the care with which we should treat our concepts and abstractions.[23] These themes are present in a passage from *Adventures of Ideas*:

> [Philosophers presuppose] that the subject-object relation is the fundamental pattern of experience. I agree with this presupposition, but not in the sense in which subject-object is identified with knower-known. I contend that the notion of mere knowledge is a high abstraction and that conscious discrimination itself is a variable factor only present in the more elaborate occasions of experience. The basis of experience is emotional. Stated more generally, the basic fact is the rise of an affective tone originating from things whose relevance is given. Thus the Quaker word "concern," divested of its suggestion of knowledge, is more fitted to express this fundamental structure.[24]

The radicality of Whitehead's metaphysics is outlined in this passage. First, he disaggregates the subject-knower and object-known equivalents. In earlier philosophy, such as that of Descartes, Locke, and Hume, these relations are assumed to be identical, yet as Whitehead argues, they imply a relationship of "mere knowledge" that abstracts the subject from the occasion of knowing so that it can become purely mental. As such, the equation of subject-object with knower-known exemplifies the fallacy of misplaced concreteness, of mistaking a high abstraction for a basic fact. The alternative conception Whitehead proffers imagines a subject-object relationship constituted through feeling, the mutual experience of the subject and object by one another. Feeling here need not be identified with high-level emotional states (though they are the result of these processes) but can be registered as concern—which Whitehead understands as a directional or vector feeling. We also might understand it as a mutual *tending toward* an object, or, following Sarah Ahmed, as an orientation toward others.[25] Ultimately, this basic fact of feeling resists any conception of subject and object as distanced. Whitehead comes to describe the emotionally involved subject and object as a "superject," which is the minimum unit of experience.[26] Another point to draw out from this passage is that feeling is not a priori. The affective tone arises through processes of feeling the world. There is no affect separate from this production of subjectivity in experience. This last point exemplifies Whitehead's ontological principle: "There is nothing which floats into the world from nowhere. Everything in the actual world is referable to some actual entity."[27] As such, affect does not exist ex nihilo as pure virtuality, nor is it ever truly separate from some feeling thing.

While Whitehead is critical of abstraction in this passage insofar as it limits our understanding and appreciation of experience, he is not opposed to abstraction. He recognizes that it is necessary—that we are, to twist a concept from Deleuze, abstracting machines experiencing the world. Yet, as Isabelle Stengers has noted, Whitehead asks that we care for our abstractions and attend to what they lure us into thinking, feeling, and speaking.[28] Most of all, Whitehead insists that we refuse to follow a line of flight to some Archimedean point that will give us a perfectly objective view.[29] We are each capable of achieving only a partial perspective, the richness of the world being an inexhaustible source of change and novelty. The revision of our perspectives and abstractions thus becomes the work of politics, which I understand as the affective maintenance of collectives and relational communities.

With the persistent novelty of these concepts, it is no surprise that Whitehead has been taken up in late twentieth- and early twenty-first-century affect theory and science studies. And Deleuzian resonances abound in Whitehead's corpus. Consider, for example, Whitehead's statement that "philosophy can exclude nothing. Thus it should never start from systematization. Its primary stage can be termed assemblage."[30] "Assemblage," of course, is how Gilles Deleuze and Félix Guattari's concept of *agencement* has been translated into English, and it would be interesting to speculate on the potential connections here, yet Whitehead's use of the word is rare and does not attain the consistency or specificity of a concept in his philosophy.[31] But the term is suggestive. Beginning our work from assemblage—from parts and ingredients of events—avoids the other fault of forging too high an abstraction, which would "bifurcate experience" into what is real appearance and that which might be construed as semblance—or, as John Locke would write, primary and secondary qualities. In *The Concept of Nature*, Whitehead argues: "For natural philosophy everything perceived is in nature. We may not pick and choose. For us the red glow of the sunset should be as much part of nature as are the molecules and electric waves by which men of science would explain the phenomena. It is for natural philosophy to analyze how these various elements of nature are connected."[32] To ascribe truth to one event over another would be to commit the fallacy of misplaced concreteness—to endow a high abstraction with a concrete force not proper to it.

Whitehead seems to set up an impossible task for any scholar—"we may not pick and choose." And yet we must. We need abstractions in order to communicate our feeling of the world. Whitehead's point, as I understand it, is that we need to attend to the performativity of our abstractions, their real effects on the world. Abstraction is not the same as bifurcation, nor is abstraction necessarily an arena for misplaced concreteness. In advance of my fuller discussion of Whitehead's theory of feelings and music, the concepts developed so far—the emotional basis of experience and the injunction to avoid misplaced concreteness and bifurcation—afford a vantage point to critique Massumi's formulation of affective autonomy. In *Parables for the Virtual*, he writes:

> The autonomy of affect is its participation in the virtual. *Its autonomy is its openness*. Affect is autonomous to the degree to which it escapes confinement in the particular body whose vitality, or potential for interaction, it is. Formed, qualified, situated perceptions and cognitions fulfilling functions of actual connection or blockages are the capture and closure of affect. Emotion is the most intense (most contracted) expression of that capture and of the fact that something has always and again escaped.[33]

Notice what it is that affect does: it "escapes confinement," it is both virtual and potential. It is "arrested," "captured," and subject to "closure." Subjectivity, evinced by emotion and cognition, is produced through blockages of affect. Affect's political force lies in its capacity to resist subjectivity—or, as in the passage quoted above, its power lies in filling up fragmented moments outside our experience. Affect is a priori, existing before subjectivity and stanching its flow. Compare this with Whitehead's understanding of emotion. The affective tone of experience arises from the mutual feeling of subjects and objects. Affect arises out of relations, through productions of subjectivity. With his desire for deferral, escape, and circulation, Massumi gives the concept of affect a false concreteness that places the potential capacity for change and novelty off limits for us. We are always already outside of affect, even though it surrounds us; we may be in it, but we are certainly not of it. In what follows, I ask if the kind of bifurcation produced by Massumi's affect theory is worth holding on to, or if Whitehead's theory of feelings offers us another way to think of affect relationally and communally through the experience of music.

II

Whitehead's argument that "the basis of experience is emotional" is all well and good, yet the passage from *Adventures of Ideas* discussed above does not tell us much about what feeling is, how it works, and what forms it takes. Whitehead's theory of feeling is part of a larger metaphysical system that he calls "the theory of prehensions."[34] Prehensions are the relations between subjects and objects discussed above that take the form of affective tones. In Whitehead's philosophy, the words *feeling, prehension, event, emotion,* and *affect* are largely interchangeable. Yet, while Whitehead finds the terms equivalent, he does understand there to be "gradations of feeling"—from simple vector feeling to complex emotions to cognition, what Susanne Langer refers to when she articulates feeling and thought as contiguous.[35] This theory of prehensions is developed at length in *Process and Reality*. Of particular interest for musical thought is that Whitehead's example of feeling is the audition of a musical tone: "As a simple example of this description of feeling, consider the audition of sound. In order to avoid unnecessary complexity, let the sound be one definite note. The audition of this note is a feeling. The feeling has first an auditor, who is the subject of the feeling. But the auditor would not be the auditor he is apart from this feeling of his."[36] Here we should bear in mind Whitehead's insistence that "we may not pick and choose" what aspects of experience really count—any failure to begin from the mangle of experience that is listening (for example to imagine "sound itself" as a falsely concrete idea) and imagine an objective position from which we might audit sonic experience would immediately bifurcate our integrated feeling into primary and secondary qualities—or, more to the point, produce a high abstraction whose conceptual utility would be impoverished by its marked rejection of qualia.

Take, for example, a specific tone heard later in Wubbels's Viola Quartet (fig. 12.3). Here the four players arrive at a hard-won unison. The struggles of the opening minutes give way to the uneasy repose and stasis of this passage. As Whitehead remarks, "A feeling bears on itself the scars of its birth; it recollects as a subjective emotion its struggle for existence."[37] The feeling as subjective form is the particular relationship between me as a listener as part of the event of the quartet—a nexus producing emotion through the mutual feeling of subjects and objects drawn together in the musical performance. When I

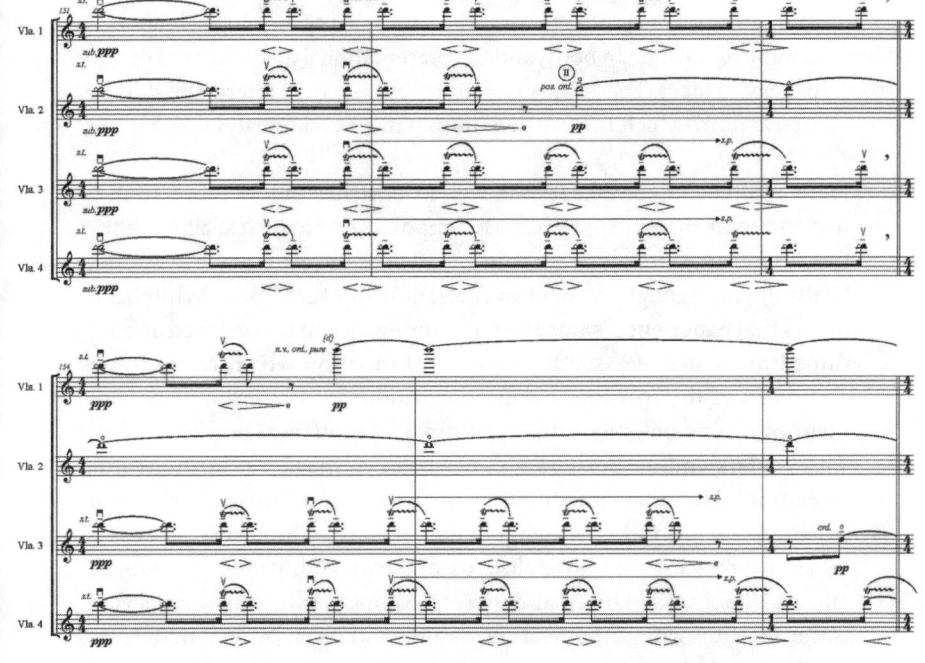

Fig. 12.3. Pitch unison between violas. Wubbels, Viola Quartet, p. 18. Reprinted with permission of the composer.

asked earlier, "Where are we when we feel?" it was the relationality of the *we* that was of greatest interest to me. The quartet forges a fragile nexus, and we as listeners are enrolled within that nexus, feeling with and through it. Affect does the work of mediation, marking the passages and movements of our production of subjectivity, but doing so through coproduction. The many are become one—not one as a singular unity, but as a concrescent diversity. The affective tone arising from this occasion is something we are both in and of, for it would not have come into existence had we not felt it. Its feeling is the result of our becoming-with the sounds we experience.

As Whitehead's elaboration of sound-as-feeling continues in *Process and Reality*, he conceptualizes an aural event as a nexus:

> Secondly, there is a complex ordered environment composed of certain other actual entities which, however vaguely, is felt by reason of this audition. The environment is the datum of this feeling. It is the external world, grasped systematically in this feeling. In the audition, it is felt under the objectification of vague spatial relations and as exhibiting musical qualities. But the analytic discrimination of the

datum of the feeling is in part vague and conjectural so far as consciousness is concerned: there is the antecedent physiological functioning of the human body, and the presentational immediacy of the presented locus. There is also an emotional sensory pattern, the subjective form, which is more definite and more easily analyzable.[38]

Here Whitehead complicates as well as enriches our sense of sound, noting the nexus of experience as composed of processes, actual entities, and events already at work in advance of the experience of sound, but suddenly brought into a novel relationship through it. Whitehead insists that experience is not atomic—though it can be analyzed as continued processes of assembly and transformation which enroll more and more of the world in experience. Audition is an exemplary moment of feeling one's world in gradations of vagueness and specificity. This understanding bolsters a conception of music as, in the words of Antoine Hennion, "mediation itself"—the constant gathering and sowing, weaving and unweaving of experience.[39] These very processes make us what we are, entangling us together with sound, the world, and one another: "The final concrete component in the satisfaction is the audition with its subject, its datum, and its emotional pattern as finally completed. It is a particular fact not to be torn away from any of its elements."[40]

III

In view of these passages, what kind of affect theory emerges from Whitehead's philosophy, and what concepts might they provide for our understanding of the particular musicality of emotional experience—that is, its affective tone? At first blush, there seems to be a potential conformity with some aspects of Deleuzian affect theory as presented by Massumi, at least on the matter of distinguishing gradations of emotion. Deleuze's forms of intensity and sensation seem at first to align with Whitehead's sense of bare feeling having a vector character that does not rise to the level of conscious discernment. This bare feeling's vectoral quality is a kind of brute awareness or perception:

> The crude aboriginal character of direct perception is inheritance. What is inherited is feeling-tone with evidence of its origin: in other words, vector feeling-tone. In the higher grades of perception vague feeling-tone differentiates itself into various types of sense—those of touch, sight, smell, etc.—each transmuted into a definite prehension of tonal contemporary nexus by the final percipient.[41]

Yet there is a crucial difference between Whitehead's understanding of the process of feeling and the Deleuzian-Massumian version. In the latter, for affect to be felt as emotion is for it to be captured in ingrained patterns of thought and culture, to be arrested in subjectivity. Emotion is then bound to the logic of representation whose value for the more radical empiricism that Massumi advocates is limited.[42]

Whitehead's theory of feeling makes no such distinctions between feeling, affect, and emotion, as they are all emergent from a process of subject-object interaction—of actual entities feeling the world. For Whitehead's theory of feeling to conform to Deleuzian-Massumian affect (understood as prepersonal or nonsubjective), it would have to bifurcate experience through deterritorialization, tearing feelings away from the actual entities generating it, blocking processes before a final satisfaction has been achieved.[43] Such a rending of affect from subjectivity is untenable for Whitehead, who in section 2 of his theory of feelings writes, "A feeling cannot be abstracted from the actual entity entertaining it.... Thus, a feeling is a particular in the same sense in which each actual entity is a particular. It is one aspect of its own subject."[44] Or, to put it more bluntly, "Feelings are inseparable from the end at which they aim; and this end is the feeler."[45] An affective event, then, is a line not of flight out of an assemblage into the virtual but toward concrescence.[46]

Despite the tension I've identified between Whitehead and Deleuzian affect, Deleuze draws upon Whitehead to bolster his view of deterritorializing musical affect. Deleuze's references to Whitehead are infrequent. In *Difference and Repetition* (1964), Deleuze calls *Process and Reality* "one of the greatest books of modern philosophy."[47] Only in his study on Leibniz, *The Fold* (1988), does he produce a sustained commentary on Whitehead's philosophy. The brief chapter, titled "What Is an Event?," evokes the scene of musical performance in order to join Whitehead's thought to his own. *Event* is the word Whitehead offered as an equivalent concept for his ideas of "prehension," "feeling," and "actual entity"—all concepts that refer to a spatiotemporal unity, an "occasion of experience" giving rise to a specific affective tone. Deleuze stages his encounter with Whitehead by musical means: "A concert is being performed tonight. It is the event. Vibrations of sound disperse, periodic movements go through space with their harmonics or submultiples. The sounds have inner qualities of height, intensity, and timbre." Deleuze's account begins abstractly in a play of forces—vibrations, movements, dispersion. We're in a world of sensation prior to subjectivity. Gradually, though, the event materializes. He continues: "The sources of the sounds, instruments or vocal, are not content only to send the sounds out: each one perceives its own and perceives the others while perceiving its own."[48] The sensational event is gradually given physical form, and its elements come into relation with one another—relations of perception, based in autoaffection and observation. After laying out the conditions of the event, Deleuze translates his concert into the language of Whitehead by means of *Swann's Way*: "These are active perceptions that are expressed among each other, or else prehensions that are prehending one another: 'First the solitary piano grieved, like a bird abandoned by its mate; the violin heard its wail and responded to it like a neighboring tree, it was like the beginning of the world.'"[49]

Deleuze's adoption of Whitehead's term *prehension* marks his swerve toward affect in thinking of musical experience, as does the quotation of the concert scene from *Swann's Way*. However, for Deleuze, this affect is not an emotional tone giving rise to concrescence of subjectivity, but a translation of the concert event into its vibrations and virtuality. As the Proust quotation seems to suggest, musical affect is a deterritorialization of sound, a becoming-animal that arrives at "pure virtualities that are actualized in the origins, but also pure possibilities that are attained in vibrations or flux."[50] My reading of this passage is admittedly a close one, but the distinctions between Whitehead and Deleuze's accounts of affect emerge when the fuller contours of Whitehead's theory of feelings are taken into account. Deleuze invokes Whitehead's concepts to convey musical experience as an unraveling of the material conditions and a movement toward sensation itself, figured here as "vibration" and "flux." The ultimate satisfaction is not, as for Whitehead, the creation of novel feelingful entities, but rather the production of a line of flight toward undifferentiated, free-flowing affect. The political utility of this conception of affect remains the same as in Massumi: to derealize current matters of concern, to return to states of flux prior to subjectivity, and to escape representational forms. Novelty, for Deleuze, cannot be created through productions of subjectivity, though it is a point that Whitehead insists upon when he argues, as I noted at the beginning of this essay, that "creativity is the ultimate" and that "the basis of experience is emotional."

By way of conclusion, I'd like to consider the alternatives Whitehead offers us for rethinking affect not as foreclosed upon by processes of subjectivity, but as produced by them. Novelty emerges through these processes, and it does not depend upon their undoing for political agency. His thought also provides a mode of working with abstractions and concepts that understands their performative effects and leaves them open to revision. This latter mode becomes the real work of politics. To open up these lines of thought, I wish to pursue the Proustian path marked out by Deleuze. The brief passage from *Swann's Way* quoted in *The Fold* continues:

> Was it a bird, was it the soul of the little phrase [of Vinteuil's sonata] not yet fully formed, was it a fairy—this creature invisibly lamenting, whose plaint the piano afterward tenderly repeated? Its cries were so sudden that the violinist had to leap to his bow to collect them. Marvelous bird? The violinist seemed to want to charm it, tame it, capture it. Already it had passed into his soul. Already the violinist's body, truly possessed, was shaking like a medium's with the summoned presence of the little phrase.... Like a rainbow, whose brilliance weakens, fades, then rises again, and before dying away altogether, flares up a moment more brilliant than ever.... The ineffable word of one man who was absent, perhaps dead (Swann did not know if Vinteuil was still alive, breathing out above the rites of these officiants), was enough to hold the attention of three hundred people, and made of this dais, where a soul had thus been summoned, one of the noblest altars on which a supernatural ceremony could be performed.[51]

Proust here seems to be a process philosopher. Musical performance does the work of ordering the assemblage of things, sounds, instruments, and people. In performance, Vinteuil's sonata "holds" together three hundred audience members, linking up the past and the future, animating community through the interaction with sound. For a moment, a moment Swann desires not to break, "the many become one and are increased by one," as Whitehead has written. I spoke earlier of music being a form of mediation. What Whitehead, by way of Proust and Wubbels, allows us to conceptualize is that music is a form of affective mediation producing modes of feeling that compose our common world. This is not a utopian vision. Novelty itself is not an intrinsic good, nor are all forms of emotional belonging egalitarian or desirable.[52] If anything, Whitehead allows us to conceptualize the affective mediation of the world not as something to be celebrated in itself, but as an ontological condition to be attuned to in hopes of building better bonds and composing better worlds:

> Music elicits some confused feeling into distinct apprehension. It performs this service, or disservice, by introducing an emotional clothing which changes the dim objective reality into a clear Appearance matching the subjective form provided for its prehension.

There is then the vague truth-relation, *via* community of subjective form, between the music and the resulting Appearance. There is also the truth-relation between Appearance and the Reality—the Reality of National Life, or of Strife between nations, or of the Essence of God. This complex fusion of truth-relations, with their falsehoods intermixed, constitutes the indirect interpretative power of Art to express the truth about the nature of things.[53]

The modifications to affect theory that Whitehead offers are an end to both autonomy and modes of theorizing that attribute good politics to conceptions of affect that escape the world, exceed subjectivity, and revel in the break between content and effect. Whitehead's theory of feeling retains the creativity and plurality of Deleuzian affect theory while directing it toward the work of recognizing and modifying the "emotional clothing" of our experience, which is entangled with our abstractions, symbolic codes, and modes of representation. As I see it, the work of affect theory is to assist in "the fearlessness of revision" that Whitehead called for, not to idealize sensation beyond our selves.[54]

Notes

Thanks for reading to Christopher Hasty, Kyle Kaplan, and Sianne Ngai. Jamie Currie gave helpful feedback on an early version of this essay. I'm also grateful to the receptive audiences at SUNY Stony Brook, Northwestern University, and the University of Kansas who helped think through Whitehead's philosophy with me. Many of these ideas were further developed in my seminar "Sound, Affect, and Signification" in the winter of 2015, and I extend my thanks to the students who participated. All shortcomings are, of course, my own.

1. Alfred North Whitehead, *Process and Reality*, corrected ed., ed. David Ray Griffin and Donald W. Sherburne (New York: Free Press, 1978), 21.
2. Ibid., 21.
3. Ibid., 21.
4. Alfred North Whitehead, *Adventures of Ideas* (New York: Free Press, 1967), 176.
5. Eric Wubbels's Viola Quartet is included on Alex Mincek, Jeff Snyder, Alex Ness, Kate Soper, Jim Altieri, Eric Wubbels, Clara Latham, and Sam Pluta, *The Language Of*, Quiet Design CD 700261255088 (2008).
6. Eric Wubbels, quoted in Ryan Dohoney, "Proximity to a Notion of Fusion: An Interview with Alex Mincek and Eric Wubbels of the Wet Ink Ensemble," *Dissonance: Swiss Music Journal for Research and Creation* 116 (December 2010): 22.
7. Brian Massumi, *Semblance and Event: Activist Philosophy and the Occurrent Arts* (Cambridge, MA: MIT Press, 2011), 65.
8. Massumi makes his case for a Deleuzian-Spinozist conception of affect in "The Autonomy of Affect," in "Politics of Systems and Environments, Part II," *Cultural Critique* 31 (Autumn 1995): 83–109; later published in Massumi, *Parables for the Virtual: Movement, Affect, Sensation* (Durham, NC: Duke University Press, 2002), 23–45.

9. See Jasbir K. Puar, *Terrorist Assemblages: Homonationalism in Queer Times* (Durham, NC: Duke University Press, 2007); and Kathleen Stewart, *Ordinary Affects* (Durham, NC: Duke University Press, 2007).

10. Massumi, *Parables for the Virtual*, 24.

11. Massumi develops this line of thought further to suggest that because affect is autonomous and virtual, there is a fundamental discontinuity in experience such that "all relations are virtual." See Massumi, *Semblance and Event*, 64. Whitehead's point, as I understand it, is that affects only emerge from concrete relations and mutual feeling of subjects and objects. Feelings are, in a quite literal sense, facts.

12. On Massumi's use of scientific data, see Constantina Papoulias and Felicity Callard, "Biology's Gift: Interrogating the Turn to Affect," *Body and Society* 16, no. 1 (2010): 29–56; and Ruth Leys, "The Turn to Affect: A Critique," *Critical Inquiry* 37, no. 3 (2011): 434–72. On the white privilege of affective autonomy, see Claire Hemmings, "Invoking Affect: Cultural Theory and the Ontological Turn," *Cultural Studies* 19, no. 5 (2005): 548–67.

13. See esp. Gilles Deleuze and Félix Guatarri, *A Thousand Plateaus: Capitalism and Schizophrenia*, trans. Brian Massumi (Minneapolis: University of Minnesota Press, 1987).

14. See Susanne K. Langer, *Feeling and Form: A Theory of Art, Developed from "Philosophy in a New Key"* (New York: Charles Scribner's Sons, 1953). See also Langer, "The Process of Feeling," in *Philosophical Sketches* (New York: Mentor, 1964), 11–29. For commentary on Langer, see Eldritch Priest, "Felt as Thought," in *Sound, Music, Affect: Theorizing Sonic Experience*, ed. Marie Thompson and Ian D. Biddle (London and New York: Bloomsbury Academic, 2013), 45–64.

15. F. David Martin, "The Power of Music and Whitehead's Theory of Perception," *Journal of Aesthetics and Art Criticism* 25, no. 3 (1967): 313–22.

16. Christopher Hasty, *Meter as Rhythm* (Oxford and New York: Oxford University Press, 1997); Hasty, "Broken Sequences: Fragmentation, Abundance, Beauty," *Perspectives of New Music* 40, no. 2 (2002): 155–73; and Jonathan W. Bernard, "Elliott Carter and the Modern Meaning of Time," *Musical Quarterly* 79, no. 4 (1995): 644–82.

17. Richard Elfyn Jones, "A Whiteheadian Aesthetic and Musical Paradigm," *Canadian Aesthetics Journal* 8 (2003), accessed February 12, 2017, http://www.uqtr.uquebec.ca/AE/Vol_8/libres/jones.html. See also Jones, "A. N. Whitehead and Music: Real Time," *Musical Times* 141, no. 1873 (2000): 47–52.

18. On misplaced concreteness, see Whitehead, *Process and Reality*, 7–8.

19. Steve Goodman, *Sonic Warfare: Sound, Affect, and the Ecology of Fear* (Cambridge, MA: MIT Press, 2010), 91–98.

20. My interest in emotion as mediation aligns my work with that of Richard Grusin, who has turned to Whitehead to develop his concept of "radical mediation." See Grusin, "Radical Mediation," *Critical Inquiry* 42, no. 1 (2015): 124–48.

21. Whitehead, *Process and Reality*, xi.

22. Ibid., 113.

23. On caring for abstractions, see Isabelle Stengers, "A Constructivist Reading of *Process and Reality*," *Theory, Culture & Society* 25, no. 4 (2008): 91–110, reprinted in *The Lure of Whitehead*, ed. Nicholas Gaskill and A. J. Nocek (Minneapolis: University of Minnesota Press, 2014), 43–64. See also Stengers, *Thinking with Whitehead: A Free and Wild Creation of Concepts* (Cambridge, MA: Harvard University Press, 2011).

24. Whitehead, *Adventures of Ideas*, 175–76.

25. Sarah Ahmed, *Queer Phenomenology* (Durham, NC: Duke University Press, 2006), passim.

26. See Whitehead, *Process and Reality*, 151 and passim.
27. Ibid., 244.
28. Stengers, *Thinking with Whitehead*.
29. For the classic critique of the desire for the Archimedean point—which also references Whitehead—see Hannah Arendt, *The Human Condition* (Chicago: University of Chicago Press, 1958), 257–68.
30. Alfred North Whitehead, *Modes of Thought* (New York: Free Press, 1966), 2.
31. On *agencement* vs. assemblage see John Phillips, "*Agencement*/Assemblage," *Theory, Culture, and Society* 23, nos. 2–3 (2006). Alfred North Whitehead uses the term "assemblage" in his description of the event: "[Prehension] was introduced to signify the essential unity of an event, namely, the event as one entity, and not as a mere assemblage of parts or of ingredients. It is necessary to understand that space-time is nothing else than a system of pulling together of assemblages into unities. But the word *event* just means one of these spatio-temporal unities. Accordingly, it may be used instead of the term 'prehension' as meaning the thing prehended." Alfred North Whitehead, *Science and the Modern World* (New York: Free Press, 1967), 72. A potentially analogous term for *agencement* in Whitehead's thought could be "nexus," which implies particular relationships between a given set of things. For further ruminations on the connections between Deleuze and Whitehead, see Steven Shaviro, *Without Criteria: Kant, Whitehead, Deleuze, and Aesthetics* (Cambridge, MA: MIT Press, 2009).
32. Alfred North Whitehead, *The Concept of Nature: The Tarner Lectures Delivered in Trinity College, November 1919* (1920; New York: Dover, 2004), 29.
33. Massumi, *Parables for the Virtual*, 35.
34. Whitehead, *Process and Reality*, 219–82.
35. Whitehead, *Modes of Thought*, 10; and Langer, "The Process of Feeling," 18.
36. Whitehead, *Process and Reality*, 233–34.
37. Ibid., 226.
38. Ibid., 234.
39. Antoine Hennion, "The History of Art—Lessons in Mediation," trans. Liz Libbrecht, *Réseaux: Communication—Technologie—Société* 3, no. 2 (1995): 238.
40. Whitehead, *Process and Reality*, 234–35.
41. Ibid., 119.
42. Massumi, *Semblance and Event*, 39–86.
43. See the feminist elaboration of this point in Hemmings, "Invoking Affect."
44. Whitehead, *Process and Reality*, 221.
45. Ibid., 221.
46. For more on Deleuzian musical experience as virtuality and flux, see Michael Gallope, "Is There a Deleuzian Musical Work?" *Perspectives of New Music* 46, no. 2 (2008): 93–129.
47. Gilles Deleuze, *Difference and Repetition*, trans. Paul R. Patton (New York: Columbia University Press, 1994), 284–85.
48. Gilles Deleuze, *The Fold: Leibniz and the Baroque*, rev. ed. (London and New York: Continuum, 2006), 91.
49. Ibid., 91.
50. Ibid., 91.
51. Marcel Proust, *Swann's Way*, trans. Lydia Davis (New York: Penguin, 2002), 365–66.
52. This echoes Hemmings's point in her critique of Massumi and Eve Sedgwick when she notes the asymmetrical production of negative affect among women and people of color

in Western society. Some do not have the luxury of escaping or disassociating from the affects they are involved in producing. See Hemmings, "Invoking Affect."

53. Whitehead, *Adventures of Ideas*, 249.

54. Alfred North Whitehead, *Symbolism: Its Meaning and Effect* (New York: Capricorn Books, 1959), 88.

PART 6

Theorizing the Affections

CHAPTER 13

Delivering Affect

MERSENNE, VOICE, AND THE BACKGROUND
OF JESUIT RHETORICAL THEORY

André de Oliveira Redwood

Marin Mersenne has received ample recognition for his contributions to the history of music theory. His lengthy and wide-ranging *Harmonie universelle* (1636–37) stands as an unrivaled summa of erudite musical knowledge in the seventeenth century. Despite the breadth of his treatise, however, music scholars past and present tend to examine his output for one of two reasons: he is known to us on the one hand as the author of a magisterial work of organology, and on the other as a key figure in the seventeenth-century shift toward a quantitative and experimental approach to the study of musical sounds. Indeed, it is chiefly in his role as a scientist that he is best known; anybody wishing to consider the tectonic shift in the foundations of musical knowledge that occurred in the seventeenth century must come to grips with the work of the French Minim.[1]

Far less frequently discussed, among music scholars at least, are the ways in which Mersenne's project participates in his wider mission of reforming natural philosophy in a manner conformable with the orthodoxies of his beloved Catholic Church. As far as could be managed, he hoped and worked for intellectual and religious conciliation. Mersenne's catholicity, in both large-C and small-c senses, was inevitably bound up with his scientific aspirations.[2] It is for this reason, for example, that the first three books of *Harmonie universelle* are given over entirely to the study of mechanics, not only in connection with the nature of sound and the behavior of sound-producing bodies, but also with a whole range of other mechanical topics.[3] So too, however, is his mission bound up with the ecclesiastical imperative to propagate the faith. To be sure, the Minims of the convent at the Place Royale enjoyed a well-earned reputation for their scientific activities. But just as important, they were an order of preachers, daily presenting themselves to the public, often against a multitude of competing voices, and with little reason to expect a docile flock.[4] The Minims thus understood what generations of orators and rhetoricians had long taught: the importance in persuasion of moving the emotions—what the Latin writers called *movere* or *flectere*, and what since came to be thought of in terms of affect. In this area, none of the orator's resources was deemed more essential, none more efficacious, than the voice.

Mersenne's interest in the voice reflects this eminently rhetoric-centered understanding: as the primary instrument of both song and speech, it is the voice, with its dual capacity to reflect the passions and to act on them, that provides the basis of his theorization of music and rhetoric.[5] Indeed, Mersenne's conception of music and rhetoric, centering so extensively on the physical production of human sound, belongs in that universe of pulsating air, vibrating strings, and colliding bodies that so fascinated him. This dependence on knowledge of the physical world is what makes Mersenne's rhetorical theorizing so amenable to an affect-based perspective: if there is any weight to Mersenne's assertion that the preacher deserves to reap the benefits of his extensive studies more than any of his other readers, it was almost inevitable that this worked to establish an account of the affective powers and uses of the voice.[6]

To an extent neither widely recognized nor fully understood, his theorization came in the wake of an important turn in the history of rhetoric. It was precisely during the first two decades of the seventeenth century—Mersenne's formative years—that voice, and the rhetorical office of *pronuntiatio*, or delivery, began to receive unusually intense scrutiny from rhetoricians. Especially important in this regard were the Jesuit theorists, many of whom were Mersenne's fellow Frenchmen. Variously renowned and reviled for their skill and effectiveness as teachers, preachers, and missionaries, the Jesuits had every reason to take delivery seriously. Mersenne, who spent his late adolescence and early adulthood at the Jesuits' famed Collège Henri-IV in the town of La Flèche, clearly absorbed his teachers' interest in rhetoric. Inasmuch as both Mersenne and his Jesuit compatriots considered the instruction of future religious orators as essential to their goal of promoting and expanding the reach of Catholic ideology, they were joined by a shared mission. Mersenne's discussion of delivery is thus aimed not so much at his fellow *érudits*, but at the far less exalted parish preacher.[7]

My aim in this chapter is thus twofold. First, I summarize Mersenne's discussion of the voice with a view to explaining both its internal workings and its relevance to the study of voice and affect. Second, I survey the principal Jesuit rhetorical theorists active in the decades that preceded the publication of the *Harmonie universelle*. In doing so, I revisit a path traveled by literary historians, most notably Marc Fumaroli, Philippe-Joseph Salazar, and Erec R. Koch.[8] As we will see, Mersenne approaches the voice and the passions in a manner that, to varying degrees, reflects his mechanistic inclinations. As such, his approach represents a notable departure from that taken by his Jesuit predecessors. Yet, true to his polymathic syncreticism, Mersenne appears to have been unwilling fully to commit himself to the "new," purely mechanistic position. His hesitation provides an intriguing case study: in the early decades of a radical epistemological transformation, in which he himself played no small part, Mersenne shows himself on rather more difficult ground when it comes to matters of voice and affect. That our Minim (who is so often unwavering in his conviction about the explanatory power of mechanics and mathematization) hesitates here testifies to the notable challenges surrounding the subject.

Pronuntiatio, Passions, and the Physicality of the Affective Voice

Immediately apparent in Mersenne's treatment of the voice and its affective potential is his emphasis on its physicality. Significant portions of the "Livre premier de la voix, des parties qui servent à la former, de sa définition, de ses propriétés, et de l'ouïe" are taken up with propositions concerned with the formation and manipulation of vocal sounds. In Propositions 2–4 of the book, he sets out to describe the muscles involved in vocal production, specifically those of the chest and larynx; establish the direct relationship between the glottis and the voice; and explain the role of the nerves and muscles of the larynx in the production of pitch.[9] Propositions 15–19 address the vocalization of pitch, again with a continued interest in the vocal anatomy and its physical operations.[10] Early in this group of propositions, he admits that it would be difficult to understand the production of vocal pitch without a prior knowledge of the movements of reeds, which he compares to the vibrations that take place within the larynx during vocalization.[11] Proposition 21 treats the question of vocal volume, a product of the force of the air as it is pushed through the vocal tract.[12] Propositions 35 and 36 discuss various ailments that may afflict the voice, together with their cures (for clearing the throat, for example, Mersenne recommends a combination of leeks and onions; and he suggests that similar results may be obtained by mixing crushed bean sprouts with sugar, licorice juice, or tobacco syrup).[13] Finally, Propositions 53 and 54 deal with the production of consonants and vowels, and the causes and remedies associated with the production of excessively nasal vocalizations.[14]

Although Mersenne's study of the voice is clearly a product of the age, its fundamental concerns hark back to the *Institutio oratoria* of Quintilian. Early in his chapter on delivery, the Roman rhetorician describes the nature of a person's voice, which he divides into two parts, *quantitas* and *qualitas*, volume and quality. Volume refers, simply enough, to the loudness or softness of the voice. Quality, he writes, "is more complex. A voice may be clear or husky, full or thin, smooth or harsh, limited or rich, hard or flexible, resonant or dull."[15] Mersenne's propositions—addressing topics such as the volume and ailments of the voice—address both volume and quality. Like Mersenne after him, Quintilian was also concerned with vocal health, writing, for example, that "any defect... produces a voice which is muffled, harsh, or cracked."[16] But Quintilian quickly leaves aside the nature of the voice, suggesting that "it is not necessary ... to investigate the causes of all these variations—whether the difference lies in the part of the body where the breath is formed, or in the pipes, as it were, through which it passes; whether the voice has a nature of its own or just reacts to movements; and whether strength of lungs or chest or even head does more to help it."[17] These kinds of questions, which Quintilian was content to set aside, are precisely the ones that preoccupy Mersenne in the "Livre premier de la voix." Mersenne wishes to understand what *causes* the voice to be stronger or weaker, to produce one syllable or another, or to have one quality or another. For Mersenne, these are physical (and physiological) questions; as such, they are what allow his effort to theorize *pronuntiatio* to stand on terra firma.

Beyond his interest in the bodily source of vocal utterance, Mersenne's concern with the physical and physiological dimensions of rhetorical delivery is also evident in the way in which he describes passionate speech. Building on the foundations set forth in the "Livre de la voix," he attempts later in the *Harmonie universelle* to formulate a theory of vocal inflections, which he calls "accents of the passions."[18] These "accents" may be of service to either the singer or the orator; in either case, their purpose is to express and arouse the passions. After considering alternative schemes for naming and categorizing the passions, he settles on a small number of fundamental passions, ultimately focusing much of his theorization on the passion of anger (*cholere*). Of particular interest in connection with the physical dimension of the embodied passion is Mersenne's attempt to associate three ascending degrees of anger with a concomitant acceleration of the pulse. Speculating that the pulse of a person experiencing the first degree of anger may be in a sesquialtera (3:2) relationship to that of a normal resting pulse, he suggests that the pulse of a person in the second degree of anger would be double a resting pulse, which, he explains, arises from a sesquitertian (4:3) increase from the first degree. Finally, the third degree would involve an utterly tachycardic tripling of the resting pulse.[19]

If Mersenne is confident about the physical, mechanical operations of the voice, he is rather less certain about how to approach the passions. In the course of theorizing the accents of the passions, Mersenne was forced to confront questions about the nature of the passions themselves. To begin with, he had to establish the identity of the passions and their number. At first he grounds his discussion not in any new mechanistic theory, but in the long-established Thomistic explanation. In scholastic doctrine, the passions are a part of a broader theory of the soul's tendencies of attraction and repulsion, known as *appetites*.[20] As Mersenne writes, the appetites, and the passions that go with them, are thought to be connected to parts of the body: the concupiscible appetite and its passions reside in the right side of the heart and in the liver; the irascible appetite and its passions reside in the left side of the heart and in the spleen.[21] Mersenne groups these passions into pairs along the attraction–repulsion axis. Love (attraction to an essential good) is paired against Hate (repulsion from an essential evil). Love is further divided into Joy (attraction to a present good) and Desire (attraction to an absent good). Hate is divided into Sadness (repulsion from a present evil) and Aversion (repulsion from an absent evil). The five irascible passions are traditionally grouped as one singleton and two pairs—Anger (repulsion from a present evil), which has no corresponding attraction (since no present good is difficult to obtain); Hope/Courage (attraction to an absent but obtainable good, repulsion from a defeatable evil); and Despair/Fear (attraction to an unobtainable good, repulsion from an undefeatable evil).

The proposition then takes an unexpected turn and leaves the reader suspecting that Mersenne came to realize only after he had begun to write how difficult his task would be. With little explanation, he reduces the number of passions from eleven to four: joy, pain, fear, and hope. Rather than justify through analysis, however, Mersenne invokes ancient authority, citing passages from Boethius, Virgil, and Filelfo.[22] Having apparently abandoned the scholastics' eleven-passion scheme in favor of one that was both simpler and authorized by the ancients, Mersenne soon turns to a new scheme, lowering the number of principal passions from four to three—anger, joy, and sorrow—and positing three degrees of intensity for each passion, resulting in a total of nine.[23] Thus, Mersenne's initial attempt to simplify the scholastic model in favor of one supported by ancient authority quickly gives way to a selective reclaiming of the Thomistic passions (interestingly, the three that he selects have in common that each involves an attraction to or repulsion from a present good or evil). Despite his effort to simplify, then, Mersenne clearly struggled fully to free himself from the scholastic framework. His explanation for the bodily operations of the passions was similarly traditional. Mersenne retained the Galenic theory of vital spirits that predominated in the sixteenth century. Drawing a comparison to the ebb and flow of tides, Mersenne explains that in the passion of joy, the heart expands, sending the vital spirits upward in the body and producing a flushed appearance. If the vital spirits ascend to the point that the heart no longer has enough, as occurs during a great excess of joy, "we faint, and sometimes die laughing." By contrast, an excess of sorrow and similar passions causes the vital spirits to descend and smother the heart, rendering the face pale.[24]

After this lengthy discussion of the passions, he finally closes the proposition by returning to the accents, inquiring whether it is possible to establish four accents to correspond to the four passions. By this time, Mersenne has evidently given up on finding accents specific to the eleven Thomistic passions. (This after having asserted, in Proposition 9, that there are so many accents that it is hardly possible to express them all). He is reduced, it would seem, to making general statements on the question—sad accents, for example, are "slow, gloomy, and unfortunate," whereas hateful accents are "more violent." He can do little more than to conclude—defeatedly?—that "it is difficult to express all these accents."[25]

What purpose do the accents of the passions serve? They are clearly important in the performance of vocal music; hence the placement of this discussion in the "Livre de l'art de bien chanter." Yet Mersenne closes this section not with an argument for the accents' relevance to the singer, but with a claim for their utility for the *prédicateur*—the preacher. As he explains here, and again later in the *Harmonie universelle*, the preacher will benefit from familiarity with the accents because it will allow him to understand the workings of his own voice: its overall range, its notes of optimal resonance, and the characteristics of each passion.[26]

Importantly, the eloquence that Mersenne formulates here is based on the body. Nowhere in this discussion does he touch on the more familiar language-based material of rhetorical theory (e.g., topics of invention, divisions of a speech, tropes and figures). If we are to identify a foundation for the way in which Mersenne relates the science of sound to music theory and to the practice of oratory (especially of a religious kind), it may be the domain of affect, with its frank acknowledgment of the importance of the nonlinguistic elements of experience. And given Mersenne's overt mission to promote Catholic orthodoxy at a time when the dominion of the Catholic Church was no longer absolute, it is perhaps telling that he offered his readers a means of persuasion essentially unconnected from argumentative approaches.[27] Even for the highly erudite (and verbose) Mersenne, it seems, it was necessary to establish a basis for what the ancients had called *movere*—the movement of an emotional state for persuasive ends.[28] A similar emphasis on *movere* characterizes Jesuit rhetorical theory; with this emphasis on emotional rhetoric it was perhaps inevitable that they, too, would turn toward delivery as a center of attention.

Delivery in Early Seventeenth-Century Jesuit Theory

Mersenne's approach to the voice and its connection to affect clearly is shaped by his scientific predilections. In this respect, he does not immediately appear to fit the familiar mold of the rhetorician, particularly given the heavy emphasis placed by rhetoricians and historians of rhetoric on the earlier parts of the discipline (*inventio, dispositio,* and *elocutio*—invention, arrangement, and style).[29] Clearly, however, Mersenne shared with the ancients an interest in the emotions and how to move them.[30] Importantly, this interest would also be a central characteristic of Mersenne's Jesuit teachers. From 1604 to 1609, the teenaged Mersenne studied at the newly formed Collège at La Flèche, the same school that saw the young René Descartes pass through its curriculum, and where the famed rhetorician Nicolas Caussin would teach just a few years later.[31] Indeed, as Peter Dear (in the only intellectual biography of Mersenne in the English language) has shown, Mersenne's education at the hands of the Jesuits proved foundational in shaping both his program of natural philosophy and the manner in which he advanced that program: even with France proving an inhospitable environment for these papal agents, the Jesuits nevertheless "provided [Mersenne] with tools by which even an apparently revolutionary break with existing, officially sanctioned views about nature and its study could appear compatible with established learning."[32] Rhetoric, the humanist discipline par excellence, was of course at the center of this education, and Mersenne saw no need to break with his erstwhile schoolmasters on this question.[33] Nor did Mersenne need to break from his erstwhile schoolmasters when it came to the importance of rhetoric in preaching.[34]

The early seventeenth-century rhetoricians were unique in the history of their discipline precisely because of the special emphasis they placed on delivery in general and on the voice in particular. In his indispensable studies of the subject, Philippe-Joseph Salazar identifies a succession of Jesuit rhetoric treatises dating from 1600 on, each of which pays considerably more attention to the *ars pronuntiandi* than did the writings of any previous rhetorician.[35] The series begins with the Peter Ramus–inspired work of Alphonso Alvarado, whose *Artium disserendi ac dicendi libero duo* (1600) laid the groundwork for future developments in the first quarter of the seventeenth century. Evincing the Ramist passion for systemization, Alvarado divided vocal *pronuntiatio* into ever smaller categories, delimiting more than fifty ways in which the voice could be inflected—with each category of inflection assigned to a particular passion, section of a speech, or type of subject matter.[36] This represented a significant departure from traditional accounts of *pronuntiatio*, which largely relied on—and often severely abbreviated—the information provided by Quintilian.[37]

The five authors and treatises identified by Salazar as the sources of the "armature" of this newly emerging line of Jesuit texts, which provide previously unseen theorization of the *ars pronuntiandi*, are Carlo Reggio (*Orator Christianus*, 1612), Nicolas Caussin (*De eloquentia sacra et humana*, 1619), André Valladier (*Partitiones*, 1621), Pierre d'Auberoche (*Eloquentia Pantarba*, 1626), and Louis de Cressolles (*Vacationes autumnales*, 1620).[38] Just as delivery stood above all else for the great Attic orator Demosthenes, so did it take on a renewed importance for these Jesuit rhetoricians: as described by Salazar, "*pronuntiatio* is envisaged as the instrument of the passions, the 'voice of the passions,' and the heart of eloquent persuasion—more than argumentation or elocution."[39]

Particularly important in this group of treatises is Cressolles's *Vacationes autumnales*, published by Sebastien Cramoisy, the same publisher who three years later would print Mersenne's massive *Questiones celeberrimae in Genesim* (as well as the *Harmonie universelle* over a decade later). Unlike most other rhetoric treatises, the *Vacationes* is dedicated in its entirety to delivery and goes so far as to reimagine the position of delivery (*actio et pronuntiatio oratoria*) within the traditional hierarchy of rhetoric's five parts by placing it at the top.[40] As Fumaroli notes, the *Vacationes* aspires to provide "a complete pedagogy of *actio*, founded upon the teaching of the ancient rhetors."[41] Although it is difficult to imagine Cressolles's highly erudite treatise truly serving as a practical pedagogical aid for anybody involved in the day-to-day business of preaching, there is arguably more at stake in Cressolles's conceptualization of a delivery-centered rhetoric than the reorientation of rhetorical theory. With the considerable theological importance given to the notion of "divine speech" fashioned into human form, a rhetoric of the voice comes to approach the "divine archetype, render[ing] the Orator, an image of God, the incarnation on earth of the Word."[42]

Hence it comes as no real surprise that Mersenne saw delivery as the heart of eloquence and conceived of the relationship between music and rhetoric in largely vocal terms. The "Livre de la voix" thus has a special place within the overall scheme of the *Harmonie universelle*: it offers a means by which Mersenne's concern with the operations of the physical world may find its way into the musical and rhetorical domains. Further, the voice provides an important basis on which to compare musical performance and oratorical delivery. This, together with the long and venerable history of theological significance with which the voice was imbued (one need merely call to mind the central Christian doctrine of the Incarnation—*verbum caro factum est*, "the word was made flesh"), offers reason enough for Mersenne to devote a considerable number of pages to the study of its workings.[43]

What does remain an intriguing question, however, is how actively Mersenne was participating in these rhetorical conversations, if at all. Frustratingly for anybody wishing to draw a direct connection between Mersenne's thinking and that of these Jesuits, the evidence is circumstantial. Although Mersenne was known for his spectacular erudition, he does not mention any of these rhetoricians in the *Harmonie universelle*. There is, moreover, no evidence that he corresponded with any of them at any point in his long career. And yet, Mersenne's biographer and fellow Minim, Hilarion de Coste, indicates that Mersenne was visited in his friary cell by Caussin, whose lengthy *De eloquentia sacra et humana* was one of the most well-known of the Jesuit rhetoric treatises.[44] Many of these rhetoric books dating to the 1620s appeared while Mersenne was already active as an intellectual in Paris. He had not yet given his career over entirely to scientific and mathematical studies. What is more, Caussin was a well-known figure for other reasons, having played a significant role in the French royal court (including a brief stint as Louis XIII's confessor). As for Cressolles's treatise, the editors of Mersenne's correspondence note that he appears not to have been aware of it when he attempted a systematic study of the errors of pronunciation in the *Quaestiones in genesim*.[45] The *Quaestiones* is an early work, however, and the absence of any mention of the *Vacationes* does not exclude the possibility that Mersenne came to know the work at some later time.

We must take care, then, to avoid overstating the connection between the Jesuit rhetoricians and Mersenne's later theorizations. Most of Mersenne's direct references to rhetorical theory rely heavily on ancient sources—Cicero and Quintilian—rather than contemporaneous or near-contemporaneous ones. Even so, Mersenne and the Jesuits show an interest in delivery to a degree not seen since Quintilian's *Institutio oratoria*, and both shared the aim of facilitating the pragmatic education of Catholic preachers. With delivery standing out as the part of rhetoric given over entirely to nonverbal persuasion, it is a natural locus at which to consider early seventeenth-century attitudes about affect. Mersenne's study of the voice thus offers us an important source from one of the period's most prolific musical thinkers; his efforts, in turn, invite us to examine his relationship with the Jesuit rhetorical theory that began to emerge during his formative years. Nevertheless, Mersenne's and the Jesuits' shared interest in the voice, together with Mersenne's early education at La Flèche, at the very least suggest that the connection is more than coincidental. The *Harmonie universelle* differs from the Jesuit treatises in that Mersenne retained his primary interest in mathematics and mechanics, that is, in the physical properties of sound—and this remained the central focus of the "Livre de la voix." But if musical knowledge and rhetorical theory (particularly as formulated by these Jesuits) may be said to find a common ground in Mersenne's intellectual world, it is the voice that most clearly provides it.

* * *

Mersenne makes an unlikely rhetorician. With his obsessive approach to quantification, mathematization, and physical experimentation, strongly evident in virtually all his writings, one might have expected him to have paid little attention to a discipline that, since its earliest days, struggled against the charge that it trafficked in opinion, manipulation, and downright deception. Yet his clerical imperative to propagate the faith made efficacious persuasion an unquestioned necessity. Insofar as he was able to reconcile his mechanistic predilections with questions of eloquence and persuasion, it was through the physicality of the voice. Moreover, his intellectual formation under the supervision of Jesuit schoolteachers, which involved a rigorous upbringing in the humanist tradition, placed classical rhetoric in a central position in his education. Whereas thinkers such as Descartes would famously (and perhaps disingenuously) make a point of renouncing the priorities that shaped their early education, Mersenne took the somewhat gentler approach of working to assimilate, accommodate, and compromise. The result can make for confusing reading, with one approach unexpectedly giving way to another within just a few pages of text. Mersenne's "universal" aspirations, however, enabled him to include areas of activity in his thought that might have been far less at home in the hands of thinkers possessed of a more aggressively reformist bent.

There was no shortage of theological justification for such an emphasis on the vocalized utterance, if one was needed. But outside the rarefied domain of the polymaths—Mersenne, Athanasius Kircher, Robert Fludd, and others—preaching was a perilous business, the site of raging battles for souls, territory, and power.[46] In this respect, the ability to produce and move affects represented far more than a question of speculative exercise. Mersenne's activities in mechanics and music theory, however, make his contribution to rhetorical theory of a very different sort than that of his Jesuit contemporaries. The same may be said for his role in the history of music theory: his commitment to understanding the science of sound creates a situation rarely seen in the music-rhetoric exchange as it is conventionally imagined. Here it is music theory—both as an extension of mechanics and as a form of disciplining the vibrating human instrument—that has something to offer rhetoric, and not the other way around.

Notes

1. The most accessible description in English is H. F. Cohen, *Quantifying Music: The Science of Music at the First Stage of the Scientific Revolution, 1580–1650* (Dordrecht: D. Reidel, 1984), 97–114.

2. Mersenne's religious objectives serve as a foundational premise in both major intellectual biographies of him. See Robert Lenoble, *Mersenne; ou, La naissance du mécanisme...* (Paris: J. Vrin, 1943), and Peter Dear, *Mersenne and the Learning of the Schools* (Ithaca, NY: Cornell University Press, 1988).

3. See Thomas Christensen, "The Sound World of Father Mersenne," in *Structures of Feeling in Seventeenth-Century Cultural Expression*, ed. Susan McClary (Toronto: University of Toronto Press; Los Angeles: UCLA Center for Seventeenth- and Eighteenth-Century Studies and the William Andres Clark Memorial Library, 2013), 60–89.

4. Preaching occupied a central role in the Minims' earthly mission; see P. J. S. Whitmore, *The Order of Minims in Seventeenth-Century France* (The Hague: Martinus Nijhoff, 1967), 120–21.

5. This is my argument in "Mersenne and the Art of Delivery," *Journal of Music Theory* 59, no. 1 (2015): 99–119.

6. Marin Mersenne, *Harmonie universelle, contenant la théorie et la pratique de la musique* (Paris: Sebastien Cramoisy, 1636), III.11:373. The existence of multiple versions and pagination errors makes citing the *Harmonie universelle* challenging. I use the system proposed in Redwood, "Mersenne and the Art of Delivery," 102.

7. Redwood, "Mersenne and the Art of Delivery," 113–17.

8. Marc Fumaroli, *L'âge de l'éloquence: Rhétorique et "res litteraria" de la Renaissance au seuil de l'époque classique* (Geneva: Droz, 1980), esp. 233–423; Philippe-Joseph Salazar, *Le culte*

de la voix au XVIIᵉ siècle: Formes esthétiques de la parole à l'âge de l'imprimé (Paris: Honoré Champion, 1995), esp. 55–66, 95–127, and 155–70; Salazar, "La voix au XVIIᵉ siècle," in *Histoire de la rhétorique dans l'Europe moderne, 1450–1950*, ed. Marc Fumaroli (Paris: Presses Universitaires de France, 1999), 787–821; Erec R. Koch, "Voice, Aurality, and the Natural Language of Passion in Mersenne's *Harmonie universelle*," *Seventeenth-Century French Studies* 28, no. 1 (2006): 77–89; and Koch, *The Aesthetic Body: Passion, Sensibility, and Corporeality in Seventeenth-Century France* (Newark: University of Delaware Press, 2008), esp. 131–60.

9. Mersenne, *Harmonie universelle*, II.5:3–7.

10. Ibid., II.5:16–28. This section of the book is also specifically addressed to the questions on pitch height famously posed in the eleventh book of the pseudo-Aristotelian *Problems*.

11. Ibid., II.5:17.

12. Ibid., II.5:29–30.

13. Ibid., II.5:43–46.

14. Ibid., II.5:56–60.

15. [Marcus Fabius] Quintilian, *Institutio oratoria*, ed. and trans. Donald A. Russell as *The Orator's Education* (Cambridge, MA: Harvard University Press, 2002), 11.3:15.

16. Ibid., 11.3:20.

17. Ibid., 11.3:16.

18. Mersenne, *Harmonie universelle*, III.11:365–73. I give a more detailed discussion in my "Mersenne and the Art of Delivery," 108–13.

19. Mersenne, *Harmonie universelle*, III.11:370.

20. According to Thomistic doctrine, the passions arise from the specific appetite called the "sensitive." The sensitive appetite involves the body in addition to the mind and soul, and thus responds to the stimuli experienced by the senses—including sound. The sensitive appetite is divided into two categories: concupiscible and irascible. The concupiscible appetite involves attraction to and repulsion from some object that is easily available; the irascible involves attraction to and repulsion from objects that are difficult to obtain. Each appetite gives rise to a group of passions: the concupiscible appetite contains six passions (Love, Hatred, Joy, Sorrow, Desire, and Aversion); the irascible contains five (Anger, Hope, Boldness, Despair, and Fear). These divisions are summarized in the table below.

	Attraction	Repulsion
Concupiscible appetites (objects easily available)	Love (attr. to essential good) Joy (attr. to present good) Desire (attr. to absent good)	Hatred (rep. from essential evil) Sorrow (rep. from present evil) Aversion (rep. from absent evil)
Irascible appetites (objects difficult to obtain)	[None] (present good is not difficult to obtain) Hope (attr. to obtainable good) Despair (attr. to unobtainable good)	Anger (rep. from a present evil) Boldness (rep. from surmountable evil) Fear (rep. from unsurmountable evil)

See Thomas Aquinas, *Summa Theologica*, 5 vols., trans. Fathers of the English Dominican Province (New York: Benziger Brothers, 1948), I Q. lxxxi–lxxxii; I–II Q. xxiii.

21. Mersenne, *Harmonie universelle*, III.11:367.

22. Ibid., III.11:367–68. Mersenne first cites Boethius's *Consolation of Philosophy* 1.7:25–

31 (my quotation begins at line 20 in order to convey the sense): "tu quoque si vis / lumine claro / cernere verum / tramite recto / carpere callem: / gaudia pelle / pelle timorem / spemque fugato / nec dolor adsit / nubila mens est / uinctaque frenis / haec ubi regnant" (You too, if you wish to see the light of truth clearly, and to travel the straight path, drive out joy, drive out fear, and let hope and pain be fled from. The mind is clouded and fettered wherever these reign). He then cites Virgil's *Aeneid* VI:734: "metuunt, cupiuntque, dolent, gaudentque" (they fear, and desire, they grieve, and rejoice). Finally, Mersenne quotes a passage by the noted humanist Francesco Filelfo (1398–1481) from his *Satires*, V.4:4: "Hic timet, ille cupit, dolor hinc furit, inde voluptas" (The one fears, the other delights; When pain rages, pleasure then takes hold for no reason"). Mersenne is chiefly concerned with the four emotions conveyed (*timet, cupit, dolor,* and *furit*), but the overall sense of this passage, together with that of the Boethius—that the path to wisdom lies in a tranquil, reasoned serenity—likely also appealed to the clergyman in him.

23. Mersenne, *Harmonie universelle*, III.11:369–71.

24. Ibid., III.11:368.

25. Ibid., III.11:369.

26. Ibid., III.11:373.

27. By the time he had written the *Harmonie universelle*, Mersenne had already engaged in several religious and philosophical arguments, including two overtly polemical treatises: *L'impiété des déistes, athées, et libertins de ce temps* (Paris: Pierre Bilaine, 1624), and *La vérité des sciences contre les Sceptiques ou Pyrrhoniens* (Paris: Toussaint du Bray, 1625).

28. Augustine, whose *De Doctrina Christiana*, ed. and trans. R. P. H. Green (Oxford and New York: Clarendon Press, 1995), provided the Christian justification for the adoption of pagan rhetoric, replaced *movere* with *flectere* ("to bend"). Augustine's term connotes a considerably more purposeful use for emotional persuasion, suggesting that the audience's emotions can be bent, or manipulated, in one direction or another.

29. See, e.g., Brian Vickers, *In Defence of Rhetoric* (Oxford and New York: Clarendon Press, 1988), esp. 294–339. Vickers, a literary historian, locates the heart of rhetoric in the figures of *elocutio* and places particular emphasis on their role in moving the emotions. Being primarily interested in written rhetoric, Vickers has little to say about delivery. Ironically, he adduces as examples of the figures' expressive power a series of passages taken from a most performance-conceived source—Shakespeare's plays. Ibid., 335–39.

30. For an excellent argument concerning the importance of passions in both ancient rhetorical theory and early modern French thought, see Gisèle Mathieu-Castellani, *La rhétorique des passions* (Paris: PUF, 2000).

31. Mersenne studied at La Flèche from 1604 to 1609, from about the age of sixteen to twenty-one. Descartes was there from 1607 to 1614. The two-year overlap raises the possibility that the two may have encountered each other at that time. Since the two were separated in age by eight years (Mersenne was born in 1588, Descartes in 1596), it is unlikely that any contact would have been especially meaningful. There is in any case no positive evidence that they knew each other at the time.

32. Dear, *Mersenne and the Learning of the Schools*, 7.

33. Ibid., 9–22.

34. On the pragmatic importance of preaching to the Jesuits, see ibid., 22; on the spiritual importance of preaching to the Minims, see n. 4 above.

35. See Salazar, *Le culte de la voix* and "La voix au XVIIe siècle."

36. Alfonso Alvarado, *Artium disserendi ac dicendi. libero duo* (Basel: Ludwig, 1600). For a modern presentation of Alvarado's divisions, see Salazar, "La voix au XVIIe siècle," 820.

37. Cipriano Suárez, *De arte rhetorica libri tres* (Coimbra: Juan de Barreira, 1562), which

served as the elementary Jesuit school textbook and which was very likely used by the young Mersenne, is a case in point: of 141 chapters spanning three books, delivery is treated in three chapters—the last three. Of those, one introduces the subject, the second deals with voice, and the third treats gesture.

38. Salazar, "La voix au XVIIe siècle," 794. With the exception of Pierre d'Auberoche, all these authors were Jesuits.

39. Ibid., 795. Demosthenes is said to have asserted that delivery comprised the first, second, and third most important elements of oratory; the story appears several times in the fundamental rhetoric texts. See, e.g., Quintilian, *Institutio oratoria*, 11.3:5–8; Marcus Tulius Cicero, *De Oratore*, trans. James M. May and Jakob Wisse as *On the Ideal Orator* (Oxford and New York: Oxford University Press, 2001), 3.213; *Brutus*, trans. G. L Hendrickson and H. M. Hubbell (Cambridge, MA: Harvard University Press, 1939), 142; and *Orator*, ibid., 56.

40. The traditional five parts of rhetoric begin with invention and conclude with delivery, according to the imagined sequence of formulating, composing, learning, and delivering a speech, hence the ordering: *inventio* (invention), *dispositio* (arrangement), *elocutio* (style), *memoria* (memory), and *pronuntiatio/actio* (delivery).

41. Fumaroli, *L'âge de l'éloquence*, 316. For a fuller discussion, see Sophie Conte, "Louis de Cressolles: Le savoir au service de l'action oratoire," *XVIIe siècle* 237, no. 4 (2007): 653–67.

42. Marc Fumaroli, "Le corps éloquent: Une somme d'*actio* et *pronuntiatio rhetorica* au XVIIe siècle; Les *Vacationes autumnales* du P. Louis de Cressolles (1620)," *Dix-septième siècle* 132, no. 3 (1981): 264.

43. The most well-known biblical reference for the Incarnation is in John 1:1–14, which concludes, "et Verbum caro factum est" (and the Word was made flesh).

44. See Hilarion de Coste, *La vie du R. P. Marin Mersenne, théologien, philosophe, et mathématicien, de l'ordre des Pères Minimes* (Paris: Sebastien Cramoisy, 1649), 65. A complete translation of de Coste's biography can be found in F. N. David, *Games, Gods and Gambling: The Origins and History of Probability and Statistical Ideas from the Earliest Times to the Newtonian Era* (New York: Hafner, 1962), 196–228.

45. See *Correspondance du P. Marin Mersenne, religieux minime*, vol. 1, ed. Cornelis de Waard (Paris: Presses Universitaires de France, 1945), 102 n. 1.

46. See Larissa Taylor, "Dangerous Vocations: Preaching in France in the Late Middle Ages and Reformations," in *Preachers and People in the Reformation and Early Modern Period*, ed. Larissa Taylor (Boston: Brill Academic, 2003), 91–124.

CHAPTER 14

Mimesis and the Affective Ground of Baroque Representation

Daniel Villegas Vélez

The *Musurgia Universalis* as Epistemic Fold

Athanasius Kircher's 1650 *Musurgia Universalis* is one of the most quoted, yet least read, treatises on seventeenth-century theories of the affections.[1] The twelve-hundred-page tome is still one of the most ambitious and all-encompassing works on music, and its author, who published books on subjects as diverse as magnetism, Egyptology, combinatorics, and geology, today enjoys a reputation for being "the last man who knew everything," even though most of what he wrote has been disproven, refuted, or forgotten.[2] Musicology typically sees the *Musurgia* as an archive. It preserves a great number of musical examples and references to seventeenth-century organology, performance practice, and musical life in general. Yet while Kircher's actual contributions to the field are always in dispute, interest in his theoretical work on music is growing constantly, a testimony to its importance.[3]

This is not unrelated, however, to the epistemic problem that will be the focus of this essay: the *Musurgia* occupies a particularly difficult position between ancient and modern approaches to music theory. It sits, so to speak, right in between Gioseffo Zarlino and Jean-Philippe Rameau (or René Descartes, in some accounts), between two periods that Michel Foucault has described as the Renaissance and classical epistemes, or regimes of knowledge.[4] The clean epistemic cut between these moments, if it could be said to exist as such, is of crucial importance for both the historical theory of the affections as well as the strands of contemporary affect theory that emphasize the status of affect as being pre- or nonrepresentational. Kircher's theory of the affections, the influence of which continued well into the eighteenth century, could be read as a testimony of a theory of the affections where representation is not the dominant epistemic framework, and would thus be an important text, both historically and theoretically, in which to examine the relation between music and affect at the onset of modernity. In this essay, I show how contemporary affect theory—through Gilles Deleuze's and Brian Massumi's philosophy of virtuality—can help us rethink the notion of representation as a form of mimesis that unfolds out of the Renaissance episteme, by examining the heterogeneous components of Kircher's theory of the affections from the perspective of the virtual. In other words, I suggest that the epistemic problem of situating the *Musurgia* can be productively addressed by approaching it as an ontological one.

According to most accounts, it was at the moment of the transition from the late Renaissance into the long eighteenth century that the modern notion of representation arose, breaking with a cosmological conception of the world that was based on a continuous fulcrum of similarities.[5] In Foucault's well-known reading of the Renaissance, all things exist in a continuum joined by similitudes and correspondences—a mimetic ground—which are discovered through hermeneutics and manipulated by magic. In the seventeenth century, Foucault argues, this Renaissance episteme was replaced by the classical episteme, a change made explicit in the new semiotic theory, which understands signs according to a binary structure of sign and signified, with separation and mediation replacing the continuous linkage of macro- and microcosmic similarities. Gary Tomlinson offers an example of how this epistemic shift appears in musical contexts by comparing two well-known compositions by Monteverdi. For Tomlinson, the madrigalisms of "Sfogava con le stelle," on the one hand, belong to a magical episteme of similarities, their conventionality less significant than the chain of signatures that they revealed; it signifies by disclosing hidden connections. The famous descending tetrachord in the *Lamento della ninfa*, on the other hand, belongs to the classical episteme: its function is not to reveal existing similitudes but to suggest new associations and thus "a new world." Tomlinson views the tetrachord as "a musical structure filled with extramusical emblematic significance ... [the] connection [between lament and ostinato] is not founded in the given similitudes of things, in a folding-in of the world on itself ... the ostinato is an emblem that does not resemble, in short; it *represents*."[6] Instead of a stylistic or technical development in Monteverdi's compositional practices, these pieces are evidence of the epistemic shift in which the *Musurgia* is also caught.

Situated on the fault line between the Renaissance and classical epistemes, the *Musurgia* displays, more than any work of its kind, the type of unequal sedimentation, disruption, and fractures that constitute the material of an archaeology of epistemic discontinuity; its heterogeneity is more productive than any unity it may attempt. In my reading, the inconsistencies and ambiguities in Kircher's text enter in a baroque resonance with our considerations of how affect has been shaped and continues to operate in the present. My approach here—employing Deleuzian affect theory to amplify the resonances between Kircher's work and contemporary anthropological approaches to magic and mimesis—does not aim for a unified account of the *Musurgia*, nor does it simply celebrate heterogeneity as a marker of the baroque per se. I take the passages on the theory of the affections in Kircher's text as the material traces of transformations that we have inherited and continue to employ today, and rather than applying affect theory to Kircher's work, I seek to produce a transformation in both by reading one against the other. In other words, my engagement with the *Musurgia* is a reflection on a multifarious modernity as it crystallizes in the complex negotiations that occur in that work—a modernity that, in some sense, is still our own. In this way, Kircher's inconsistencies and ambiguities can be shown to be vitally relevant to our contemporary considerations of how affect has been shaped and continues to operate in the present.

Kircher's theory of the affections has received attention in the context of his classification of musical styles and his attempt to correlate affections with specific modes.[7] This has been read as entwined with musical rhetoric and *Figurenlehre*, as was common for seventeenth-century German writers, grounded in theology, magic, and Cartesian philosophy.[8] Kircher's well-known classification contains nine styles, and he offers examples for each of the twelve modes and for eight principal affections. Fig. 14.1 is one of those examples: "Baci soavi e cari," from Carlo Gesualdo's first book of madrigals (1613), presented as *paradigma affectus amoris*, exemplifying the affection of love. The example is necessarily supplemented by an analytical description of its affective qualities: "See in this brief example [*exiguo paradigmate*] how skillfully the affection of love is expressed and how the intervals languish [*languent*]. The voices are beautifully syncopated; certainly, there is nothing more apt to express the syncope of a languishing soul [*languentis animis*]."[9]

Any attempt to elaborate on Kircher's examples—or paradigms, as he calls them—will quickly require delving into the language of sympathetic magic and late Renaissance cosmology, not so much in their content but in their mode of operation, in their affective effectivity. These *paradigmata*, abstract as they are in Kircher's work, begin to attain a very specific type of autonomy when they are reproduced in

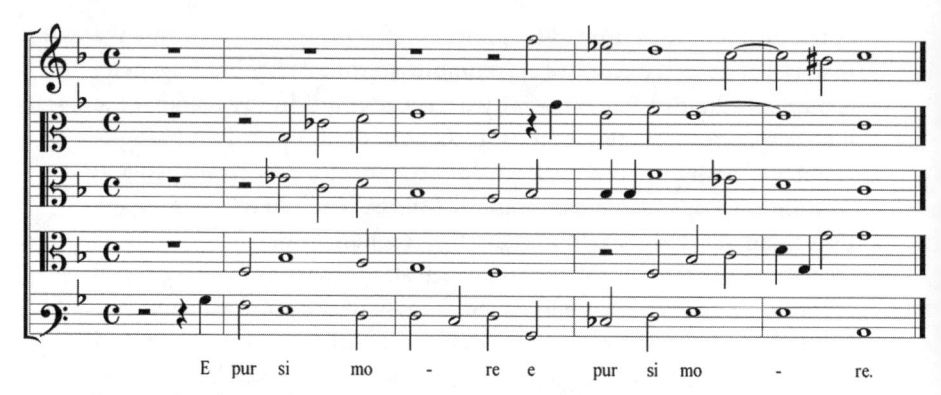

[Musical notation with text below: "E pur si mo — re e pur si mo — re."]

Fig. 14.1. *Paradigma affectus amoris.* Athanasius Kircher, *MU*, A:599

subsequent theories of the affections, whose proliferation in the eighteenth century belies an ambivalent attraction towards their explanatory power. No wonder musicologists claim that there was never a unified doctrine of the affections.[10] Kircher would have agreed.

This classification, I argue, is only the final part of a much more complex engagement with what Kircher calls the doctrine of *musica pathetica*, music composed with an aim to move the affections. The *paradigmata* are the product of this engagement, more mementos than proof. I present two related theses: first, the most interesting part of Kircher's thought lies not in these final *paradigmata* but in the acoustic assemblage of sound and theory that produces them—a very unstable mixture of Galenic humoral theory, sympathetic magic, and music theory, entirely irreducible to its components, and sitting squarely in an episteme based on similitude.[11] This mixture demands new modes of interpretation that contemporary affect theory may supply. Second, at the same time, the *paradigmata* partake of the modern, representational episteme, creating a theory that is by necessity discontinuous with itself. If archaeology is concerned with asking, "What does it mean no longer being able to think a certain thought, or to introduce a new thought?," then a corollary question would be, "How is it possible to think two thoughts at the same time?" How can we make sense of the doctrine of the affections without dismissing the incommensurability of its components, its multifarious, excessive lack of regularity? And what, besides the lack of a consistent doctrine, can we find in a bizarre treatise such as the *Musurgia Universalis* that is of philosophical relevance for affect theory today? It is difficult to gauge exactly when the passage of one episteme to another occurred, or, to borrow Daniel K. L. Chua's quip, when the world went out of tune.[12]

We can think of the *Musurgia* as situated in a particular archeological formation, a fold—at once a baroque event and a geological formation (and this figure anticipates my turn to the philosophy of Deleuze below)—in which the two epistemes overlap and pass into each other, producing a limit that is not one. That is, if Claudio Monteverdi's madrigals mark, in Tomlinson's reading, a shift from one episteme to another, Kircher's *paradigmata* belong to both the Renaissance and the classical epistemes. Even further, I suggest that this baroque fold makes readable the difference between epistemes: in Kircher's work we attend to the very moment when the Renaissance episteme based on similitude vanished and was replaced with the modern one based on representation, yet Kircher's *paradigmata* still depend on the previous episteme. With this move I attempt to understand what the nature of an epistemic discontinuity might mean in musicological terms. I suggest that mimesis and representation—the key functions of the Renaissance and classical epistemes, respectively—are similar yet different at the same time (mimesis being their common "ground"); that the seventeenth century is a crucial place for the transformation of this noncontinuity; and that we can see all of this at play in Kircher's work.[13] Most important, I argue that attending to this moment can also illuminate the stakes of modern forms of representation and subjectivity writ large, as well as the ways in which contemporary affect theory confronts these modern modes of knowledge and experience. If the seventeenth century saw the rise of representation as the principal category for modern thought, and thus also as the anchoring point of the reflexive modern subject, then much contemporary philosophy—including affect theory—has aimed to undo the primacy of representation in multiple ways. This impacts our present understanding of affect, in particular the ways in which the affective turn has sought to undo the primacy of the reflexive subject of representation by assuming affects to be autonomous, operating above or below meaning and representation.

Mimesis and the Magical Force of Affect

For musicology, Foucauldian archaeology has served as a hermeneutical aid in interpreting repertoires that rely on different understandings of subjectivity, gender, power, and meaning.[14] Yet, in Tomlinson, its use came with a warning that has now turned into historicist dogma: while we can reconstruct the forms of knowledge of the past, the nature of an epistemic discontinuity means that these are fundamentally different from our own, and this distance remains unbridgeable—a space of the other that is inaccessible to our understanding.[15] We can ask *how* magic works, but we cannot understand *that* it works. The preservation of this space, Tomlinson argues, allows the other to resist the scrutiny of the presentist, ethnocentric historian. Yet this circumspection, as I see it, also has the contradictory effect of radicalizing the Eurocentric prejudice that magic and alterity belong together, trapped in the epistemic past of the primitive, reified "other." The epistemic break remains: the historian can only represent what is ultimately inaccessible, while the affective power of the other's practices remains locked in itself.

Facing the same problem from the side of anthropology in the context of postcolonial magical practices, Michael Taussig thinks of mimesis as the very medium by which sameness and alterity are simultaneously construed, most evidently in the encounters between "the moderns" and "the primitives," where what is to be the same and what is to be the other are constantly reconfigured. Mimesis, in Taussig's refrain, "is the nature that culture uses to make second nature."[16] According to this account, representation would not simply replace a primitive mode of knowledge (based on continuity) with a modern one (based on mediated discontinuity). Rather, mimesis would produce a simultaneous reconfiguration of alterity and sameness that redistributes what is natural or original and what is cultural or artificial. Elsewhere I argue that musicking, conceived broadly as a mimetic and performative practice, is an acoustic assemblage, as defined by Ochoa Gautier, involved in negotiating the difference between the natural (what is given) and the artificial (what is made) through sound. It distributes beings into copies and originals, or more specifically, produces originals—paradigms—out of things presumed to be copies.[17] In this process of contagion, as Walter Benjamin had noted, sympathetic magic—mimesis's most notorious form in antiquity—would not simply be abandoned because it ceased to be efficacious or because of an epistemic shift. Instead, modernity would still be magical: the magical capacity of mimesis to affect at a distance would effectively be incorporated into language, including its contagious power of making the copy draw on and assume the character and power of the original.[18]

As Anna Gibbs shows, mimesis is also a crucial point of contact between the two main strands of affect theories: the intensive asubjectivity of Deleuzian Spinozism and its interest in the virtual, and the explorations of the biological and psychological conditions of affect as developed by Silvan Tomkins and his followers.[19] While the first strain focuses on the relations between the organic and the inorganic that make up a subject and its becomings, the latter theorizes a set of discrete affects that underlie all human communication. Mimesis, Gibbs writes, is "a complex imbrication of biological capacities with sociality," or more precisely "the immediacy of what passes between bodies and which subtends cognitively mediated representation, which it does not ever entirely replace or supersede."²⁰ Gibbs considers mimesis to be a mode of affective communication through contagion; it operates at every level of experience where, instead of messages, action is transmitted, joining bodies through heterogeneous networks of bodies and things.²¹

Mimesis, in this sense, would constitute an affective bond that works at a distance through contagion—just like magic—and it would remain determining of modernity in particular ways. If this mimetic link between affect and magic holds, then this would offer a way of reading Kircher's text not so much across the epistemic divide, but enabled by it, helping us appreciate its baroque heterogeneity from the present. And, more than preserving Kircher's alterity, this approach should help us see modernity itself as heterogeneous, with affect and representation vying for epistemological preeminence. Instead of understanding alterity in terms of "us and them," we can approach it by displacing the epistemological problem toward an ontological one, as I suggest here, by sketching a theory of magic that borrows from modern anthropology as much as it does from Kircher, using Deleuze's language to make their contagion possible. For Tomlinson, magic is a mode of disclosing hidden similitudes between things, but it is also a means of producing real transformations on the body—such as the healing of the *tarantati* that Kircher made famous.²² To grasp the affective role of magic, then, we need to look no further than Massumi's notion of "incorporeal materialism."²³

For Massumi, affect theory's main concern is to account for the event, asking how it is possible that something that lacks substance or attributes—something incorporeal—has real effects on the body. Massumi's critique seeks to return movement to the body in constructionist accounts, focusing less on identities conceived as points on a grid (redoubled by representation) than on possible becomings—and especially on the forces that produce or hamper such becomings; it emphasizes process over product. In a philosophy of virtuality, identity is defined as the actualization of specific segments of a multiplicity that is no less real than these actualized segments. This multiplicity is the virtual, a limit form of potential that is real yet not actualized.²⁴ Thus, incorporeal materialism focuses on the real but abstract concreteness—the virtual—that brings movement to the body. Abstractness, in this account, means not immediately present but always in passage. Quoting Giordano Bruno, Massumi suggests that magic is another name for incorporeal materialism, "the alloying of knowledge and the power to act," invoking a pragmatic understanding of magic that resists casting it as "irrational" or as the other of modernity.[25] Accordingly, it is the passage from the virtual to the actual (or, more specifically, the passing from a philosophy of signification to a philosophy of virtuality), and not just the discontinuity between antiquity and modernity, that best accounts for the role of magic between affect and representation. Unlike the later *Affektenlehre*, Kircher's theory of the affections is, after all, neither a poetics (a prescriptive guide for composition) nor an aesthetics (an analytic description of works), but a philosophy: the *Musurgia Universalis* is an examination of the cosmos in musical terms, of the musical composition of the universe (*musurgia = mousikēs ergon*, the work of music).[26] In what follows, I will use Kircher's text, read as such a philosophy of the virtual, to understand music's place in this constellation.

The Body and the Cosmos: Magical Cartographies

First, let us begin with a classic account of magic in terms of mimesis. For James George Frazer, magic is regulated by two laws: (1) similarity, or imitation; and (2) contact, or contagion. "The first one," Frazer writes, "affirms that like produces like, or that an effect resembles its cause; [the second] that things which have once been in contact with each other continue to act on each other at a distance."[27] Taussig's ethnographic evidence shows that these two types fold into each other, their distinction becoming untenable: the magic of similarity constitutes but an instance of the magic of contact.[28] To imitate is already to be in touch, and touch is already contagion. Three important conclusions follow: (1) mimesis is always a mode of contagion; (2) imitation is a means for the transformation of that which is imitated; and (3) representation, the copy, retains a specific power to act at a distance.

Mimesis, then, is the basis for the magical powers of imitation and representation. An appropriate musical formulation of this thought appears in the Renaissance philosopher and *magus* Marsilius Ficino: "[Song] imitates and enacts everything so forcefully that it immediately provokes both the singer and hearers to imitate and enact the same things."[29] Here song's affective power is based on mimetic contagion, on the magical power to act at a distance by becoming movement and affection in the body. But to relate affect, magic, and music is but a preliminary step to enter into the baroque complexity of Kircher's text, and much more could be said about this relation that can't be addressed here.

A good entry point into the theory of the affections exposed in the *Musurgia* is to examine Kircher's use of Galenic humoral medicine, a dense formation of philosophy, physiology, and magic that provides the very material fulcrum of similarities connecting the body to the cosmos. For Kircher, an avid reader of Ficino, the affections are the result of a certain combination of primary qualities: the humors. As Claude Palisca puts it, "The vapors from the four humors mix in various proportions according to the objects of the imagination."[30] The quality of each affection depends on the characteristics of the object. For example, "if the object is terrifying, sad, and tragic, the vapors rising from the receptacle of black bile endow the animal spirit with a cold and dry temperament, subjecting the soul to melancholy, sorrow, pain, lamentation, and similar affections."[31] Each of these steps involves a passage from the material (an object) to the incorporeal (the imagination), back to the body (the humors and their corresponding effects, which are both material and immaterial). We can see in this description the relation between process and event examined by Massumi. The relation between these elements is not mechanistic causality but mimetic contagion. Cast in terms of the theory of magic outlined above, the object rearranges the humors and vapors according to its own qualities, whether by contact or at a distance, transmitting its qualities to the whole body: *contagion*. Or again, the body recomposes itself according to the object of the imagination and undergoes an emotion: *imitation*. The effect of the vapors in the body then produce another effect on the soul, an emotion, which is, in a sense, doubly separated from the object that caused it. In other words, what appears as an emotional state in the soul—melancholy, for example—is the mental image of the bodily image of an object coming from the imagination: doubly mediated *representation*.

The virtual as such is inaccessible to the senses but, Massumi writes, this does not preclude figuring it, constructing images of it.[32] Galenic humoral theory is nothing other than the mapping of the body onto a cosmos that exceeds it and recomposes it with its planetary movement (see fig. 14.2).[33] Planets, temperatures, fluids, stones—all have an influence on the body at a distance or from within. The body is defined by the potential relations it can establish with other bodies, by the multiplicity of components—planets, stones, humors—that connect across it. The ensemble of these potential relations or perceptions is the virtual.[34] But the elements that define each bodily state can never be entirely accounted for until a reading is made, until the ensemble of potentialities defined by each component actualizes itself in an astrological reading or a manifest emotion.[35] A Galenic body is not a Cartesian machine: its affections are not the result of a mechanistic cause and effect. It is not by determining what kind of music is heard or what

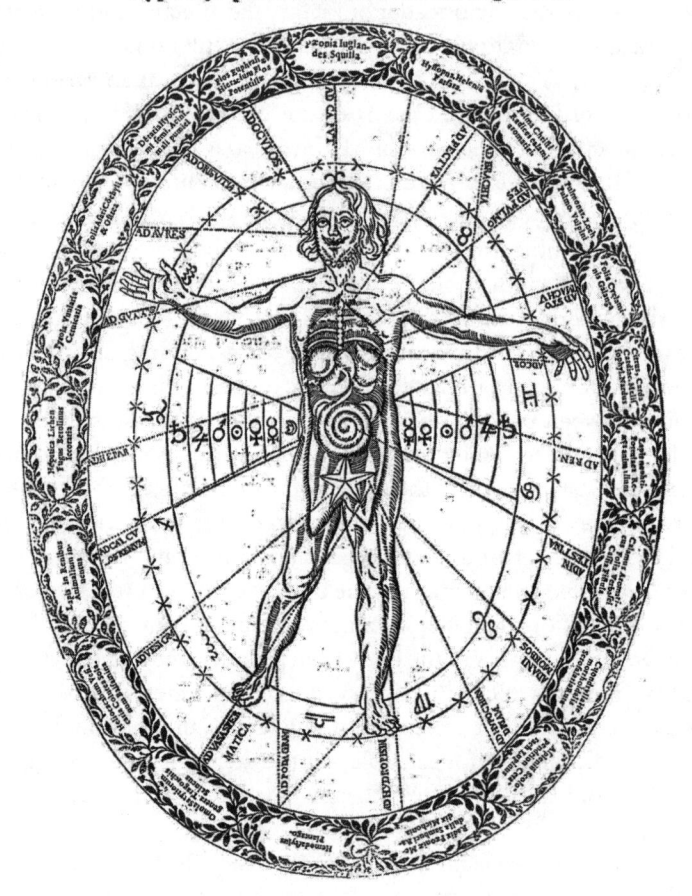

Fig. 14.2. *Typus sympathicus microcomsi cum migacosmo*

emotion it is supposed to represent that Kircher seeks to account for the affective power of music. Rather, it is by attending to the body and its affections, to the way they connect with the cosmos, that we can understand how they are susceptible to being affected by music. And it is not only a matter of determining what media are connected but also in what way, and what the result is of their connection. In Kircher's account, each affection signals a particular arrangement—an actualization—of disparate media in a determinate space and time. The virtual is felt in these actualizations as affect.[36]

An important difference between the possible and its realization, on the one hand, and the virtual and its actualization, on the other, is that the actual does not resemble the virtual, whereas the possible is always presumed to resemble the real that it produces. Hence, it is not a matter of seeking the resemblance between cause and effect, but of establishing how the virtual—the cosmic multiplicity—has differentiated itself into the affection. As Deleuze writes, it is difference that is primary in the process of actualization.[37] This would make us think that magic has no role to play here, because it relies on similitude and mimesis, or that Kircher's theory of the affections remains a philosophy of representation, but the opposite is true. Mimesis is not the repetition of similarities, but the production of difference through repetition in different media of aspects that later appear similar.[38] Music provides the limit case here, since the similarity between its object and its effects in the body has always been a matter of conception. Let us now examine how Kircher describes music's role within the affective cosmos of Galenic theory.

Affective Combinatorics: Music, Affect, and Emotion

Kircher's discussion of Galenic humoral theory is found in book 7 of the *Musurgia*. This book is divided in two parts. The first part, titled *Erotematica*, presents a series of rhetorical questions that rehearse the dispute between ancient Greek and modern music.[39] The question of the affective power of music results from this evaluation, as it did for the Florentine Camerata, and from Kircher's reluctance to declare either ancient or modern music to be better.[40] The second part focuses on modern music, the uses and abuses of harmony, and the value of ecclesiastic chant. The third part is the exposition of the actual theory of the affections under the name of *musica pathetica*. *Erotema VII*, entitled *Physiologum*, poses the question of how music moves the affections ("Quomodo numerus harmonicus affectus moveat"). Kircher determines that, insofar as the affections belong to the corporeal *appetitus sensitivus*—the material part of the soul in humoral theory—the affections must be analyzed with respect to their material conditions (*pathemata materialibus quoque conditionibus*), their physiology.[41]

Kircher's crucial move is to avoid offering a stereotypical catalog of emotions and assign them musical correspondences based on either similitude or convention. Rather, he begins with an account of what produces these emotions—process, not product. If, Kircher writes, affections are aroused by diverse mixtures of vapors produced by the sympathetic resonance of music with the humors, then, since there is an infinite variety of types of music, the affections that can be aroused are also infinite.[42] This potential infinity opens us to what we can call a theory of incorporeal materiality, in the sense outlined above, dealing with the event as the actualization of the virtual. It is not that we have a repertoire of possible emotions—just as, for Massumi, subjectivity cannot be reduced to a position within a grid—but rather that emotions are always the result of an event, produced by the interaction of infinite but ultimately traceable elements, none of them bearing any resemblance to their effects. Kircher uses humoral theory to map the infinity of affections—all the ways in which the body can be affected—and to trace their becomings and actualizations, the moment when they pass from the incorporeal (the real but abstract) into the material (the body's emotion). And if one knows how to enable these connections and follow their passages, it is impossible not to obtain the miraculous effects of music.

The rest of Kircher's "doctrine" attempts to deal with two consequences of this theory: first, one must know exactly how affections are aroused to understand how they relate to music, and second, this task has to be undertaken in a scientific mode, inquiring into their material conditions, their causes, rather than recalling the doctrines of the ancients or inferring them from the opinions of the public. To attempt to correlate modes and emotions in the way Kircher's precursors have done, especially since the modes of the ancients do not correspond to the modern ones, will be "like drinking from the glass of the Danaids"—that is, a task that can never be completed.[43] Rather, if the miraculous effects of ancient music are to be revived, modern musicians must first analyze the habits and inclinations of men today and discover which harmonies and rhythms correspond to these.[44]

We thus arrive at a working definition of Kircher's doctrine of the affections, expressed here in the language of Deleuze and Massumi. Its objects are the states of the body—infinite in number—that appear as the result of the actualization of the virtual. Its method consists in tracing the diverse media that are connected across bodies and the modes in which they are rearranged: the doctrine attempts to map the virtual as such through an affective combinatorics located on the body. One of the most concise formulations of Kircher's theory, in which the mechanistic, almost Cartesian language conceals most of what separates the two writers, reads: "The cause of the diversity of affections that are aroused [*concitationes affectum*] is none other than what we call the diverse states of the soul [*spiritus rationem*] animated in diverse ways according to varying tension and release [*intensionis ed remissionis*] of the harmonic movement imposed in the air."[45]

Affections are the discrete, local actualizations of the virtuality of tensions and releases—or relations of movement and rest, in a Spinozist language—that can be verified in a body. These affections—which, for clarity, are called emotions—can be distinguished from affect. Following Massumi, we can use the term *emotion* for the personalized content and *affect* for the continuation that exceeds both subject and object. Emotion is contextual, semiotically and semantically qualified intensity. Affect is situational, continuity across gaps that becomes actualized as emotions through specific processes—in this case the magic of musical contagion—in which the body is traversed, exceeded, made impersonal: "Impersonal affect is the connecting thread of experience. It is the invisible glue that holds the world together."[46]

Indeed, Kircher is interested in addressing the movement, passage, and continuity of affect, the excess of feeling that traverses and joins bodies, sounds, and planets, as well as the particular emotions that appear as a result of the interaction of variables whose number and mode of organization place them at the level of the virtual. As Gibbs argues, affective communication relies on mimetic contagion, on the bioneurological means—such as mirror neurons—by which particular affects (*sensu* Tomkins) are transmitted from body to body.[47] Following Massumi and Benjamin, Gibbs does not limit this transmission to similitude, medium, or signification. Mimetic communication, instead, is asubjective and amodal: it jumps across senses and media, producing "nonsensuous similarities," joining heterogeneous networks, bodies, and media into new connections.[48] Intensity, continuity, fulcrum of similarities: all of these are names for something that mimesis is not— they are what mimesis makes. If affect is the invisible glue that holds the world together, mimesis is the *vis adhesiva*—the binding power, to use the scholastic formulation—of affect, what makes affect behave as glue in the first place, by joining what is similar and making what is different appear as similar.

For Kircher, emotions are a miraculous surface effect, a ripple in the continuous fulcrum of similarity as projected on the screen of the body. They need to be analyzed and identified as and through movement, as events in an infinite but scientifically demonstrable process. To be able to account for emotions, one must also attend to affect as their correlate and condition, maintaining the distinction that makes both possible: the material condition of emotions is incorporeal materiality. Kircher's method of doing so is an affective combinatorics that mixes ancient and modern knowledges, analogy and experimentation. The body is explained as a mechanism only to show that every mechanism is a cosmos. The body is the surface of inscription of a virtual, affective continuity bonded by mimesis; the body is a cosmos because the cosmos traverses the body in music.[49] Kircher presents an experiment with diverse fluids in glasses that resonate in sympathy with each other when set in vibration to demonstrate the persistence of sympathies and antipathies in things, and to suggest that the body is itself composed of containers and media of this sort and that it works in a similar way.[50] In fact, book 10, the *Dechachordon Naturae* (*Decachord of Nature*), presents a table of the sympathetic correspondences of everything in the cosmos as well as the image of the macrocosm and microcosm presented in fig. 14.2.

Music, for Kircher, operates similarly, that is, by similitude: song moves the soul, song is air in harmonious motion, and the soul is continuous with air, while the words (re)present an object to the imagination.[51] Two parallel processes ensue: the humors are excited first through sympathy with the vibrations of the soul and then again according to the object of the imagination, producing vapors whose mixture produces a specific affection. These movements are qualified: proportionate movements will produce positive affections, disproportionate ones will produce negative affections.[52]

To account for this process of actualization Kircher formulates four conditions for *musica pathetica*, which, instead of neatly accounting for the variability of their effects into particular types, demonstrates how mimesis produces the virtual by enabling the reassembling of disparate media, by producing continuity out of the heterogeneous and amodal linkages that exceed the body.[53] They are first stated in *Erotema VI*: "The first one is harmony itself. Second is rhythm and proportion. Third is the force of the pronunciation of words in music itself, or language. Fourth is the disposition of the listener, or the capability in the subject [*subiectum*] to remember things."[54] Each element, infinite as it is, has the capacity to independently arouse the affections, yet the effect is greater when all are in accord [*congruit*]. Similitude, a common affective aim, organizes the diverse parts of music to attain a unified effect in the listener. Impersonal affect, the infinite virtuality that travels across bodies, finds its points of demarcation and actualization according to the habits and states of particular bodies. Organized by similitude, it becomes individualized—a personal, unique emotion: "I mean a [well-]disposed soul because without the fourth condition, that is, the disposition of the listener, you would more quickly move a stone than an ill-disposed subject.... Music moves thus not just any subject, but only that in whom the natural humors are in accordance [*congruit*] with the music."[55]

The listening subject is defined with respect to nationality, temperament, habits, dispositions—affective bonds that dislocate its individuality.[56] For Ulf Scharlau, here the listener is more active than in any other theory of the affections; he or she needs to be disposed *toward* the intended affection, to anticipate it.[57] In the terms I've been suggesting throughout, however, the subject appears less as a source of intention toward the affections than the place of inscription of a continuity that traverses it in multiple directions, however unified the affection might be. When these four conditions reappear in the third part of book 7, the definition of "disposition of the listener" is expanded through a consideration of space, time, temperature, the qualities of the singers and instruments, and so on. This is affective combinatorics at its extreme: the summation of variables exceeds any possible count, and the body is dislocated by the plurality of forces that attempt to locate in it a certain, specific disposition. To recall the formulation of Gibbs, mentioned above, mimesis produces a perception of the virtual as affect: it joins the disparate media of humors, vapors, and air in the body with instruments, voices, stages, and weather conditions. It brings them into determinate relations, an infinity of minute transformations that will congeal in the magical event of an emotion aroused.

From Affect to Representation: Back to the Fold

When, in the third part of book 7, Kircher attempts the classification and organization of modes and affections introduced at the beginning of this chapter, something has happened at an epistemic and ontological level. The infinite play of resemblances—mimesis—has produced a virtuality that is now once again actualized, analyzed, classified. It has been put to rest: we move to the level of representation. Similarity gives way to exemplarity. Since the affections, as he affirmed, are infinite, the only way to analyze them is to select the most important ones and then investigate their possible combinations: affective combinatorics.

But this operation—actualizing the virtual—is not an easy task. One can perform several permutations: starting with each mode, find a particular example, a *paradigma*, that shows without any admixture the affection for which the chosen mode is most appropriate. A highly controlled experiment, performed under strict conditions, the *paradigmata* are selected with the same tempo and the same measure to exhibit only the harmonic aspects of each mode (see book 7, part 3, chapter 2, "De natura Tonorum ad concitandos affectus aptorum"). One can also perform the inverse operation: starting with famous examples from the literature, isolate passages in which the principal affections are clearly expressed. These examples appear in diverse tempos and modes; they are culled from real life, so to speak, yet they require description, interpretation—such as Gesualdo's "Baci soavi e cari" (chapter 6, "Qua ratione instituenda melothesia, vt datum quemuis affectum moueat"). A third option, which Kircher abandoned because it would take too much time, would arrange a catalog of texts from Scripture describing each of the principal affections and ask composers around the world to set them to music (chapter 4, "De melothesias pathetica praxi"). The last option is a global approach, which considers musical genres instead of individual fragments. Kircher distinguishes between the *stylo impressus*, the impression that the same type of music has in each person, from a *stylo expressus*, the generic, established characteristics of different types of music. He then arranges these genres with respect to the affections they usually excite in the audience, using once again examples from famous composers: take a larger slice of the virtual, leave microscopic analysis for sociological observation, and again draw conclusions about the ways that the affections are elicited (chapter 5, "De vario stylorum harmonicorum artificio").

These *paradigmata*, it is clear, are neither affect nor affections; they are representations, slices, stoppages of the affective becoming of music. Affect is the virtual continuity that produces actual, determined emotions; the *paradigmata* are copies, magic imitations, expressions. Twice removed from the virtuality that made them possible, these *paradigmata*—"music," in a traditional sense—capture and duplicate the surface effects that allowed Kircher to select them in the first place; yet as examples they are different in nature and kind from affections as such.

In one and the same work Kircher reached the most powerful formulation of the theory of the affections and delivered it into the age of representation, which would only be interested in the taxonomy of these posterior results, that is, in the still, static, ossified *paradigmata*. At this point representation is exemplification, a production of images of the body, organized in discrete, exemplary fragments; as magical copies, they incorporate the affective power of the bodies that produced them, yet they are different in kind. The relation between the emotions and the rhythmic or harmonic qualities will soon cease to be evident, becoming nonsensuous similarity.

This is the most magical aspect of mimesis: it uses copies to produce originals. The *paradigmata* look as if they were the models after which composition must be undertaken to achieve similar effects, erasing the fact that these *paradigmata* are themselves nothing but effects. At the outset of modernity, then, a magical event happens: the copy acquires, or pretends to acquire, for the rest of the theorists interested in the affections, the powers of that which it imitates, a power of resembling, arousing, and disappearing at the same time.

Notes

1. Athanasius Kircher, *Musurgia universalis, sive ars magna consoni et dissoni in X libri digesta* (Rome: Corbelletti, 1650). There is a facsimile edition, Athanasius Kircher, *Musurgia Universalis*, ed. Ulf Scharlau (Hildesheim and New York: G. Olms, 1970). Hereafter cited as *MU*. There is an abridged German translation from 1662, also published in facsimile: Athanasius Kircher, *Kircherus Jesuita Germanus Germaniae Redonatus Sive Artis Magnae de Consono & Dißono Ars Minor Das Ist Philosophischer Extract Und Auszug, Aus Deß Welt-Berühmten Teutschen Jesuitens Athanasii*, trans. Andreas Hirsch (Kassel: Bärenreiter, 1988). According to the scholarship on the *Musurgia* and after Kircher's own practice, the two volumes of the *Musurgia* will be referred to as A and B, respectively.

2. Paula Findlen, ed., *Athanasius Kircher: The Last Man Who Knew Everything* (New York: Routledge, 2004).

3. The most recent and significant works in English focusing on the *Musurgia Universalis* are John McKay, "Universal Music-Making: Athanasius Kircher and Musical Thought in the Seventeenth Century" (Ph.D. diss., Harvard University, 2012); and Eric Bianchi, "Prodigious Sounds: Music and Learning in the World of Athanasius Kircher" (Ph.D. diss., Yale University, 2011). The reference works on the *Musurgia Universalis* are still Ulf Scharlau, *Athanasius Kircher (1601–1680) als Musikschriftsteller: Ein Beitrag zur Musikanschauung des Barock* (Marburg: Görich & Weiershäuser, 1969), and Rolf Dammann, *Der Musikbegriff im deutschen Barock* (Cologne: A. Volk, 1967). See also Melanie Wald, *Welterkenntnis aus Musik: Athanasius Kirchers "Musurgia Universalis" und die Universalwissenschaft im 17. Jahrhundert* (Kassel: Bärenreiter, 2006); Tiziana Pangrazi, *La "Musurgia Universalis" di Athanasius Kircher: Contenuti, fonti, terminologia* (Florence: Leo S. Olschki, 2009); Markus Engelhardt and Michael Heinemann, eds., *Ars magna musices: Athanasius Kircher und die Universalität der Musik; Vorträge des deutsch-italienischen Symposiums aus Anlass des 400. Geburtstages von Athanasius Kircher (1602–1680); Musikgeschichtliche Abteilung des Deutschen Historischen Instituts in Rom, in Zusammenarbeit mit der Hochschule für Musik "Carl Maria von Weber" in Dresden, Rom, Deutsches Historisches Institut, 16.–18. Oktober 2002* (Laaber: Laaber-Verlag, 2007); Penelope Gouk, *Music, Science and Natural Magic in Seventeenth-Century England* (New Haven, CT: Yale University Press, 1999); Daniel Stolzenberg, ed., *The Great Art of Knowing: The Baroque Encyclopedia of Athanasius Kircher* (Stanford, CA: Stanford University Libraries, 2001); John Edward Fletcher, *A Study of the Life and Works of Athanasius Kircher, "Germanus Incredibilis": With a Selection of His Unpublished Correspondence and an Annotated Translation of His Autobiography*, ed. Elizabeth Fletcher, Aries Book Series 12 (Leiden and Boston: Brill, 2011); Fletcher, ed., *Athanasius Kircher und seine Beziehungen zum gelehrten Europa seiner Zeit*, WolfenbüttelerArbeiten für Barockforschung 17 (Wiesbaden: Harrassowitz, 1988); and Cecilia Campa, *Musicista filosofo e le passioni: Linguaggio e retorica dei suoni nel Seicento Europeo* (Naples: Liguori, 2001). As Fletcher notes, scholars interested other aspects of Kircher's diverse output are seldom interested in writings about music. Of these, see esp. Thomas Leinkauf, *Mundus combinatus: Studien zur Struktur der barocken Universalwissenschaft am Beispiel Athanasius Kirchers SJ (1602–1680)* (Berlin: Akademie Verlag, 1993); Felicia Englmann, *Sphärenharmonie und Mikrokosmos: Das politische Denken des Athanasius Kircher (1602–1680)* (Cologne: Böhlau Verlag, 2006); Anna Maria Partini, *Athanasius Kircher e l'alchimia: Testi scelti e commentati* (Rome: Edizioni Mediterranee, 2004); Ingrid Rowland, *The Ecstatic Journey: Athanasius Kircher in Baroque Rome* (Chicago: University of Chicago Library, 2000); Siegfried Zielinski, *Deep Time of the Media: Toward an Archaeology of Hearing and Seeing by Technical Means*, trans. Gloria Custace (Cambridge, MA: MIT Press, 2006);

and Joscelyn Godwin, *Athanasius Kircher: A Renaissance Man and the Quest for Lost Knowledge* (London: Thames & Hudson, 1979).

4. Michel Foucault, *The Order of Things: An Archaeology of the Human Sciences* (London and New York: Routledge Classics, 2002). See also Jairo Moreno, *Musical Representations, Subjects, and Objects: The Construction of Musical Thought in Zarlino, Descartes, Rameau, and Weber* (Bloomington: Indiana University Press, 2004) and Gary Tomlinson, *Music in Renaissance Magic: Toward a Historiography of Others* (Chicago: University of Chicago Press, 1993).

5. For an overview of this metanarrative, see Suzannah Clark and Alexander Rehding, eds., *Music Theory and Natural Order from the Renaissance to the Early Twentieth Century* (Cambridge and New York: Cambridge University Press, 2001); and the review of this volume by Karl Braunschweig, *Music Theory Spectrum* 25, no. 1 (2003): 142–51. Alongside the New Historicism, this Foucauldian framework has replaced earlier musicological approaches to the relation between affect, emotions, and meaning. The first one, elaborated mainly by Dietrich Bartel and George Buelow, consider affect under the tradition of *musica poetica*, namely the use of figures borrowed from rhetoric to guide musical analysis and composition. The second highlights the centrality of Descartes's treatise on the passions — culminating in Mattheson's theories — in displacing earlier magical accounts of the power of music to argue for a mechanistic theory of the affections that belongs to the Scientific Revolution. The main debate in the first of these approaches concerns the unity of its discourse, while the other centers on the issue of disenchantment and the influence of magical practices in the Scientific Revolution. For an overview of these and other trends, see Penelope Gouk, "In Search of Sound: Authenticity, Healing and Redemption in the Early Modern State," *Senses & Society* 2, no. 3 (2007): 303–28.

6. Tomlinson, *Music in Renaissance Magic*, 240.

7. For a succinct and influential account of Kircher's classification, see Lorenzo Bianconi, *Music in the Seventeenth Century* (Cambridge and New York: Cambridge University Press, 1987), 51 ff. For an account of the passages I explore below, with translations, see Claude V. Palisca, *Music and Ideas in the Sixteenth and Seventeenth Centuries, Studies in the History of Music Theory and Literature 1* (Urbana: University of Illinois Press, 2006), 193–95.

8. For *Figurenlehre*, see Dietrich Bartel, *Musica Poetica: Musical-Rhetorical Figures in German Baroque Music* (Lincoln: University of Nebraska Press, 1997), 106–11. For theology, magic, and Cartesianism in Kircher, see Scharlau, *Athanasius Kircher*; and Susanne Schaal-Gotthardt, "Musica pathetica: Kirchers Affektenlehre," in *Ars magna musices: Athanasius Kircher und die Universalität der Musik; Vorträge des deutsch-italienischen Symposiums aus Anlass des 400. Geburtstages von Athanasius Kircher (1602–1680); Musikgeschichtliche Abteilung des Deutschen Historischen Instituts in Rom, in Zusammenarbeit mit der Hochschule für Musik "Carl Maria von Weber" in Dresden, Rom, Deutsches Historisches Institut, 16.–18. Oktober 2002*, ed. Markus Engelhardt and Michael Heinemann (Laaber: Laaber-Verlag, 2007), 141–54.

9. "Vides in hoc exiguo paradigmate, cum quanto ingenio affectus amoris expressus sit, interualla quomodo langueant; quam pulchre voces se syncopent, certe ad languentis anim syncopen exprimendam nihil aptius assumere poterat." *MU*, A:600. All translations are mine except as noted.

10. George J. Buelow, "Johann Mattheson and the Invention of the *Affektenlehre*," in *New Mattheson Studies*, ed. George J. Buelow and Hans Joachim Marx (Cambridge: Cambridge University Press, 2006), 393–408. For a reconsideration of eighteenth-century theories of the affections in light of contemporary affect theory (and their discontents), see Roger Mathew Grant, *Peculiar Attunements: How Affect Theory Turned Musical* (New York: Fordham University Press, 2020).

11. I borrow the phrase "acoustic assemblage" from Ana María Ochoa Gautier, *Aurality: Listening and Knowledge in Nineteenth-Century Colombia* (Durham, NC: Duke University Press, 2014), 22–23: an acoustic assemblage is "the mutually constitutive and transformative relation between the given and the made that is generated in the interrelationship between a listening entity that theorizes about the process of hearing producing notions of the listening entity or entities that hear, notions of the sonorous producing entities, and notions of the type of relationship between them." The importance of magic and alchemy in Kircher's writings has been well noted, especially in Anna Maria Partini, *Athanasius Kircher e l'alchimia: Testi scelti e commentati* (Rome: Edizioni Mediterranee, 2004); Penelope Gouk, *Music, Science, and Natural Magic in Seventeenth-Century England* (New Haven, CT: Yale University Press, 1999; and Gary Tomlinson, *Music in Renaissance Magic: Toward a Historiography of Others* (Chicago: University of Chicago Press, 1993). These approaches are indebted to Frances Yates, *Giordano Bruno and the Hermetic Tradition* (Chicago: University of Chicago Press, 1964).

12. Daniel K. L. Chua, "Vincenzo Galilei, Modernity and the Division of Nature," in Clark and Rehding, *Music Theory and Natural Order*, 22.

13. "Ground" appears here in scare quotes because mimesis, in all rigor, cannot be called a ground. The essence of mimesis—if it had one—would lie in the fact that it doesn't have anything proper to it, that it doesn't have any essence other than "absolute vicariousness, carried to the limit (but inexhaustible), endless and groundless—something like an infinity of substitution and circulation." Philippe Lacoue-Labarthe, *Typography: Mimesis, Philosophy, Politics*, ed. Christopher Fynsk, introduction by Jacques Derrida (Cambridge, MA: Harvard University Press, 1989), 116.

14. See the introduction to Clark and Rehding, *Music Theory and Natural Order*. Susan McClary and Suzanne Cusick's work comes to mind with respect to issues of gender and power addressed through a Foucauldian lens.

15. Tomlinson, *Music in Renaissance Magic*, 247.

16. Michael T. Taussig, *Mimesis and Alterity: A Particular History of the Senses* (New York: Routledge, 1993), xiii.

17. Villegas Vélez, *Mimetologies: Mimesis and Music 1600–1850* (Oxford University Press, forthcoming).

18. Taussig, *Mimesis and Alterity*, xiii. For Benjamin's theory of mimesis, see "On the Mimetic Faculty," in *Selected Writings, 1931–1934*, vol. 2, pt. 2 (Cambridge, MA: Belknap Press, 2005), 720; "Doctrine of the Similar," in special Walter Benjamin issue, *New German Critique* 17 (1979): 65–69, and Anson Rabinbach, "Introduction to Walter Benjamin's 'Doctrine of the Similar,'" in special Walter Benjamin issue, *New German Critique* 17 (1979): 60–64.

19. Silvan S. Tomkins, *Affect Imagery Consciousness: The Complete Edition*, 2 vols. (New York: Springer, 2008); Daniel Lord Smail, *On Deep History and the Brain* (Chicago: University of Chicago Press, 2009); Eve Kosofsky Sedgwick, Adam Frank, and Irving E. Alexander, eds., *Shame and Its Sisters: A Silvan Tomkins Reader* (Durham, NC: Duke University Press, 1995); and Sedgwick, *Touching Feeling: Affect, Pedagogy, Performativity* (Durham, NC: Duke University Press, 2003). For an account of the two currents of affect theory and a criticism of the appropriation of scientific research for cultural theory, focusing on the work of Brian Massumi and William E. Connolly, see Ruth Leys, "The Turn to Affect: A Critique," *Critical Inquiry* 37, no. 3 (2011): 434–72.

20. Anna Gibbs, "After Affect: Sympathy, Synchrony, and Mimetic Communication," in *The Affect Theory Reader*, ed. Melissa Gregg and Gregory J. Seigworth (Durham, NC: Duke University Press, 2010), 193.

21. Ibid., 187. Similarly, William E. Connolly refers to the work of the neuroscientist Giacomo Rizzolatti on mirror neurons to argue that "social experience is not merely mediated by the web of language, it is also infused by the ability humans and monkeys have to read and mimic the intentions of others before and below language." Connolly, "Materialities of Experience," in *New Materialisms: Ontology, Agency, and Politics*, ed. Diana Coole and Samantha Frost (Durham, NC: Duke University Press, 2010), 183. For the relation between mimetic theory and the neurosciences, see Nidesh Lawtoo, "The Mimetic Unconscious: A Mirror for Genealogical Reflections," in *Imitation, Contagion, Suggestion: on Mimesis and Society*, ed. Christian Borch (New York: Routledge, 2019). Gary Tomlinson assimilates the role of mimetic capacities relying on deep-brain structures for technological transmission with the capacity for entrainment capacities that underlie the more developed synchronies of musicking. Tomlinson, "Evolutionary Studies in the Humanities: The Case of Music," *Critical Inquiry* 39, no. 4 (2013): 647–75.

22. *MU*, B:221–24. The literature on the tarantella is too broad to report on here, but see Tomlinson, *Music in Renaissance Magic*, 154–70; and Ernesto De Martino, *The Land of Remorse: A Study of Southern Italian Tarantism*, trans. and annotated Dorothy Louise Zinn (London: Free Association Books, 2005).

23. Brian Massumi, *Parables for the Virtual: Movement, Affect, Sensation* (Durham, NC: Duke University Press, 2002), 5 ff. Massumi borrows the term "incorporeal materialism" from the appendix to Michel Foucault, *Archaeology of Knowledge* (London and New York: Routledge, 2002), and suggests that it is equivalent to Deleuze's "transcendental empiricism."

24. In the classic Aristotelian account, the distinction between potentiality and actuality is a theoretical one. Everything is always actualized, and hence what is *in potentia* is not real, yet we need to presume it in order to account for movement and change. For Deleuze, however, in order to account for movement, difference, and becoming, we must be able to show that the real does not entirely coincide with what is actual; in fact, the real exceeds the actual. What is real without being actual is the virtual. See Gilles Deleuze, *Bergsonism*, trans. Hugh Tomlinson and Barbara Habberjam (New York: Zone Books, 1988), 97. For the difference between the virtual and the potential, see Massumi, *Parables for the Virtual*, 98 and 133 ff.

25. Massumi, *Parables for the Virtual*, 247–48 n. 8. Gibbs also suggests rethinking magic and mimesis together as a form of overcoming Eurocentric prejudices for which these are the preserve of children, "primitives," and animals. Gibbs, "After Affect," 189.

26. See Villegas Vélez, *Mimetologies*, 422.

27. James George Frazer, *The Golden Bough*, quoted in Taussig, *Mimesis and Alterity*, 47.

28. Marcel Mauss had already argued this point. For Mauss, the two laws tend to be confused because they are abstractions of a more general magical intuition that understands nature to be a continuous whole. Mauss, *A General Theory of Magic* (New York: W. W. Norton, 1975), 72.

29. Ficino, quoted in Tomlinson, *Music in Renaissance Magic*, 112.

30. Palisca, *Music and Ideas*, 194. Cf. *MU*, A:551–52.

31. Ibid.

32. Massumi, *Parables for the Virtual*, 134.

33. This representation of the microcosm and macrocosm, as often happens with Kircher, is by no means his original creation, and it is reprinted in several of its works. It is found in Cornelius Aggripa's *Three Books of Occult Philosophy* and has an evident counterpart in Leonardo da Vinci's "Vitruvian Man," a version of which also appears in the *Musurgia*. Panel B of Aby Warburg's *Mnemosyne* consists of several versions of this image, of which

the earliest is an illumination from Hildegard of Bingen's *Liber Divinorum Operum*. Aby Warburg, *Der Bilderatlas: Mnemosyne*, vol. 2, 1 of *Gesammelte Schriften*, 3rd ed., ed. Martin Warnke with Claudia Brink (Berlin: Akademie Verlag, 2008). See also Fritz Saxl, "Macrocosm and Microcosm in Medieval Pictures," in *Lectures*, vol. 1 (London: Warburg Institute, 1957), 58–72.

34. Massumi, *Parables for the Virtual*, 98.

35. Benjamin discusses the mimetic relation between reading, writing, and astrology in Benjamin, "Doctrine of the Similar (1933)," 66.

36. Massumi, *Parables for the Virtual*, 133.

37. Deleuze, *Bergsonism*, 98.

38. For mimesis as the production of difference, see Villegas Vélez, "Mimetologies: Aesthetic Politics in Early Opera" (Ph.D. diss., University of Pennsylvania, 2016), 95; and Luiz Costa Lima, *Control of the Imaginary: Reason and Imagination in Modern Times* (Minneapolis: University of Minnesota Press, 1988).

39. *MU*, A:532–617.

40. "Accedo tandem ad maximam illam, nullo non tempore inter Musicos agitatam controuersiam; Vtrum videlicet musica Veterum nostra moderna perfectior fuerit; & vtrum illa tantae perfectionis, & excellentiae fuerit, vt omni ad eam pertingenispe moderni frustrentur." *MU*, A:543.

41. "Cum παθημάτων, quas affectiones, seu passiones Ethici appellant υποκείμενον, sive subiectum sit appetitus sensitivus corporeus, et materialis: necessario dicta pathemata materialibus quoque conditionibus, ut in Ethica musica fuse dicetur, substabunt; consistunt enim in certa quadam primarum qualitatum elementarium combinatione, vaporesque dici possunt, quatuor humorum varie, et varie pro phantasticae facultatis obiectis commistorum." *MU*, A:551.

42. "Quemadmodum igitur harmonicorum motuum infinita varietas est, ita & affectionum inde resultantium; quorum rationem si quis perfecte nosset, is haud dubie maxima nature miracula in suscitandis animi passionibus vi musicae efficere posset; Nil enim aliud facere oporteret, nisi harmonicos numeros metricosque spiritui affectione aliqua praegnanti perfecte accordare; hoc facto, impossibile est, ut intentus effectus non sequatur." *MU*, A:552.

43. "Quod antequam faciamus, mirari fatis non possum, vaum & inutilem quorundam Musica strorum in recta tonorum assignationi laborem. Videntur mihi huiusmodi perpetuo in vase Danaidum aqua replendo occupari & eum nihil nom agant, quo magnum aliquid mundo se detexisse demonstrent, per actis tamen omnibus & re bene considerata, quod omnes alij, in aeresepiscatos & cerebro & crumena vacuos reperiunt." *MU*, A:565.

44. "Hinc igitur, si veterum musicorum miracula renouare velint, respicere debent musici nostri, ut primo alicuis subiecti inclinationem & naturalem habitudinem explorent, deinde iuxta eandem numeros harmonicos verborumque thema ijs congruum adaptent, & non dubitent quin eosdem, quos veteres, effectus sint causaturi." *MU*, A:551.

45. "Ex hoc discursu luculenter patet, causam diversae concitationis affectum aliam non esse, nisi quam diximus diversam spiritus rationem pro diversis intensionis et remissionis motus harmonici gradibus in aere impressis aliter incitatam." *MU*, A:568.

46. Massumi, *Parables for the Virtual*, 217.

47. Gibbs, "After Affect," 191.

48. Ibid., 193.

49. It could be argued that the centrality of music for the cosmos seems gratuitous in this place. Indeed, if the body is such "a series of media," then music would have to be counted as just one of them. The answer to this lies in the Neoplatonic orientation of the *Musurgia*,

most prominently expressed in the hermetic dictum found in Book X: "Music is nothing other than understanding the order of everything" (Musica nihil aliud est, quam omnium ordinem scire; *MU*, B:2). It is not that the cosmos is musical, although it is held to be organized musically — i.e., by musical proportions and correspondences — but, most important, music is a mode of understanding of the cosmos: *philosophia musica*. In the end, however, it can be argued that the idea of the cosmos *is* produced as music through mimesis.

50. "Contingit enim idem in diuersa complexione hominum, quod in pulcherrimo illo experimento, quod libro 9. exhibimus, vbi in vitreis scyphis diuersi liquores infuisi agitantur iuxta numerorum & proportionum diuersam habitudinem.... Hinc etiam sit, ut dum choreas agentes cernimus, in similes motus animemur, ex similitudine videlicet harmonicarum proportionum numerorumque spiritum nostrum similiter afficientium similitudine & Sympathia." *MU*, A:551.

51. "Granted that a musical tone is a movement that communicates to the air a motion exactly proportionate, that the air is in a continuum with the animal spirit, which itself is in perpetual motion, it follows that at the same time as the soul ... is excited by song and the fantasy by the object represented by the words, the air excites a natural humor altogether equivalent and proportional to the object and to the sonorous movements. As to the vapor, it rises and mixes with the animal spirit already excited by the sonorous numbers of the song and the air that is continuous with it. Finally, by its movement the spirit impels the soul to affections proportionate to the numbers and to the words" (MU A 552). Translation in Palisca, *Music and Ideas*, 195.

52. Palisca, *Music and Ideas*, 194.

53. Gibbs, "After Affect," 201. It would be more precise to say that mimesis allows for the virtual incorporeality of the virtual to be felt across the connections, since the virtual never appears as such. To "produce," here, might then be understood as to produce a perception of it — an affect.

54. "Nisi quatuor conditiones annexas habeat, quarum vna deficiente, desideratus effectus minime obtinebitur: Prima est ipsa harmonia. Secunda, numerus & proportio. Tertia, verborum in ipsa musica pronunciandorum vis, & efficacia, siue ipsa oratio. Quarta audientis dispositio, siue subiectum memoratarum rerum capax." *MU*, A:550.

55. "Dici animos dispositos, quia nisi quarta conditio, hoc est audientis dispositio praesserit, citius saxum quam hominem indispositum incapacemque moqueris ... oquerisigitur ut moueat, non qualecunque subiectum vult, sed illud cuius humor naturalis musicae congruit." Ibid.

56. "Omnia agenio patriae, ab inclinatione, & temperamento particulari, & a consuetudine introducta dependent." *MU*, A:554. Erotema V discusses the preference of different peoples, ancient and modern, for their own music, which he says is due as much to weather conditions as to nationalism (*filopatridos*; *MU*, A:542), as well as to the particular temperaments of individuals, which account for deviations from the national tendencies.

57. Scharlau, *Athanasius Kircher*, 236. This analysis of the four conditions is taken directly from Zarlino, *Istitutioni harmoniche*, book II, chap. 8, which in turn draws from Bishop Jacopo Sadoleto, *De liberis recte instituendis* (Venice, 1533). Scharlau also suggests that Kircher takes these conditions directly from Zarlino (Scharlau, *Athanasius Kircher*, 237). For the role of passage in Zarlino, see Moreno, *Musical Representations, Subjects, and Objects*, 45.

CHAPTER 15

Affect and the Recording Devices of Seventeenth-Century Italy

Emily Wilbourne

Giulio Caccini, writing "to the readers" in the preface to his *Le nuove musiche* (1602), was deeply concerned with affect, in particular with the ideal of *cantare con affetto*.[1] Translated by H. Wiley Hitchcock as "affective singing," *cantare con affetto* meant to sing in such a way that an auditor could be palpably affected by the song, an effect—in Caccini's account—of artful text setting and precise techniques of musical declamation.[2] Hitchcock is quick to note that Caccini uses the word *affetto* frequently, yet deploys it in two very different senses: in the first instance, *affetto* describes a "state of mind-*cum*-emotion"; in the second, it refers to the vocal ornaments (or *affetti*) with which a given melody might be embellished. "The double meaning," Hitchcock explains, "arises from the Baroque theory that music's aim is to 'move the affect' (first meaning) by embodying itself an affect (first meaning), often in particular, even stereotyped idioms or affects (second meaning)."[3] It is the relationship between these two "affects" with which this essay is concerned.

For modern scholars of seventeenth-century aesthetics, the tension between the *affetti* and the codified, clichéd gestures with which they were associated has bedeviled interpretation.[4] The citations and reiterations of such a system are inimical to modern historiographic methods, which prioritize stylistic evolution and compositional innovation over a large-scale reliance on existing formal procedures, and stand in a problematic relationship to "genuine" emotional expressivity, which in modern affective schema presupposes a resistance to the generic and the cliché. The language available to describe the *affetti*, musical and otherwise, is freighted with derogatory value judgments— "formulaic," "conventional," "derivative,"—that make it difficult to write about how and why such material was prized by contemporary audiences. And yet the most popular musics of the seventeenth century, both vocal and instrumental, trafficked heavily in precisely such features. In this essay I consider the generic conventions of mid-century Venetian opera in relation to the doubled nature of affect. Inspired by the work of Monique Scheer (following Pierre Bourdieu),[5] whereby emotions are understood as "a kind of practice"—actions performed by habituated bodies—I theorize the repetitions and clichés of this repertoire as a form of recording device: a technique by which to store and repeat information, and a means of disseminating or consuming aesthetic content.[6] My understanding of these musical-affective techniques as a form of recording technology runs counter to commonly accepted definitions of the process of audio recording. Jonathan Sterne, for example, in his foundational text, *The Audible Past*, defines recording technology as the transduction of sound into some other medium—including therein vibrations, grooves on a disc, the ones and zeros of digital code, and conceivably also the graphic representations of musical notation, but not the formulae and codified musical gestures for which I am using the term here.[7] Thinking about such content as recording devices defamiliarizes our modern understanding of audio fidelity to an original (and now past) performance, and indeed, of the fleeting, ephemeral status of performance itself. Understood as a technology of audio reproduction, the "particular, even stereotypical idioms" of early modern *affetti* can be understood to constitute both the means and the message of seventeenth-century affective song.

The *dramma per musica* of the mid-century Venetian stage is typified by the works of Francesco Cavalli (1602–1676). Born in the short few months between the signing of Caccini's dedication and the appearance in print of *Le nuove musiche*, Cavalli was to become the foremost opera composer of his generation, penning at least forty-one operas, of which scores for twenty-seven have survived—several in the composer's own hand. Cavalli's music is notable for the codification of musical and dramatic standards; in the words of Ellen Rosand, his "works made their impact more through repetition than as individual aesthetic objects, demonstrating and reinforcing their successful formulas season after season."[8] Such formulae operated on many levels—textual, linguistic, narrative, characterological, and gestural, in addition to musical—and most were adopted virtually unchanged from the conventions of the contemporary vernacular theatre, the commedia dell'arte.[9] Where opera differs from other theatrical genres is in the pervasive presence of notated music and thus, in cases where the scores survive, of incontrovertible evidence for the pitched and rhythmic outlines of theatrical (and musical) declamation: in opera, *cantare con affetto* links specific musical *affetti* to the embodiment of affect. The repeatability of this process is crucial. In this essay I want to discuss Cavalli's best-known and most widely performed work, *Il Giasone*, specifically the laments sung by one of the two lead female characters, Isifile. The success of Isifile's final lament relies on a rich coagulation of affect enabled by precisely the repetitions and citations that this essay seeks to foreground. The character, her words, her music, her gestures, and ultimately her ability to move her onstage and offstage listeners depends on the precise manipulation and reinhabitation of clichéd and thus highly anticipated material. This example illustrates how the formulaic elements of operatic music and of opera and Italian theater more broadly facilitated the goals of *cantare con affetto*, "mov[ing] the affect" by "embodying itself an affect" through "stereotyped idioms or affects."

Il Giasone, with a libretto by Giacinto Andrea Cicognini, was first performed in 1649.[10] It is widely considered to be the most-performed opera of the seventeenth century. The plot is based on characters from the myth of the Argonauts: the eponymous Giasone (Jason) is charged with capturing the Golden Fleece, though the treatment of this incident is fleeting, and the actual narrative of the opera is newly elaborated and relies on a conflation of several temporally distinct episodes from the mythical Jason's life. When the show opens, the young hero is enamored of a secret lover, later revealed to be Medea, Queen of Colchis, and Giasone's obsession with the feminine delights of lovemaking are proving worrisome for his fellow soldiers. Once Medea reveals her identity to Giasone, confessing her love and the existence of identical-twin sons—borne and birthed in secret over the course of their attenuated affair—their indulgent lovemaking intensifies, and Medea promises to help Giasone capture the Golden Fleece, which she does. Circumstances are complicated by the arrival of Giasone's previous lover, Isifile, Queen of Lemnos, who brings with her another set of twin boys, also fathered by the remarkably fertile hero (cast, ironically or not, as a castrato). The main arc of the story is concerned with these two women and their respective claims on Giasone's attention.

Giasone, who prefers Medea's ardent embraces to Isifile's lamentations, arranges for the captain of his unit, Besso, to murder the unfortunate woman—or, more accurately, arranges for Besso to murder the person who comes to him and inquires whether Giasone's orders have been carried out. Giasone then sends Isifile to Besso charged with this message. Medea, however—impatient to know the fate of her rival—arrives first and asks precisely the wrong question. Besso throws Medea into the sea. When Isifile arrives moments later, Besso balks at killing more than one queen a day.

Medea, for her part, does not drown, and is pulled from the waves by her jilted ex-lover, Egeo. With her warm feelings for Giasone quashed by his apparent murder attempt, her rescue reignites her former passion, freeing Giasone for an eventual reconciliation with Isifile. Along the way to the *lieto fine*, various secondary characters—soldiers, servants, and an elderly nurse—crisscross the stage, facilitating the convoluted plot machinations and providing numerous opportunities for comic set pieces.

The plot, the characters, and their interactions have clear links to commedia dell'arte precedent. The combined presence, for example, of comic servants and serious lovers is a quintessential element of the commedia dell'arte canon, and the servants themselves fit stock tropes of the genre's practice. Isifile's servant, Oreste—who tracks down her errant lover and helps to resolve the events of the drama—fills the role of the *primo zanni*; Egeo's servant, Demo—a stuttering, hunchbacked, boastful coward—is a classic *secondo zanni*.[11] The two pairs of lovers are similarly arranged according to dell'arte norms, both through chains of unrequited affection (Isifile loves Giasone who loves Medea; Egeo loves Medea who loves Giasone) and their ultimate resolution into couples. Furthermore, the *donne innamorate* represent the two standard types of leading ladies cast in commedia dell'arte productions, with Isifile, on the one hand, the adamant innamorata who refuses to give up a lover who betrayed her—lamenting all the while—and Medea, on the other, the ardent innamorata preoccupied with the delights of love and her consuming desire for passionate fulfillment.[12] The complementarity of the two *innamorata* characters is such that the appearance of one elicits the arrival of the other, with important implications for their characterization and affective potential.

The presence of an ardent *innamorata* is presaged in the opening two scenes: first when Ercole bemoans Giasone's preoccupation with feminine charms, and then when the hero himself enters and sings the aria "Delizie, contenti," describing his almost unbearable delight in love. When Medea appears in scene 4, the audience is primed to anticipate either ardent effusions or adamant refusals: her aria, "Se dardo pungente," however, defers the moment of recognition through both textual and musical means, exploiting the citational nature of contemporary theatrical convention and playing with representational norms in a manner entirely dependent on highly stereotyped categories of characterization and emotional expression.

In "Se dardo pungente," two verses of ten lines in *versi senari* are arranged into paired tercets and couplets through the positioning of punctuating *troncò* lines; the same music is used for each verse. The entire first strophe foregrounds the "sharp dart" of love, Medea's "wounded breast," and the "struggles of [her] heart" to "resist," and thus it is only in the second verse that her ardent nature is confirmed: the second verse reveals the futility of the struggle against love, rhyming Medea's "love" and "ardor" for her paramour with a description of her swooning response to passion. Only here can the listener be sure that this character is the lover referenced by Ercole and Giasone, and not the adamant innamorata they would presume must also soon make an entrance. Musically, Cavalli crafts a similarly ambiguous setting (see ex. 15.1). The bass line emphasizes the chromatic inflections of the A minor mode, as well as the descending tetrachord, from scale degree 8 down to 5, long associated with the genre of lament.[13] The rhythmically limited vocabulary of the vocal line magnifies the abrupt span of the poetic meter. The aria is in triple time and Medea's obsessively dotted second beats mark a repeated stepwise descent to dissonant intervals with the bass, producing a palpable lurch away from the downbeat. Wendy Heller describes this as "a persistent throbbing on beat two, marked by a suggestively caressing lower neighbor," though in truth the sexualized tone of her descriptive adjectives is appropriate only in retrospect: Cavalli's music, like Cicognini's text, is cleverly constructed to seem mournful on the first hearing, and is revealed as representative of erotic tension only on the second.[14] For the listener seeking to categorize Medea as the ardent or the adamant innamorata, "Se dardo pungente" delays the moment of confirmation, feinting toward lament before dissolving into sexual pleasure.

It is the sedimented conventions of the operatic endeavor—the repetitions and citations of plot, character type, and characteristic vocal sound—that make the affective experience of "Se dardo pungente" so successful. Through the use of "particular, even stereotyped idioms" associated with lament, Cavalli moves the affects of his audience throughout the first verse, engendering sympathetic pangs. This affect is then released with the semantic shift into the second verse—presumably articulated in performance with a suggestively different set of vocal ornaments over the repeated melodic line—creating, on a larger scale, a sense of release and even amusement at the successful exploitation of audience expectations. Taken together, the two verses of the aria produce the structural equivalent of the offbeat suspensions in the melody, deferring a pleasurable resolution in order to enjoy the friction of dissonant and sexual tension as long as possible.[15]

By the time Isifile makes her appearance in the penultimate scene of act 1, the audience has witnessed Giasone and Medea declare their love openly, sealing proceedings with a duet, and the arrival of the other

Ex. 15.1. Medea, "Se dardo pungente." Francesco Cavalli, *Il Giasone*, act I, scene iv.
Text: If the prickling dart of a luminous gaze wounded my heart; If by love's delights my heart is consumed both night and day; If a divine face stole this soul away; If [my] fate is to love, who can resist? // If when I saw you, Beautiful, murderous eyes, I lost all vigor; If I love you and adore you, If I faint, if I die of noble ardour; If Cupid, from heaven, established my beloved; Then I should love: It is meant to be.

innamorata is hotly anticipated. As the audience might expect, Isifile laments, and she does so in physical and musical settings familiar from other lament texts. The opening lines of the recitative situate Isifile on the shore, calling—largely in vain—after the sails of a ship, much like Arianna, Dido, and Olimpia had before her.[16] The poetry makes use of anaphora, fragmentation, and elaboration (for example, "È il mio cor, la mia vita, il mio desio, / È Giasone, il mio ben, il mio ben, lo sposo mio")—all classic elements of lament poetry—to help portray her disturbed state. Isifile's opening words—"Stop, stop, cruel one! Return, unfaithful one!" (Ferma, ferma, crudele; Ritorn'in dietro, infido)—render her position clear as the abandoned-yet-still-enamored archetype. Like most introductory operatic scenes, Isifile's lament explicitly names her character and explicates the indebtedness of her emotional state to the unfolding story.

This poetry can be fruitfully compared to the improvisatory style of commedia dell'arte actresses; see, for example, the passages from Marina Dorotea Antonazzoni *detta* Lavinia (1593–1639) quoted at some length in my book on the commedia dell'arte.[17] Like the text for Isifile quoted here, Antonazzoni's poetry relies heavily on the generative principle that Robert Henke labels "copiousness," where each line of verse elaborates on the content of the previous line, generating a list of descriptive epithets that can reach exhaustive, poetically excessive proportions.[18] In the excerpt reproduced in ex. 15.2, phrases such as "sposa solo di nome / moglie senza marito" emphasize Isifile's point and express her distress without offering new content. The closing couplet condenses the entire verse, and the final rhyme (*ristoro/adoro*) serves as punctuation to an otherwise unrhymed text.

In Cavalli's declamatory setting, the resonance of this text with the laments of the spoken theater would have been very clear, and Isifile's recitative vocabulary would have emphasized her adamant qualities, throwing Medea's capacity for ardent aria into relief. As the piece opens, eight measures of a held D in the bass give the singer maximum flexibility and all but ensure that the text is comprehensible. The only moment of ornamentation in five pages of music decorates the word "adore," in the phrase "servant, follower, and lover to that Giasone whom I adore despite myself"—illustrating Giasone's powers of seduction as he moves Isifile to amorous behaviors against her better judgment. Further representational signs of lament are thrown in for good measure: when Isifile shifts temporarily into triple meter, at "S'ei non torna," the central section of the lament (see ex. 15.3), a descending bass tetrachord features prominently. In the last section, "Così ad un tempo istesso" (not shown), the bass line descends through an entire seventh before leaping an octave to resolve down once again.

In this scene, location, narrative circumstance, long-standing performance traditions, poetry, and music work together to position Isifile's outburst as inevitable. Importantly, the citation of familiar tropes provides the affective weight that renders her lament moving. While it might seem to go without saying, the presence of such tropes

Ex. 15.2. Isifile, "Isifile infelice." Francesco Cavalli, *Il Giasone*, act 1, scene 13.
Text: Unhappy Isifile, unfortunate exile from the beautiful throne of Lemnos; queen without a realm, mother to illegitimate children before being a wife; wife only in name, wife without a husband, martyr to fortune, disconsolate wanderer, deprived of every comfort; servant, follower, and lover to that Giasone, whom I adore despite myself.

raises audience expectations that Isifile will be distressed and primes the audience as sympathetic listeners even before she arrives. Without the framework of tradition and repetition, gestures such as Isifile's placement on the shore or her poetic and musical idioms would have lacked the rich history of their previous instantiations, and the librettists, composers, and performers would have needed to work much harder to conjure the same affective response.[19] Indeed, the operas of mid-century Venice inhabited a reception context strongly dissimilar from that of opera today, where the emergence of the canon, and later of literal recording technologies, has prepared audiences to view each work as a masterpiece, available for repeated listening, and expected to differentiate itself from the horizon of preceding works though innovation and compositional genius. Instead, the operas of Cavalli and his contemporaries are more similar to the episodic conventions of long-running television shows: full appreciation for *The Simpsons* or *Seinfeld* comes not from a single viewing of a single episode, but from long

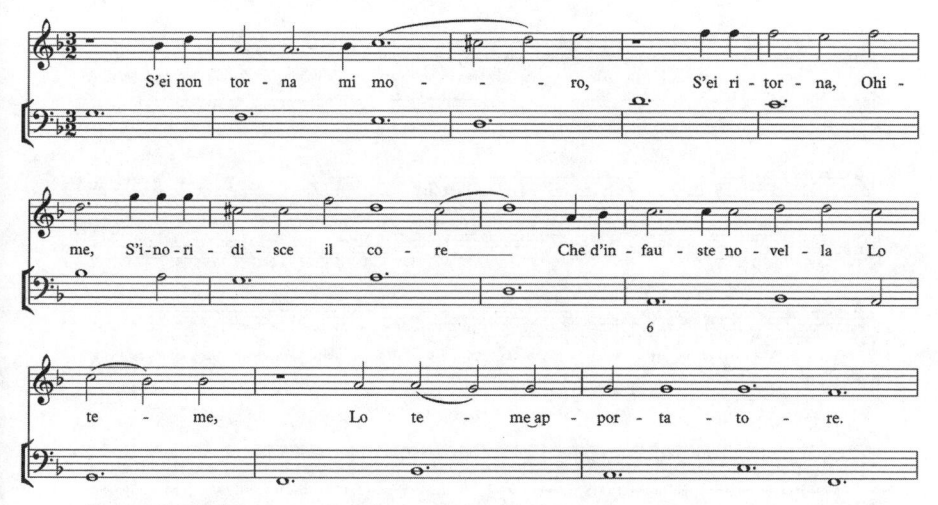

Ex. 15.3. Isifile, "S'ei non torna." Francesco Cavalli, *Il Giasone*, act I, scene xiii.
Text: If he doesn't return, I will die. If he does return, alas, my heart falters; I fear he is the bearer of dire news!

familiarity with the characters, the typical plot arcs, and the ways in which particular episodes combine the tropes and clichés of the genre in appreciably new and different ways.

In this context, Isifile's role in *Il Giasone* can be understood as a masterpiece of the *cantare con affetto*: not because it breaks with tradition, but precisely for the way in which it rehearses and combines generic tropes. This can be seen with particular clarity in the work's finale, and in Isifile's final lament.[20] In several ways this later lament is gratuitous, for, with Medea's affections transferred back to Egeo, Giasone is romantically unencumbered, and the audience knows that his return to Isifile is merely a matter of time. Yet even after Isifile saves Giasone's life (from an irate Egeo, bent on revenge for Giasone's presumed attack on Medea), and after Egeo and Medea proclaim their love in a tuneful duet, Giasone remains petulant and ill-disposed toward his erstwhile paramour. Thus, Isifile — already cast and coded in the adamant mode — laments once again.

Musicological commentators have noted the degree to which Isifile's "Infelice, ch'ascolto?" (reproduced in its entirety as ex. 15.4) samples existing lament conventions. We can point, for instance, to the discontinuous, sectional nature of the piece. Each new emotional twist in a multifaceted recitation is marked by a melodic, modal, or textural contrast to the proceeding material, exemplifying the "varij affetti" Margaret Murata has named as typical of operatic soliloquies.[21] We could

Ex. 15.4. Isifile, "Infelice, ch'ascolto?" Francesco Cavalli, *Il Giasone*, act 3, scene 21. (continued caption on opposite page)

Text: Unhappy one, what do I hear? Do not grieve, Jason, for, if my life was, as I understand it, a miscarriage of errors that produces your pain, I come to sacrifice it to your fury. If I had died in the sea, such a quick death would not perhaps have satisfied your rage. Now since I am alive, cheer up, o cruel one, for you will be able, with repeated deaths, to unleash the cruel desire of your proud heart. Yes, yes, my tyrant, cut right through these abhorrent limbs; tear apart, little by little, my unhappy flesh; dissect my chest; rend me at your pleasure; torment my senses; and might my long death prolong my torment, and your joy. But, if in the end you [have] lost the cherished memories of being my husband, be sure that the name "father" survives
your cruelties intact!
Do not forget, Jason, that you are a father and that my children are a part of you. If natural laws oblige even the wild beasts to feed their offspring, let your generous hand give to them, at the least, the sustenance they beg! And do not permit that your sceptered sons, languishing for hunger, would expire their innocent souls.
Queen [Medea], Egeo, friends! Plead for me with this cruel one, so that while wounding me he leaves these breasts untouched by his blows; so that I could, at least, nourish my sons with the cold milk of the dead maternal breast. Beg him, o merciful ones, such that those infant angels can be present at the martyrdom of their betrayed mother, and that with every wound that he will imprint on my chaste chest, they could drink my dripping blood; so that it [my blood], in passing into their pure veins, will be embodied in them, and their breast will become, in some way, an innocent tomb to my innocence.
Farewell earth, farewell sun; farewell my queen and friend; friends, farewell. Farewell scepters, farewell country; farewell my children! Your mother, undone from her terrestrial veil, will wait in heaven to see you again. Now come, come, my sons, my dear treasures; it is time that I consign you to the adored monster who is my executioner and your father.
Children, I die and wait for you [in heaven]; and you, Jason, though you kill me, I adore you.

point, as well, to the declamatory rhythms, evident throughout the common-time passages; to the cadential collapse, seen at the ends of phrases such as "fuori," "l'aque," and "sì breve" in the second and third systems; or to the piece's intensifying chromaticism. In the sixth and seventh systems, the tessitura, the rhythms, and the repeated use of the imperative tense recall the *concitato* genera of Monteverdi's lament for Arianna, similarly celebrated for its epitomizing function in relation to lament tropes. Ellen Rosand cited Isifile's "Infelice, ch'ascolto?" as a culminating moment in lament composition, drawing on and combining sections of recitative soliloquy along with the descending-tetrachord lament aria: "The intensity of recitative becomes all the more expressive as it breaks free from the restraints of measured aria style, and the restraint of aria style in turn earns tension from having succeeded in reining in an emotional outburst."[22] Wendy Heller goes so far as to say that in this particular scene, "Isifile uses *every available* lament gesture" (emphasis added).[23]

As Heller also notes, "Infelice ch'ascolto?" differs from most of its precedents—and certainly from the mythical narrative on which the story is nominally based—in that Isifile gets to deliver her lament directly before its intended recipient. Though rejected, Isifile is able to display her emotional response to Giasone himself, and not just to the sails of his distant and fast-disappearing ship. "Isifile transforms a private lament-monologue into a performance," writes Heller, "both deadly serious and steeped in irony, engaging our sympathy for the heroine's desperation while at the same time underscoring the impossibility and absurdity of her predicament."[24] While lament was almost always a performance witnessed by both on- and offstage audiences— think again of the archetypal Arianna, whose vain pleas are observed by an entire crowd of fisherfolk, or Penelope, attended by her nurse—in singing to Giasone, Isifile is provided with a rare opportunity for persuasive song. The self-consciousness of her outpouring helps magnify the effect of the scene, for the watching audience sees and hears Isifile, but also sees and hears Giasone respond to Isifile, as well as to the other characters who stand as witnesses.

The multiple audiences of this song have left important gestural traces in Cicognini's text and Cavalli's music, foregrounding moments of shifting address and the turns of the performer's body, moments that Mauro Calcagno would label *diexis*.[25] The text consists of sixty-seven lines of *versi sciolti*, divided, as Rosand points out, into three distinct sections of music. A recitative opening notated in common time; a triple-meter central section beginning at "Regina, Egeo, amici," characterized by a recurrent descending tetrachord in the bass line; and a return to the recitative texture at "Assistino ai martiri." The broad sectional divisions line up with Isifile's appeal to various sections of her audience: after the rhetorical question of the opening line, addressed as much to herself as to any would-be listener, the first section of the lament is directed at Giasone; at "Regina, Egeo, amici," Isifile calls upon her other listeners to intervene with Giasone on her behalf; at "Assistino ai martiri," she unfolds a long subjunctive clause detailing the consequences for her children of her distress at Giasone's hand. The alignment of linguistic, bodily, and musical shifts is emphasized by other, less frequently noted sectional divisions. First, the flatward hexachordal shift at "Non ti scordar, Giason, che padre sei" (Do not forget, Giasone, that you are a father), when Isifile moves from a discussion of her fractured rapport with Giasone to focus on their children, and second, the double bar line at "Addio terra" (Goodbye, world), where Isifile begins to take leave of the world and of each of her interlocutors in turn.[26] A final double bar line sets off the final two lines of text, which sum up the content of the entire lament in aphoristic fashion: "Children, I die and wait for you [in heaven]; and you, Jason, though you kill me, I adore you."

The affective kernel of this piece can be found in Isifile's appeal to her status as mother, and to the success with which she locates her maternal importance within the flesh of her body. Isifile's challenge to Giasone—"Go ahead, rend me limb from limb"—such that he could wring maximum pleasure from her long, slow, agonizing death reaches a hyperbolic climax as she imposes one condition on her dismemberment, and calls upon the watching bystanders to hold Giasone accountable: "Leave these breasts [*mammelle*] untouched by his blows; so that I could, at least, nourish my sons with the cold milk of the dead maternal breast [*seno*]." This is a wonderfully rich—affective and effective—moment of rhetorical brilliance, against which Giasone has no recourse. He is moved, as have been generations of audiences, both contemporary and modern. It is, however, important to note that the power of this scene relies on precisely those rehearsals and citations that are so easy to dismiss as conventional, formulaic, or derivative: librettist and composer have managed to unite and reincorporate an extraordinarily dense nexus of clichéd gestures—textural, musical, and physical.

Nothing about this aria is completely original. The central image, of Isifile and Giasone's sons nursing from their mother's severed breasts, gains energy from the literary tradition of the poetic blazon, in which feminine beauty is always already understood as an assemblage of parts. Isifile's paean to fragmentation emphasizes this point, while the suspensions—at "lento, lento" and elsewhere—depict both her own pain and Giasone's presumed enjoyment, playing once again on the multiple referents of well-placed dissonance. At the work's climax, the phrase "these breasts"—importantly, not the relatively sedate *seno*, but the plural and explicitly maternal *mammelle*—stages an unveiling. The plural noun references the morphology of the specifically female body, while the resonant double vowels conjure up the sounds of the *mamma* or *mammana* (wet nurse) and of the act of *mammellare* (to breastfeed). The pronoun, *queste*, calls attention to the singing, breathing body of the performer and demands that the character of Isifile put her breasts quite literally on view—thus incorporating into her lament both the physical evidence of her maternity and the quintessential gesture of the lamenting woman: the woman who laments was expected to expose her breasts. She rends her clothes, beats her chest, and tears her hair—embodied actions confirming her distress. These gestures form the repertoire of motions associated with the emotion of lament, by definition the register of a woman pushed beyond the bounds of propriety and driven by despair to lose control. As described in the Scala scenario *La pazzia d'Isabella*, for example, published in 1611 and indicative of Italian theatrical norms, the distressed title character "becomes entirely mad, tears off all her clothing, and as if out of her senses runs through the streets."[27] In short, she laments. Thus, in "Infelice, ch'ascolto?," the audience's surprise lies not in the fact that Isifile exposes her body to view, but in the way that Cicognini has justified the exposure as part of the drama.

For viewers and auditors versed in Italian theatrical conventions, the final lament scene should have been immediately recognizable, ideally eliciting an "Ooh, I love this bit!" even at the first performance. Everything is a repeat: Isifile's words, Isifile's sound, Isifile's movements across and on the stage. These repetitions, the recourse made by librettist, composer, and performer to preexisting *affetti*, are an important structural device, but also, I would argue, a recording device. They provide a playback technology that enables the recall of emotions and affects with which the audience is already intimately familiar. For me, as a modern scholar attempting to think about the affective resources of such works within a historically relevant context, I find it both liberating and productive to think of these repeats as literal, material devices; as, that is, the technology that enables a particular musical theatrical experience. To do so short-circuits the deprecating value judgments of the traditional descriptive vocabulary. A reliance on existing technological devices is not "formulaic," "generic," or "conventional" in the widely understood sense of the terms. As recording devices, the repetitions and clichéd gestures (musical, textual, and physical) of seventeenth-century theatrical music are not compositional choices at all, but rather the infrastructure that permits the dissemination of the material and delivers it to the listening and watching audience in the most effective and efficient way. For me, thinking of these iterations as a literal technology rather than as hackneyed techniques reduces a reliance on persistent habits of modern musical aesthetics whereby originality is prized over other compositional gifts. Freed, even if only partially or temporarily, from the insidious logic of the post-Romantic canon, I find myself better able to appreciate the ingenuity and brilliance with which composers and librettists such as Cavalli and Cicognini were able to manipulate the devices at their disposal, moving their audiences to affect by their use of extant *affetti*.

Furthermore, the tension between the *affetti* and the more familiar recording devices of late modernity frays productively at the edges of some tightly knit yet thoroughly modern assumptions about what it means to faithfully reproduce sound. Importantly, the *affetti* do not permit the playback of musical or visual material in the absence of originary bodies, nor do they facilitate the kinds of exact repetition characteristic of our current recording technologies. Instead, bodies must be understood as the hardware on which such recordings can be replayed, and the repetitions and citations of their reproduction as the process by which they gain affective power. Scheer, arguing that emotions are a practice, executed by a "knowing body," quotes Bourdieu's theory of symbolic force: "A form of power that is exerted on bodies ... on the basis of the dispositions deposited, like springs, at the deepest level of the body. If it can act like the release of a spring, that is, with a very weak expenditure of energy, this is because it does no more than trigger the dispositions that the work of inculcation and embodiment has deposited in those who are thereby primed for it."[28] Both the means and the message, the affective tropes and gestures of the Italian stage, ran in well-worn but highly effective grooves, enabling composers, poets, and performers to communicate with their audiences in poignant, powerful, and economical ways. They offer us a technology whereby we can reanimate the affective potential of early modern performance, learning to listen past the invocative or citational nature of such gestures and toward their evocative, affective power.

The new musics of the seventeenth century privileged a specificity of expressive techniques, rushing into print with idiomatic material suited to particular instruments or contexts: Giulio Caccini, for example, wanted "to avoid that old style of *passaggi* formerly in common use (one more suited to wind and stringed instruments than to the voice)."[29] Modern scholars have tended to view the embrace of print as a way to record the ephemeral experience of performance, yet to do so they must continually justify the "apparently formulaic approach" that underlies both vocal and instrumental genres.[30] If the *affetti* were recording devices, however, then musical performance was less ephemeral and far more easily repeatable than we might have imagined. Revaluing the formulaic repetitions of this music allows us to ask new questions about these repertoires, prioritizing the faithful reproduction of both *affetti* and affect, and resisting the assumption—foreign to early modern audiences—that the music of performance, once past, was lost to time. The *affetti* were available for repeated listenings. Their practice, through repetition, was both action and affect, motion and emotion. Through the use of such devices, music successfully moved its audience, "embodying itself an affect (first meaning)," through "particular, even stereotyped idioms or affects (second meaning)."

Notes

Earlier versions of this essay were presented at the "Sound and Affect: Voice, Music, World" Conference, Stony Brook University, NY; at the UCLA Musicology Department's Distinguished Lecture Series; and at the Baroque Opera Workshop, Queens College, CUNY—though the auditors of those early versions may find this one changed to the point of unrecognizability. I would like to thank Gary Tomlinson, in particular, for his helpful and encouraging words after a rehearsal of some of these ideas, and one of the anonymous reviewers of my book manuscript for some chance comments that steered this other text in new and profitable directions. I would also like to thank Thomas Marks for his comments on a draft of this essay, Thomas Hedrick for his work in typesetting the musical examples, and Lucia Marchi for her comments on and improvements to the Italian translations.

1. Giulio Caccini, "To the Readers," in *Le nuove musiche* (Florence, 1602), ed. and trans. H. Wiley Hitchcock (Madison, WI: A-R Editions, 1970), 43–56.

2. Ibid., 47.

3. Ibid., 45 n. 12.

4. The concept of *Affektenlehre*, popularized in English-language history texts as the "Doctrine of the Affections," has been the subject of taxonomic explanations in both contemporary and historiographic sources, redoubling the general presumption that the baroque *affetti* were mechanical or superficial correlations between signs and emotional content. See, e.g., Isabella van Elferen, "Affective Discourse in German Baroque Text-Based Music," *Tijdschrift voor muziektheorie* 9, no. 3 (2004): 217–33, who makes a similar point about the historiographical treatment of baroque affects.

5. Monique Scheer, "Are Emotions a Kind of Practice (And Is That What Makes Them Have a History)? A Bourdieuian Approach to Understanding Emotion," *History and Theory* 51, no. 2 (2012): 193–220.

6. Presciently, perhaps, Hitchcock suggested that "in its second meaning, *affetto* approaches the modern English 'device.'" Caccini, *Le nuove musiche*, 45 n. 12.

7. Jonathan Sterne, *The Audible Past: Cultural Origins of Sound Reproduction* (Durham, NC: Duke University Press, 2003).

8. Ellen Rosand, *Opera in Seventeenth-Century Venice: The Creation of a Genre* (Berkeley and Los Angeles: University of California Press, 1990), 4.

9. Emily Wilbourne, *Seventeenth-Century Opera and the Sound of the Commedia dell'Arte* (Chicago: University of Chicago Press, 2016).

10. Rosand describes *Il Giasone* as "probably the most frequently performed opera of the entire seventeenth century," citing multiple libretti published between 1649 and 1690 and the survival of no fewer than nine European manuscripts of the score; Rosand, *Opera in Seventeenth-Century Venice*, 275 n. 39. The extant sources for *Il Giasone* and for Cavalli's other works are listed in Thomas Walker and Irene Alm, "Cavalli, Francesco," *Grove Music Online* (Oxford University Press), accessed July 10, 2017, http://www.oxfordmusiconline.com/sub scriber/article/grove/music/05207.

11. I discuss the comic characters of *Il Giasone* in Emily Wilbourne, "Demo's Stutter, Subjectivity, and the Virtuosity of Vocal Failure," in "Colloquy: Why Voice Now?," ed. Martha Feldman, *Journal of the American Musicological Society* 68, no. 3 (2015): 659–63.

12. The *adamant* and *ardent innamorate* are discussed at length in my *Seventeenth-Century Opera*; see chap. 4, "Penelope and Poppea as Stock Figures of the Commedia dell'Arte."

13. See Ellen Rosand, "The Descending Tetrachord: An Emblem of Lament," *Musical Quarterly* 65, no. 3 (1979): 346–59.

14. Wendy Heller, "Hypsipyle, Medea, and the Ovidian Imagination: Taming the Epic Hero in Cavalli's *Giasone*," in *Readying Cavalli's Operas for the Stage: Manuscript, Edition, Production*, ed. Ellen Rosand (Farnham England, and Burlington, VT: Ashgate, 2013), 176.

15. Susan McClary has argued repeatedly for the sexual tension of dissonance treatment in seventeenth-century music; see, e.g., *Desire and Pleasure in Seventeenth-Century Music* (Berkeley and Los Angeles: University of California Press, 2012).

16. Tim Carter suggests Olimpia as a precedent for Rinuccini's Arianna, a circumstance that explains Arianna's repeated references to the wild beasts and deserted shore (despite the crowd of fisherfolk who watch and comment on her performance). Carter, "Lamenting Ariadne?," *Early Music* 27, no. 3 (1999): 395–405, esp. 399.

17. *La paccia d'Arianna* or *The Madness of Arianna*, written by the commedia dell'arte actress Marina Dorotea Antonazzoni *detta* Lavinia (1593–1639), survives in a manuscript dated 1622 at the Biblioteca Braidense in Milan (Racolto Morbio 2). The play is discussed in my book *Seventeenth-Century Opera and the Sound of the Commedia dell'Arte* (Chicago: University of Chicago Press, 2016); see chap. 2, "Ma meglio di tutti Arianna comediante."

18. Robert Henke, *Performance and Literature in the Commedia dell'Arte* (Cambridge and New York: Cambridge University Press, 2002), 31–49.

19. Mary Ann Smart makes a related point about physical gestures and audience reception in *Mimomania: Music and Gesture in Nineteenth-Century Opera* (Berkeley and Los Angeles: University of California Press, 2004).

20. I have discussed this final lament, "Infelice, ch'ascolto?," in another context: see my "Breastmilk, Exposed Bodies, and the Politics of the Indecent," *Echo: A Music-Centered Journal* 14, no. 1 (2016): http://www.echo.ucla.edu/volume-14-1-2016/article-breastmilk-exposed-bodies-politics-indecent/.

21. See Margaret Murata, "The Recitative Soliloquy," *Journal of the American Musicological Society* 32, no. 1 (1979): 45–73.

22. Rosand, *Opera in Seventeenth-Century Venice*, 374.

23. Heller, "Hypsipyle, Medea, and the Ovidian Imagination," 181.

24. Ibid., 185.

25. Mauro Calcagno, *From Madrigal to Opera: Monteverdi's Staging of the Self* (Berkeley and Los Angeles: University of California Press, 2012).

26. Heller compares this section to Monteverdi's *Orfeo*, specifically the title character's farewell to the earth and sun before his departure for the underworld, see Heller, "Hypsipyle, Medea, and the Ovidian Imagination," 184.

27. Flaminio Scala, *Il teatro delle favole rappresentative, overo La ricreatione comica, boscareccia e tragica: Divisa in cinquanta giornate* (Venice: Gio. Battista Pulciani, 1611), fol. 117v: "diventa pazza affatto, si straccia tutte le vestimenta d'attorno, e come forsennata se ne corre per strada."

28. Pierre Bourdieu, *Masculine Domination*, trans. Richard Nice (Stanford, CA: Stanford University Press, 2001), 38; quoted in Scheer, "Are Emotions a Kind of Practice?," 208.

29. Caccini, *Le nuove musiche*, 43.

30. The quote comes from Rebecca Cypess, *Curious and Modern Inventions: Instrumental Music as Discovery in Galileo's Italy* (Chicago: University of Chicago Press, 2016), where it appears with notable frequency, particularly during her discussions of Biago Marini's *Affetti musicali* of 1617.

CHAPTER 16

Immanuel Kant and the Downfall of the *Affektenlehre*

Tomás McAuley

The eighteenth-century *Affektenlehre*. The words roll easily off the tongue: the temporal qualifier ("eighteenth-century") is so closely associated with the noun (*Affektenlehre*) that their joining into one phrase seems almost inevitable.[1] The same could not be said of the seventeenth-century *Affektenlehre*. The phrase might still be used, but any such talk would be peppered with qualifications, with careful mention of origins and developments, or of the doctrine's not having reached its fullest instantiation. Talk of the nineteenth-century *Affektenlehre*, though, would be far worse. If the *Affektenlehre* had yet to reach its zenith in the seventeenth century, it was undoubtedly past its prime in the nineteenth. For sure, versions of such a doctrine persisted in some circles and continue to do so to this day.[2] But the *Affektenlehre* in the nineteenth century was a pale imitation of its former self. Aestheticians, critics, and theorists alike were far slower to draw on it—and when it did appear, it had lost the strident confidence that it had carried for much of the previous century. When Eduard Hanslick complained in 1858 that "it is affirmed daily that the *affects* are the sole aesthetic foundation of music," yet described this view nonetheless as an "old phantom," he spoke both to the continuing power of the doctrine and to its waning.[3] The doctrine had, in a word, lost its intuitive—one might say, its affective—resonance.

But why was this? How had a theory so intimately associated with musical thought in the eighteenth century fallen so far from grace by the nineteenth? Does this century periodization, with its elevation of the years around 1800, reflect the reality of the downfall of the *Affektenlehre*—or does it distract from a process with less convenient dates? And what is an *Affektenlehre* anyway?

On Definitions

I start with the last question, for there are those for whom the notion of an eighteenth-century *Affektenlehre*—or doctrine of the affects—would be just as troublesome as talk of such a doctrine in the seventeenth century or the nineteenth century. Most famously, George Buelow wrote in the early 1980s that

> many German Baroque writers on music were fond of saying that the expression of the Affections in music was a subject as vast as the bottomless ocean. We shall not come closer to understanding this important aspect of Baroque music if we insist, like so many writers of the past and present, in condensing the uncharted, watery expanses of Baroque expressivity into a single raindrop labelled the *Affektenlehre*.[4]

There can be no doubting that Buelow is correct: there was no single, universally held statement of the *Affektenlehre*. This premise, however, in no way entails the conclusion that there was no doctrine at all. There were, rather, multiple systems that all shared the same basic conception of music.[5]

According to this conception, music should move the affects (or affections, *Affekte*) of the listener, for their moral, spiritual, or physical betterment, for their pleasure, or for a combination of these. The exact meaning of *Affekt* inevitably changed over time and was in any case often left unstated, but the word referred in general to what we might now call a physically rooted emotion or feeling. Whilst twenty-first-century theories of affect are quick to emphasize its indeterminacy, eighteenth-century theorists of the *Affektenlehre* delighted in accuracy. *Affekte* were, in principle, delineable, specifiable, and ripe for categorization—even if theorists could never quite agree on how to delineate, specify, and categorize them.

The various versions of the *Affektenlehre* were united in their holding fast to two key tenets. The first was that in moving the affects there was a causal relation at play between musician (whether performer or composer) and listener. The second was that particular musical means could, at least in principle, be linked to particular affective responses. The various systems based around the *Affektenlehre*, however, also differed in two related aspects. First, explanations of the causal link between musician and listener varied widely. Second, attempts to define the specific musical means available to the musician failed consistently to reach any kind of consensus. Nonetheless, their shared premises are sufficient to be able to talk simply of the *Affektenlehre*, without needing always to talk of multiple *Affektenlehren*.

This general conception of music was common across much European literature. There was also, however, what Dietrich Bartel has identified as a "specifically German view"—a view based, at least in part, "on an attempt to rationally understand and explain the underlying physiological phenomena."[6] It is to this German view that I refer in my use of the term *Affektenlehre*—without, however, claiming any single aspect of this view as exclusively German.[7]

On Methods and Dates

What, then, of the date? Did the *Affektenlehre* really meet its downfall at so convenient a date as 1800? Well, almost. The *Affektenlehre* was deposed not at the start of the nineteenth century, but at the start of what is more usually called the long nineteenth century—the period from the beginning of the French Revolution (1789) to the beginning of the World War I (1914). In fact, I shall propose an almost exact date. The *Affektenlehre* died in April 1790. How could I possibly justify such a precise claim? To answer this question, I need to turn to the broader question: What led to the downfall of the *Affektenlehre*?

There are two ways one might set about answering this broader question. The first would be to examine a wide range of music criticism and related primary sources in order to see when, where, and to what extent the doctrine really did fall out of fashion. One could then work backward from there to seek the ultimate cause, if any, of this. This would make for good history—but I don't do it here. Or, at least, I don't go much beyond general observations of this kind.[8] The second way to set about explaining the downfall of the *Affektenlehre* would be to ask a more logical question: When—and where—did the doctrine stop making sense?

Prima facie, this might seem like a less obvious route of investigation—but I suggest that it also makes for good history. It is, in any case, the route that most previous scholarship on this topic has taken, if not self-consciously so. In asking when the doctrine stopped making sense, such scholarship has customarily turned to musical factors. In particular, such scholarship proposes (or presumes) that the *Affektenlehre* had been an adequate response to most eighteenth-century music but failed to explain the newfound depth, complexity, and sublimity of music from the late eighteenth century onward—and of the mature instrumental works of Haydn, Mozart, and Beethoven in particular. In this picture, these works demanded (or revealed) a whole new conception of music, one in which music's purpose was no longer simply to move the affects of the listener mechanically, but rather to offer nonlinguistic knowledge or insight into the listener's inner life—or into the nature of being itself.[9]

Such a new view of music did indeed come into being in this period, and I have written elsewhere about the causes of its emergence.[10] Here, though, I want to focus not on the emergence of this newer view, but on the downfall of the *Affektenlehre*. This very separation of downfall and emergence betrays my departure from previous scholarship on the topic, for in this scholarship, the undoing of the *Affektenlehre* and the rise of a newer view of music are customarily seen as but two sides of the same coin. Just as the *Affektenlehre* failed to do justice to the profundity of the music of Beethoven and his contemporaries, according to this story, a new view of music arose that could do just this. Indeed, scholarship in this tradition tends to focus heavily on the emergence of the newer view of music—and the music that supposedly inspired it. The implication is that the *Affektenlehre* was so much fluff waiting to be swept away.

In the present essay, however, I argue that the downfall of the *Affektenlehre* was a relatively self-contained process, separable in principle from the emergence of the newer view of music that arose around the same time. I argue also that the *Affektenlehre* met its final collapse in response not to changes in musical composition, but rather to changes in contemporary philosophy. In particular, I will suggest, the *Affektenlehre* met its downfall in the philosophy of Immanuel Kant. In order to show how this was the case, I will examine the place of music in Kant's *Kritik der Urteilskraft* (*Critique of the Power of Judgment*) of—yes, April—1790.[11]

Where it has been addressed in Anglophone scholarship of the past few decades, Kant's discussion of music has frequently been written off as derivative and confused.[12] For the same reason, no doubt, much recent scholarship on the musical thought of this era has overlooked Kant altogether.[13] In what follows, however, I argue that this very combination of derivation and confusion embodies the downfall of the *Affektenlehre*—a downfall playing itself out precisely in the *Kritik der Urteilskraft*.

On Listeners and Philosophers

That my investigation is into the question of when and where the *Affektenlehre* stopped making sense, rather than into when and where it stopped being held, is crucial. There is no suggestion, rare instances aside, that listeners in 1790—not even well-educated, German-speaking listeners—were familiar with Kant's *Kritk der Urteilskraft*. Similarly, there is no suggestion that any given listener suddenly changed their way of hearing music, that under the influence of Kant they switched overnight to a new mode of perception. Rather, I claim here only to have identified, in what was initially a relatively obscure intellectual context (the *Kritik der Urteilskraft* was hardly a best seller), the point— or at least, one key point—at which the *Affektenlehre* stopped making sense.[14]

That said, Kantian philosophy did undergo a remarkable process of popularization—in relative terms, at least—in the later 1780s, a process in which Karl Leonhard Reinhold's widely read *Briefe über die Kantische Philosophie* (*Letters on the Kantian Philosophy*) played a crucial role.[15] I do not attempt here to quantify what effect this popularization of Kantian philosophy might have had on attitudes to music more generally, though in a place and age saturated with ideas of *Bildung* (roughly, self-cultivation) and *Popularphilosophie* (popular philosophy), it is surely worth entertaining the possibility that there might have been some. More importantly in the present context, Kant's philosophical system was to be of unprecedented influence on subsequent German philosophy. Practically every major German philosopher of the nineteenth and twentieth centuries, from Hegel to Adorno, was responding in some fundamental way to the philosophical challenges laid out by Kant. And I do, in the conclusion to this essay, suggest that Kant's undermining of the *Affektenlehre* had a direct, immediate, and substantial impact on the place of music in subsequent philosophical thought.

On Derivation and Confusion

With that, I turn now to Kant's discussion of music in the *Kritik der Urteilskraft*. In this work, Kant uses the terms *Musik* (music) and *Tonkunst* (literally, the art of tone) to refer primarily to instrumental music, considering vocal music to be a combination of music and poetry. As such, he begins his most extensive discussion of music by comparing this art to poetry. Music, claims Kant, "speaks through mere sensations without concepts," meaning that, unlike poetry, it does not "leave behind something for reflection." In this respect, music is inferior to poetry. In another respect, however, music is potentially superior to poetry, because "it moves the mind in more manifold and, though only temporarily, in deeper ways." Music's ability to move the mind, to arouse a "play of thought" is, however, "merely the effect of an as it were mechanical association."[16] Kant explicates this mechanical association:

> [Music's] charm ... seems to rest on this: that every expression of language has, in context, a tone that is appropriate to its sense; that this tone more or less designates an affect of the speaker and conversely also produces one in the hearer ... just as modulation is as it were a language of the sensations [*Empfindungen*] universally comprehensible to every human being, the art of tone puts that language into practice for itself alone, in all its force, namely as a language of the affects [*Affecten*].[17]

This, in microcosm, is Kant's view of music. It is thoroughly typical of the eighteenth-century *Affektenlehre*.

Such is the derivation. What, though, of the confusion? In a word, although Kant is clear on his basic conception of music, he dithers on the value that music so conceived might have. In particular, Kant cannot decide whether music is a beautiful art or merely an agreeable one. The two types of art share, for Kant, the aim of arousing pleasure in the spectator (or listener) but differ in the types of pleasure they offer. If the aim of an art is pleasure as "mere sensations" (*Empfindungen*), then it is agreeable. If, however, the aim of an art is pleasure as "kinds of cognition," then it is beautiful.[18]

At one point, Kant discusses music as a beautiful art.[19] Elsewhere, however, he says explicitly that music is not a beautiful art.[20] Still elsewhere, Kant gives serious thought to the question of whether music is a beautiful art but does not come to a firm conclusion.[21] For a thinker so logical, rigorous, and confident on almost every subject, Kant's indecision on the value of music is remarkable. On balance, however, Kant seems to lean toward the conclusion that music is not a beautiful art, for he is clear that music "speaks through mere sensations."[22] In this sense, the pleasure that music provides is not fully cognitive in the way that Kant demands.

Although earlier eighteenth-century thinkers commonly assigned music a lowly place within the beautiful arts, music's place *as* a beautiful art was never seriously threatened.[23] Compared to this broadly positive assessment of music as a beautiful art, Kant's (tentative) conclusion that music is merely agreeable displays a broadly negative assessment of music. Despite having the same basic conception of music as previous thinkers, then, Kant's assessment of music differs sharply from theirs. Hence Kant's confusion: he tries to follow previous thinkers in his explanation of music but does not reach the same conclusion as to music's value.

But why is this? Why does Kant, still conceiving of music in terms of the *Affektenlehre*, reach a negative assessment of this art? A literal answer to this question—and one that took Kant at his word—would trace closely Kant's own intermittent digressions on music, attempting to show in each instance how Kant holds music up against his criterion for beauty and for beautiful art, only to find music ultimately lacking. Or, perhaps more simply, it would note merely that Kant takes our experience of beauty to be cognitive and music's affective power to be noncognitive. Job done.

I would like, however, to propose a less literal approach to the question of why Kant reaches a negative assessment of music. This approach asks—beyond what Kant himself may or may not have said—how music *should* be judged, when conceived according to the *Affektenlehre*, but held within the philosophical context that Kant provides. I suggest that Kant undermines three key premises of earlier *Aufklärung* (German Enlightenment) philosophy, premises that are necessary for a positive evaluation of music according to the *Affektenlehre*. The first concerns Kant's notion of disinterested beauty. The second concerns his views on rhetoric. The third—and most fundamental—returns to Kant's belief that the pleasure taken in beautiful art must be cognitive.

On Interest

Kant opens the main body of the *Kritik der Urteilskraft* with four interlocking definitions of the beautiful. The first of these is as follows:

> **Taste** is the faculty for judging an object or a kind of representation through a satisfaction or dissatisfaction **without any interest**. The object of such a satisfaction is called **beautiful**.[24]

Kant thus separates beauty and interest, interest being any use or purpose that an object or representation might be perceived to have. This is not to say that objects (or representations) with a use or purpose cannot be beautiful, but merely that they can be considered beautiful only insofar as they are considered apart from any such use or purpose.[25]

Although anticipated by a small number of Enlightenment thinkers, Kant's separation of beauty and interest is at odds with the mainstream of earlier eighteenth-century notions of beauty, which customarily link beauty with virtue.[26] Even David Hume, who severed the link between beauty and virtue, and who Kant famously declared had awoken him from his dogmatic slumbers, still defines beauty in part by utility:

> It is evident, that one considerable source of *beauty* in all animals is the advantage which they reap from the particular structure of their limbs and members, suitably to [their] particular manner of life.... Ideas of utility and its contrary, though they do not entirely determine what is handsome or deformed, are evidently the source of a considerable part of approbation or dislike.[27]

The *Affektenlehre* is rooted in interest, for it specifies a use for music, namely the moving of the affects for primarily moral, spiritual, or medical purposes. Because of this, Kant's notion of disinterested beauty can only lead to a negative assessment of music conceived in accordance with the *Affektenlehre*.

On Rhetoric

Given the kinds of uses that the *Affektenlehre* specified for music, it should come as no surprise that this doctrine was rooted in contemporary theories of rhetoric. It took from rhetoric both the abstract idea that it is possible and desirable for one person to arouse set (and potentially involuntary) responses in another and the outlines of the specific means for so doing. In this, the *Affektenlehre* drew on a relationship between music and rhetoric that was especially strong in German-speaking countries.[28]

Kant, however, is damning of rhetoric. He has two reasons for his position. The first is that rhetoric can be used "for glossing over or concealing vice or error."[29] The second is that it corrupts peoples' motivations even for good actions. Kant writes that "even if [rhetoric] can sometimes be applied to purposes that are in themselves legitimate and praiseworthy, it is nevertheless still objectionable that the maxims and dispositions be subjectively corrupted in this way, even if the deed is objectively lawful: for *it is not enough to do what is right, but it is also to be performed solely on the ground that it is right.*"[30] Kant's belief that "it is not enough to do what is right" flies in the face of conventional Enlightenment justifications of rhetoric, of the arts in general, and of music in particular, namely that it *is* enough to do what is right, and that rhetoric and the rhetorically inspired arts can aid in directing people to correct thoughts, feelings, and behaviors. In his influential *Allgemeine Theorie der schönen Künste* (*General Theory of the Fine Arts*) (1771–74), for example, Johann Georg Sulzer states that "the most important service the fine arts can offer to man consists without doubt in the well-ordered dominating desires that it can implant, by which the ethical character of man and his moral worth is determined."[31]

It might be asked, however, *why* Kant believes that "it is not enough to do what is right." In his *Grundlegung zur Metaphysik der Sitten* (*Groundwork of the Metaphysics of Morals*, 1785), Kant contrasts his (supposedly successful) moral theory to all previous (supposedly unsuccessful) moral theories:

> If we look back upon all previous efforts that have ever been made to discover the principle of morality, we need not wonder now why all of them had to fail. It was seen that the human being is bound to laws by his duty, but it never occurred to them that he is subject *only to laws given by himself but still universal* and that he is bound only to act in conformity with his own will, which, however, in accordance with nature's end is a will giving universal law.[32]

In this work, and in the *Kritik der praktischen Vernunft* (*Critique of Practical Reason*, 1788), Kant characterizes the principle of acting in accordance with self-given laws as "autonomy" and that of acting in accordance with externally imposed maxims as "heteronomy."[33] Kant believes that all previous moral theories were based on the principle of heteronomy, but that his own moral theory is based on the principle of autonomy. Although it is always wise to treat his historical claims with suspicion, Kant's formulation does hold true for his relationship with earlier eighteenth-century thinkers at least. Prior to Kant, it had generally been presumed that the source of morality lay outside of the individual, either in God, or, for a few radical Enlightenment thinkers, in a universal natural order or human nature.[34] Kant undoes this premise: although, fortuitously, every human will is bound by the same law, that law is always created by the individual human will, never given to it.

An externally given law, suggests Kant, would need only to be heeded; a self-given law, however, needs to be followed for its own sake. If simply acting in accordance with the law is sufficient, then any art (be it rhetoric or rhetorically inspired music) that persuades people to act in accordance with the law is likely to be seen in a positive light. If it is necessary to act in accordance with the law for the sake of so doing, however, then not only does rhetoric not help morality, it positively hinders it. For at the very moment that it is persuading people to act in accordance with the law, rhetoric is stopping those same people from acting in accordance with the law for the sake of so doing. Given the reliance of the *Affektenlehre* on a rhetorical conception of music, Kant's rejection of rhetoric can only lead to a negative assessment of music conceived in accordance with the *Affektenlehre*.³⁵

On Freedom

I want to return now to that central Kantian criterion for beautiful art: that the pleasure to which it gives rise must be a kind of cognition. Again, Kant's views contrast sharply with those of earlier Enlightenment thinkers. To return again to the *Allgemeine Theorie der schönen Künste* as a touchstone, Sulzer here defines beauty as "that perfection one senses [*fühlt*] or feels [*empfindet*]."³⁶ Kant, however, complains explicitly that the pleasures to which music gives rise to are mere *Empfindungen* (sensations). But why, in the first place, does Kant hold that the pleasure to which beautiful art gives rise must be cognitive?

This is a question that goes to the heart of Kant's aesthetics. As such, there are two ways of addressing it. The first is to treat Kant's aesthetics as a distinct and relatively self-contained sphere of his philosophy; the second is to consider the place of Kant's aesthetics within his broader philosophical enterprise. The first, typical of contemporary analytic philosophy, encourages clarity of thought in making sense of Kant's ideas about art, nature, and beauty, and so facilitates the use of these ideas in ongoing debates in philosophical aesthetics. The second, however, comes closest to Kant's own intentions — or his stated intentions, at least. It also explains most convincingly how Kant came to his belief that the pleasure taken in beautiful art must be cognitive. It is, in a word, the most historically telling perspective and, as such, the one that I take up here.

It is also, however, a perspective beset by two problems. First, it is far from clear how Kant's philosophical system is *supposed* to fit together. The problem is so intractable that generations of Kant scholars have made but halting progress on its resolution, leading to a panoply of possible interpretations. Second, regardless of the interpretive angle one might choose, this system remains notoriously difficult, not to mention philosophically troublesome. As such, the brief outline of Kant's philosophical system that follows of necessity takes a particular interpretive angle on Kant's philosophy, simplifies complex matters, and remains incomplete.³⁷ Nonetheless, I suggest that any other plausible interpretation of Kant's philosophy — presented in whatever level of detail — would facilitate similar conclusions to those I reach here. I have simply chosen that which most clearly highlights the relevant issues.

From a historical perspective, Kant's philosophy is best seen as an attempt to respond to problems in earlier Enlightenment thought.[38] Chief amongst these problems was a perceived conflict between freedom and necessity. Both were in their way central goals of the Enlightenment, a movement that sought, amongst other things, to free people from oppression and superstition.[39] One of the ways in which it strove to do so was through rational explanations of human morality (to free people from oppression) and of the natural world (to free them from superstition). Such explanations of human morality were based largely on the principle of individual freedom. Explanations of the natural world, on the other hand, were based primarily on the model of mechanical causation: events in nature should, according to this model, be explained by recourse to prior events, rather than by recourse to ultimate purposes or to the supernatural. Yet this model contained the seeds of a danger: that the very human freedom so cherished by Enlightenment thinkers would itself prove, in the face of mechanical explanations, to be illusory. If everything in nature is explainable in purely mechanical terms, why should human actions be any different?

Kant responds to this difficulty by suggesting that the natural world around us is a world of mere appearances (*Erscheinungen*). It is a world of appearances because we cannot know it apart from our own modes of human perception, chief among them space and time, which are not aspects of an independently existing nature but are instead imposed upon nature by the human subject. These appearances are real from the standpoint of human perception—that is to say, they are real *to us*—and as such are to be distinguished from mere illusions (*Scheine*). They are not, however, real considered apart from the standpoint of human perception. In this world of appearances, necessity rules supreme. Alongside this world of appearances, however, Kant also posits a world of things as they are in themselves. The human subject must of necessity exist in this world of things-in-themselves (*Dinge-an-Sich*), for it is from this world that they impose the order of human perception. In this world, Kant believes, humans are free—free, in particular, to make moral decisions.

But how can a subject live in two such radically different worlds at the same time? Kant answers by distinguishing between different cognitive faculties. There is a faculty of understanding, which provides the laws that govern the world of appearances; and a faculty of reason, which makes free decisions in the more fundamental world of things-in-themselves. In the wake of the *Kritik der reinen Vernunft* (*Critique of Pure Reason*, 1781; 2nd ed., 1787) and the *Kritik der praktischen Vernunft* (1788), Kant's critics quickly picked up on the question of how the subject connects the faculty of understanding and the faculty of reason.

This question holds within it two still deeper questions. First, how are the worlds of appearances and of things-in-themselves connected? Second, what is the relation between freedom and necessity?

In the *Kritik der Urteilskraft*, Kant proposes a solution. His solution is to describe a third cognitive faculty, which he calls the power of judgment. This faculty mediates between the faculty of understanding and the faculty of reason.[40] It does so through its judgment of beauty, for the judgment of beauty is neither moral nor mechanistic, and as such lies outside of the domains of the faculties of reason and of understanding. In mediating between the faculty of understanding and the faculty of reason, the judgment of beauty connects the world of appearances and that of things-in-themselves — and, by extension, mediates also between freedom and necessity.[41]

Kant proposes that one of the things that we can judge as beautiful is art. To judge something as beautiful is, for Kant, to take pleasure in it. For the cognitive faculties fully to be engaged, however, the pleasure taken in art must itself be cognitive. If this pleasure is mere sensation (*Empfindung*), the cognitive faculties are not fully engaged, and the power of judgment is not able to play its mediating role. Here, then, we have an answer to our question: why must the pleasure taken in beautiful art be cognitive? The answer is that only in this way can the judgment of beauty mediate between the faculties of reason and of understanding — and between freedom and necessity. We have seen how, according to Kant's statement of the *Affektenlehre*, music moves us mechanically and speaks through "mere sensations": the pleasure taken in it is not cognitive (or it is cognitive on a merely superficial level). As such, music, unlike other arts such as poetry, does not provide substance for the mediation between cognitive faculties.

This desire for beauty to mediate between the faculties of reason and of understanding — and between freedom and necessity — also motivates, at a deeper level, Kant's views on the disinterestedness of art and on rhetoric. For Kant, beauty is able to mediate between the faculties by virtue of the fact that it is neither moral nor mechanistic. If beauty is to be neither moral nor mechanistic, though, it must remain separate from both virtue and utility. That is to say, the pleasure taken in beauty must remain disinterested.

Furthermore, in the specific context of his postulate of a faculty of reason distinct from the faculty of understanding, Kant's doctrine of moral autonomy is itself an attempt to square the circle between freedom and necessity, suggesting that we must all follow the same moral law, but that so doing does not constrain our freedom, because each human subject creates that same moral law for themselves. The doctrine of moral autonomy, as we saw, is responsible for Kant's rejection of rhetoric. This rejection of rhetoric, then, stems again from Kant's desire to mediate between freedom and necessity. Further, his particular theory depends in this context on his postulate of a world of things-in-themselves, beyond the world of appearances—in other words, it is bound up again in Kant's philosophical system as a whole.

We can now see how all three premises on the basis of which music can, in the context of Kant's philosophy, only be negatively assessed—his notion of disinterested beauty, his rejection of rhetoric, and his insistence that the pleasure taken in art must be cognitive—all stem from his overall philosophical system and his desire to mediate, through art in particular, between freedom and necessity.

We might sum this up by saying that a key purpose of art was, for Kant, to mediate between freedom and necessity. Yet, in positing a causal—and potentially involuntary—relation between musical means and affective outcomes, music as conceived according to the *Affektenlehre* involved no freedom, but only necessity. We might also return to Kant's comparison of music and poetry. Kant writes of poetry that "it strengthens the mind by letting it feel its capacity to consider and judge of nature, as appearance, freely, self-actively, and independently of determination by nature."[42] Music, by contrast, "speaks through mere sensations without concepts, and hence does not, like poetry, leave behind something for reflection."[43] The implication, though not quite stated explicitly, is that music, unlike poetry, does not escape the world of appearances. Again, music, on this reading of the *Affektenlehre*, involves no freedom, only necessity.

More generally, Kant clearly valued the principle of freedom: his entire mature philosophical project might be described as an attempt to rescue human freedom from a purely mechanistic worldview. But music's perceived disaffinity with freedom was not just a lack: the affective power of this art was a positive *threat* to human freedom. Whilst this was a long-standing danger of the doctrine—and of rhetorical thought more generally—Kant's reflections on disinterested beauty, on moral autonomy, and on cognitive engagement in human judgments of art each in their own way highlighted this danger more acutely than had previous philosophical investigations.

On Endings

The key point in all this is that Kant, quite unintentionally, shifted the philosophical landscape in such a way that, in his philosophy, the *Affektenlehre* no longer made sense in the same way that it did to previous thinkers. More precisely, the doctrine had always been intended to provide a positive role for music, yet in the context of Kant's philosophy it can lead only to a negative assessment of this art. It is certainly possible to continue to hold the doctrine in a Kantian philosophical context. Indeed, Kant himself did exactly that. But once its ability to provide a positive role for music was taken away, the *Affektenlehre* was bound to fall out of use. This is exactly what happens with thinkers who follow in Kant's footsteps: Kant is the first and the last major thinker in the tradition of German Idealism—the tradition that he himself founded—to conceive of music this way. The downfall of the *Affektenlehre*, from this perspective, was driven primarily not, as most previous scholarship has suggested, by musical factors, but rather by philosophical ones.

This is not to say that the broader downfall of the *Affektenlehre* is attributable *only* to Kantian philosophy. Indeed, the popularity of the doctrine was already waning by the time that Kant wrote his *Kritik der Urteilskraft*. Yet three things are worth noting. First, the doctrine remained sufficiently strong in the late 1780s, as Kant was writing his *Kritik der Urteilskraft*, for it to be the natural conception of music for a thinker such as Kant, someone without an especially robust musical background, to reach for. Second, though Kant's philosophical system as a whole was radically new, many of the problems it confronted, most especially the conflict between freedom and necessity, were longstanding concerns of Enlightenment thinkers. In this sense, Kant encapsulated, intensified, and accelerated intellectual movements that were already undermining the *Affektenlehre* more generally.

Third, the downfall of the *Affektenlehre* within the tradition of German Idealism in particular opened the door for the birth of a newer conception of music in this same tradition—one in which music is believed able to offer insight into the inner life of the listener, or even into the ultimate nature of being. As I suggested earlier in this essay, the birth of this newer view of music is separable from the downfall of the *Affektenlehre*: the older doctrine was not swept out of the way by a newer view of music, but rather simply stopped making sense in a new philosophical context. Yet, within the tradition specifically of German Idealism, the downfall of the *Affektenlehre* in Kant opened the door for the birth of this newer conception of music in thinkers who followed him, most notably Friedrich Schlegel, Novalis, and Friedrich Wilhelm Joseph Schelling.

Whilst this new conception of music was sharply distinguished from the *Affektenlehre*, and from the deterministic, mechanistic conception of affective action on which it was based, this did not rule out the possibility of other conceptions of musical affect. On the contrary, the downfall of the *Affektenlehre*, with its strikingly deterministic vision of affect, may itself have been the impetus for, or at the very least have helped to clear space for, thinkers of Kant's and subsequent generations to propose new, more indeterminate theories of music's affective power. This may have been the end of the *Affektenlehre*, in other words, but that does not mean that it was the end of affect.

Notes

1. For their invaluable comments on previous versions of this material, in various forms, my thanks go to Michael Fend, Mark Evan Bonds, Andrew Bowie, Julian Johnson, Víctor Durà-Vilà, Friedlind Riedel, Matthew Pritchard, Alexander Wilfing, Elizabeth Swann, and the editors of the present volume. An early version of a portion of this material was presented at the 2011 meeting of the American Musicological Society (San Francisco); my thanks go to the audience at that event for their insightful questions and comments. Work toward the final version of the essay was funded by the British Academy (in the form of a postdoctoral fellowship) and was greatly aided by the research assistance of Ariana Phillips-Hutton, whose own position was funded, on my return from a period of parental leave, by the University of Cambridge's Returning Carers Scheme. Any errors or omissions remain my own.

2. One place in which variants of this doctrine have—as part of a critical dialogue—resurfaced in recent decades is the philosophy of music in its "analytic" guise. These debates themselves have often drawn on work in empirical music psychology. For an overview, see Derek Matravers, "Arousal Theories," in *The Routledge Companion to Philosophy and Music*, ed. Theodore Gracyk and Andrew Kania (Abingdon and New York: Routledge, 2011), 212–22.

3. The phrase "old phantom" was present from the first edition of Eduard Hanslick, *Vom Musikalisch-Schönen: Ein Beitrag zur Revision der Ästhetik der Tonkunst* (Leipzig: Rudolph Weigel, 1854)., but the reference here to "affects" was added only in the second edition, published in 1858. A very similar sentiment, however, can be found in the equivalent passage of the first edition, where Hanslick refers to the ongoing prominence of *Gefühle* (feelings), rather than *Affecte* (affects), in music-aesthetic investigations. Hanslick, *Vom Musikalisch-Schönen: Ein Beitrag zur Revision der Ästhetik in der Tonkunst*, Teil 1: Historisch-kritische Ausgabe, ed. Dietmar Strauß (Mainz: Schott, 1990), 24–25. Translation taken from *Eduard Hanslick's On the Musically Beautiful: A New Translation*, trans. Lee Rothfarb and Christoph Landerer (New York: Oxford University Press, 2018), 3.

4. George J. Buelow, "Johann Mattheson and the Invention of the *Affektenlehre*," in *New Mattheson Studies*, ed. George J. Buelow and Hans Joachim Marx (Cambridge and New York: Cambridge University Press, 1983), 404. On other previous scholarship on the *Affektenlehre*, alongside new insight into the relationship between music and rhetoric in this period, see Bettina Varwig, "One More Time: J. S. Bach and Seventeenth-Century Traditions of Rhetoric," *Eighteenth-Century Music* 5, no. 2 (2008): 179–208, esp. 179–81; and Varwig, "'Mutato semper habitu': Heinrich Schütz and the Culture of Rhetoric," *Music & Letters* 90, no. 2 (2009): 215–39, esp. 215–16.

5. Roger Mathew Grant makes a similar point, noting in response to Buelow that there was indeed no "cohesive" doctrine, but describing the *Affektenlehre* as "bigger and messier" than Buelow and others had taken it to be. Grant, "Music Lessons on Affect and Its Objects," *Representations* 144, no. 1 (2018): 35.

6. Dietrich Bartel, *Musica Poetica: Musical-Rhetorical Figures in German Baroque Music* (Lincoln: University of Nebraska Press, 1997), 29–30. It is important to note, however, that this physiological focus was not premised on a clean break between body and mind or body and soul. Rather, as Bettina Varwig has shown, the "affective motions" that music was believed to arouse "engaged a subject's physical and psychological faculties simultaneously" and so "evinced a human soul-body continuum that challenged any meaningful distinction between blood and nerves on the one hand, and morality and virtuous action on the other." Varwig, "Heartfelt Musicking: The Physiology of a Bach Cantata," *Representations* 143, no. 1 (2018): 42.

7. For recent studies that highlight the crucial role played by non-German, and especially French, sources in affective discourses in this period, see André Redwood, "Mersenne and the Art of Delivery," *Journal of Music Theory* 59, no. 1 (2015): 99–119; Roger Mathew Grant, "Peculiar Attunements: Comic Opera and Enlightenment Mimesis," *Critical Inquiry* 43, no. 2 (2017): 550–69; and Grant, 'Music Lessons on Affect and Its Objects.'

8. For an investigation of this broad intent covering an impressively wide range of contemporary reviews of instrumental music to offer insight into changes in musical thought in the later eighteenth century, see Mary Sue Morrow, *German Music Criticism in the Late Eighteenth Century: Aesthetic Issues in Instrumental Music* (Cambridge and New York: Cambridge University Press, 1997).

9. John Neubauer, for example, has suggested that "the gradual growth of instrumental music in the eighteenth century, culminating in the production of sonatas, symphonies, and chamber music, forced an aesthetic revaluation of major import." Neubauer, *The Emancipation of Music from Language: Departure from Mimesis in Eighteenth-Century Aesthetics* (New Haven, CT: Yale University Press, 1986), 2.

10. See Tomás McAuley, "Rhythmic Accent and the Absolute: Sulzer, Schelling and the Akzenttheorie," *Eighteenth-Century Music* 10, no. 2 (2013): 277–86.

11. A second edition of the *Kritik* appeared in 1793, and a third in 1799. The main substantive changes between first and second edition were in the Introduction; the third edition contained only minor corrections. On the various editions, see the editors' introduction to Immanuel Kant, *Critique of the Power of Judgment*, ed. Paul Guyer and Allen W. Wood (Cambridge and New York: Cambridge University Press, 2000), xlv–xlvi.

12. See Neubauer, *The Emancipation of Music from Language*, 182–92; Enrico Fubini, *History of Music Aesthetics* (London: Macmillan, 1990), 220–21; and Peter Kivy, *The Fine Art of Repetition: Essays in the Philosophy of Music* (Cambridge and New York: Cambridge University Press, 1993), 250–64. For a compelling account of how thinkers in the wake of Kant attempted to build a more coherent "Kantian music aesthetics," see Matthew Pritchard, "Music in Balance: The Aesthetics of Music After Kant, 1790–1810," *Journal of Musicology* 36, no. 1 (2019): 39–67.

13. This is the case, at least, with English-language scholarship. In Italian-language scholarship, one full monograph (Piero Giordanetti, *Kant e la musica* [Milan: CUEM, 2001]) has been devoted to Kant's views on music. It has also been translated into German, in a revised version, as *Kant und die Musik* (Würzburg: Königshausen & Neumann, 2005). For more general—and less purposive—introductions to Kant's views on music than that provided here, see Christel Fricke, "Kant," in *Music in German Philosophy: An Introduction*,

ed. Stefan Lorenz Sorgner and Oliver Fürbeth, trans. Susan H. Gillespie (Chicago: University of Chicago Press, 2011), 27–46, itself translated from German; and, focused on the place of music in Kant's broader aesthetics, Hannah Ginsborg, "Kant," in *The Routledge Companion to Philosophy and Music*, ed. Theodore Gracyk and Andrew Kania (Abingdon: Routledge, 2011), 328–38.

14. On the dangers of making broad claims about changes in listening practices in this period, see Nicholas Mathew, "The Tangled Woof," [review of] Mark Evan Bonds, *Music as Thought: Listening to the Symphony in the Age of Beethoven*; David Wyn Jones, *The Symphony in Beethoven's Vienna*; and Melanie Lowe, *Pleasure and Meaning in the Classical Symphony*, *Journal of the Royal Musical Association* 134, no. 1 (2009): 133–47; and Matthew Head, "Music with 'No Past?' Archaeologies of Joseph Haydn and *The Creation*," *19th-Century Music* 23, no. 3 (2000): 191–217.

15. Originally published in installments in *Der teutsche Merkur* in 1786–87, then in a revised, expanded book edition in 1790. For the latter, see Karl Leonhard Reinhold, *Briefe über die Kantische Philosophie*, ed. Raymund Schmidt (Leipzig: Reclam, 1923). The *Briefe* are also available in English translation as Karl Leonhard Reinhold, *Letters on the Kantian Philosophy*, ed. Karl Ameriks, trans. James Hebbeler (Cambridge and New York: Cambridge University Press, 2005). On role of the *Briefe* in popularizing Kantian philosophy, see the introduction to that latter volume, esp. ix–xiii.

16. In referencing Kant's works I cite (in the format GS, volume:page) the standard German collected edition (Kant, *Gesammelte Schriften*, ed. Royal Prussian [subsequently German, then Berlin-Brandenburg] Academy of Sciences [Berlin: Georg Reimer, subsequently Walter de Gruyter, 1900–]). When referencing the *Kritik der reinen Vernunft*, however, I cite, following standard practice the original first (A) and second (B) editions. English translations are taken from the relevant volumes of the authoritative Cambridge edition (i.e., Kant, *Critique of the Power of Judgment*; Kant, *Critique of Pure Reason*, ed. and trans. Paul Guyer and Allen W. Wood [Cambridge: Cambridge University Press, 1998]; and Kant, *Practical Philosophy*, trans. and ed. Mary J. Gregor [Cambridge: Cambridge University Press, 1997]). These editions include marginal references to the standard German numberings. All of the preceding citations of Kant on music are taken from GS, 5:328.

17. GS, 5:328.

18. GS, 5:305. Emphases in original text removed. Kant does not accept Baumgarten's account of sensory experience as confused cognition: "For two components belong to cognition: first, the concept, through which an object is thought at all (the category), and second, the intuition, through which it is given." (B146).

19. GS, 5:328–30.

20. In a passing comment from the "Remark" that follows §53, Kant writes of the art of the joke that it deserves "*like music* . . . to be counted as agreeable rather than as beautiful art." GS, 5:332, my emphasis. One might object that Kant thinks in §14 that a tone is capable of beauty. This may well be the case, but Kant is here talking about tone (*Ton*) and beauty (*Schönheit*), not music (*Tonkunst*) and beautiful art (*schöne Kunst*). GS, 5:224.

21. GS, 5:324–25.

22. GS, 5:328.

23. For the classic account—albeit one that has been extensively critiqued—of the formation of the system of beautiful arts, see Paul Oskar Kristeller, "The Modern System of the Arts: A Study in the History of Aesthetics, Part I," *Journal of the History of Ideas* 12, no. 4 (1951): 496–527; and Kristeller, "The Modern System of the Arts: A Study in the History of Aesthetics, Part II," *Journal of the History of Ideas* 13, no. 1 (1952): 17–46.

24. GS, 5:211.

25. More precisely, the issue is whether we have an interest in the "existence" of an object: "If the question is whether something is beautiful, one does not want to know whether there is anything that is or that could be at stake, for us or for someone else, in the existence of the thing, but rather how we judge it in mere contemplation." GS, 5:205.

26. An especially striking forerunner to Kant in this regard is Karl Philipp Moritz, who in a 1785 public letter to Moses Mendelssohn combines the notion of aesthetic disinterest with that of "internal purposiveness," so anticipating Kant's concept of "purposiveness without an end" (or "purposiveness without a purpose" [Zweckmäßigkeit ohne Zweck]). Moritz writes: "I have to take delight in a beautiful object just for its own sake; thus, the lack of external purposiveness has to be substituted by internal purposiveness; the object has to be perfect in itself." Cited in and trans. Alexander Wilfing, "Hanslick, Kant, and the Origins of Vom Musikalisch-Schönen," Musicologica Austriaca, accessed February 18, 2020, http://www.musau.org/parts/neue-article-page/view/47. For Kant's discussion of purposiveness without an end, see GS, 5:219–36.

27. David Hume, Enquiries Concerning Human Understanding and Concerning the Principles of Morals, 3rd ed. (Oxford: Clarendon Press, 1975), 244.

28. As Mark Evan Bonds has observed, the art of rhetoric was renewed in the eighteenth century "with special vigor in German-speaking lands." Bonds, Wordless Rhetoric: Musical Form and the Metaphor of the Oration (Cambridge, MA: Harvard University Press, 1991), 60.

29. GS, 5:327.

30. Ibid.

31. Johann Georg Sulzer, Allgemeine Theorie der schönen Künste in einzeln, nach alphabetischer Ordnung der Kunstwörter auf einander folgenden, Artikeln abgehandelt, Erster Theil (Leipzig: M. G. Weidmanns Erben & Reich, 1771), 313. Translation from Sulzer and Heinrich Christoph Koch, Aesthetics and the Art of Musical Composition in the German Enlightenment: Selected Writings of Johann Georg Sulzer and Heinrich Christoph Koch, ed. and trans. Nancy Kovaleff Baker and Thomas Street Christensen (Cambridge and New York: Cambridge University Press, 1995), 31. Although the Allgemeine Theorie was a multiauthored work, it is clear that Sulzer himself is the author of this particular article.

32. GS, 4:432.

33. GS, 4:433–34 and 5:33.

34. My usage of the phrase "radical Enlightenment" follows Jonathan Israel. See Israel, Radical Enlightenment: Philosophy and the Making of Modernity, 1650–1750 (Oxford and New York: Oxford University Press, 2001), 3–13.

35. For a broader contextualization of this ethical perspective within a "narrative of nineteenth-century musical ethics," Tomás McAuley, "Ethics," in The Oxford Handbook of Music and Intellectual Culture in the Nineteenth Century, edited by Paul Watt, Sarah Collins, and Michael Allis, 481–506 (New York: Oxford University Press, 2020).

36. Sulzer, Allgemeine Theorie, Teil 1, 302; and Sulzer and Koch, Aesthetics and the Art of Musical Composition, 43. Again, it is clear that Sulzer is the author of this particular article.

37. Of the many topics that have been set aside here, one especially notable omission is any discussion of the role of the imagination in Kant's philosophy. For an authoritative treatment of this topic, see Jane Kneller, Kant and the Power of Imagination (Cambridge and New York: Cambridge University Press, 2007).

38. For a more detailed yet still pithy examination of how Kant and philosophers who followed him were responding to problems in Enlightenment philosophy, see Frederick Beiser, "The Enlightenment and Idealism," in The Cambridge Companion to German Idealism,

ed. Karl Ameriks (Cambridge and New York: Cambridge University Press, 2000), 18–36. For a defense of the Enlightenment as an international phenomenon, see John Robertson, *The Case for the Enlightenment: Scotland and Naples, 1680–1760* (Cambridge and New York: Cambridge University Press, 2005). In the case of Kant in particular, the international nature of the philosophical scene that he confronted is most clear in his responses to David Hume and Jean-Jacques Rousseau.

39. On the Enlightenment as a quest for betterment of the human condition, see the introduction to Israel, *Radical Enlightenment*.

40. *GS*, 5:195–98.

41. On "the ground of the unity" of "the concept of nature" and "the concept of freedom," see esp. *GS*, 5:175–76.

42. *GS*, 5:326.

43. *GS*, 5:328.

ACKNOWLEDGMENTS

The editors offer their most heartfelt thanks to the authors for sharing their brilliant research, and for their patience and dedication throughout the long production of this volume. This collection grows from a conference of the same name held at Stony Brook University on April 18–19, 2014. We thank all the scholars who participated in that event as presenters, session chairs, and members of the audience. The conference would not have been possible without the logistical and financial support of Stony Brook's Department of Music and Department of Philosophy, as well as a grant from Stony Brook's research fund for the Faculty in Arts, History, and lettered Social Sciences (FAHSS). It was organized in conjunction with the Music and Philosophy Study Groups of the American Musicological Society and the Royal Musical Association. We thank the conference committee—Amy Cimini, Tomás McAuley, Jairo Moreno, and Lorenzo Simpson—for their help in planning this event, and we thank Felipe Ledesma-Nuñez, Hayley Roud, Alissa Betz, and Martha Zadok, for their work in making it happen. The publication of the present volume has been supported financially by Pennsylvania State University's Department of Philosophy, and by a second grant from Stony Brook's FAHSS. We thank Stony Brook's Department of Music for providing funds to assist in the editing of this collection, and we thank Gui Hwan Lee and Ilan Marans for their diligent and careful editorial work. Finally, we offer our sincere thanks to Barbara Norton for her superb work in copyediting this volume, to Judi Gibbs for her expert indexing, and to Tristan Bates, Dylan Montanari, and Marta Tonegutti from the University of Chicago Press for their exemplary professionalism.

Chapter 3 was previously published as Gary Tomlinson, "Sign, Affect, and Musicking Before the Human," boundary 2, 43, no. 1, 143–72. © 2016, Duke University Press. All rights reserved.

CONTRIBUTORS

JAMES CURRIE, associate professor of music, University at Buffalo

RYAN DOHONEY, associate professor of musicology, Northwestern University

CHRISTOPHER HAWORTH, lecturer in music, University of Birmingham

DON IHDE, professor emeritus of philosophy, Stony Brook University

ROBIN JAMES, associate professor of philosophy, University of North Carolina at Chapel Hill

ADAM KNOWLES, assistant teaching professor of philosophy, Drexel University

JUDITH LOCHHEAD, professor of music history and theory, Stony Brook University

TOMÁS MCAULEY, assistant professor of music and Ad Astra Fellow, University College Dublin

EDUARDO MENDIETA, professor of philosophy, Pennsylvania State University

MICHAEL BIRENBAUM QUINTERO, associate professor of music, Boston University

ANDRÉ DE OLIVEIRA REDWOOD, assistant professor of music and theater, University at Albany

MARTIN SCHERZINGER, associate professor of media, culture, and communication, New York University

LORENZO SIMPSON, professor of philosophy, Stony Brook University

STEPHEN DECATUR SMITH, associate professor of music history and theory, Stony Brook University

GARY TOMLINSON, John Hay Whitney Professor of Music and the Humanities, Yale University

DANIEL VILLEGAS VÉLEZ, postdoctoral researcher, Institute of Philosophy, Leuven

EMILY WILBOURNE, associate professor of musicology, Queens College and the Graduate Center, City University of New York

JESSICA WISKUS, professor of music, Duquesne University

BIBLIOGRAPHY

Adkins, Lisa. *The Time of Money*. Stanford, CA: Stanford University Press, 2018.
Adorno, Theodor. "On Jazz." Trans. Jamie Owen Daniel. *Discourse: Journal for Theoretical Studies in Media and Culture* 12, no. 1 (1990): 45–69. https://digitalcommons.wayne.edu/discourse/vol12/iss1/4.
Adorno, Theodor W. *Aesthetic Theory*. Edited by Gretel Adorno and Rolf Tiedemann. Translated by Robert Hullot-Kentor. New York: Continuum, 2002.
———. *Current of Music: Elements of a Radio Theory*. Translated by Robert Hullot-Kentor. English edition. Cambridge, UK, and Malden, MA: Polity Press, 2009.
———. *Mahler: A Musical Physiognomy*. Translated by Edmund Jephcott. Chicago: University of Chicago Press, 1992.
———. *Minima Moralia: Reflections from Damaged Life*. Translated by E. F. N. Jephcott. London and New York: Verso, 1994.
———. *Prisms*. Translated by Samuel Weber and Shierry Weber Nicholsen. Cambridge, MA: MIT Press, 1981.
———. *Sound Figures*. Translated by Rodney Livingstone. Stanford, CA: Stanford University Press, 1999.
———, with George Simpson. "On Popular Music: III. Theory about the Listener." *Journal on Media Culture* 2 (January 2000). http://www.icce.rug.nl/~soundscapes/DATABASES/SWA/On_popular_music_3.shtml.
Ahmed, Sara. *Queer Phenomenology: Orientations, Objects, Others*. Durham, NC: Duke University Press, 2006.
———. *The Cultural Politics of Emotion*. 2nd ed. 2004; Edinburgh: Edinburgh University Press, 2014.
Alvarado, Alfonso. *Artium disserendi ac dicendi. libero duo*. Basel: Ludwig, 1600.
Amoore, Louise. *The Politics of Possibility: Risk and Security beyond Probability*. Durham, NC: Duke University Press, 2013.
Antonazzoni, Marina Dorotea. "La paccia d'Arianna." Milan, 1622. Racolto Morbio 2. Biblioteca Braidense.
Appelbaum, David. *Voice*. Albany: State University of New York Press, 1990.
Arendt, Hannah. *The Human Condition*. Chicago: University of Chicago Press, 1958.
———. *The Origins of Totalitarianism*. New York: Harcourt Brace Jovanovich, 1976.

Aristotle. *Aristotle's Politics*. Translated and with an introduction, notes, and glossary by Carnes Lord. 2nd ed. Chicago: University of Chicago Press, 2013.

———. *The Complete Works of Aristotle: The Revised Oxford Translation*. Edited by Jonathan Barnes. Princeton, NJ: Princeton University Press, 1984.

———. "Poetics" and "Rhetoric." Translated by S. H. Butcher and W. Rhys Roberts. Introduction and notes by Eugene Garver. New York: Barnes & Noble Classics, 2005.

Atlas of Plucked Instruments. Accessed February 13, 2020. http://www.atlasofpluckedinstruments.com/index.htm.

Atlas of Plucked Instruments—Lutes. Accessed February 13, 2020. http://www.atlasofpluckedinstruments.com/lutes.htm.

Attali, Jacques. *Bruits: Essai sur l'economie politique de la musique*. Paris: Presses Universitaires de France, 1977.

———. "Interview with Jacques Attali." Interviewed by Fredric Jameson and Brian Massumi. *Social Text* 7 (Spring–Summer 1983): 3–18.

———. *Noise: The Political Economy of Music*. Translated by Brian Assumi. Minneapolis: University of Minnesota Press, 1985.

Augoyard, Jean-François, and Henri Torgue. *Sonic Experience: A Guide to Everyday Sounds*. Montreal: McGill–Queen's University Press, 2014.

Augustine. *De Doctrina Christiana*. Edited and translated by R. P. H. Green. Oxford and New York: Clarendon Press, 1995.

Badiou, Alain. *Logics of Worlds: Being and Event, 2*. Translated by Alberto Toscano. London and New York: Continuum, 2009.

Barenboim, Daniel. "In the Beginning Was Sound." Transcript. *Reith 2006—Daniel Barenboim: In the Beginning Was Sound*. BBC Radio 4, April 7, 2006. Accessed August 24, 2017. www.bbc.co.uk/radio4/features/the-reith-lectures/transcripts/2000/#y2006.

———. "Meeting in Music." Transcript. *Reith 2006—Daniel Barenboim: In the Beginning Was Sound*. BBC Radio 4, April 28, 2006. Accessed August 24, 2017. www.bbc.co.uk/radio4/features/the-reith-lectures/transcripts/2000/#y2006.

Baricco, Alessandro. *The Barbarians: An Essay on the Mutation of Culture*. New York: Rizzoli, 2014.

———. *An Iliad*. Translated by Ann Goldstein. New York: Vintage International, 2007.

Bartel, Dietrich. *Musica Poetica: Musical-Rhetorical Figures in German Baroque Music*. Lincoln: University of Nebraska Press, 1997.

Barthes, Roland. *Image, Music, Text*. Essays selected and translated by Stephen Heath. New York: Hill & Wang, 1977.

Baudrillard, Jean. *Selected Writings*. Edited by Mark Poster. Stanford, CA: Stanford University Press, 1988.

Bauman, Zygmunt. *Wasted Lives: Modernity and Its Outcasts*. Malden, MA: Polity/Blackwell, 2004.

Becker, Gary S. "A Theory of the Allocation of Time." *Economic Journal* 75, no. 299 (1965): 493–517.

———. "Irrational Behavior and Economic Theory." *Journal of Political Economy* 70, no. 1 (1962): 1–13.

Beer, David. "Power through the Algorithm? Participatory Web Cultures and the Technological Unconscious." *New Media & Society* 11, no. 6 (2009): 985–1002.

Beiser, Frederick. "The Enlightenment and Idealism." In *The Cambridge Companion to German Idealism*, edited by Karl Ameriks, 18–36. Cambridge and New York: Cambridge University Press, 2000.

Benjamin, Walter, "Doctrine of the Similar (1933)." Translated by Knut Tarnowski. Special Benjamin issue, *New German Critique* 17 (1979): 65–69.

———. "On the Mimetic Faculty," in *Selected Writings*, vol. 2, pt. 2, *1931–1934* (Cambridge, MA: Belknap Press, 2005), 720–22.

Benjamin, Walter. *Selected Writings*, vol. 2, pt. 2, *1931–1934*. Edited by Michael William Jennings, Howard Eiland, and Gary Smith. Cambridge, MA: Belknap Press, 2005.

Benkler, Yochai. Voluntary Payment Models." Boston, MA: Berkman Center for Internet & Society at Harvard University, 2011. https://cyber.harvard.edu/sites/cyber.law.harvard .edu/files/Rethinking_Music_April-25-2011_hi-res.pdf.

———. *The Wealth of Networks: How Social Production Transforms Markets and Freedom.* New Haven, CT: Yale University Press, 2006. "

Berenstein, Nadia. "Flavor Added: The Sciences of Flavor and the Industrialization of Taste in America." Ph.D. diss., University of Pennsylvania, 2018.

Bergo, Bettina. "Philosophy as *Perspectiva Artificialis*: Merleau-Ponty's Critique of Husserlian Constructivism." In Maurice Merleau-Ponty, *Husserl at the Limits of Phenomenology: Including Texts by Edmund Husserl*, edited by Leonard Lawlor with Bettina Bergo, 155–82. Evanston, IL: Northwestern University Press, 2002.

Bergson, Henri. *Laughter: An Essay on the Meaning of the Comic*. Translated by Cloudesely Brereton and Fred Rothwell. Rockville, MD: Arc Manor, 2008.

———. *Matter and Memory*. Translated by Nancy Margaret Paul and W. Scott Palmer. North Chelmsford, MA: Courier, 2012.

Berlant, Lauren. *Cruel Optimism*. Durham, NC: Duke University Press, 2011.

———. *The Female Complaint: The Unfinished Business of Sentimentality in American Culture.* Durham, NC: Duke University Press, 2008.

———. *The Queen of America Goes to Washington City: Essays on Sex and Citizenship.* Durham, NC: Duke University Press, 1997.

Berliner, Paul. *Thinking in Jazz: The Infinite Art of Improvisation*. Chicago: University of Chicago Press, 1994.

Bernard, Jonathan W. "Elliott Carter and the Modern Meaning of Time." *Musical Quarterly* 79, no. 4 (1995): 644–82.

Bernet, Rudolf, Iso Kern, and Eduard Marbach. *An Introduction to Husserlian Phenomenology*. Evanston, IL: Northwestern University Press, 1993.

Bernhard, Thomas. *Correction*. Translated by Sophie Wilkins. New York: Vintage International, 2010.

Bianchi, Eric. "Prodigious Sounds: Music and Learning in the World of Athanasius Kircher." Ph.D. diss., Yale University, 2011.

Bianconi, Lorenzo. *Music in the Seventeenth Century*. Cambridge and New York: Cambridge University Press, 1987.

Blake, David. "Musicological Omnivory in the Neoliberal University." *Journal of Musicology* 34, no. 3 (2017): 319–53.

Bloch, Ernst. *Essays on the Philosophy of Music*. Translated by Peter Palmer. Cambridge and New York: Cambridge University Press, 1985.

Boddice, Rob. *The History of Emotions*. Manchester: Manchester University Press, 2018.

Böhme, Gernot. *Der Typ Sokrates*. Frankfurt am Main: Suhrkamp Verlag, 2002.

Boltanski, Luc, and Eve Chiapello. "The New Spirit of Capitalism." Paper presented at the Conference of Europeanists, March 14–16, 2002, Chicago.

Bonds, Mark Evan. *Music as Thought: Listening to the Symphony in the Age of Beethoven.* Princeton, NJ: Princeton University Press, 2006.

———. *Wordless Rhetoric: Musical Form and the Metaphor of the Oration*. Cambridge, MA: Harvard University Press, 1991.

Born, Georgina. *Music, Sound and Space: Transformations of Public and Private Experience*. Cambridge and New York: Cambridge University Press, 2013.

Bourdieu, Pierre. *Language and Symbolic Power*. Edited by John B. Thompson. Translated by Gino Raymond and Andrew Adamson. Cambridge, MA: Harvard University Press, 1991.

———. *Masculine Domination*. Translated by Richard Nice. Stanford, CA: Stanford University Press, 2001.

———. *Outline of a Theory of Practice*. Cambridge: Cambridge University Press, 1977.

Boysen, Benjamin. "The Embarrassment of Being Human: A Critique of New Materialism and Object-Oriented Ontology." *Orbis Litterarum* 73, no. 3 (2018): 225–42.

Braidotti, Rosi. *The Posthuman*. Cambridge, UK, and Malden, MA: Polity Press, 2013.

Braunschweig, Karl. Review of *Music Theory and Natural Order from the Renaissance to the Early Twentieth Century*. *Music Theory Spectrum* 25, no. 1 (2003): 142–51.

Brennan, Teresa. *The Transmission of Affect*. Ithaca, NY: Cornell University Press, 2003.

Brothers, Thomas David. *Louis Armstrong: Master of Modernism*. New York: W. W. Norton, 2014.

Bucher, Taina. *If . . . Then: Algorithmic Power and Politics*. New York: Oxford University Press, 2018.

Buck-Morss, Susan. "Aesthetics and Anaesthetics: Walter Benjamin's Artwork Essay Reconsidered." *October* 62 (Autumn 1992): 3–41.

Buelow, George J. "Johann Mattheson and the Invention of the Affektenlehre." In *New Mattheson Studies*, edited by George J. Buelow and Hans Joachim Marx, 393–408. Cambridge and New York: Cambridge University Press, 1983.

Burtner, Matthew. "Sounding Art Climate Change." In *The Routledge Companion to Sounding Art*, edited by Marcel Cobussen, Vincent Meelberg, and Barry Truax, 287–304. New York: Routledge, 2017.

Butler, Judith. *Bodies That Matter: On the Discursive Limits of "Sex."* New York: Routledge, 1993.

Byrne, James M., and Donald J. Rebovich, eds. *The New Technology of Crime, Law and Social Control*. Monsey, NY: Criminal Justice Press, 2007.

Caccini, Giulio. *Le nuove musiche*. Florence, 1602. Edited and translated by H. Wiley Hitchcock. Madison, WI: A-R Editions, 1970.

Calcagno, Mauro P. *From Madrigal to Opera: Monteverdi's Staging of the Self*. Berkeley and Los Angeles: University of California Press, 2012.

Calvino, Italo. *Under the Jaguar Sun*. Translated by William Weaver. New York: A Harvest Book, Harcourt, 1988.

Campa, Cecilia. *Il musicista filosofo e le passioni: Linguaggio e retorica dei suoni nel Seicento Europeo*. Naples: Liguori, 2001.

Carson, Anne. *Glass, Irony and God*. New York: New Directions, 1995.

Carter, Tim. "Lamenting Ariadne?" *Early Music* 27, no. 3 (1999): 395–405.

Caussin, Nicolas. *De eloquentia sacra et humana parallela, libri XVI*. Paris: Chappelet, 1619.

Cavarero, Adriana. *For More than One Voice: Toward a Philosophy of Vocal Expression*. Translated by Paul A. Kottman. Stanford, CA: Stanford University Press, 2005.

Cavell, Stanley. *A Pitch of Philosophy: Autobiographical Exercises*. Cambridge, MA: Harvard University Press, 1994.

Christensen, Thomas. "The Sound World of Father Mersenne." In *Structures of Feeling in Seventeenth-Century Cultural Expression*, edited by Susan McClary, 60–89. Toronto: University of Toronto Press; Los Angeles: UCLA Center for Seventeenth- and Eighteenth-Century Studies and the William Andres Clark Memorial Library, 2013.

Chua, Daniel K. L. "Vincenzo Galilei, Modernity and the Division of Nature." In *Music Theory and Natural Order from the Renaissance to the Early Twentieth Century*, edited by Suzannah Clark and Alexander Rehding, 17–29. Cambridge and New York: Cambridge University Press, 2001.

Chude-Sokei, Louis. *The Sound of Culture: Diaspora and Black Technopoetics*. Middletown, CT: Wesleyan University Press, 2016.

Cicero, Marcus Tullius. *Brutus; Orator*. Translated by G. L Hendrickson and H. M. Hubbell. Cambridge, MA: Harvard University Press, 1939.

———. *On the Ideal Orator*. Translated by James M. May and Jakob Wisse. Oxford and New York: Oxford University Press, 2001.

Clark, Suzannah, and Alexander Rehding, eds. *Music Theory and Natural Order from the Renaissance to the Early Twentieth Century*. Cambridge and New York: Cambridge University Press, 2001.

Clough, Patricia Ticineto, and Jean O'Malley Halley. *The Affective Turn: Theorizing the Social*. Durham, NC: Duke University Press, 2007.

Clover, Joshua. *1989: Bob Dylan Didn't Have This to Sing About*. Berkeley and Los Angeles: University of California Press, 2010.

Cohen, Alix, and Robert Stern, eds. *Thinking about the Emotions: A Philosophical History*. 1st ed. Oxford: Oxford University Press, 2017.

Cohen, H. F. *Quantifying Music: The Science of Music at the First Stage of the Scientific Revolution, 1580–1650*. University of Western Ontario Series in Philosophy of Science 23. Dordrecht: D. Reidel, 1984.

Conard, Nicholas J. "A Female Figurine from the Basal Aurignacian of Hohle Fels Cave in Southwestern Germany." *Nature* 459 (June 2009): 248–52.

Connolly, William E. "The Complexity of Intention." *Critical Inquiry* 37, no. 4 (2011): 791–98.

———. "Materialities of Experience." In *New Materialisms: Ontology, Agency, and Politics*, edited by Diana Coole and Samantha Frost, 178–200. Durham, NC: Duke University Press, 2010.

Conte, Sophie. "Louis de Cressolles: Le savoir au service de l'action oratoire." *XVII*e *siècle* 237, no. 4 (2007): 653–67.

Cook, Jill, ed. *Ice Age Art: Arrival of the Modern Mind*. London: British Museum Press, 2013.

Cooper, Melinda. *Life as Surplus: Biotechnology and Capitalism in the Neoliberal Era*. Seattle: University of Washington Press, 2008.

Coste, Hilarion de. *La vie du R.P. Marin Mersenne, theologien, philosophe et mathématicien de l'ordre des Pères Minimes*. Paris: Sebastien Cramoisy, 1649.

Cottrell, Stephen. *The Saxophone*. New Haven, CT: Yale University Press, 2012.

Cox, Christoph. *Sonic Flux: Sound, Art, and Metaphysics*. Chicago: University of Chicago Press, 2018.

Critchley, Simon. *On Humour*. London and New York: Routledge, 2002.

Crouch, Stanley. *Considering Genius: Writings on Jazz*. New York: Basic Books, 2006.

Cumming, Naomi. *The Sonic Self: Musical Subjectivity and Signification*. Bloomington: Indiana University Press, 2000.

Cypess, Rebecca. *Curious and Modern Inventions: Instrumental Music as Discovery in Galileo's Italy*. Chicago: University of Chicago Press, 2016.

Dahlhaus, Carl. *The Idea of Absolute Music*. Translated by Roger Lustig. Chicago: University of Chicago Press, 1989.

———. *Nineteenth-Century Music.* Translated by J. Bradford Robinson. Berkeley and Los Angeles: University of California Press, 1989.

Damasio, Antonio. *Descartes' Error: Emotion, Reason, and the Human Brain.* New York: G. P. Putnam's Sons, 1994.

———. *The Feeling of What Happens: Body and Emotion in the Making of Consciousness.* San Diego, CA: Harcourt, 2000.

———. *Looking for Spinoza: Joy, Sorrow, and the Feeling Brain.* Orlando, FL: Harcourt, 2003.

Dammann, Guy. "Rules of Engagement." *Guardian,* May 13, 2006. Accessed August 22, 2017. https://www.theguardian.com/music/2006/may/13/classicalmusicandopera.

Dammann, Rolf. *Der Musikbegriff im deutschen Barock.* Cologne: A. Volk, 1967.

Darwin, Charles. "A Biographical Sketch of an Infant." *Mind* 2, no. 7 (1877): 285–94.

———. *The Expression of the Emotions in Man and Animals.* London: J. Murray, 1872.

David, F. N. *Games, Gods and Gambling: The Origins and History of Probability and Statistical Ideas from the Earliest Times to the Newtonian Era.* New York: Hafner, 1962.

De Landa, Manuel. *Deleuze: History and Science.* New York: Atropos, 2010.

———. *A Thousand Years of Nonlinear History.* New York: Zone Books, 1997.

De Martino, Ernesto. *The Land of Remorse: A Study of Southern Italian Tarantism.* Translated and annotated by Dorothy Louise Zinn. London: Free Association Books, 2005.

Deacon, Terrence W. "Beyond the Symbolic Species." In *The Symbolic Species Evolved,* edited by Theresa Schilhab, Frederik Stjernfelt, and Terrence W. Deacon, 9–38. Biosemiotics 6. Dordrecht: Springer Netherlands, 2012.

———. "The Hierarchic Logic of Emergence: Untangling the Interdependence of Evolution and Self-Organization." In *Evolution and Learning: The Baldwin Effect Reconsidered,* edited by Bruce H. Weber and David J. Depew, 273–308. Cambridge, MA: MIT Press, 2003.

———. "The Symbol Concept." In *The Oxford Handbook of Language Evolution,* edited by Kathleen R. Gibson and Maggie Tallerman, 393–405. Oxford and New York: Oxford University Press, 2011.

———. *The Symbolic Species: The Co-Evolution of Language and the Brain.* New York and London: W. W. Norton, 1997.

Dean, Jodi. "Affective Networks." *Media Tropes* 2, no. 2 (2010): 19–44. https://mediatropes.com/index.php/Mediatropes/article/view/11932.

Dear, Peter. *Mersenne and the Learning of the Schools.* Ithaca, NY: Cornell University Press, 1988.

Deleuze, Gilles. *Bergsonism.* Translated by Hugh Tomlinson and Barbara Habberjam. New York: Zone Books, 1988.

———. *Difference and Repetition.* Translated by Paul R. Patton. New York: Columbia University Press, 1994.

———. *The Fold: Leibniz and the Baroque.* Revised ed. London and New York: Continuum, 2006.

———. "Postscript on the Societies of Control." *October* 59 (1992): 3–7.

———. *Two Regimes of Madness: Texts and Interviews, 1975–1995.* Edited by David Lapoujade. Translated by Ames Hodges and Mike Taormina. Los Angeles, CA: Semiotext(e), 2006.

Deleuze, Gilles, and Félix Guattari. *Anti-Oedipus: Capitalism and Schizophrenia.* Translated by Robert Hurley, Mark Seem, and Helen R. Lane. Minneapolis: University of Minnesota Press, 1983. First published as *L'Anti-Oedipe,* vol. 1 of *Capitalisme et schizophrénie* (Paris: Éditions de Minuit, 1972).

―――. *A Thousand Plateaus: Capitalism and Schizophrenia*. Translated by Brian Massumi. Minneapolis: University of Minnesota Press, 1987. First published as *Mille plateaux*, vol. 2 of *Capitalisme et schizophrénie* (Paris: Éditions de Minuit, 1980).

―――. *A Thousand Plateaus: Capitalism and Schizophrenia*. New ed. London: A&C Black, 2004.

―――. *What Is Philosophy?* Translated by Hugh Tomlinson and Graham Burchell. New York: Columbia University Press, 1994.

DeNora, Tia. *Music in Everyday Life*. Cambridge, and New York: Cambridge University Press, 2000.

DeRiso, Nick. "Revisiting Judas Priest's Subliminal Lyrics Trial." Ultimate Classic Rock. Accessed July 10, 2018. https://ultimateclassicrock.com/judas-priest-suicide-trial/.

Derrida, Jacques. *Of Grammatology*. Translated by Gayatri Chakravorty Spivak. Baltimore, MD: Johns Hopkins University Press, 1976.

―――. *Of Spirit: Heidegger and the Question*. Translated by Geoffrey Bennington and Rachel Bowlby. Chicago: University of Chicago Press, 1989.

―――. *Monolingualism of the Other, or, The Prosthesis of Origin*. Translated by Patrick Mensah. Stanford, CA: Stanford University Press, 1998.

DeVeaux, Scott. *The Birth of Bebop: A Social and Musical History*. Berkeley and Los Angeles: University of California Press, 1999.

de Warren, Nicolas. *Husserl and the Promise of Time: Subjectivity in Transcendental Phenomenology*. Cambridge and New York: Cambridge University Press, 2009.

―――. "Time." In *The Routledge Companion to Phenomenology*, edited by Sebastian Luft and Søren Overgaard, 190–201. London: Routledge, 2014.

Dilts, Andrew. "From 'Entrepreneur of the Self' to 'Care of the Self': Neo-Liberal Governmentality and Foucault's Ethics." *Foucault Studies* 12 (October 2011): 130–46.

Diogenes Laertius. *Lives of Eminent Philosophers*. Translated by R. D. Hicks. Cambridge, MA: Harvard University Press, 1925.

Dixon, Thomas. *From Passions to Emotions: The Creation of a Secular Psychological Category*. Cambridge: Cambridge University Press, 2003.

Dohoney, Ryan. "Proximity to a Notion of Fusion: An Interview with Alex Mincek and Eric Wubbels of the Wet Ink Ensemble." *Dissonance: Swiss Music Journal for Research and Creation* 116 (December 2010): 18–24.

Drott, Eric A. "Music as a Technology of Surveillance." *Journal of the Society for American Music* 12, no. 3 (2018): 233–67.

du Gay, Paul. *Consumption and Identity at Work*. Thousand Oaks, CA: Sage, 1996.

Eidsheim, Nina Sun. *Sensing Sound: Singing and Listening as Vibrational Practice*. Durham, NC: Duke University Press, 2015.

―――. "Sensing Voice: Materiality and the Lived Body in Singing and Listening." *Senses and Society* 6, no. 2 (2011): 133–55.

Engelhardt, Markus, and Michael Heinemann, eds. *Ars magna musices: Athanasius Kircher und die Universalität der Musik: Vorträge des deutsch-italienischen Symposiums aus Anlass des 400. Geburtstages von Athanasius Kircher (1602–1680); Musikgeschichtliche Abteilung des Deutschen Historischen Instituts in Rom, in Zusammenarbeit mit der Hochschule für Musik "Carl Maria von Weber" in Dresden, Rom, Deutsches Historisches Institut, 16.–18. Oktober 2002*. Laaber: Laaber-Verlag, 2007.

Englmann, Felicia. *Sphärenharmonie und Mikrokosmos: Das politische Denken des Athanasius Kircher (1602–1680)*. Cologne: Böhlau Verlag, 2006.

Escudero, Jesús Adrián. "Heidegger's *Black Notebooks* and the Question of Anti-Semitism." *Gatherings: The Heidegger Circle Annual* 5 (2015): 21–49.

Eshun, Kodwo. *More Brilliant than the Sun: Adventures in Sonic Fiction.* London: Quartet Books, 1998.
Fanon, Frantz. *Black Skin, White Masks.* Rev. ed. London: Pluto Press, 2008.
Farin, Ingo, and Jeff Malpas, eds. *Reading Heidegger's "Black Notebooks 1931–1941."* Cambridge, MA: MIT Press, 2016.
Faye, Emmanuel. *Heidegger: The Introduction of Nazism into Philosophy in Light of the Unpublished Seminars of 1933–1935.* Translated by Michael B. Smith. New Haven, CT: Yale University Press, 2009.
Feld, Steven. "Acoustemology." In *Keywords in Sound,* edited by David Novak and Matt Sakakeeny, 12–21. Durham NC: Duke University Press, 2015.
———. *Sound and Sentiment: Birds, Weeping, Poetics, and Song in Kaluli Expression.* 2nd ed. Philadelphia: University of Pennsylvania Press, 1990.
Fiala, Andrew. *The Philosopher's Voice: Philosophy, Politics, and Language in the Nineteenth Century.* Albany: State University of New York Press, 2002.
Findlen, Paula, ed. *Athanasius Kircher: The Last Man Who Knew Everything.* New York: Routledge, 2004.
Fink, Bruce. *The Lacanian Subject: Between Language and Jouissance.* Princeton, NJ: Princeton University Press, 1995.
Fletcher, John Edward. *A Study of the Life and Works of Athanasius Kircher, "Germanus Incredibilis": With a Selection of His Unpublished Correspondence and an Annotated Translation of His Autobiography.* Edited by Elizabeth Fletcher. Aries Book Series 12. Leiden and Boston: Brill, 2011.
Fletcher, John Edward, ed. *Athanasius Kircher und seine Beziehungen zum gelehrten Europa seiner Zeit.* WolfenbüttelerArbeiten für Barockforschung 17. Wiesbaden: Harrassowitz, 1988.
Fodor, Jerry A. *A Theory of Content and Other Essays.* Cambridge, MA: MIT Press, 1990.
Foucault, Michel. *Archaeology of Knowledge.* London and New York: Routledge, 2002.
———. *The Birth of Biopolitics: Lectures at the Collège de France, 1978–79.* Edited by Michel Sennelart. Translated by Graham Burchell. Basingstoke and New York: Palgrave Macmillan, 2008.
———. *Discipline and Punish: The Birth of the Prison.* Translated by Alan Sheridan. 2nd ed. New York: Vintage Books, 1995.
———. *The Order of Things: An Archaeology of the Human Sciences.* London and New York: Routledge Classics, 2002.
———. *The Use of Pleasure.* Vol. 2 of *The History of Sexuality.* Translated by Robert Hurley. New York: Vintage Books, 1988.
Fox-Brewster, Thomas. "Location, Sensors, Voice, Photos?! Spotify Just Got Real Creepy with the Data It Collects on You." *Forbes,* August 20, 2015.
Fricke, Christel. "Kant." In *Music in German Philosophy: An Introduction,* edited by Stefan Lorenz Sorgner and Oliver Fürbeth, 27–46. Chicago: University of Chicago Press, 2011.
Fubini, Enrico. *History of Music Aesthetics.* London: Macmillan, 1990.
Fumaroli, Marc. *L'âge de l'éloquence: Rhétorique et "res literaria," de la Renaissance au seuil de l'époque classique.* Hautes études médiévales et modernes 43. Geneva: Droz, 1980.
———. "Le corps éloquent: Une somme d' *actio* et *pronuntiatio rhetorica* au XVIIe siècle; Les *Vacationes autumnales* du P. Louis de Cressolles (1620)." *Dix-septième siècle* 132, no. 3 (1981): 237–64.
"Future Soldier 2030 Initiative." *Wired,* 2009. https://www.wired.com/images_blogs/dangerroom/2009/05/dplus2009_11641-1.pdf.

Gadamer, Hans-Georg. *Truth and Method*. Translation revised by Joel Weinsheimer and Donald G. Marshall. London and New York: A & C Black, 2013.

Gallope, Michael. "Is There a Deleuzian Musical Work?" *Perspectives of New Music* 46, no. 2 (2008): 93–129.

Galloway, Alexander R. "Peak Analog." March 22, 2019. http://cultureandcommunication.org/galloway/peak-analog.

Garcia, Luis-Manuel. "Beats, Flesh, and Grain: Sonic Tactility and Affect in Electronic Dance Music." *Sound Studies* 1, no. 1 (2015): 59–76.

Garofalo, Reebee. "From Music Publishing to MP3: Music and Industry in the Twentieth Century." *American Music* 17, no. 3 (1999): 318–54.

Gibbs, Anna. "After Affect: Sympathy, Synchrony, and Mimetic Communication." In *The Affect Theory Reader*, edited by Melissa Gregg and Gregory J. Seigworth, 186–205. Durham, NC: Duke University Press, 2010.

Giddens, Anthony. *Modernity and Self-Identity: Self and Society in the Late Modern Age*. Cambridge: Polity Press, 1991.

Gilbert, J. "Signifying Nothing: 'Culture,' 'Discourse' and the Sociality of Affect." *Culture Machine* 6 (2004). Accessed August 19, 2014. https://culturemachine.net/deconstruction-is-in-cultural-studies/signifying-nothing/.

Ginsborg, Hannah. "Kant." In *The Routledge Companion to Philosophy and Music*, edited by Theodore Gracyk and Andrew Kania, 328–38. Abingdon: Routledge, 2011.

Giordanetti, Piero. *Kant e la musica*. Milan: CUEM, 2001. Revised and translated into German as *Kant und die Musik* (Würzburg: Königshausen & Neumann, 2005).

Gleason, Maud W. *Making Men: Sophists and Self-Presentation in Ancient Rome*. Princeton, NJ: Princeton University Press, 1994.

Glinsky, Albert. *Theremin: Ether Music and Espionage*. Urbana: University of Illinois Press, 2000.

Goddard, Michael, Benjamin Halligan, and Paul Hegarty. *Reverberations: The Philosophy, Aesthetics and Politics of Noise*. London and New York: Continuum, 2012.

Godwin, Joscelyn. *Athanasius Kircher: A Renaissance Man and the Quest for Lost Knowledge*. London: Thames & Hudson, 1979.

Goehr, Lydia. *Elective Affinities: Musical Essays on the History of Aesthetic Theory*. New York: Columbia University Press, 2011.

Goldie, Peter, ed. *The Oxford Handbook of Philosophy of Emotion*. Oxford and New York: Oxford University Press, 2010.

Gonzalez, Francisco. "And the Rest Is *Sigetik*: Silencing Logic and Dialectic in Heidegger's *Beiträge zur Philosophie*." *Research in Phenomenology* 38, no. 3 (2008): 358–91.

Goodman, Steve. *Sonic Warfare: Sound, Affect, and the Ecology of Fear*. Cambridge, MA: MIT Press, 2010.

Gopnik, Adam. "The Information: How the Internet Gets Inside Us." *The New Yorker*, February 14 & 21, 2011.

Gossett, Che. "We Will Not Rest in Peace: AIDS Activism, Black Radicalism, Queer and/or Trans Resistance." In *Queer Necropolitics*, edited by Jin Haritaworn, Adi Kuntsman, and Silvia Posocco, 31–50. New York: Routledge, 2014.

Gouk, Penelope. "In Search of Sound: Authenticity, Healing and Redemption in the Early Modern State." *Senses and Society* 2, no. 3 (2007): 303–28.

———. *Music, Science, and Natural Magic in Seventeenth-Century England*. New Haven, CT: Yale University Press, 1999.

Gracyk, Theodore, and Andrew Kania, eds. *The Routledge Companion to Philosophy and Music*. New York: Routledge, 2011.

Grant, Roger Matthew, *Peculiar Attunements: How Affect Theory Turned Musical*. New York: Fordham University Press, 2020.

———. "Music Lessons on Affect and Its Objects." *Representations* 144, no. 1 (2018): 34–60.

———. "Peculiar Attunements: Comic Opera and Enlightenment Mimesis." *Critical Inquiry* 43, no. 2 (2017): 550–69.

Gregg, Melissa, and Gregory J. Seigworth, eds. *The Affect Theory Reader*. Durham, NC: Duke University Press, 2010.

Groff, Elizabeth, and Tom McEwen. "Identifying and Measuring the Effects of Information Technologies on Law Enforcement Agencies." Washington, DC: U.S. Department of Justice, Office of Community Oriented Policing Services, 2008.

Gross, Daniel M. *The Secret History of Emotion: From Aristotle's "Rhetoric" to Modern Brain Science*. Chicago: University of Chicago Press, 2006.

———. *Uncomfortable Situations: Emotion between Science and the Humanities*. Chicago: University of Chicago Press, 2017.

Gross, Daniel M. *Uncomfortable Situations: Emotion between Science and the Humanities*. Chicago: University of Chicago Press, 2017.

Grosz, Elizabeth, Z. *Chaos, Territory, Art: Deleuze and the Framing of the Earth*. New York: Columbia University Press, 2008.

Grusin, Richard. "Radical Mediation." *Critical Inquiry* 42, no. 1 (2015): 124–48.

Gumbrecht, Hans Ulrich. *Production of Presence: What Meaning Cannot Convey*. Stanford, CA: Stanford University Press, 2004.

Habermas, Jürgen. *Between Naturalism and Religion: Philosophical Essays*. Translated by Ciaran Cronin. Cambridge, UK, and Malden, MA: Polity Press, 2008.

Haddad, Darren, Sharon Walter, Roy Ratley, and Megan Smith. "Investigation and Evaluation of Voice Stress Analysis Technology." Final Report, February 13, 2002. https://www.ncjrs.gov/pdffiles1/nij/193832.pdf.

Hägglund, Martin. "Radical Atheist Materialism: A Critique of Meillassoux." In *The Speculative Turn: Continental Materialism and Realism*, edited by Levi Bryant, Nick Srnicek, and Graham Harman, 114–29. Melbourne: re:press, 2011.

Hainge, Greg. *Noise Matters: Towards an Ontology of Noise*. New York: Bloomsbury Academic, 2013.

Halberstam, Jack. *Gaga Feminism: Sex, Gender, and the End of Normal*. Boston: Beacon Press, 2012.

Hall, Stuart. "Encoding, Decoding." In *The Cultural Studies Reader*, edited by Simon During, 477–87. London and New York: Routledge, 1993.

Hanslick, Eduard. *The Beautiful in Music: A Contribution to the Revisal of Musical Aesthetics*. Translated by Gustav Cohen. London: Novello, 1891.

———. *Eduard Hanslick's On the Musically Beautiful: A New Translation*, trans. Lee Rothfarb and Christoph Landerer (New York: Oxford University Press, 2018).

———. *On the Musically Beautiful: A Contribution towards the Revision of the Aesthetics of Music*. Translated and edited by Geoffrey Payzant. Indianapolis, IN: Hackett, 1986.

———. *Vom musikalisch-Schönen: Ein Beitrag zur Revision der Ästhetik der Tonkunst*. Leipzig: Rudolph Weigel, 1854; 2nd ed., 1858.

Haraway, Donna J. "A Cyborg Manifesto: Science, Technology, and Socialist-Feminism in the Late Twentieth Century," In *Simians, Cyborgs, and Women: The Reinvention of Nature*. New York: Routledge, 1991.

———. *Staying with the Trouble: Making Kin in the Chthulucene*. Durham, NC: Duke University Press, 2016.

Hardt, Michael. "Affective Labor." *boundary 2* 26, no. 2 (1999): 89–100.
Harman, Graham. *The Quadruple Object*. Winchester, UK, and Washington, DC: Zero Books, 2010.
Hasty, Christopher. "Broken Sequences: Fragmentation, Abundance, Beauty." *Perspectives of New Music* 40, no. 2 (2002): 155–73.
———. *Meter as Rhythm*. Oxford and New York: Oxford University Press, 1997.
Head, Matthew. "Music with 'No Past?' Archaeologies of Joseph Haydn and *The Creation*." *19th-Century Music* 23, no. 3 (2000): 191–217.
Hearn, Alison. "'Meat, Mask, Burden.': Probing the Contours of the Branded 'Self.'" *Journal of Consumer Culture* 8, no. 2 (2008): 197–217.
Hegarty, Paul. *Noise/Music: A History*. New York: Continuum, 2007.
Hegel, Georg Wilhelm Friedrich. *Aesthetics: Lectures on Fine Art*. Translated by T. M. Knox. Oxford: Clarendon Press, 1975.
Hegel, Georg Wilhelm Friedrich. *Philosophy of Mind*. Revised and with an introduction by Michael Inwood. Translated by W. Wallace and A. V. Miller. Oxford and New York: Clarendon Press, 2007.
Heidegger, Martin. *Anmerkungen I–V (Schwarze Hefte 1942–1948)*. Vol. 97 of *Gesamtausgabe: IV. Abteilung; Hinweise und Aufzeichnungen*. Edited by Peter Trawny. Frankfurt am Main: Vittorio Klostermann, 2015.
———. *Being and Time: A Translation of "Sein und Zeit."* Translated by Joan Stambaugh. Albany: State University of New York Press, 2010.
———. *Being and Truth*. Translated by Gregory Fried and Richard Polt. Bloomington: Indiana University Press, 2010.
———. *The Fundamental Concepts of Metaphysics: World, Finitude, Solitude*. Translated by William McNeill and Nicholas Walker. Bloomington: Indiana University Press, 1995.
———. *Plato's "Sophist."* Translated by Richard Rojcewicz and André Schuwer. Bloomington: Indiana University Press, 1997.
———. *Ponderings II–VI: Black Notebooks, 1931–1938*. Translated by Richard Rojcewicz. Bloomington: Indiana University Press, 2016.
———. *Überlegungen II–VI (Schwarze Hefte 1931–1938)*. Vol. 94 of *Gesamtausgabe: IV. Abteilung; Hinweise und Aufzeichnungen*. Edited by Peter Trawny. Frankfurt am Main: Vittorio Klostermann, 2014.
———. *Überlegungen VII–XI (Schwarze Hefte 1938–1939)*. Vol. 95 of *Gesamtausgabe: IV. Abteilung; Hinweise und Aufzeichnungen*. Edited by Peter Trawny. Frankfurt am Main: Vittorio Klostermann, 2014.
———. *Überlegungen XII–XV (Schwarze Hefte 1939–1941)*. Vol. 96 of *Gesamtausgabe: IV. Abteilung; Hinweise und Aufzeichnungen*. Edited by Peter Trawny. Frankfurt am Main: Vittorio Klostermann, 2014.
Heller, Wendy. "Hypsipyle, Medea, and the Ovidian Imagination: Taming the Epic Hero in Cavalli's *Giasone*." In *Readying Cavalli's Operas for the Stage: Manuscript, Edition, Production*, edited by Ellen Rosand. Farnham, England, and Burlington, VT: Ashgate, 2013.
Hemmings, Clare. "Invoking Affect." *Cultural Studies* 19, no. 5 (2005): 548–67.
Henke, Robert. *Performance and Literature in the Commedia dell'Arte*. Cambridge and New York: Cambridge University Press, 2002.
Hennion, Antoine. "The History of Art—Lessons in Mediation." Translated by Liz Libbrecht. *Réseaux: Communication—Technologie—Société* 3, no. 2 (1995): 233–62.
Henriques, Julian. *Sonic Bodies: Reggae Sound Systems, Performance Techniques, and Ways of Knowing*. New York: Continuum, 2011.

Hochschild, Arlie Russell. *The Managed Heart: Commercialization of Human Feeling*. Berkeley and Los Angeles: University of California Press, 2012.

Hogle, Linda F., ed. *Regenerative Medicine Ethics: Governing Research and Knowledge Practices*. New York: Springer, 2014.

Homer. *The Odyssey*. Edited by Bernard Knox. Translated by Robert Fagles. Bibliotheca Homerica Langiana. New York: Viking, 1996.

Horkheimer, Max, and Theodor W. Adorno. *Dialectic of Enlightenment*. London: Allen Lane, 1973.

———. *Dialectic of Enlightenment*. New York: Continuum, 1997.

———. *Dialectic of Enlightenment: Philosophical Fragments*. Edited by Gunzelin Schmid Noerr. Translated by Edmund Jephcott. Stanford, CA: Stanford University Press, 2002.

Hulse, Brian Clarence, and Nick Nesbitt, eds. *Sounding the Virtual: Gilles Deleuze and the Theory and Philosophy of Music*. Farnham, England, and Burlington, VT: Ashgate, 2010.

Hume, David. *Enquiries Concerning Human Understanding and Concerning the Principles of Morals*. 3rd ed. Oxford: Clarendon Press, 1975.

Ihde, Don. *Acoustic Technics*. Lanham, MD: Lexington Books, 2015.

———. *Experimental Phenomenology: Multistabilities*. 2nd ed. Albany, NY: State University of New York Press, 2012.

———. *Listening and Voice: Phenomenologies of Sound*. 2nd ed. Albany, NY: State University of New York Press, 2007.

Israel, Jonathan I. *Radical Enlightenment: Philosophy and the Making of Modernity, 1650–1750*. Oxford and New York: Oxford University Press, 2001.

James, Robin. "Cloudy Logic." *New Inquiry*. January 27, 2015. https://thenewinquiry.com/cloudy-logic/.

———. *Resilience and Melancholy: Pop Music, Feminism, and Neoliberalism*. Alredsford, Hants: Zero Books, 2017.

———. *The Sonic Episteme: Acoustic Resonance, Neoliberalism, and Biopolitics*. Durham, NC: University Press, 2019.

Jameson, Fredric. "Wagner as Dramatist and Allegorist." *Modernist Cultures* 8, no. 1 (2013): 9–41.

Jamieson, Kathleen Hall. *Cyberwar: How Russian Hackers and Trolls Helped Elect a President; What We Don't, Can't, and Do Know*. New York: Oxford University Press, 2018.

Jones, Richard Elfyn. "A. N. Whitehead and Music: Real Time." *Musical Times* 141, no. 1873 (2000): 47–52.

———. "A Whiteheadian Aesthetic and Musical Paradigm." *Canadian Aesthetics Journal* 8 (2003). http://www.uqtr.uquebec.ca/AE/Vol_8/libres/jones.html.

Jorgensen, Larry M. "Descartes on Music: Between the Ancients and the Aestheticians." *British Journal of Aesthetics* 52, no. 4 (2012): 407–24.

Kane, Brian. "Sound Studies without Auditory Culture: A Critique of the Ontological Turn." *Sound Studies* 1, no. 1 (2015): 2–21.

———. *Sound Unseen: Acousmatic Sound in Theory and Practice*. Oxford and New York: Oxford University Press, 2014.

Kant, Immanuel. *Critique of Pure Reason*. Edited and translated by Paul Guyer and Allen W. Wood. Cambridge: Cambridge University Press, 1998.

———. *Critique of the Power of Judgment*. Edited by Paul Guyer and Allen W. Wood. Cambridge and New York: Cambridge University Press, 2000.

———. *Gesammelte Schriften*. Edited by Royal Prussian (subsequently German, then Berlin-Brandenburg) Academy of Sciences. Berlin: Georg Reimer, subsequently Walter de Gruyter, 1900–.

---. *Practical Philosophy*. Edited by Paul Guyer and Allen W. Wood. Cambridge: Cambridge University Press, 2006.

Karpf, Anne. *The Human Voice: How This Extraordinary Instrument Reveals Essential Clues about Who We Are*. New York: Bloomsbury, 2006.

Kassabian, Anahid. *Ubiquitous Listening: Affect, Attention, and Distributed Subjectivity*. Berkeley and Los Angeles: University of California Press, 2013.

Kauffman, Stuart A. *Investigations*. Oxford and New York: Oxford University Press, 2000.

---. *The Origins of Order: Self-Organization and Selection in Evolution*. Oxford and New York: Oxford University Press, 1993.

---. *Reinventing the Sacred: A New View of Science, Reason, and Religion*. New York: Basic Books, 2008.

Kelley, Robin D. G. *Thelonious Monk: The Life and Times of an American Original*. New York: Free Press, 2009.

Kelly, Caleb. *Sound*. London and Cambridge, MA: MIT Press, 2011.

Kelly, Thomas Forrest. *Capturing Music: The Story of Notation*. 1st ed. New York: W. W. Norton, 2014.

Kim-Cohen, Seth. *In the Blink of an Ear: Toward a Non-Cochlear Sonic Art*. New York: Continuum, 2009.

Kindy, Kimberly, and reported by Julie Tate, Jennifer Jenkins, Steven Rich, Keith L. Alexander, and Wesley Lowery. "Fatal Police Shootings in 2015 Approaching 400 Nationwide." *Washington Post*, May 30, 2015. https://www.washingtonpost.com/national/fatal-police-shootings-in-2015-approaching-400-nationwide/2015/05/30/d322256a-058e-11e5-a428-c984eb077d4e_story.html.

Kircher, Athanasius. *Kircherus Jesuita Germanus Germaniae redonatus, sive Artis Magnae de Consono & Dißono Ars Minor: Das ist Philosophischer Extract und Auszug, aus deß Weltberühmten Teutschen Jesuitens Athanasii Kircherii von Fulda, Musurgia universali*.... Translated by Andreas Hirsch. Facsimile ed. Kassel: Bärenreiter, 1988.

---. *Musurgia Universalis*. Edited by Ulf Scharlau. Hildesheim and New York: G. Olms, 1970.

---. *Musurgia Universalis, sive Ars magna consoni et dissoni, in X. libros digesta*. Rome: Ex typographia Hœredum Francisci Corbelletti, 1650.

Kisiel, Theodore. "The Siting of Hölderlin's 'Geheimes Deutschland' in Heidegger's Poetizing of the Political." In *Heidegger und der Nationalsozialismus II: Interpretationen*, edited by Alfred Denker and Holger Zaborowski, 145–54. Heidegger-Jahrbuch 5. Freiburg: Karl Alber, 2009.

Kivy, Peter. *The Fine Art of Repetition: Essays in the Philosophy of Music*. Cambridge and New York: Cambridge University Press, 1993.

---. *Introduction to a Philosophy of Music*. Oxford and New York: Oxford University Press, 2002.

Kneller, Jane. *Kant and the Power of Imagination*. Cambridge and New York: Cambridge University Press, 2007.

Knowles, Adam. "Steresis and Silence: The Aristotelian Origins of Heidegger's Thinking of Silence." In *Sources of Desire: Essays on Aristotle's Theoretical Works*, edited by James Oldfield. Newcastle upon Tyne: Cambridge Scholars, 2012.

---. "A Genealogy of Silence: *Chōra* and the Placelessness of Greek Women." *PhiloSOPHIA: A Journal of Continental Feminism* 5, no. 1 (2015): 1–24.

Koch, Erec R. *The Aesthetic Body: Passion, Sensibility, and Corporeality in Seventeenth-Century France*. Newark: University of Delaware Press, 2008.

———. "Voice, Aurality, and the Natural Language of Passion in Mersenne's *Harmonie Universelle*." *Seventeenth-Century French Studies* 28, no. 1 (2006): 77–89.

Kockelman, Paul. *Agent, Person, Subject, Self: A Theory of Ontology, Interaction, and Infrastructure*. Oxford and New York: Oxford University Press, 2013.

———. "Biosemiosis, Technocognition, and Sociogenesis: Selection and Significance in a Multiverse of Sieving and Serendipity." *Current Anthropology* 52, no. 5 (2011): 711–39.

Kraut, Robert. "Why Does Jazz Matter to Aesthetic Theory?" *Journal of Aesthetics and Art Criticism* 65, no. 1 (2005): 11–12.

Krell, David Farrell. "Heidegger's *Black Notebooks, 1931–1941*." *Research in Phenomenology* 45, no. 1 (2015): 127–60.

Kristeller, Paul Oskar. "The Modern System of the Arts: A Study in the History of Aesthetics, Part I." *Journal of the History of Ideas* 12, no. 4 (1951): 496–527.

———. "The Modern System of the Arts: A Study in the History of Aesthetics, Part II." *Journal of the History of Ideas* 13, no. 1 (1952): 17–46.

Kull, Kalevi. "An Introduction to Phytosemiotics: Semiotic Botany and Vegetative Sign Systems." *Sign Systems Studies* 28, no. 1 (2000): 326–50.

LaBelle, Brandon. *Acoustic Territories: Sound Culture and Everyday Life*. London: Continuum, 2010.

———. *Lexicon of the Mouth: Poetics and Politics of Voice and the Oral Imaginary*. New York: Bloomsbury, 2014.

Lacan, Jacques. *The Seminar of Jacques Lacan, Book VII: The Ethics of Psychoanalysis, 1959–1960*. Edited by Jacques-Alan Miller. Translated by Dennis Porter. New York: W. W. Norton, 1997.

Lacoue-Labarthe, Philippe. *Typography: Mimesis, Philosophy, Politics*. Edited by Christopher Fynsk. Introduction by Jacques Derrida. Cambridge, MA: Harvard University Press, 1989.

Langer, Susanne K. *Feeling and Form: A Theory of Art, Developed from "Philosophy in a New Key."* New York: Charles Scribner's Sons, 1953.

———. *Philosophy in a New Key: A Study in the Symbolism of Reason, Rite, and Art*. Cambridge, MA: Harvard University Press, 1942.

———. "The Process of Feeling." In *Philosophical Sketches*, 11–29. New York: Mentor, 1964.

Larmore, Charles E. *Patterns of Moral Complexity*. Cambridge and New York: Cambridge University Press, 1987.

Lash, Scott. "Power after Hegemony: Cultural Studies in Mutation?" *Theory, Culture & Society* 24, no. 3 (2007): 55–78.

"Layered Voice Analysis Test Report Finds Arjul Rai Guilty." Webindia123, 2013. Accessed November 23, 2018. https://news.webindia123.com/news/Articles/India/20131113/2283258.html.

Le Dœuff, Michèle. "Philosophy in the Larynx." In *The Philosophical Imaginary*, 129–37. Translated by Colin Gordon. London and New York: Continuum, 2003.

Leinkauf, Thomas. *Mundus combinatus: Studien zur Struktur der barocken Universalwissenschaft am Beispiel Athanasius Kirchers SJ (1602–1680)*. Berlin: Akademie Verlag, 1993.

Lenoble, Robert. *Mersenne; ou, La naissance du mécanisme . . . .* Paris: J. Vrin, 1943.

Levanon, Yoram, and Lan Lossos-Shifrin. System and Method for Determining a Personal SHG Profile by Voice Analysis. US Patent 7917366 B1, filed September 28, 2006, and issued March 29, 2011.

———. System for Indicating Emotional Attitudes through Intonation Analysis and Methods Thereof. US Patent 8078470 B2, filed December 20, 2006, and issued December 13, 2011.

Levenson, Robert W. "Emotion and the Autonomic Nervous System: A Prospectus for Research on Autonomic Specificity." In *Social Psychophysiology and Emotion: Theory and Clinical Applications*, edited by Hugh Wagner, 17–42. Chichester and New York: John Wiley & Sons, 1988.
Leys, Ruth. *The Ascent of Affect: Genealogy and Critique*. Chicago: University of Chicago Press, 2017.
———. *From Guilt to Shame: Auschwitz and After*. Princeton, NJ: Princeton University Press, 2007.
———. *Trauma: A Genealogy*. Chicago: University of Chicago Press, 2000.
———. "The Turn to Affect: A Critique." *Critical Inquiry* 37, no. 3 (2011): 434–72.
Lima, Luiz Costa. *Control of the Imaginary: Reason and Imagination in Modern Times*. Minneapolis: University of Minnesota Press, 1988.
Lochhead, Judy I. "Music Places: Imaginative Transports of Listening." In *The Oxford Handbook of Sound and Imagination*, vol. 1, edited by Mark Grimshaw-Aagaard, Mads Walther-Hansen, and Martin Knakkergaard, 683–700. Oxford and New York: Oxford University Press, 2019.
Long, A. A. *Stoic Studies*. Berkeley and Los Angeles: University of California Press, 1996.
Lotman, Juri. "On the Semiosphere." Translated by Wilma Clark. *Sign Systems Studies* 33, no. 1 (2005): 205–26.
Ludacris. "Rest of My Life" (music video). Featuring Usher and David Guetta. The Island Def Jam Music Group, 2012.
Luft, Sebastian, and Søren Overgaard, eds. *The Routledge Companion to Phenomenology*. London: Routledge, 2014.
Mader, Mary Beth. *Sleights of Reason: Norm, Bisexuality, Development*. Albany: State University of New York Press, 2011.
Maffesoli, Michel. *The Time of the Tribes: The Decline of Individualism in Mass Society*. Translated by Don Smith. London and Thousand Oaks, CA: Sage, 1996.
Malpas, Jeff. "On the Philosophical Reading of Heidegger: Situating the *Black Notebooks*." In *Reading Heidegger's "Black Notebooks 1931–1941,"* edited by Ingo Farin and Jeff Malpas, 3–22. Cambridge MA: MIT Press, 2016.
Martin, F. David. "The Power of Music and Whitehead's Theory of Perception." *Journal of Aesthetics and Art Criticism* 25, no. 3 (1967): 313–22.
Marx, Karl, and Frederick Engels. "Manifesto of the Communist Party." Marxists Internet Archive. Accessed November 23, 2018. https://www.marxists.org/archive/marx/works/download/pdf/Manifesto.pdf.
Massumi, Brian. "The Autonomy of Affect." In Politics of Systems and Environments, part 2, *Cultural Critique* 31 (Fall 1995): 83–109.
———. *Parables for the Virtual: Movement, Affect, Sensation*. Durham, NC: Duke University Press, 2002.
———. *Semblance and Event: Activist Philosophy and the Occurrent Arts*. Cambridge, MA: MIT Press, 2011.
Mathew, Nicholas. "The Tangled Woof." [Review of] Mark Evan Bonds, *Music as Thought: Listening to the Symphony in the Age of Beethoven*; David Wyn Jones, *The Symphony in Beethoven's Vienna*; and Melanie Lowe, *Pleasure and Meaning in the Classical Symphony*. *Journal of the Royal Musical Association* 134, no. 1 (2009): 133–47.
Mathiesen, Thomas J. *Apollo's Lyre: Greek Music and Music Theory in Antiquity and the Middle Ages*. Lincoln: University of Nebraska Press, 2000.
Mathieu-Castellani, Gisèle. *La rhétorique des passions*. Paris: PUF, 2000.

Matravers, Derek. "Arousal Theories." In *The Routledge Companion to Philosophy and Music*, edited by Theodore Gracyk and Andrew Kania, 212–22. New York: Routledge, 2011.

Mattheson, Johann, and Reinhard Keiser. *Das neu-eröffnete Orchestre, oder Universelle und gründliche Anleitung, wie ein Galant Homme einen vollkommenen Begriff von der Hoheit und Würde der edlen Music erlangen . . . möge*. Hamburg: Benjamin Schillers Witwe, 1713.

Maturana, Humberto R., and Francisco J. Varela. *Autopoiesis and Cognition: The Realization of the Living*. Dordrecht and Boston: D. Reidel, 1980.

Mauss, Marcel. *A General Theory of Magic*. New York: W. W. Norton, 1975.

McAuley, Tomas. "Rhythmic Accent and the Absolute: Sulzer, Schelling and the Akzenttheorie." *Eighteenth-Century Music* 10, no. 2 (2013): 277–86.

McAuley, Tomás. "Ethics." In *The Oxford Handbook of Music and Intellectual Culture in the Nineteenth Century*, edited by Paul Watt, Sarah Collins, and Michael Allis, 481–506. Oxford and New York: Oxford University Press.

McAuley, Tomas, and Nanette Nielsen, eds. *The Oxford Handbook of Music and Philosophy*. Oxford and New York: Oxford University Press, forthcoming.

McClary, Susan. *Desire and Pleasure in Seventeenth-Century Music*. Berkeley and Los Angeles: University of California Press, 2012.

McConnell, Ivana. "Identity Labor and Online Communities." *The Learned Fangirl: A Critical Look at Pop Culture and Technology* (blog). August 19, 2016. http://thelearnedfangirl.com/2016/08/identity-labor-personal-brand/.

McDonald, Glenn. "Every Noise at Once." EveryNoise (website). Accessed February 14, 2020. http://everynoise.com/engenremap.html#otherthings.

McKay, John Zachary. "Universal Music-Making: Athanasius Kircher and Musical Thought in the Seventeenth Century." Ph.D. diss., Harvard University, 2012.

McLuhan, Marshall, and Barrington Nevitt. *Take Today: The Executive as Dropout*. New York: Harcourt Brace Jovanovich, 1972.

Meillassoux, Quentin. *After Finitude: An Essay on the Necessity of Contingency*. Translated by Ray Brassier. London and New York: Continuum, 2008.

Mendieta, Eduardo. "The Jargon of Ontology and the Critique of Language: Adorno and Philosophy's Motherless Tongue." In *The Aesthetic Ground of Critical Theory: New Readings of Benjamin and Adorno*, edited by Nathan Ross, 47–65. Lanham, MD: Rowman & Littlefield, 2015.

———. "The Sound of Race: The Prosody of Affect." *Radical Philosophy Review* 17, no. 1 (2014): 109–31.

Merleau-Ponty, Maurice. *Husserl at the Limits of Phenomenology: Including Texts by Edmund Husserl*. Edited by Leonard Lawlor with Bettina Bergo. Evanston, IL: Northwestern University Press, 2002.

———. *Nature: Course Notes from the Collège de France*. Translated by Robert Vallier. Evanston, IL: Northwestern University Press, 2003.

———. *Phenomenology of Perception*. Translated by Colin Smith. London: Routledge, 1981.

———. *The Visible and the Invisible: Followed by Working Notes*. Edited by Claude Lefort. Evanston, IL: Northwestern University Press, 1968.

Mersenne, Marin. *Correspondance du P. Marin Mersenne, religieux minime*. Vol. 1. Edited by Cornelis de Waard. Paris: Presses Universitaires de France, 1945.

———. *Harmonie universelle, contenant la théorie et la pratique de la musique*. Paris: Sebastien Cramoisy, 1636.

———. *L'impiété des déistes, athées, et libertins de ce temps*. Paris: Pierre Bilaine, 1624.

———. *Quaestiones celeberrimae in Genesim: cum accurata textus explicatione*. Paris: Sebastien Cramoisy, 1623.

---. *La verité des sciences contre les Sceptiques ou Pyrrhoniens.* Paris: Toussaint du Bray, 1625.

---. *La verité des sciences contre les Sceptiques ou Pyrrhoniens.* Edited and annotated by Dominique Descotes. Paris: Honoré Champion, 2003.

Meštrović, Stjepan G. *Postemotional Society.* London and Thousand Oaks, CA: Sage, 1997.

Meyer, Leonard B. *Emotion and Meaning in Music.* Chicago: University of Chicago Press, 1956.

Mincek, Alex, Jeff Snyder, Alex Ness, Kate Soper, Jim Altieri, Eric Wubbels, Clara Latham, and Sam Pluta. *The Language Of.* Quiet Design CD 700261255088, 2008.

Mitropoulos, Angela. *Contract and Contagion: From Biopolitics to "Oikonomia."* New York: Minor Compositions, 2012.

Modell, Amanda. "'Only God Can Make a Genome': Pandora Internet Radio, God Tricks and 'The Music Itself.'" Paper presented at the Society for Ethnomusicology National Meeting, Austin, TX, December 8, 2015.

Montiglio, Silvia. *Silence in the Land of Logos.* Princeton, NJ: Princeton University Press, 2000.

Moran, Dermot. *Introduction to Phenomenology.* London and New York: Routledge, 2000.

Moreno, Jairo. *Musical Representations, Subjects, and Objects: The Construction of Musical Thought in Zarlino, Descartes, Rameau, and Weber.* Bloomington: Indiana University Press, 2004.

Morrow, Mary Sue. *German Music Criticism in the Late Eighteenth Century: Aesthetic Issues in Instrumental Music.* Cambridge and New York: Cambridge University Press, 2006.

Murata, Margaret. "The Recitative Soliloquy." *Journal of the American Musicological Society* 32, no. 1 (1979): 45–73.

Musk, Elon. "Is Life a Video Game?" Code Conference 2016. Accessed November 23, 2018. https://www.youtube.com/watch?v=2KK_kzrJPS8.

Nagel, Mechthild. *Masking the Abject: A Genealogy of Play.* Lanham, MD: Lexington Books, 2002.

Nancy, Jean-Luc. *Listening.* Translated by Charlotte Mandell. 1st ed. New York: Fordham University Press, 2007.

Nattiez, Jean-Jacques. *Music and Discourse: Toward a Semiology of Music.* Translated by Carolyn Abbate. Princeton, NJ: Princeton University Press, 1990.

Neubauer, John. *The Emancipation of Music from Language: Departure from Mimesis in Eighteenth-Century Aesthetics.* New Haven, CT: Yale University Press, 1986.

Ngai, Sianne. *Ugly Feelings.* 1st Harvard University Press paperback ed. Cambridge, MA: Harvard University Press, 2007.

Nietzsche, Friedrich Wilhelm. *Untimely Meditations.* Edited by Daniel Breazeale. Translated by R. J. Hollingdale. Cambridge: Cambridge University Press, 1997.

North, Helen F. "The Concept of *Sophrosyne* in Greek Literary Criticism." *Classical Philology* 43, no. 1 (1948): 1–17.

Nussbaum, Charles O. *The Musical Representation: Meaning, Ontology, and Emotion.* Cambridge, MA: MIT Press, 2007.

Nussbaum, Martha C. *Anger and Forgiveness: Resentment, Generosity, Justice.* New York: Oxford University Press, 2016.

---. *The Fragility of Goodness: Luck and Ethics in Greek Tragedy and Philosophy.* First published 1986. Rev. ed. Cambridge and New York: Cambridge University Press, 2001.

---. *Political Emotions: Why Love Matters for Justice.* Cambridge, MA: Belknap Press, 2013.

———. *Upheavals of Thought: The Intelligence of Emotions*. Cambridge and New York: Cambridge University Press, 2001.

Nye, William P. "Theodor Adorno on Jazz: A Critique of Critical Theory." *Popular Music and Society Popular Music and Society* 12, no. 4 (1988): 69–73.

Ochoa Gautier, Ana María. *Aurality: Listening and Knowledge in Nineteenth-Century Colombia*. Durham, NC: Duke University Press, 2014.

Olson, Michael P. "Thomas Bernhard, Glenn Gould, and the Art of the Fugue: Contrapuntal Variations in *Der Untergeher*." In "Form and Style in Contemporary Austrian Literature," special issue, *Modern Austrian Literature* 24, no. 3/4 (1991): 73–83.

O'Neal Irwin, Stacey. *Digital Media: Human-Technology Connections*. Lanham, MD: Lexington Books, 2016.

Ott, Hugo. *Martin Heidegger: A Political Life*. Translated by Allen Blunden. London: HarperCollins; New York: Basic Books, 1993.

Page, Will, and Eric Garland. "The Long Tail of P2P." *Economic Insight* 14 (2008): 1–8.

Palisca, Claude V. *Music and Ideas in the Sixteenth and Seventeenth Centuries*. Studies in the History of Music Theory and Literature 1. Urbana: University of Illinois Press, 2006.

Pangrazi, Tiziana. *La "Musurgia Universalis" di Athanasius Kircher: Contenuti, fonti, terminologia*. Florence: Leo S. Olschki, 2009.

Papandrea, Dawn. "Spotify's CMO on Using Data to Create Content Marketing Hits." *NewsCred Insights*, June 5, 2017. https://insights.newscred.com/spotify-cmo-data-content-marketing/.

Papoulias, Constantina, and Felicity Callard. "Biology's Gift: Interrogating the Turn to Affect." *Body and Society* 16, no. 1 (2010): 29–56.

Parr, Adrian, ed. *The Deleuze Dictionary*. New York: Columbia University Press, 2005.

Partini, Anna Maria. *Athanasius Kircher e l'alchimia: Testi scelti e commentati*. Rome: Edizioni Mediterranee, 2004.

Pasick, Adam. "The Magic That Makes Spotify's Discover Weekly Playlists So Damn Good," *Quartz*, December 21, 2015. https://qz.com/571007/the-magic-that-makes-spotifys-discover-weekly-playlists-so-damn-good/.

Peirce, Charles S. *The Essential Peirce: Selected Philosophical Writings*. Vol. 2. *1898–1913*. Edited by the Pierce Edition Project. Bloomington: Indiana University Press, 1998.

———. *Philosophical Writings of Peirce*. Selected and edited with an introduction by Justus Buchler. New York: Dover, 1955.

———. *Selected Writings (Values in a Universe of Chance)*. Edited with an introduction and notes by Philip P. Wiener. New York: Dover, 1966.

Peraino, Judith. *Listening to the Sirens: Musical Technologies of Queer Identity from Homer to Hedwig*. Berkeley and Los Angeles: University of California Press, 2005.

Peterson, Richard A. "Why 1955? Explaining the Advent of Rock Music." *Popular Music* 9, no. 1 (1990): 97–116.

Phillips, John. "*Agencement*/Assemblage." *Theory, Culture and Society* 23, nos. 2–3 (2006):108–9.

"Philosoph Günter Figal tritt als Vorsitzender der Martin-Heidegger Gesellschaft zurück: Kritische Forschung nötig" [radio interview, WDR3]. Accessed September 20, 2015. http://www.wdr3.de/zeitgeschehen/guenterfigal106.html.

Pinch, Trevor, and Karin Bijsterveld, eds. *The Oxford Handbook of Sound Studies*. Oxford and New York: Oxford University Press, 2012.

Pinch, Trevor J., and Karin Bijsterveld. "'Should One Applaud?': Breaches and Boundaries in the Reception of New Technology in Music." *Technology and Culture* 44, no. 3 (2003): 536–59.

Pinch, Trevor, and Frank Trocco. *Analog Days: The Invention and Impact of the Moog Synthesizer*. Cambridge, MA: Harvard University Press, 2002.

Plamper, Jan. *The History of Emotions: An Introduction*. Translated by Keith Tribe. Oxford: Oxford University Press, 2015.

Plato. *The Republic*. London: Penguin, 1987.

Plato. *Republic*. In *The Complete Works of Plato*. Translated by Benjamin Jowett. Kindle ed. Kirkland, WA: Latus ePublishing, 2012.

Plato. *Republic*. Translated by C. D. C. Reeve. Indianapolis, IN: Hackett, 2004.

Pollan, Michael. "The Intelligent Plant." *The New Yorker*, December 23, 2013. https://www.newyorker.com/magazine/2013/12/23/the-intelligent-plant.

Polt, Richard F. H. *The Emergency of Being: On Heidegger's Contributions to Philosophy*. Ithaca, NY: Cornell University Press, 2006.

———. "The Secret Homeland of Speech: Heidegger on Language, 1933–34." In *Heidegger and Language*, edited by Jeffrey Powell, 63–85. Bloomington: Indiana University Press, 2013.

Powell, Devin. "A Flexible Circuit Has Been Injected into Living Brains." Smithsonian Magazine. Accessed November 23, 2018. https://www.smithsonianmag.com/science-nature/flexible-circuit-has-been-injected-living-brains-180955525/.

Priest, Eldritch. "Felt as Thought." In *Sound, Music, Affect: Theorizing Sonic Experience*, edited by Marie Thompson and Ian D. Biddle. London and New York: Bloomsbury Academic, 2013.

Pritchard, Matthew. "Music in Balance: The Aesthetics of Music After Kant, 1790–1810." *Journal of Musicology* 36, no. 1 (2019): 39–67.

Proust, Marcel. *Remembrance of Things Past*. 3 vols. Translated by C. K. Scott Moncrieff, Terence Kilmartin, and Andreas Mayor. New York: Vintage Books, 1981.

———. *Swann's Way*. Translated by Lydia Davis. New York: Penguin Books, 2002.

Prum, Richard O. *The Evolution of Beauty: How Darwin's Forgotten Theory of Mate Choice Shapes the Animal World—and Us*. 1st ed. New York: Doubleday, 2017.

Puar, Jasbir K. *Terrorist Assemblages: Homonationalism in Queer Times*. Durham, NC: Duke University Press, 2007.

Quintilian, [Marcus Fabius]. *Institutio oratoria*. Edited and translated by D. A. Russell as *The Orator's Education*. Cambridge, MA: Harvard University Press, 2002.

Rabin, Nathan. "I'm Sorry for Coining the Phrase 'Manic Pixie Dream Girl.'" *Salon*, July 16, 2014. Accessed June 1, 2015. https://www.salon.com/2014/07/15/im_sorry_for_coining_the_phrase_manic_pixie_dream_girl/.

Rabinbach, Anson. "Introduction to Walter Benjamin's 'Doctrine of the Similar.'" In special Walter Benjamin issue, *New German Critique* 17 (1979): 60–64.

Radano, Ronald M. *New Musical Figurations: Anthony Braxton's Cultural Critique*. Chicago: University of Chicago Press, 1993.

Rainie, Lee, Janna Anderson, and Jonathan Albright. "The Future of Free Speech, Trolls, Anonymity and Fake News Online." Pew Research Center: Internet, Science & Tech, Washington, DC. March 29, 2017. https://www.pewresearch.org/internet/2017/03/29/the-future-of-free-speech-trolls-anonymity-and-fake-news-online/.

Rancière, Jacques. *Disagreement: Politics and Philosophy*. Minneapolis: University of Minnesota Press, 1999.

Ratliff, Ben. *Coltrane: The Story of a Sound*. New York: Farrar, Straus & Giroux, 2007.

Read, Jason. "A Genealogy of Homo-Economicus: Neoliberalism and the Production of Subjectivity." *Foucault Studies* 6 (February 2009): 25–36.

———. *The Micro-Politics of Capital: Marx and the Prehistory of the Present*. Albany: State University of New York Press, 2003.

Redwood, André. "Mersenne and the Art of Delivery." *Journal of Music Theory* 59, no. 1 (2015): 99–119.

Rée, Jonathan. *I See a Voice: Deafness, Language, and the Senses; A Philosophical History*. New York: Metropolitan Books, 1999.

Reguillo, Rossana. "Errant Surfing: Music, YouTube, and the Role of the Web in Youth Cultures." Translated by Peggy Westwell and Pablo Vila. In *Music and Youth Culture in Latin America: Identity Construction Processes from New York to Buenos Aires*, edited by Pablo Vila, 106–31. New York: Oxford University Press, 2014.

Reinhold, Karl Leonhard. *Letters on the Kantian Philosophy*. Edited by Karl Ameriks. Translated by James Hebbeler. Cambridge and New York: Cambridge University Press, 2005.

Reinhold, Karl Leonhard. *Briefe über die Kantische Philosophie*. Edited by Raymund Schmidt. Leipzig: Reclam, 1923.

Reiter, Andrea. "Thomas Bernhard's 'Musical Prose.'" In *Literature on the Threshold: The German Novel in the 1980s*, edited by Arthur Williams, Stuart Parkes, and Roland Smith, 187–207. New York: Berg, 1990.

Revelli, Marco. "Worker Identity in the Factory Desert." Translated by Ed Emory. In *Radical Thought in Italy: A Potential Politics*, edited by Paolo Virno and Michael Hardt, 116–22. Minneapolis: University of Minnesota Press, 1996.

Rifkin, Jeremy. *The Age of Access: The New Culture of Hypercapitalism, Where All of Life Is a Paid-For Experience*. New York: Jeremy P. Tarcher/Putnam, 2000.

Rimbaud, Arthur. *Selected Poems and Letters*. Translated by Jeremy Harding. London: Penguin, 2004.

Robertson, John. *The Case for the Enlightenment: Scotland and Naples, 1680–1760*. Cambridge and New York: Cambridge University Press, 2005.

Robinson, J. Bradford. "The Jazz Essays of Theodor Adorno: Some Thoughts on Jazz Reception in Weimar Germany." *Popular Music* 13, no. 1 (1994): 1–25.

Robinson, Joseph. "What I Learned in the Lenoir High School Band." *Wilson Quarterly* 19, no. 4 (1995): 102–9.

Ronson, Jon. "Josh Ostrovsky: 'The Internet Is Like a Giant Weird Orgy.'" *Guardian*, November 7, 2015. Accessed June 13, 2017. https://www.theguardian.com/technology/2015/nov/07/josh-ostrovsky-fat-jew-jon-ronson-instagram.

Rorty, Amélie Oksenberg. "From Passions to Emotions and Sentiments." *Philosophy* 57, no. 220 (1982): 159–72.

Rosand, Ellen. "The Descending Tetrachord: An Emblem of Lament." *Musical Quarterly* 65, no. 3 (1979): 346–59.

———. *Opera in Seventeenth-Century Venice: The Creation of a Genre*. Berkeley and Los Angeles: University of California Press, 1991.

Rosen, Christine. "The Age of Egocasting." *New Atlantis* 7 (2004–5): 51–72.

Rosenwein, Barbara H., and Riccardo Cristiani. *What Is the History of Emotions?* Cambridge, UK, and Malden, MA: Polity Press, 2018.

Ross, Andrew. *Nice Work If You Can Get It: Life and Labor in Precarious Times*. New York: New York University Press, 2009.

Rousseau, Jean-Jacques. *Essay on the Origin of Languages and Writings Related to Music*. Translated by John T. Scott. Hanover, NH: University Press of New England, 1998.

Rowland, Ingrid D. *The Ecstatic Journey: Athanasius Kircher in Baroque Rome*. Chicago: University of Chicago Library, 2000.

Rumbaugh, Duane M., James E. King, Michael J. Beran, David A. Washburn, and Kristy L. Gould. "A Salience Theory of Learning and Behavior: With Perspectives on Neurobiology and Cognition." *International Journal of Primatology* 28, no. 5 (October 2007): 973–96.

Sacks, Oliver. *Musicophilia: Tales of Music and the Brain*. New York: Vintage Books, 2008.

Safranski, Rüdiger. *Martin Heidegger: Between Good and Evil*. Cambridge, MA: Harvard University Press, 1998.

Salazar, Philippe-Joseph. *Le culte de la voix au XVIIe siècle: Formes esthétiques de la parole à l'âge de l'imprimé*. Paris: Honoré Champion, 1995.

———. "La voix au XVIIe siècle." In *Histoire de la rhétorique dans l'Europe moderne: 1450–1950*, edited by Marc Fumaroli, 787–821. Paris: Presses Universitaires de France, 1999.

Sardashti, Hasti. *"Short Cuts" and American Life and Society in the Early Nineties*. Central Milton Keynes, UK: AuthorHouse, 2011.

Saxl, Fritz. "Macrocosm and Microcosm in Medieval Pictures." In *Lectures*, vol. 1, 58–72. London: Warburg Institute, 1957.

Scala, Flaminio. *Il teatro delle favole rappresentative, overo La ricreatione comica, boscareccia, e tragica: Divisa in cinquanta giornate*. Venice: Gio. Battista Pulciani, 1611.

Schachter, Stanley, and Jerome Singer. "Cognitive, Social, and Physiological Determinants of Emotional State." *Psychological Review* 69, no. 5 (1962): 379–99.

Schafer, R. Murray. *The Tuning of the World: A Pioneering Exploration into the Past History and Present State of the Most Neglected Aspect of Our Environment—the Environment*. 1st ed. New York: A. A. Knopf, 1977.

Scharlau, Ulf. *Athanasius Kircher (1601–1680) als Musikschriftsteller: Ein Beitrag zur Musikanschauung des Barock*. Marburg: Görich & Weiershäuser, 1969.

Scheer, Monique. "Are Emotions a Kind of Practice (And Is That What Makes Them Have a History)? A Bourdieuian Approach to Understanding Emotion." *History and Theory* 51, no. 2 (2012): 193–220.

Scherer, F. M. *Quarter Notes and Bank Notes: The Economics of Music Composition in the Eighteenth and Nineteenth Centuries*. Princeton, NJ: Princeton University Press, 2004.

Scherzinger, Martin. "Alchemies of Sanctioned Value: Music, Networks, Law." In *Artistic Citizenship: Artistry, Social Responsibility, and Ethical Praxis*, edited by David J. Elliott, Marissa Silverman, and Wayne D. Bowman, 359–80. Oxford and New York: Oxford University Press, 2016.

———. "Algorithmic Audition: Modeling Musical Perception." In *Imagined Forms: Modeling Material Culture*, edited by Martin Brueckner, Sandy Isenstadt, and Sarah Wasserman. Chicago: University of Chicago Press, 2020.

———. "The Executing Machine: Deleuze, Boulez, and the Politics of Desire." In *The Dark Precursor: Deleuze and Artistic Research*, edited by Paulo de Assis and Paolo Giudici, 36–55. Leuven: Leuven University Press, 2017.

———. "On Sonotropism." *Contemporary Music Review* 31, nos. 5–6 (2012): 345–51.

———. "Political Economy of Music Streaming: Distributed Networks, Surveillance, and Automation." In *The Cambridge Companion to Music in Digital Culture*, edited by Nicholas Cook, Monique Marie Ingalls, and David Trippett, 274–97. Cambridge and New York: Cambridge University Press, 2019.

———. "Toward a History of Digital Music: New Technology, Business Practices, and Intellectual Property." In *The Cambridge Companion to Music in Digital Culture*, edited by Nicholas Cook, Monique Marie Ingalls, and David Trippett, 33–57. Cambridge and New York: Cambridge University Press, 2019.

Schopenhauer, Arthur. *The World as Will and Representation*. 2 vols. Translated by E. F. J. Payne. New York: Dover, 1969.

Schüll, Natasha Dow. *Addiction by Design: Machine Gambling in Las Vegas*. Princeton, NJ: Princeton University Press, 2014.

Scott, David. *Gilbert Simondon's Psychic and Collective Individuation: A Critical Introduction and Guide*. Edinburgh: Edinburgh University Press, 2014.

Seabrook, John. "Spotify: Friend or Foe?" *The New Yorker*, November 24, 2014. https://www.newyorker.com/magazine/2014/11/24/revenue-streams.

Sebeok, Thomas A. *Global Semiotics*. Bloomington,: Indiana University Press, 2001.

———. *Signs: An Introduction to Semiotics*. 2nd ed. Toronto: University of Toronto Press, 2001.

Sedgwick, Eve Kosofsky. *Touching Feeling: Affect, Pedagogy, Performativity*. Durham, NC: Duke University Press, 2003.

Sedgwick, Eve Kosofsky, and Adam Frank. "Shame in the Cybernetic Fold: Reading Silvan Tomkins." *Critical Inquiry* 21, no. 2 (1995): 496–522.

Sedgwick, Eve Kosofsky, Adam Frank, and Irving E. Alexander, eds. *Shame and Its Sisters: A Silvan Tomkins Reader*. Durham, NC: Duke University Press, 1995.

Self, Robert T. *Robert Altman's Subliminal Reality*. Minneapolis: University of Minnesota Press, 2002.

Semel, Beth Michelle. "Listening Like a Computer: Computational Psychiatry and the Re-Coding of Psychiatric Screening." Presentation delivered at the Science, Technology and Society Seminar: STS Circle at Harvard, December 2, 2019.

Serafin, Andrzej. "A Reception History of the *Black Notebooks*." *Gatherings: The Heidegger Circle Annual* 5 (2015): 118–42.

Shannon, C. E. "A Mathematical Theory of Communication." *Bell System Technical Journal* 27, no. 3 (1948): 379–423. http://cm.bell-labs.com/cm/ms/what/shannonday/shannon1948.pdf.

Shaviro, Steven. "Consequences of Panpsychism." http://www.shaviro.com/Othertexts/Claremont2010.pdf.

———. "Post-Cinematic Affect: On Grace Jones, Boarding Gate and Southland Tales." *Film-Philosophy* 14, no. 1 (2010): 1–102.

———. *The Universe of Things: On Speculative Realism*. Minneapolis: University of Minnesota Press, 2014.

———. *Without Criteria: Kant, Whitehead, Deleuze, and Aesthetics*. Cambridge, MA: MIT Press, 2009.

Sheff, David. "Phil Collins Interview." *Playboy*, October 1986. Accessed September 24, 2011. https://www.davidsheff.com/phil-collins.

Shirky, Clay. "The Music Business and the Big Flip." January 21, 2003. "Networks, Economics, and Culture" Mailing. Accessed November 23, 2018. http://www.shirky.com/writings/music_flip.html.

Shouse, Eric. "Feeling, Emotion, Affect." *MC Journal* 8, no. 6 (December 2005). http://journal.media-culture.org.au/0512/03-shouse.php.

Silver, Nate. *The Signal and the Noise: Why So Many Predictions Fail—But Some Don't*. New York: Penguin Press.

Silverstein, Michael. "Indexical Order and the Dialectics of Sociolinguistic Life." *Language and Communication* 23, no. 3 (July 1, 2003): 193–229.

———. "Metapragmatic Discourse and Metapragmatic Function." In *Reflexive Language: Reported Speech and Metapragmatics*, edited by John A. Lucy, 33–58. Cambridge and New York: Cambridge University Press, 1993.

Simpson, Lorenzo C. *The Unfinished Project: Toward a Postmetaphysical Humanism.* New York: Routledge, 2001.
"Sitar." Wikipedia. Accessed May 17, 2016. https://en.wikipedia.org/wiki/Sitar.
Smail, Daniel Lord. *On Deep History and the Brain.* Chicago: University of Chicago Press, 2009.
Smart, Mary Ann. *Mimomania: Music and Gesture in Nineteenth-Century Opera.* Berkeley and Los Angeles: University of California Press, 2004.
Smith, Dorothy E. *The Everyday World as Problematic: A Feminist Sociology.* Boston: Northeastern University Press, 1987.
Solomon, Robert C. *The Passions: Emotions and the Meaning of Life.* Indianapolis, IN: Hackett, 1993.
Spence, Lester K. *Stare in the Darkness: The Limits of Hip-Hop and Black Politics.* Minneapolis: University of Minnesota Press, 2011.
Stalley, Richard. "Sophrosyne in Symposium." In *X Symposium Platonicum: The "Symposium"; Proceedings I, Pisa, 15th–20th July, 2013,* 201–4. Pisa, 2013.
Stallman, Richard. "The Gnu Manifesto." gnu.org. First published 1983. Accessed November 23, 2018. https://www.gnu.org/gnu/manifesto.en.html.
Stengers, Isabelle. "A Constructivist Reading of Process and Reality." *Theory, Culture & Society* 25, no. 4 (2008): 91–110.
———. "A Constructivist Reading of Process and Reality." In *The Lure of Whitehead,* edited by Nicholas Gaskill and A. J. Nocek, 43–64. Minneapolis: University of Minnesota Press, 2014.
———. *Thinking with Whitehead: A Free and Wild Creation of Concepts.* Cambridge, MA: Harvard University Press, 2011.
Sterne, Jonathan. *The Audible Past: Cultural Origins of Sound Reproduction.* Durham, NC: Duke University Press, 2003.
———. *MP3: The Meaning of a Format.* Durham, NC: Duke University Press, 2012.
Stewart, Kathleen. *Ordinary Affects.* Durham, NC: Duke University Press, 2007.
Stoller, Paul. *The Taste of Ethnographic Things: The Senses in Anthropology.* Philadelphia: University of Pennsylvania Press, 1989.
Stolzenberg, Daniel, ed. *The Great Art of Knowing: The Baroque Encyclopedia of Athanasius Kircher.* Stanford, CA: Stanford University Libraries, 2001.
Stringer, Omari. "The Sound of Politics: An Examination of Political Orientations and Musical Preferences among College Aged Adults." Honors undergraduate thesis, University of Central Florida, 2017. https://stars.library.ucf.edu/honorstheses/159.
Suárez, Cipriano. *De arte rhetorica libri tres.* Coimbra: Juan de Barreira, 1562.
Sulzer, Johann Georg, and Heinrich Christoph Koch. *Aesthetics and the Art of Musical Composition in the German Enlightenment: Selected Writings of Johann Georg Sulzer and Heinrich Christoph Koch.* Edited and translated by Nancy Kovaleff Baker and Thomas Street Christensen. Cambridge and New York: Cambridge University Press, 1995.
Sulzer, Johann Georg, Johann Abraham Peter Schulz, and Johann Philipp Kirnberger. *Allgemeine Theorie der schönen Künste in Einzeln: Nach alphabetischer Ordnung der Kunstwörter auf einander folgenden, Artikeln abgehandelt, Erster Theil.* Edited by Christian Friedrich von Blankenburg. Hildesheim: G. Olms, 1967–70.
Sulzer, Johann Georg. *Allgemeine Theorie der schönen Künste in einzeln, nach alphabetischer Ordnung der Kunstwörter auf einander folgenden, Artikeln abgehandelt, Erster Theil.* Leipzig: M. G. Weidmanns Erben & Reich, 1774.
Tapscott, Don. *The Digital Economy: Promise and Peril in the Age of Networked Intelligence.* New York: McGraw-Hill, 1995.

Taussig, Michael T. *Mimesis and Alterity: A Particular History of the Senses*. New York: Routledge, 1993.
Taylor, Larissa. "Dangerous Vocations: Preaching in France in the Late Middle Ages and Reformations." In *Preachers and People in the Reformations and Early Modern Period*, edited by Larissa Taylor, 91–124. Boston,: Brill Academic, 2003.
Than, Ker. "Stone Age Art Caves May Have Been Concert Halls." *National Geographic News*, October 28, 2010, 1.
Thomas Aquinas. *Summa Theologica*. Edited by Fathers of the English Dominican Province. 5 vols. New York: Benziger Brothers, 1948.
Thompson, Emily. *The Soundscape of Modernity: Architectural Acoustics and the Culture of Listening in America, 1900–1933*. Cambridge, MA: MIT Press, 2002.
Thompson, Marie, and Ian D. Biddle, eds. *Sound, Music, Affect: Theorizing Sonic Experience*. New York: Bloomsbury Academic, 2013.
Thrift, Nigel. "Intensities of Feeling: Towards a Spatial Politics of Affect." *Geografiska Annaler: Series B, Human Geography* 86, no. 1 (2004): 57–78.
Tomkins, Silvan S. *Affect, Imagery, Consciousness*. 4 vols. New York: Springer, 1962–92).
Tomkins, Silvan S. *Affect Imagery Consciousness: The Complete Edition*. 2 vols. New York: Springer, 2008.
Tomlinson, Gary. *Culture and the Course of Human Evolution*. Chicago: University of Chicago Press, 2018.
———. "Evolutionary Studies in the Humanities: The Case of Music." *Critical Inquiry* 39, no. 4 (2013): 647–75.
———. *A Million Years of Music: The Emergence of Human Modernity*. 1st ed. New York: Zone Books, 2015.
———. *Music in Renaissance Magic: Toward a Historiography of Others*. Chicago: University of Chicago Press, 1993.
Trawny, Peter. *Freedom to Fail: Heidegger's Anarchy*. English ed. Cambridge, UK, and Malden, MA: Polity Press, 2015.
———. *Heidegger and the Myth of a Jewish World Conspiracy*. Translated by Andrew J. Mitchell. Chicago: University of Chicago Press, 2015.
———. "Heidegger, 'World Judaism,' and Modernity." *Gatherings: The Heidegger Circle Annual* 5 (2015): 1–20.
Tucker, Mark, ed. *The Duke Ellington Reader*. Oxford and New York: Oxford University Press, 1993.
Turino, Thomas. *Music as Social Life: The Politics of Participation*. Chicago: University of Chicago Press, 2008.
———. "Peircean Thought as Core Theory for a Phenomenological Ethnomusicology." *Ethnomusicology* 58, no. 2 (2014): 185–221.
———. "Signs of Imagination, Identity, and Experience: A Peircian Semiotic Theory for Music." *Ethnomusicology* 43, no. 2 (1999): 221–55.
Uexküll, Jakob von. *"A Foray into the Worlds of Animals and Humans," with "A Theory of Meaning."* Translated by Joseph D. O'Neil. Minneapolis: University of Minnesota Press, 2010.
"Understanding People through Music: Millennial Edition." Spotify. Accessed September 14, 2017. https://www.spotifyforbrands.com/sv-SE/news/understanding-people-through-music-millennial-edition/.
Valladier, André. *Partitiones oratoriae, seu De oratores perfecto*. Paris: Pierre Chevalier, 1621.
Vallega-Neu, Daniela. *Heidegger's "Contributions to Philosophy": An Introduction*. Bloomington,: Indiana University Press, 2003.

———. "Heidegger's Poietic Writings: From *Contributions to Philosophy* to *Das Ereignis*." In *Heidegger and Language*, edited by Jeffrey Powell, 119–45. Bloomington: Indiana University Press, 2013.

———. "Heidegger's Reticence: From *Contributions* to *Das Ereignis* and toward *Gelassenheit*." *Research in Phenomenology* 45, no. 1 (2015): 1–32.

Van Breda, H. L. "Le sauvetage de l'héritage husserlien et la fondation des Archives-Husserl." In *Husserl et la pensée moderne/Husserl und das Denken der Neuzeit*, edited by H. L. Van Breda and J. Taminaux. The Hague: Martinus Nijhoff, 1959.

van Elferen, Isabella. "Affective Discourse in German Baroque Text-Based Music." *Tijdschrift voor muziektheorie*. 9, no. 3 (2004): 217–33.

Vandenberghe, Frédéric. "Deleuzian Capitalism." *Philosophy and Social Criticism* 34, no. 8 (2008): 877–903.

Varwig, Bettina. "Heartfelt Musicking: The Physiology of a Bach Cantata." *Representations* 143, no. 1 (2018): 36–62.

———. "'Mutato Semper Habitu': Heinrich Schütz and the Culture of Rhetoric." *Music & Letters* 90, no. 2 (2009): 215–39.

———. "One More Time: J. S. Bach and Seventeenth-Century Traditions of Rhetoric." *Eighteenth-Century Music* 5, no. 2 (2008): 179–208.

Vickers, Brian. *In Defence of Rhetoric*. Oxford and New York: Clarendon Press, 1988.

Villegas Vélez, Daniel. "Mimetologies: Aesthetic Politics in Early Modern Opera." Ph.D. diss., University of Pennsylvania, 2016.

Virno, Paolo. "Post-Fordist Semblance." Translated by Max Henninger. *SubStance* issue 112 (vol. 36, no. 1) (2007): 42–46.

Voegelin, Salomé. *Listening to Noise and Silence: Towards a Philosophy of Sound Art*. New York: Continuum, 2010.

Wackenroder, Wilhelm Heinrich. *Confessions and Fantasies*. Translated by Mary Hurst Schubert. University Park: Pennsylvania State University Press, 1971.

Wagner, Richard. *Richard Wagner to Mathilde Wesendonck*. Translated by William Ashton Ellis. 2nd ed. New York: Charles Scribner's Sons, 1905.

Wald-Fuhrmann, Melanie. *Welterkenntnis aus Musik: Athanasius Kirchers "Musurgia Universalis" und die Universalwissenschaft im 17. Jahrhundert*. Kassel: Bärenreiter, 2006.

Walker, D. P. *Spiritual and Demonic Magic: From Ficino to Campanella*. 2nd ed. Notre Dame, IN: University of Notre Dame Press, 1975.

Walker, Thomas, and Irene Alm. "Cavalli, Francesco." *Grove Music Online*. Oxford University Press. Accessed July 10, 2017. http://www.oxfordmusiconline.com/subscriber/article/grove/music/05207.

Warburg, Aby. *Der Bilderatlas Mnemosyne*. Vol. 2, 1 of *Gesammelte Schriften*. Edited by Martin Warnke and Claudia Brink. 3rd ed. Berlin: Akademie Verlag, 2008.

Weil, Simone, and Rachel Bespaloff. *War and the Iliad*. Translated by Mary McCarthy. Introduction by Christopher Benfey. Afterword by Herman Broch. New York: New York Review of Books, 2005.

Welton, Donn, ed. *The Body: Classic and Contemporary Readings*. Malden, MA: Blackwell, 1999.

Whitehead, Alfred North. *Adventures of Ideas*. New York: Free Press, 1967.

———. *The Concept of Nature: The Tarner Lectures Delivered in Trinity College, November 1919*. Mineola, NY: Dover, 2004.

———. *Modes of Thought*. New York: Free Press, 1966.

———. *Process and Reality: An Essay in Cosmology*. Corrected ed. Edited by David Ray Griffin and Donald W. Sherburne. New York: Free Press, 1978.

———. *Science and the Modern World*. New York: Free Press, 1967.
———. *Symbolism: Its Meaning and Effect*. New York: Capricorn Books, 1959.
Whitmore, P. J. S. *The Order of Minims in Seventeenth-Century France*. The Hague: Martinus Nijhoff, 1967.
Wilbourne, Emily. "Breastmilk, Exposed Bodies, and the Politics of the Indecent." *Echo: A Music-Centered Journal* 14, no. 1 (2016). http://www.echo.ucla.edu/volume-14-1-2016/article-breastmilk-exposed-bodies-politics-indecent/.
———. "Demo's Stutter, Subjectivity, and the Virtuosity of Vocal Failure." In "Colloquy: Why Voice Now?," edited by Martha Feldman. *Journal of the American Musicological Society* 68, no. 3 (2015): 659–63.
———. *Seventeenth-Century Opera and the Sound of the Commedia dell'Arte*. Chicago: University of Chicago Press, 2016.
Wilfing, Alexander. "Hanslick, Kant, and the Origins of *Vom Musikalisch-Schönen*." *Musicologica Austriaca*. Accessed February 18, 2020. http://www.musau.org//parts/neue-article-page/view/47.
Williams, Raymond L. "Structures of Feeling." In *Marxism and Literature*, 128–35. Oxford and New York: Oxford University Press, 1977.
Winnubst, Shannon. "The Queer Thing about Neoliberal Pleasure: A Foucauldian Warning." *Foucault Studies* 14 (September 2012): 79–97.
———. *Way Too Cool: Selling Out Race and Ethics*. New York: Columbia University Press, 2015.
Wiskus, Jessica. *The Rhythm of Thought: Art, Literature, and Music after Merleau-Ponty*. Chicago: University of Chicago Press, 2013.
Wittgenstein, Ludwig. *Tractatus Logico-Philosophicus*. Translated by C. K. Ogden. London: Routledge & Kegan Paul, 1922.
Wolfe, Cary. *What Is Posthumanism?* Posthumanities 8. Minneapolis: University of Minnesota Press, 2010.
Wynter, Sylvia. "Unsettling the Coloniality of Being/Power/Truth/Freedom: Towards the Human, after Man, Its Overrepresentation—An Argument." *CR: The New Centennial Review* 3, no. 3 (2003): 257–337.
Yates, Frances A. *Giordano Bruno and the Hermetic Tradition*. Chicago: University of Chicago Press, 1964.
Zielinski, Siegfried. *Deep Time of the Media: Toward an Archaeology of Hearing and Seeing by Technical Means*. Translated by Gloria Custance. Cambridge, MA: MIT Press, 2006.
Žižek, Slavoj. *Organs without Bodies: On Deleuze and Consequences*. New York: Routledge, 2004.
Zuboff, Shoshana. *The Age of Surveillance Capitalism: The Fight for a Human Future at the New Frontier of Power*. London: Profile Books, 2019.
Zupančič, Alenka. *The Odd One In: On Comedy*. Cambridge, MA: MIT Press, 2008.

INDEX

Page numbers with an *f* refer to a figure or a caption.

Abbate, Carolyn, 214
Acoustic Technics (Ihde), 104
Acoustocene, definition of, x
Adderley, Cannonball, 241–42
Adkins, Lisa, 37
Adorno, Theodor W., 213; background of, 14–15, 159–60; DeNora contrasted with, 167, 169–70; *Dialectics of Enlightenment*, 163; on emotional listeners, 164–65; homogenization of 1930s/40s, 171; on jazz, 163, 166, 239–40; Kantian philosophy impact on, 346; on mass-mediated cultural meanings, 169–70, 178; on mass-scale production/uniformity, 171, 176–77; political effects of, 166–67; on popular music, 185; "On Popular Music," 164; on rhythmically obedient listeners, 165–66; on standardization under monopoly capital, 208
Adventures of Ideas (Whitehead), 273
affect: affections vs., 314–15; and affective turn, 1–2; *affetto*, 325; algorithmic management of, 188; autonomy of, 18–19, 271, 275, 282, 283n11; in Beethoven's Fifth Symphony, 11; behaviors influenced by, 8; decline of, 344–45, 354–55; definition of, 318; and emotion, 159–60; evolution of, 212–13; evolution of emotions/values over time, 20, 32n63; felt vs. attributed, 162; individual vs. transpersonal, 9–10; infant/childhood development of, 147–48; and key/chord taxonomy, 8–9; Kircher on, 313; listener's inner life vs., 345; mimesis and (*see* mimesis); as *musica poetica*, 320n5; and negative impact on women and people of color, 284n52; polarization of, 21; as raw experiences/intensities of sensation relationship, 161; in Renaissance thought, 6; role of pitch in, 8; since World War II, 17; tonally moving forms in, 12; "two-factor" theory of, 162. See also *Affektenlehre*; Galenic humoral medicine
affect (and Bernhard's *Correction*), 231–33; refuting subjectivization of, 224–27; subjectivity and life course, 227–30; "subliminal messages/subliminal reality, 231, 236n25; summary, 27, 233–34. See also Massumi, Brian
affect (labor): background of, 27–28; in emotional/personality tests, 216; and empiricism, 218; industrialized, 215–19; and lie detection, 216; and Marxism, 207–9; and materialism, 217–18; and military-industrial complex, 215–16; in music studies, 217; networked, 198; and semiophobia, 218; social media/online music, 201–4; as sonotropic

affect (labor) (*continued*)
  default, 211–15; user surveillance and preference profiles (*see* users); virtual reality (*see* virtual reality); as weapon, 197
affect, Merleau-Ponty on. *See* Merleau-Ponty, Maurice
affect, nonhuman: causal covariance, 83; coevolutionary feedback, 79; conventionalization, 84; difficulties of ubiquitous agency, 81–84; of flowers and animal pollinators, 79–81; human-nonhuman discontinuity, 81; panpsychism, 84, 85; prehensions, 80, 84; of rocks/inanimate objects, 84–86; semiosis limited to humans, 81; sign and information, 76–79; and signification, 87; and territorialization/deterritorialization/reterritorialization, 88
affect concepts and debates: history of, 20–22; landmarks, 18–19; publications of, 22–25
affections: affect vs., 314–15; Scharlau on, 316–17; theory of, 305, 314
affective domain, 18, 22
"Affective Labors" (Hardt), 23
affective sonic intensity, 109–10
affect studies/theory, ix–x, 1–3; as academic fad, 108–9, 133–34; forerunners of, 16; Leys's critique of, 82; Massumi on, 309; and neoliberalism, 134; and representation, 304, 307
affect theory, modifications to. *See* Whitehead, Alfred North
Affektenlehre (Doctrine of Affects), 8–9, 14; background of, 340n4, 342; Buelow on, 343; date of decline, 344–45; definition of, 343–44; evolution of, 212–13; German Idealism as replacement for, 355, 357n11; German view of, 344; Grant on, 356n5; Kantian philosophy impact on, 345–46, 354–55; rhetoric in, 349–50; sonatas, symphonies, chamber music as forcing reevaluation of, 357n7; as twentieth-century concept, 30n22. *See also* Kant, Immanuel
After Finitude (Meillassoux), 91, 93
"Against Interpretation" (Sontag), 214

Ahmed, Sara, 1–2, 24, 273; *The Cultural Politics of Emotions*, 22
"Alright" (Lamar), 232
alternate reality. *See* virtual reality
Althusser, Louis, 163, 208
Altman, Robert: *Nashville*, 227, 231, 232
Alvarado, Alphonso: *Artium disserendi ac dicendi libero duo*, 296
Amoore, Louise, 37
Analog Days (Pinch and Trocco), 105
Antonazzoni, Marina Dorotea, 331
Apel, Karl-Otto, 17, 145
Apple Music, 220n8
Arendt, Hannah, x, 207
Argos (dog), 146–47
Aristotle, 3; on aesthetic education, 5; on music as respite, 135n4; on musical education, 5–6; *Poetics*, 4–5, 19; *Politics*, 5, 19, 135n4; on potentiality vs. actuality, 321n11; *Rhetoric*, 19, 24; on tragedy, 4–5; voice of, 143
Armstrong, Louis: "Potato Head Blues," 248–49
Arnold, Matthew, 179
Artium disserendi ac dicendi libero duo (Alvarado), 296
Ascent of Affect, The: Genealogy and Critique (Leys), 21
Attali, Jacques, 15, 39; on historical change, 181; on music stockpiling, 183; *Noise* or *Bruits*, 45; on statistical modeling of noise, 45–46
Auberoche, Pierre d', 296
Audible Past, The (Sterne), 16, 326
Augoyard, François, on anamnesis (loss of forgetfulness), 227, 230, 233
"Autonomy of Affect, The" (Massumi), 18–19

Badiou, Alain, 91, 214, 218
Barenboim, Daniel: Anglo-American musicology role, 112–13; as buffoon, 120; coherence of, 126; on expression, 130–31; humor of, 122; language of, 111–12, 123–24, 127–28; music as profession/music as way of life, 26, 112, 128; on music as respite, 113–14; music as weapon, 115–18; musical life

vs. extramusical life, 110–11, 114, 118, 126; professionalism or lack of, 113–15; Reith Lectures, 110, 113, 119, 122, 126; as Romantic Existentialist, 110; sonic gravity theory (musical performance theory), 110–11, 129
Baricco, Alessandro, 145, 173
Bartel, Dietrich, 320n5, 344
Barthes, Roland, 144, 213
Baudelaire, Charles, 13
Baudrillard, Jean, 177; *Simulacra and Simulation*, 210
Beauvoir, Simone de, 17
Becker, Gary, 37, 44, 45–46, 47–48
Beethoven, Ludwig van, 203, 344–45
Being and Time (Heidegger), 58, 60, 66
Benjamin, Walter: on contagion, 308; "The Work of Art in the Age of Technical Reproducibility," 214
Benkler, Yochai, 203
Bentham, Jeremy, 244
Berenstein, Nadia, 163
Bergson, Henri, 1–2, 18, 19, 229; influence on Whitehead, 273
Berio, Luciano, 214
Berlant, Lauren, 1–2; *Cruel Optimism*, 23–24; historical affect of, 10; *The Queen of America Goes to Washington City: Essays on Sex and Citizenship*, 23
Berlinger, Joseph, 11
Bernard, Jonathan, 272
Bernhard, Thomas: *Correction*, 227–30, 234
Beyond Verbal, 216
Biddle, Ian, 214
Bijsterveld, Karin, 106
Billboard Top 40, 175
"Biographical Sketch of an Infant, A" (Darwin), 147–48
Bloch, Ernst, 15, 213
Boddice, Rob, 20
Boethius, 293
Bostrom, Nick, 209
Boulez, Pierre, 214
Bourdieu, Pierre, 29, 143, 151–52, 208, 326, 339
Boysen, Benjamin, 218
Brentano, Franz, 86

Brown, Clifford, 239
Bruno, Giordano, 309–10
Brunschvicg, Léon, 253
Bucher, Taina, 187
Buelow, George, 8–9, 30n22, 320n5, 343
Burrower, The (Kafka), 225
Butler, Judith, 153, 163

Caccini, Giulio: expressive techniques used by, 325, 339; as foremost opera composer, 326; *Le nuove musiche*, 325, 326
Calcagno, Mauro, 336
Calvino, Italo, 152–53
Cantor, Georg, 91
capitalism, 187–89; deliberate shaping of consumer taste, 163–71, 176; developing user preference profiles, 176–86; diversification/niche markets, 171–73; homogenization of musical taste, 159–61; human/nonhuman-technology blurring, 188; labor-leisure blurring of, 178–79; Marxism vs., 207–8; and mass-scale marketing/production, 171; modernity/cultural impact on vision, 161–63; music ownership/relinquishment of, 173–74, 191n57; selling listeners to advertisers, 182; streaming (*see* streaming); technology changes, 173–76; user surveillance, 178. See also Adorno, Theodor W.; DeNora, Tia; social media
Carney, Harry, 242
Carson, Ann, 41
Carter, James, 243
Cassirer, Ernst, 75
cathedral music, prehistoric cave parallels to, 100
Caussin, Nicolas, 23, 295, 296–97
Cavalli, Francesco: *Il Giasone* (opera), 327–39, 330*f*, 332–34*f*; musical and dramatic standards codified by, 326
Cavarero, Adriana, 156
cave art, 100, 105
Cavell, Stanley: *A Pitch of Philosophy*, 150
censorship, Plato on, 4
Chion, Michel, 213
Chua, Daniel K. L., 306–7

Chude-Sokei, Louis, 188
Cicero, 298
Cicognini, Giacinto Andrea, 327, 336
Clément, Catherine, 87–88
Clough, Patricia Ticento, 1–2, 214
Clover, Joshua, 232
Cogito, 216
Cohen, Alix: *Thinking About the Emotions: A Philosophical History*, 21–22
Cohen, Leonard, 1, 51
Coleman, Ornette, 241–42
Collins, Phil, 27, 227, 233; "Doesn't Anybody Stay Together Anymore?," 232; *Face Value* (album), 232; *Hello I Must Be Going* (album), 232; "In the Air Tonight," 27, 232; *No Jacket Required* (album), 232
Collins, Suzanne: *The Hunger Games*, 204
Coltrane, John, 241–42
Compendium musicae (Descartes), 6
Concept of Nature, The (Whitehead), 274–75
Concerto for Cootie (Ellington), 243
Condillac, Étienne Bonnot de, 149
Connolly, William, 82–84
consciousness, 254–55, 265n11; and depth perception, 255–57; flesh as embodiment of, 260; as lack of separation, 255–56; music and affect, 262–64; past, present, and future, 258–59; and rhythm, 261; separation and depth, 256–58; Swann and Odette as symbols in, 262–64; transcendence and time, 258–62. *See also* Merleau-Ponty, Maurice
Cooper, Melinda, 37; *Life as Surplus*, 54n29
copyright issues, 159, 174–76
Correction (Bernhard), 227–30, 234
cost/benefit analysis: neoliberalism, 37–39; in rap music, 39, 48–50
Coste, Hilarion de, 296–97
covariance, causal, 78
Cox, Christoph, 225
Cramoisy, Sebastien, 296
Cressolles, Louis de: *Vacationes autumnales*, 296, 297

Crisis (Husserl), 253
Cristiani, Riccardo: *What Is the History of Emotions?*, 21
Critique of Practical Reason (*Kritik der praktischen Vernunft*; Kant), 350, 352
Critique of Pure Reason (*Kritik der reinen Vernunft*; Kant), 352
Critique of the Power of Judgment (*Kritik der Urteilskraft*; Kant), 345–46, 352–53, 355, 357n11
Cruel Optimism (Berlant), 23–24
Cultural Politics of Emotions, The (Ahmed), 22
Cumming, Naomi, 75, 226–27

Dahlhaus, Carl, 9–10, 12
Damasio, Antonio, 1–2; *Descartes' Error: Emotion, Reason, and the Human Brain*, 19
Dammann, Guy, 120, 121
dancing: evidence of, 102; jitterbug dancers, 165–66
Darwin, Charles, 20–21, 132; "A Biographical Sketch of an Infant," 147–48; shortcomings of, 98n49; on variation-with-selection, 92–93
Das neu-eroffnete Orchestre (Mattheson), 8
Davis, Miles, 239
Da vita coelitus comparanda (Ficino), 7
Dean, Jodi, 199–200
Dear, Peter, 295
Deee-Lite (band): "Groove Is in the Heart," 232
Deleuze, Gilles, 1–2, 16, 18, 19, 130, 131–32; on animal affect, 87; on assemblage, 87–88, 274; on closing off, 131; on controls, 181; on desiring machines, 211; on "desiring-production," 200; on deterritorializing musical affect, 279; *Difference and Repetition*, 279; on events, 279–80; *The Fold: Leibniz and the Baroque*, 279; intensity of, 124; on past and present, 233–34; philosophy of virtuality, 304; on societies of control, 179; on *Swann's Way*, 280–81; *A Thousand Plateaus: Capitalism and Schizophrenia*, 72, 76, 80, 87, 224–25; trans-

position of modernist musical terms by, 214
Demosthenes, 296, 302n39
DeNora, Tia, 159–60, 185–86; Adorno contrasted with, 167, 169–70; on deliberate shaping of consumer taste, 177; interviews by, 167, 187; on listener practices, 167–68; on mass-mediated cultural meanings, 169–70; on music as magic mirror, 226; on music as prosthesis, 184; *Music in Everyday Life*, 16, 17, 167; on production flexibility, 171–72; on self-identity/self-making, 167–69, 190n32; on self-regulation, 167–68
Derrida, Jacques: on accents, 153–54; on "danger" of Heidegger, 67n9; *Monolingualism of the Other*, 156; *Of Grammatology*, 150; in the public sphere, 156
Descartes, René: about, 273; *Compendium musicae*, 6; dualism of, 254; education of, 295, 301n31; Merleau-Ponty's critique of, 255; on musical structure, 9; *On the Passions of the Soul*, 8; on physiological responses to music, 212
Descartes' Error: Emotion, Reason, and the Human Brain (Damasio), 19
de Warren, Nicolas, 266n32
Dialectics of Enlightenment (Adorno and Horkheimer), 163
Difference and Repetition (Deleuze), 279
Discipline and Punish (Foucault), 199
Discourse on the Origin and Basis of Inequality (Rousseau), 148
Dixon, Thomas, 8, 19, 20
Djibo (Songhay teacher), 162–63
Doctrine of Affects (*Affektenlehre*). See *Affektenlehre*
"Doesn't Anybody Stay Together Anymore?" (Collins), 232

Echo Nest (music quantification program), 183
Eidsheim, Nina: "Sensing Voice: Materiality and the Lived Body in Singing and Listening," 16–17
Ek, Daniel, 175
Elias, Norbert, 208

Ellington, Duke: as composer, 242–43; *Concerto for Cootie*, 243
embodiment relations, definition of, 105
emotion: algorithmic management of, 188; definition of, 314–15. *See also* affect
Emotion and Meaning in Music (Meyer), 75
Engels, Friedrich, 207
Erlmann, Veit: *Reason and Resonance: A History of Aurality*, ix
Eryximachus, 42
Eshun, Kodwo, 233
"Essay on the Origin of Languages" (Rousseau), 148, 150
Ethics (Spinoza), 87
Every Noise at Once (website), 182–83

Facebook, 178, 201–2, 220n8
Face Value (album; Collins), 232
Fanon, Franz, 163
Fantasies on Art (Wackenroder), 11
Faye, Emmanuel, 65–66
Feld, Steven, 2
Ferrell, Jonathan, 50
Ficino, Marsilio: on affective power of music, 7–8; *Da vita coelitus comparanda*, 7–8; on song's affective power, 310–11; Tomlinson on, 30n14
Figal, Günter, 56
Filelfo, 293
Fink, Eugen, 17
Firth, Colin, 142
Flaubert, Gustave, 13
Fludd, Robert, 299
Fodor, Jerry, 78
Fold, The: Leibniz and the Baroque (Deleuze), 279
Forkel, Johann Nicolaus, 12
Foucault, Michel: on channeling labor, 181; and Derrida, 154; on discipline, 208; *Discipline and Punish*, 199; on entrepreneurship limits, 47; on neoliberalism, 43; on Renaissance vs. classical regimes of knowledge, 29, 303, 304, 320n5; on sophrosyne (moderation), 40–41, 52n7; voice of, 143–44
Fragility of Goodness, The (Nussbaum), 25

Frank, Adam, 19, 21; on bodily/materialist perspective on affect, 18; "Shame in the Cybernetic Fold: Reading Silvan Tomkins," 18

Frazer, James George, 310

From Guilt to Shame: Auschwitz and After (Leys), 24

Fumaroli, Marc, 291, 296–97

Gadamer, Hans-Georg, 227, 250

Galenic humoral medicine, 6–7, 310–13, 314

Galloway, Alexander, 218

Garcia, Luis-Manuel, 232

Gehlen, Arnold, 17

General Theory of the Fine Arts (*Allgemeine Theorie der schönen Künste*; Sulzer), 349, 351

George VI, King of England, 142

German Idealism, as *Affektenlehre* replacement, 355

Gesualdo, Carlo, 305, 317–18

Get Out (film), 209

Getz, Stan, 242

Giacomini, Lorenzo, 212

Giasone, Il (opera), 327–39; Besso (male character), 327; Demo (servant), 328; Egeo (male character), 328, 333; Ercole (character), 328, 329; Giasone (Jason; lead male character), 327–31, 333, 336–37; Isifile (lead female character), 327–33, 332–34f, 335–38; Medea, Queen of Colchis (lead female character), 327–31, 330f, 333; as most frequently performed opera of seventeenth century, 340n10; musical crafting of emotion in, 329, 331, 335–37; Oreste (servant), 328; status as mother (plot), 337–38; unfaithful lovers/unrequited love (plot), 327–36

Gibbs, Anna, 308–9, 315, 317, 322n25, 324n53

Gilbert, Jeremy, 88

Gilroy, Paul, 249–50

Glass, Philip, 104–5

GNU ("Gnu's not Unix!") Manifesto, 202

Goldie, Peter: *The Oxford Handbook of Philosophy of Emotion*, 21–22

Goodman, Steve (Kode9), 214; on affect and conscious experience, 225; on human receptivity, 224; influence on Whitehead, 272; *Sonic Warfare: Sound, Affect, and the Ecology of Fear*, 16

Google+, 201

Gopnik, Adam, 200

Gordon, Dexter, 241–42

Gossett, Che, 55n45

Gouk, Penelope, 6, 8

Grant, Roger Mathew, 212, 356n5

"Groove Is in the Heart" (Deee-Lite), 232

Gross, Daniel M., 19; on political rhetoric, 20; *Uncomfortable Situations: Emotion between Science and the Humanities*, 24

Grosz, Elizabeth, 124, 129–30, 131–32

Groundwork of the Metaphysics of Morals (*Grundlegung zur Metaphysik der Sitten*; Kant), 350

Guattari, Félix, 16, 130; on animal affect, 87; on assemblage, 87–88, 274; on closing off, 131; on desiring machines, 211; on "desiring-production," 200; *A Thousand Plateaus: Capitalism and Schizophrenia*, 72, 76, 80, 87, 224–25; transposition of modernist musical terms by, 214

Guetta, David, 50

Guiraud, Pierre, 152

Gumbrecht, Hans-Ulrich, 211–12

Habermas, Jürgen, 17, 154–56

Hainge, Greg, 225

Hanslick, Eduard: on *Affektenlehre*, 342, 356n3; Cassirer's philosophy reconciled with, 75; *On the Musically Beautiful*, 12; on power of feeling, 12

Haraway, Donna, 183, 187, 188

Hardt, Michael: "Affective Labors," 23

Harman, Graham, 85, 86, 91

Harmonie universelle (Mersenne), 289, 292, 296

harmony: ancient Greek vs. contemporary Western views on, 41–43, 54n22; geometric ratios vs. frequency ratios, 47; as mathematical relationships among interacting sound frequen-

cies, 45; as relationship among sound waves, 38
Harper, Adam, 214
Harrison, George, 106
Hasty, Christopher, 272
Haydn, Franz Joseph, 344–45
Hearn, Alison, 178–79
Hegel, G. W. F., 72; on crucifixion, 10–11; Kantian philosophy impact on, 346; *Phenomenology of Spirit*, 11; *Philosophy of Mind*, 12–13
Heidegger, Martin
  Being and Time, 58, 60, 66
  "Being and Truth" lectures, 57–58
  Black Notebooks: anti-Semitism in, 25–26, 56; background of, 25–26, 56–58; capacity for silence, 57–61; as difficult reading, 61, 68n15; as performance of silence, 61–65; on World War II destruction as emergency, 62
  correlationism, 72
  dangerous thinking of, 67n9
  ethics of, 66
  implementation of Aryanization laws by, 57
  on language as distinguishing humans from animals, 59
  mention, 1–2, 17, 72
  political involvement of, 62–63, 65
  sigetics (silent thinking), 26, 56–57
  on silence as circular argument, 58–59
  on silence of the hidden Germans, 57
  tool analysis of, 86
  voice of, 64, 143–44
Heinichen, Johann David, 212
Heller, Wendy, 329, 335–36
Hello I Must Be Going (album; Collins), 232
Henke, Robert, 331
Hennion, Antoine, 278
Henriques, Julian, 214
History of Emotions, The (Plamper), 20–21
Hitchcock, H. Wiley, 325
Hitler, Adolf, ix
Hobbes, Thomas: *Leviathan*, ix
Hochschild, Arlie Russell: *The Managed Heart: Commercialization of Human Feelings*, 22–23
Hodges, Johnny (Rabbit), 241–42
Hoffmann, E. T. A., 11, 12–13
Homer: *Iliad*, 145–46; *Odyssey*, 145–47
Horkheimer, Max: *Dialectics of Enlightenment*, 163; on mass-scale production/uniformity, 171, 176–77; on standardization under monopoly capital, 208
Hulse, Brian, 214
Hume, David, 273; on beauty and utility, 348–49; on causality, 91; influence on Whitehead, 273; Kant's response to, 359n38
Hunger Games, The (book; Collins), 204
Hunger Games, The (film), 204–6
Husserl, Edmund, 17, 86; *Crisis*, 253; critique by Merleau-Ponty, 265n9; de Warren on, 266n32; *Ideas*, 253; influence on Merleau-Ponty, 253, 259

Ideas (Husserl), 253
Ihde, Don, 2, 15–16; *Acoustic Technics*, 104
Iliad (Homer), 145–46
Inception (film), 209
incorporeal materialism: Kircher on, 313–14; Massumi on, 309–10
Instagram, 220n8
institutioni harmoniche, Le (Zarlino), 8
Institutio oratoria (Quintilian), 292, 298
instruments: ancient, 101–2; in cliff paintings, 101; digital/electronic, 104–5, 106; flutes/woodwinds, 41–42, 54n22, 100, 105; harmony produced by, 41–42, 54n22; keyboards, 102–3, 105, 106–7; playing skills, 102, 103, 105, 106; prehistoric, 100; recent, 102–3; resonators, 101, 102; stringed, 54n22, 101, 106; studiolike control board as, 105; synthesizers, digital/Moog/Buchla/hybrid, 103–5; theremin, 103; tuning, 100, 102, 105
Interspeed, 216
"In the Air Tonight" (Collins), 232
Italian opera, 17th century: *affetto* (affect) and gestures in, 325–26, 338–39; background of, 325–27; commedia dell'arte in, 328, 331; copiousness of, 331; *Il Gia-*

Italian opera, 17th century (*continued*) sone (see *Giasone, Il*); print as recording device, 339
Izambard, Georges, 125

James, Robin: *Resilience and Melancholy*, 49; *The Sonic Episteme: Acoustic Resonance, Neoliberalism, and Biopolitics*, 2
James, William, 273
Jameson, Fredric, 13–14, 45
Jaspers, Karl, 67n9
jazz improvisation: Adorno's diatribes against, 15; aesthetic contract in, 249; African American values in, 241–42; as collaborative, 249; ethics of, 246, 249–50; fitting response, 239, 243–46, 247–48, 250; freedom vs. constraint, 243–46, 247–48; graphocentrism, 241; learning by example, 247; "legit" sound, 250n6; moral rules/judgment, 244–45; musician's "sound," 239; negotiation in, 249; performer's sound as central component, 239, 242–43; phronesis/judgment, 244–45; pitch as sound type, 240–41; rule-based approaches, 244–46; social positioning in, 242; timbre/timbral improvisation, 240, 241, 242, 243, 251n8; tonal criteria, 250n6; tone color in, 243, 251n8; vocalized tonal qualities in, 242. See also notation/score
Jesuit rhetoric: accents, 294; affective voice, 291–95; background of, 289–91; body language, 294–95; delivery of, 295–98, 302nn39–40; emotional persuasion in, 295, 301n28; passions, 293–94, 296; physical/physiological dimensions of, 291, 292–93; pulse and anger in, 292–93; summary, 288–89; Thomistic doctrine in, 293–94, 300n20; vocal inflections, 292, 296; vocal sounds and pitch, 291; volume and quality, 292. See also Mersenne, Marin
Jones, Richard Elfyn, 272

Kafka, Franz: *The Burrower*, 225; "Silence of the Sirens," 146
Kane, Brian, 225

Kant, Immanuel: on aesthetics, 351; *Affektenlehre* decline under, 344–45, 354–55; on beauty and interest, 348, 353, 358n26; conflicted views of music, 346–48; *Critique of Practical Reason* (*Kritik der praktischen Vernunft*), 350, 352; *Critique of Pure Reason* (*Kritik der reinen Vernunft*), 352; *Critique of the Power of Judgment* (*Kritik der Urteilskraft*), 345–46, 352–53, 355; on freedom and necessity, 351–54; *Groundwork of the Metaphysics of Morals* (*Grundlegung zur Metaphysik der Sitten*), 350; influence on Whitehead, 273; on interest, 348–49; on jokes, 358n20; on morality, 243–44, 350; on music, 354–55; on the natural world, 352; on poetry, 346, 354; responses to Hume and Rousseau, 359n38; on rhetoric, 349–50, 353–54; on taste, beauty, and interest, 348–49; transcendental idealism of, 91; on understanding, reason, and judgment, 352–53. See also *Affektenlehre*
Kantian philosophy, popularization of, 346
Karpf, Anne, 151
Kauffman, Stuart: on definition of agency, 82–83, 85; on meaning of information, 78–79; *Reinventing the Sacred: A New View of Science, Reason, and Religion*, 82
Kierkegaard, Søren, 213
King's Speech, The (film), 142–43
Kircher, Athanasius, 299; on emotions, 315; on incorporeal materiality, 313–14; on music, 316; on *musica pathetica*, 306, 316; *Musurgia Universalis*, 29, 303–4, 305, 306–7, 310, 313, 316; *Paradigma affectus amoris*, 306*f*; theory of affections, 305, 314; use of Galenic humoral medicine, 310–11
Kivy, Peter, 251n8
Koch, Erec R., 291
Kode9 (Goodman, Steve), 214

LaBelle, Brandon, 143
Lacan, Jacques, 119, 208

INDEX

Laertius, Diogenes: *Lives of Eminent Philosophers*, 143
Lamar, Kendrick: "Alright," 232
Lamento della ninfa (Monteverdi), 304
Langer, Susanne: on feeling and thought as contiguous, 271–72; influence of Whitehead, 276; *Philosophy in a New Key*, 75
Lash, Scott, 179, 181
Lefebvre, Henri, 208
Leibniz, Gottfried Wilhelm, 91
Letters on the Kantian Philosophy (*Briefe über die Kantische Philosophie*; Reinhold), 346, 358n15
Leviathan (Hobbes), ix
Lévi-Strauss, Claude, 135n17
Leys, Ruth: *The Ascent of Affect: Genealogy and Critique*, 21; critique of affect theory, 82; *From Guilt to Shame: Auschwitz and After*, 24; *Trauma: A Genealogy*, 24
Life as Surplus (Cooper), 54n29
Lives of Eminent Philosophers (Laertius), 143
Locke, John, 274; about, 273
logos: in the *Iliad* and the *Odyssey*, 145–46; as proportionate, 40; voices of, 152–57. *See also* voice/language
Lowrie, Victor, 268–69
Ludacris: on cost/benefit analysis, 49, 50; "healthy" risk-taking by, 51; "The Rest of My Life," 39, 48–50
Lyotard, Jean-François, 213

MacLean, Jackie, 241–42
Mader, Mary Beth, 46–47
Malpas, Jeff, 66, 68n15
Managed Heart, The: Commercialization of Human Feeling (Hochschild), 22–23
Mandel, Max, 268–69
Marpurg, Friedrich Wilhelm, 12, 212
Martin, F. David, 272
Marx, Karl, 207
Massumi, Brian, 1–2, 16, 20–21; on affect/intensity/emotion/qualification, 18–19, 161–62, 164, 168; agentless affect of, 80–81; on autonomous system of affect, 76–77; on autonomy of affect, 18–19, 271, 275, 283n11; "The Autonomy of Affect," 18–19; on content and effect gap, 224, 231, 271, 282; goals of, 160; on human receptivity, 224; on incorporeal materialism, 309–10; interview with, 45; philosophy of virtuality, 304; on physiological responses to music, 211–12; on virtual reality, 206; on Whitehead, 270–71
Mathiesen, Tobias, 54n22
Matrix (film), 209–11
Matheson, Johann, 12; *Affektenlehre* (Doctrine of Affects), 212–13; *Das neu-eroffnete Orchestre*, 8; Hanslick on, 13; key/chord taxonomy developed by, 8–9; Palisca on, 30n22
Maus, Marcel, 208
Mei, Girolamo, 8
Meillassoux, Quentin, 72; *After Finitude*, 91, 93; on correlationist historicism, 92; on mathematics, 92, 93
Merleau-Ponty, Maurice, 1–2, 17; background of, 28, 253–56; consciousness (*see* consciousness); and phenomenology, 253, 264n4; *Phenomenology of Perception*, 253–54, 259–60; *The Visible and the Invisible*, 254–55, 257–58, 259–62
Mersenne, Marin: background of, 28, 298–99; *Harmonie universelle*, 289, 292, 296, 298; Jesuit education of, 290, 295, 298, 301n31; *Questiones celeberrimae in Genesim*, 296, 297; scientific research of, 289, 295. *See also* Jesuit rhetoric
Messiaen, Olivier, 214
Mestrovic, Stepjan: *Postemotional Society*, 177
Meyer, Leonard: *Emotion and Meaning in Music*, 75
Mill, John Stuart, 244
mimesis: Adorno on, 14–15; affect and, 307–10; as binding power, 315; essence of, 321n13; and magic, 322n25; outcome of, 315, 316; and virtual incorporeality, 317, 324n53
Minims (Catholic preachers), 289–90
Minton's Playhouse, 249
Mitropoulos, Angela, 51

Modell, Amanda, 183
moderation. *See* sophrosyne
Monk, Thelonious, 129, 249
Monolingualism of the Other (Derrida), 156
Monroe's Uptown House, 249
Montesquieu, 149
Monteverdi, Claudio: *Lamento della ninfa*, 304; "Sfogava con le stelle," 304; Tomlinson on, 307
Moritz, Karl Philipp, 358n26
Mozart, Wolfgang Amadeus, 344–45
Murata, Margaret, 333, 335
music: affective power of, 8; of ancient Greece, 54n22; ancient/modern approaches to theory, 303; backlash against, 106; capitalist influence on (*see* capitalism); democratization of, 174; digital, 103–4; harmony (*see* harmony); hybridization of, 106; Kant's views of, 346–48; Kircher on, 316; listener practices, 167–68; notation, 102, 105–6; physical effects, 88–89; physiological responses to, 212; poetry vs., 346; political effects of, 166–67; rationalization in seventeenth and eighteenth centuries, 8–9; remuneration for, 202–3; Renaissance/classical epistemic discontinuity, 304–5; semiotics in, 75; silence as preceding/following, 128–29; statistical modeling in, 45; streaming (*see* streaming); streaming governed by algorithms, 161; technology evolution, 159; transition from *Affektenlehre* to German Idealism, 355–56
music, human: Ice Age music, 26, 99–101; instruments, evolution of (*see* instruments); summary, 105–7
musical education: Aristotle on, 5–6; Plato/Socrates on, 3–4
Musica practica (Ramis de Pareia), 7
music discovery tools, 182, 183
Music in Everyday Life (DeNora), 16, 17, 167
musicking, nonhuman/prehuman: background of, 26, 71–73; biosemiosis/prelinguistics, 73–76, 83, 87–90; causal covariance, 78; history vs. historicism, 91–94; index and indexicality, 75–76, 90; information and meaning, 78; intentionality, 74; interpretants, 73–75, 76, 77; Kantian philosophy impact on, 72; music vs. language and symbolic cognition, 71; niche construction, 74; paradox of manifestation, 92; semiosphere, 74; "Shannon information," 78; sign and information, 76–79; signification process, 73; speculative materialism/speculative realism, 72, 91; symbolism, 75; thirdness, 73, 78–79
Musk, Elon, 209
Musurgia Universalis (Kircher), 29, 303–4, 305, 306–7, 310, 313, 316
Myspace, 201

Nancy, Jean-Luc, 185
Napster, 174
Nashville (Altman), 27, 227, 231, 232
Nattiez, Jean-Jacques, 75
Nemesysco, 216
neoliberalism, 2–3, 25; in capitalism, 23–24; cost/benefit analysis of, 37–39, 44; and entrepreneurial investment, 43–44; in late 1990s, 171–72; Plato's influence on, 43; probabilist and postprobabilist, 54n29, 55n49; race as risk in, 50, 51; statistical/mathematical tools in, 48. *See also* sophrosyne
Neubauer, John, 357n9
New Aesthetic of Musical Impotence, The (Pfitzner), 239
Newton, Isaac, 273
Ngai, Sianne: *Ugly Feeling*, 24–25
Nice Work If You Can Get It: Life and Labor in Precarious Times (Ross), 204
Nietzsche, Friedrich, 14, 48, 211, 213
Noise or *Bruits* (Attali), 45
No Jacket Required (album; Collins), 232
North, Helen, 53n17
notation/score: performance vs., 240–41; pitch, 241–42
nuove musiche, Le (Caccini), 325
Nussbaum, Charles, 75
Nussbaum, Martha, 1–2; *The Fragility of*

Goodness, 25; *Upheavals of Thought: The Intelligence of Emotions*, 25

Ochoa Gautier, Ana María, 308, 321n11
Odysseus, 146–47
Odyssey (Homer), 145–47
Of Grammatology (Derrida), 150
"On Popular Music" (Adorno), 164
On the Musically Beautiful (Hanslick), 11–12
On the Passions of the Soul (Descartes), 8
Ordinary Affects (Stewart), 22
Organs without Bodies (Žižek), 231–32
Ostrovsky, Josh, 206, 207
Oxford Handbook of Philosophy of Emotion, The (Goldie), 21–22

Palisca, Claude, 6, 30n22, 311
Pandora, 159, 174, 179, 182
Paradigma affectus amoris (Kircher), 306*f*
Parr, Adrian, 88
Payton, Nicholas, 239
peer-to-peer (P2P) file sharing ("piracy"): availability of, 175; onset of, 174; recovery from, 159
Peirce, Charles Sanders, influence of, 73–75, 88
Peraino, Judith, 53n15
performances, multi-media, 104–5
Pfitzner, Hans: *The New Aesthetic of Musical Impotence*, 239
Phaedrus (Plato), 157n10
Phenomenology of Perception (Merleau-Ponty), 253–54, 259–60
Phenomenology of Spirit (Hegel), 11
Philosophy in a New Key (Langer), 75
Philosophy of Mind (Hegel), 12–13
philosophy style, 153
Pinch, Trevor: *Analog Days*, 105; on backlash against changes, 106
Pitch of Philosophy, A (Cavell), 150
Plamper, Jan: *The History of Emotions*, 20–21
Plato: on anamnesis (loss of forgetfulness), 233; divided line of, 38, 40, 52n10, 52n13; on harmony, 41–42, 47; on Kallipolis, 3–4, 51; mathematics used by, 47–48; on musical education, 3–4; *Phaedrus*, 157n10; philosophy style, 153; *Politeia*, 19; *Republic*, 3, 38, 40, 52n13, 53n15; on sophrosyne (moderation), 38, 40–41; *Timaeus*, 7; voice of, 143
Plessner, Helmut, 17
Poetics (Aristotle), 4–5, 19
Politeia (Plato), 19
Politics (Aristotle), 5, 19
Popoff, Tawnya, 268–69
postdemocracy. *See* neoliberalism
Postemotional Society (Mestrovic), 177
"Potato Head Blues" (Armstrong), 248–49
privacy issues, 199, 220n3
Process and Reality (Whitehead), 80, 268, 276, 277–78
Protevi, John, 1–2
Proust, Marcel, 28, 263–64; as process philosopher, 281; *Swann's Way*, 262, 280–81
Prum, Richard, 79
Puar, Jasbir, 271
Pythagoras, 38, 42

Quantz, Johann Joachim, 212
Questiones celeberrimae in Genesim (Mersenne), 296, 297
Quintilian, 296; *Institutio oratoria*, 292, 298; on vocal health, 292

Rameau, Jean-Philippe, 303
Ramis de Pareia, Bartolomeo: on affective power of music, 7–8; *Musica practica*, 7
Ramus, Peter, 296, 299
Rancière, Jacques, 37–38, 39, 47, 52n13
Rawls, John, 143–44
Read, Jason, 37, 179
Reason and Resonance: A History of Aurality (Erlmann), ix
record companies/music labels: declining monopolies, 174; Facebook, 201; Google+, 201; Myspace, 201; production/marketing by, 171
recorded music, 103–4
Reggio, Carlo, 296
Reguillo, Rossana, 173, 178, 183

Reich, Steve, 104–5
Reinhold, Karl Leonhard: *Letters on the Kantian Philosophy* (*Briefe über die Kantische Philosophie*), 346, 358n15
Reinventing the Sacred: A New View of Science, Reason, and Religion (Kauffman), 82
Reith Lectures. *See* Barenboim, Daniel
Republic (Plato), 3, 38, 40, 52n13, 53n15, 121
Resilience and Melancholy (James), 48
"Rest of My Life, The" (Ludacris), 39, 48–50
Revelli, Marco, 207
Reznikoff, Iegor, 100
rhetoric: in *Affektenlehre* (Doctrine of Affects), 349; Gross on, 20; Jesuit (*see* Jesuit rhetoric); Kant on, 349–50, 353–54
Rhetoric (Aristotle), 19, 24
Riefenstahl, Leni: *The Triumph of the Will*, ix
Rifkin, Jeremy, 181
Rimbaud, Arthur, 125
Rorty, Amélie Oksenberg, 20
Rosand, Ellen, 326, 335, 336, 340n10
Rosen, Christine, 178–79
Rosenwein, Barbara H.: *What Is the History of Emotions?*, 21
Ross, Andrew: *Nice Work If You Can Get It: Life and Labor in Precarious Times*, 204
Rossini, Gioachino, 9–10
Rousseau, Jean-Jacques: Derrida on, 150; *Discourse on the Origin and Basis of Inequality*, 148; "Essay on the Origin of Languages," 148, 150; on evolution of language, 148–50; Kant's response to, 359n38; *The Social Contract*, 150
Rush, Geoffrey, 142

Salazar, Philippe-Joseph, 291, 296
Sartre, Jean-Paul, 17, 255, 265n10
Schachter, Stanley, 162, 184
Schaeffer, Pierre, 213
Schafer, R. Murray, 2
Scharlau, Ulf, 316–17
Scheer, Monique, 29, 326, 339

Schelling, Friedrich, 213
Scherer, Frederic M., 202
Schopenhauer, Arthur, 13–14, 179, 213, 243–44, 245–46
Schumann, Robert, 9
Schumpeter, Joseph A., 202
Sedgwick, Eve Kosofsky, 19, 21; "Shame in the Cybernetic Fold: Reading Silvan Tomkins," 18; *Touching Feeling: Affect Pedagogy Performativity*, 23
Semaine, 216
"Sensing Voice: Materiality and the Lived Body in Singing and Listening" (Eidsheim), 16–17
"Sfogava con le stelle" (Monteverdi), 304
Shafer, R. Murray, 15
"Shame in the Cybernetic Fold: Reading Silvan Tomkins" (Sedgwick and Frank), 17, 18
Shankar, Ravi, 106
Shannon, Claude, 78
Shaviro, Steven, 80–81, 85
Shepherd, John, 241
Shirky, Clay, 202
Shouse, Eric, 89
Shrimshraw, Will, 214
Sielaff, Miranda, 268–69
Signal and the Noise, The (Silver), 47
"Silence of the Sirens" (Kafka), 146
Silver, Nate: *The Signal and the Noise*, 47
Silverstein, Michael, 75–76
Simondon, Gilbert, 27, 227, 235n15
Simulacra and Simulation (Baudrillard), 210
Singer, Jerome, 162, 184
Sloterdijk, Peter, x
Snapper, Juliana, 16–17
Social Contract, The (Rousseau), 150
social media: acquisitions/mergers of, 201; binding technique of, 200; "egocasting," 178; feedback loop on, 200; financial risks of, 220n3; labor-leisure blurring with, 178; liabilities, 220n3; music discovery tools, 182, 183; playlists, 176, 179, 180, 181, 182–83, 184, 193n91; social networks replaced by, 200–201; user-generated content for, 220n3. *See also specific social media*

Socrates: on employment, 121; on musical education, 4; on Plato, 143
Songza, 159, 182, 184
sonic affective regimes, 2–3; as a bodily presence, 17; contributors to, ix; Napoleonic wars' impact on, 10; and Plato/Aristotle, 3–4, 6; Renaissance thought in, 6–7
Sonic Episteme, The: Acoustic Resonance, Neoliberalism, and Biopolitics (James), 2
Sonic Warfare: Sound, Affect, and the Ecology of Fear (Goodman), 16, 17
Sontag, Susan: "Against Interpretation," 214
sophrosyne (moderation), 51; acoustic harmony, 38–39; as ancient Greek concept, 38; Christianity as dividing line, 43; diminishing returns in, 39, 44, 47, 48–49; as freedom from enslavement, 39–40; musical harmony in, 41–43, 47, 53n17; neoliberal cost-benefit analysis, 37–39, 44; neoliberal market modeling, 44–48; noise as beneficial, 39; Platonic, 38, 39–44, 47–48; probabilist math, 37, 51, 54n29, 55n49; ratio/divided line in, 40; rap music cost-benefit analysis, 39, 48–50. *See also* neoliberalism
sound: within chaos, 129, 130; as experienced within the womb, 148; as a vibratory force, 9
sound-affect concepts and debates: landmarks, 18–19; terminology, 17–18, 22
sound-affect relationship, historical periods, 1–3; affect (*see* affect); ancient philosophies, 3–6; early modernism, 6–9; Romanticism, 9–15; sound studies, 15–17
"Sound and Affect: Voice, Music, World" (conference, 2014), 1
Soundscapes of Modernity (Thompson), 16
sound studies, 2, 15–17; ontological turn in, 234, 235n5
sound waves: acoustic harmony as relationship among, 38–39; as mathematical relationships, 45; in water, 17
speech impediments, 142–43, 144

speech therapy, 142–43
Spence, Lester, 50
Spinoza, Baruch, 1–2, 18, 19, 88, 224, 229; *Ethics*, 87; ethics of, 112
Spotify, 159, 174, 175, 176, 179, 180, 182, 183, 184, 201–2
Stalley, Richard, 42
Stallman, Richard, 202
Stengers, Isabelle, 274
Stern, Robert: *Thinking About the Emotions: A Philosophical History*, 21–22
Sterne, Jonathan, 2; *The Audible Past*, 16, 326; on noise as beneficial, 39
Stewart, Kathleen, 271; *Ordinary Affects*, 22
Stoller, Paul, 162–63
Stravinsky, Igor, 15, 129
streaming: about, 26–27, 189, 202; algorithmic, 161, 176, 180, 182, 184–85; algorithmic code, 187; detailed data from, 182; gatekeeping, 174–75; homogenizing mass impact of, 180; lean-in/lean-out listening, 179–80; platforms for, 159, 174, 220n8; YouTube videos (*see* YouTube). *See also* social media; *and specific platforms*
"Stronger" (West), 48
"Structures of Feeling" (Williams), 22
Sulzer, Johann Georg: *General Theory of the Fine Arts* (*Allgemeine Theorie der schönen Künste*), 350, 351
Swann's Way (Proust), 262, 280–81
symphonies: standardization/tonal variation allowable in, 250–51n6; tonal criteria for, 250n6

Taine, Hippolyte, 147
Taussig, Michael, 308, 310
technology: criminology/policing techniques, 199, 219n2; disinformation propagated by, 197, 209, 219n1; industrialized, 215–19; of 1930s/40s, 171; for personal profiles (*see* users); for social media (*see* social media); for spyware, 199, 207; for streaming (*see* streaming); for surveillance, 178, 197–200, 207, 215; for virtual reality (*see* virtual reality)

Theremin, Leon, 103
Thinking About the Emotions: A Philosophical History (Cohen and Stern), 21–22
Thompson, Emily, 2; *Soundscapes of Modernity*, 16
Thompson, John B., 151
Thompson, Marie, 214
Thousand Plateaus, A: Capitalism and Schizophrenia (Deleuze and Guattari), 72, 76, 80, 87, 224–25
Thrift, Nigel, 108
Timaeus (Plato), 7
Tomkins, Silvan, 18, 19, 308
Tomlinson, Gary, 6; on affect and consciousness, 225–27; on Ficino's musical magic, 7–8, 30n14; on Renaissance/classical shift, 304, 307–8
Tompkins, Silvan, 1–2
Toop, David, 214
Torgue, Henri, on anamnesis (loss of forgetfulness), 227, 230, 233
Touching Feeling: Affect Pedagogy Performativity (Sedgwick), 23
Trauma: A Genealogy (Leys), 24
Tristan und Isolde (Wagner), 128
Triumph of the Will, The (documentary), ix
Trocco, Frank: *Analog Days*, 105
Turino, Thomas, 75
"turn to affect," 19, 21
Turrentine, Stanley, 241–42

Uexküll, Jacob von, 87, 88, 89–90
Ugly Feeling (Ngai), 24–25
Uncomfortable Situations: Emotion between Science and the Humanities (Gross), 24
Upheavals of Thought: The Intelligence of Emotions (Nussbaum), 25
users: personal preference profiles for, 176–86, 198–99; spyware, 199, 207; surveillance of, 178, 197–200, 207, 215
Usher (rap musician), 48

Vacationes autumnales (Cressolles), 296, 297
Valladier, André, 296

Vandenberghe, Frédéric, 187
Virgil, 293
Virno, Paolo, 202
virtual reality, 204–7, 209–11; *Get Out* (film), 209; *The Hunger Games* (film), 204–6, 209; *Inception* (film), 209; *The Matrix* (film), 209–11; *Westworld* (television), 209–11
Visible and the Invisible, The (Merleau-Ponty), 254–55, 257–58, 259–62
voice/language: accents, 26, 142, 152, 153–54, 156–57; articulatory style, 152; bodily hexis, 26, 141, 151–52; Calvino on, 153; Darwin and Rousseau on, 147–50; evolution of, 148–49; geographic impact on, 149, 150; at home, 155–56; infant/childhood development of, 147–48; linguistic habitus, 151, 152; literacy impact on, 150; mother tongue, 156–57; physiognomy of, 142–44; prosody, 152; and the public sphere, 154–56; qualities of, 144–45; speech/body language, 151–52; speech muscles, 151; syntactical variations, 152; transition from oral to written, 145–47; Ulysses's voice, 147; uniqueness of, 147. *See also* logos

Wackenroder, Wilhelm Heinrich: *Fantasies on Art*, 11; on music as divine miracle, 213; technical metaphors of, 12–13
Wagner, Richard, ix; Adorno's diatribes against, 15; letter to Mathilde Wesendonck, 13; predilection for Schopenhauer's thought, 13–14; *Tristan und Isolde*, 128
Webster, Ben, 241–42
Weil, Simone, 145
Wesendonck, Mathilde, 13
West, Kanye: "Stronger," 48
Westworld (television), 209–11
What Is the History of Emotions? (Rosenwein and Cristiani), 21
Whitehead, Alfred North, 278–82; on abstractions, 274, 275; *Adventures of Ideas*, 273, 276; on assemblage, 274, 284n31; on autonomy of affect, 282; career of,

272–73; "category of the ultimate," 268; *The Concept of Nature*, 274–75; creating unisons, 268–69; Deleuzian-Massumian affect vs., 278–79, 280; on events, 279; on experience as emotional, 276; on feeling (emotion), 85, 97n35; on feelings (prehensions), 80, 84, 86, 91, 272, 276, 284n31; influences, 271–72, 273; "many becoming one," 268; on music as mediation, 281; on nexus of emotions, 276–78, 284n31; periods of, 272–76; *Process and Reality*, 80, 268, 276, 277–78, 279; sound as feeling, 276–78; on subject-object relationship, 273; on "superject," 274; Wubbels's Viola Quartet as example, 268–72. *See also* Wubbels, Eric, Viola Quartet

Williams, Charles Melvin "Cootie": Ellington's composition for, 243; as second composer, 251n16

Williams, Raymond: "Structures of Feeling," 22

Windt, Herbert, ix

Winnubst, Shannon, 43, 52n8, 54n35

Wittgenstein, Ludwig, 72, 122–23

"Work of Art in the Age of Technical Reproducibility, The" (Benjamin), 214

Wubbels, Eric, Viola Quartet: gestural enmeshments of violas, 269*f*; performances by, 268; pitch unison between violas, 277*f*; rhythmic/pitch unison with hocketing, 270*f*; unison during, 276–77. *See also* Massumi, Brian

Wynter, Silvia, 188

Young, Lester, 241–42

YouTube, 159, 173, 175, 178, 179

YouTube Red, 220n8

Zarlino, Gioseffo, 303; *Le institutioni harmoniche*, 8; on musical structure, 9

Žižek, Slavoj, 214; *Organs without Bodies*, 231–32